Advance praise for *The Cos*

The key to Chip Smith's book, *The Cost of Privilege,* *Taking On The System of White Supremacy and Racism*, which signals that this is the work of a social justice activist. Yet, it is also meticulously researched and based on wide reading. As a teacher, I see this book as a dream text for a high school or university course on racism; as an activist myself, I see it as an organizing manual. But, the general reader can be assured that this is a well written and reliable book on a subject that everyday is becoming more urgent.

—**Roxanne Dunbar-Ortiz**, historian, writer, and activist

The *Cost of Privilege* is a fine activists' primer for understanding racism in the US from a revolutionary, democratic, working-class perspective. Writing in a down-to-earth style, Smith weaves theoretical insight, political history, and organizing practice together, shows how capitalism, racism, and patriarchy interconnect, and offers excellent ideas for movement building.

—**Johanna Brenner**, author of *Women and the Politics of Class*

This book will be an eye-opener for union leaders trying to unite the movement. It challenges those who hope to avoid divisions in the U.S. working class by simply changing the subject to "common interests". And it will no doubt help white union leaders in particular reflect differently on their own history and position in society. It is a colossal effort, bringing together – probably for the first time – race theory, labor history, analyses of patriarchy and intersectionality, and personal reflections on race and social activism, between the covers of a single volume. Read it, change the way you organize, change the world.

—**Jeff Crosby**, President, North Shore Labor Council, Lynn, Massachusetts

Chip Smith and the large cast of characters who engaged in the production of *The Cost of Privilege* have given us a book of enormous power, scope, and analytic/practical insight. It locates white supremacy and racism as central to the systems of power within the United States and the larger world-system. But it points as well to race, class, and gender as interlocking forms of oppression, as opposed to viewing them as separate but related systems of oppression.

Even more important this work not only locates these systems of oppression within a historical social system, it explains the role of oppressed strata in the development of knowledge about the social world, and strategies for changing that world. Smith and his comrades who have been in the forefront of the struggle against racism and white supremacy for some thirty years have given us an exemplary work which I place on a par with classics such as Robert Allen's *Black Awakening in Capitalist America* (1970), Bob Blauner's *Racial Oppression in America* (1972), and James Boggs's *Racism and the Class Struggle* (1970).

—**Rod Bush**, author of *We Are Not What We Seem: Black Nationalism and Class Struggle in the American Century*

The *Cost of Privilege* makes it clear that the struggle for racial equality must be at the very heart of a movement to replace a system based on exploitation with one based on cooperation. Historical and future oriented, theoretical and practical, global and local, social and personal, it encourages reflection, organization, and strategic action.

—**Meizhu Lui**, Executive Director, United for a Fair Economy

In *The Cost of Privilege,* Chip Smith and his associates have done something I never thought possible: they've combined a solid analysis of race and racism in the US with a training manual for white anti-racists. Their work is deep: accounts of past struggles inform their thinking about 21st-century racism. The book is both readable and humane: while teaching and challenging white anti-racists, it also respects and honors their struggles and accomplishments. *The Cost of Privilege* will be an excellent text for a practice-oriented course on race, and it also speaks eloquently to all whites committed to racial justice. Highly recommended!

—**Howard Winant**, University of California, Santa Barbara, and author of *The World Is a Ghetto: Race and Democracy since World War II*

As a white anti-racist organizer, I've been looking for an analysis of white privilege that is grounded in the historical development of the intersecting systems of white supremacy, capitalism, and patriarchy in the U.S. I've been seeking strategies that challenge white privilege in the context of working to build a revolutionary multi-national movement: one whose politics support the self-determination of peoples of color; the struggles of working class people of all colors against the capitalist system; the liberation of all women, especially women of color; and the efforts of nations in the Global South to free themselves from the tentacles of U.S. imperialism.

The Cost of Privilege is a book I've been waiting for. I think it's written by revolutionary anti-racist organizers for social justice activists who aspire to be anti-racist organizers and revolutionaries. At a time when the white anti-racist movement is growing and searching for ways to do more principled and effective political work, this book is a "must read" for all those committed to challenging white supremacy.

—**Sharon Martinas**, co-founder of the Challenging White Supremacy Workshop

The *Cost of Privilege* provides a comprehensive and thoughtful examination of the emergence and evolution of white supremacy. This book does so in a manner that reckons with the complexity of this history in the intertwining of patriarchal and capitalist class structure of society while maintaining clarity about the overriding social forces at work. The *Cost of Privilege* balances discussion of systemic and institutional structuring of white supremacy in U.S. and global society with rich evidence of people's struggles throughout history to resist and challenge these realities as well as concrete examples for reflecting upon assumptions and actions. In doing so, this book offers the reader cause for hope in the face of the brutality that white supremacy has rendered throughout the last five centuries.

—**Melanie E. L. Bush**, Assistant Professor, Adelphi University

The *Cost of Privilege* represents a significant contribution to our understanding of the integral link between capitalism, race, and white supremacy. The book plays a unique role in that it is written from the standpoint of the practitioner or the organizer, rather than from the standpoint of the observer. This is a book that not only must be read, but can serve as a basis for anti-racist work in existing struggles and movements. I am keeping my copy of the book very nearby!

—**Bill Fletcher, Jr.**, labor and international writer and activist

The Cost of Privilege

The Cost of Privilege

Taking On the System of White Supremacy and Racism

Chip Smith

With

Michelle Foy, Badili Jones, Elly Leary,
Joe Navarro, and Juliet Ucelli

Art and graphic design by

Malcolm Goff

Camino  Press

Second printing, 2007

Single and bulk orders available from publisher:

Camino Press
PO Box 87941
Fayetteville, NC 28304
910 670-0891

www.CostofPrivilege.com

ISBN-13: 978-0-9791828-0-8
ISBN-10: 0-9791828-0-8

Library of Congress Control Number: 2007900543

Printed by Linemark Printing, Inc., Largo, MD

To the memory of three freedom fighters who passed away as this book was being written…

Ted Allen

…whose groundbreaking work on white privilege helped lay the foundation for the analysis in these pages

Sanjulo Ber

…whose tireless commitment to the people – in Pittsburgh's workplaces, on the street, and at the heart of the African American community – advanced a working class perspective in the struggle

Anne Braden

…whose unflagging drive, patience, and compassion showed other white people what is possible in the struggle to end white supremacy

White Privilege Working Group

Michelle Foy was introduced to organizing as a student at the University of Colorado during the 1994 struggle to create an Ethnic Studies Department. With Critical Resistance she worked to defeat Proposition 21, California's youth criminalization initiative, and helped found the California Prison Moratorium Project. Currently she is the coordinator of the Bay Area Center for Political Education.

Badili Jones was a founding member of In the Life Atlanta, the largest Black LGBTQ pride celebration in the U.S. He joined the black liberation movement as a 14-year old in Newark, New Jersey – and has written about and fought against racial privilege, patriarchy, and class oppression from an intersectional standpoint ever since. He is currently a core team member of Queer Progressive Agenda.

Elly Leary served as national co-chair of the New Directions Movement – a caucus in the United Auto Workers – and has written about the U.S. workers' movement for *Monthly Review* and other publications. As a worker, rank and file organizer, union officer, and labor educator, she has struggled against white supremacy in U.S. labor unions for 35 years.

Joe Navarro, a teacher, writer, and community activist, recently earned a Masters degree in Mexican American Studies at San Jose State University – researching racist educational practices in California's public schools. Active in the Chicano movement since the late 1960s, he is the author of seven chapbooks of poetry – including *Ambidextrous In Two Languages* – and is also a member of *Apoyo Tarahumara*.

Juliet Ucelli, a New York City public school social worker, helped initiate Italian Americans for a Multicultural U.S. (IAMUS) – an organization that joined native peoples and others in opposing the 1992 Columbus commemorations. She has written on Eurocentrism, school reform, and Italian-American identity and is a co-founder of the New York Marxist School.

Art and graphic design

Malcolm Goff is a painter, printmaker, and graphic designer, who combines abstraction, African motifs, and social realism in his art. Goff's work appears in numerous private and corporate collections – and his murals, in the halls and on the walls of public buildings in the South. He teaches art in the public schools of Durham, NC.

Website

The website associated with *The Cost of Privilege* is
www.CostofPrivilege.com

Contents

Boxed Inserts

Illustrations

The Cost of Privilege

Introduction

Land was the bait used to hook poor Europeans into suppressing the Indian peoples and enforcing the slave system. Usually it was not even very good land, since that had been monopolized by the ruling elite. For 300 years and with native peoples' land and the slave system as the foundation, systematic racial advantages have worked to prevent a combined popular challenge to the ruling establishment. The downplaying, neglect, and sometimes outright denial of the need to overcome systematic racial privileges has doomed many struggles, large and small. The system is pervasive – reaching into people's most intimate personal and family relations – and suffocatingly dominant in the media and society's cultural habits.

Nonetheless, people have also struggled – and from time to time have won victories. There have been slave revolts, resistance to settler expansion and annexation, multiracial strikes, heroism in war, mass pressure for civil rights, and urban rebellions. People persevered with strength and resilience drawn from their communities, from the land, and from their shared experience of oppression. A section of the European American community has contributed positively over the centuries to this history of struggle – most notably during the Civil War, during the unionization battles of the 1930s, and in the upsurge of the national movements during the 1960s and '70s.

The United States is the richest of the world's developed industrial countries, yet it has the greatest inequality in the distribution of that wealth – the top being reserved, with few exceptions, to a white, male-dominated ruling class. The United States is the only industrial country without a national health program. It has the highest incarceration rate, and illiteracy and infant mortality rates that compare unfavorably with some of the world's poorer countries, not just the developed ones.

Given this reality, there is no question why the top 1% of society maintains the system of racial preferences as a means of social control. Rather, the question is, why has this system proved so effective? Why in the 1860s did hundreds of thousands of non-slave owning Southern white people give up their lives to preserve a system that monopolized the land and kept them poor? Why were oppressed Irish immigrants in the North often hostile to the Union goals in the Civil War? In the late 1940s, why were white-supremacist arguments so successful in combating Southern labor organizing? Since the 1980's why have so many white union members, the so-called "Reagan Democrats," supported programs that go against their interests as wage earners?

The current period

In 1981 Roxanne Mitchell and Frank Weiss's *A House Divided: Labor and White Supremacy* answered these questions by focusing on the role of white privilege in U.S. history. Their analysis strongly influenced the current author and the working group responsible for this present volume. For us, Mitchell and Weiss's insights have stood up well over the past twenty-five years. At the same time, we believe an updated assessment of the importance of white privilege is timely for several reasons:

- Social justice activists need anti-racist theory to help sustain the movement of young people who, in fits and starts, are raising struggle around the war in Iraq, the environment, violence against women, educational access, sweat shops, and the prison system. Such an analysis must be unsparing in its criticism of white supremacy. It should reflect the central importance of struggles by people of color and provide a theoretical foundation for unity among such movements. And it should draw out the historical and material basis for European Americans' joining the struggle.
- Many people active in the social justice movement today were born after the civil rights and national liberation movements of the 1960s. Activists can benefit from learning how white supremacy helped derail those movements – as well as those of earlier periods in U.S. history. White organizers, in particular, can gain insight into questions like: When should I speak up, and when listen? When should I take initiative and offer leadership, and when follow? What is my responsibility to white working class people? Providing some practical answers to these questions is an important goal of this book.
- Since September 11, 2001, the U.S. ruling elite has increased its drive to control the world's resources and people. Contributing to these developments are economic pressures at home, resistance by Third World countries abroad, and competition from other capitalist powers. Externally, the wars in Iraq and Afghanistan, counter-insurgency programs in Colombia and the Philippines, and the spread of U.S. military bases around the world are evidence of heightened U.S. militarism. Internally, cutbacks in resources for education, health care, and housing assistance, the ex-

port of manufacturing and service jobs, increased spending for prisons, and the abandonment of Gulf Coast hurricane survivors – all have hit communities of color the hardest. Given this situation, opposing imperialist war has become a key task for the social justice movement. Our hope is that this book will help make clear the link between white supremacy and U.S. imperial interests across the globe.

- There have been important changes in the terrain of struggle in the 25 years since the publication of *A House Divided*:
  - Immigration is changing the face of the working class in the United States.
  - The center of gravity of the economic system has shifted out of the northern rust belt to the South and Southwest.
  - Academic studies of whiteness have broadened awareness of the role of privilege; yet, at the same time, other studies have suggested the reduced importance of race in social analysis.
  - The trade union movement had a change of leadership in the mid-1990s and then split in 2005.
  - Many union organizers have a new understanding of the need to organize immigrants, both documented and undocumented. Nonetheless, the percentage of workers organized into unions continues to decline – even if at a slower rate – and unorganized workers make up nearly 90% of the workforce.

  Understanding these developments is critical for the struggle against white supremacy in this period.
- Various initiatives across the United States are looking to reconstitute, or refound, the revolutionary left in this country. The goal is to develop theory, program, and organization that can bring millions of people into motion and wield real influence in national and local affairs – pointing toward a new society without race, class, or gender privileges. Among the various left organizations, as well as within the broader progressive movement, there are wide differences on how to fight white supremacy – what it consists of, its significance, and how, when, or even if the system should be confronted. Our hope is that by contributing to the debate on this key question of revolutionary strategy, we can help move the left toward greater unity.

Approach to the study

Our approach to the study of white privilege focuses first, in Section I, Chapters 1-4, on the white race – the historic source, and current center of problems related to race in the United States. Then in Section II we examine the development of the people of color movements on the other side of the color line. And in Sections III and IV we look at social class and gender and how they interact with and influence the central dynamic of color.

We base the analysis on history – describing the origin of the white race at the onset of slavery, and then the deepening of racial oppression to national oppression in the period when the United States became a world power a hundred years ago. We come at this history from different angles – from the perspectives of race, class, and gender – to get a multilayered sense of how white supremacy functions. Each section brings the story up to the current period – and points to ways people can organize today to confront systematic oppression.

In the second half of the book, Sections V-VII build on the earlier discussion to suggest a strategic alignment of forces with the potential to overcome white supremacy. Overall, the main conclusion calls for a broad strategic alliance of 1) people of color movements struggling for national liberation and an end to institutionalized racism, 2) women and lesbian-gay-bisexual-transgender/questioning (LGBTQ) people seeking to end the system of patriarchy, and 3) the multinational U.S. working class fighting to overturn capitalism and replace it with the democratic rule of the popular classes and their allies. Central to this conclusion is the understanding that when women of color and their working class sisters succeed in organizing to improve their lives, the whole society changes for the better.

Section VIII presents a multilevel program – personal, organizational, and social – aimed at helping activists build the core strategic alliance against white supremacy and racism. And Section IX sums up the argument of the book with an overall assessment of the social cost of white privilege – while pointing to a future where new kinds relationships can flourish, relationships nurtured in the course of today's struggle.

Acknowledgments

Many people have written on the subject of race in the United States. Hundreds, even thousands of books discuss its history, psychology, and underlying social theory – and they come from a range of different perspectives. We – the author and the White Privilege Working Group who supported this writing project – want to begin by honoring this work. There are references to many writers in the pages that follow – and in the bibliography at the back of the book. But we also recognize that there are many others whose writings we have not been able to review, benefit from, or include in this discussion.

We have tried to be inclusive and multi-sided in our approach. But what we bring in particular to this study is our association – some of us closer than others – with the Freedom Road Socialist Organization/*Organización Socialista del Camino para la Libertad* (FRSO/*OSCL*), with its decades of organizing centered on the struggle against white supremacy. Our hope is that this organization's practical standpoint helps ground the overall analysis and makes the book useful to both new and veteran activists.

The author is a white man, and an old one at that. This attempt to understand the system of white supremacy and point a way out seems to me to be both an impossible task and, at the same time, a compelling responsibility. Fortunately, many people have provided support along the way. First, the working group of Michelle Foy, Badili Jones, Elly Leary, Joe Navarro, and Juliet Ucelli helped with planning and feedback at each stage of the writing process. Second, a broader group of people contributed early drafts of certain sections and made critical recommendations that helped deepen the content of the book. These people include John Allocca, Steve Backman, Cameron Barron, Ajamu Dillahunt, Martin Eder, Bill Gallegos, Fernando Gapasin, Stan Goff, Tom Goodkind, Bruce Hobson, Steve Hollis, Thandabantu Iverson, Bob Lederer, Jon Liss, Paul McLennan, Becky Minnich, Doug Mónica, Eric Odell, Dennis O'Neil, Charlie Orrock, Lou Plummer, Bryan Proffitt, John Riley, Mark Schulz, Juan Taizán, Claire Tran, and Garret Virchick. All these people gave generously of their time and energy to make this book as accurate and useful as possible.

Special thanks go to Malcolm Goff for his illustrations and cover design; to Dasan Ahanu, Yolanda Carrington, and Joe Navarro for the use of their poetry to introduce sections III, VI, VII, and IX; and to Bill Gallegos for his description of the League for Revolutionary Struggle.

A still broader circle of family and friends supported the work through their conversations, expressions of interest, and patient inquiries over the nearly six years from beginning to end of the project. Included here are friends in and around Fayetteville: Andrew Bryant, Jr., Bridgette Burge, Roderick Lewis, Darlene Hopkins, Myra Kinderknecht, Tina Plummer, Nancy Shakir, Jim Stolz, and Carol Wadon, as well as participants in the Opened Gates Book Club, Wanda Hunter, Dorothy Fielder, and Frances Huggins; friends in Philadelphia: Amadee Braxton, D Chou, Fred Engst, Eric Joselyn, and Ellen Somekawa; and family members: Nick, Nikki, Nate and Nina Smith, as well as Malia Kulp and Alan Yottey.

Special gratitude goes to Kim Eng Koo, MD, for her presence and patience throughout the project; and to the group of Freedom Road activists, as well as the broader left in North Carolina, who helped keep the book's discussion anchored in social practice.

After so much help from so many people, the hope is that any remaining errors are minor – and the author takes full responsibility for those that do remain.

We hope this book contributes to discussion, debate, and action by the many organizations and individuals who want to end white supremacy in the United States. Our conviction, which we hope these pages make clear, is that the system of racial preferences is the main barrier to forming a broad movement that can fundamentally transform U.S. society. We hope to be able to join with you, the reader, and with many, many others in carrying out this righteous struggle.

"Is not the slave trade entirely at war with the heart of man? And surely that which is begun by breaking down the barriers of virtue, involves in its continuance destruction to every principle, and buries all sentiments in ruin! When you make men slaves, you...compel them to live with you in a state of war."

—Olaudah Equiano, former slave

I

The White Race

In order for there to be white supremacy, there has to be a white race. But up until about three hundred years ago, there was no such thing.[1] It is hard for us today to imagine what it must have been like – a world where color did not carry the same social weight as it does today. The Nordic, Germanic and Slavic races, for example, were three separate families of European peoples. The last group, the Slavs, were so named because historically Russia, Germany, and traders at the western end of the Mediterranean Sea viewed these peoples as a good source of slaves.

For Europeans color carried with it various cultural meanings – *white* conveyed a sense of purity, and *black* a sense of evil. In Northern Europe where there was little social diversity, these meanings generally did not carry over to judgments about people based on their skin color. Desdemona's purity, for Shakespeare in the early 1600s, had more to do with her feminineness than her whiteness, while the African Othello was portrayed as both a respected warrior and king.

Nonetheless, color did attach to people – in Spain and Portugal, for example – where there was an array of skin colors and the colors roughly lined up with a person's social position. Slavery, dating back to Roman times, died out in Northern Europe around the 10th century, but it remained a lively part of the economies bordering the Mediterranean. Muslims and Christians captured each other's soldiers in the Crusades, for example, and then sold them to their respective upper classes to use in their personal service and in their workshops. Owning and showing off one's slaves was a mark of distinction. Relationships with slaves tended to be personal. Slaves were often freed after years of service or on the death of an owner; and intermarriage with members of the dominant culture was common.

Slaves were often brought to market from distant regions – where presumably they had been captured in a just war – and sold in Genoa, Venice, Naples, and Cádiz. Ships carried their human cargo from Greece and Turkey at the eastern shore of the Mediterranean, while overland trade routes brought Africans from regions south of the Sahara. With the upper classes abstaining from all work, and with Africans among those laboring at the other social extreme, the poles of color aligned with leisure and compulsion became a part of people's consciousness in Southern Europe. Given the degree of intermarriage, a highly refined spectrum of colors, each with its own name, came to be identified between the two poles. Adding to the social complexity was the fact that money tended to increase a person's social status. "Money whitens" – as they still say in much of Latin America today. This hierarchy of color in Spain and Portugal, which carried over to their colonies in New Spain and Brazil, differed sharply from the polar black-white pattern that developed in the English colonies of North America.

In Chapter 1 we will take the story from the time of the European conquest of North America to the creation of the white race in the decades around 1700. The English are central to this story as they experimented in the South first with indentured English labor and then shifted to a system of slavery. Chapter 2 then deepens the content of what it means to be white by looking at the contributions of various European powers – along with the newly formed United States – in their treatment of Indians, Mexicans, and, later, Asian immigrants. The cultural dimension of whiteness – how white people have seen themselves over the centuries – is the topic of Chapter 3. And we conclude this section in Chapter 4 with a brief survey of the steps required to reverse the policies that created and continue to maintain the white race.

Chapter 1

Origins of the White Race

The main difference between the English and other European colonizers is that the English tried at first to settle their colonies with independent farmers and tenants from home. By contrast the Spanish who arrived in the Americas a century earlier were military men who had no intention of doing any work. They turned to forced Indian labor to mine the silver in Potosí, Peru, and to enslaved Africans to produce sugar on the Caribbean islands and in New Spain (Mexico).[1]

When the Spanish took over an established empire, as with the Aztec and Inca peoples, they relied on the existing relations of power to compel villagers to work for them. Where indigenous villages were more scattered, as on the Caribbean islands, the Spanish killed or drove off all the native peoples – the Taino Indians in Puerto Rico, for example – and replaced them with enslaved Africans. In both types of colonies, since very few women came from Spain, the conquistadors and their soldiers tended to marry local women. And while the survival rate for Africans working the sugar fields was appallingly low, over time the percentage of slaves freed in the Spanish and Portuguese colonies was much higher than in the English colonies – as was the level of intermarriage. As a result, the Latin colonies developed a *mestizo* or mixed culture – part European, part native, part African.

The English were relative latecomers to the colonizing business. By the time they set up their first permanent colony in Jamestown in 1607, the slave trade from Africa to the Americas had been underway for almost 100 years. The Pope had given his blessing to this inhuman transport by conferring on the Portuguese the *Asiento*, an exclusive contract to provide slaves to the Spanish and Portuguese colonies in the New

World. Meanwhile, British seamen during this period – like Jack Hawkins and Francis Drake – were little more than pirates. They raided Portuguese slave ships but had no access to a regular supply of slaves from the African coast. Spain and Portugal dominated the Atlantic until going into decline around the time the British defeated the Spanish Armada in 1588. Then during the 1600s the Dutch trading economy rose to prominence – settling Manhattan Island and northern Brazil, as well as territories along the sea routes to the East Indies. Meanwhile, the English built up their sea power. By 1713 when the *Asiento* passed from the Dutch to the English at the treaty of Utrecht, England "ruled the waves" – and dominated a brutal trade in slaves during the 18th century that dwarfed other periods.

The Jamestown settlement

All that was to come later. In 1607 there were just English immigrant farmers and tenants along the James River – several hundred of them – and almost everyone died in the first couple years. Provisions had to be supplied by the Virginia Company owners in England, and survival depended on help from the native Powhatan people. The colonists were lucky this time. A Spanish settlement in 1526 along the coast of today's South Carolina, and an English one on Roanoke Island in the 1580s, had failed after provoking the hostility of the native peoples. Given the Europeans' approach to non-Christian peoples, this outcome is not surprising. The rapacious pillaging of Hernando De Soto from 1539 to 1542 extended from Florida northward to what became North Carolina and then westward to the Mississippi. DeSoto left a trail of disease, kidnapping, rape and death – as well as a cold hatred among the native peoples for the invaders. Vásquez de Coronado's expedition into the Southwest in this same period used similar methods – and had similar results.

The Jamestown settlers, however, managed to hang on. At one point survivors loaded up their ship and were heading back to England, when a supply ship arrived and they had to turn back to Jamestown. An important, but historically ominous development was the shift to tobacco farming in the mid-1610s. Initial returns on the crop sales in England were high and, as a result, all the farmers, tenants, and developing plantation owners shifted their fields almost exclusively to tobacco. The company directors in England called for a more balanced economy, and the colonial governors mouthed similar phrases. But as the market became glutted and the price of tobacco fell, the colonists responded by increasing the area devoted to tobacco production to try to make up the difference. This pattern of tobacco monoculture and persistent overproduction played a key role in the development of the Virginia colony's labor system.

The first Africans arrived in Jamestown in 1619, brought by a Dutch ship that had taken its cargo from a Portuguese slave trader. The Africans were welcomed by the labor-poor colony and contracted to work for a period of years in the same way the English were at that time. Due to the harsh conditions, very few workers, whatever their background, survived the period of their contract. Nonetheless, labor relations at this time were governed by an English law put in place by Queen Elizabeth in 1563. This "Statute of Artificers and Compulsory Assessment" spelled out the rights of workers – minimal as they were – and the boundaries that employers could not go beyond. In this sense, workers were "free." They could not be shifted to another employer against their will. They could bring charges against an employer for harsh treatment or for failure to fulfill the employer's side of the contract. Workers were free to marry, and employers could not extend the period of a worker's contract.

All these provisions were overturned in the early 1620s. English laborers, as well as the handful of Africans among them, lost all the rights afforded English workers by the Elizabethan law of 1563. They were reduced to *chattel bond* laborers – tradable the same as goods or property (chattel), and bound to an employer without pay for a period of time enforced by the courts (bonded).

This dramatic change in the labor system occurred in 1622. Powhatan Chief Opechancanough, heading an alliance of 32 native peoples, attacked the Jamestown colony and killed a quarter of the settlers. Thirty-five years earlier, Opechancanough's father had wiped out the English colony on Roanoke Island. In the early years of the Jamestown settlement, however, the marriage of Princess Pocahontas to the colonial governor John Rolfe had papered over the shaky Indian-English relations. Then Pocahontas died while in England, followed by her father's death a few years later. Increasing numbers of English arrived – 5,000 in 1619 alone – and the land they farmed continued to expand. For the English, this land being turned into tobacco fields was empty; for the Powhatan, it was filled with resources sustaining their way of life. The Englishmen's drive for material gain also conflicted with the more settled system of mutual recognition and gift-giving practiced by the Indians. By 1622 Opechancanough had had enough.

What seems amazing today is neither the Indian attack nor their eventual defeat by the settlers. It is the way the colonial elite heartlessly turned the attack to their own monetary advantage. The Virginia-based governing council called on surviving farmers and tenants to regroup in and around Jamestown from their remote homesteads. Then they prohibited the planting of corn, using the excuse that the cornfields gave cover to attacking Indians. In this situation of scarcity, the governing elite owned the only small boats available to obtain corn from friendly

Indians across the Chesapeake. The landowners were thus able to completely control the market for corn, and they used their advantage mercilessly. The cost of food increased dramatically. With tobacco growing restricted, the tenant farmers lacked the wherewithal to pay for food. Many starved or died from related diseases. Others resorted to crime, and most lost all that they owned and found themselves pressed into debt servitude. The landowners dispensed with the pretense of hiring free workers. Laborers could now be assigned wherever the master wanted. They could be rented out, or passed from one owner to another. Employers extended the terms of servitude for relatively minor infractions, and whipping and mutilation were common punishments.

As the labor system grew harsher, new workers arriving from England found themselves being merged into this system – on the pretext of owing five years labor to their master for the cost of their transport to Virginia. It was no longer a case of the Virginia Company sponsoring an immigrant – paying their way with the promise of contract work or tenancy for a set period. Petty criminals were given the choice of "jail or transport to Virginia." Also, a *headright* system encouraged upper class landowners to import laborers: each person brought in from England allowed the contractor to claim an additional 50 acres of land. Ship captains press-ganged drunks and beggars, and in return for the voyage they claimed the headright on their victims – which they then sold to local landowners. In this way free tenancy gave way to chattel bond servitude. For the period of their indenture, servants belonged to their owners the same as if they were tools or livestock. Employers' only obligation was to feed their workers, provide them a set of clothes, and at the end of five years give them a customary, but unspecified, "freedom dues" – usually a bushel of corn and a rifle.

These conditions of chattel servitude applied to women as well as men. But the number of women imported was much smaller. The governing elite had conflicting motives to contend with. They complained about the large number of deaths among tenant workers – and the loss in income that resulted – and looked to women to help care for and sustain the labor force. At the same time, the period required for pregnant women to come to term, give birth and care for children was viewed as a total waste. For this reason, bond laborers were not allowed to marry or have sexual relations during the time of their servitude. Punishments for doing so were severe, including extending the years of their contract.

Women's powerless position in English society carried over to the colonies, where they remained under the control of their master, their employer – once beyond the period of indenture – or their husband. Coverture – the right of a man to be "king of his castle" – applied in Virginia only among free workers. This traditional male privilege helped tie men into the colony's labor system and keep them available to serve in the militia. Women could shorten their period of servitude by marrying a free man. But the power imbalance often worked to make bondswomen vulnerable to male promises. And hovering over every immigrant servant woman was the built-in potential for sexual exploitation by the master.

Beginnings of slavery

English indentured servants performed almost all the work done in Virginia during the 1600s. Some 90,000 laborers were carried to Virginia, mainly to work in the tobacco fields and to serve on the plantations of the colonial elite. An owner ruled over everyone on his land as if they belonged to a single family. This social system contrasted sharply with the traditional English farm system being developed in the northern colonies of New England. Ironically, however, it was in New England that slavery first became legal. The successful use of English bond workers in Virginia and Maryland delayed the onset of legalized slavery there. In New England, by contrast, the Pequot War of 1636-1637 resulted in significant numbers of Indian captives. Legalizing slavery gave community approval to retaining these captives as lifetime servants or, more commonly, trading them to the English colony on the island of Barbados for enslaved Africans. Though slavery began earlier in New England, the small-farm character of the economy there kept slavery from becoming central to its labor system.

In *The Shaping of Black America*, Lerone Bennett, Jr. comments that the English developed their slave-trading ways by practicing first on the English lower classes:

> [W]hite servitude was the proving ground for the mechanisms of control and subordination used later in African American slavery. The plantation pass system, the slave trade, the sexual exploitation of servant women, the whipping-post and slave chain and branding iron, the overseer, the house servant, the Uncle Tom: all these mechanisms were tried out and perfected on white men and women....[I]t is plain that nothing substantial can be said about the mechanisms of black bondage in America except against the background and within the perspective of white bondage in America.[2]

Today, it is hard to believe that such things actually happened: "What, you're saying white people were treated like slaves? You've got to be kidding!" The key point is that during this period, despite the white skin color of the English immigrants, *white people* – in the sense people understand the term today – *didn't really exist yet*. They were just lower class English people who had been pushed off their farms in England and turned into a landless, wandering workforce – some of whom got transported to the Virginia colony. The British ruling class treated the common people in their country with contempt. In England people starved for lack of work and food. Families fled their home districts when the parishes were too poor to provide either work or support. When brought before the city courts for being vagabonds, unemployed workers found themselves sent back to their impoverished home districts. If people turned to theft to survive, the penalties were harsh, including execution for minor offenses.

Poverty of this inhuman kind was relatively new in England. Beginning in the early 1500s landlords decided it was more profitable to raise sheep than to have tenants grow crops. Before this period hardship was shared, and landlords felt a measure of obligation toward their tenants during difficult times. The coming of capitalism to agriculture brought modern-style poverty with it, and along with it as well came the fear and loathing of the ruling class.

A hundred years of acting on their greed had hardened the British upper class rulers to the suffering in their own country. Next door, in Ireland, during the Tyrone War that opened the 1600s, the British army subdued the Irish population by burning crops and starving people into submission, enforcing a famine that lasted three and a half years. Given this history, the treatment of the lower class people transported to Virginia makes more sense.

Once the British economy picked up after the mid-1600s English Civil War, the wandering unemployed in England began to find work. It became harder to fill the ships heading to Virginia. Also, during the 1660s the British established the Royal Adventurers as a slave-trading monopoly – later replaced by the Royal African Company. English ships seized from the Dutch the Cape Verde Islands and their territories along the African Gold Coast. Setting up their command post at Cape Coast, in today's Ghana, the English for the first time had a secure source of slaves to supply their colonies in the West Indies and Virginia.

Rebellion and white privilege

The new system of indentured servitude put in place in the 1620s reduced production costs for the developing planter class. It enabled them to profit from tobacco farming even when overproduction resulted in low prices in England. This arrangement remained reasonably stable for about 50 years.

Then in the mid-1600s things began to change. An African run-away received an extension to lifetime servitude, while the two Europeans who had escaped with him had just a few years added to their contracts. In the 1660s, a law declared that children should be considered slave or free depending on the status of their mother. And in 1670 free Africans were forbidden to employ European indentured servants. Since it was still cheaper to employ bondservants than to purchase slaves, this law aimed mainly to prevent Africans from accumulating property.

Land became scarcer in this period too, with more servants surviving their contract period and clearing out farms for themselves. New land claims were at the edge of the colony, in territory contested by nearby Indian peoples. Meanwhile, vast areas closer to the coast remained undeveloped because they belonged to the plantation elite, having been acquired by headright during previous decades. By pushing the newly freed servants to the outskirts, the planters set up a buffer between themselves and their potentially hostile neighbors.

Meanwhile, the ferocious exploitation of the servant class had been met with resistance over the years. Court records testify to the many instances of cooperation and solidarity among the servants. Edmund Morgan writes in *American Slavery/American Freedom: The Ordeal of Colonial Virginia* that European servants and enslaved Africans "initially saw each other as sharing the same predicament. It was common, for example, for servants and slaves to run away together, steal hogs together, get drunk together. It was not uncommon for them to make love together. White, black and native workers, bonded and free, cooperated to counter the harsh class oppression of the plantation elite."[3]

Not only did this developing solidarity threaten profits, it created a profound sense of physical insecurity in the planter class. Their backs were against the Atlantic. They were living on stolen land next to dispossessed native peoples. And they were outnumbered by exploited, abused, and resentful servants and slaves – along with poor freemen who were little better off. Virginia's governor described the situation as he saw it: "How miserable that man is that Governes a People where six parts of seven at least are Poor Endebted Discontented and Armed."[4]

Bacon's Rebellion

Howard Zinn, in his *People's History of the United States*, describes the "complex chain of oppression" that existed in 1676 Virginia: "The Indians were plundered by white frontiersmen, who were taxed and controlled by the Jamestown elite. And the whole colony was being exploited by England, which bought the colonists' tobacco at prices it dictated and made 100,000 pounds a year for the King."[5]

These antagonisms finally erupted in rebellion in 1676 – beginning with a dispute between a frontiersman and a native, escalating to the seizure of a hog, then to a retaliatory murder, a militia massacre of natives, and finally guerrilla war.

The House of Burgesses in Jamestown learned that further north in New England, Indians were building a military alliance to attack the settlers in what became known as King Philip's or Metacom's War. The Virginia elite decided to try to cut deals with some of the threatening nations. The anti-Indian frontierspeople reacted, adding a sense of settler betrayal to the massive grievances already charged to the Anglo-

American elite. Nathaniel Bacon, a member of the ruling class in Virginia, engaged in a public debate with Governor Berkeley on the conduct of the war against the natives. Bacon hated and feared the indigenous peoples and harbored notions of political power himself. He employed populist rhetoric against first the Indians, and then the colonial establishment. Berkeley underestimated Bacon's influence on the frontierspeople and had him arrested.

Two thousand people marched on the capital in Jamestown. Berkeley released Bacon, who then organized an independent militia and attacked a peaceful native community, the Pamunkey. Berkeley's official colonial militia then mobilized against Bacon, whose forces now included both Europeans and Africans, the latter seizing the opportunity to join the rebellion. Bacon burned down Virginia's government buildings to drive home the demand for more native land. Berkeley appealed to the British Navy; but help came slowly, due in part to royal resistance to the cost of the military expedition.

The rebellion mobilized popular anger for a time but then lost momentum. Desertions quickly became common among both Bacon's and the official militia. Bacon himself fell ill and died in the fall of 1676. The rebellion sputtered out when the Royal Navy finally showed up and disarmed the last band of rebels – a mixed group of eight Negroes and twenty English bondsmen. Twenty-three people were hanged.

Despite the unjust expansionist goal of the rebellion, black and white laborers, both bonded and free, had made clear their potential for united action. This experience demonstrated the instability of the tobacco colonies, where the ruling class faced a mass of impoverished laborers and slaves internally and dispossessed native peoples externally. Finally, the local ruling class discovered that in a crisis they could not reliably turn to Britain to help suppress a rebellion.

Establishing the colonial system of privilege in North America

The terror experienced by the plantation ruling class led them to search for a better system of social control than military power. In doing so they drew on the British experience in Ireland earlier in the 1600s. There the British had imported Protestant immigrants from Scotland into Ulster, the northernmost province in Ireland, to serve as a buffer class. All Scottish settlers, no matter how lowly, benefited from privileges denied to all classes of the native Irish Catholics. This so-called Protestant Ascendancy allowed Britain to significantly reduce their military costs of occupation. Only Ulster Protestants had representation in Parliament. Only Protestants served in the local militias that enforced order on the island. Protestants received favored treatment in the courts and in employment. And only Protestants could vote – but just those who owned property. Political and economic power rested with the Ulster upper class – an extension of the British aristocracy. The solid Protestant front against the Catholics thus proved useful in obscuring the deep class division in Ulster. Protestant laboring people's anger targeted Catholics and not their own upper class oppressors.

In a fashion similar to Ireland, the Virginia planters began to force divisions between European and African workers. They made life a little easier for European servants, and they intensified the repression of black laborers, both slave and free. The landowning class passed legal sanctions against intermarriage in 1691 – and over the years had to repeatedly reinforce these laws, because people kept on loving each other.

It took decades to alternately reward and punish Europeans into becoming white – into acting reliably in the interests of the European ruling elite, rather than out of solidarity with their class sisters and brothers from Africa. The colonies one by one legally consolidated the slave system – lifetime bondage, severe penalties for running away, distinctions based on color for a whole range of offenses, and the banning of intermarriage. A 1691 law barred any owner from setting a black bonded laborer free. In 1705 the colony confiscated all property owned by slaves, including the livestock raised for personal use and sale.

The 1705 code also made clear the many privileges for "Christian white"[6] limited-term bond laborers. One provision kept the master from whipping or beating a white Christian laborer without a court order. And freedom dues of guns, corn, and money went only to white workers, since they alone could serve out their period of indenture.

The planter class also restricted the rights of free black people. Laws banned people of African descent from holding public office, from bearing witness in court against a white person, from "lifting his or her hand" against a white person, and from holding a gun or other weapon whether "offensive or defensive."[7]

The sanction against the possession of weapons – and thus the right to self-defense – had a gender dimension to it as well. Theodore Allen notes, "The denial of the right of self-defense would become a factor in the development of the peculiar American form of male supremacy, white male supremacy, informed by the principle that any European American male could assume familiarity with any African American woman. That principle came to have the sanction of law…Free African American women had practically no legal protection in this respect, in view of the general exclusion of African-Americans, free or bond, from giving testimony in court."[8]

This period shaped the European American workers' new, specifically white identity in the context of a developing settler state. The system of laws and practices slowly and forcibly socialized Europeans into aligning themselves with the ruling class and not with their black peers.

Destroying the natural connection between European and African laborers required extreme levels of repression – "rivers of blood" to use Lerone Bennett, Jr.'s graphic phrase.[9] The colonial rulers' solution, according to Allen, provided "a new birthright not only for Anglos but for every Euro-American, the 'white' identity that 'set them at a dis-

English methods of social control

Around 1700 the word *white* began to appear in Virginia and Maryland official documents, referring to all European Americans, both rich and poor. This usage of *white* was bound up with a set of privileges defined in contrast to the conditions of black people. Whiteness centered on being "not black." Its social function centered on social control.

In Britain, by contrast, small independent farmers of the yeoman class became the social buffer after the enclosures in the 1500s. The ownership of land, specifically provided for by the ruling elite of the time, successfully bound this rural sector to the emerging capitalist social system. This same pattern developed in New England; and the Jamestown colony tried this option during its first decade or so, as well. The shift to indentured servitude in the 1620s, however, closed off the small farmer option for the southern colonies.

Two other English colonies of this same period help illustrate the English approach to social control. On the West Indian island of Barbados, colonization started out with a sizable number of British small-scale farmers and tenants. There, however, the ready availability of slaves transported by Portuguese and Dutch traders turned farming quickly toward a slave-driven plantation system. Independent farmers found themselves squeezed out, and a number of them moved to South Carolina in the later 1600s. As a result, black people came to predominate in the population of Barbados. There the pattern of social control looked much like that of the Spanish colonies of the Caribbean: a small European elite ruling over a large majority of Africans. To resolve the problem of the buffer class, in Barbados black people moved into the overseer-soldier-craftsman-small shop-owner class. This black middle class continues to exist in majority black Caribbean island societies today, while the wealthy tend to be either white or light-skinned in color.

In Ireland, by contrast, the English imported into Ulster a whole population of Protestant Scots during the 1600s to serve as a social buffer. This settler population stood in for the British, making it possible to reduce military expenses. The white race served this same social control function in the English colonies of North America. Forcing privileges on the white laborers cost a little more up front – in wages, in freedom dues, and in land allotments. But the payback was much greater in the long run. White people now willingly served on slave patrols and in the anti-Indian militias. And white working people, despite their impoverished conditions, never again rose up against the plantation system and its ruling class.

—*source: Allen,* The Invention of the White Race

tance'...from the laboring class African-American, and enlisted them as active, or at least passive, supporters of lifetime bondage of African Americans."[10]

This structure of privilege and oppression based on skin color was historically new. In Ireland the racial divisions centered on religion and nationality, not on color. In both Ireland and the southern colonies, however, all members of the favored race, even the worst off, benefited from privileges that were denied even the best-off members of the subject race.

It is significant that once this system of white racial oppression took hold in the South – once the white race came into existence – Southern white workers never again rose up against the plantation system. White people's anger – due to their poor land and their being shut out of work as craftsmen on the plantations – targeted the slaves as the cause of their misery, rather than the slave system and its white ruling class. Poor white people embraced white supremacy and in doing so condemned black people to generations of inhuman bondage. They also condemned themselves, their children, and grandchildren to lives of bitter hardship and brutality.

Chapter 2

Shades of Whiteness

The color white has a peculiar character when applied to skin color. It takes on new shades of meaning depending on the colors of the people white supremacy oppresses. Given that the native peoples were the first ones to feel the brunt of the European invaders, it stands to reason that "anti-red" would have been the first shade of whiteness. But that is not how the history of the English colonies unfolded. Both in New England and later in the Carolinas the English found that survival required allying with certain native peoples in order to neutralize the attacks of others. The English had superior manufactured goods that they could trade for animal skins – and later for Indian captives whom they turned into slaves. In much the same way as in Africa, indigenous peoples captured traditional enemies and offered them to the colonists in return for clothing, jewelry, cooking utensils, and weapons.

Despite the steady displacement of the native peoples from their land, both sides – Indian and English, at least in the early years – viewed the attacks and counterattacks, the alliances and trade relations as being among equals. Colonists distinguished different Indian nations by names – Pequot, Wampanoag, and Narragansett in New England; Savannah, Creek, and Yamasee in the Carolinas. Treaties were made and broken, traders moved among the different peoples learning their ways, and joint- raiding parties attacked common enemies.

That there was a level of respect, even if grudging, between Europeans and the native peoples did not save the Indians from being turned into slaves. It was found, however unsurprisingly, that Indian slaves tended to run away to rejoin their people. And unless pushed nearly to extinction, the indigenous nations had the power to retaliate against systematic enslavement. Also, the native peoples tended to be susceptible to

European diseases, while Africans were immune, due to centuries of exposure along the overland trade routes between Europe and Central Africa. Given this overall situation, New England and Carolina traders opted to ship captive Indians to Barbados in exchange for Africans and sugar. Some 50,000 indigenous people were sold in this way in the first century of colonization, mostly between 1670 and 1720. In fact, more Indians were shipped out of the English colonies during this period than Africans brought in.[1]

Native peoples and whiteness

The English described Indians as having "tawny" colored skin. French and Spanish Catholics, and English Protestants as well, viewed the indigenous people as potential converts to Christianity. The colonists also paid attention to the social structures of the communities they dealt with. They commented, for example, on the relative social equality of women, the organizational complexity of the Iroquois Federation, and the democratic discussion that characterized policy-making in the towns that made up the Creek Nation of the Southeast.[2]

For over a hundred years during a long 18th Century, the English and French allied with different nations around the Great Lakes and along the Mississippi to fight each other – all reflecting wars centered in Europe. It made a difference to the Europeans which community was which. The indigenous peoples of the southeast, however, began to view themselves as "red" beginning around 1720.[3] Leaders from various nations saw themselves in contention with the European powers – the "white people" from France and England. Europeans, however, did not pick up on this language until later – the French in the 1730s, and the English in the 1750s – and its usage was at first restricted to the language of diplomacy.

By comparison, in Europe the Swedish naturalist Linnaeus in the 1740 edition of his *Systema Naturae* grouped humans for the first time into four "varieties" – white, red, yellow and black. By 1758, the 10th edition had added evaluations to these groupings, ranking Indians – in the tradition of the "noble savage" – higher than Asians and Africans. Yet during this same time period the English essayist Samuel Johnson in his authoritative *Dictionary* defined *race* as applying to the "families of mankind" – and made no reference to color.

Native usage of *red* may have come in response to the colonists' beginning to refer to themselves as *white* in the early 1700s. In this way the Indians could distinguish themselves as a group from white colonists and black slaves. By contrast, *red* was seldom used as a descriptor in the northern colonies or in the Great Lakes region, either by native peoples or Europeans. Indian nations in the Southeastern United States used the color red to denote war, and there were origin stories linking their people to the "red earth." The French encountered a number of communities along the Mississippi who identified themselves as red when they first met. The French in turn were quicker to adopt this terminology in referring to native peoples, while they were slower to identify themselves as "white," preferring "French," compared to the English usage in the southern colonies.

By the 1750s the Indians' use of *red* clearly centered on the need for coalition building to resist the European advance. Nancy Shoemaker quotes the Delaware and Shawnee appeal to the Iroquois to "take up the Hatchet against the White People, without distinction, for all their Skin was of one Colour and the Indians of a Nother, and if the Six Nations wou'd strike the French, they wou'd strike the English." This spirit was clear in the preaching of the Delaware Prophet Neolin, as well as in his disciple Pontiac's call for a "cleansing war against 'the Whites'" in 1763.

In this same year, the "Paxton Boys," speaking in the name of "Distressed and Bleeding Frontier Inhabitants" living on the eastern side of the Susquehanna began a private war to exterminate all the Indians in the Pennsylvania colony. They attacked settlements in Conestoga, near Lancaster, and later moved against the Delaware Indians around Philadelphia. While the Paxton Boys' attempts were thwarted, Indian hating continued in the frontier area and helped consolidate a new sense of whiteness in the North. This period saw a hardening of the lines of color between red and white on both sides, with the British striking a pose of peacemaker between the two worlds.

In the years leading up to the War of 1812, indigenous and white forces once again opposed each other, but this time on a more extensive scale. On the native side, Tenskwatawa and Tecumseh in the north and the Creek prophet Hillis Hadjo in the south built an alliance aimed at the encroaching settlers backed by their state militias. They called for a spiritual rejuvenation of the native peoples, as had Neolin 50 years before. On the United States side Andrew Jackson embodied the hatred of all Indians that had driven the Paxton Boys' earlier attacks. Divisions between Indian *nativists* and *accommodationists* gave Jackson the opportunity to unite with Cherokee, Choctaw, and Chickasaw forces against the Creek and Seminole. Later, as president, Jackson drove all these peoples – allies and enemies alike – from their homelands. As the 19th century proceeded, Indians became fully assigned to the derogatory category "Redskin," as settlers moving west jumped at the chance to seize native lands and resources.

The European powers

The red-white color line may have followed the creation of the white race, but the expropriation and destruction of native peoples extends back to the first European settlements: the French, near the St. Lawrence

River at Charlebourg-Royal (1541) and later their trading center at Quebec (1608); the Spanish, at St. Augustine (1565) – after driving out French Protestants who had landed in the area a year earlier – and in New Mexico (1598); the English, at Jamestown (1607) and Plymouth (1620); the Dutch in New Amsterdam (1612); and the Russians, trading for furs in Alaska after 1741. For three hundred years the European powers, and later the United States, fought amongst themselves and against the North American native peoples to control the continent. These battles were just one part of the worldwide European struggle for colonies – and for the slaves that produced their wealth.

Contending slave powers

More than 11,000,000 slaves were transported from Africa to the Americas, and another 9 million died miserably at some point along the journey from inland villages to the stockades and dungeons along the African coast, or on crossing the Atlantic to points of entry and resale in the Americas. Some 500,000 souls arrived in what eventually became the United States. Another 250,000 went to Mexico – half before the first black people disembarked in Jamestown in 1619.

The largest portion of this human traffic occurred over the two centuries from 1650 to 1850. Sugar was the main crop African people gave their lives for – after coffee, tea, and cocoa captured the taste buds of European consumers in the early 1600s. In the North American colonies the early cash crops were tobacco in Virginia, rice in the Carolinas, and sugar in Louisiana. Later, with the patenting of the cotton gin in 1794, the South turned to cotton.

The pay-off for slave-driven colonization was immense. Gold filled the royal treasuries of Spain and Portugal during the 1500s and into the 1600s. It stimulated economic activity throughout Europe with its inflationary impact. The trade in slaves and later the work the slaves performed drove industrialization in England and the United States. U.S. slave trading ships set off from New England beginning in the early 1700s. Later, during the early to mid-1800s, New York City became a thriving center based on profits from slavery. The majority of the ships that ran slaves illegally – after the United States outlawed the slave trade in 1807 – were fitted out in New York. The last 50 years of the trade saw some two million people transported from Africa to the West. New York's business class also profited by handling all the export and import trade connected to the cotton industry in the South.

Over four centuries beginning in the mid-1400s, the European ruling classes' lust for empire destroyed tens of millions of people – native peoples and Africans in the first place, but European laboring people too. Each power contributed something to the whiteness of white supremacy. The Dutch stole Manhattan for a handful of beads. In California the

Franciscan mission system disguised their exploitation with religious paternalism. And the Russians used their superiority in arms to suppress fierce resistance by the Aleut, Inuit, and Tlingit peoples, reaching as far south as Fort Ross near Bodega Bay in California to advance their fur trade.

The Dutch left first, when England took over New Amsterdam in the 1660s. The Russians left last, growing tired of Tlingit attacks and a declining fur market and finally selling Alaska to the United States in 1867. The French stayed until 1803, but then gave up the attempt to expand their foothold in Baton Rouge and New Orleans at the mouth of the Mississippi. Shortly before their control ended, the Bourbon elite got a boost from planters escaping the slave revolution in Haiti. Besides their cultural influence on language, food, and architecture, the French left behind a significant Creole class of land (and slave) owners and merchants – considered black by the U.S. system of color-coding. The French also left the South's largest slave market in New Orleans. Over the following decades, Africans illegally shipped through Cuba and Mexico passed through the New Orleans market to the booming cotton and sugar cane plantations in nearby states. New Orleans was also the destination for the legal coastal transport of young people born and raised in Virginia or Maryland and then sold away from their families to labor in the Deep South.

Spain and the Southwest

Aside from England, Spain had the largest impact – though mostly indirect – on the character of white supremacy in the United States. First, there was the slave labor itself, as well as the slave trade to the American colonies. The Spanish were there at the start, in 1518, when they first imported slaves to work the fields in Hispaniola. And they were there at the end, keeping Cuba's slave-killing sugar fields running as an enticement to illegal traders into the mid-1800s. The *Asiento*, the centerpiece of the trade for two hundred and fifty years, regulated the supply of slaves specifically to the Spanish colonies.

Second, there was the relative openness of the Spanish to racial intermingling and their higher rate of freeing slaves. The term *relative* here is in reference to the English. It does not deny the Spaniards' exquisite sense of color gradations, their greed, or their inhumanity toward their fellow humans. One can say that the English – and later the white men of the United States – "intermingled" too. Only the laws in the English colonies made clear that children of slaves were slaves regardless of who the father was. And the laws also discouraged the freeing of slaves. The difference in the Spanish and English influences is clear today in the white culture of the United States and what came to be the *mestizo* culture of Latin America.

Those who accompanied Juan de Oñate in 1598 in the founding of New Mexico were of varied backgrounds and colors.[4] The majority were native people, as was the case overwhelmingly in the whole of Mexico. The Spanish who came to Mexico were roughly the same in number as the slaves kidnapped and imported from Africa. Some of the *conquistadors* were of African origin as well – the result of the pre-Columbian history of slavery in Spain.

A third difference separating the Spanish from the English – and especially from white North Americans – was their attitude toward native laborers. The labor system imposed on New Mexico by Oñate was the same as the one further south at Tenochtitlán, the center of the conquered Aztec empire. The Spanish *repartimiento* system – where villages provided workers for the Spanish mines and fields – was a forced labor system, and it was harshly enforced. But at least there was a place for the native peoples in the Spaniards' worldview. For the English the native people were best when they were out of sight – pushed out beyond the borders of their colonies. Once the United States had a free hand, the white ruling class, the miners, the homesteaders, and the military simply wanted the indigenous people gone – for good. This genocidal mindset became overwhelming and played itself out most clearly in California.

The somewhat more benevolent picture of the Spanish needs to be qualified by the horrors visited on the native peoples under their control during the 1500s. The peaceful Arawak peoples of the northern Caribbean islands were maimed, murdered and driven to extinction – through disease, suicide, and women's refusal to bear children. Then after burning at the stake the Mayan and Inca leaders of Central and South America, tens of thousands of common people found themselves rounded up and sent to slavery and death in the silver mines of Perú. This dreadful carnage finally led the Dominican priest Bartolomé de las Casas – a former Indian fighter and slave-owner himself – to agitate for an end to the enslavement of indigenous peoples in the American colonies. Reflecting the mindset of the times, however, Las Casas initially recommended that African people be used in their place. His campaign to abolish Indian slavery achieved formal success in 1542. But under various guises the impressment of native people into the mines and fields continued for almost 300 years – often under the watchful eye of the church.[5]

Spanish missionaries and soldiers moved into Upper California – now part of the United States – beginning in 1763, rather late in colonial history. Over the next fifty years, they set up a series of missions stretching from San Diego to the Bay Area, with the administrative center in Carmel.[6] Junípero Serra, the Franciscan monk who led the colonizing venture, is currently a candidate for sainthood in the Catholic Church. His defenders point to the protection of the Indian workforce from the *presidio* soldiers and settlers who lived near the missions. Serra was deeply religious, whipped himself and otherwise mortified his flesh, and was relentless in his efforts to convert the native populations. At the same time, he enticed people into signing a statement declaring their Christian beliefs – a statement written in a strange language and marked by people who had no writing in their own culture. Once converted in this way, there was no turning back. If people tried to flee – back to their people or to the freedom of the forest and their traditional ways – colonial troops would track down the run-aways and return them to the mission. There priests and armed guards compelled the native people to give up their language, rise early for prayer services, and spend their days laboring on the mission farms.

The harshness of mission life shows up in declining birth rates and the early deaths of women. By 1830 the sex ratio with men was down to 42%. Young women lived in locked dormitories, and they could only escape through marriage after becoming adults at age 12. Once married, divorce was forbidden. Armed guards watched over all aspects of mission life. The contrast with native cultures was total: California Indians did not resort to physical punishment and seldom even raised their

Pueblo Uprising against the Spanish in New Mexico, 1680

In 1607, the Franciscans succeeded in forcing [Juan de] Oñate's resignation [because of his cruelty and exploitation of the indigenous peoples]. Spanish commitment to New Mexico again wavered: the colony was troublesome, unproductive, and separated from the major centers of New Spain by a large unconquered territory where supply convoys and reinforcements were preyed on by bands of Native Americans. In 1609, however, under Franciscan pressure, the Crown agreed to retain the area as a field for missionary activity....For the next seventy years, cut off from developments elsewhere in North America, the Franciscans were to dominate and reshape the Pueblo world.

The friars' assault on native culture, and particularly the merciless beatings they administered to offenders, left a legacy of bitterness and resentment. When the Church accused settlers of corruption and of exploiting Indians economically and sexually, the colonists riposted that the missionaries' excessively harsh treatment of dissenters risked provoking a full-scale rebellion against Spanish rule.

They were right. In 1680, exacerbated by a long period of drought and an increase in raids by Apaches, the tensions in the Pueblo world erupted in violence. The last straw was the trial for "sorcery" of forty-seven pueblo people, four of whom were sentenced to death and the rest to imprisonment or lashing. Led by one of the men who had been whipped, Popé, the outraged Indians turned on the friars – who, by some accounts, were given the choice of leaving peacefully – and killed twenty-one of them. Then, in a

voices with children.

In time, retired Spanish soldiers received land grants and the mission labor system served as a model for working their lands. The presidio soldiers commandeered non-Christian Indians to grow crops and provide personal services to the officers. The Franciscan friars, in their self-identified role as protectors of the native peoples, objected to the land seizures and the forced labor in the forts and on private farms. In theory, once the native Christian workers were prepared to farm and live on their own, the mission land was to be turned over to them. Spain actually passed a law in 1787 that required self-rule by the mission Indians. The self-serving paternalism of the friars, however, got in the way of this transfer of power. Meanwhile private landholding grew and the ties with Spain weakened – especially during the Mexican independence struggle beginning in 1810 – and the missions and the surrounding estates became more commercially oriented. New settlements increasingly had difficulty finding converts, so raiding parties replaced baptism as a way to meet the demand for labor.

Mexico won independence in 1821 and made Indians citizens, giving

well-planned campaign, they stole or killed the horses and mules that were the conquerors' "principal nerve of warfare," and finally, after destroying most of the outlying Spanish settlements one by one, they surrounded Santa Fe.

Unlike the Indians in King Philip's War, who, almost at the same moment, were desperately trying to expel the English from New England, Popé and his Pueblo and Apache followers still massively outnumbered their European enemies. At the time of the revolt, there were fewer than 2,500 people living in Spanish households in the whole of New Mexico, most of them servants or slaves, and only around 170 colonists who were capable of bearing arms. Against them were ranged some 8,000 Native American troops. As they tightened their hold on the "kingdom's" capital by cutting off the water supply, the Indians were heard to exult, in words echoing the missionaries' jibes against their own deities: "Now the God of the Spaniards, who was their father, is dead, and Santa Maria who was their mother, and the saints...were pieces of rotten wood."

After nine days, the Spanish survivors used their superior firepower to break out of Santa Fe and escape south towards Mexico. On the way, they found not only bodies, but in the smoking ruins of churches, a mirror image of the desecrated *kivas* [Pueblo holy places]: statues smeared with excrement, chalices thrown into a basket of manure, a crucifix stripped of paint by a whip. And – a bizarre glimpse of how Christian symbolism had entered the Pueblo psyche – lying at the feet of the martyred Fray Pedro De Avila y Ayala, three lambs with their throats cut.

—from: Wilson, The Earth Shall Weep

them the right to vote and hold office. But the Mexican policy of encouraging colonization through land grants meant that expropriation and exploitation of native labor actually increased in the decades leading up to the 1846-1848 Mexican-American War. In 1833 the Mexican government secularized the mission system, emancipated the Indian laborers, and directed that half the land and farm implements be turned over to them. The other half went to local administrators, who were also given the right to use forced indigenous labor to work their land. In this situation, most of the native people who escaped working the officials' estates ran away. The various mission industries – producing soap, shoes, saddles, and wines – disappeared, and with them went the skilled trades of the missioners.

Anglos from the United States began colonizing California during this period of Mexican rule. In Texas, the pressure to expand the slave system led to large-scale homesteading, a war for Texas independence in 1836, and eventually the U.S. war to annex all of northern Mexico. When Mexico abolished slavery in 1830, Mexican territory became a haven for run-away slaves, just as Florida under Spanish rule had been up to 1818. The Seminole Wars in Florida were wars to secure and expand the slave system. In Texas, "Remember the Alamo" drew attention away from the deeper message: "Remember the white man's right to hold slaves."

The annexation of the northern half of Mexico in 1848, followed by the gold rush to California in 1849, added a new shade to the white race: not-Mexican, not Spanish-speaking, not-brown. The hard-edged racism of this new wave of colonizers targeted the native peoples for extinction and the *mestizo* Mexicans for expropriation through legalized theft. African slavery never existed in California; and after much debate in Washington centered on the extension of the slave system, California entered the union in 1850 as a free state. Nonetheless, genocidal attacks on Indians took on a ferocity that surpassed anything to the east. After all, there was now no place for the Indians to flee to. And for the Anglo settlers and fortune hunters, there was no place for Indians in their society either. While a few landowners opted to continue the forced labor system of earlier years, the state legislature, reimbursed by the federal government, paid the expenses of white raiding parties that destroyed Indian villages, murdering thousands.

As for Mexican landowners from San Francisco to Texas, the new capitalist legal and commercial banking system, focused on investment and growth, worked against the *hacendados* and their more relaxed approach to production for use. Whether defrauded by lawyers, expropriated by debt-collecting bankers, taken over through intermarriage, or violently moved on by Anglo posses, Mexican land holdings passed almost entirely to a new white ruling class in the Southwest in the 60 years to 1910. Though legally assured "all the rights of citizens" – and thereby, by implication, included as white people – by the Treaty of Guadalupe-Hidalgo in 1848,* Mexican inhabitants of the annexed region found themselves reduced to social conditions similar to those of black people in other parts of the country.

Asians and Pacific Islanders

The final color in the rainbow of non-whiteness came from Asian newcomers to the West Coast beginning in the gold rush years. First came the Chinese, followed in later years by Japanese and Filipino immigrants. While initially tolerated in the mining towns, Chinese became the target of white fortune hunters who grew frustrated with the returns on marginal sites.[7] The earliest law targeting Chinese, passed in 1854, classified Chinese with Indians and ruled out both citizenship and their right to testify in court. Anti-miscegenation laws, prohibiting mixed race marriages, and the restriction of immigration to males only followed later. In California the Workingman's Party headed the fight for Chinese exclusion. And as anti-"coolie" sentiment spread across the country, the campaign led to passage of the federal Chinese Exclusion Act in 1882.† Then over the next 40 years anti-Asian movements targeted Japanese, Filipino, Korean, and South Asian labor – and succeeded, for example, in banning mixed marriages with Japanese in 1906, as well as limiting their immigration.[8]

The period at the turn of the 20th century saw the closing of the frontier at the same time that Jim Crow segregation took hold throughout the

---

* Article IX of the Treaty of Guadalupe-Hidalgo guaranteed the annexed inhabitants "the enjoyment of all the rights of citizens of the United States according to the principles of the Constitution" – thereby signaling that this new population conformed with the Naturalization Act of 1790, which held that "any alien, being a free white person" could become a citizen. Once the Johnson-Reed Immigration Act of 1924 tightened requirements, however, the 1930 Census identified Mexican Americans as a non-white race. After protests, officials changed the wording; and the 1940 census began the practice of dividing Mexican Americans by color, separating out Mexican Indians and Mexicans of African descent as non-white. In 1970 the "ethnic" category *Hispanic,* together with specific countries of origin, appeared for the first time – being tested on just 5% of the questionnaires that year. *(Acuña,* Occupied America, *p. 54; Allen,* The Invention of the White Race, Vol. 1, *p. 185; Allen, "'Race' and 'Ethnicity'"; U.S. Census Bureau, "The Hispanic Population")*

† The Chinese Exclusion Act of 1882 banned entry into the United States by Chinese contract laborers. In 1888 the law expanded to include "all persons of the Chinese race" – but allowing temporary admission for people in government, professional, and business occupations. Congress renewed the act in 1892 – and then again in 1902 for an indefinite period. Chinese people, only .002% of the U.S. population in 1880, dropped "from 105,465 in 1890...to 61,639 in 1920." In 1943 under pressure from the war with Japan, Congress repealed the act – but in doing so allowed just 105 people to enter each year. Only with the Immigration Act of 1965 did the barriers truly come down – permitting 20,000 immigrants per year from each Asian country, and exempting family members from the count. *(Takaki,* Strangers from a Different Shore, *quotes on pp. 111-112)*

country. California was the leading example of a white ruling and laboring class front arrayed against native peoples, Mexicans, Asian immigrants, and the freedmen and descendants of slaves who ventured that far west. Whiteness here carried with it many shades of excluded color.

This fully developed white supremacist outlook accompanied the U.S. push beyond its shores in the 1890s. Hawai'i, strongly influenced by U.S. sugar and pineapple interests, became an outright colony in 1898. A cabal of Americans, Britons, and Germans had moved against the nationalist-minded Queen Liliuokalani in 1893, forming a "republic" similar to Texas before being annexed. Puerto Rico, the Philippines, and Guam followed after the Spanish-American war and the bloody 3-year suppression of the Filipino resistance struggle. The United States gained an outpost in Panama with the construction of the canal (1904–1914) using mostly black West Indian workers; sent troops to occupy Haiti (1915–1934) and Nicaragua (1926–1933); and intervened in Cuba, Honduras and Guatemala. As the Klu Klux Klan was reborn, Woodrow Wilson preached the gospel of "self-determination" – for white, European countries only. White supremacy stood at the pinnacle – and in opposition to all the colored peoples of the world. White privileges had become the privileges of empire.

Overview

The white race emerged out of the dynamics of social control in Virginia around 1700. All white people came to have rights that no black person could share. Even at this point whiteness had an anti-Indian aspect: in return for their access to land, white farmers on the outskirts of the colonies served as a buffer against nearby indigenous peoples. White people paid for their privileges with insecurity and sometimes with their lives. But there was no clear white-red color line at this time, since friendly nations also served as buffers for the colonies.

In the 1800s the Indian Wars and the officially sanctioned movement of land grabbers into Florida and Texas helped keep land central to white privilege. The Homestead Act of 1862 opened western territories to settlement by white people at almost the exact time former slaves were first given arms and admitted into the Union army. Later, white farmers in the South began to feel their privileges slip as black people gained limited access to land, which they worked mainly as sharecroppers. Taking advantage of this situation, factory owners set up the textile industry in the South and made a conscious decision to hire white people only – while keeping wages at a subsistence level. Also, the trade unions of the period excluded black craftsmen. So while the content of the privileges changed, the reality of white workers' complicity in systematic racial oppression continued.

California's experience makes the same point. Black people were a very small percentage of the state's population until a wave of migration in the 1930s. Nonetheless, white racism was virulent, targeting Indians, Chinese, and Mexicans. White privileges centered on land, preferential treatment by the courts and bankers, and access to jobs. As in the South, white men also had privileged access to women of color.

Across the country, the white race – the multi-class front of white people united against peoples of color – served as the guarantor of the U.S. brand of capitalism. Racial privileges were essential to keeping this front together – through the ravages of economic depression, monopoly pricing, and financial expropriation. By the late 1800s the Robber Barons ruled – and stole from everyone. Meanwhile most ordinary white folks, even as they fought the monopolists through the 1880s and '90s, never let go their belief that the hardships and insecurity they faced were in part due to workers of color.

Chapter 3

Images of Whiteness

Up to this point we have looked at how the white race came into existence and the ways white privileges gained new meaning as the United States grew, enveloping different communities of color in the process. Now we shift to the ideas in white peoples minds – the systems of thought or ideology – that have helped sustain white supremacy for so long. To understand what the white race is, one must grasp not only its material reality, but also the ways people process that reality in their minds.

This world of ideas – as reflected in conversation, letters, the press and culture generally – both reflects and distorts what is going on in the social system. It serves to justify the way life is and make the inhumanity around us seem both natural – as if ordained by God – and unchallengeable.* This ideological side of white supremacy reinforces the system of inequality and lets the hard-edged enforcement powers of the state move more to the background. It is certainly true that the courts, the police, and the prison system play a huge role in maintaining white supremacy – as does the U.S. military on a world scale. But the complicity of the majority of white people in this system of oppression requires that they feel good about themselves. The constant use of force can disrupt the appearance of naturalness that keeps the system running smoothly.

We will look briefly at three periods of U.S. history to highlight the role of ideology in the social construction of the white race. Much impor-

---

* The Italian political theorist Antonio Gramsci called this ideological form of domination *hegemony*, and identified it as key to understanding how a numerically small owning class can rule over a much larger subject population.

tant work has been done in this area over the past decade and more. We will be able to touch here on only a few of the themes that writers like Alexander Saxton, David Roediger, Michael Omi and Howard Winant, and Ruth Frankenberg have developed.[1] We encourage readers to consult these authors for a full treatment of the subject.

The 1700s

In colonial times the tools available for shaping people's ideas were limited. Community assemblies, the laws and courts, the church, and the press informed public discourse. Nonetheless, the ruling elite was able to unfold a massive campaign of disinformation to confuse and reorient people's thinking about skin color. Local vigilante groups then reinforced the racist message. It was white men, and propertied ones at that, who spoke at public meetings and proclaimed the laws that forced the separation of white and black working people. Preachers read the laws aloud from the pulpit on Sundays. The press publicized the laws and ran ads for the return of runaway slaves. As Lerone Bennett, Jr. notes, official documents referred to people who were not white with terms like "abominable mixture," "barbarous," and "savage."[2] Church leaders preached slavery, some bought and sold slaves, and sermons identified "black people with Ham* and Indians with the devil."[3]

As the plantation system developed, the images of what it meant to be a man or woman took shape in relation to race. The white patriarch embodied whiteness as a paternal figure, wielding power over his wife, children and slaves. The white mistress, presumed to be pious and pure, led a life separate from any kind of labor, aside from bearing the next generation of slave owners. Black women personified sexuality and lust – and felt the mistress's jealous anger – except when patronized as dutiful servants, tending to household chores and caring for white children. From early on, black women's images served the warped needs of the plantation culture – either justifying the attacks of white men, or comforting the fears that come from forcing oppressed people to wait on you in the most personal ways. Meanwhile, black men lacked the most basic English right of coverture afforded even the poorest white man – the right to marry, to protect his wife and family, and to be "lord of his manor," even if it was no more than a shack. The planter's aura of patriarchal manhood caused a deep sense of inferiority in laboring class white men, feeding their anger and eagerness to strike out – at black people or Indians, at their wives and each other. Whiteness came at the expense of almost everyone in the community – black men and women in the first

* Ham, a son of Noah, was said to have been cursed by his father with black skin and to be a "servant of servants," thereby justifying slavery – although this association of blackness with Noah's curse appears nowhere in the Bible.

place, but with white women of all classes held in their own subject places as well. Meanwhile poor white men fed their own hard-edged racism and image of self-worth by working as overseers on the plantations and taking part in slave patrols and in the Indian-fighting militias.

Later during the Revolutionary War period, public discourse centered on the demand for "freedom and equality." These words, spoken by and for propertied white men in relation to the English, resonated with broad sectors of the people. Many poor white men interpreted them as an invitation to move westward onto Indian lands. By contrast, Abigail Adams, the wife of the second president of the United States, asked that the laws of the new country "not put such unlimited power into the hands of the husbands. Remember, all men would be tyrants if they could."[4] And Benjamin Banneker – the self-taught inventor, scientist, and astronomer – spoke out against the hypocrisy of revolutionary leaders who proclaimed the "Self-Evident" truth "that all men are created equal," while "detaining by fraud and violence so numerous a part of my brethren under groaning captivity and cruel oppression, that you should at the same time be found guilty of that most criminal act, which you professedly detested in others, with respect to yourselves."[5]

During this period in both Virginia and the Northern states, popular opinion moved in the direction of ending slavery. A wave of Christian evangelism also helped contribute to a sense of common humanity. Vermont abolished slavery in 1777 and Massachusetts followed in 1781. By 1804 other Northern states had all provided for children of slaves to be free once they reached the age of 28.

In the Upper South during a brief opening until 1800, owners had the opportunity to legally free their slaves. Many did so, particularly in parts of Maryland and Delaware where "three-quarters of all blacks were free by 1810."[6] Also, in 1785 Thomas Jefferson offered a bill in the Virginia House of Delegates to gradually abolish slavery in the state – but it was defeated. The great mass of slaves throughout the South remained in bondage. Then Gabriel's Rebellion in Richmond, Virginia, in 1800 – drawing inspiration from both the U.S. Revolutionary War and Haiti's current struggle for independence – sent shock waves throughout the South. Free black people now had to leave Virginia within six months or risk re-enslavement. Over the following decades as white public opinion turned strongly pro-slavery, Jefferson retreated from his public opposition to the system. By the time of his death in 1826 he had freed only 2% of his slaves – all members of his common law wife's family, the Hemings.

The U.S. Constitution adopted in 1787 foreshadowed this shift in public opinion. A conservative, compromise document, the Constitution actually confirmed the dominant power of the slaveholders. The Constitution's infamous "three-fifths of a man" provision gave Southern politicians control over federal politics for 70 years. The slave trade received a two-decade grace period before being made illegal in 1807. These years saw the South import more slaves from Africa than during any other two decades in history. During this same period the invention of the cotton gin dramatically cut the processing costs of cotton farming – and made cotton "King." With it came a resurgence and redefinition of the white race.

The pre-Civil War period

In the North a white sector of the working class began to take shape as industry started to grow in the 1820s.[7] Previously the urban workforce had primarily been artisan workshop owners and their apprentices. In the late 1820s and 1830s, however, this developing sector began producing its own "penny" newspapers, as well as theater and blackface minstrel shows. James Fenimore Cooper's books promoted the image of the rugged woodsman and Indian fighter – at once independent yet deferential to upper class figures. Davey Crockett fit this same mold of a "Western Hero" – fighting Indians and clearing the frontier, while at the same time serving as a promotional icon of elitist Whig book publishers. The dominant figure of the age, however, was President Andrew Jackson, who made his name by massacring indigenous peoples throughout the Southeast. Jackson and his Democratic Party, popularly known as The Democracy, represented both the rabid hatred of native peoples and a white populist, grassroots democratic ideology aligned with the Southern slaveholders.

The Jacksonian movement dominated politics in the decades before the Civil War. It projected both *egalitarianism* – for white people – and *republicanism* – in the sense of being an expression of white popular power. In this view, everyone who counted within the United States was a *producer* – a category that included farmers, workers, and capitalists. Male workers tended to see their employment by a capitalist as transitional – until they could buy some land and become financially independent. And women workers did factory work only until they could find a husband. In neither case did the culture support a sense of class – especially one that included slaves, free black people, and women as full members of the working class.

This producer-oriented republicanism brought with it a built-in tendency toward racism and male supremacy. Anyone not independently productive in a capitalist sense – be they native peoples, slaves, marginalized free black people, or dependent women – automatically deserved their inferior status. In addition, the white republicanism considered marginal sectors susceptible to manipulation by the aristocratic, moneyed elite – represented politically by the Whig party. The Constitution provided support for this view by giving Southern landowners additional voting power based on the three-fifths count of their slaves.

The program of the Jacksonian White Republic gave all white men, regardless of property ownership, the right to vote – and at the same time moved systematically to deprive free black people of their voting rights. Connecticut took action in 1818. New York imposed a property requirement that excluded nine out of ten potential black voters in 1821. In subsequent years North Carolina, Tennessee, and all the Northwest states of that time except Wisconsin denied black people the suffrage. As more white laboring class people gained the vote, the slave owners found themselves compelled to shift from their earlier unity with the elitist Northern Whigs to supporting the Democrats. In return, The Democracy – both North and South – became a firm advocate for the slave system. It promoted war with Mexico in order to expand the slave territory, and opposed both protective tariffs, which tended to limit agricultural markets abroad, and corporate access to land.

The Democracy embraced all European immigrants, recognizing them to be white people even when discriminated against. The press pictured the Irish, the largest immigrant group in the pre-Civil War period, as lazy drunkards – comparing them, sometimes unfavorably, with black people. At times in the South, Irish work gangs labored on jobs considered too dangerous for the monetarily more highly valued slaves. But there were two things Irish workers had, or could get, that set them apart from free black people: citizenship and ready access to jobs. The Naturalization Law of 1790 explicitly restricted citizenship and the vote to white men. As to jobs, most Irish people coming to the United States were destitute. They were willing to take any kind of work, often at lower wages than the current standard. As a result, Irish workers displaced free black workers from household service and from the most menial laboring positions.

Even though the Irish people brought with them a centuries-old history of racial oppression in religious form, they tended to adapt to white cultural pressures and privileges and fought any identification with the darker races. Irish voters became the social base of the Democratic Party in New York City – where the Catholic Church and trade unions lined up with pro-slavery financial and shipping interests to oppose abolitionism. In later decades, Irish workers in San Francisco helped drive the Chinese out of urban manufacturing jobs.

The underside of white republicanism also showed itself in the movement of working class white people in and out of roles identified with people of color. The harsh discipline of factory life was new for many, since most workers came from local farms or straight from the rural districts of Ireland. One way to relieve the class tension at the workplace was to take on either the carefree attitude popularly associated with black people, or the wild and independent aura of the native peoples. Street gangs put on blackface both as a disguise and as a way to free themselves temporarily from social restraints – in order to go out and attack the black sections of town. Such rioting might start out as a protest against a bank or other ruling class target – but then the mob would find it easier to vent their anger on black people.

The upsurge of racial violence in the 1830s came as public authorities moved to officially discourage association between black and white people. In the early 1800s "Negro Election Day"* festivities were often multiracial. Now these gatherings were shut down. Police raided entertainment places in working class neighborhoods where black and white people socialized together. Instead of a limited but direct human contact between the races, blackface street gangs and minstrel shows took center stage.

The mild anti-elitism of minstrel humor safely disguised and defused class antagonisms. Over the course of its half-century of existence into the 1890s, minstrel shows defended the staid, quiet ways of the storybook Old South – in contrast to the constant movement and insecurity of white workers' lives. This pattern held true before, during and after the Civil War – although appropriate pro-Union phrases were added as a cover during the war. The wildly popular minstrel shows targeted all people of color for ridicule – African, Chinese, native peoples and Mexicans – thereby reinforcing white workers' feeling of superiority despite the hard conditions of their lives.

During the 1850s the white republicanism of the Jackson era shifted among some workers to a "free white labor" outlook, opposed to the extension of slavery. While remaining firmly anti-black – Oregon's constitution, for example, excluded all black people from the state – the goal of limiting competition from slavery stood in contradiction to the plantation system. Sections of working class white people, including women textile workers, broke from the Democratic Party in the 1850s and backed the new, free-soil oriented Republican Party. During the Civil War and its aftermath, a few Radical Republican voices pushed free white labor advocates to become genuinely egalitarian. They called for full social equality for freedmen based on land ownership – advancing a demand for "40 acres and a mule." Unfortunately, the material reality, habits, and

---

* "From about 1750 to 1850, long before [winning] the right to vote under the U.S. Constitution, African Americans living in such New England communities as New Haven, Boston, Newport and Portsmouth held their own elections to choose regional black kings, governors or sheriffs. ...Originally, Black Election Day coincided with colonial elections. African Americans were released from work for the voting and victory celebrations, which included food, singing, dancing and games. Those elected held lifelong ceremonial titles and exercised some judicial power as well." *(Yale Bulletin, "The historic tradition of "Black Election Day")*

mindset of white privilege sustained the working class base of white supremacy through this period – despite the revolutionary challenge to people's thinking. W. E. B. DuBois's later commented: "The...emotional and intellectual rebound of the nation made it nearly inconceivable in 1876 that ten years earlier most men had believed in human equality."[8]

Looking ahead

During the 1700s and pre-Civil War periods, people's images of the white race shifted in response to social struggle and changing material conditions. In the 1700s, the challenge to the thought patterns of white supremacy came in the form of the Revolutionary War and its ideology promoting freedom and equality. In the 1800s, it arose from the demand for free soil and opposition to the power of the planter class.

After the Civil War, as we will discuss at more length in Chapter 9, both white privilege and the exclusionary perspective of free white labor found a home in trade unions organized on a craft basis. Public discourse in this period included a verbal commitment to political equality and civil rights, as a legacy of the Civil War. It was harder to be outright triumphalist about white supremacy after so much blood had been spilt. Instead, the actual practice of exclusion tended to be hidden behind commitments to "organizing all workers" and "separate but equal." Meanwhile lynch mobs and rioting enforced real life inequality across the country. In time the old triumphalism returned. John Brown went from being the hero and martyr of the pre-Civil War Harper's Ferry raid to being pictured in textbooks as a deranged old man. Then President Woodrow Wilson segregated all federal offices and commented favorably on *Birth of a Nation*, the 1915 movie extolling the virtues of the terrorist Klu Klux Klan.

As Karl Marx and Fredrick Engels, the European social critics of the Civil War era, noted, "The ruling ideas of each age have ever been the ideas of its ruling class."[9] But these ideas – among which are the images people use to comprehend race – can be challenged. The 1960s provides a third such example in the shaping and reshaping of the white race.

The 1960s peoples' movements

From President Wilson's time through the 1950s, whiteness came packaged as inclusively multi-ethnic – a "nation of (white) immigrants." Black people, native peoples, Latinos, and Asians were all but invisible publicly. Movies featured an occasional black maid, Charlie Chan, Tonto, and now and then a Mexican bandit. Cub Scouts and Boy Scouts extolled "Indian ways" at the same time that they ignored the existence of real native peoples. At the same time, despite elements of discrimination directed against Southern and Eastern Europeans, and Jewish people, public discourse celebrated the diversity of immigrant America. During the

1950s TV portrayed white people as hard working and headed to the suburbs, like Ozzie and Harriet. Those workers stuck in city apartments, like Jackie Gleason's *The Honeymooners*, were aspiring but a little backward (Ralph), or just plain dumb (Norton). Women stayed at home, and could either be ditzy like Lucy, in *I Love Lucy*, or the center of domestic rationality, as with Alice in *The Honeymooners*. Wherever they were, white people were just normal folks. In fact, white people hardly even noticed they were white at all. That is what happens when everyone who is not white is made to disappear.

The social movements of the 1960s changed all that – not wholesale, but by appropriating existing imagery and expanding it to accommodate the new developments.[10] The upsurge forced open the concept of ethnicity to include black people and then other peoples of color. The Voting Rights and Civil Rights Acts of the mid-1960s provided a measure of formal equality, while cultural images changed dramatically and with lasting effect. These conditions compelled white people to begin seeing themselves as part of a multiracial society. And the Vietnam War brought home an awareness of people of color in other parts of the world. The common denominator underlying these dramatic changes was popular struggle – open resistance to the white supremacist power structure both at home and abroad.

The broader worldview coming out of the 1960s, along with the accompanying changes in the legal structure, were major accomplishments. But this new dominant understanding remained shallow – not really rooted in history. One day people of color were invisible; a short time later they were equal – at least in many white folks' minds. Looking backwards, it helps to remember that the Treaty of Guadalupe-Hidalgo formally included Mexican Americans as full citizens – and indirectly as white people – in 1848. But that did not keep Mexicans from losing their land or being denied access to parks and public accommodations. It did not keep Mexican children from being sent to segregated schools. And it did not protect people from degrading slurs or from being treated as second-class citizens in their own homeland. History shows that legal recognition alone does not count for much.

In the 1970s the corporations countered the 1960s upsurge with a media-driven backlash against the freedom movements. While social scientists counterposed a policy of "benign neglect" to affirmative action, big companies took steps to shift their industrial base to the non-union and politically backward Sunbelt states. Subjected to police repression and political cooptation, the peoples' movements faltered and public discourse shifted once again. Instead of a core of dynamic inclusiveness, what remained was a shell of formal equality. White folks could still feel comfortable believing that everyone was equal. But at the same time, in real life white people enjoyed their privileges – better jobs and more access to promotion, better housing, better schools and control of police departments. While affirmative action made some inroads into this pattern of privilege, the political reaction that fully took hold under Reagan in the 1980s worked to reverse the earlier gains.

People in the United States today are still living in this era of multicultural colorblindness. Lacking a sense of history, while at the same time claiming full equality for everyone, the dominant discourse shifts the blame for glaring inequalities onto those who are suffering from oppression. "Everyone is equal – so if you can't make it, it must be your fault." Pseudo-scientists back this perspective with bell-curve* statistics and theories of genetic determinism. And academics carry the argument worldwide by promoting and justifying the new "white man's burden" – a civilizing mission to bring U.S. style democracy, along with corporate domination, to the darker-skinned peoples of the world. White privilege continues, and with it – reflecting the vast inequalities of real world power politics – comes the conviction that the white race is the first among equals.

---

* *The Bell Curve*, published in 1994 by Richard Herrnstein and Charles Murray, uses faulty statistical reasoning to argue against affirmative action programs that aim to correct historic injustices.

Chapter 4

Beyond the White Race

We have looked at how the white race was created 300 years ago, and how real privileges along with shifting sets of ideas have helped keep the white race – and the underlying system of capitalism it supports – in place since then. This story not only describes an effective mechanism for ruling class domination, however. It also suggests ways that people can work to overcome racial privileges. Doing so requires that people eliminate both 1) the concrete reality of systemic inequality, and 2) the racial images – the racist ideology – that flows from and reinforces that reality.

First we want to set out some conclusions from the preceding chapters to help orient the discussion:

• ***Human beings created the white race as a means of social control.*** Whiteness is socially constructed, not biologically determined by white people's genes. In Chapter 1 we recounted the evidence linking the emergence of the white race to social processes – to solidarity and rebellion on the one side, and to the ruling class drive for social control and wealth accumulation on the other. This account is very different from the scientific racist viewpoint that dominated public opinion just a hundred years ago. Then, biological factors and "the survival of the fittest" were said to have resulted in the ascendance of the white race – both in the United States and, together with the European powers, across the globe. Proponents twisted the new science of genetics to make the hierarchy of races seem natural and permanent.

Science actually demonstrates that the opposite is the case.[1] Archeological and genetic records show that all humans (*Homo sapiens*) are related. We developed in Africa about 140,000 to 200,000 years ago; and all the peoples of the world have descended from groups who migrated out of Africa about 50,000 years ago. Skin color basically comes down to how far north or south of the equator your ancestors lived many thousands of years ago. For people living near the equator, the melanin in darker skin is protective against ultra-violet rays that destroy folates, essential for reproduction. For those living more north or south, there is a trade-off in benefits from Vitamin D production that led to people's color shading off into brown and then white.

What has actually been natural for humanity is for people to interact, to marry, and for their genetic markers to spread through neighboring populations. This pattern is true both for *Homo sapiens* and for our predecessors (*Homo erectus*) who spread across the globe almost two million years ago. It is rare for a human population to be totally isolated. And even in a situation like Australia, cut off by wide expanses of water since the last ice age, the number of generations without contact was but a blink of an eye in evolutionary time.

Two human beings are about 99.9% genetically the same – which makes sense given that humans and chimpanzees share about 98% of their genetic material. "The human genome comprises about 3 x 10^9 [3 billion] base pairs of DNA.... Between any two humans, the amount of genetic variation – biochemical individuality – is about 0.1 percent. This means that about one base pair out of every 1,000 will be different between any two individuals."[2] If we focus on just this .1% – the tiny amount that accounts for all human variation – about 85% of this variation shows up as differences within a given population. This figure means that people within a settled village or distinct national grouping vary much more among themselves than they do with other population groups. Another 9% of human variation is shared across populations that include more than one racial grouping. So that leaves only 6% of human variation – or less than .006% of human genetic material – to be connected in some way with race. These differences, which have evolved only in the last 50,000 years since our ancestors left Africa, include blood group markers, physical changes associated with temperature, altitude and diet, and protections against germs of various kinds. And even here, the differences overlap and blend into one another, as genes interact in complex ways with each other and with the environment. *The bottom line is that there is no clear genetic marker for race.*

Take blood types, for example. While there are different percentages of type A, B, and O – or Rh^+ and Rh^- – in different parts of the world, one can find each blood type in all regions. Looked at more generally, each population linked by skin color includes within it a great deal of variation from one individual to another. And all human populations share this complex variation in the ways genes manifest themselves. It takes many generations for genetic material to disappear in the process of natural selection and in the formation of new species. But it takes only a few individuals to (re)introduce genetic information into a population's gene pool. The molecular anthropologist Jonathan Marks comments:

> ...a global cataclysm that killed or sterilized every human being except the Uzbeks or the Dinka would still leave the vast majority of the major genetic variants of the species represented in the gene pool. This is true for Rh, for ABO, and for nearly all human genes...Racial variation has now been shown to be scientifically, mathematically trivial.[3]

• ***Since the white race was socially constructed, it can be socially deconstructed.*** Ordinary human beings put in place this social system based on skin color. It is reasonable to expect, therefore, that we can disassemble it as well.

• ***The content of whiteness in the United States has contributions from many sources*** – both European but, more importantly, from the suppression and denial of people of color in U.S. history, both past and present. Whiteness is defined by, and only has meaning in relation to, the negation and appropriation of the lives of people of color. A strategy for a thoroughgoing, revolutionary transformation of the social system requires an appreciation of the many histories of struggle against white supremacy – and identifying with them, making them our own.

• ***There is a material advantage to being white.*** These privileges are afforded in varying degrees to all members of the white race. Even the worst off white person has benefits – social and psychological – that come from being born white. The privileges are dispensed and enforced by the dominant social power, the ruling class beneficiaries of white supremacy. Once in place the structure tends to be self-reinforcing – until conditions change and the system is thrown into crisis. Such periods of struggle open the possibility for social transformation and movement toward ending all racial privileges.

• ***The images of whiteness – and their negative distortions of people of color – culturally reinforce the system of privilege.*** The broad social discourse around race that we all participate in has an independent dynamic. It can develop in all kinds of directions, based on the technology available, the skills and creativity of cultural workers, and the contested terrain of power relations. At the same time, discourse is linked in complex ways to the underlying material reality of privilege and domination – sometimes helping to clarify these relations, but more often obscuring them and making oppression by the ruling class more manageable.

• ***The white race came into being at a time when capitalism was taking root in North America.*** The emerging capitalist class made use of the white race to control the laboring people, and later to safeguard their seizure of land and resources from the native peoples, Mexicans, Puerto

Ricans, Hawai'ians, and others. There is a strategic link between the struggle against capitalism – for a society controlled by and centered on the needs of working people – and overcoming white supremacy.

• ***The construction of whiteness is closely linked to the images and privileges determined by a system of male domination.*** What it means, and has meant, to be a man or a woman in the United States has often been related to people's skin color – and vice versa. Being fully respectful of each other requires that people appreciate the particular ways men and women of different races have each lived their lives. Out of this wealth of individual experience, a movement for social justice can then develop a holistic understanding of the ways white supremacy impacts every person at a personal level.

• ***There have been times when white people have struggled alongside people of color.*** The joint resistance of laboring people in the 1600s was a natural human response to oppression in the absence of a color line. Examples of solidarity and joint sacrifice also occurred during the Revolutionary War and Civil War periods. In more recent times we can look to the civil rights and freedom movements of the 1960s.

• ***There is a huge human cost to the system of racial privileges.*** The clearest cost is in the mind-numbing record of subjugation of people of color – the millions of native peoples destroyed and the genocidal impact on their ways of life; the countless victims of the slave trade and the system of lifetime bondage based on race; the dispossession and degradation of Mexican Americans; the racial attacks, along with immigration and marriage restrictions directed at Asian immigrants; the unjustified imprisonment and dispossession of Japanese Americans during World War II; the unnatural isolation and exclusion of all peoples of color from the main currents of national life; the continuing crimes of poor education and health care, substandard housing, and disproportionate imprisonment. This history – truly an ocean of pain and suffering – has swallowed up untold years of human energy, beauty and creativity. At the same time, the majority of laboring class recipients of white privilege have led narrow, constricted lives; conspired in the soul-rotting subjugation of their brothers and sisters of color; and gratefully served the white supremacist ruling class, even as they were being bled dry. This vast tally, drawn from both sides of the color line, sums up the shameful, wretched, incalculable costs of white privilege.

It is past time that we move together to collect on this debt to our common humanity. In order to encourage such action, we list here some steps people can take to end white privilege, based on the bulleted points listed above. We include in parentheses the chapters where you can read more about each proposed step:

- ***Make an effort to understand the way the white race has been constructed.*** (Chapters 1-4, 10)
- ***Criticize all the ways that social discourse favors white people*** and distorts the lives of people of color. (Chapters 3, 16-17)
- ***Study the resistance to white supremacy by people of color,*** and understand this history in the context of the worldwide struggle for liberation. (Chapters 1-2, 5-8, 21-23)
- ***Study the links between the system of capitalism and white supremacy,*** and seek out ways to target both these mutually supporting systems. (Chapters 9-11, 23, 26)
- ***Grasp the connections between patriarchy and the fight against white privilege.*** Work to eliminate male privilege and the social discourse that maintains it. (Chapters 12-15, 23)
- ***Focus attention on the current structure of white privilege and the ways white supremacy divides people of color from one another.*** Work to overcome these divisions and promote the leadership of people of color in the struggle. (Chapter 16, 21-23, 25-26)
- ***Criticize the greed, shortsightedness and betrayal wrapped up in the sordid history of white privilege.*** Recall and learn from the examples of white people joining in the fight against white supremacy. (Chapters 1-3, 16-20)
- ***Work to turn the system of privilege around,*** **by** directing the resources of privilege to the struggle, linking up white people with the movements of people of color, and building a world without privileges one relationship at a time. (Chapters 24-27)

Tiger

The white man is a tiger at my throat,
Drinking my blood as my life ebbs away,
And muttering that his terrible striped coat
Is Freedom's and portends the Light of Day.
Oh white man, you may suck up all my blood
And throw my carcass into potter's field,
But never will I say with you that mud
Is bread for Negroes! Never will I yield.

Europe and Africa and Asia wait
The touted New Deal of the New World's hand!
New systems will be built on race and hate,
The Eagle and the Dollar will command.
Oh Lord! My body, and my heart too, break—
The tiger in his strength his thirst must slake!

—Claude McKay

II

RACE, NATIONS, AND EMPIRE

In the United States European Americans make up an informal white alliance that encompasses people from all social classes. A white, male, business-owning elite runs the country and exploits working people on both sides of the color line. At the same time, white workers possess material and psychological privileges that tend to keep them passive, vaguely uneasy, and generally unresponsive to the demands of people of color for justice.

The core problem in this racial struggle is white supremacy – historically rooted in the creation of the white race and white privileges some 300 years ago. Racial oppression occurs when all members of the dominant group have social and psychological advantages over everyone in the subject group. This definition clearly applied to the white race in relation to peoples of color in the United States at the close of the 19th Century. In the 1890s, for example, members of indigenous nations were murdered, robbed of their land, and treated as social oddities – regardless of people's standing in their own communities. In this same period, African Americans experienced segregation and disfranchisement – whether sharecropper, skilled worker, or college professor. Mexicans lost their land and social standing; Asians, their right to marry and raise a family. The poorest white people felt entitled to their privileges, while all people of color found themselves pushed to the margins of society.

W.E.B. DuBois wrote in 1903, "The problem of the twentieth century is the problem of the color-line."[1] As we will detail in Chapter 16, the color line is still with us, even though conditions have changed significantly in 100 years. Moreover, as the United States developed into a world power, the character of the struggle against white supremacy took on an added, national dimension. The domination of countries overseas had its counterpart at home. The United States invested its imperial expansion with white supremacy as it colonized Hawai'i, seized Puerto Rico, Guam, and the Philippines from Spain, and intervened in China and Central America. At home white supremacy joined with monopoly power to grind down peoples of color and, in response, generated freedom struggles centered on achieving political power and self-determination. This new character to the struggle, its national character, took shape in the run-up to World War I – at the same time that the United States joined the European powers in subjugating the less developed countries of the world. Decolonization movements later gained strength and won independence after World War II. Inside the United States national consciousness blossomed in the 1960s and '70s – in a climate of victorious liberation struggles in Africa (Algeria, Guinea-Bissau, Angola, and Mozambique), Latin America (Cuba), and Asia (China and Vietnam).

Chapter 5 highlights conditions inside the United States that accompanied its emergence as an economic and military world power. We center discussion on the Reconstruction period after the Civil War, roughly from 1865 to 1877. During this pivotal moment for democracy in the United States, black leadership in the South set in place a program that is progressive even by today's standards. Reactionary forces eventually subverted and crushed this social revolution. Then in subsequent years Reconstruction's defeat impacted all the subject peoples in the United States – through suppression of the indigenous peoples, expropriation of Mexican landowners, exclusion of Chinese immigrants, and the development of a nationwide system of segregation. While taking an immense human toll, this consolidation of white supremacist monopoly capitalism in time led to a new sense of peoplehood among the various oppressed peoples of color. Resistance never ceased, even in the worst of times. People fought back with strikes, emigration, community building, armed self-defense, cultural affirmation, political analysis, and organizations of all kinds.

Chapter 6 reviews the record of the United States as a new imperialist power – controlling subject nations both inside and outside the country. The right of oppressed nations to self-determination is the focus of Chapter 7. Here we examine the demand for self-determination in relation to 1) race-based struggles, 2) national minority demands for autonomy, and 3) the U.S. government's version of self-determination imposed on and resisted by the indigenous First Nations. We conclude this section in Chapter 8 by looking at the practical consequences of the analysis for organizing today – by placing the national movements in the context of the worldwide fight for global justice.

Chapter 5

Reconstruction

At the end of the Civil War, the United States began an unprecedented experiment in democracy. Policies during the Reconstruction period enfranchised former male slaves and lifted them to a position of economic and political power. The United States for the first time attempted to be true to documents like the Declaration of Independence and Bill of Rights. New guarantees took the form of the Thirteenth, Fourteenth and Fifteenth Amendments – abolishing slavery, enforcing equality before the law by the federal government, and prohibiting denial of the vote on racial grounds. At the same time, however, the word *male* made its entry into the Constitution for the first time, explicitly excluding women from the franchise. And while the Civil Rights Bill of 1875 banned discrimination in public accommodations, it lacked enforcement powers and by 1883 had been ruled unconstitutional.

Revolution and counter-revolution

During Reconstruction over 600 black men won elected office as Republicans – the "Party of Lincoln" – in the legislatures of the 11 former Confederate states.[1] Nineteen black men represented the South in the U.S. House of Representatives, including eight who served after Reconstruction's formal end in 1877. Two black senators, Hiram R. Revels and Blanche K. Bruce, represented Mississippi in the U.S. Senate. The era closed when Congressman George H. White from North Carolina completed his second and final term in 1901.

At the state level, 18 black men held leading positions in five states: South Carolina, Louisiana, Mississippi, Florida and Arkansas. P.B.S. Pinchback briefly served as governor of Mississippi; while other elected leaders held the posts of Lieutenant Governor (LA, MS, SC), Treasurer

(LA, SC), Superintendent of Education (AK, FL, LA, MS), and Secretary of State (FL, MS, SC). Often more important for grassroots people were the local positions filled throughout the South – such as sheriff, county supervisor, and tax collector.

This newly gained political power also enabled black people to leverage economic power as well. Republican legislatures passed laws making credit available to poor people. They passed measures that protected the rights of tenants, favored renters and sharecroppers, and shifted the tax burden to the wealthy. New possibilities in every area of economic life opened for Southern working people of all races.

Driven by the freedmen's desire for schooling, Reconstruction governments set up many of the first public education systems in the South. By 1870, 50% of white children and 40% of black children were in school. Half of the nine thousand teachers teaching in the region's 4,000 schools were black. More than 20 major black colleges were founded during this period, including Fisk (1866), Howard and Morehouse (1868), and Meharry (1876). Graduates from these schools helped fill the demand for black teachers and elected officials.

Republican Reconstruction governments were activist in outlook – taxing land and property, and implementing policies that addressed the needs of their impoverished constituencies. Eric Foner notes, "Public schools, hospitals, penitentiaries, and asylums for orphans and the insane were established for the first time or received increased funding. South Carolina funded medical care for poor citizens, and Alabama provided free legal counsel for indigent defendants...Nashville expanded its medical facilities and provided bread, soup, and firewood to the poor...Washington itself embarked on a public works program, including the laying of much-needed sewer lines."[2] These expenditures drew heated criticism from plantation owners, the Democratic Party, and racists across the country. What really stirred their anger was something very different, however. As Lerone Bennett, Jr., says, "The monstrous crime of Reconstruction was equality."[3]

Even after the bloody defeat of Reconstruction in the mid-1870s, both races could be found eating in the same restaurants and burying their loved ones in the same graveyards. While most classrooms remained segregated, Mississippi, Louisiana, and South Carolina passed laws creating interracial school systems, and New Orleans "witnessed an extraordinary experiment in interracial education."[4] It was only in 1881 that a Tennessee Jim Crow* railroad law began the policy of segregating public facilities. Then in 1890 Mississippi moved a step further by drawing

* The term *Jim Crow* originated in a 19th-century minstrel song stereotyping African Americans and over time came to represent government-sanctioned racial segregation in the United States.

up a new constitution that effectively barred black voters from the polls. In following years this Mississippi Plan became the model for all the Southern states.

Growth of black institutions

In just two years after the surrender of the Confederate Army in 1865, black civic and political organizations blossomed throughout the South – especially in the Black Belt region, the plantation low country known for its rich, dark soil. As Foner points out, under the protection of Northern occupying troops, many of whom were black, the newly liberated slaves created self-help organizations and schools, became active members of the Republican Party and Union Leagues, published newspapers and organized banks, established "burial societies, debating clubs, Masonic lodges, fire companies, drama societies, trade associations, temperance clubs, and equal rights leagues."[5]

As during slavery, black people also established their own churches – enriched by a musical and oral tradition going back to African origins. White churches refused to give up the markers of white privilege and physically segregated white and black worshippers. Black churches stood at the heart of community life and nurtured social, economic, and political leadership. Churches linked "blacks across lines of occupation, income, and prewar status...offered the better-off the opportunity for wholesome and respectable association, provided the poor with a modicum of economic insurance, and opened positions of community leadership to men of modest backgrounds."[6]

More than any other factor, the intractable nature of white supremacy maintained the solidarity of these new institutions through all their internal tensions. The recognition that black people would never be allowed an equal partnership with white people – even with white allies – helped advance the trend of Black Nationalism historically. National consciousness grew out of the lived experience of the black masses – people who were still partly African, but forged together by generations of toil into a new people, with a culture of resistance linked to the land of North America.

The early development of black civil society in the post-Civil War years was a heady and hopeful time. People demonstrated a sophisticated grasp of issues and organization – and asserted these abilities often in the face of furious and violent reaction. Then a counter-revolutionary alliance of nightriders, Democrats, preachers calling for Southern "Redemption," newspaper editors, New South businessmen, and white craft workers took shape. And remnants of the defeated planter elite never missed an opportunity to inflame and alarm whites of every class about the perils of what they called "Negro domination."

From Presidential to Congressional Reconstruction

After Lincoln's assassination in April, 1865, Andrew Johnson became president. Johnson represented the white mountain people of Eastern Tennessee who hated the planters' domination of the South. Yet as Johnson's example makes clear, the mountain folks' attitude toward black people was uneven, at best. During the two years that Johnson controlled post-war policy – the period of Presidential Reconstruction – the planters moved to retake power and establish the plantation system as before, but without calling it slavery. Confederate leaders resumed their positions in state governments, and state legislatures passed Black Codes – laws aimed at forcing people back into their former work roles.

In celebrating their newly won freedom, the freed slaves took to the road to reunite with family members, explore new possibilities, and simply to assert their right to move about. When at work, people would stop to attend political or community meetings. Women refused to return to the fields, devoting time to their children and to campaigning for public education. In these exhilarating times, the Black Codes attempted to turn back the clock. Vagrancy laws meant people could be picked up for no reason, put in jail, and then leased out to local planters to work the fields under guard. Southern society as a whole became the collective slave master. Armed vigilantes roamed the countryside enforcing the codes, and white rioters attacked black people in New Orleans and Memphis.

General William Tecumseh Sherman's Special Field Order No. 15 granted the liberated slaves of the South Carolina low country 40 acres and the loan of army mules to help with plowing. Also, the head of the Freedmen's Bureau, O.O. Howard, ordered 40-acre allotments to be set aside for distribution. But President Johnson rescinded both these measures in the summer of 1865 – as he moved to reinstate the property of the plantation owners. Johnson's goal during this period was to consolidate a coalition of Democrats in the North with white workers, small farmers, and a reined-in planter class in the South.

The Republican Party responded slowly to this threat. Reports from black people and their allies in the federally sponsored Freedmen's Bureaus, along with a spontaneous strike wave by Southern black labor in 1866-67, made clear that conciliation with the racists was not an option. Then when President Johnson vetoed the Civil Rights Act of 1866, the Republicans knew they had to take action. Led by the most principled anti-slavery advocates in Congress – Thaddeus Stevens, Charles Sumner, and other "Radical Republicans"* – the Congress quickly 1) overturned

* The Radicals were the wing of the Republican Party with roots in the abolitionist movement. Leaders in the Senate included Sumner, Benjamin Wade, and Henry Wilson; and in the House, Stevens, George Julian, and James Ashley. (*Foner,* Reconstruction) Radical Benjamin Wade: "The radical men are the men of principle: they are the men who feel

Johnson's veto, 2) passed the 14th Amendment penalizing the South if they did not extend the franchise to black people, 3) drew up a set of punitive laws that overturned the Black Codes and removed Confederate sympathizers from the state governments, and 4) impeached President Johnson. While Johnson retained his position by one vote in the Senate, this new program of Congressional Reconstruction in the spring of 1867 opened a period of truly revolutionary change in the South.

The dramatic shift in Reconstruction policy, however, also gave rise to a counter-offensive. Opponents moved quickly to organize the Klu Klux Klan, and cracks opened in the Republican front that eventually contributed to Reconstruction's defeat. Armed terror directed at black people had already taken a heavy toll since the close of the war. Then in April 1867 former Confederate officers and planters formally organized the KKK. Hooded nightriders targeted local black political leaders and their white Southern ("scalawag") and transplanted Northern ("carpetbagger") allies. For three years the Klan ran amok. White-led Republican governments in the South generally lacked the resolve to suppress the terrorists. In Texas and Arkansas, however, the governors declared martial law and relied on the state militia (Arkansas) and state police (Texas), both of which had large numbers of black ex-soldiers in their ranks. These forces broke up the armed gangs, made hundreds of arrests, tried and hung three leaders, and drove the stragglers across state lines. Finally, in 1870-71 the federal government passed the Enforcement and the Klu Klux Klan Acts. These laws empowered federal troops to intervene when state governments refused to take action. Committed Attorneys General, Amos T. Ackerman and George H. Williams, pursued the Klan, prosecuted its leaders, and sent federal troops into nine South Carolina counties – forcing thousands of racists to flee the state. Ackerman also carried out an educational campaign throughout the North that mobilized public opinion behind these actions.

The Republicans, however, did not fully unite behind this campaign to suppress the Klan. Some balked at the exercise of federal power. Others used the post-war climate of scandal-ridden business expansion to promote government by the "best men," in place of President Grant's Reconstruction agenda. The party began to fracture into *stalwarts*, aligned with President Grant and Republican machine politics, and *liberals*, promoting non-interference by the federal government and reliance on the elite to rule. Radical Republicans could be found in both camps – some alignments resulting from personal animosity directed at President Grant, particularly after his attempt to annex the Dominican Republic in 1871. The divisions among Republicans led to a Liberal Republican Con-

---

what they contend for. They are not your slippery politicians who can jigger this way or that, or construe a thing any way to suit the present occasion." (*Simkin, "Radical Republicans")*

vention in 1872 – and a subsequent alliance with Democrats to oppose Grant's reelection. Grant won by a large margin, and Reconstruction remained in place for four more years. But the Liberals singled out the Reconstruction governments of the South – and the strong role of black leadership there – for particularly vehement abuse.

Over time white paternalism toward the South's black people showed its true character. Northern capital gained control of the Republican Party's mix of Unionists, abolitionists, liberal elitists, utopian socialists, machine politicians, and free black people. Much like the Democratic Party of today – with its 1990s Welfare Reform and Effective Death Penalty laws – the Republican Party of the 1870s ratcheted to the right. While courting black voters, the party betrayed black interests when it came time to deliver on election promises. Meanwhile, the Democrats of the 1870s, after toying with more tolerant "New Departure" politics, fully committed themselves to open white supremacy. Echoes of this anti-federal government outlook have persisted in the South to this day in calls for "states' rights."

Counter-revolution and federal retreat

By the early 1870s, only South Carolina, Mississippi, Louisiana and Florida – states with majority or near-majority black populations – still retained Reconstruction governments. The planter controlled Democratic Party had successfully "redeemed" the others, beginning in 1867 with Maryland. Then in 1873 an economic depression hit the country, which pushed concern for the treatment of black people out of public consciousness. Charles Sumner on his deathbed made an appeal for the passage of the Civil Rights Act of 1875. A watered-down version became law – after dropping the section that desegregated the schools – but it was essentially an empty gesture. That same year Grant drew public condemnation for blocking the forced seating of Democratic legislators in Baton Rouge, Louisiana. Liberal, free-market oriented Republicans joined the Democrats in citing Louisiana as an example of excessive federal intervention in state affairs. This Republican backsliding undermined Grant's efforts to move against electoral violence and thereby safeguard black people's voting rights.

Then in the summer of 1876, Grant received news that the Oglala Sioux leader Crazy Horse had joined with the Cheyenne to defeat federal troops at the Battle of the Rosebud in Montana. Crazy Horse then linked his forces with the Hunkpapa Sioux chief, Sitting Bull, and on June 25th they trapped and destroyed General George Armstrong Custer's 7th Cavalry in the valley of the Little Big Horn. This indigenous threat, when combined with recession-driven worker unrest in the East, convinced the ruling class that Federal forces could no longer be spared for the increasingly ineffective occupation of the South.

Meanwhile, white vigilante violence had become commonplace in all the elections in the Reconstruction states. When combined with the planters' economic power over black voters, Democrats were able to take power state by state across the Deep South. By the time the Republicans agreed to the Hayes-Tilden Compromise in 1877, which kept the presidency in Republican hands, Reconstruction was essentially already dead. The Republicans simply formalized Reconstruction's end by pledging not to interfere with Democratic governments across the South. President Hayes withdrew the federal troops to their barracks – and later redeployed them against striking railroad workers in Pittsburgh and against the Nez Percé people resisting forced relocation in the Northwest.

President Grant later commented that he "found the events of 1877 'a little queer.' During his administration...the entire Democratic Party and the 'morbidly honest and "reformatory" portion of the Republican' had thought it 'horrible' to employ federal troops 'to protect the lives of Negroes. Now, however, there is no hesitation about exhausting the whole power of the government to suppress a strike on the slightest intimation that danger threatens.'"[7]

The struggle continues

Migration movements

While 1877 marked the close of Reconstruction, it by no means ended the self-organization and initiative of the African American people. In 1879 a mass movement out of the South drew on Biblical imagery of the Exodus to mobilize tens of thousands to flee economic hard times and political oppression.[8] Planters, in turn, mobilized vigilante squads to turn these "Exodusters" back from the Mississippi River. They bribed steamboat captains and threatened reprisals if crowds eager to emigrate gained passage. Plantation owners saw their labor force fleeing before their eyes and resolved to stop the exodus. But because of the hard economic times, poor white workers were not so inclined to terrorize black people into returning to a crowded labor market, and violence was limited.

Steven Hahn reports that the total number of black people who moved to Kansas was in the range of 20,000 to 25,000. Another thousand migrated from the upper South to Indiana – and then possibly on to other states. In subsequent years, with the breakup of Indian Territory in Oklahoma after the 1887 Dawes Act, those lands too became a destination. A black "town-building" movement established more than 20 communities in Oklahoma. And together with descendants of slaves owned by the territory's native peoples in pre-war times, the newcomers formed the social basis for the emergence of Tulsa's "Black Wall Street," destroyed by white rioters in 1921.*

Meanwhile, the white-led African Colonization Society received inquiries in waves, depending on social conditions, during each of the closing decades of the 19th Century. The number of actual emigrants tended to be in the hundreds during each peak period. But many others made plans to move to Africa, with organizing often centered on their church and its pastor. Emigration was a major undertaking, and expensive. The timing had to be right and the harvest and sales adequate to pay off debts, purchase tickets, and still have enough left to get to embarkation points in New Orleans, Charleston, Norfolk, or Baltimore. Then there were the costs of setting up once in Liberia. A developing sense of peoplehood and self-affirmation drove these emigration efforts. Hahn reports that "there is to be seen in the letters, petitions, and testimonies about emigration the articulation of a deep sense of identity among those who simultaneously shared African descent and suffered white oppression, of an incipient popular nationalism, and of a desire for social separatism."[9]

Post-Reconstruction alliances

Even in the difficult post-Reconstruction period, however, people seized on opportunities to advance issues of local concern to the black community. In the Deep South, for example, *fusion* politics aligned certain black politicians and their voting base with elements in the Democratic Party, thereby maintaining a measure of local political control within the overall white supremacist structure. A second type of alliance, linked with white agrarian insurgencies, aimed to reduce debts and provide easier access to credit. Independents and Greenbackers led such campaigns in Eastern Texas, Louisiana, Mississippi, and the northern counties of Georgia and Alabama. To appeal to black voters, these parties often called for increased school funding and an end to voter fraud.

Readjusters: In Virginia an alliance of black people in the east together with white mountain people in the west took control of the state government from 1879 to 1883. Once in power, the reformers reduced

---

* A false newspaper report on the rape of a white woman set off the worst race riot in U.S. history in the segregated Greenwood section of Tulsa Oklahoma on Monday, May 30, 1921. Rioters torched over a thousand homes and killed up to 300 people. The Tulsa Race Riot Commission set up in 1997 recommended that compensation be paid to survivors – as had happened in 1994 with survivors of the Rosewood, FL, massacre of 1923 – but the city and state failed to follow through. Four hundred plaintiffs, including 150 survivors, then filed suit in federal court in 2003 with the help of a team of lawyers led by Harvard Law Professor Charles Ogletree. On May 16, 2005, the Supreme Court rejected without comment an appeal of the lower court's ruling that a two-year statute of limitations could not be extended. *(Askia Muhammad,* Final Call, *June 1, 2005)*

the burden of bank debt, put money into education – a major demand of the movement's black constituency – and founded a black state college, the Virginia Normal and Collegiate Institute. Hahn reports that in the four years the Readjusters were in power, "black schools multiplied from 675 to 1,715, and the students enrolled increased from 35,768 to 90,948."[10]

Faced with these electoral gains, the Democratic Party responded with a racist campaign aimed at dividing the hill people from their black allies. The Readjusters failed to meet this challenge head-on and refused to put forward black candidates above the local level. Meanwhile, black people grew tired of providing the voting muscle for the alliance while seeing all the major positions going to white politicians. The result was a defeat for the Readjusters in 1883. Eastern Virginia pushed on, however, forming political clubs that included non-voting women, founding a newspaper, and building an electoral machine that in 1888 sent former slave and Union League organizer John Mercer Langston to Washington.

Knights of Labor: The Knights of Labor, which we will discuss in some detail in Chapter 9, organized Worker Assemblies and mounted bi-racial electoral campaigns that overlapped other insurgent movements of the period. The Knights actively organized black people – but in the South usually into segregated assemblies. Nonetheless, in 1886 the Knights held an integrated national convention in Richmond, Virginia – reflective of the interracial politics in the state during the 1880s. Black people also were active in the 1877 national railroad strike, and supported union organizing on the New Orleans waterfront, in coalmines, and in cotton and sugar cane fields across the South.

Broken promise of Populism

Populism – North Carolina: In the 1890s, black initiative contributed to the agrarian upsurge known as the Populist Movement. In North Carolina an alliance of white and black small farmers mounted a Populist-Republican fusion campaign that gained control of the state legislature in 1894. Once in power the alliance gave local voters the right to select county officials and took steps to protect the black franchise. These measures paid off in 1896 with the election of a Republican governor and George H. White as Congressional representative from the "Black Second." Even more important was the upsurge in black office-holders at the local level. Hahn quotes the outraged comments of white supremacist Furnifold Simmons: "Negro CONGRESSMEN, NEGRO SOLICITORS, NEGRO REVENUE OFFICERS, NEGRO COLLECTORS OF CUSTOMS, NEGROES in charge of white institutions, NEGROES in charge of white schools,...NEGRO CONSTABLES arresting white women and men, NEGRO MAGISTRATES trying white women and men, white convicts chained to NEGRO CONVICTS, and forced to social equality with them."[11] The emphasis given here to "white women" and "social equality" is a forerunner of the Democrats' racist campaign that succeeded in smashing the fusion movement two years later.

North Carolina's interracial politics stood out as an exception during these years. But the lack of resistance by white allies to the ensuing Democratic onslaught fit the dominant pattern of the period. Georgia's Populist leader Tom Watson moved from courting black votes in the 1890s to actively promoting segregation a few years later. Populist platforms across the South made gestures toward black people's concerns, but once in power the party bent over backward to prove it had no interest in social equality. Robert Allen notes that Virginia Populist conventions were segregated, while Alabama's had no black delegates.[12] Populists proclaimed their opposition to lynching – but took no action when a lynching actually occurred. Populists failed to oppose, and even supported, segregationist legislation being passed throughout the South in these years. They offered a promise of jury duty as an enticement to black voters – but then refused to open the rolls in Populist-controlled counties. Populists opposed racially mixed education and refused to support federal aid to either black or white schools out of a concern to preserve states' rights.

The movement lost momentum when the Populist Party merged nationally with the Democrats in 1896. In North Carolina during the 1898 electoral campaign, Democratic newspapers carried hysterical denunciations charging black men with raping white women. Editors claimed that with black politicians in power, black people were "taking over" even the most intimate aspects of white people's lives. Defense of "white womanhood" became the rallying cry for the assault on North Carolina's fusion politics – and with it, on black political rights generally. The violent defeat of fusion came in Wilmington, North Carolina, in 1898. White mobs shot down black people in the street, drove hundreds from their homes, and seized the mayor's office. Desperate appeals to the Republican governor and to President William McKinley, also a Republican, went unanswered.

Populism – Eastern Texas: In Eastern Texas, Grimes County remained the country's last outpost of interracial politics. Here German settlers had joined with black Republicans to wield significant local power for decades. But by the late 1890s the Southern tradition of "White Capper" gangs and rural "Regulators" emerged in the form of the local White Man's Union. Vigilantes roamed Eastern Texas, intent on suppressing the last vestiges of black political power. The story repeated itself here as it had elsewhere over the previous 30 years – a history of armed outrages against striking sugar workers in Louisiana (1887), against Colored Alliance boycott leaders in Mississippi (1889), and against striking cotton pickers in Arkansas (1891), as well as lynch mob terror that became commonplace in the South from the 1880s on. In 1900, the last biracial post-Reconstruction government passed into history. In the small town of Anderson, Texas, the White Man's Union gunned down "much of the Populist leadership, beginning with the blacks."[13]

Overview and a look ahead

Intense struggles marked the 35 years from Lee's surrender at Appomattox in 1865 through Reconstruction to the defeat of fusion politics in Eastern Texas in 1900. Throughout these years and into the 20th Century, as one front of struggle closed down, another opened up. Acting through the Republican Party, black people held power in parts of the South for less than a decade. But during this time they turned the world upside down, putting "the bottom rail on top."[14] Social legislation – in matters affecting land and labor, education, civil rights, and the public sphere generally – benefited all working class people. The social order the former slaves created compares favorably with today's rampant inequality, overflowing prisons, and shrinking opportunities for people in the poorer sectors of the workforce. After 1875 people's creativity continued to break through in reform movements driven by the same aspirations that shaped the Reconstruction program.

With the suppression of fusion politics in the 1890s, new forms of struggle emerged. At Tuskegee University from 1895 to 1915, Booker T. Washington represented a new class of black businessmen who preached class peace, self-improvement, and an alliance with white monopoly power. Counterposed to Washington were W.E.B. DuBois and William Monroe Trotter, editor of the *Boston Guardian*, who together with 25 others founded the all-black Niagara Movement in 1905. While this organization was short-lived, the Niagara Movement projected the voice of northern black intellectuals – independent and clear in their denunciation of the unjust racial order. Publisher and anti-lynching campaigner Ida B. Wells supported the Niagara Movement and joined in the 1909 call to found the National Association for the Advancement of Colored People (NAACP). Black workers organized within the Mineworkers Union and in the International Workers of the World (IWW) – and later formed the Union of Sleeping Car Porters, led by A. Philip Randolph. Black intellectual Hubert Harrison, originally from St. Croix in the Virgin Islands, struggled within the white left, challenging the Socialist Party to recognize the advanced character of black people's struggle – as did Cyril Briggs, leader of the African Blood Brotherhood, in relation to the Communist Party USA.

Ida B. Wells founded the first black women's suffragette organization, the Alpha Suffragette Club, in 1913. Black women fought for women's suffrage, even though the racist pragmatists in the leadership of the movement discounted their support. W.E.B. DuBois published trailblazing studies of black life; edited *The Crisis*, the independent organ of the NAACP founded in 1910; and built on H. Sylvester-Williams 1900 London Pan African Conference to call together the first Pan-African Congress in 1919. As the Great Migration of black people to the North took shape during the World War I labor shortage, Marcus Garvey brought national consciousness into the streets of New York and into organized chapters of the United Negro Improvement Association (UNIA) across the South. Taken together, these businessmen, intellectuals, workers, and women – the broad masses of black people, North and South – represented the stirrings of a nation that was seeking its authentic voice and its place in history.

The rejection of Reconstruction's attempt at multiracial democracy also impacted other people of color across the country. Federal troops redeployed westward to fight the Indian wars. White homesteaders followed, with their settler consciousness no longer challenged by the reality of black political power in a reconstructed South. Lynchings, which enforced white supremacy in the South after Reconstruction, targeted Mexicans in the Southwest as well. After being reconstituted in 1874, the Texas Rangers resumed their role as the main enforcers of racial inequality in Texas. Their actions contrasted sharply with those of the Reconstruction state police who had suppressed the Klan just a few years earlier. Many black soldiers, veterans of the Civil War and Reconstruction, found themselves transported to the border with Mexico in a conscious effort by authorities to foment hostility between black people and Mexicans. Contradictions later erupted in Beeville, near Corpus Christi, in a riot between black and Mexican workers in 1894. Finally, anti-Chinese agitation, the Democratic Party's secret weapon in undermining the Republican's Reconstruction program, helped turn the 1877 railroad strike in San Francisco into an anti-Chinese riot.

Overall, the closing decades of the 19th Century were a time of turmoil – featuring economic centralization, hardship for workers and farmers, deflation, and widespread anti-monopoly struggles. Race was central to this process of capitalist consolidation. White people gained privileged access to land and jobs; but in return the majority of them found themselves squeezed by debt and having little control over work conditions, farm prices, or credit rates. Such tensions fed the white agrarian movements of the 1880s and '90s – at the same time that Indian wars, lynch mobs, exclusionary legislation, and segregation tended to govern relations among the masses of working people. In this climate of division and violence, the bankers, monopolists, and land speculators rose to dominate the country. They embodied capitalism's drive to accumulate – at any cost – while politicians cleared the way. Elite institutions justified expansion across the continent and beyond with theories of white racial superiority – and dressed it up as social science.

In the environment of industrial expansion after the Civil War, the democratic aspirations of the freed slaves had stood in practical opposition to the drive for monopoly and, later, imperial power. Even in defeat, as Lerone Bennett, Jr. comments, "Long before the rise of Afro-Asia, long before the emergence of the United Nations, black Americans struck a blow – in the heart of the Western World – for all the peoples of the [Third]* World."[15] The defeat of Reconstruction represented a decisive step away from a society based on political and social equality. Instead, the dominant forces in society used legal and illegal terror to reestablish the color line – and extend it through the further dispossession of indigenous peoples and Mexicans, and the exclusion of Chinese immigrants.

White workers and farmers fought the new monopolists. But, with few exceptions, they also accepted, if not participated in, the brutal treatment of peoples of color. These divisions among laboring people made possible the accumulation of vast fortunes, the reorganization of society on a foundation of extreme differences of wealth and power – within a shell of self-righteous, liberal, democratic institutions – and the projection of the white owning class onto the world stage. Reconstruction had been a period of opportunity and hope. Its defeat moved the question of political power – and the question of nationhood – more to the center of oppressed peoples' struggles inside the United States. In this way a basis developed for political unity with the oppressed nations of Latin America, Asia, and Africa that were to come under U.S. influence in the 20th Century.

---

* Bennett actually refers to the "First" world – giving precedence of order to the majority people of color across the globe.

Chapter 6

Imperialism and National Oppression

The monopoly power of the Robber Barons soon made clear its tendency toward imperialist expansion. In 1898 the United States seized on the break-up of the Spanish Empire to take over Puerto Rico and Guam, intervene in Cuba, and launch a bloody colonial war against resistance fighters in the Philippines. Shortly thereafter, the United States joined several European powers in suppressing the Boxer Rebellion in China – an uprising of Chinese nationalists against foreign occupation. These events marked the entrance of the United States into the club of countries holding overseas colonies. Internationally the actions of the United States reflected the Jim Crow system of national oppression taking shape at home.

This new imperialist role came at a time of sharpening contradictions among the European powers, as they competed to partition the world into economic spheres of influence. At the 1884 Berlin Conference, for example, the Europeans tried to avoid war by parceling out Africa's wealth of human and natural resources among themselves – this after 400 years of sponsoring tribal conflict and slave trading on the continent.

Modern imperialism differs from capitalist colonialism mainly because it 1) is powered by the expansion drive of industrial monopolies, 2) centers on financial institutions' exporting investment capital, and 3) features a struggle by transnational corporations to control the resources of the world when the world has already been divided up among the industrial powers.[1] These high-pressure economic conditions tend to push the world toward war. Eventually the tension between a rising Germany and Great Britain, the dominant empire of the period, erupted into World War I.

The United States mainly tried to sidestep this big power contention by calling for an "Open Door" into the wealth of the colonial world. While keeping a firm hold on the former Spanish colonies, as well as the recently acquired Hawai'ian Islands, the United States centered its policy on indirect control – economic exploitation through investment and trade. The United States maintained a pretense of local self-government, supplemented as needed by gunboat diplomacy. As Howard Zinn points out in his *People's History of the United States,* U.S. relations with Latin America were typical of this approach:

> Between 1900 and 1933, the United States intervened in Cuba four times, in Nicaragua twice, in Panama six times, in Guatemala once, in Honduras seven times. By 1924 the finances of half of the twenty Latin American states were being directed to some extent by the United States. By 1935, over half of U.S. steel and cotton exports were being sold in Latin America.[2]

As the United States took steps to dominate nations abroad, conditions at home hardened into a system of national oppression as well. The legal apparatus of Jim Crow segregation marginalized all people of color in the United States. At the same time social reformers indoctrinated European immigrants in the finer points of democracy – more accurately understood as white privilege. During what historians call the Progressive Era, Presidents Roosevelt, Taft, and Wilson instituted the Civil Service, federal standards, professional licensing, and a progressive income tax…along with the segregation for the first time of all federal facilities.

In this context African American, Mexican, and Asian peoples came to assert their collective humanity over against the dominant system. Being communities apart – dependent only on themselves for survival and development – people turned oppression into a source of strength, and a community's own power into the surest guarantor of democratic rights.

Oppressed nations of the Sunbelt

The African American Nation

Expressions of a nationalist outlook appear in the writings of Booker T. Washington, W.E.B. DuBois, Hubert Harrison, and in the Garvey movement during and after World War I. But the process of becoming a nation is not just a matter of a few decades' development. For centuries African people shared the experience of being uprooted and forced into slavery. Then a history of institution building in the North from 1787 to 1837 later flowered into the mass activism of the Reconstruction period.

Going back to the earliest roots of a developing national consciousness, Lerone Bennett, Jr. notes in *The Shaping of Black America:*

> Pioneer blacks began early in the eighteenth century to develop a sense of themselves as Africans separated from Africa and from the Europeans, who excluded them and mocked their aspirations. This dawning sense of peoplehood was stimulated by external exigencies, by segregation on the plantations and in the towns; but it was stimulated also by internal exigencies, by the need to be together, by the need to express a different worldview, by the need to see beyond the blocked horizon...And out of it all there finally emerged the first shoots of a new synthesis, neither European nor African."[3]

Later, once the brief window of the Revolutionary War period had closed, free black people set about creating their own institutional infrastructure in the North – beginning in 1787 with Richard Allen's founding the Mother Bethel AME Church in Philadelphia. Then came the Free African Society, "which DuBois called 'the first wavering step of a people toward a more organized social life.' The society was a mutual aid group, an embryonic church, and a political structure. It also contained the germ of a major black business, the insurance company.... Simultaneously with these initiatives, black leaders founded educational and cultural institutions.... With the organization of the first newspapers and magazines, the different organizations and colonies of Black America began to coexist in the same time zone."[4]

In 1829 David Walker in his *Appeal* laid claim to the soil on which the slaves had labored:

> The Americans say, that we are ungrateful – but I ask them for heaven's sake, what should we be grateful to them for – for murdering our fathers and mothers? – Or do they wish us to return thanks to them for chaining and handcuffing us, branding us, cramming fire down our throats, or for keeping us in slavery, and beating us nearly or quite to death to make us work in ignorance and miseries, to support them and their families. They certainly think that we are a gang of fools....
>
> Let no man of us budge one step, and let slaveholders come to beat us from our country. America is more our country, than it is the whites – we have enriched it with our *blood and tears*. The greatest riches in all America have arisen from our blood and tears: – and will they drive us from our property and homes, which we have earned with our *blood*? They must look sharp or this very thing will bring swift destruction upon them. The Americans have got so fat on our blood and groans, that they have almost forgotten the God of armies.[5]

With the end of slavery, the 95% of U.S. black people living in the South, some four million strong, could construct their own institutions in the Black Belt region – drawing on the complex social networks built up under slavery, as well as on the experience of earlier generations in the North. With the reassertion of white supremacist rule after Reconstruction, the path of separate national development became more central to the struggle. Economically, psychologically and culturally, African

Americans consolidated themselves as a people during this period – on land Africans and their descendents had paid for with centuries of unpaid labor and suffering.

Then during the 1920s activists from the Communist Party-USA, both black and white, reviewed the situation of African Americans with revolutionaries from around the world. Meeting in Moscow as part of the Communist International, or Comintern, representatives looked at developments like the Great Migration to the North of African Americans during and after World War I, the impact of the war on returning black GIs, the dramatic upsurge of the Garvey nationalist movement as a counter to Jim Crow segregation, and the stirrings around the world of national liberation movements – including Pan-Africanism. As a result, the Comintern in 1928 adopted the "Resolution on the Negro Question in the United States." Here for the first time working class revolutionaries set themselves the task "to come out openly and unreservedly for the right of the Negroes to national self-determination in the southern states, where the Negroes form a majority of the population."[6] In addition, the resolution pointed to the link between national oppression inside the United States and African people oppressed by imperialism elsewhere in the world: "The Negro race everywhere is an oppressed race. Whether it is a minority (USA, etc.), majority (South Africa) or inhabits a so-called independent state (Liberia, etc.), the Negroes are oppressed by imperialism. Thus, a common tie of interest is established for the revolutionary struggle of race and national liberation from imperialist domination of the Negroes in various parts of the world."[7]

This theoretical perspective is important because 1) it gave precedence for the first time to the African American freedom movement within a working class socialist framework; 2) it opened the way to broad organizing gains by the Communist Party-USA during the 1930s; and 3) it helped broaden and deepen among non-African peoples the appreciation of black people's liberation struggle inside this country. That African American people in the South constitute a nation – a "Nation within the Nation," to use W.E.B. DuBois' phrase[8] – is not as immediately clear as compared, say, to the indigenous peoples of North America. African Americans never controlled a territory within what is now the United States. Their language, English, is the same as that of European Americans – even though it has distinctive characteristics that fueled the 1990s Ebonics debate. And due to the ferocious racial oppression in this country, economic classes within the Black Nation developed in a distorted way. Teachers, a few doctors, news publishers, clergymen, morticians, and other small service shops historically could survive within a segregated society. Other roads to economic development, however, were blocked.

The Comintern Resolution helped sweep away the confusion. More than anything, the resolution publicly validated the integrity of the African American people's freedom struggle in its own right. The position drew on two profound understandings: first, the African American's near super-human history of resistance to oppression in the United States; and, second, the relatively recent ascendance of U.S. capitalism to the heights of world power. Inside the United States, this dual recognition informed the Communist Party USA's organizing approach to the labor and popular struggles of the 1930s. These core understandings came to the fore again in the black liberation movement of the 1960s and '70s – and remain valid, if largely outside of public consciousness, today. An appreciation of the deeply rooted national character of the black freedom struggle is a key element in making sense of our 21st Century world.

The Chicano Nation

The path to national consciousness developed differently for the

African Blood Brotherhood

The African Blood Brotherhood (ABB) was the first organized force in the United States to link the issues of race, class, self-determination and the fight for socialism. Long after the organization's eventual merger with the Communist Party USA in the 1920s, the ABB continued to influence revolutionary activists – especially impacting Black Power forces in the 1960s.

Cyril Briggs, an immigrant from the Caribbean island of Nevis, founded the ABB as a secret organization in 1917. The ABB's magazine, *The Crusader* (1918-1922), identified itself with the militant Black Nationalist Hamitic League of the World. Only in 1921 did *The Crusader* make clear its role as the organ of the ABB. The magazine addressed themes like "Africa for the Africans", "the renaissance of Negro power and culture throughout the world," "race patriotism," and "government of the Negro, by the Negro, and for the Negro." Armed self-defense against lynchings stood at the heart of the ABB agenda, along with demands for universal suffrage, equal rights for blacks – including no discrimination on the job or in hiring – and an immediate end to segregation. Although a few women such as Grace Campbell and Bertha de Basco held important posts in the organization, the ABB's military style tended to make it more welcoming to men.

The Russian Revolution electrified Briggs and the members of the ABB. It was not long before they combined their unique analysis of race and class with an advocacy for socialism. In 1919, for example, Briggs drew a parallel between the forced removal of black workers from a Pennsylvania steel town – where they had migrated during the wartime labor shortage – and the notorious Palmer raids of that year aimed at the deportation of white foreign-born radicals. The ABB saw both these repressive measures as clear examples of "the mailed fist of capitalism."

Mexican people whose territory the United States annexed in 1848. To put things in perspective, the Northern 45% of Mexico taken by the United States "included the immense riches of the Texas oilfields and the California gold areas, as well as more than 100,000 people."[9] This subject population already constituted a people – but now a conquered people – on land where they had lived for a hundred years and more. The Spanish-speaking residents, having indigenous roots themselves, had worked out a relatively peaceful pattern of coexistence and intermarriage with the native peoples.

The incoming white settlers, however, were different. Gilberto Lopez y Rivas comments that "the unarmed Spanish-Americans with their traditions of peaceful community life came to regard the American cowboys as worse than the Comanches and Apaches [with their raiding parties]. These ranchers treated the Spanish-Americans as though they were not human beings and had no rights that needed to be respected. They refused to accept them socially, dispossessed them of their lands, scat-

Despite the entrenched racism of most labor unions, the ABB declared, "the Negro's place is with labor." In the ABB's view, black people would benefit most from "the triumph of Labor and the destruction of parasitic Capital Civilization with its Imperialism incubus that is squeezing the life-blood out of millions of our race." The group's program centered on black self-organization – the "race first" principle – with the black working class in the lead. On this foundation the movement could then build multiracial alliances – especially with "advanced" white workers in the labor movement.

In the early 1920s, Briggs and others in the ABB grew closer to the newly formed Workers (Communist) Party. Black communists like Claude McKay and Otto Huiswood came into the political flow of the ABB. They connected socialism to self-determination for black people in both Africa and the Americas – including inside the United States. In their vision of socialism, a distinct black agenda would continue throughout the post-capitalist period.

The closeness with the Communist Party became a two-way street. Up to then socialists and communists had little understanding of the way race shaped class struggle in the United States. The ABB's political agenda became influential inside the party – especially its understanding that any lasting alliances within the labor movement required rooting out racism among white workers. With the support of communists from abroad, the ABB's viewpoint won out in the form of the 1928 Comintern Resolution on the Black Nation in the South. These developments finally cemented the relationship between the ABB and the CP-USA.

—*sources: Solomon,* The Cry was Unity; *Kelley,* Freedom Dreams

tered their sheep, and drove off their cattle."[10]

From the 1850s to the 1870s in Texas, people the Anglos labeled "bandits" fought against Yankee power. Juan Gonzalez notes that Juan "Cheno" Cortina in 1859 "raised an army of twelve hundred Mexicans and ...declared a war against the Anglo settler minority. For the next two decades, Cortina's band launched sporadic guerilla raids into Texas from safe havens on the Mexican side."[11]

Resistance struggles also broke out in the New Mexico territory in the 1880s and '90s. Clark S. Knowlton describes how Anglos and the U.S. government used violence, technicalities around land grants, property taxes, overgrazing, fences, railroads, creation of forest reserves, and homestead laws to steal Mexican lands and disrupt the people's way of life. "Since 1854, the Spanish-Americans have lost over 2,000,000 acres of private lands, 1,700,000 acres of communal land, 1,800,000 acres taken by the state, and vast areas lost to the federal government."[12]

The impact of these attacks together with the imposition of a segregated social structure resulted in "the collapse of the village economy...and an accelerated cultural breakdown."[13] At the same time, a countertrend developed in the form of 1) mutual aid societies and 2) workplace organizing that led to major strike activity. The strengthening of personal ties in these new social forms helped reconstitute community life under difficult conditions.

Developments in Mexico also reinforced this process of breakdown and renewal. From 1876 on, U.S. companies bought up land and resources and built railroads with the help of the Porfirio Díaz dictatorship. Rail networks in Northern Mexico connected at the border with the new tracks crisscrossing the U.S. Southwest. From 1890 to 1910 immigration to the North took off, as migrant workers began to follow the railroad lines all the way to Chicago. In the decade after 1910, the Mexican Revolution shook the oligarchy and millions died in the struggle – leading workers to bring their families north to settle. By 1920 the eugenics movement* in the United States urged the closing down of immigration from Eastern Europe, Asia, and other "non-white" regions to preserve the purity of the white gene pool. Nevertheless, Anglo ranchers in Texas – and increasingly in California as well – agitated successfully to keep their supply of Mexican labor flowing smoothly.

Mexican people's situation inside the United States has been closely tied both to developments in Mexico and to economic conditions in the

---

* Francis Galton, a cousin of Charles Darwin, came up with the word *eugenics* in 1883 to describe a social policy that restricts reproduction to weed out people he considered "unfit." Henry Laughlin, one of the founders in 1922 of the American Eugenics Society, later became president of the Pioneer Fund, a "white supremacist organization that is still functioning today." *(Cavanaugh-O'Keefe, "Introduction to Eugenics")*

United States. In the 1930s, U.S. authorities deported millions of people back to Mexico as depression and drought ravaged the Southwest. Ten years later, the landowners once again wanted their workers – and the doors reopened, until the 1953 recession and Operation Wetback forced people back across the border. For U.S. capitalism, the preferred arrangement is for Mexican workers to be available only when needed – temporarily and on demand. Farm owners today who hire H2-A and H2-B contract labor to work their fields support similar "guest worker" policies.

The Southwest's links to Mexico go back a thousand years. Legend, linguistic and archeological evidence indicate that the Aztecas migrated south from Aztlán – the Colorado River region of the United States – to found their capital Tenochtitlán, which in time became Mexico City. Centuries later the oldest non-native trade route in the United States, the *Camino Real,* ran from Santa Fe, founded in 1610, to the Mexican city of Chihuahua. During the mid-1800s, business people in the Arizona portion of the New Mexico territory looked to the port of Guaymas on the Gulf of California as the preferred route for their commercial links to the world. Anglo expansionists in 1857 carried out a failed invasion into Northern Mexico from California, angry that the Gadsden Purchase four years earlier had not included the rich mines of Sonora. And President Buchanan followed with some gunboat diplomacy outside Guaymas in 1859. Mexican workers – depending on the state of relations with Anglo settlers and the Apache people – moved back and forth across the border to work in Arizona's silver and gold mines, and later in the copper mines. And in the opening years of the 20th Century, the anarchist movement contributed to the revolutionary ferment in Mexico from bases in Los Angeles and South Texas.* In 1916 Pancho Villa attacked Columbus, New Mexico, and General John "Black Jack" Pershing – who had earlier battled Muslim resistance fighters in the Philippines – carried out his Punitive Expedition through northern Mexico, unsuccessfully chasing the rebel general and his troops for months. Economically, politically, and demographically the Southwest and Mexico have a special connection that over hundreds of years repeatedly shifted and reconstituted itself in new forms.

The Southwest includes descendants of 19th Century residents – around San Antonio and along the Rio Grande/Bravo, in northern New

---

* The *Partido Liberal Mexicano* a revolutionary party of both anarchists and socialists, struggled against the Porfirio Díaz dictatorship, supported worker organizing in the mines of Arizona and northern Mexico, formally recognized the rights of women, published the newspaper *Regeneración* with a circulation of 30,000, opposed police brutality and the lynching of Mexicans, and organized three invasions into Mexico. Party leaders included the well-known anarchist journalist Ricardo Flores Magón and the socialist organizer Lázaro Gutiérrez de Lara. *(Acuña,* Occupied America*)*

Mexico and on the high plains of southern Colorado, and in the mining region of Arizona and on farms in California. In addition, there are generations of immigrants from Mexico and their descendants living throughout the Southwest. All these people share a common language that the dominant culture barely tolerates. Through sheer numbers a good portion of the territory annexed by the United States 150 years ago has already been reclaimed. In towns, cities, and rural areas, people of Mexican ancestry – many of whom identify themselves as *Chicano/a* – carry out a whole range of economic and social functions. They are workers, predominantly, but also intellectuals, businesspeople, small proprietors, politicians, ranchers, and farmers. The Chicano people manifest a rich cultural heritage – connected to Mexico and, deeper still, to indigenous peoples and enslaved Africans in a region running from the Yucatán to the Red River and up the Pacific Coast to San Francisco Bay. Driven out by invading white settlers, Mexicans later returned as a dependent labor force – and then created a place for themselves despite the discrimination and contempt of white society. The Southwest remains connected to Mexico by millions of personal and economic ties – but the region also has its own history. Conquest and forced dispersion, immigration and deportation, settlement and self-validation together have combined to create a people – the Chicano Nation – living inside the United States, linked to Mexico, and rooted historically among the indigenous and African peoples.

A people's national rights – their right to self-determination – cannot be taken away as a result of the disruption of community life by expansionist capitalism and white supremacy. An early political expression of the demand for national independence appeared after the economic take-over of South Texas at the start of the 20th Century. Commercial developers moved into the region south of the Nueces River about 1905 – disturbing the more easy-going bicultural climate that existed in the Rio Grande/Bravo border region during the last decades of the 19th Century. Railroads, land subdivisions, planned towns, and white immigrants changed the character of the area. Settlers brought with them their Jim Crow mentality and, acting like imperialist foot soldiers, treated previously respected Mexican leaders with contempt. It is not simply a coincidence that the 1915 *El Plan de San Diego* [*] surfaced at the same time the

---

[*] *El Plan de San Diego*, named after a town in South Texas, arose out of the turmoil within the Mexican Revolution and the land grabs and marginalization of Mexicans in the Rio Grande/Bravo valley. During 1915 and 1916 there were some 30 raids into South Texas by parties supporting the two major contending forces in Mexico – "most of them with roots in the United States." Some 21 European Americans died during this period, while U.S. authorities used the uprising as an excuse for a reign of terror along the border. Official reports gave the number of Mexicans beaten, hanged, or shot to death as 300 – in a climate

United States was setting itself up as an imperialist world power. The *Plan* expressed an authentic Chicano call for the "independence and segregation of the States bordering upon the Mexican Nation, which are: Texas, New Mexico, Arizona, Colorado and upper California [the U.S. state of California], of which states the Republic of Mexico was robbed in most perfidious manner by North American imperialism." The *Plan* also recognized the national rights of native peoples and "Orientals," and called for the formation of an African American republic in the U.S. South.

Native peoples at the close of the 19th Century

The year 1890 marked the final conquest of North America by the U.S. Army. The massacre at Wounded Knee capped nearly three centuries of genocidal expropriation of the native peoples by slaughtering of over 200 people, mostly women and children. In 1871 the U.S. government had stopped making treaties with the Indian peoples – thereby ceasing to recognize their existence as separate nations. Between then and 1900 two waves of land seizures reduced Indian land holdings by half. James Wilson describes these episodes of massive theft in *The Earth Shall Weep*: "In the first 13 years of the Dawes Act [1887 to 1900] alone, the government forced through nearly 33,000 allotments and 'released' some 28,500,000 acres of 'surplus' land – an achievement of which Andrew Jackson himself might have been proud."[14]

Earlier, seven major land grabs had involved "only a relatively small number of tribes – in 1880, the Utes of Colorado, for instance, were forced to surrender 12 million acres at a stroke…"[15] By the 1930s Indian holdings had been reduced to some 47 million acres.

Along with land seizures came a policy of forced assimilation: children taken from their homes and sent to Christian mission schools, given new names, and forbidden to speak their own language. At the Carlisle, PA, Indian School the toll was enormous. Luther Standing Bear comments: "The change in clothing, housing, food, and confinement combined with lonesomeness was too much, and in three years nearly one half the children from the Plains were dead."[16]

Yet the policy continued, and "by 1900 there were more than 300 Indian schools across the country, with a combined enrolment of nearly 22,000."[17]

Native Americans experienced forced assimilation, while people of African, Mexican, and Asian descent experienced segregation. Vine Deloria, Jr. in *Custer Died for Your Sins* describes this contrast in policy:

---

with no legal restraints on either the Texas Rangers or vigilante murders. *(Acuña,* Occupied America, *p. 177)*

> The white man adopted two basic approaches... He systematically excluded blacks from all programs, policies, social events, and economic schemes....
>
> With the Indian the process was simply reversed... Indians were...subjected to the most intense pressure to become white. Laws passed by Congress had but one goal – the Anglo-Saxonization of the Indian....
>
> The white man forbade the black to enter his own social and economic system and at the same time force-fed the Indian what he was denying the black. Yet the white man demanded that the black conform to white standards and insisted that the Indian don feathers and beads periodically to perform for him.[18]

From the time national recognition ended in 1871, there has been a constant struggle to reclaim the full rights of sovereignty – despite U.S. policies of assimilation, termination, and, most recently, self-administration. The First Nations have the most obvious historic claim to nationhood inside the United States – and to the territorial and political rights that come with it.

Colonized nations

Hawai'i, Puerto Rico, Cuba, and the Philippines historically were a bridge the United States crossed in asserting its economic and political power around the globe. Home to peoples of color, these nations fit well with the U.S. ruling class's "civilizing" mission – used to justify the imperialist exploitation of foreign land and labor. Native Hawai'ians and the indigenous peoples of Alaska were a kind of nuisance for white U.S. settlers intent on getting rich on what they considered to be empty lands. There is nothing new in this story. Hawai'i and Alaska repeated the history of the West by gaining statehood as white settler dominated societies in 1959. The Philippines, Cuba, and Puerto Rico, however, proved more difficult to deal with.

The Philippines

The war to suppress the Philippines lasted from 1899 to 1903, required 70,000 U.S. troops and killed hundreds of thousands of Filipinos. Howard Zinn quotes Senator Albert Beveridge in an address that reflects the war's motivation:

> Mr. President, the times call for candor. The Philippines are ours forever.... We will not renounce our part in the mission of our race, trustee, under God, of the civilization of the world....
>
> The Pacific is our ocean.... The Philippines give us a base at the door of all the East....
>
> No land in America surpasses in fertility the plains and valleys of Luzon. Rice and coffee, sugar and cocoanuts, hemp and tobacco.... The wood of

> the Philippines can supply the furniture of the world for a century to come....
>
> My own belief is that there are not 100 men among them who comprehend what Anglo-Saxon self-government even means, and there are over 5,000,000 people to be governed.
>
> It has been charged that our conduct of the war has been cruel. Senators, it has been the reverse.... Senators must remember that we are not dealing with Americans or Europeans. We are dealing with Orientals.[19]

For the next 44 years, the Philippines remained an outright colony of the United States – and later served as a U.S. military base in the war against Vietnam. The Filipino people succeeded in throwing out the U.S.-supported dictator Ferdinand Marcos in 1986. And then in 1991 they forced the closing of all U.S. military installations in the country, including the huge Clark and Subic Bay bases. Since September 11, 2001, however, the United States has used the War on Terror as an excuse to reintroduce troops – officially in a training capacity.

Dominated economically by the United States, the Philippines send thousands of nurses, housekeepers, and farmworkers to this country every year. Poverty is such that some people in the capital city of Manila survive in makeshift shelters built on huge trash dumps, eking out an existence by picking through the trash. In these conditions, the struggle for national liberation from U.S. imperialism continues. The peasant-based New People's Army, led by the Communist Party of the Philippines, holds power in much of the countryside. Labor and student struggles unfold in the cities, targeting U.S. economic and political control. Progressive social movements fight women's oppression and militarism, demand schools and health care, and struggle for the social supports necessary to free children from labor so they can attend school. And in the summer of 2004 the resistance movement won a significant victory when it forced the government of Gloria Macapagal Arroyo to withdraw support from the U.S. occupation of Iraq.

Cuba

The continuing neocolonial* status of the Philippines today has clear similarities and contrasts with Cuba – also wrested from Spain in 1898 and dominated by U.S. economic interests for 50 years. First the United States occupied Cuba militarily; and then it compelled the adoption of the Platt Amendment as part of the 1901 Constitution, permitting the United States to intervene as it saw fit. Only after the revolutionary guerilla movement headed by Fidel Castro and Che Guevara kicked U.S. corporations and the mafia off the island in 1959 were the Cuban people

---

* *Neocolonial* status refers to a situation where a country is dominated economically and politically by an outside power but retains formal independence.

able to win true independence. With it has come more than 45 years of unremitting U.S. hostility – including a continuing economic blockade, a military base on Cuban soil at Guantánamo, restricted travel in and out of the island (while encouraging illegal flight), and support for armed invasion and assassination attempts. Cuba's experience shows how staunch a people must be to achieve true self-determination in the face of U.S. political and economic pressures.

Puerto Rico

Puerto Rico continues to be a U.S. colony to this day – as recognized by the U.N. Special Committee on Decolonization. Committee resolutions in 1991 and 1998 "reaffirmed the inalienable right of the people of Puerto Rico to self-determination." And in 2004 the committee "called on the United States to expedite a process allowing the people of Puerto Rico to fully exercise" this right.[20]

The current unstable *commonwealth* status affords the Puerto Rican people neither the rights of national recognition nor full citizenship in the United States. Juan Gonzalez in *Harvest of Empire* describes the island's political, military and economic domination by its colonial master:

- ***Politically*** the people are subject to federal laws passed without representation from the island. The Puerto Rican Constitution can be amended by the U.S. government, which also must approve any agreements made with third countries. Puerto Ricans can be drafted to serve in the U.S. army but cannot vote for the president.
- ***Militarily*** the island is located strategically at the entrance to the Caribbean. The United States has bases on 14% of the island, a higher concentration than anywhere inside the borders of the United States. Only on May 1, 2003, did the United States finally relinquish its use of Vieques* – a small island off Puerto Rico's east coast – for naval target practice.
- ***Economically*** Puerto Rico is a treasure house – at the same time that some 60% of the island's population lives in poverty. Net in-

---

* The U.S. Navy took over the small island of Vieques in 1941 and began using the seaward side for target practice. Protests against the military occupation occurred in the late 1970s and then again in April 1999 after shells missed the target and killed David Sanes Rodríguez. On May 1, 2003, the Navy closed down the site after four years of demonstrations, civil disobedience, and the arrest of thousands. Instead of returning the island to Puerto Rico, however, the Navy gave the property to the U.S. Department of Interior's Fish and Wildlife Service. The following year with the closing of the Roosevelt Roads naval base, the Puerto Rican national movement had achieved the first of its four demands for Vieques: the "Four D's" of demilitarization, decontamination, devolution, and development. *(Becker, "Vieques"; U.N., "Decolonization Committee Calls for Expediated Process of Self-Determination for Puerto Rico")*

> come from direct U.S. investment tops all countries in the world. The island accounts for 40% of all profits taken from Latin America. "Puerto Rico is among the most industrialized and most captive economies in the Third World – 99.3 percent of its exports are manufactured goods, and 90 percent of all those exports go to the United States." [21] In addition, Puerto Ricans are the highest importers of U.S. goods per person in the world.

Besides the current commonwealth status, there are three other possibilities that the Puerto Rican people might choose to resolve their colonial position: *statehood, total independence* and *free association*. The latter two options both allow for full national sovereignty.

Gonzalez argues that free association might prove to be the best solution. The prospect of statehood is probably ruled out because the Puerto Rican people insist on retaining Spanish as their principal language. The United States has made English a condition for statehood – not surprising, given its history of discrimination against the Spanish-speaking people of the Southwest. Another difference of principle centers on the Puerto Rican Constitution's rejection of the death penalty. Nevertheless, the Puerto Rican people tend to value their U.S. citizenship status – granted as part of the Jones act in 1917 and strengthened by the U.S. Immigration and Nationality Act of 1952. Today, with almost as many Puerto Ricans living on the U.S. mainland as on the island – 2.8 vs. 3.3 million in 2000 – Gonzalez and other observers feel that the Puerto Rican people are unlikely to voluntarily give up their access to the powerful U.S. economy or their right to travel easily between the island and the *barrios* of urban North America.

Free association is a relationship that could preserve bi-national citizenship while affirming Puerto Rico's national identity and independence. Examples of the free association approach are the Marshall Islands and Micronesia in the South Pacific. Both countries gained their independence from the United States in 1986 and are now members of the United Nations. Formerly, they were part of the U.S. Pacific Island Trust Territories. The official currency of the islands is the U.S. dollar; and by the treaty of free association, the United States is responsible for defense. As to the question of citizenship, a freely associated Puerto Rico could allow its citizens dual citizenship. And since the Puerto Rican people today are U.S. citizens, by U.S. law their offspring would be as well.

Total independence is the third possible choice. Nationalism has a long history in Puerto Rico, and a majority of the people supported independence into the 1940s, even after the U.S. government began to criminalize the independence struggle. The Nationalist Party rose to prominence in the 1930s. In 1937 police killed 22 members of the party and wounded almost a hundred at a peaceful demonstration in Ponce. Authorities arrested Harvard-trained lawyer, Pedro Albizu Campos, and other party leaders for sedition and jailed them for nearly ten years. Then in the early 1950s armed attacks on President Truman's residence at Blair House and on the U.S. Congress sent four liberation fighters to jail for 25 years, and one for 29. The U.S. government held Albizu Campos responsible for these actions and returned him to prison until shortly before his death in 1965.

As of 2004, five Puerto Rican political prisoners still remained incarcerated: Oscar Lopez Rivera, Haydee Beltran Torres, Carlos Alberto Torres, Juan Segarra Palmer, and Antonio Camacho Negrón. These prisoners, together with 11 others whom President Clinton released in 1999, were charged with armed actions linked to the Fuerzas Armadas de Liberación Nacional (FALN) and the Ejército Popular Boricua, also known as the Macheteros. On September 23, 2005, the FBI assassinated Filiberto Ojeda Rios, the leader of the Macheteros. (See box for the story.)

For perspective on the armed struggle for independence in Puerto

The Murder of Filiberto Ojeda Rios

On Friday, September 23, [2005], scores of FBI agents surrounded a house in semi-rural Hormigueros, Puerto Rico. They attacked, and a sniper shot Filiberto Ojeda Rios, the Responsible General of Los Macheteros, a revolutionary organization fighting for the independence of Puerto Rico. Wounded, Filiberto was left to bleed to death before the Feds moved in the next day.

This assassination sparked a wave of protest in Puerto Rico. Though some news stories appeared in the US media, they faded fast. In fact, this murder has three stories.

The first is the immediate story of imperialist vengeance and arrogance. Filiberto Ojeda Rios had taken up arms against the colonialist occupiers of his homeland, and had been set free by Puerto Rican juries for charges stemming from actions which had appropriated millions of dollars from the likes of Wells Fargo, actions which had resulted in the wounding of an FBI agent and others. Still a target of the US, Filiberto had eluded capture for 15 years. The FBI chose to open their assault on the fugitive on the day of *El Grito de Lares*, the patriotic holiday celebrating the 1868 uprising against Spanish colonialism.

The second is the underlying story of Puerto Rican anger and resistance. Thousands gathered the first night in San Juan and other cities across the island. Politicians and public figures soon denounced the murder and its timing, not only independentistas but also leading folks from the Commonwealth and Statehood parties. Filiberto's funeral motorcade was saluted by hundreds of thousands, as schools flying the Machetero flag emptied out. Anxious elected officials convened their own hearings on the crime.

The third is the unfolding story of broad-based actions and organization. Over the last decade the people of Puerto Rico have waged several rounds

Rico, consider the U.N. General Assembly resolution passed in 1978, which recognizes "the legitimacy of the struggle of peoples for independence, territorial integrity, national unity and liberation from colonial domination, particularly armed struggle." The United States has a clear choice in dealing with such armed patriots: jail them and kill them, as has been done up to now, or allow the Puerto Rican people to exercise their right to self-determination.

The Puerto Rican Independence Party (PIP) led the early legal struggle for independence from its founding in 1945. Until the 1970s the PIP had a sizable following on the island and among Puerto Ricans in the United States. During the 1970s the Young Lords Party, *MINP-El Comité,*[*] and the Puerto Rican Socialist Party (PSP) took up the banner of independence. The PSP originated from the *Movimiento Pro-Independencia*, a split-off from the PIP under the leadership of Juan Mari Bras. At its high point, the PSP drew 20,000 people to Madison Square Garden on October

of struggle. The unsuccessful mass strike[*] of 1998 trained them in mass civil disobedience. The successful battle to drive the US Navy off the island of Vieques followed, developing highly effective flexible tactics and the coordination of front-line struggle with building bases of support. This year, over 80% of the members of the Puerto Rican teachers union voted to uphold disaffiliation from the furious American Federation of Teachers, its US-based "parent," and run their own union. Lessons and leaders from all of these struggles came to the fore as word of the standoff spread. Respected lawyers and doctors demanded to cross the FBI cordon and arrange a peaceful arrest; they were refused. When the FBI insisted that power to the besieged house be shut off, the head of the electrical workers union warned on radio and television that any member who did so would be thrown out of the union forever.

This historic moment should serve as a blunt reminder to the US left, as it is to the US ruling class, that Puerto Rico remains a captive nation under the heel of colonial domination. And as Mao Zedong pointed out, "Where there is oppression, there is resistance." With the FBI's murder of Filiberto Ojeda Rios, new fuel has been added to the burning flames of resistance in Puerto Rico.

—from: FRSO/OSCL, "They can kill a revolutionary, but they can't kill the revolution"

[*] On July 7 and 8, 1998, a general strike of more than 500,000 workers protested the privatization of the island's telephone company under the slogan "*Puerto Rico No Se Vende*" – "Puerto Rico is not for sale." (*Torres,* "Cien Años de Lucha")

---

[*] *Movimiento de la Izquierda Nacional Puertorriqueño*

27, 1974, for a pro-independence rally. After violent rightwing attacks, electoral setbacks, and internal disagreements over tactics, the PSP disbanded in 1993. The PIP continues as an electoral voice for independence; but it won just 4.8% of the popular vote in the 2000 elections for Puerto Rico's non-voting representative to the U.S. Congress. Also, in the most recent of three popular referendums since 1952 on Puerto Rico's status, independence took just 4.4% of the vote. The figures for commonwealth status were 48.4%; and for statehood, 46.25%.[22]

During the late 1990s a bill sponsored by Alaska Republican Don Young called for a plebiscite to resolve the question of Puerto Rico's status. The options proposed were *commonwealth, statehood,* and *separate sovereignty.* The latter category included both *complete independence* and *free association.* If commonwealth status were to win out, then a vote would be held every ten years until either statehood or separate sovereignty eventually gained a majority. By passing this bill, Congress would have finally recognized the island's colonial reality.

Unfortunately, while the House passed the Young Bill in 1998, it never came to a vote in the Senate. A December 2005 White House task force report, however, called for a vote up or down on the current commonwealth status – followed by the choice of statehood or independence, if the commonwealth option is defeated.[23] Whether this approach will finally resolve Puerto Rico's status or simply perpetuate the commonwealth colonial relationship remains unclear.

Insular Areas

In the Pacific, Guam and American Samoa are the largest island territories controlled by the United States that remain on the U.N.'s decolonization list.[24] The Virgin Islands in the Caribbean have a similar status. In addition there are nine small islands and atolls – like Wake and Midway, familiar from World War II battles – that today are uninhabited or serve as wildlife preserves, after once housing military installations. In the Caribbean, in addition to claiming the small island of Nawassa between Haiti and Jamaica, the United States disputes control over the Serranilla Bank and Bajo Nuevo with countries like Jamaica, Colombia, Honduras and Nicaragua. Mostly claimed under the Guano Islands Act of 1856, the insular territories' real significance is military. They extend the reach of the United States far beyond its borders, giving its ships an excuse to roam throughout the Pacific and Caribbean. Taken together with United States military bases in more than a hundred countries worldwide, and its military budget equal to all other countries' combined, U.S. imperialism maintains a global military presence unequaled by any previous empire in history.

Chapter 7

The Right to Self-Determination

Our approach to identifying the national character of movements inside the United States relies on 1) the history of a people's development in North America, 2) the record of their resistance to white patriarchal capitalism, and 3) the inherent character of U.S. imperialism. We now want to approach the question in a more theoretical way, while relying on the earlier discussion to ground the discussion concretely. We draw out the meaning of *self-determination* and its link to *national oppression* by focusing on the question of political power. But we also try to sharpen these concepts by showing their relation to 1) racial oppression, 2) changing social conditions, 3) national minorities, and 4) the U.S. government's dealings with the indigenous First Nations. The goal is not so much to work toward a set definition of an oppressed nation – although we make use of a commonly recognized definition in our discussion. It is more to highlight a range of elements that go into an overall assessment of nationhood – as well as to highlight the difference this judgment makes in practical organizing work.

Racial vs. national oppression

We have been using a definition of *racial oppression* that centers on the across-the-board character of domination – where even the worst-off members of the dominant group have privileges in relation to the subject group. Theodore Allen develops this definition in his two-volume study *The Invention of the White Race*. He then contrasts *racial* oppression with *national* oppression – where members of the upper class of the oppressed group are afforded recognition and privileges, and politically brought into the dominant group's ruling coalition. Allen uses Ireland as a historic example, contrasting the racial oppression of the 1700s Protestant Ascendancy with the national oppression of the later Irish Union period.

While accepting the basic thrust of Allen's analysis, his definition of national oppression seems too restrictive, particularly in a hegemonic imperialist power like the United States. In the early 20th Century European left parties, particularly the Russians, took a different position in light of developments leading up to World War I. Later, as mentioned in the previous chapter, the Communist International in consultation with African American and other U.S. revolutionaries applied their analysis to the situation of African Americans in the United States.

By this widely recognized definition, a nation is *"A historically constituted, stable community of people, formed on the basis of a common language, territory, economic life and psychological make-up, manifested in a common culture."*[1] These criteria can serve as a useful guide to understanding the historic reality of subject peoples in the United States. The difference with Allen's definition centers on his requiring that the upper class of the subject nation be given a measure of power and class privilege that set them apart from their social base – while maintaining sufficient ties to the common people to be useful in controlling them. In the United States white supremacy linked to monopoly economic power has blocked and distorted the development of upper classes among the subject peoples. In addition, the defeat of Reconstruction tended to close off assimilation into the existing structure of society as a pathway to full economic, political, and social equality. As a result, achieving political power as a people – as a nation – moved more to the center of the freedom agenda. Here the demand is for self-determination. By contrast, when racial oppression dominates, people tend to look to assimilation as the path to equality. An assimilationist vision informed both the 1865–1877 Reconstruction period and the 1950s–60s civil rights movement. National liberation struggles, however, focus on achieving political power as a people in areas of national concentration. Democratic rights then flow from and are guaranteed by the exercise of this political power – up to and including the nation's right to secede and form its own country if necessary.

While racial and national struggles have their distinctive characteristics, they are also deeply interconnected. There is no need to pit one type of struggle against the other. Both are defined in relation to the color line – so fighting discrimination and demanding affirmative action to correct historic injustices are of common concern. Also, both types of struggle in a sense can give rise to the other. For example, the civil rights movement of the 1960s passed over into the black power movement. The nationalist upsurge then resulted in profound cultural changes that, while having a definite national character to them, also brought black people more into the mainstream of U.S. life.

The unity and tension between racial and national struggles are together built into the demand for the right to self-determination. Self-determination is a basic democratic right; it is not a demand for separation. The right to self-determination provides a nation with an option that it may or may not wish to exercise. It is like the right to divorce: having the right to divorce does not mean that every marriage has to break up – far from it. Unity is primary – but the option to split remains latent even in the best of marriages. The essential point is that there is free choice – at least formally. Free choice is a necessary condition for people to live together on the basis of equality and mutual respect. But it is not enough to legally assure this outcome. Economic conditions, for example, can keep women bound in unhappy, or even abusive, relationships. And economic conditions can likewise maintain independent nations under imperialist control. Basic justice and thoroughgoing democracy require full equality – political, social, and economic. The long-term goal is a community of freely associating women and men of all races and nations, where national groupings have full access to political power – but retain the right to secede if necessary.

While unity is the desired outcome, the reality of national oppression today carries with it certain consequences for the movement – consequences that flow from the national character of the subject peoples. Among these are:

- ***Demands*** – National demands aim for organized political power in areas of concentration – be it as a representative on city council, in the sheriff's or mayor's office, on the school board, or leading a county, reservation, or independent state. Such demands for power do not imply exclusion of other nationalities, who can and should play an important role as allies. One example of a national struggle centers on the reconstruction of New Orleans after Hurricane Katrina – including the right of return and the retention of political power by the city's black majority. (See the end of this chapter and the next for more examples.)

- ***Forms of organization*** – Oppressed nationalities have the right to caucuses within larger organizations, distinct organizations within an alliance, and a leading revolutionary organization linked to the nation's homeland. Black Workers for Justice (BWFJ), based in North Carolina, is an example of a national form of organization within the broader workers movement. (For a discussion of related organizational questions, see Chapters 23 and 25.)

- ***Leadership*** – The necessity of a leading role for oppressed nationality people is most evident in their own national liberation struggle. But also, given the centrality of national oppression to U.S. imperialism – along with the corrupting influence of white privilege – oppressed nationality peoples can be expected to play a leading role in the overall social justice movement as well. (For some practical implications of this understanding of oppressed nationality leadership, see Chapters 20, 23, 25, and 26.)

These consequences of an oppressed nation analysis are clearest when contrasted with organizations that include race as just one of a number of concerns, or that subordinate race to other oppressions like class or gender, rather than keeping each struggle central in its own way. In these situations, special demands (*special* in the sense that the dominant group does not view them as essential), caucuses, or claims on leadership tend to challenge the control of the usually white, often male individuals holding power in the group or movement. Various left organizations, for example, over the years ruled out nationality caucuses on the basis that they were divisive both to their organizations and to the working class. In reality, however, such caucuses, special demands, and affirmative action in leadership are measures that help build unity in an organization – as well as in the working class. It is the unacknowledged blindspot of white leadership on issues of race that is the real source of division.

While recognizing the existence of oppressed nations and their right to self-determination, it is also important to note that not all forms of nationalism are progressive. The attempt of the white supremacist U.S. ruling class to consolidate its nation's domination of the world is the purest example of reactionary nationalism. Other national struggles that serve the interests of imperialism also share this oppressive character: Israel's suppression of the Palestinian nation and Great Britain's hold over Northern Ireland are two examples. Also, tendencies toward *narrow*, or *reactionary nationalism* can work against the unity of oppressed peoples, pitting one national grouping against another. In addition, national movements, due to their multi-class character, can end up replacing one set of exploiters with another of a different color. The struggle for working class leadership of the national movements is critical in this regard – while at the same time uniting with the national sentiments of other classes, and supporting their contributions to community building. Overwhelmingly the nationalism of the oppressed peoples of color inside the United States is progressive and has the potential to strike at the root of the imperialist system.

Changing social conditions

In the two previous chapters we drew out the national character of the African American struggle as manifested in 1) the history of slavery and discrimination centered in the Black Belt South; 2) the religious and cooperative institutions set up in the North in the late 1700s and in the South during Reconstruction; 3) the system of white supremacy that, in defeating Reconstruction, suppressed and denied black people access to land, employment, and capital; 4) the migrations, urbanization process, and struggles of the early 20th century that brought with them class differentiation and a flowering of black culture*; and 5) the imperialist character of the U.S. social system, which has national oppression as a cornerstone.

Over the intervening period since the 1920s, small-scale black capitalists first grew in numbers, with the loosening of segregation's racial strictures, but then lost out as white corporations took over every corner of the U.S. market.† Sharecropping on large plantations, still common in the South in the 1920s and '30s, dropped off sharply with the mechanization of agriculture and the migration of rural workers to northern urban centers. Black workers moved into industry during and after World War II – aided by the more inclusive labor organizing of that period – but then deindustrialization and globalization squeezed people out in more recent decades. (See Section III, "Race and Class" for more detail on these periods.) Sports and entertainment figures, who in the 1920s seldom broke through to the mainstream, today occupy a prominent, but still largely distinct sector of these industries – while the commanding heights remain under white control. And Jesse Jackson's presidential campaigns of the 1980s were in a different league from the 1940s Harlem-based victory of Benjamin Davis, Jr., elected as a Communist to the New York City Council, or Adam Clayton Powell, Jr.'s 25 year run in Congress.

The 1960's and '70s upsurge in the national movements gave evidence of the changes that had taken place since the 1930s – while reinforcing the validity of the Black Nation analysis. As Komozi Woodward points out: "the chief sources of contemporary black nationality formation are urban. African American nationalism has spread quickly in the cities because of the nature of urban bureaucratic competition and conflict in a multiethnic capitalist society. As blacks migrated to the North, they were not absorbed into White America: instead they developed a distinct national culture and consciousness....African Americans were urbanized and modernized in a very separate manner, which laid the foundations for a distinct black national political community."[2] In addition, the various class forces within the nation made clear their social existence in the struggle for political primacy – poorer sector workers in

---

* The Harlem Renaissance was a black arts movement of the 1920s identified with intellectuals such as Langston Hughes, James Weldon Johnson, and Claude McKay. *(Bush,* We Are Not What We Seem*)*

† Even during segregation, when there was a captive market for black companies, a survey of Chicago's businesses in 1938 showed that white businesses outnumbered black businesses, and "less than one-tenth of the money spent by the black consumer went to black businesses."*(Ofari,* The Myth of Black Capitalism, *pp. 41, 44-45)*

the Black Panther Party; industrial workers in the League of Revolutionary Black Workers and the Black Workers Congress; the Southern mass base of the voting rights movement in SNCC (Student Non-Violent Coordinating Committee) and SCLC (Southern Christian Leadership Conference); and the emerging cultural, intellectual, and political intelligentsia in the National Black Power Conferences from 1966 to 1969, and the 1972 National Black Political Convention in Gary, Indiana. As we will discuss in Section IV, "Patriarchy and Privilege," contradictions around gender also developed during this period. Tensions arose within existing organizations and led to new formations like the Third World Women's Alliance and the National Black Feminists Organization. All these forces drew on the national sentiments and energy at the base of the movement among the masses of black people both north and south.

In assessing today the validity of the Black Nation analysis, one might ask: "If the CP-USA analysis was correct and a nation existed in the late 1920s, and if despite significant changes in class structure by the 1960s and '70s, the nation still existed in that period, what has happened since then that might have caused the nation to disappear?" To ask the question is to answer it: nothing of such a qualitatively significant character has happened. Since African Americans continue to make up some 12% of society, the only possibility is that they might have become fully assimilated. But the opposite is true. Since 1980 the society has stagnated or moved backward with respect to segregated housing patterns, affirmative action, and economic inequality.* What has succeeded during this period, however, as mentioned in Chapter 3, is an ideological offensive that has persuaded many – mostly white – people that equality has been achieved. Aiding in this effort also has been the small but visible business-oriented black elite, partially integrated into the corporate, political, and opinion-molding sectors of society.

Overall, black people's consciousness of being part of an oppressed nation today is nowhere near what it was in the 1960s and '70s. Nationhood is both objective (existing independently in the external world) and subjective (reflected in the outlook and understanding of the people themselves). The criteria set out in the definition of nation above are a first pass at a social science guide to the concrete, real-world existence of nations. The subjective side is more difficult to determine – and only gains full expression in an organized movement for national liberation. From time to time national consciousness has taken political forms – in demands for community or tribal control of schools, for bilingual education, or for local electoral power. Higher-level demands may focus on land claims, reparations, or the recognition of the sovereign status of,

---

* We will examine the continuing record of white privilege – and white denial – in Chapters 16 and 17.

say, Hawai'i, Aztlán (the former northern states of Mexico), or the old plantation country of the South – the Black Belt. In each case, a nation has its homeland, where the main concentration of its people lives – along with individuals from other nationalities who may inhabit that same territory. Members of the oppressed grouping may also live in other regions, dispersed by capitalist market pressures to distant cities in search of work. Descendants of Mexicans living in Chicago are still Chicanos, just as Puerto Ricans in New York are Borinqueños. Land is central to nationhood – be it the historic homeland or the generally urban areas of the North and West where peoples of color live in concentrated communities. As Malcolm X pointed out, land and the question of political power are closely connected: "land is the basis of all independence, land is the basis of freedom, justice, and equality."[3]

Short of such national movements or demands, a people can demonstrate their loyalty to the common identity in many ways. It is not necessary to proclaim oneself a "Black Nationalist" for national sympathies and commitments to be part of one's life. People often express these sentiments through institutional forms like the family, church, or school – or through community and issue organizations, sororities and fraternities, reunions, book clubs, or holiday celebrations. Music, dance, hairstyles and other cultural forms are a powerful uniting force. These common social and emotional experiences, along with common group ideals, goals, and political aspirations, when shared by millions, add up to a sense of group identity.

A majority of black people still live in the South – 55.3% as of 2002. In addition, the 1990s saw the greatest movement of black people back to the South since this return migration began in the 1970s.* People often retire to the South and families hold reunions that celebrate their Southern roots. All these facts together indicate that black people can be considered a historically rooted community of people, having a common language (English), culture, and internal network of economic relationships, and that they constitute a nation whose homeland is the Black Belt South. As a nation black people should enjoy the democratic right to self-determination, up to and including the right to secede from the United States if the people so choose.

---

* A survey of top cities for African Americans in 2004 listed seven in the old South (Atlanta, Dallas, Nashville, Houston, Charlotte, Birmingham, and Memphis) and one in a border state (Baltimore). *(www.businessenterprise.com)* Georgia's African American population passed that of California and Florida between 1990 and 2000. The 35% increase of 603,000 was the greatest of any state. Latino and Asian populations also grew significantly during the 1990s to 5% and 2% respectively. Atlanta's greater metropolitan saw the white population decline from 77% to 55% between 1970 and 2000, with the shift due mainly to the growth of African Americans. *(Georgia Office of Planning and Budget, "Georgia Population Trends 1990 to 2000")*

In addition to African Americans, a similar overall analysis holds for the Chicano people, with their historic homeland in the Southwest, and for the indigenous peoples, with their disputed land claims throughout the country. It can be easier to see the Chicano and native peoples as nations 1) because their languages are distinct from English and 2) because for a long period in the past they functioned as separate political entities on territory now held by the United States. At the same time, the ravages of history have left many indigenous peoples in depressed conditions, dispersed from their homelands, and with nowhere near a normal, capitalist class structure. The common bond shared with the African American nation is a history of forced subjugation and cultural domination by white supremacy.

In the end one must step back and look at the whole pattern of oppression, resistance, and development through the various stages of U.S. history. It is not enough to count the number of counties where black people are a majority, or the number of capitalists from a particular indigenous community. Land, language, culture, economic life, and a people's history of common suffering and struggle – all must be weighed as a whole, in their entirety. Together they yield a deeply rooted sense of the reality today of national oppression under U.S. imperialism.

National minorities

Many Puerto Rican people living in the United States support self-determination for their island country. In similar fashion, millions of Palestinians dispersed from their homeland by Israel – many of whom now live in the United States – identify with the Palestinian national struggle and yearn to return home. These peoples, like millions of other immigrants from oppressed nations of the global South, belong to *oppressed national minorities* inside the United States. Similarly, African Americans concentrated in parts of the United States outside the South can be viewed as national minorities in those areas. Nations and national minorities have the same core demand for political power. In homeland territories this demand for power takes its highest form: the democratic right of a nation to secede if it wishes and form its own country – the right to self-determination. In other parts of the United States, the comparable demand for national minorities is *autonomy* – control of local institutions within the larger society.

Relations among the various oppressed nationalities are complicated and we will examine them in some detail in Chapter 22. There are tensions between African Americans and Latinos in LA, in the Black Belt South, and elsewhere where capitalists can manipulate competition for scarce jobs to keep people divided. Also, throughout the Sunbelt region, many native peoples live on reservations historically forced on them by the U.S. government. These territories function in some ways like the official black homelands of the former apartheid South Africa, or the enclosures of today's West Bank Palestine. Indian lands usually are marginal and lacking in natural resources – leftovers from the pickings by railroad, mining, and agricultural interests, as well as by white settlers. Self-determination for the many native peoples will require an extended period of negotiation to identify appropriate homeland territories, taking into account the long history of displacement and broken treaties. With these difficult issues in mind, the demand for self-determination nonetheless has the potential to unite all the oppressed nations of the South and Southwest – along with the justice-loving European Americans and others who end up residing in the various national territories.

The interrelations among oppressed nationalities become even more complex on taking the various immigrants of color into account. Each new grouping, driven to immigrate by the workings of the imperialist system, has its own particularities of language and history. On the one hand, resistance to the overall racist character of the system tends to bind people together. On the other, the relatively low level of national consciousness inside the United States today often leads progressive newcomers – say, from the *Dominican Republic* or the *Philippines*[4] – to orient primarily to the social struggles in their home countries. *Puerto Ricans* in New York City are part of the U.S. social reality and subject to discrimination on the basis of race, language, and nationality. But they are also just a short trip over the "air bridge" to their homeland, and Puerto Rican flags are everywhere in the *barrios* – not just at the annual parade down 5th Avenue. The dominant culture accords *Haitians* the status of African American as soon as people set foot in the United States. Yet inside the black community they form a distinct minority, and tensions can arise around assimilation into this community.[5] *Cape Verdeans* also assimilate in a distinctive way into African America, retaining a strong sense of their island roots and their connection to Portuguese culture. Similarly for *Honduran* or *Mexican* nationals in relation to the Chicano people. In this regard, the broad-based upsurge of Latino workers demanding immigration rights in the spring of 2006 marks a new stage in the development of the Chicano national liberation struggle.

South Asians and *Palestinians* do not fit into the major national groupings inside the United States; and *Muslim people* from many countries became the target of government profiling and repression after 9/11. Each such community carves out its own niche – finding its own ways to resist and flourish, creating yet another piece of the oppressed nationality tapestry. Within this complex pattern immigrant peoples carry out local campaigns against white supremacy, while linking everyone more closely to the national and anti-imperialist struggles in their homelands.

Pan-ethnic organizing took shape in the 1960s, as 1) the indigenous peoples of the United States jointly organized for greater decision-making power; and 2) people of Chinese, Japanese, Korean and other national backgrounds, both immigrant and native born, grouped together to fight discrimination and violence against Asian-Pacific Island peoples as a whole. Before that era, these various peoples occupied largely separate social spaces inside the United States.[6] Today the more inclusive categories are commonly understood – appearing in names of organizations like the American Indian Movement or Asian Americans United. At the same time, nations carry out their own independent struggles for recognition, land, and economic development – and some individuals resent the loss of identity in the pan-ethnic term *Indian*. Among Asian-Pacific Islander people groups like the Korean Independent Workers Organization (KIWA) and the Filipino Workers Center carry out targeted organizing campaigns in Los Angeles. How these different outlooks and forms of organization will develop – both interrelatedly and independently – is unclear. The only certainty is that, regardless of the framework used, organizers have to pay attention to the specific language, culture, and history of the people they are engaged with – while keeping in mind the overall context of a white supremacist superpower 300 years in the making.

Indigenous peoples and self-determination

It is ironic that during the past quarter-century, the U.S. government has actually begun using the term *self-determination* in its dealings with the indigenous peoples. It is the term favored in describing the current status of the more than 500 officially recognized Indian tribes and nations. American Indian Movement (AIM) leader Russell Means, however, prefers to call the status "self-administration."[7] The United Nations has made clear in its formal decolonization guidelines that self-determination is a right belonging to the oppressed people themselves. There are safeguards to assure that the former colonizing power cannot control a subject people's decision on its status.

James Wilson, in *The Earth Shall Weep*, describes the contradictory conditions Indian people find themselves in today. Indian culture is recognized as never before – as evidenced by the opening in 2004 of the Smithsonian Museum in Washington DC dedicated to native history. Education is improving – but with it comes the slipping away of young people into the social mainstream, accomplishing what decades of assimilationist boarding schools could not. Economic power is in the hands of tribal councils – but usually still with a trust clause reserving final authority to U.S. authorities. Poor land, lack of access to water, the absence of capital and credit, and reliance on the free market together mean that actual economic power often lies with outside business investors. Along with the gains in native political power have come cutbacks in federal money, which then lead to increased competition among the indigenous peoples for the funds that remain. As a result, while there are exceptions, conditions on reservations remain oppressive: "there are soaring rates of drug and alcohol abuse, suicide (particularly among teenagers), homicide, family violence and 'accidental death.'"[8]

Even the most basic question of who is an Indian is contested. Federal criteria center on who has the proper percentage of "blood" – cutting against traditional, relation-based approaches to inclusion in the community. Ward Churchill talks of the "identity monitors" and "purity police" who emerged as a result of these restrictive policies – checking the documentation of Indian artists and "buttonhole[ing] and order[ing]...children as young as eight years of age...to prove they were 'genuine' Indians."[9] In addition, the manipulation of census categories has resulted in the loss of more than 10 million native people – half disappearing into the Hispanic/Spanish category; and the other half, of mixed native and African descent, lost due to the "way census questions were asked and answers tallied."[10] The Cherokee Nation of Oklahoma has dealt with this situation by doing away with the blood quantum criterion entirely – relying instead on traditional criteria that govern outsiders' becoming members of the nation. As a result the number of Cherokee people in Oklahoma increased from fewer than 10,000 in the 1950s to over 300,000 today.[11]

Hawai'i

Hawai'i is an important example of the struggle for self-determination. In 1993 President Clinton apologized to the native Hawai'ians for the 1898 seizure of the islands without any vote by the native inhabitants. The United States at that time was looking for a Pacific base to launch a military expedition against Spain in order to suppress the Philippine resistance. In 1946 the U.N. included Hawai'i on its list of colonized territories. Once Hawai'i became a state in 1959, however, the islands were considered to have exercised their right to self-determination. The problem is that everyone in Hawai'i voted in the statehood plebiscite – settlers as well as the native Hawai'ians, the Kanaka Maoli. This approach contradicts explicit international procedures for resolving colonial questions that specify the native inhabitants alone should decide their status. In addition, the only options offered on the referendum were statehood or a continuation of the territorial status.

In the 1990s, organizations like Ka Laui Hawai'i and Ka Pakaukau initiated a campaign for Hawai'ian decolonization. As a first step these organizations counted the native population in the traditional way, thereby raising the number of Kanaka to 138,742 in 1990, instead of the less than 10,000 in the official count. Second, the organizations developed a *Master Plan* that calls for reparations and "sovereign jurisdiction over some 1.6 million acres."[12]

So far, the U.S. government refuses even to recognize the Kanaka people as an official tribe or nation. When the issue of *self-determination* comes up, the United States qualifies it by referring to *internal* self-determination. According to a 2001 statement of the National Security Council, this phrase means "tribal self-government and autonomy" but "it is not necessarily synonymous with more general understandings of self-determination under international law." Given the U.S. stalling and clouding of the issues, Ka Laui Hawai'i decided to take their case to the United Nations. The U.S. role in that body, however, suggests that not much can be expected. Churchill believes, however, that a moral intervention by that body "would likely generate a tangible enhancement of the Kanaka Maoli negotiating position...[and] expose...the truth lurking behind the shopworn U.S. façade of being a 'nation of laws.'"[13]

Native claims

In 1966 the indigenous peoples of Alaska came together to form the Alaska Federation of Natives (AFN). Five years later the AFN won from the United States control of 44 million acres and $1 billion under the Alaska Native Claims Settlement Act (ANCSA) of 1971. This first major land agreement put the land under the control of native corporations – that is, business entities – and not the communities themselves. The CEO of one of these corporations commented in 2003, "ANCSA was really the first real settlement between Native Americans and the federal government that was an act of self-determination. The previous treaties and settlements involved land and assets held in trust for Native people by the government and controlled by the Bureau of Indian Affairs."[14]

In 1980, however, Willie Hensley, keynote speaker at the AFN Convention that year offered a deeper perspective: "Unfortunately, our identity as people – our tribal soul – now has an uneasy resting place: That land [is] now owned by our business corporations....We cannot look to corporate life or politics to fill the void of a century of psychological repression. Business and politics are not an *end*. They are simply a *means* to the primary task of tribal renewal and survival."[15]

This contradiction between means and fundamental goals is a recurrent theme in the struggle for indigenous self-determination. It also takes the sharper form of tension between tribal representatives recognized by the U.S. government – and at times appointed by it – and the traditional leaders of the people. A particularly vexing example is the ongoing Hopi and Navajo dispute over land rights at Big Mountain, Arizona. Here Peabody Coal Company has profited for decades, strip-mining coal and using precious underground aquifer water to carry coal slurry to distant power plants. Traditional leaders of both nations have been a force for unity in working through the issues of native sovereignty, traditional land use, and shared benefits from coal deposits. But federal acts in 1974,

1980, and 1996 have mainly worked to keep the coal profits flowing in the name of energy independence – while imposing a relocation plan on thousands of Navajo sheep farmers that has kept the territorial dispute between the communities festering. Tribal representatives recognized by the U.S. government negotiated the lease agreements with Peabody – at disadvantageous terms for both nations – and many native, mostly Navajo, workers mine the coal. But the economic benefits from the land use cut against traditional values, destroy the environment, and encroach on sacred lands. This trade-off does not add up to true sovereignty or self-determination.[16]

In similar fashion, the U.S. government negotiated the release of Western Shoshone land rights with a particular group within that nation – rights that gave legal cover to nuclear and conventional bomb testing, open-pit gold mining using cyanide leeching, the blocking of access to and destruction of ancestral lands, the digging up and transfer of human remains, the pollution of water and destroying of hot springs, and the construction of the monster Yucca Mountain storage facility for nuclear waste – which the state government of Nevada also opposes. Leaders of the Western Shoshone claim six million acres in four states, as ceded in the original treaty of 1863. When the people rejected an offer of payment for the land, the U.S. government accepted payment from itself – and placed the funds in trust. Legal avenues through the court system have been blocked – with U.S. negligence or incompetence causing delays, and the government throughout evidencing contempt and disrespect for the native claims. As a result, the Western Shoshone took their case to international tribunals and won two historic judgments: one by the Inter-American Commission on Human Rights in 2002,[17] and then in May 2006 by the United Nations' Committee on the Elimination of Racial Discrimination.[18] These decisions carry no enforcement power, but they demonstrate to the world both the oppressive conditions inside the United States and the First Nations' righteous determination to achieve justice.

A strong voice advancing native claims in the courts since 1970 has been the Native American Rights Fund (NARF). In 1996 NARF filed the largest class action suit ever against the Interior Department for the mismanagement of individual Indian trust accounts holding rights to mining, oil, and timber resources. *Cobell vs. Norton* seeks an accounting and resolution of these claims, and in 2005 the indigenous nations suggested a possible settlement figure of $27.5 billion. U.S. District Judge Royce Lambeth has observed that Interior "demonstrated an unprecedented level of defiance" in the case, and "made numerous illegitimate representations, failed to correct known misrepresentations, and failed to inform the court about self-inflicted obstacles to comply with its discovery obligations." In December, 2005, Judge Lambeth awarded the NARF attorneys $7 million in fees and expenses to that point in the case. Lambeth concludes: for anyone "harboring hope that the stories of murder, dispossession, forced marches, assimilationist policy programs, and other incidents of cultural genocide against the Indians are merely the echoes of a horrible, bigoted government past that has been sanitized by the good deeds of more recent history, this case serves as an appalling reminder" of the continuing disregard of the indigenous peoples' basic human rights.[19]

Chapter 8

National Struggles and the Fight for Global Justice

Looking back a century, the concepts *imperialism* and the *national question* both became critical questions for left social analysis in the years leading up to the First World War. As the imperialists struggled to redivide the world, stirrings among the colonized people foreshadowed their emergence as actors in their own right. First the revolution in Mexico in 1910, then the first Pan-African Congress in 1919, followed by anti-colonial revolutions in China, India, Vietnam, and in many other countries – all helped mobilize national consciousness against the rule of finance capital worldwide.

Then with the collapse of direct colonialism after World War II, anti-imperialist struggles increasingly focused on economic structures of domination and the military power that keeps them in place. The historic Bandung Conference in 1955 brought representatives from 29 African and Asian nations. Later the Non-Aligned Movement led by Yugoslavia's Josip Broz Tito sought a path of development independent of both the western imperialists and the bloc of countries identified at the time with the Soviet Union. In the 1980s many of these same forces pushed for a New Economic Order that would permit favorable terms of trade and access to capital from the rich – that is to say, imperialist – powers of the United States, Europe, and Japan.

Neoliberalism

The U.S. ruling class resisted tenaciously each of these efforts at leveling the playing field. With the election of Ronald Reagan in 1980, the more open rule of money in world markets replaced the post-World War II system of welfare-state capitalism. Since then free-market ideology – often called *neoliberalism* (see box on next page) – has taken hold almost everywhere. The institutions charged with aiding economic development worldwide – the International Monetary Fund (IMF) and World Bank – imposed harsh "structural adjustment," and more recently "poverty reduction" programs in the service of western banking and industrial interests. The result: debt burdens weigh down developing countries, and billions of dollars flow out to the rich countries that supposedly are the poor countries' benefactors. Crises in Mexico (1994), Asia (1997), and in Russia, Brazil and Argentina in the early years of the 21st Century reveal a fragile – but highly adaptive – world system.

If you happen to be part of the capitalist elite, this system is working just fine. The *Wall Street Journal* reported in June 2004 that the US leads industrialized countries in wealth inequality, with the top 1% controlling over one third of the country's assets.[1] As to income inequality, Steven Rattner in the *Washington Post* writes, "Income inequality in the United States is now not only at a record level and not only the greatest since we began measuring it – it is also on a par with that of a Third World country."[2] For low and middle-income countries not including China, IMF

Neoliberalism

The main points of neoliberalism include:

1) ***The rule of the market.*** Liberating "free" enterprise or private enterprise from any bonds imposed by the government (the state) no matter how much social damage this causes. Greater openness to international trade and investment, as in NAFTA [see footnote on p. 100]. Reduce wages by de-unionizing workers and eliminating workers' rights that had been won over many years of struggle. No more price controls. All in all, total freedom of movement for capital, goods and services….

2) ***Cutting public expenditure for social services*** like education and health care. ***Reducing the safety-net for the poor***, and even maintenance of roads, bridges, water supply – again in the name of reducing government's role...

3) ***Deregulation.*** Reduce government regulation of everything that could diminish profits, including protecting the environment and safety on the job.

4) ***Privatization.*** Sell state-owned enterprises, goods and services to private investors. This includes banks, key industries, railroads, toll highways, electricity, schools, hospitals and even fresh water. Although usually done in the name of greater efficiency, which is often needed, privatization has mainly had the effect of concentrating wealth even more in a few hands and making the public pay even more for its needs.

5) ***Eliminating the concept of "the Public Good" or "Community"*** and replacing it with "individual responsibility." Pressuring the poorest people in a society to find solutions to their lack of health care, education and social security all by themselves – then blaming them, if they fail, as "lazy."

—from: Martínez and García, "What is 'Neoliberalism'?"

and World Bank policies have reduced the rate of growth, while increasing economic instability, dependence on foreign capital, and the overall number of people in poverty.[3] And at the same time that neoliberalism succeeded in increasing the Third World's share of world manufacturing exports, these countries' share of world income went down.* As Martin Hart-Landsberg points out, "neoliberalism is not so much a bad policy choice as it is a forced structural response on the part of many third world states to capitalist generated tensions and contradictions."[4] Meanwhile at the high end, wealth is becoming obscenely concentrated: "The 497 billionaires in 2001 registered a combined wealth of $1.54 trillion,... well over the combined gross national products of all the nations of sub-Saharan Africa ($929.3 billion) or those of the oil-rich regions of the Middle East and North Africa ($1.34 trillion). 'This collective wealth of the 497 is also greater than the combined incomes of the poorest half of humanity.'"[5]

Then after the events of September 11, 2001, the U.S. ruling class moved to strengthen its hold on world resources and establish a presence in Central Asia. The collapse of the Soviet Union in 1991 had left the United States the sole superpower. And unlike a century ago, the European and Japanese imperialists of today no longer contend militarily with the United States. They resort to an occasional U.N. resolution, NATO objection, or World Trade Organization ruling as a way to compete for spheres of influence. While France opposed the U.S. invasion of Iraq in 2003, for example, it then joined the United States in removing President Jean-Bertrand Aristide from power in Haiti less than a year later.

Meanwhile, structural adjustment programs are not reserved only for workers overseas. Job insecurity, privatization of public resources, budget cuts everywhere but in military spending, and a free rein to big business are the daily reality of life in the United States. While there are certain advantages to living in this country – national privileges, which like white privileges cut both ways (see Chapter 16) – the same system squeezes working people both at home and abroad.

Global justice movement

Given the common conditions facing working people around the world, it is not surprising that the global justice movement burst onto the

---

* For Mexico, between 1980 and 1997, the share of world manufacturing exports increased by a factor of ten – suggesting remarkable growth and development. But Mexico's actual share in the value contributed to final products decreased by one third during this period, and its share of world income decreased by 13%. In other words, while exports rose sharply, much of what went into those exports came from other countries, as part of production networks controlled by multinational corporations in the industrial countries – and in the United States in particular. *(Hart-Landsberg, "Neoliberalism")*

world stage in Seattle in December 1999. This upsurge was an outgrowth of – and heavily influenced by – the Zapatista uprising against NAFTA* in 1994 and the various international *encuentros* led by the Zapatista support movement during the 1990s. After Seattle, tens of thousands took to the streets in Washington, Quebec, Genoa, and in hundreds of smaller demonstrations around the world. While derailed temporarily by the events of September 11, 2001, the movement reemerged at the end of 2002 with a huge anti-war/global justice demonstration in Florence, Italy.

In this same flow – and after years of pressure from people of African descent worldwide – the United Nations convened the August 2001 World Conference Against Racism (WCAR) in Durban, South Africa. Here the agenda centered on the historic debt owed to the developing nations by the former slave-trading countries and colonialists of the North. And while recognizing the crimes of the past, the conference also paid attention to the current reality of racist domination. Rejecting U.S. protests, the WCAR sided overwhelmingly with the Palestinian people's struggle to regain their national rights. Conference attendees also joined South African activists to challenge the host government's tendency to rely on neoliberal policies – privatization, restriction of basic services for the people, and making economic development dependent on the interests of foreign investors.

WCAR represented a breakthrough comparable to Seattle because of the way it brought oppressed nationality consciousness to bear on issues of imperialist globalization. U.S. arrogance was clear for all to see: the United States sent only low-level functionaries and then withdrew from the conference before the final vote on resolutions. Unfortunately, the events of 9/11 overshadowed the WCAR and played into U.S. hands. Later in 2001, for example, the United States bullied everyone at the World Trade Organization meeting in Doha, Qatar – by threatening retaliation as part of "the fight against terrorism," if countries refused to fall in line with its neoliberal trade program.

Meanwhile the Workers Party of Brazil had initiated in January 2001 the World Social Forum (WSF) movement. Yearly meetings in Porto Alegre, Brazil – and later in other cities of the Global South – brought grassroots activists together at the same time the world elite's World Economic Forum met in Davos, Switzerland. From 10,000 people at the first gathering, the convergences grew to over 100,000 in later years. The movement generated regional and sub-regional gatherings in Europe,

---

* The North Atlantic Free Trade Agreement (NAFTA) reduces trade barriers between the United States and both Mexico and Canada. It works to the advantage of capital and against workers 1) by opening markets for cheap agribusiness produce – like corn, a staple in Mexico – which drives farmers off the land, creates unemployment, and puts downward pressure on wages; and 2) by encouraging investment in Mexico's export sector, which undercuts jobs in U.S. plants.

Africa, and Latin America – and "polycentric" meetings in January 2006 in Caracas (Venezuela), Bamako (Mali),* and Karachi (Pakistan). Increasing participation by activists from the United States led to the formation of Grassroots Global Justice (GGJ), which brought over 100 delegates from more than 60 organizations to Porto Alegre in 2003 – with similar representation in subsequent years. While the majority of participants from the United States have been from policy groups and non-profits of various kinds, GGJ's delegation was noteworthy for being "predominately people of color, and the majority of the delegates were women. There was a vibrant representation of young people, as well as long-time community organizers...GGJ also had a strong labor contingent of rank-and-file workers."[6] GGJ's *Mission* reads in part: "We believe that as U.S.-based organizations, we must be committed to building a strong enough movement to prevent the U.S. government and U.S. corporations from suppressing popular movements and interfering in the internal affairs of other countries." Plans are in place for U.S. Social Forum regional meetings during 2006, and then a full USSF gathering in Atlanta, GA, in the summer of 2007.[7]

Resistance to empire

A main force opposing the drive to empire in the world today is the resistance of oppressed nationality peoples. We have highlighted some of these struggles in earlier pages – in Puerto Rico, Cuba, and the Philippines, for example, and among the indigenous peoples of North America and Hawai'i. Here we want to survey other centers of resistance. In a period of general ebb in the movements of people of color, struggles continue to break out. Some raise sharp political criticisms in a period of neoliberal domination. Others mark solid advances for the social movements in a period of right wing rule.

Latino upsurge

On March 25, 2006, over a million Latino people marched through the center of Los Angeles. Similar marches had taken place in Chicago and other cities across the country earlier in the month. "For one brief and glorious moment, the streets belonged to us – not to the craven developers and rich Euro-Americans who are gentrifying the poor and homeless out of all affordable living space, nor to the crass politicians who pretend that providing drivers licenses to immigrants threatens our national security, not even to the shit-mouthed talk radio dummies with their gutless refrain about controlling 'our' borders and protecting 'our' culture.

---

* The Bamako gathering produced a ten-point program, the *Bamako Appeal*, with the potential to unite and give a public face to social justice movements worldwide. The appeal is available at http://mrzine.monthlyreview.org/BamakoAppeal.pdf.

On this one day, for the entire day, the streets belonged to domestic workers, garment workers, busboys, janitors, day laborers, and farm workers – people with dark skins and a Spanish language."[8]

Demonstrations and high school walkouts followed on the "National Day of Action," April 10, and again on May 1, a "Day without Immigrants." This movement of millions – which as it grew, brought in immigrant peoples of other nationalities as well – targeted repressive legislation passed by the House of Representatives at the end of 2005, HR 4437.* It was primarily a workers movement, demanding full rights and a path to citizenship for everyone. But it also drew support from other social classes within *la raza*: radio personalities – along with their bosses and advertisers, Catholic Church leaders, and the broad middle class. In addition, the movement reflected within the United States the assertive, independent spirit of Latin American leaders like Hugo Chávez in Venezuela and Evo Morales in Bolivia. In the early marches, and especially in Los Angeles, Mexican flags were common and signs stated clearly "This is our homeland" – referring to the Northern half of Mexico taken by the United States in 1848. Leaders shifted tactics, however, and in later marches people carried only U.S. flags. This change reflects tensions over the direction of the movement and its grassroots core demands: 1) citizenship for everyone, including no "guest worker" programs; and 2) an end to repressive laws that criminalize immigrants, including Muslims and Arabs. The emergence of a strong left pole within the movement – one that is able to connect the question of immigration to U.S. foreign policy, and the Latino people's struggle to that of African Americans – will be important to advancing this program. Otherwise people's energy may end up being channeled into minor rearrangements of the U.S. racial hierarchy.

Katrina reconstruction

Rebuilding New Orleans to meet the needs of the pre-hurricane, August 2005 black majority is the central struggle for self-determination in the current period. The shameful record of the event cries out for justice and righteous retribution: at least 1300 people dead due to official and racist neglect; survivors displaced through no fault of their own and then dispersed throughout the country to undermine their ability to resist; labor laws undermined and immigrant workers brought in to work un-

---

* HR 4437, also known as the Sensenbrenner-King Bill, named after its main sponsors, James Sensenbrenner (R-WI) and Peter King (R-NY), 1) made it an "aggravated felony" not to have proper immigration documents or to help someone who is undocumented, even unknowingly, 2) turned state and local police into immigration agents, 3) required employers to enforce proper documentation, 4) sharply increased the budget of the border patrol, and 5) called for the building of a 700-mile two-layered fence on the border with Mexico. *(National Immigration Forum, "The Sensenbrenner-King Bill's 'Greatest Misses'")*

protected and often unpaid in hazardous, even poisonous conditions; disenfranchisement of hundreds of thousands in the 2006 spring elections; hand-outs to shipping lines and security companies; no-bid clean-up and construction contracts that ignore the local workforce and local companies; and control in the hands of the white wealthy minority, who plan to rebuild the city in their own image.

Overall the progressive forces suffered from divisions and internal contradictions in the aftermath of the flooding. This situation prevented organizers from mounting a sustained and powerful response in the first nine months. Major energy went into meeting survivors' immediate needs – in the region around New Orleans, in southern Mississippi, and in cities around the country where survivors found themselves relocated. A Survivors Assembly in December, along with local Survivor Councils, did not succeed in mounting a political challenge to the white supremacist agenda. Malcolm Suber, an organizer for the People's Hurricane Relief Fund, commented in early April 2006 that African Americans' response to Katrina should have been at the same level as the massive immigrants' rights marches.[9] Saladin Muhammad of the Black Workers for Justice pointed out that the government's actions "brought about the largest displacement of African Americans in the U.S. South since the end of the post-Reconstruction period. It represents the most extreme example in the current period of the U.S. policy of gentrification and ethnic cleansing." And in relation to the Latino upsurge, the policy "also made clear that even with 'full' citizenship, non-white oppressed nationalities inside the United States will be treated like oppressed nations – considered expendable and a threat to U.S. national security, with little to no funding in infrastructure to protect lives and communities, super-exploitation of labor, subject to special laws, racial profiling and police harassments."[10] The struggle for the reconstruction of New Orleans and for the self-determination of the African American people is far from over – especially as links are built with the rising Latino resistance.

Labor struggles

Oppressed nationality people are the most dynamic sector of the workers movement and are the main source of new organizing gains. For example,

- *1999:* 74,000 home health care workers in California – mostly black, Latina, and Asian women – organize with the help of the Service Employees International Union (SEIU).[11]
- *2004:* The Million Worker March Movement rallies in Washington DC on October 17, 2004. Initiated by black workers in the International Longshore and Warehouse Union (ILWU) Local 10, the demonstration challenges the Democratic Party and AFL-CIO

leadership just weeks before the 2004 presidential elections. Demands included a national healthcare system, bring the troops home now, repeal the U.S. Patriot Acts, and amnesty for all undocumented workers.[12]

- *2004:* The Ohio-based Farm Labor Organizing Committee (FLOC) successfully concludes its 5-year Mt. Olive Pickle Boycott and signs up 8,000 H2-A contract farm laborers in North Carolina.
- *2005:* Latino, Haitian, and Mayan Indian farmworkers in Florida, led by the Coalition of Immokalee Workers, declare victory in their 4-year campaign to have Taco Bell increase pay for picked tomatoes by one cent per pound.[13]
- *2005:* The International Worker Justice Campaign holds hearings and files a complaint with the International Labor Organization (ILO) over the lack of public worker bargaining rights in North Carolina, led by the mostly black workers of the UE-150 Public Workers Union.
- *2006:* The United Food and Commercial Workers union (UFCW) continues their three-year campaign to organize the 60% Latino and 35% African American workforce at the Smithfield hog-processing plant in Tar Heel, North Carolina, the largest in the world. Smithfield shuts down the plant on both April 10 and May 1 for "repairs," since so many workers planned to take part in the immigrant rights demonstrations those two days.

Against male violence

- Aishah Simmons's film *No!* focuses a spotlight on the experiences of black women survivors of rape – in an overall social context where 1) the white media uses alleged rapes in the Superdome in New Orleans in September 2005 to dehumanize the hurricane survivors; and 2) following the official discounting of these rumors, no action is taken around those rapes that actually did occur – thereby making black women and their pain disappear, once again.[14]
- A young black mother and student, working as an exotic dancer in the spring of 2006 at a Duke University lacrosse team party in Durham, NC, finds herself at the cross-hairs of race, class, and male privilege – sparking a grand jury indictment, community vigils, attacks by the news program "60 Minutes" and other media, the re-election and later forced recusal of the District Attorney, and an upsurge in organizing against sexual violence regardless of the outcome of the case.

Other forms of struggle

- ***Antiwar organizing*** – Black Solidarity Against War (BSAW) on the East Coast and *Guerrero Azteca* in California, build opposition to the Iraq war and occupation.
- ***Black land loss*** – Farmers in the Black Farmers and Agriculturalist Association, after an inadequate court settlement, continue their struggle to win justice for years of discriminatory treatment by the U.S. Department of Agriculture.[15]
- ***Economic development*** – National Black Unity Convention in Gary, Indiana, in March 2006 calls for a focus on economic development, building on the original Gary convention of 1973, which focused on gaining political power.[16]
- ***Electoral arena*** – Black and Latino candidates campaign for local offices – mayor, sheriff, school board – throughout the South and

SWOP Takes on Environmental Racism in New Mexico

Recognition of environmental racism and its tactics has been a long time coming. An organization that did much to pave the way in the 1980s was the Southwest Organizing Project (SWOP) of Albuquerque, New Mexico....Born in 1981 and funded primarily by church groups at that time, SWOP is a multiracial, multi-issues community organization working "to empower the disenfranchised in the Southwest to realize social, racial, and economic justice."

SWOP became involved in fighting pollution when it started organizing in the Sawmill barrio of Albuquerque in 1984 and heard families complain of health problems they attributed to a particleboard company in the area. Ponderosa Products Inc was polluting the groundwater, generating sawdust everywhere, and making intolerable noise. In the struggle that followed and the victory it produced, we can see key aspects of SWOP's general strategy.

A first, basic goal was to demystify policymaking. "Have you ever wondered how decisions are made as to which streets get paved, how our community is zoned, or who receives loans to purchase homes? Who plans the way our neighborhood is developed? Everyone, it seems, makes plans for our community except sawmill area residents!" Those were headlines – in both English and Spanish – on one of the many leaflets distributed by SWOP. They set the tone for a process that included door-to-door surveys of residents' complaints; community meetings to inform people about the technical and legal aspects of the struggle; setting up a neighborhood organization (in this case, the Sawmill Advisory Council); and voter registration so that residents could hold elected officials accountable.

In 1987 Ponderosa Products finally signed an agreement to pump out bad

Continued on next page

Southwest; and Hmong and South Asian immigrants work to build grassroots electoral power.[17]

- ***Environment*** – The NC Environmental Justice Network fights waste dumps in the black communities of North Carolina; and the Southwest Workers Union empowers residents to compel the Department of Defense to clean up Kelly Air Force Base, near San Antonio, Texas.[18]
- ***Mass mobilizations*** – Millions More Movement marks the ten-year anniversary of the Million Man March, with a rally in Washington DC on October 15, 2005.
- ***Reparations*** – Thousands rally for reparations in Washington, DC, on August 27, 2002.
- ***And many other struggles*** – for affirmative action in hiring and promotion, educational equality, bilingual education and other

Continued from previous page

water and reduce noise emission. That document stands as the first urban cleanup agreement between industry, government, and the community in New Mexico – and probably in the whole Southwest.

Exposing the problems and educating the public has been essential in all of SWOP's efforts. For example, SWOP and the National Council of Churches' Eco-Justice Task Force co-sponsored hearings in 1989 where a dozen New Mexicans and borderland Mexicans told personal stories of being sickened in their workplaces. Unforgettable testimony came from Virginia Candelaria, one of many workers exposed to poisonous solvents and wastes in Albuquerque's General Telephone and Electronics (GTE) plant. Candelaria suffered severe damage to her central nervous system after nine years of cleaning circuit boards. Other women had children with birth defects, and eventually 465 workers filed suit. When asked if GTE had changed the process, Candelaria had difficulty speaking; her attorney replied for her, "Most of the dangerous processes, most of the dangerous chemicals, have been moved to Juárez, Mexico. There is a plant across the border now." All too often such transfers have been the so-called solution to a pollution problem.

As Virginia Candelaria's testimony indicated, women workers of color are especially vulnerable to contamination....Those who attended the hearings where Candelaria spoke were taken on tours to see the contamination by Albuquerque paint factories, gas refineries, sewage treatment centers and a dog food factory where unused animal parts were heaped outdoors to rot. It became nauseously evident that communities inhabited by people of color are targeted for toxin-producing industries and facilities that wouldn't be allowed in other neighborhoods. For people of color, then, environmental issues are issues of social, economic and racial justice."

—*from: Martínez, De Colores* Means All of Us

language rights, prison reform and against racial profiling, housing, health care, quality child care, and full voting rights.

Resistance abroad

The war in Afghanistan, declared over in December 2001, has continued as a low-intensity conflict. The poppy crop has made a huge comeback, and periodic U.S. bombing missions take a costly toll in civilian casualties. The invasion and occupation of Iraq in 2003 dramatically undermined the U.S. position in the world and squandered the reserves of good will extended after the bombing of the World Trade Center in 2001. The U.S. empire faces challenges on a number of fronts: countries on the U.N. Security Council remain opposed to preventive wars; socialist and populist leaders in Bolivia, Brazil, Cuba, Ecuador, and Venezuela stake out more independent economic positions; revolutionary struggles continue in the Philippines, Nepal, and Colombia; the World Trade Organization's Doha Round of negotiations bogged down; and China grows as an Asian economic power – though appearing less and less socialist in its internal practices.

Finally, the struggles of the First Nations inside the United States are closely interwoven with challenges to U.S. militarism worldwide. Who can teach more lessons about the U.S. history of conquest, occupation, and regime change? About the enforcement of corporate-led, U.S.-style democracy on subject peoples? About the testing and after-effects of conventional and nuclear armaments? Or about the appropriation of native culture – "Blackhawk and Apache helicopters, Tomahawk missiles"[19] – for imperialist ends? These lessons also carry with them the promise – or better, the certainty – of resistance to imperialist domination by nations inside the United States, as well as by those in Central Asia, Latin America, and in every other corner of the empire.

Overview and look ahead

U.S. militarism and empire building push people to resist all around the world. Driving today's developments is the same lethal mix of white supremacy and economic monopoly that initially took hold in the closing decades of the 19th Century. U.S. imperialism grew up in conditions made possible by the defeat of Reconstruction and the distribution of native peoples' land to corporations and white settlers. Imperialism means national oppression – controlling peoples' economies, exploiting their labor power, and distorting their development to fit the dominant power's needs. Inside the United States imperialism created conditions for national consciousness and movements for national liberation to arise, centered on demands for political power and self-determination. The democratic promise of Reconstruction, though defeated and suppressed, later reappeared in the Garvey Movement after World War I, in the communist-led organizing of the 1930s, and in the modern liberation movements of the 1960s and '70s. African American, Chicano, native peoples, Asian communities – all came to assert their identity and connect their demands to those of oppressed peoples of color around the world, fighting the same system of white supremacist patriarchal capitalism.

Race and nationality are central to the way U.S. society functions. Social class and gender are also critical to its operation. The next section, "Race and Class," looks at white privilege in a working class context, emphasizing traditional workplace organizing outside the home. The following section, "Patriarchy and Privilege," then broadens the perspective to include the interrelations of white privilege with patriarchy, the system of male domination. The concept *intersectionality* helps bring together the multiple ways each person oppressed by capitalism relates to society – by seeing people as whole human beings, more than the sum of race, class, gender, sexual orientation, age, and physical capabilities. A vision of liberation worth fighting for requires that all the oppressed see themselves fully in the new society the social justice movement is struggling to build.

Stemmer

(Dedicated to the millions who smoke the treat that kills.)

It's a hot, sweaty, steamy day.
Gonna be a real long day today.
I'm standin' rigid as a pole at my station, my place t'be 'xact
Strippin' these leaves, fast as I can go—No, faster than I
can go, or should go

I'm a machine, and so is the rest of the girls—we're here to get the job done.
It's too hot in here, cain't he see that?
He keeps looking at me, holdin' his clipboard, tappin' his pencil.
I'm going fast as I can, boss.

Boss's face is Hell-red: face sweats, eyes sweat, hair bleeds sweat and reeks of sweat
It's a long, hot, stuffy-ass day here.

I keep on going, I keep on going, my hands are torn up, dry as a bone, I've nicked myself a few times too.

I'm going as fast as I can, boss.

Damn you girl/nigger/wench (Whatever!) his eyes say
He knows he don't want to be here, why is he here?
Time is money, money is time.
That's the way it is here in Bull Durham
I live and die on His Time, and on my dime.

—*Yolanda Carrington*

III

RACE AND CLASS

Why should we talk about class at all in this book? After all our central focus is racism and white privilege. There are two main answers to this question: First, as we saw in Section I, the dominant force involved in setting up the racist system of preferences in colonial times was the planter class. Later, after the Civil War, Northern industrialists formed a *de facto* alliance with white supremacists in the South to crush Reconstruction and extend the color line. And together the Northern and Southern ruling elites promoted imperial expansion. To understand race in the United States, there is no getting away from the dominant economic class, be it slave-owning or industrial.

Second, where there's a ruling class, there are the ruled: slaves, small farmers, artisans, storeowners, and workers – workers in factories and offices and at home with the children. People in different social classes struggle in various ways to make a better world for themselves. They create political parties, push forward leaders to represent their interests, form alliances, and contest for power. The movement of history, at least in its broad strokes, can often be understood best as a history of struggles among these different classes and class alliances.

In this section we approach the relationship of race and class in three ways – historically, theoretically, and strategically. In Chapter 9 we look at two critical periods in U.S. history – the years after the Civil War, and the decades from 1930 to 1950. In both these periods white workers passed up working class unity for the opportunity to gain white privileges. After the Civil War there were white only craft jobs, homesteads in the West, and a segregated textile industry in the South. After World War II there were GI Bill education grants and redlined suburban real estate loans. The consequences of the organizing defeats in both these periods still weigh heavily on people today, impacting the whole country but especially the Sunbelt region of the South and Southwest.

In Chapter 10 we draw on these historic lessons, as well as on material from earlier chapters, to highlight three theoretical conclusions relating white privilege and the state of U.S. working class consciousness. We begin by reviewing what we mean by the word *class*. Then we look at how different working class leaders in the past understood the relationship between race and class in the United States. We finish by assessing the different positions put forward by the political left in the 1970s on this question. Along the way we summarize three points, concerning 1) the low level of working-class consciousness in the United States, 2) the class dynamics driving white privilege and racism, and 3) certain essential steps necessary to end the system of racial preferences.

In the final chapter of this section, Chapter 11, we return to the South and Southwest, but now updating the discussion with an analysis of the period from the 1970s to the present. We point to a strategy for left organizers today grounded in both history and current conditions – namely, "Organize the South and Southwest." Then in a concluding review we show how our perspective on race, class, and class-consciousness – as developed in Chapters 9-11 – underlies the argument of the entire book. The bottom line is that for partisans of the working class, there is no reason why a small minority should control all of society and benefit from the misery of others.

Chapter 9

Missed Opportunities

W.E.B. DuBois commented in *Black Reconstruction* that the problem for white workers was their inability to "see in black slavery and Reconstruction, the kernel and meaning of the labor movement."[1] White workers' consciousness could not get past the privileges given Europeans on arriving in the United States. Despite experiencing extreme exploitation, miserable working conditions, and beatings by nativist, anti-immigrant gangs, white people in the 19th Century still possessed relative privileges: minimal human rights, access to paid work, and the opportunity to become citizens and vote. Immigrants were never viewed as property; and no abuse of people from Europe could compare to the dehumanization of African Americans, slave or free.[2]

Trade unions during and after the Civil War

The Civil War totally disrupted the Southern economy, but at the same time it unleashed tremendous economic forces in the North.[3] Especially affected were industrial sectors directly connected to the war – railroads, iron and steel, textiles and meatpacking. Meanwhile, as capitalists made their fortunes, conditions for workers deteriorated.

The iron molder William H. Sylvis spent the war years traveling through the North, Midwest, and parts of Canada, building local unions in iron foundries and bringing them together into the centralized Iron Molders International Union. At the same time, a movement in northern and western cities united locals from different industries into citywide central labor bodies, called trades assemblies. Together these efforts sought to blunt the increased power and aggressiveness of wartime industrial employers.

The National Labor Union and the struggle in the South

Following the South's surrender in 1865, a combination of trades assemblies and newly organized unions formed the National Labor Union (NLU). The main issue at the founding convention was the fight for an eight-hour workday. From its beginning the NLU reflected internally the opposing forces in the fight for democracy in the South. Abolitionists, Radical Republicans, and workers transformed by their Civil War experiences together made up a minority of the organization. "Copperheads" – pro-Confederate Northerners and the anti-Civil War wing of the Democratic Party – dominated the labor movement.

During the war Copperhead leaders had sought to unite white northern workers behind the interests of Southern slaveholders. They fanned class resentment over the 1863 Union Conscription Act, which allowed the wealthy to buy their way out of service in the Union army. They also encouraged Northern union leaders to spread fear of job competition from newly freed slaves.

All but one union forming the NLU excluded black workers from membership.[4] Also, none of the unions – and only one newspaper, the *Boston Daily Evening Voice* – appreciated what Reconstruction was all about, or the vital stake all workers had in the outcome of the struggle. NLU President William Sylvis shared the understanding that African Americans "number four million strong, and a greater proportion of them labor with their hands than can be counted from among the same number of any other people on earth."[5] Also, a few labor newspapers and organizers argued that excluding the black sector of the laboring population would force the excluded "in self-defense, to underwork their brethren or class...and oblige them to become co-operators with the enemy."[6]

Out of deference to the majority, Sylvis never argued against the affiliates' exclusion of black workers – while he had taken such a stand in defense of women workers. The most notorious example of exclusion occurred when the National Typographical Union barred from membership the son of the great abolitionist leader Frederick Douglass. The NLU's National Executive Board shared in the shame by turning down the case on appeal.

Sylvis expressed a desire to organize black workers during an organizing tour of the South just months before his death in 1869. But at the same time he opposed the Freedmen's Bureau, "was offended by the social intermingling of black and white under the new regime in the South,"[7] and misunderstood the Reconstruction governments' fight for land, public education, and social legislation for all. Instead, he argued that black workers should fight for an independent labor party. In the South the votes of the former slaves made the difference in the continued electoral victories of the Republican Party. Despite its serious limitations and lack of long-term commitment to the goal of democracy, the Republican Party at that time represented black people's best hope for the future.

The National Colored Labor Union (NCLU) – formed in 1869 and led by the shipbuilder Isaac Myers – promoted pro-Reconstruction views that contrasted with the NLU's. Three experiences shaped this new organization's orientation: First, in 1866 the all-white NLU, despite its call to organize all workers, excluded black workers from its founding convention in Baltimore. Second, Myers, who had been a caulker in the Baltimore shipyards, witnessed a strike by white workers in 1865 that led to the firing of a thousand black workers. And third, white businessmen helped Myers and other black workers set up their own shipyard after the mass firing. Such experiences contributed to the NCLU's suspicion of labor militancy and their openness to working with capitalists – a view similar to that of Booker T. Washington a generation later. While the NCLU represented a wide range of occupations and trades, it also included religious leaders, professionals, and others with a concern for labor. The NCLU focused on Reconstruction issues, such as employment, equal treatment before the law, access to land in the South, and education. And it sought to organize all workers, in contrast to the NLU's emphasis on the skilled trades. According to Philip Foner's *Organized Labor and the Black Worker*, the NCLU included men and women of all races, including Chinese workers who were not contract laborers – "thus becoming the only labor organization of the period to open its ranks to the Chinese immigrant."[8]

Motion toward bridging the gulf between the NLU and NCLU began with a handful of black workers' attending the 1868 and 1869 meetings of the NLU. Then in 1870 the fourth convention of the NLU opened with the prospect of a united movement. The gathering quickly deteriorated, however, when white delegates rejected the admission of ex-slave and Union League organizer John Mercer Langston, based on his ties to the Republican Party. While progress toward some kind of an alliance seemed possible around most economic issues, politically the two organizations diverged. The NCLU remained committed to the Republican Party; the NLU pushed for the formation of a labor party.

In retrospect, it is clear that Sylvis' abstract call for an independent labor party missed the real opportunity to unite with the freedmen in a solid block behind the Radical Republicans – the section of the party committed to thoroughgoing democracy. The NLU instead flirted with the elitist opposition within the party, the Liberal Republicans. Labor reform efforts ran aground at the 1872 Liberal Republican Convention when, as one NLU leader stated, the Liberals "could not reach over the gulf that divides capital and labor."[9] Despite the NLU's emphasis on its working class constituency – in comparison to the NCLU's more open membership policy – the NLU turned out to prefer the white capitalists of the Liberal Republicans over their class brothers and sisters in the NCLU. Had the NLU forces recognized their class interests and struggled to bridge the gap with black labor, the dream of a true labor party might in time have become a reality. Pro-democracy forces might have split off to form a labor party during the mid-1870s when industrialists took full control of the Republican Party and sold out Reconstruction. Instead, white labor proved over time that it preferred the "white man's party" – the Democratic Party* of that period – to other options that came along, whether Republican, socialist, populist, or fusion.

W.E.B. DuBois saw this lost opportunity for a unified national labor movement as a great tragedy: "The South, after the war, presented the greatest opportunity for a real national labor movement which the nation ever saw. Yet the labor movement, with but few exceptions, never realized the situation....As the Negroes [in the NCLU] moved from unionism toward political action, white labor in the North not only moved in the opposite direction..., but also evolved the American Blindspot for the Negro and his problems. It lost interest and vital touch with Southern labor and acted as though the millions of laborers in the South did not exist."[10] Instead of Reconstruction consolidating a movement for democracy rooted among all laboring people, its defeat – as we saw in Chapter 5 – led to the victory of Jim Crow segregation by the turn of the century.

Chinese exclusion

Chinese workers first arrived in California during the Gold Rush in 1848. Then the building of the transcontinental railroad in the late 1860s escalated the demand for Chinese labor. Thousands took part in the dangerous work of bridging and tunneling through the western mountain ranges. But when the economic Panic of 1873 struck, white workers turned to scapegoating immigrants, murdering many Chinese, and terrorizing their communities. Unions played a major role in building this hysteria and spreading it across the country – despite the fact that in 1870 there were only 368 Chinese living outside the West.[11]

The Union Label had its sordid beginnings in 1874 as the Cigar Makers International Union (CMIU) in California drove Chinese labor out of the trade. The CMIU, under the leadership of future American Federa-

---

* Party alignments have shifted dramatically over the past hundred years and more. From Reconstruction until the 1930s, African Americans in the main stayed loyal to the Republican Party. It is only since Franklin Delano Roosevelt's presidency that African Americans shifted their support to the Democratic Party. The Dixiecrats, the open white supremacists in the party, stayed in Roosevelt's coalition for another thirty years or so but then moved to the Republicans as part of that party's "Southern Strategy." With the racists went a good section of white labor – still chasing their white privileges despite Republican-led attacks on trade unions, safety regulations, overtime pay, and Social Security.

tion of Labor President Samuel Gompers, devised a white label for boxes of cigars made by white workers. Even some proponents of African American equality and otherwise liberal organizations joined in scapegoating the immigrant workers.

Michael Goldfield, in *The Color of Politics*, describes how Chinese exclusionism provided a wedge issue for the Democratic Party to make a comeback after the Civil War. The Democrats had little following then outside the South because of their alignment with the defeated Confederacy. But in the 1870s abolitionists and Radical Republicans found themselves increasingly isolated when they spoke out against Chinese exclusion. The Democrats managed to regain their influence with northern and western white workers by posing as the defenders of white worker interests. They claimed – along with later labor historian John R. Commons – that "the Country might have been overrun by Mongolian labor."[12] To this issue the Democrats added promises of support for the eight-hour day and other working class demands. None of these promises were kept, however – except for the exclusion of Chinese immigrants.

Craft unionism and the Knights of Labor

The depression years of the 1870s and '80s rivaled in their impact the later Great Depression of the 1930s. The impoverishment of many factory and farming families led to resistance to capitalists among broad sectors of the population. Crushing this resistance became an urgent necessity for leaders of the increasingly monopolized economy. The ruling class resorted to the army, judicial repression including executions, state militias, local police, private police and spy networks (the most notorious being the Pinkerton Agency), vigilante mob violence, and lynchings.

Any serious labor challenge to the monopolists' agenda also gained the label "anarchist" or "communist,"* especially after the 1871 Paris

---

* The words *communist* and *anarchist* refer to two historic trends in the working class movement. Both trends generally share an analysis of society divided into economic classes and a vision of the future where the state, with its repressive police and army, no longer exists. They differ, however, on the need for revolutionary organization, which communists emphasize, as well as on the weight given to direct action tactics by small groups, which some anarchists stress. Other anarchists support mass action, as communists do, but tend to think primarily in terms of worker "self-activity" and "self-organization." In the wake of the collapse of the Soviet Union, the term *communism* for many people today has taken on a meaning that runs counter to its original liberatory impulse.

The word *socialist* can be used to describe a wide range of people sharing a vision of thoroughgoing democracy – including, 1) Communist Party members in, for example, South Africa or the Philippines; 2) revolutionary socialists more generally, who struggle for working class power based on inherent contradictions in capitalist society; 3) people who hold to a reform path for putting "people before profits"; and 4) those who form model communities based on shared ownership and social equality.

Commune* uprising in France. What later came to be known as "redbaiting" claimed that all resistance to wage cuts, layoffs, and anti-worker, anti-farmer legislation was the work of revolutionary troublemakers. The United States saw similar propaganda in the 1950s and '60s – claiming that outsiders, mostly communists, were stirring up contented Negroes in the South.

In the repressive conditions of the 1870s and '80s, skilled workers organized along craft lines and in 1881 formed what later became the American Federation of Labor (AFL). Rather than bring all workers in a particular industry into the union, this "guild" approach tended to foster an exclusionary mentality. Socialists in the AFL still retained strong notions of solidarity. But the majority focused on protecting the privileges of the skilled membership – white males, usually American-born, and often Protestant.

What happened in the railroad brotherhoods during this period is typical of the craft unions' stance. The leadership of the brotherhoods joined proponents of a "New South" to build a segregated labor system after Reconstruction. In some railway trades African Americans had been a near majority after the Civil War. By the 1900s the Brotherhood of Locomotive Engineers was all white – and had an exclusionary white supremacy clause in its constitution to keep it that way. The other brotherhoods followed suit, until African Americans found themselves confined to track maintenance gangs and other segregated, unskilled or servant-type work.

Challenging this trend toward craft unionism, the Order of the Knights of Labor organized a competing broad-based movement within the working class. Founded in 1869 by garment workers, the Knights expanded during the 1870s into the coal and iron regions of western Pennsylvania, and later into virtually every corner of the country. In many non-urban areas, workers from all trades and industries joined together in one assembly. While segregated locals predominated in the South, assemblies in other parts of the country often were interracial – and after 1881 open to women. Rodolfo Acuña contrasts the Knights of

---

* The working class of Paris formed the Paris Commune on March 18, 1871. People seized the city in defense of the six-months old Republic, as the French government capitulated to the Germans in the closing days of the Franco-Prussian War. The workers elected the Commune's leadership based on universal suffrage. The newly formed government then armed the citizens and disbanded the official army, set government pay scales no higher than workers' wages, opened educational institutions to everyone, declared the separation of church and state and returned priests to private life, banned pawn shops, and turned the city's factories over to their workers. The French government, under the watchful eye of the German army, then attacked the city, and the people of Paris held out until the end of May. The indiscriminate bloodbath that finally suppressed the workers' uprising counted many thousands of men, women, and children among its victims – while the upper classes danced in the streets. *(Marx,* The Civil War in France*)*

labor in the Southwest with the AFL: "except for the Knights of Labor, Euroamerican labor institutions either ignored the Mexicans or excluded them."[13] Chinese workers were the one exception to the Knights' inclusive approach – foreshadowing policies that eventually would destroy the Order in the 1890s. The Knights campaigned for the 1882 Chinese Exclusion Act and hailed its passage as a victory.

The biggest jump in the Order's growth came with the great railroad upheavals of the 1880s. The craft-based railway brotherhoods proved useless in the face of the starvation and homelessness suffered by thousands of laid-off workers and their families during the depression years. The Knights gained their greatest victory in 1885, when striking workers on the Wabash Railroad in Texas – including Mexican and black laborers – forced the notorious robber baron Jay Gould to rescind a wage cut. In the following year, workers poured into the Order and increased its membership seven-fold to 700,000.

Meanwhile, the movement for the eight-hour workday had grown to involve hundreds of thousands in political and workplace actions. The AFL proved to have a far more focused and consistent approach to this central issue than the Knights. In 1884 the Federation set the date for a nationwide general strike, including marches and demonstrations, for May 1st, 1886.

Decline of the Knights of Labor

While the Knights generally supported strikes once the workers went out, the leadership preferred non-confrontational methods and were quick to brand militants in the union with the label *anarchist*. In keeping with this outlook, Grand Master Workman Terrence Powderly tried to distance the Order from the 1886 May Day actions. Rank and file Knights, however – both black and white – participated in large numbers throughout the country. Then a bomb of unknown origin exploded among the ranks of Chicago's mobilized police force, killing one officer – in what became known as the Haymarket Affair. Four anarchist leaders were hung – though to this day no one knows the identity of the bomber – and the decline of the Knights followed a few years later. Not only had the Knights disavowed the biggest unifying issue of the time, but they also failed to escape the savage repression that followed the mass demonstration. Police enforced anti-labor laws and curfews, raided the Order's offices and meeting halls, and destroyed their printing presses. Despite the Knights' protestations – and their internal purges of suspected anarchists – the authorities dealt with them as just another unacceptable threat to the system.

Even with the vicious repression during this period, however, the Knights broke new ground in the South with their interracial organizing. From time to time the Order took forthright stands opposing segregation. One example is the fall 1886 National Convention held in Richmond, VA, where national leaders insisted that all hotels and theaters admit the convention's African American delegates. The interracial solidarity flowing from this gathering built upon the May Day rallies earlier in the year and carried over into the organization's internal culture. Philip Foner reports that Newark and Boston had large multiracial May Day marches in 1887. And in the South, African American journalist Ida B. Wells wrote from Memphis that same year: "I was fortunate to attend a meeting of the Knights of Labor...I noticed that everyone who came was welcomed and every woman from black to white was seated with the courtesy usually extended to white ladies alone in this town. It was the first assembly of the sort in this town where color was not the criterion to recognition as ladies and gentlemen."[14]

Despite these stands and the Knights' growth in previously labor-hostile areas of the South, the only true challenge to the Southern labor regime came from below – in the form of black-led plantation and urban worker organizing. The longshoreman and other waterfront workers in the southern ports are one example of such struggles. In New Orleans city leaders resorted to violent military actions to crush waterfront strikes. Later they memorialized these actions with a statue to white supremacy that stood prominently in New Orleans until the 1970s.

The Knights' overall membership dropped off sharply with the repression of the late 1880s, but African American workers continued to join in large numbers. Philip Foner attributes the Order's popularity to 1) its emphasis on land reform, education, and worker cooperatives; 2) the union's mutual benefit associations and social functions; and 3) the opportunity for African Americans to develop as leaders within the organization. Nonetheless, Powderly and other top leaders proved themselves wavering in their support of black-led struggles. When racists shot South Carolina organizer H.F. Hoover while he spoke to black workers in Georgia, the Knights' executive board simply requested an investigation into the murder. During a sugar workers strike in Thibodaux Louisiana in 1887, white vigilantes killed more than twenty workers and lynched the strike leaders – but the national leadership did nothing. Then when an investigation showed that members of the Order actually participated in white militia raids in nearby Berwick, LA, Powderly refused to act. When African American editors complained, Powderly "lectured the black editors about the evils of strikes, assured them that he never would endorse a walkout, and urged them to tell black Knights that 'cooperation is the true remedy for the ills of industry.'"[15]

Similarly in the Southwest, the division between union militants and the Powderly forces resulted in a split in the New Mexico workers assemblies in the late 1880s. Under the leadership of district organizer Juan José Herrera, the Knights fought the railroads' theft of public lands.

Rodolfo Acuña points out, "The land, in accordance with Mexican law and traditions, was held in common by the people and could not be sold."[16] But Anglo land grabbers claimed huge tracts and began fencing them in. Speculators hoped to sell land at inflated prices to the railroads and to white settlers coming into the area. In response militants formed *Las Gorras Blancas* (the White Caps) and cut fences at night and destroyed railroad property. *Las Gorras* enjoyed wide support among the Mexican people, who marched in support of arrested leaders and put pressure on the courts to protect people's land grant rights. Later the New Mexico Knights leadership helped found the People's Party, which dominated the Las Vegas County elections in 1890. The land struggle succeeded in suppressing speculation for a couple years; but it eventually lost momentum as the movement got tied up in the courts and state legislature. Better off sectors of the community worked to isolate the Knights' leadership, and Powderly expelled Herrera from the Order in the early 1890s.

Not surprisingly, after this record of betrayal, including purges of suspected anarchists, black and Mexican workers began to leave the Knights in increasing numbers. By the early 1890s, membership was down to 200,000. Then in 1894, as segregation took hold throughout the country, the Knights called for the deportation of black people to Africa. A year later membership stood at 20,000 and the Order ceased to function as a viable organization.

Looking back on this history, the Knights failed on two fronts: first, by not uniting whole heartedly behind grassroots struggle – be it for the eight-hour day, in support of striking sugar workers, or against settler expansion in the Southwest. Second, the Knights failed to consistently oppose, and eventually colluded in setting up, the emerging segregationist Jim Crow system in the South.

The AFL gains control

The American Federation of Labor, in contrast to the Knights, managed to survive the post-1886 period of repression. The AFL grew, first, because of its central role in the eight-hour movement and, second, because of the enormous expansion of skilled trades brought about by the rapid industrialization of the U.S. economy. This increase in skilled labor is one example of how the developing productive forces caused huge changes in social relations across the country. The spread of the railroads is another. Indigenous peoples suffered from the disruption of buffalo grazing lands. Mexican teamsters and their horse-drawn wagons lost out to the "iron horse." And wherever the railroads went, white settlers followed in growing numbers. Industrialization pushed up a new monopoly ruling class; and the high stakes at play help explain the vicious labor repression of the period. The violent shift to a segregated society – enforced by lynch mobs in the South and Southwest – also nurtured an exclusionary, pro-capitalist labor movement.

By representing skilled workers exclusively, the AFL gained a short-term organizational advantage and its leaders, a barely tolerated acceptance into the upper circles of capitalist society. This personal and sectoral advancement, however, came at the cost of disunity and powerlessness for the working class as a whole. The AFL was the first major labor organization in the United States to proclaim itself pro-capitalist. It was openly white supremacist, with many of its affiliates having constitutional clauses barring membership to workers of color. While supporting the strategic concept of federation – where different skilled trades support each other's struggles – the AFL opposed class-wide solidarity, particularly with unskilled and semi-skilled immigrants,

The Japanese-Mexican Labor Association

A century ago the fields around Oxnard were the center of the sugar beet industry in California. Initially sugar farmers used Mexican and Chinese contract labor, but that ended with the extension of the Chinese Exclusion Act in 1902. The growers then turned to aggressively recruiting Japanese workers. The beet industry used a system of subcontractors, usually racially based, to supply their workers. In the spring of 1902, however, the American Sugar Beet Company joined a number of prominent businessmen and bankers in Oxnard to set up a new contracting company, the Western Agricultural Contracting Company (WACC). Industry leaders feared that the growing number of Japanese subcontractors would use their control of the labor market to raise wages and improve working conditions. With farmer and refinery backing the WACC simply declared that all subcontractors now had to go through them.

The Mexican and Japanese subcontractors were furious – as were the workers. With the WACC in control, wages dropped to nearly half their previous level. In February 1903 roughly 800 Japanese and Mexican workers met and formed the Japanese-Mexican Labor Association (JMLA). The new organization had three groups among its members: subcontractors, workers, and temporary student laborers. The leadership of the union came from the subcontractors and, to a lesser extent, from the students. Some of the students had been active in the socialist movement among the Japanese people in San Francisco and Oakland.

The JMLA moved quickly, by voting to stop working through the WACC – which basically meant a vote to strike. The JMLA demanded an end to WACC's monopoly, a return to their former wage levels, and an end to the WACC company store. The JMLA chose a strategic time for their action – the "thinning" season, when workers thin out the beet seedlings by hand to allow the hardiest to grow.

The WACC met this challenge by forming the Independent Agricultural

and with people of color.

Except for one year, Samuel Gompers held onto power in the AFL from 1886 to his death in 1924. Gompers's control did not simply flow from his wily use of bureaucracy to stamp out democratic challenges. He had a base among white craft workers committed to preserving their privileged position. And while Gompers tried to exclude women from the cigar industry, once 20,000 women struck the garment shops of New York City in 1909, he supported organizing the needle trades – but under male leadership. For over 60 years Gompers and his successors cultivated a climate of entitlement – as opposed to a consciousness of class. An infusion of people of color and the unskilled would have required an entirely new approach to holding power in the federation. It might also have forced the unions into an unnerving new stance – confronting capi-

Labor Union (IALU). As with all company unions, the IALU's aim was not to eliminate abusive treatment or raise wages. Rather its goal was to "secure and maintain harmonious relations between employees and employers." The IALU began recruiting strikebreakers immediately – and the JMLA fought back. The strikers had some success in stopping new recruits from scabbing. And some of the recruits even joined the JMLA. Then violence erupted on March 23, 1903, when the JMLA tried to put their union banner on a truck filled with scabs. Several union members were killed, and the bloodshed in turn led to showdowns at some of the area's largest ranches.

Soon the local farmers were at the negotiating table, and the JMLA succeeded in winning all its demands. Two Anglo socialist union organizers affiliated with the Los Angeles County Council of Labor (LACCL) joined the Mexican and Japanese union heads at the table. The support of these Anglos was important and groundbreaking since most of the labor movement was engaged in rabid anti-Asian campaigns. Although the LACCL had passed a resolution supporting the JMLA, that same resolution reaffirmed the council's staunch opposition to further Asian immigration.

Soon after the successful strike the JMLA applied to join the AFL. Most forces inside the AFL were hostile to both the union and the request. Samuel Gompers, the president of the AFL, granted the union a charter on the condition that Asians could not become members. The JMLA was furious and rejected the charter saying, "We would be false to them and to ourselves and to the cause of unionism if we accepted privileges for ourselves which are not accorded to them."

As a result of the AFL's betrayal, local agricultural business elites managed to isolate the JMLA. Without allies, the union in time was unable to function and dissolved. The unique class alliance and rejection of race privilege that Mexican and Japanese immigrants achieved in the California beet fields had demonstrated its power. But the corporate-labor white front won out in the end.

—*source: Almaguer,* Racial Fault Lines

tal class to class – as actually began to take shape later during the labor upsurge of the 1930s.

Overview of the period

From the Civil War through Reconstruction and after, the country experienced great upheavals, but the multiracial working class failed to forge a common bond of solidarity in these struggles. Privileges, both imposed and seized, shaped the lives of white workers, both native born and immigrant. Unions minimized job competition by driving Chinese workers out of the labor market; and craft jobs went to white workers, while the unions protected their privileged status. At the same time, the AFL's exclusionary policies undercut class unity and weakened labor's ability to resist the rising monopolies. The new textile mills in the South became the near-exclusive domain of low-wage white workers.* European immigrants took over Northern city governments and the accompanying patronage jobs – and then primarily served the interests of the moneyed elite, while keeping the lower classes in tow. Homesteading opportunities enlisted white people in suppressing the First Nations; and credit flowed to these homesteaders, even if it later was subject to recall when convenient for the bankers. Mexicans lost their land, and debt peonage tied down black farmers in the old plantation South. For most Europeans the United States was "a land of opportunity" – at least until the next depression – no matter how harsh the social reality they became part of. For people of color, the country increasingly became a prison house of nations.

During this same period the U.S. army moved against striking railroad workers, monopolies grew up on the backs of the divided workforce, and urban and rural poverty impacted white workers, as well as workers of color. Long workdays, hazardous conditions, and insecurity were the common lot of all laboring people. But despite this common oppression, the solidarity achieved during the Civil War gave way to a violently enforced system of privileges. A climate of heightened racism grew up within the emerging monopoly-dominated economy. And the proudly worn badge of "free, white labor" actually marked a defeated proletarian army – doomed, despite its militancy, for attacking its allies and accepting the enemy's gifts.

Tenant organizing, Operation Dixie, and the 'red scare'

It was not until 1928 that the Communist Party USA (CP) adopted the position that African Americans constitute an oppressed nation and that fighting national oppression is central to the success of the working class

---

* Before 1965, only some 2% of textile employees were black, filling laboring jobs at the fringe of the industry. (*Lyons, reviewing Minchin,* Hiring the Black Worker)

struggle in the United States. The CP called for political self-determination for African Americans living in the majority-black counties in the South. It launched its Southern organizing campaign with a strike and interracial organizing in the textile mills in and around Gastonia, NC, in 1929.* In subsequent years, the party concentrated on Birmingham and the surrounding rural counties in Alabama.

The best treatment of the CP's work with Alabama sharecroppers and workers in the 1930s and '40s is Robin D. G. Kelley's *Hammer and Hoe.* Two other books, *Black Worker in the Deep South* by Hosea Hudson, and *All God's Dangers*, the story of Nate Shaw, provide oral histories of a worker from Birmingham and a sharecropper from Tallapoosa County. These two freedom fighters helped lead the resistance to the South's apartheid system. On the other side, Alabama's rulers – the owners of U.S. Steel and the coalmines, the planters, and their enforcers in the police departments, sheriffs' offices, and Ku Klux Klan – unleashed a murderous attack on Alabama's working-class movement.

The Alabama CP, being mostly black and rural, or first-generation urban, differed in their demographics from the national organization. The party built organizations of sharecroppers, steelworkers, coal and iron ore miners, and anti-repression and legal defense organizations that persevered through a decade of official and vigilante terror – through murders, floggings, mutilations, and dynamitings. Only rarely were victories won – improvements in working conditions, wages, and share prices. But people demonstrated once again, as they had so often over the years since Reconstruction, that workers and tenant farmers in the South could stand up and fight.

CP organizing in the Southwest

A similar spirit fed communist organizing among farmworkers in the Southwest. Militant strikes broke out in 1933 among berry workers in El Monte, California, and in the cotton fields of the San Joachín Valley. CP organizers with the Cannery and Allied Workers International Union (C&AWIU) led battles against growers, the police, and their backers in the press and industrial associations. Chicana women organized an infrastructure in the labor camps to support the strike. The workers devised methods like roving pickets to outmaneuver company goons – who nonetheless got away with gunning down a half-dozen workers over the course of the strike. Eventually the state ended the confrontation with a compromise increase in wage rates, along with a fact-finder's

---

* One early incident in the Gastonia strike made clear the importance of not giving in to white workers' racism. Responding to such pressure, a white organizer in Bessemer City, near Gastonia, strung a rope down the middle of a hall to divide the white and black workers at a union meeting. The black workers refused to return. *(Weisbord, "Gastonia 1929")*

toothless condemnation of the growers' violations. In the following months police raided the CP headquarters in Sacramento and sent eight organizers to jail for criminal syndicalism, effectively shutting down the C&AWIU.

This experience in California shared many features with the CP-led struggle in the South: large numbers of people in motion, courageous organizers, and violent repression. One important difference, however, was the CP's lack of attention to the national character of the struggle among the Chicano workers. Acuña comments, "the C&AWIU leadership can be criticized for promoting unnecessary fights with Mexican unions, which they attempted to discredit by describing them as nationalist or reactionary... C&AWIU organizers... did not understand the history of the people they were attempting to lead...Few understood Spanish or bothered to learn it."[17]

United front work and the CIO

In the mid-1930s two events greatly affected the CP's organizing efforts in Alabama. First, the international communist movement changed its core strategy in order to counter the victories of fascism in Germany, Italy, and Japan. The Popular Front approach called for communists to focus less on their revolutionary base building and more on forming united fronts with other anti-fascist forces. Second, John L. Lewis, president of the United Mine Workers, started the Committee for Industrial Organization within the AFL in 1935 – and later split to form the Congress of Industrial Organizations (CIO) in 1938. The CIO committed itself to organizing whole industries – and not just craft workers – in auto, steel, rubber, electrical, textile, and other major industries.

Facing its own brand of fascism in Birmingham, the united front approach created mostly problems for the Alabama CP. Black people had enthusiastically joined the CP-led fight against segregation; but the party's abandonment of its revolutionary position on the Black Nation eroded its support. The Popular Front policy favorably adjusted the party's go-it-alone style of the preceding years. But instead of retaining a base in their earlier work, the party shifted all its limited resources into reaching out to Southern white liberals – most of whom proved slow to respond. Along with this shift in resources, the CP also tended to downplay the struggle against racism, although its multiracial internal culture remained a model for the times.

CIO organizing campaigns demanded the energy and skill of many CP cadre. The Steel Workers Organizing Committee (SWOC) hired 60 CP organizers in the Midwest alone. In the Southwest, prominent communists led the industrial union UCAPAWA*, building on a history of Mexican worker organizing in Texas, especially around San Antonio and along the Rio Grande. In the South, the CP led CIO organizing drives in lower-paid and majority-black sectors like tobacco, food processing, and laundries. In Memphis, St. Louis, and Winston-Salem, left-led CIO industrial union victories also advanced the African American freedom struggle.

The greatest face-off between socially progressive unionism and conservative accommodationism to white supremacy occurred in Birmingham, Alabama. U.S. Steel – in Ensley, Fairfield, Bessemer, and other Birmingham area towns – strongly backed the Klan-police axis that enforced the Jim Crow status quo. City commissioner and later police commissioner Bull Conner bossed this axis for decades, beginning as a radio announcer and vigilante recruiter for the "Big Mules" at U.S. Steel. Connor drew on workers in the steel mills and at the B. F. Goodrich plant in Tuscaloosa to fill the ranks of his white terrorist goons. And while some unions, especially those where communists were active, opposed Connor, others helped fund his election campaigns.[18]

After the 1937 CIO victory in the auto plants of Flint, Michigan, U.S. Steel shocked the industrial world by signing a nationwide agreement with SWOC – which from then on became the United Steelworkers of America (USWA). The agreement saved much sweat, blood, and money; and the USWA was then able to turn its attention to the more stubborn "Little Steel" companies. U.S. Steel also saved a lot – by not facing a strike, not having their work force radicalized in an organizing campaign, and not seeing the left emerge as the grass-roots leadership of the union.

In Birmingham, the payoff for U.S. Steel was even greater. While new seniority procedures took away a little of the company's management prerogative, the company was able to preserve a highly segregated departmental seniority system – along with its separate lines of promotion. With these white privileges in place, the steelworkers' locals around Birmingham and across the country developed their own brand of white unionism. Black workers could rise only so far within the organization – shut out from powerful positions like president or head of the grievance committee.

A. Philip Randolph's Negro American Labor Council, set up in 1960, worked to change such practices in organized labor. But it was only in 1974 that black steelworkers succeeded in forcing the federal government to issue a "Consent Decree," overturning the Jim Crow departmental seniority system. The Decree targeted several of the biggest U.S.

---

* Union of Cannery, Agricultural, Packing and Allied Workers of America. See box on p. 130 for a description of UCAPAWA/FTA.

steelmakers, including U.S. Steel, along with the USWA, which had colluded in the arrangement for more than 30 years. Even this remedy, however, failed to open up bricklayer, carpenter, and electrician jobs to black workers – given that the USWA and big steel together administered the agreement. As to the $31 million distributed in back pay, someone with 30 years received about $900. In return for this one time payment, workers had to sign an agreement forgiving the company and promising not to sue – not just for past discrimination, but for discrimination in the future as well. Steelworker Ray Henderson commented, "There were a lot of guys that never signed those checks – just tore them up. They were truly insulted by it. The union played a role in that. They knew what they were doing [by not protecting us equally]. I've always been bitter about that even though I like the union: it gives you more flexibility to get the things you want. I'm a union man, still."[19]

Operation Dixie

The CIO launched Operation Dixie in 1946 with the professed aim to organize all Southern workers. The first target chosen for the campaign, however, was the nearly all-white Southern textile industry, the bulwark of white privilege in the South since the 1880s. Employers had offered poor white people an opportunity to set themselves apart from the black laboring population by moving into the mills. The industry demonstrated both white exclusiveness, on the one side, and low pay and poor working conditions, on the other – an inseparable package of privilege and misery that has characterized the lot of Southern white workers.

In 1934 these workers erupted in rebellion across the South. People responded in part to an opening provided by President Roosevelt's call for workers to form unions. But more basic was the mill owners' refusal to go along with federal guidelines on improving wages and hours as a way to pull the economy out of the recession. The United Textile Workers (UTW), an AFL craft union, headed up the campaign. The AFL's attitude toward black workers contrasted sharply with that of the CP's multiracial organizing approach in Gastonia five years earlier. One black laborer commented that if he had joined a massive demonstration by white striking textile workers in 1934, he was "afraid he'd be lynched."[20] Also, a couple years later the CIO charged that AFL members cooperated in vigilante attacks when the CIO tried to organize black and white workers together.

Under UTW leadership at least 400,000 workers went out on strike for 22 days in the "Uprising of '34." In the end politicians served the mill owners well by crushing the strike. The Georgia National Guard beat and bayoneted workers – and then herded them into World War I detention camps. A coordinated action by authorities across the South arrested all the strike leaders. Five strikers died, and many workers found themselves blackballed from the industry – despite an agreement that the strikers would be rehired. Families lost their company-owned housing, and those workers who returned to the mills did so with broken spirits. The failure of the national union to put up a fight – the national vice-president hailed the "victorious end" of the strike[21] – gave unionism a bad name for decades.

In addition to this history of failed struggle in the 1930s, the conditions Operation Dixie faced after the war differed significantly from those during the time of the CIO's greatest organizing successes. In the late 1930s corporate hegemony had been discredited by years of depression. Workers were wide open to organizing, and a leftwing infrastructure could be found in many workplaces and communities. Also, unlike the CP organizers of the 1930s, organizers sent by the CIO in 1946 had been trained in the North, with its multi-ethnic, but primarily white workforce. They had no sense of the South's racial dynamics, nor how to forge unity in a principled way. The communists, by contrast, had sunk roots during the battles of the early 1930s and were well positioned for the upsurge later in the decade. Finally, CIO president Philip Murray rejected the center-left alliance approach that produced the successful drives of the 1930s. Instead, he appointed Van Bittner as campaign director – a right-winger from his own steelworkers union – and loaded up the organizing staff with anti-communists.

Michelle Brattain's *The Politics of Whiteness* details Operation Dixie's problems in organizing Southern textile. The CIO's Textile Workers Union of America (TWUA) succeeded in organizing several Floyd County, GA, mills during World War II. Given the anti-fascist character of the war, anti-Semitism and Aryan superiority – two traditional anti-union talking points – were somewhat muted during this period. The Floyd County locals developed a very active union culture, but with a serious drawback: their embrace of white unionism. This stance left the union vulnerable to a resurgence of white supremacy at the end of World War II, in a climate of carefully cultivated anti-communism directed against the Soviet Union.

Once Operation Dixie announced its plan to target the textile industry, County Commissioner William H. Lewis began a yearlong campaign of anti-union radio and newspaper editorializing. "Operation Dixie: The Iron Curtain Descends" headlined one of his many front-page articles.[22] Even as the CIO became more anti-communist and began identifying and purging left-wingers, Lewis jumped on this practice as vindication of his charge that the CIO was full of "reds." Moving on to racebaiting, Lewis wrote, "the South is Anglo-Saxon; the North is mixed races."[23] In another article he warned the national vice-president of the TWUA, "You do not know the South. The Klan can rise again, to restore to our people their rights and again drive out the carpetbaggers. You do well to fear the Klan because you cannot destroy its spirit."[24]

Lewis's voice was just the loudest of a growing chorus of anti-CIO hysteria. The organizing drive at Floyd County's Lindale Pepperell Mills went down to defeat, a loss that echoed across the South. Demoralization from the defeats in textile subsequently led to Operation Dixie's overall collapse. Some early noteworthy exceptions, however, stand out. Up to December 1946, the left-led Food, Tobacco and Agricultural union (FTA) had been involved in 62 Operation Dixie organizing drives – winning 52 of them for a net gain of 12,616 workers. These advances disappeared, however, when the CIO and AFL later moved together to crush the FTA and other left-led unions in 1949. The overall result of the 1946 to 1953 Operation Dixie campaign was a setback for unionism in the South – and a major loss of organizational strength and resources for the African American people.

UCAPAWA and the FTA

Founded in 1937, UCAPAWA [United Cannery, Agricultural, Packing, and Allied Workers of America] represented a model of democratic trade unionism and offered unprecedented opportunities for local leadership. The union made its greatest gains among Mexican cannery and African American tobacco workers. In 1939, led by veteran organizer and Communist Party activist Dorothy Ray Healey, over four hundred cannery operatives, the majority Mexican and Russian Jewish women, staged a successful strike at the California Sanitary Canning Company. Two years later, UCAPAWA's vice president, Luisa Moreno, expanded organizing campaigns throughout southern California. Los Angeles rank and file formed Local 3, the second-largest UCAPAWA affiliate. In 1943 twelve of the fifteen elected positions in Local 3 were held by women, eight by Mexicanas. They negotiated innovative benefits, such as a hospitalization plan, free legal advice, and at one plant, management-financed day care.

In 1944 UCAPAWA became the Food, Tobacco, Agricultural, and Allied Workers of America (FTA). In many respects, UCAPAWA/FTA was a women's union. By 1946 66 percent of its contracts nationwide had equal pay for equal work clauses and 75 percent provided for leaves of absence without loss of seniority (e.g., maternity leave). Nationally, women held 44 percent of elected union posts in food-processing locals and 71 percent in tobacco units. After World War II, virulent redbaiting by rival unions, management, and politicians eviscerated the union. In 1950 UCAPAWA/FTA was one of ten unions expelled from the CIO for alleged Communist domination.

UCAPAWA/FTA, however, has left a legacy of unwavering commitment to democratic trade unionism for people of color and for women.

—from: Ruiz, "UCAPAWA and the FTA"

The red scare

With the Cold War intensifying in the late 1940s, white unionism received a huge boost in the form of government intervention against left-led unions. The nation's media joined in – praising the patriotism of white unionism and its reserves of Klan nightriders. The racist forces claimed the role of defending Southern values and traditions. They branded social unionism, with its tradition of fighting for black equality, as unpatriotic, communistic, un-American, and terroristic.

Leaders of the largest CIO unions used the red scare to settle scores with left opponents contending for power in the industry. The USWA raided CP-led Mine, Mill and Smelter Workers locals – aided by increased vigilante terrorism, police repression, House Un-American Activities Committee subpoenas, and a secessionist movement of conservative white miners within the locals themselves. By the early 1950s, Mine-Mill no longer existed in Birmingham – and the Alabama CP had disbanded.

Anti-communist CIO raids also succeeded in destroying left unions where workers of color had gained leadership positions. Particularly devastating was the crushing of FTA Local 22, which had built a strong base among black workers at the R.J. Reynolds tobacco plants in Winston-Salem, NC. Another ominous defeat during this period was the crushing by the United Auto Workers (UAW) of the Farm Equipment (FE) Local at the International Harvester plant in Louisville, KY. Before being raided by the UAW, the FE had organized multiracial locals with black leadership and had ended segregated locker rooms in Southern plants.

Robin Kelley's *Hammer and Hoe* raises the question whether the Birmingham CP could have weathered this Cold War repression if the party had not abandoned its working class base in the black neighborhoods. After all, the Party had survived and grown during the difficult years of the early 1930s. Even with the lynching of party cadre along with their staunchest supporters, the CP persevered in revolutionary base building. Also, Mine-Mill managed to survive similar all-out attacks on their base among metal miners in New Mexico, even after being thrown out of the CIO in 1949. The movie classic *Salt of the Earth*, for example, shows Mexican mineworkers and their wives winning a legendary 17-month strike – by finally forcing the Empire Zinc Company to settle in February 1952.*

---

* *Salt of the Earth* came out in 1954, the same year as Elia Kazan's *On the Waterfront*. Its director, Herbert Biberman, was one of the Hollywood Ten – people who served time for refusing to respond to Congress about their communist convictions. Hollywood blacklisted *Salt of the Earth* and Biberman had great difficulty completing the film. Then only a dozen or so theaters nationwide agreed to screen it. *On the Waterfront*, by contrast, won Oscars for Kazan and the film's screenwriter Bud Schulberg, both of whom cooperated with the House

During this anti-communist period the CIO's tainted victories – sometimes won through collusion with employers – proved disastrously hollow for its organizing in the South. By resorting to redbaiting and racebaiting tactics in their confrontations with left-led locals, the CIO destroyed the most effective organizing ever carried out in the region. White trade unionism reinforced the hostile conditions that contributed to the CIO's humiliating defeat in Operation Dixie. The experience brings to mind the Knights of Labor some sixty years before, when white supremacy and attacks on anarchists destroyed the Order and left workers of color without organized labor's support.

Looking more broadly, we can see the power of the state – government power at all levels – standing behind the CIO. The union purges were just part of a larger process of class rule that reestablished the system of racial preferences in the post-World War II period. W.E.B. DuBois and Paul Robeson had their passports taken from them because of their leftist views and their worldwide popularity. A resurgence of violence in the South went unopposed, even as it targeted black soldiers returning from the war. Federal authorities approved the segregation of new housing developments to keep black people out of the booming suburbs. And the GI Bill opened higher education overwhelmingly to white workers, by not challenging segregationist practices at colleges and universities, nor assuring the local availability of federally backed loans. Renewed segregation in the South had its counterpart in racist company and union practices in the North. In the Detroit auto industry, for example, white workers with a high school education got the good jobs – but at the cost of pollution in their neighborhoods and lax safety standards on the job. Meanwhile federal and state governments turned a blind eye to discrimination both inside the plants and in the UAW.

Passage of the 1947 Taft-Hartley Act had the most lasting impact of all the federal measures of the period. It marked the reassertion of ruling class hegemony that the upsurge of the 1930s had contested. White supremacist Democratic congressmen and senators – the so-called Dixiecrats – consolidated an alliance with the Republican Party to pass this bill. Anti-union "right-to-work"* – actually right-to-fire – laws then took

---

Un-American Affairs Committee by informing on others in the film industry. *(Boisson, "Salt of the Earth")*

* Section 14(b) of the National Labor Relations Act (NLRA) of 1947, also known as the Taft-Hartley Act, permits states to do away with the "union shop" – where a majority vote determines whether all the workers in a bargaining unit belong to the union. In right-to-work states unions that win a majority vote must represent all the workers, but only those workers who voluntarily join pay dues. The result is either higher dues for members, driving people away, or reduced resources for organizing and struggle, both on the job and in the community. With union strength undermined, workers in right-to-work states have little bargaining power on the job and weak protections in state law. Essentially employers have a free hand to "fire at will" – except where federal law intervenes. Even in such cases, how-

hold in conservative southern and western states. These laws greatly curtailed the clout of organized labor – and are still a tremendous burden for the working class today. The indifference of the dominant CIO leadership, combined with the hostility of the AFL to African American voting rights in the South, virtually guaranteed the political victories of the Dixiecrats. In later decades this alliance would reinvent itself under Richard Nixon as the Republican Party's "Southern strategy."

Overview of the period

The 1930s and '40s saw both great gains and great losses for the working class in the United States. First, it is hard to overemphasize the breakthrough represented by having a revolutionary party committed to organizing all the workers in the U.S. working class. For the first time in history, the left seriously organized among African Americans in the South and Chicano workers in the Southwest. The CPUSA with its Black Nation analysis played a leading role in this effort – along with the newly formed CIO and a few independent organizations like the Highlander School in Eastern Tennessee. Together these forces built working class organizations centered among the oppressed nationality peoples – and in the process confronted the racist ideology that corrupted the thinking of white coworkers. Multiracial organizing in the South and Southwest created a new social reality that challenged the existing structure of privilege.

Second, the red purges throughout organized labor had a devastating impact on the ability of the left to maintain an institutional left pole within the union movement. The CIO purged 11 national and international unions in 1949 and opened the door to USWA, UAW, and other unions' raiding of left-led locals. In addition, the CIO unions added anti-communist clauses to their constitutions, screening out the left opposition internally. Both actions crippled attempts to form alliances between left and pragmatic unionists within the labor movement. Bill Fletcher and Fernando Gapasin point out that the victories of the 1930s resulted from just such an alliance: "Change was brought about by an alliance between pragmatists and a broadly-defined Left, which advocated an inclusive unionism from a variety of socialist perspectives....Since the creation of the CIO, leftists have had most impact on the union movement when they were able to influence the direction of pragmatic trade unionists."[25]

Third, after World War II the ruling class took actions that reestablished their time-tested system of white racial preferences. Worried that the militancy of the pre-war years would reassert itself – especially after

---

ever – taking discrimination as an example – proving intent is very difficult and judgments seldom bring satisfaction in a timely manner. In reality, "right-to-work" means "right-to-fire."

the largest strike wave in U.S. history in 1946 – the country's power elite turned to the same reward and punishment approach that had proved so effective in earlier periods. This time, instead of homesteading, white workers gained access to suburban home ownership. Redlining – so-called from the marks drawn on maps by government policymakers and later implemented more informally by real estate agents – kept new development tracts, like the Levittowns of the Northeast, lily white. Meanwhile in the South, the mechanization of agriculture disproportionately drove black farmers off their land – and north into the decaying central cities. The GI bill opened up opportunities for white returning GIs, while black soldiers found themselves largely excluded from the program. And a national media campaign pushed women of all races out of the World War II factories – with women of color going first, just as they had been the last to be hired. White women went back to their traditional jobs – or to their homes and the cult of domesticity. For many women of color, however, being "domestic" still meant taking care of other people's homes and children.

Finally, the top leadership of the CIO – President Philip Murray (USWA), along with Vice-President and successor Walter Reuther (UAW) – took an active part in reestablishing the relations of privilege. They failed to challenge white workers' racist practices during Operation Dixie. They expelled the militant left unions and organizers who had made possible the multiracial struggles of the 1930s and '40s. And they failed to block passage of Taft-Hartley. Unions lost strength in the South and Southwest. With union losses went the only social force capable of raising regional wage scales and overcoming the inequalities favoring white workers. Organized labor largely gave up its role as champions of oppressed nationality concerns. And the South and Southwest became a sinkhole undermining labor's strength for generations with the threat of plant relocation.

Chapter 10

Race, Class, and Privilege

Based on the lessons from working class history recounted in Chapter 9, together with insights from earlier chapters, we now want to highlight some theoretical points concerning race, class, and privilege. Here we focus on *class*, using a definition centered on people's relationship to the system of production – and to the relations of distribution and exchange that flow from it. In this view, social class centers on how people earn their livelihood and the degree of control they have over their working conditions. Sometimes people use the word *class* in a more general sense to refer to broad groupings of people – based, for example, on income level, age, or gender. Our usage comes from the 19th Century social theorist Karl Marx, who in studying history realized that society's first task is to reproduce itself – to provide for the basic material needs of its citizens. In doing so, societies develop relations among its various classes that carry with them implications for how the society functions.

In early civilizations, where people hunted and gathered their food and other resources, little surplus remained beyond what the tribe, or other social grouping, required to survive. With technological development came the capacity to produce more – and to accumulate social and personal wealth in different forms. As certain people could now live off the wealth produced by others in the community, non-producing classes dealing with government, religion, and the military could now emerge to play a role in society. Early examples of such societies are the Mayan and Aztec civilizations, Rome and ancient Greece, and China's succession of dynasties. This epoch lasted several thousand years, and the forms of social organization varied. Essentially, however, societies during this period organized themselves around the laboring classes' paying tribute to the upper classes. These relations were open and clear for all to see –

whether based on slavery, as in Greece, or on peasant taxes paid to a lord or king, as in medieval times.

About five hundred years ago, this tributary system began to undergo a profound change. Trade and then production for exchange in the marketplace began to take hold. Here the central concept was no longer tribute, but an exchange of equals in the marketplace – with workers being paid a wage for the hours they work. Marx's great insight was that under capitalism, it is actually workers' *labor power* that is bought and sold for wages. Workers receive enough wages to keep themselves alive from day to day and to reproduce themselves in the next generation. Meanwhile workers create *value* in production – proportional to the time-units of labor power, adjusted for skill level, that they expend over the course of a workday. The value of what people produce in a day, however, far exceeds the cost of meeting their basic needs. This difference in value – between what people produce and what they require to reproduce themselves – is *surplus value*, the source of the factory owners' *profit*. In this situation, the fact that some people live off the labor of others comes to be disguised behind the wage system. Working people still pay tribute, but now it is in the form of surplus value. And the dominant culture works to keep people confused about what is going on.

This new *capitalist* system – named after *capital*, the money/value-producing relationship that binds together employers and workers – turned out to be very dynamic. It generated great wealth and expanded from the slave-trading centers of Europe to countries all over the world. This system is also remarkable for its hypocrisy. Workers are free – they are neither slaves nor tied to the land of a feudal* lord. No one is compelled to work – except for the fact that if you don't work, you starve or end up in jail, or in the military. In addition, Marx describes the struggle in the early years of capitalism to uproot workers from the land, so that they could be put to work in the new factories. The former peasants became "sellers of themselves only after they had been robbed of all their

---

* *Feudal* refers to the social system that came before capitalism in Europe. It consisted of large landed estates whose owners often held honorific titles and together loosely ruled over a larger territory – England, say, or France – often through a weak king. Later as capitalism began to develop, strong monarchies evolved in alliance with the rising *bourgeois* class *(see next footnote)*. Peasant farmers, or serfs, were bound to the land for life and paid tribute to the local lord with agricultural products or their labor. The nobility in turn had the obligation to protect their serfs or vassals from attacks by outsiders, as well as to help people through hard times. The church, holding a position second only to the landed aristocracy, demanded burdensome contributions from the peasants as the price of happiness in the next world. Church leaders helped maintain the system by preaching that everyone occupied a place on the ladder of creation, and everyone should be content to live out their assigned role. Local rulers often abused their position – taking excessive rents, compelling military service to attack other lords, or demanding sexual access to their subjects – and peasant revolts were not uncommon.

own means of production, and of all the guarantees of existence afforded by the old feudal arrangements. And the history of this, their expropriation, is written in the annals of mankind in letters of blood and fire."[1]

This process of forced recruitment, along with the amassing of resources to build the first factories, Marx called *primitive accumulation*. It covered an extended period of "conquest, enslavement, robbery, murder, briefly force.... The discovery of gold and silver in America, the extirpation, enslavement and entombment in mines of the aboriginal population, the beginning of the conquest and looting of the East Indies, the turning of Africa into a warren for the commercial hunting of black-skins, signalized the rosy dawn of the era of capitalist production. These idyllic proceedings are the chief momenta of primitive accumulation."[2] Primitive accumulation appropriates directly, backed up by force, and without any pretense of exchange for something equal in the marketplace. Once capitalism is up and running, however, these direct means of appropriation move more to the background. Force is held in reserve, always there supplementing the normal workings of the system, and called out especially at a time of crisis.

Mainly capitalism relies on the illusion of freedom and equality to maintain itself. The wage system disguises the fact that capitalists appropriate surplus value. The brutal record of primitive accumulation disappears from children's textbooks – repackaged as "discovery," "manifest destiny," and "progress." And the hypocrisy of disguised exploitation carries over into the political system. Formal, capitalist, democracy ignores the vast differences in resources people bring to the political process. It is not for nothing that the U.S. Senate is called "a millionaires' club."

The concept *class*, in addition to revealing the inner reality of the capitalist system, also prompts consideration of what a society without exploitation would be like – and how to organize to achieve it. For the working class to hold power – in an alliance with progressive-minded people from the professional, small business, small farm, and other classes – the masses of the dispossessed must organize to express themselves politically in their own, deeply rooted, revolutionary party. Then in the course of widespread popular struggles aimed at resisting, and in time overturning, the rule of capital, people develop their ability to govern in a new way. Relationships become direct, cooperative, and based on a sense of social solidarity – rather than being motivated by money or personal gain. And political democracy is genuine, since it reflects in the political arena a thoroughgoing economic democracy – where workers control the conditions of production, and the social surplus is the property of the whole society.

Early theorists of the U.S. working class

Marx's class analysis drew mainly on his study of European history.[3] Once transplanted to the United States in the mid-19th Century, however, Marx's ideas did not find wide acceptance. In Europe the industrial working class gravitated to Marx's ideas and created political parties aimed at contesting for power. The clearest example is Germany, where in the run-up to World War I, representatives of working class parties held strong positions in both national and local governments.

In England, the dominant colonial power at the time, Marx's friend Frederick Engels complained that the working class had formed a "*bourgeois*[*] labor party." By this phrase Engels meant that labor advocates had little independence and initiative in putting forward a clear class politics. V.I. Lenin, the leader of the Russian Social Democratic Party, later to become the Communist Party of the Soviet Union, suggested that England's problem lay in the fact that the British working class shared in the spoils of the British Empire. Working class representatives finally succeeded in forming the British Labour Party in the first years of the 20th Century – and elected 29 representatives to Parliament in 1906. The party's program – though the basis for much struggle over the years – has deteriorated in recent decades. Today we need only recall that Labour Party Prime Minister Tony Blair has been the biggest cheerleader for the U.S. invasion and occupation of Iraq.

In the United States we have never had a mass electoral labor party representing all sectors of the working class.[†] Yet labor historians have pointed to a history of U.S. working class militancy unmatched by most European countries with Labor Parties – mass strikes in industries like railroads, maritime, mining, steel, and meatpacking; the historic struggle by women textile workers in Lawrence, Massachusetts, in 1912 that

---

[*] *Bourgeois* is a French word for businessperson (plural, *bourgeoisie*), and it is related to the German word *burgher*, or townsman. These words describe people in the early "middle class," situated between land-owning aristocrats and people who worked the land, the peasant class. As capitalism developed in Europe, the *bourgeois* class gained strength through its economic dealings, particularly in the slave trade, and eventually took power from the aristocracy. The *bourgeois* class gained control of state power in the English (1688) and French (1789) revolutions. Today's small businesspeople can be referred to as *petite bourgeoisie* – small *bourgeoisie* – while the *bourgeoisie* make up today's capitalist ruling class. The United States never had a true landed aristocracy. The historic question settled by the U.S. Civil War was whether *industrial*- or *slave*-based capitalism would dominate the country. In the quote above, Engels suggests that ruling class ideas dominated the English workers' organizations of his day.

[†] The modern U.S. Labor Party held its founding convention in 1996. During its first eight years the US-LP followed a party building strategy that did not contest elections. Instead the party focused on gathering strength through grassroots campaigns for "Just Health Care" and free higher education. See www.thelaborparty.org.

raised the slogan "give us bread, but give us roses, too"; and the struggle for the 8-hour day, the Haymarket massacre, and the birth of May 1 as the International Workers Holiday. The problem is that historians are usually talking about the white sector of the working class – but they treat this sector as if it were the whole class. In doing so they obscure the segregationist practices of most U.S. unions from the Civil War through World War I and after.

Early socialist theories

Early socialist leaders largely shared the views on black labor held by white trade unionists of the late 1800s. While struggling to ground a Marxist analysis in U.S. conditions, early socialists tended to place the blame for the divided condition of the U.S. working class on African American workers. For example, Socialist Labor Party (SLP) leader Daniel DeLeon considered black people to be like feudal serfs – due to their being bound to the land as sharecroppers – and this status, in his view, kept people from fully understanding the class question. Other leaders, despite their outspoken advocacy of social reforms, were quite direct in their racism. The first Socialist Party (SP) Congressman, sent from Milwaukee to Washington in 1912, said that there was "no doubt that the Negroes and mulattoes constitute a lower race."[4] Even the militant socialist fighter Eugene Debs commented that social intercourse and equality "is pure fraud and serves to mask the real issue which is not social equality but economic equality...The Negro, given economic equality, will not ask the white man any social favor; and the burning question of 'social equality' will disappear like mist before the sunrise."[5]

These views reflect the dominance of Jim Crow thinking in the organized left of the early 20th Century. Nevertheless, both DeLeon and Debs joined in the formation of the International Workers of the World (IWW)* in 1905, which went on to have a proud history of interracial organizing. Pulp workers in Louisiana, loggers in the Northwest, migratory labor in the Midwest, women textile workers in New England, and black longshoreman along the East Coast all came under the Wobblies' "One Big Union" banner. Like the Knights of Labor, and in contrast to the AFL's craft centered unionism, the IWW organized everyone in an industry.

---

* The IWW is often considered to be *anarcho-syndicalist* – *anarcho* for "anarchist," and *syndicalist* meaning "union." Nicknamed the "Wobblies," the IWW saw the need to organize the whole working class – often through direct action – but generally opposed other, non-union forms of class organization as oppressive. IWW members envisioned their "One Big Union" growing to include all of society – and becoming the future workers' democracy. Organizers led over 150 strikes in the decade or so of their greatest influence, and Wobblies controlled the docks of Philadelphia up to the Great Depression. But the IWW often found it difficult to maintain a presence in workplaces after a struggle, because the organization opposed written contracts as a matter of principle.

Though generally anarchist in outlook, many IWW members also were members of the Socialist Party. Wobbly membership peaked at around 100,000 just before the United States entered World War I – at a time when the AFL had 2.7 million members. The IWW's industrial union approach was a forerunner of the Trade Union Education League* in the 1920s and the CIO organizing drives of the 1930s. Together with Debs and the left wing of the Socialist Party, the IWW faced fierce repression in leading opposition to United States entry into World War I. These forces understood the war to be a fight among European imperial powers over how to divide the world. Organizers of later following benefited greatly from the example of these early fighters. But from our vantage point of a hundred years later, both the SLP and the early SP suffered from a "white blindspot" in their assessment of workers of color.

One way to understand Debs and DeLeon's views is that they tended to identify with the sector of the working class they lived among – within a larger segregated society. In doing so, the concerns of this white sector came to represent for them the interests of the whole class. From this position, socialist leaders then tried to explain why other members of the class – workers of color – did not take part in economic struggles and become socialists. Such a perspective can be called *economism* – a viewpoint that sees everything in terms of class and discounts the privileged position of white workers within the working class. As we describe below, this approach has had its modern supporters, though the language used in more recent years is often less direct.

Today we benefit from having a long history of working class and national struggles to learn from. Even a century ago and earlier, however, other observers – from outside the United States and among the oppressed nationalities internally – were clear on the corrupting influence of racism and privilege in the U.S. workers movement. Karl Marx, for example, stated in *Capital*, "In the United States of North America, every independent movement of the workers was paralyzed so long as slavery disfigured a part of the Republic. Labor cannot emancipate itself in the white skin where in the black it is branded."[6]

---

* The Trade Union Education League (TUEL) united left and progressive activists in the AFL unions from 1922 through 1929. The TUEL's program centered on amalgamating craft unions into industrial unions and countering dual unionist *(see note on p. 142)* sentiments that kept workers out of the mainstream of organized labor. TUEL activists focused on 1) developing new leadership, 2) engaging in struggles at the workplace – in mines, textile mills, and the needle trades, in particular, 3) organizing the unorganized, and 4) demanding U.S. recognition of the Soviet Union (finally achieved in 1933). The experience and training provided by the TUEL in the 1920s helped create conditions in the workers' movement that made possible the explosive organizing gains of the 1930s. *(Foster,* American Trade Unionism*)*

W.E.B. DuBois, the great black intellectual, warned in his statement on leaving the Socialist Party in 1913, "The Negro problem...is the great test of the American socialist."[7] And Hubert Harrison also challenged the SP to confront racism in the United States. "Socialism," he wrote, "is here to put an end to the exploitation of one group by another, whether that group be social, economic or racial.... [T]he affirmation of this is the present duty of the Socialist Party." He added, "The ten million Negroes of America form a group that is more essentially proletarian than any other American group"[8] And from within the ranks of progressive labor, Ben Fletcher, a leading black IWW organizer, commented: "Organized labor, for the most part be it radical or conservative, thinks and acts, in the terms of the White Race."[9]

Finally, the Russian revolutionary leader Lenin, who viewed black people in the United States as an oppressed nation, noted in *Socialist Revolution and the Right of Nations to Self-Determination*, "There is only one solution to the national problem (insofar as it can, in general, be solved in the capitalist world, the world of profit, squabbling, and exploitation) and that solution is consistent democracy...The national programme of working-class democracy is: absolutely no privileges for any one nation or for any one language."[10]

Early communist theories

Communist Party-USA (CP) writers provided a range of explanations for the relatively low level of working class consciousness in the United States. For example, in *A House Divided* Roxanne Mitchell and Frank Weiss survey the theories proposed by CP leader William Z. Foster:

- The existence of the right to vote and other democratic liberties from the very founding of the state;
- The heterogeneity of composition of the United States working class, a conglomeration of many tongues and kindreds;
- The "safety valve" for social discontent provided by the availability of homesteading opportunities in the West;
- The "social mobility" factor, the relative ease with which poor persons could rise on the economic ladder to become not only property owners, but entrepreneurs;
- The relative shortage of labor, resulting in the higher level of wages, as compared with that of other countries;
- The institutionalization of "pure and simple trade unionism," in the form of a dominant labor aristocracy using its organizational authority to prevent the development of independent political action by labor.

In addition, Mitchell and Weiss list "dual unionism"*; the "decentralized character of the American government, which scattered the political efforts of the workers"; and "the notoriously corrupt American politics which disgusted many workers with political action generally."[11]

With the benefit of hindsight, we can see that many of these explanations involve, or are manifestations of white privilege – for example, the right to vote, homesteading, social mobility, higher levels of wages, and a labor aristocracy linked to craft unionism. Race and privilege run through these explanations like a white thread.

The CP's adoption of the 1928 position on the Black Nation, along with its struggles against racism inside and outside the party during the 1930s, marked a qualitative advance over earlier socialist analysis and practice – and contain deep lessons for revolutionaries today. Nonetheless, even after the 1930s heightened conditions of struggle, party leader William Z. Foster continued to see the racial divide as secondary – as a symptom of working class weakness flowing from other more primary causes. The historical record presented in Chapter 9, by contrast, supports Mitchell and Weiss in their viewing the "policy of compromise with the system of preferences for white labor and the national oppression of black, Chicano and other peoples – as being a major *cause* of this backwardness."[12]

Summarizing the perspective of the first century of left analysts, Mitchell and Weiss note, "Like the principal representatives of socialism in this country – Hillquit, Debs, DeLeon, and Norman Thomas – Foster, the principal representative of communism, never saw a causal connection between the oppression of the black people and other nationalities, the privileges of white labor, and what he termed 'the weakness of the American labor movement, its lack of social vision and its general backwardness politically and industrially, as compared with the labor movements of other countries.'"

Drawing on this discussion and on material presented in earlier chapters, we want to highlight the first of three conclusions on white privilege and the U.S. working class:

> *Conclusion 1:* **The main reason for the low level of class-consciousness in the United States, one form of which is the absence of a mass-based labor party, is that the system of white privileges has distorted the understanding of white workers, keeping them from seeing workers of color as their class brothers and sisters.**

---

* *Dual unionism* is the practice of organizing workers into separate "advanced" or "pure" unions rather than struggling inside an existing union to change its character and make it more active, more inclusive, and more responsive to its members.

The authors of *A House Divided* explain this point as follows: "Opportunism* towards the institutions of white supremacist national oppression is not simply one among a number of shortcomings: it constitutes the key political and ideological weakness of the workers' movement in this country. The strength of this opportunism, its deep roots within labor's ranks, indicates that its influence does not stem merely from the inherent appeal of any set of ideas. The main significance of white supremacy for white people does not lie in ideas of European superiority, but rather in a system of white-skin privileges, a system of preferences for white labor and other white people in employment, land usage and ownership, housing, immigration, and society generally. This system of relative advantages for whites forms the material basis for white supremacist thinking and for actions carried out by some backward sections of the white masses in defense of national oppression."[13]

As a result of these deep-rooted attitudes and practices, white workers historically have tended to lose sight of the great moral imperative of working class culture: "An injury to one is an injury to all." Conditions that people of color have been forced to endure instead come to be identified by white workers with the oppressed nationalities themselves. "Blaming the victim" becomes a reflex habit instead of targeting the social system that creates the injustices. And the fundamental ability to distinguish friends from enemies disappears in the confusion of white consciousness.

Other pitfalls in assessing the U.S. working class

During the 1930s and then again in the 1960s and '70s, certain left forces came closer to identifying the central role of racism in the working class movement. For example in the late 1920s and 1930s, the Communist Party USA stated: "There is no surer touchstone of the revolutionary understanding… of any member or section of our Communist Party, than the degree to which he [sic] understands the struggle for the national liberation of the Negroes as part and parcel of the struggle for the emancipation of the working class."[14]

Also, by the 1970s, Mitchell and Weiss note, "with the exception of a very few small sects, all left organizations in the United States currently hold that the weakness of the working class movement is somehow bound up in the relations between white labor and the oppressed nationalities as a whole. Whether they ascribe this fact to the 'cancer of racism,' 'the ruling class policy of divide-and-conquer,' white chauvinism, or the oppression of the Black Nation, most implicitly reject Foster's mild treatment of white chauvinism in the labor movement, including in its

---

* *Opportunism* refers to attitudes and actions that are unprincipled, where a person seeks narrow personal or small group advantages at the expense of a larger collection of people.

Marxist wing. Such a rejection represents an *historic advance* for the U.S. left, even if it largely consists in a strictly passive reflection of the revolutionary struggles of black people, the Chicano people, and other oppressed nationalities since the last World War."[15]

While acknowledging this advance, *A House Divided* then goes on to assess the various positions advanced by the left in the 1970s. We now want to review five of those left perspectives. The goal is to gain insight into the ways an unrecognized system of racial preferences can divert activists from a principled working class outlook.

The labor aristocracy

One perspective on the U.S. labor movement's weakness blames the misleadership of the top trade union leaders for white workers' backwardness. The problem is said to lie in the fact that when U.S. imperialism began to establish itself around 1900, the system funneled superprofits earned from exploiting other countries into the pockets of top union leaders. These "misleaders" then served their imperialist masters by fostering divisions in the working class around race.

As mentioned in Chapter 9, Samuel Gompers, the first president of the American Federation of Labor (AFL), had a long history of anti-Asian racism. He leveraged his leadership of the Cigar Workers and their racist Union Label campaign to gain the top position in organized labor. There he presided over segregated locals, nurtured an exclusionist craft mentality, and – as just one example – tried to split Mexican from Japanese berry workers in the 1903 Japanese Mexican Labor Association strike in Oxnard California.*

There is no dispute over the racist character of the AFL and its leadership – or the negative role played by many top leaders of the trade unions throughout the 20th Century. The question is, can the backward ideas and practices of white workers be blamed only on these leaders?

For one thing, this perspective seems to suggest that white workers did not really act in racist ways before the onset of imperialism and the creation of the labor aristocracy. While the superprofits gained from imperialist plunder may contribute to the bribing of an upper layer of the working class, the main dynamic is that these resources work to reinforce *already existing* divisions within the working class, and tend to differ from country to country. Lenin talks about "the home brand [of opportunism] in each particular country."[16] In England, the result was Engels's "*bourgeois* labor movement." In the United States it was, and is, a working class divided by racial preferences, by a system of advantages based on skin color.

---

* See the box describing the strike on p. 122.

At bottom, this theory of the labor aristocracy is not well grounded in U.S. history. It tends to substitute a leftist belief in the inherent revolutionary character of the working class for the real attitudes of white workers. It then finds an excuse for the workers' not acting in line with the theory by shifting the blame to the trade union leadership. This is one form of the theory that "bad ideas" have gained a hold on white workers' minds – in this case ideas coming from the labor aristocracy. In other cases, the bad ideas are blamed on the "bosses" or the "capitalists." These explanations never get to the question of why the workers are so slow that they can never manage to figure out what is really going on. If it were just a matter of bad ideas – from whatever source – one would expect that the truth would eventually win out.

As we discussed in Chapter 9, the process of rapid industrialization in the context of white supremacy shaped the development of the U.S. labor aristocracy. The National Labor Union opted to throw its lot in with the Liberal Republicans instead of defending Reconstruction. Later the inconsistently multiracial Knights of Labor lost out to a segregated, pro-capitalist craft unionism. In the absence of a class-conscious workers movement, social forces produced a top labor stratum that fit neatly into the emerging monopoly capitalist system. Gompers and his successors clearly played their role in furthering divisions in the working class. But their role – their position and outlook – was socially constructed. It was not simply a matter of their having made some lucky, if self-serving and vicious, personal choices. They grew to power in the soil of system-wide preferences for white people, nurtured by the defeat of Reconstruction.

Capitalists earn superprofits

While true as far as it goes, the capitalist superprofits viewpoint does not really get to the bottom of racial divisions in the U.S. working class. *A House Divided* labels this perspective *economism,* since it offers a purely economic explanation and motive for the system of white privileges. This explanation misses the essential fact that the only thing more important to capitalism than making profits today is... guaranteeing that they can make profits tomorrow and every day thereafter.* To do so requires social control – and in the United States social control fundamentally depends on the system of racial preferences.

The economist viewpoint starts out with the true statement that there is inequality in the life conditions of people of color compared to white people in the United States. These material differences are then said to

---

* In the powerful anti-colonial film *Burn*, Marlon Brando makes this point clearly in reprimanding the squeamishness and bean-counting attitude of the British Sugar Co.'s representative, who complained about the level of destruction required to put down the cane workers' rebellion.

work to the advantage of the capitalists because, by paying workers of color less than white workers, the capitalists are able to capture superprofits. The capitalists therefore have a stake in maintaining the system as it is.

The problem with this argument is that it is hard to explain why the unemployment rate of black and Latin workers consistently runs about double that of white workers. If capitalists can make superprofits from workers of color, why would they not hire as many of these workers as possible? Also, if this were all that was going on, one would expect that the arguments presented in introductory economics textbooks would hold true: competition in the market would eventually bid away the differences in pay between white and oppressed nationality workers. Capitalists would hire as many workers of color as possible until they became scarce – and their unemployment rate would drop very low. The capitalists would then have to start paying people of color more to attract them away from other employers, and eventually the two unemployment rates and the two pay scales would be the same.

White workers are bribed

Here the view is that capitalists earn superprofits either 1) from people of color at home generally, 2) in the U.S. South in particular, or 3) from imperialist exploitation abroad. Whichever way the capitalists extract their excessive earnings, they then distribute a portion to white workers to give them part ownership in the system. As a result, there is a material basis for the existing racist system that makes it so difficult to overcome.

A House Divided gives this perspective the label *left economism*. We are back at the superprofits theory, but with an added twist: the white workers have been bought off. Those who held to this basic analysis then drew differing conclusions as to what to do about it. Here are three:

- *Support national liberation movements overseas* until the source of the superprofits are done away with. Then you can organize white workers along with people of color.
- *Organize the oppressed nationalities at home* until the conditions for earning superprofits are overcome.
- *Organize workers of color and white workers separately*, because their material interests are different.

The common denominator in all three approaches is that they abandon the task of organizing all U.S. workers as part of the multinational working class in the United States. While the spoils of imperialist rule and super-exploitation in the homelands of the African American and Chicano nations are facts of life, it does not follow that the masses of white working people come out ahead by sharing in the superprofits.

The privileges that bind white workers to the capitalists are not so great that these workers escape being exploited by the system.

The difference between being "bribed" or "bought off," on the one hand, and being the recipient of white-skin privileges, on the other, is a key distinction. Research has shown that *where the system of racial privileges divides workers the most, the average wage level for both white workers and workers of color tends to be lowest.*[17] As an example, consider the South historically, where the sharp differences in white and black pay tended to obscure the fact that white workers received significantly less – in textiles, for example – than in other parts of the country. Mitchell and Weiss link this overall wage difference to the relative strength of the labor movement in the different regions: "The basic cause of the low industrial wage level in the South lies in the weakness of the Southern labor movement. The aggravated form of white favoritism in the South, the other side of the ferocious national oppression of the black people, has so far succeeded in crippling the Southern labor movement." [18] Privileges for white workers divide the workforce, weaken the labor movement, and cause the overall wage floor to drop for everyone. As a result, white workers who seem to benefit the most from their privileges actually lose out. This picture drives home the inner reality of white privilege: "Every worm has a hook."[19]

Racial differences are not significant

This perspective holds that while there may be differences in the conditions of life between white workers and workers of color, to focus on those differences is divisive and weakens the class. Instead, workers of all nationalities should organize around a common program that reflects their shared concerns.

Two things can be said about this perspective:

- *It is never the right time to talk about racism and white privilege.* If you are building up for a struggle, according to this view, you want to focus on what unites people to help bring them together. Then once you are in the thick of a battle, to bring up differences around race would be divisive. And in the aftermath of a struggle, people should celebrate their victories or, if defeated, not point fingers.
- *The struggle against racism and white privilege is not considered an issue of common concern* for workers of color and white workers alike. At bottom this view denies, first, the historic role of racism in dividing the U.S. working class; and, second, the insight that white workers pass up a better life by settling for being white.

In contrast to these four perspectives, we can draw out a second conclusion concerning white privileges and the U.S. working class:

Conclusion 2: **Throughout U.S. history the ruling class has carried out a series of political and economic policies – backed by state power – that have established and maintained a system of racial preferences favoring white workers. Flowing from these policies – linked to the institution of slavery in colonial times, to the defeat of Reconstruction, to the extension of the color line a century ago, and to ongoing national oppression today – the life conditions of white workers and workers of color differ significantly.**

The main material benefits to the ruling class from this system of preferences come from the ability to 1) lower the wage level across the board because of the low level of organization of the class, and 2) prevent the growth of movements for working class power and for national liberation.

The actual material differences in workers' lives imposed by this preference-centered system and its supportive culture have fed the racism in white people's minds. As a result, white workers for the most part have been unable to see past their relative advantages to make common cause with their class brothers and sisters of color.

White blindspot

A House Divided also addresses a fifth viewpoint: the *white skin privilege* analysis originally developed by Ted Allen and Noel Ignatin (Ignatiev) [A&I] during the 1970s.[20] While uniting with many of Allen and Ignatin's views, Mitchell and Weiss point to the following problems in their "white blindspot" perspective:

- A&I make little acknowledgement of the need for organization in overcoming white people's acceptance of their privileges.
- A&I's approach suffers from a kind of "individualistic moralism." Rather than seeing the struggle in class terms, people are asked to repudiate privilege as individuals. "Instead of popular appeal, this emphasis promises almost a form of personal redemption; instead of a guide to class struggle, a code of moral behavior."[21]
- A&I speak of the "actual guilt" of white people, with little attention given to the tactics required to combat the system of privilege. Allen states in *Can White Radicals Be Radicalized?*: "First, face the problem of the necessity to repudiate the white-skin privilege. Second, act: repudiate the privilege by violating the white 'gentleman's agreement' as completely as you can at every opportunity. Once radicals adopt such an approach to radicalizing the white masses, the implications for particular areas of activity will

not be hard to find. If in doubt at first, just make a list of the privileges and start violating them."[22]

By contrast, Mitchell and Weiss comment, "Left activists will not win the masses of white workers to consistent opposition to white supremacy except through participation in the day-to-day struggle, where the fight against white supremacy must be linked to the masses' other immediate needs."[23]

- A&I picture the social system and "The White Skin Privilege" in a monolithic way. This approach can get in the way of a worker grasping how different privileges show up concretely in different specific settings: "a differential in discipline within the shop; a differential in promotion; police terror against oppressed nationalities... In specific cases, many workers see the role of particular privileges in holding back the struggle of all. With time, experience and leadership, they will reject and fight to abolish these privileges, and come to see them as a part of a systematic form of domination."[24]
- A&I have a tendency to fall into a "clear the decks" outlook. This approach is counter to the way tactical struggle against white privilege should be carried out. Quoting Allen from *The Most Vulnerable Point*: "The indispensable condition of the participation of the white workers in revolutionary struggle is the repudiation of the white-skin privileges, privileges which are ruinous to the short-range and long-range interests of the entire proletariat, of whites no less than Blacks and other proletarian victims of national oppression."[25]

  The suggestion here is that white people's privileges must be repudiated – the decks cleared – before working class struggle can unfold. But this outlook obscures the close interconnection of white supremacy to the capitalist system. It separates the fight against white privileges from other aspects of the class struggle to transform U.S. society.

Based on this analysis we highlight a third conclusion concerning white privilege and the U.S. working class – a conclusion we will develop further in Chapter 11, and then more completely in Chapters 24-27:

> *Conclusion 3:* **The fight against the system of racial privileges must be *organized*. It needs to take into account the *system's inseparable connection to capitalism*. It should be *tactically sensitive* and unfold as *part of the U.S. multinational working class struggle* to meet people's basic needs – including the need to be free of national privileges of any kind.**

In summary, the central conclusion to be drawn from this theoretical overview is the following:

White privileges exist, they are significant, and they can be overcome through struggle.

BARN – Brooklyn Anti-Bias Response Network

Announcing that she "hadn't moved all the way from South Africa just to support apartheid in New York," Ann Van Zyl, a white woman, blew the whistle on her employer, Park West Realty. Park West was deliberately steering people of color away from certain apartments in Park Slope, a mainly white middle-class neighborhood in Brooklyn.

In coalition with other neighborhood groups, the Brooklyn Anti-bias Response Network (BARN) organized a weekend picket line at the real estate agency. Gary Goff delivered the following speech at a rally in front of Park West one busy Saturday afternoon. The speech was picked up by a local progressive minister and used as the text for his sermon the next day. Congregants from his largely white church then developed a "Pledge against Steering," which they circulated among area real estate agents for signature. Shortly after the rally, Park West Realty went out of business.

"BARN has a button that says 'Unity in the Community.' Now, when we say unity in the community, we don't mean that everybody should be the same. That's more like what racist and homophobic real estate agents and landlords are saying.

"One thing I've learned from the environmental movement is that the more diverse an ecosystem is, the stronger it is. I think this goes for human society too. But being diverse, all by itself, isn't nearly enough. There can't be any meaningful equality between those who have power and those who don't – between those who have privileges and those who don't. Each of us, as individuals, could – and should – decide that we were going to treat everyone fairly. But this isn't nearly enough. Some of us have unearned privileges thrust on us by society, and we need to reject them. I know this isn't the way we usually look at things, but if you think about it, it isn't really such an odd concept. Some of us who are here today are straight. Some of us are white. That means we had the privilege of renting any apartment or buying any house in this neighborhood. By being here today, we are rejecting that privilege. We're saying, 'I know I didn't ask for this privilege, but I also know I have to deal with it. And I'm simply not going to accept it.'

"This idea of privilege isn't just another interesting way of looking at prejudice. It's really important for understanding how things work. Those areas of the country that have the greatest differences between what whites are paid and what Blacks are paid are also the areas where wages in general are the lowest. Where whites have clung most tenaciously to their privileges, those same whites are paid less than whites in other areas. This is because privileges at the expense of others divide people – they weaken our ability to fight back against common oppression. At a time when our schools and hospitals and community services are under attack – now, more than ever, we need to reject those things that divide us. We need to be united.

"And that's why we say, 'Unity in the Community.'"

—from: Goff, "We Need to Reject Those Things That Divide Us"

Chapter 11

The Sunbelt Strategy

We now want to return to the South and Southwest, the Sunbelt region, but update the discussion to the current period. Reconstruction's defeat and the failure of Operation Dixie continue to impact people today – in the form of the conservative shift in ruling class policy of recent decades. In light of this long history, as well as the more recent developments outlined below, we support a strategy for working class organizing today that focuses on the South and Southwest.

Mid-1980s – the Sunbelt and capitalist restructuring

By the late 1960s and early '70s the economy of the United States began to undergo a marked shift from the pattern of the post-WW II expansion years.[1] The crisis showed up in declining profit rates beginning in 1965, a monetary crisis that led to devaluing the dollar in August 1971, and the U.S. defeat in Southeast Asia in 1975. Contributing to the crisis were 1) independence and national liberation struggles throughout the Third World, 2) urban rebellions and broad social movements at home, 3) contention with the bloc of countries led by the Soviet Union, and 4) strengthened competition from imperialist centers in Europe and Japan.

Given this increase in economic and political pressures, U.S. corporate and government leaders groped for solutions. The pattern that emerged included:

- *shifting the industrial core of the economy* out of its longtime Northeast/Midwest centers to the South and Southwest – to the Sunbelt;
- *undermining existing unions* and fighting new union organizing; and
- *dismantling the welfare state.*

The impact of this all-around attack fell disproportionately on people of color – the main social force in the popular movements of the 1960s and '70s. Real* wages began declining after 1973 and continued to do so until the mid-1990s, as the ruling class moved to reestablish corporate profit rates.

By shifting to the South and Southwest, capitalists managed to both stabilize production and firm up the social base for a rightward shift in national politics. The depressed conditions in the African American, Chicano, and many native peoples' homelands held the rest of the country hostage to the threat of plant closings and relocation. Specifically, the Sunbelt region during the 1970s and '80s offered capitalists the following "favorable business climate":

- ***Low union density*** – 14 (out of a total 22) right-to-work states with a lower-than-average percentage of union members and, as a result, lower wage levels
- ***Low corporate taxes***
- ***Weak regulations on business*** – including weak environmental controls
- ***Low employer insurance costs*** – for unemployment, workers compensation, and disability insurance coverage
- ***Large influx of federal spending*** – government dollars going to the 140 military installations across the South and Southwest, to highway construction, and to increased federal civilian employment in the area

Geography of the Sunbelt

- *Sixteen states, or portions of states*, running from southern Virginia and the Carolinas in the east to California in the west
- *623 Black Belt counties* stretching from Virginia to Texas – making up the core territory of the Black Nation, where the majority of black people in the South live today
- *Most of the territory taken from Mexico* in the Mexican American war of 1846-48 – corresponding roughly to the territory of the Chicano Nation, Aztlán
- *Many of the resource-poor lands* assigned as reservations to the native peoples

---

* The term *real* in front of *wages* or *interest rates* means that inflation – an increase in the overall price level – has been taken out of the picture. For example, the dollar amount of

- ***Lack of popular control*** – large-scale disenfranchisement of oppressed nationality voters, gerrymandering of districts, and lack of political power generally[*] – despite important gains from the civil rights and oppressed nationality freedom movements in the 1960s and '70s.

In addition to giving capitalists a way to stabilize their profit margins, the Sunbelt met three other strategic objectives:

- ***Geopolitical*** –
  - securing the border with Mexico – with an eye to Mexico's oil reserves, the *maquiladora* low-wage manufacturing sector, and the population flows into the United States to meet varying labor demand
  - expanding investment and trade on the Pacific rim
- ***Energy*** – exploiting the oil, coal, and uranium deposits in the region
- ***Militarization*** – taking advantage of the reserves of white supremacist ideology and national chauvinism to support basing the majority of U.S. armed forces in the region.[†]

The impact of the Sunbelt strategy on workers in the region shows up in:

- ***High levels of exploitation*** – of labor, natural resources, and the environment; and of youth drawn into the military to expand and defend the empire
- ***Depressed living conditions*** compared to other parts of the country – higher rates of poverty, rural unemployment, school dropouts, poor housing, infant mortality and other health measures; police brutality, attacks on the Spanish language, and harassment from Immigration and Customs Enforcement (ICE – formerly the INS, Immigration and Naturalization Service)

---

wages in people's paychecks might go up, but their real wages might decline if inflation eats up all the wage increase.

[*] Florida during the 2000 presidential election, and Georgia's attempt in 2005 to institute a modern poll tax, together demonstrate ongoing efforts to disenfranchise African American voters. The recurring threat of local and state laws targeting African American and Latino electoral power prompted the successful drive to renew the Voting Rights Act in July 2006.

[†] For example, as of September 2003, 70.2% of active duty personnel were based in 11 states of the South and Southwest. *(U.S. Department of Defense, "Percent Distribution of DoD Military and Civilian Population by State – Sept. 30, 2003)*

Into the 21st Century

The basic picture of the capitalists' strategy for the South and Southwest has not changed since the mid-1980s:

- **Population trends** show that the South grew at an average rate of 6% every year from 1991 through 1998 – a rate more than double the national average for the period.[2] From July 2004 to July 2005, 23 of the 25 fastest growing cities in the country with more than 100,000 people were in the South and Southwest.[3] And a summary of population projections states, "Three Sunbelt states – Florida, California and Texas – will account for nearly half of U.S. population growth between 2000 and 2030."[4]
- **Employment growth** in large metropolitan areas favored the South and Southwest. Between 1998 and 2003 seven of the ten fastest growing city-centered economies were in California, Nevada, Florida, Texas, and Arizona, with another two in the Northern Virginia/DC area.[5] For the ten-year period from 1993 to 2003, 20 of the top 25 metropolitan centers for job-growth were in these same states plus Louisiana and Oklahoma.[6]
- **The Pentagon's reorganization plan** will create 35,000 new jobs in Florida, Georgia, South Carolina, and Alabama. "The military is moving south, it's moving west," commented a military think tank analyst at the Lexington Institute.[7]
- **Union density** has continued to stagnate or decline despite the change in leadership in the AFL-CIO in 1995. What effect the splitting away of the Change To Win federation in 2005 will have on organizing is unclear. The table and two maps[8] of the United States that follow show the impact of the capitalists' Sunbelt strategy on union density in the South and Southwest since the mid-1980s.[9]

Today, the goods and services produced by the South make it the fourth largest economy in the world – while capital's position remains protected by Taft-Hartley, militarism, and white supremacy.

Note to table on next page: Sunbelt states are in italics; right-to-work states are marked by an asterisk. The only right-to-work state not on the list is Iowa. Source for the table and this note: is Hirsch and Macpherson, "Union Membership, Coverage, Density and Employment"

Union membership percentage and rankings by state, 2005 and change since 1983

State	2005 Percent Unionized	2005 Ranking	1983 Percent Unionized	Change in Percentage
*S. Carolina**	2.3	50	5.9	-3.6
*N. Carolina**	2.9	49	7.6	-4.7
*Arkansas**	4.8	47	11.0	-6.2
*Virginia**	4.8	47	11.7	-6.9
Utah*	4.9	46		
*Georgia**	5.0	45	11.9	-6.9
Idaho*	5.2	44		
*Texas**	5.3	43	9.7	-4.4
*Florida**	5.4	40	10.2	-4.8
*Oklahoma**	5.4	40	11.5	-6.1
*Tennessee**	5.4	40	15.1	-9.7
S. Dakota*	5.9	39		
*Arizona**	6.1	38	11.4	-5.3
*Louisiana**	6.4	37	13.8	-7.4
Kansas*	7.0	36		
*Mississippi**	7.1	35	9.9	-2.8
N. Dakota*	7.3	34		
Wyoming*	7.9	33		
New Mexico	8.1	32	11.8	-3.7
Colorado	8.3	30		
Nebraska*	8.3	30		
Kentucky	9.7	29		
*Alabama**	10.2	28	16.9	-6.7
*Nevada**	13.8	18	22.4	-8.6
California	16.5	8	21.9	-5.4
United States	12.5		20.1	-7.6
Right-to-work states	6.4			

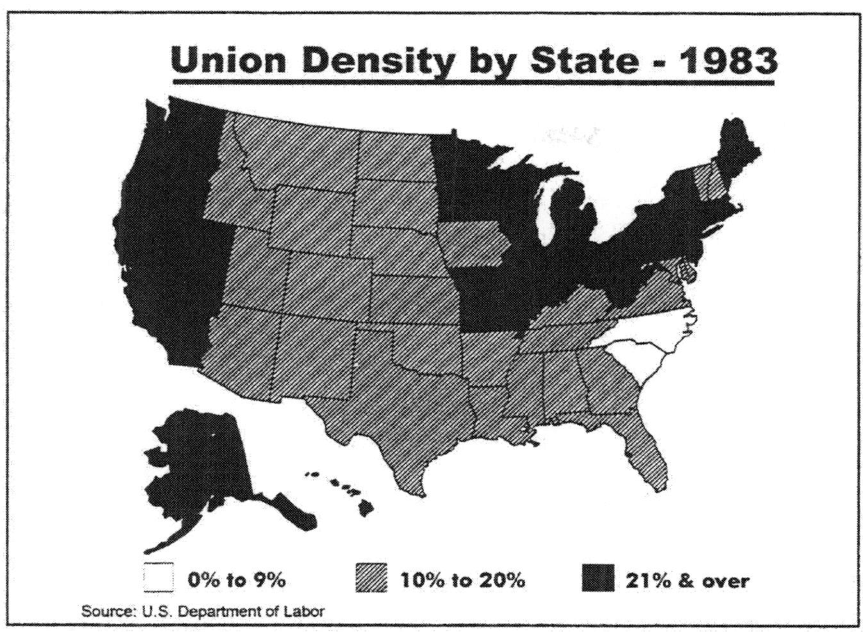
Union Density by State - 1983
0% to 9%
10% to 20%
21% & over
Source: U.S. Department of Labor

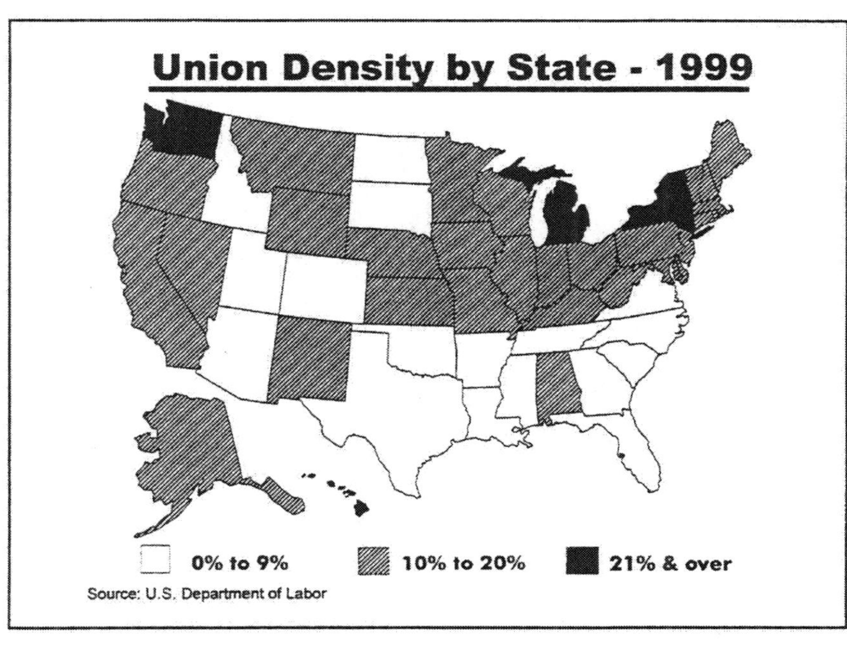
Union Density by State - 1999
0% to 9%
10% to 20%
21% & over
Source: U.S. Department of Labor

Notes on the maps on previous page:

- The data in the table on page 156 match the map for 1983, when figures are rounded to the nearest whole number.
- The following adjustments are required to bring the 1999 map up to 2005:

Improved –	Alaska (to solid black, with 22.8%)
Worse off –	Kansas (to white, with 7.0%)
	Nebraska (to white, with 8.3%)
	New Mexico (to white, with 8.1%)
	Washington (to gray from black, with 19.1%)
	Wyoming (to white, with 7.9%)
	And Michigan and New Jersey on the edge between black and gray, both with 20.5%

—source: Hirsch and Macpherson

Globalization and the Sunbelt region

Two major differences distinguish the developments of recent years from the 1980s: 1) the increased importance of foreign investment in the Sunbelt region, and 2) the increased immigration from both Mexico – as a result of the NAFTA treaty and the neoliberal restructuring of Mexico's economy – and from Asia.

First Union Bank, headquartered in Charlotte, North Carolina, boasted in 1998: "The Southeast is far and away the leader in attracting investments from overseas, accounting for close to half of all new facilities built in the United States by foreign companies during the 1990s."[10] And Saladin Muhammad, chairman of Black Workers for Justice, based in Rocky Mt., North Carolina, points out that "66 of the 75 most industrialized U.S. counties are located in the eleven Black Belt states."[11] Data on manufacturing by state show that between 1977 and 1996, the Sunbelt states increased their share of the national manufacturing total as the Northeast and Midwest portions declined. In 2001 California led the country in manufacturing with a 10.38% share. And Los Angeles was the undisputed top metropolitan area with 720,000 manufacturing workers – 125,000 more than second place Chicago.[12]

Meanwhile conditions for working people nationally remained difficult even after a long period without a recession during the 1990s. While real wage levels increased after 1996, they remained below levels achieved in the 1960s. Then the 2001 recession hit, driving unemployment rates up and keeping them there for several years. During this period the rate of job creation dropped off sharply, and *BusinessWeek* commentator Michael Mandel noted in October 2004, "the robust job growth of the 1990s [is] unlikely to return anytime soon."[13] Even high-end technical and information workers took a hit during the recession, and job creation centered on low-wage service jobs. Most affected, however, were black and other workers of color, mostly younger and less educated, who had entered the labor market in the late 1990s. Middle class black workers with long-tenure jobs also lost ground.[14]

Internationally, the Asian economic crisis of 1997 and its repercussions in Latin America and Eastern Europe took a severe toll on millions of people's lives. Then in 2001-02 a decade of neoliberal policies in Argentina came to a head and average income dropped 64% compared to five years earlier.[15] Those who have benefited from the high-velocity capital flows are the industrial and financial centers in the global West. Meanwhile, the adjustment shocks from imperialist globalization are absorbed by the working class – and by Third World* people in particular, both inside and outside the United States.

The UE Public Workers Union Local 150 summarized the situation in the U.S. South for working people in June of 2005: "The South has 28 percent of the U.S. population and close to 40 percent of U.S. poverty; has the largest number of the working poor; has the largest number of minimum wage workers; has more than 50 percent of all U.S. temporary workers; has 13 million people with no health insurance; has the highest infant mortality rate; has the least number of doctors per patient; spends 20 percent less per student in public schools; and has over 50 percent of U.S. toxic waste sites."[16]

At the same time, local and state government handouts to corporations can reach obscene levels – witness North Carolina's quarter-billion giveaway to Dell Computer in 2004. And Southern capital is building up its position with the help of foreign and domestic investment. One example is Wachovia Bank, based in Charlotte, which formed out of a succession of mergers that included CoreStates and First Union. Wachovia is currently the fourth largest bank holding company in the United States. When paired with the country's largest bank, Bank of America, the two institutions anchor a financial center in Charlotte that is second only to New York City's.

With workers from Mexico and Asia joining people driven off the welfare rolls, competition for low-wage jobs has increased throughout the South and Southwest. NAFTA opened the border to cheap U.S. agribusiness corn; and the only way out for many Mexican farmers has been to uproot themselves, divide their families, and move north.

---

* The use of the term *Third World* to describe people of color inside the United States developed during the late 1960s. It signifies both people's connection to the oppressed nations of the Global South and unity in the face of white supremacy and imperialism.

NAFTA has also had an impact that might seem to undermine the thrust of the Sunbelt analysis – namely, plant closings in the South. Many thousands of jobs have been lost in the textile and furniture industries in North Carolina, for example. What this picture shows, however, is just another dimension of dependency and powerlessness. Without organization, the majority of workers in the South and Southwest are either currently being super-exploited – or are unemployed and waiting to be super-exploited. Either way, they are at the mercy of capital.

Ruling class strategy or opportunity for the left?

The above tables and diagrams support the conclusion that the South and Southwest have provided a base for U.S. imperialism to consolidate its rule after the crisis of the 1960s and '70s. This strategy hit hardest the oppressed nationality peoples in the former industrial centers of the North and in the African American, Chicano, and native homelands of the Sunbelt region. These developments in turn have provided the material underpinnings for the rightward shift in politics and ideology of recent decades.

The implications of this picture in some respects are more important for people living outside the Sunbelt than inside. For people inside the region the need to struggle is self-evident. The consequences of national oppression are clear – but fear and hopelessness can take their toll on people's ability to fight. People outside the South, however, might say, "Yeah, that's all true, but we're up against it here, too." What's missing in this view is an appreciation of just how much what happens in the Sunbelt region influences the situation elsewhere in the country. Recall how the civil rights movement of the 1950s and '60s impacted the oppressed nationality, women's, and anti-Vietnam War movements. For over a hundred years – from the defeat of Reconstruction in the 1870s, to the passage of Taft-Hartley in the 1940s, to the ruling class reorganization of the 1980s – this region has been the bedrock of imperialism. As Saladin Muhammad says, "It's the anchor."[17]

The positive aspect in this situation, however, is that if the social justice movement can challenge imperialism in its base area, the South and Southwest – especially if linked to developments in the Global South – it will shake things loose unlike anywhere else in the United States. A classwide movement centered in the oppressed nations of the Sunbelt can point the way forward for the whole country.

Implementing a Sunbelt strategy

The overall situation in the South and Southwest, along with the ferment in the Global South described in Chapter 8, suggest that progressive forces should give strategic prioritization to the Sunbelt and its international connections. Not only would such an approach help build popular power in oppressed nationality areas of the United States and undermine white privilege, it could also limit imperialism's ability to impose its will on nations outside the United States.[18]

Key elements of a Sunbelt Strategy include:

- *Concentrating organizers* in the South and Southwest, and choosing specific locations strategically
- *Focusing work* among African American, Chicano/Latino, indigenous, and Asian/Pacific Islander workers – both U.S.-born and immigrants
- *Building collaborative relations* with progressive and revolutionary forces outside the country
- *Organizing for full immigrant rights* as part of the fight for political power – including the right to vote (even if not a citizen), as well as the fight for equality of languages (often expressed as a demand for bilingual education)
- *Paying attention to the land struggle* – fighting black land loss in the South and supporting the land claims of Chicanos in the Southwest and native peoples across the region

Concentration: Having a concentration strategy means that as people join the movement in other, non-strategic areas of the country, they would be encouraged to relocate to targeted geographical areas in the South and Southwest. Specific locations to focus on might include:

Los Angeles: The Alameda Corridor and the Alameda Corridor East – networks of shipping, warehouses, air transport, railroads and truck routes passing through LA – transport 70% of the manufactured goods from the Pacific Rim distributed inside the United States. Huge investments have gone into infrastructure to support these transportation corridors. City-sized warehouses store products in the desert just east of LA for "just in time" distribution throughout the United States. The corridors contain within them major political centers of black and Chicano struggle. "Gateway" cities with predominantly Chicano/Latino or African American populations have challenged for local political power – as a component of the struggle for self-determination.

I-85 corridor from Atlanta to North Carolina: Similar considerations apply to the arc of industry and population running up I-85 from Atlanta to Charlotte and across to Southeastern North Carolina. Here one finds auto manufacturing, including foreign companies like BMW and Mercedes-Benz; meatpacking, anchored by Smithfield's huge hog processing plant in Tar Heel, NC, together with its network of contract farms; high concentrations of black and Latino workers;

and a history of struggle among farmworkers and among public workers in North Carolina's state university system, in social services, and in government.

Southern Mississippi to Houston: The struggle for the Reconstruction of New Orleans and the Gulf Coast after Hurricanes Katrina and Rita is the central struggle for African American self-determination in this period.*

In each of these locations, a key criterion for left concentration is the presence of organizations with a history of struggle in the area. Each such organization would play a critical role in assessing forces and drawing up a strategic plan for the region, orienting newcomers and placing them in targeted industries, helping to coordinate organizing campaigns, and over time developing new grassroots leaders. In the three areas listed above, such organizations include:

Los Angeles: The Labor Community Strategy Center; as well as the Pilipino Workers Center and other member organizations of MIWON (Multi-ethnic Immigrant Workers Organizing Network), including Coalition for Humane Immigrant Rights in LA (CHIRLA), Garment Workers Center, and Korean Immigrant Workers Alliance (KIWA)

Atlanta to NC: Project South in Atlanta, and the Black Workers for Justice in North Carolina

Gulf Coast: the People's Hurricane Relief Fund and Oversight Committee, People's Organizing Committee/IFCO, Common Ground, and ACORN

In addition to these three locations, consideration might begin instead from where dynamic organizations already are active – for example:

South Florida: the Miami Workers Center and the Coalition of Immokalee Workers

I-35 corridor centered in San Antonio, stretching from the Rio Grande to Austin, Texas: Southwest Workers Union

Albuquerque, New Mexico: South West Organizing Project

Left organizations could select areas of national concentration consciously – through collective discussion – instead of letting the flow of practical work direct activities, as so often happens now. New people coming into targeted areas would follow the lead of established groups, while rooting themselves in local unions and the social movements. In time, these organizers would also join in creating new institutions that could give structure to the core oppressed nationality and immigrant

---

* See the discussion of Gulf Coast organizing in Chapter 8.

communities. By institutionalizing mass movements – and linking them up with the union movement – organizers would be able to create working class bases that survive over time.

In this scenario unionization has broader implications than simply "organizing the unorganized." Issues related to nation building and political power – such as pollution, public transportation, education, segregation, and economic development policy — would also take on strategic importance. And in the process of building their bases, organizers could reach out to other, broader forces on a solid strategic foundation.

The next three elements of a Sunbelt Strategy would hold in whichever areas people choose to concentrate:

International collaboration: One example where international connections are necessary is in "sweatshop" organizing. Low-wage manufacturers squeeze their mostly immigrant and undocumented workforce by threatening to run away to other countries. One solution has been the formation of the Workers Rights Consortium (WRC), dedicated to monitoring sweatshops for workers' rights internationally. The WRC accomplishes this task through nongovernmental agencies, worker organizations, and unions. If a particular company inside the United States violates workers' rights, the international network is alerted and organizations like Sweatshop Watch go into action to persuade consumers internationally not to purchase the company's products.

A second example looks to building relationships with progressive and revolutionary forces in Mexico. The movements in the two countries could come to function as each other's "rear guard" – U.S. forces' providing support for organizing in *maquiladora* industries along the border in northern Mexico, for example. Also, since many Mexican immigrant workers live part of the year in each country, a goal could be to maintain organized links with people year round – as the Farm Labor Organizing Committee (FLOC) has done by opening an office in Monterrey, Mexico. The Border Social Forum in Juarez, Mexico, in the fall of 2006 – part of the World Social Forum movement – offered an opportunity to strengthen such links as well.

The auto industry centered in the Charlotte–Atlanta corridor has also been a focus of international cooperation. In the fall of 1999 autoworkers and organizers from Europe, Latin America, and the United States spent a weekend together at the 2nd International Workers School, hosted by the Brisbane Institute in Atlanta. Mexico's *Frente Auténtico del Trabajo* (FAT) participated in this meeting. FAT has been a leader in establishing cross-border solidarity with workers in the United States – most notably with the independent United Electrical and Radio Workers of America (UE).

Finally, a concentration in LA potentially could disrupt in a major way the flow of imported goods from the Pacific Rim. By organizing transport centers linking shipping, rail, and trucking, for example, the movement could gain leverage against imperialist hegemony in the Pacific.* Support actions here might aid national liberation or workers' struggles in the Philippines or Colombia. And in return, U.S. organizers could expect a measure of support from workers overseas – while making allowance for the difficult conditions faced by many low-wage, often women, manufacturing workers in Third World countries.

Immigrants' rights: Fighting for full immigrants' rights is a key part of oppressed nationalities' struggle for political power and self-determination. The right to vote and equality of languages are necessary for immigrants to participate democratically as equals in the U.S. political process. Language rights often take the form of a demand for bilingual education; but they go deeper to challenge white supremacy and the Eurocentric† assumptions behind "Standard English" in schools, businesses, and culture generally.‡

Land struggles: The fight to gain or maintain control of national territory in the South and Southwest centers on African American farms, rural Mexican land grants, and native land claims. While such struggles at times involve relatively few people, they have tremendous political and symbolic meaning – as shown by the impact of Reies López Tijerina's courthouse raid in 1967.§ Such actions, carried out under the slogan

---

* The longshore strike in the fall of 2002 demonstrated the potential power of such actions – as it forced maritime companies and retail giants into a new formal alliance (the West Coast Waterfront Coalition) and drew threats of federal intervention and the possible use of military strikebreakers against the ILWU (International Longshore and Warehouse Union). *(Jobs with Justice, "Victory on the Puget Sound Waterfront")*

Wal-Mart has countered this threat to their operations by building a huge warehouse outside of Houston – "big enough to hold 30 downtown city blocks or 70 football fields" – enabling a Panama Canal route for the entry of Asian merchandise. Similarly, port operations and transport are being relocated to Mexico, with the planned construction of two mammoth NAFTA corridors in the United States that will connect to Mexican highway and rail systems at Laredo, Texas. *(Vogel, "Wal-Mart's End Run around Organized Labor" and "The NAFTA Corridors)*

† *Eurocentrism* is the outlook and set of practices that take European culture as the standard for what is useful, valuable, beautiful, or worthy of emulation.

‡ See Chapter 8 for a discussion of the immigrant upsurge in the spring of 2006.

§ Reies López Tijerina organized *La Alianza Federal de Mercedes* (The Federal Alliance of Land Grants) in 1963. Over the next four years *Alianza* members first protested and then physically occupied land granted by the Treaty of Guadalupe-Hidalgo to the town of San Joaquín de Chama. One highpoint in the struggle came when *Alianza* members entered the courthouse of Tierra Amarilla to make a citizens' arrest of the district attorney. *(Acuña,* Occupied America*)*

Tierra y Libertad (Land and Freedom), have generated broad support – among urban Chicanos/as, for example – as did the seizure of Alcatraz by American Indian Movement activists in 1969.

Organizational forces

To carry out a Sunbelt strategy will likely require high levels of organization. The goal, after all, is to focus the movement's resources on organizing the base territory of U.S. financial and corporate power. Given the largeness of the task and the relative smallness of movement forces and their low level of organization, carrying out a Sunbelt Strategy will require increased cooperation among left organizations in order to magnify the movement's impact. Recruiting and training new organizers, encouraging people to relocate to strategic areas, building the work together instead of at cross-purposes – all these steps are likely to require unprecedented levels of discussion, debate, mutual support, and collective evaluation. One possible outcome of such an effort would be a more unified, broad-based, and influential socialist front or alliance.

A national strategy has the potential to set forces in motion that can re-radicalize broad sectors of the movement. It can help center the energies of the "Newest Left" by orienting young people in particular to the struggles of the oppressed nationalities and the working class. It can also help combat tendencies in the movement that discount either the need for organization or the need for an analysis targeting imperialism. Finally, implementing a Sunbelt Strategy can give organizers a sense that their day-to-day work at the grassroots really connects with a long-term plan to transform the whole society.

On the one hand, the Sunbelt Strategy has a large scope, a long-run character, and places heavy – even possibly unrealistic – demands on the left. On the other, it is well grounded in history, as well as in an analysis of current reality. It has an international dimension. And it has the potential to link working class struggles in critical industries to the freedom movements of the oppressed nationalities in the South and Southwest. Finally, the strategy has the advantage that it builds on organizing work already being carried out – even if now only on a relatively small scale.

Most social justice activists would probably agree on the organizing challenge represented by the Sunbelt region. Many appreciate its importance as a bastion of conservatism – while discounting perhaps the positive forces already at work in the region. Finally, most activists understand that the fight against white supremacy is a key strategic task. The Sunbelt Strategy unites with these not always well-formed areas of agreement and gives people a worked out reason to get involved for the long haul – with the promise of major benefits for the movement and for themselves as organizers in return for their long-term commitment.

Overview of race and class

In this section, Chapters 9-11, we have looked at class in a very particular way – focusing 1) on workplaces outside the home, and 2) on the role of white privilege in undercutting working class unity. Our emphasis has been almost exclusively on the material aspects of this system of preferences – a standpoint fundamental to understanding how white supremacy is structured in the United States. At the same time, the reflection of these underlying material differences in people's minds and in the broader culture – that is, racist ideology – is what people often are most conscious of, even if they do not recognize its racist character. These ideas then directly shape how people in the working class relate to one another.

The interconnection of race and class also influences the perspective of the people writing this book – in particular, our viewing the struggle against white supremacy from the standpoint of the multinational working class in the United States. We have a frankly partisan outlook, one that seeks to advance the interests of a particular class – and with it the prospects for all humanity. From this class standpoint, we attempt to see reality just as it is and in an all-sided way. In this sense we aim for objectivity in our discussion of white supremacy – a perspective free from any investment in the way society is currently organized. It is our belief that this kind of working class outlook comes closest to providing the intellectual tools grassroots people need to transform society.

Finally, race and class intersect in the conviction that social revolution is necessary to overcome white supremacy. Because of their close interconnection over 300 years, ending white supremacy requires ending capitalism. And to bring an end to capitalism, the multinational working class must lead in the revolutionary transformation of society.

An awareness of these four elements of the race-class relationship – material differences, ideology, standpoint, and social revolution – adds up to class-consciousness under U.S. conditions. In this sense, the concept *class* runs as an underlying theme throughout this book. But contradictions around race – and around gender, too – cannot simply be reduced to aspects of social class. The challenge is to understand each set of social relations – involving race, class, and gender – in its own right; and, at the same time, to gain a sense of the way all three interrelate with each other.

Surveying briefly the nine sections of the book, we can see the ways class plays out within our primary focus on the struggle against white supremacy:

- *Section I* shows how white supremacy arose as a ruling class method of social control in response to a multiracial, working class – but anti-indigenous – challenge to its rule in colonial Virginia in

1676. We then traced over time the development of this ruling class social control mechanism. In Chapter 3, "Images of Whiteness," we reviewed ways that white privilege has played out in the minds and culture of white working class people over 300 years.

- *Section II*, "Race, Nations, and Empire," highlights struggles fought primarily by working class people of color. The large majority of oppressed nationality people inside the United States belong to the working class. While movement leaders have often come from the more educated strata, and national struggles have their own distinct goals and class dynamics, the driving force of the national movements has come from the grassroots. Also, today the most active sector of the labor movement is oppressed nationality workers. The conditions of people of color are the touchstone of progress in the United States; and oppressed nationality workers are the surest guarantor that the labor movement will remain true to its emancipatory goals.
- *Section III*, the current section, examines directly certain aspects of the class/race relationship.
- *The next section*, Section IV on "Patriarchy and Privilege," specifically integrates class with other aspects of people's identities, using the concept *intersectionality*. Patriarchy pre-dates capitalism, but capitalism has appropriated patriarchal relations and kept them central to the way the system runs. As with white supremacy, fighting patriarchy undermines capitalist social relations – and in doing so, takes on a class quality. At the same time, such struggles advance an intersectional vision of a society that will only become a reality once power is held by the multinational working class – with women and oppressed nationality peoples in the lead.
- *Section V* looks at the current state of white working class privilege at the start of the 21st Century. We also survey the ideas in the minds of the majority of white people – what we call "white consciousness"– that blinds people to the reality of the color line. For example, the "psychological wage" identified by W.E.B. DuBois[19] gives white workers an emotional boost that can take the edge off class oppression.
- *Section VI* reviews the history of white people's alliances with people of color – highlighting moments of both solidarity and betrayal – and focuses particularly on working class struggles.
- *Section VII* develops a strategic alignment to end white supremacy: a united front centered among oppressed nationality peoples –

with women and working class forces in the lead – and turned into a broad mass movement by the participation of white workers, women, students, and other progressive-minded people. Working class leadership, particularly among the oppressed nationality peoples, is essential to this vision – as is participation by a section of class-conscious white workers sympathetic to the perspective presented in this book.

- *Section VIII*, "Overcoming White Supremacy and Racism," brings everything together in a personal, organizational, and social program aimed at achieving a social revolution that will end white, patriarchal capitalism. Overcoming white supremacy requires a class-conscious movement – a movement 1) encompassing all the dimensions along which working people suffer under capitalism; and 2) capable of building a new society where all working class and progressive-minded people, without exception, can develop together to their fullest.
- *Section IX* summarizes the vast historic cost of white privilege – first to the oppressed nationality peoples, but also to white working class people as well. By viewing U.S. history from three perspectives – past, present, and future – one can get a sense of what a society without race, gender, and class privilege might look like: a society led by and for the multinational working class, with oppressed nationality workers and women at its center.

Our discussion of "Race and Class" in Chapters 9-11 has examined what we believe to be the central mechanism holding the U.S. system of race and class oppression in place: white privilege. Chapter 9 looked at the post-Civil War era and the years around World War II. Both these periods provided opportunities for classwide struggle, but the system successfully undercut the threat by offering racial privileges to white workers. In doing so white people gave up the opportunity to achieve a society that actually could meet their needs, as part of meeting the needs of all working people.

Chapter 10 reviewed the analysis of white privilege originally developed in *A House Divided: Labor and White Supremacy* by Roxanne Mitchell and Frank Weiss. Supported by the historical lessons of earlier chapters, we generalized three points relating white privilege to the U.S. working class movement:

- White privilege is the principal cause of disunity in the working class.
- A series of ruling-class instituted political and economic decisions created the system of privilege; and racist ideas reflect the inequality that results from these policies.

- Defeating white privilege requires an organized struggle linked to meeting people's immediate needs – including the need for social solidarity free of national privileges of any kind.

Based on these points, and keeping in mind that the goal of the working class movement is a new society organized around meeting working people's needs, we can draw the following conclusion:

In order for the struggle for working class power in the United States to be successful, the fight against white privilege must be at the center of the movement's strategic outlook.

Restated another way: in the United States the fight against white supremacy, while carried out in its own right and specifically directed at racial and national oppression, nonetheless is a form of class struggle. It undermines capitalism's main social support. And absent this perspective, the working class is certain to remain divided and weak.

Finally, the current chapter encourages the social justice movement to adopt a geographical strategy for the working class struggle today – one that takes the post-Civil War and World War II periods as a backdrop. Given the setbacks of these earlier periods – as well as the positive experiences from victories won during Reconstruction and during the 1930s and '40s – we believe today's movement should take up the historic challenge to organize the South and Southwest. Doing so will require 1) centering the movement's classwide organizing on the resistance of the oppressed nationalities in the Sunbelt region, 2) encouraging newly recruited forces to concentrate in this region, and 3) within the Sunbelt focusing on key industrial corridors where organization – both in workplaces and in communities jointly – can have the capacity to undermine imperialism at its foundation.

This strategic approach has the potential to place the freedom movements of the oppressed nationalities and the working class movement together at the core of a broad united front, or historic bloc – an alliance with the power to confront the whole system of white supremacist patriarchal capitalism. Carrying out a Sunbelt Strategy will require a deep and abiding awareness of white privilege and its corrupting influence on white workers. Great class struggles have occurred in the United States, and there will be more such struggles in the future. But they almost certainly will end in defeat for the popular forces so long as the system of racial privileges remains in place.

In the next section, Chapters 12-15, we look at the interconnections of white supremacy with patriarchy – the systematic oppression of women and people whose sexual orientation do not fit the heterosexual norm. In doing so we find that a Third Wave women's movement must be at the core of the historic bloc opposing U.S. imperialism. Women's struggles cut across both the national and working class movements, just as these two movements help set the conditions for women's liberation.

If it TAke's A Bloodbath

LET'S GET it OVER WITH.

Each form of oppression is part and parcel of the larger political strategy of capitalist and racist patriarchy. What women of color suffer in our families and relationships is, in some way, inherently connected to the rape of women in neighborhoods, the high suicide rate of American Indians on reservations, attacks on Black gays and disabled people in New York City bars, and the war in El Salvador. Whether one death is sexually motivated and the other the result of US imperialism, women of color are always potential victims.

—*Cherríe Moraga, 1983,* Loving in the War Years

IV

PATRIARCHY AND PRIVILEGE

Up to now we have focused on *race* and then in the last section on *race and class*. We also touched on aspects of male supremacy in these earlier pages – on ways that race has been wrapped up with what it means to be a man or woman in the United States, as well as on the way whiteness developed within a context of male privilege. Here we want to look more closely at the system of *patriarchy* – the system of male domination – and how it intersects with and reinforces white supremacy. This discussion points to the central role women will likely – and, in fact, must – play in the struggle for national liberation, working class power, and an end to patriarchy.

In Chapter 12 we look at ways that patriarchy has impacted U.S. history, from the time of the earliest invaders until the conservative counter-attack on the social justice gains of the 1960s and '70s. We examine various forms of patriarchal oppression, the lethal mix of race and sex under the distorted conditions of white supremacy, and the larger political uses of patriarchy for capitalist rule.

Chapter 13 surveys the impact of patriarchal oppression on women and lesbian-gay-bisexual-transgender/questioning (LGBTQ) people in today's society. We divide the discussion into three parts, focusing on 1) male violence, 2) patriarchal culture, and 3) the structural oppression of working class women.

The concept *intersectionality* is the focus of Chapter 14. We highlight the emergence of women of color feminism during the 1970s and '80s – with roots extending back to the 1960s national movements, as well as to Second Wave feminism and gay liberation.

Chapter 15 concludes by reviewing a number of today's currents that together have the potential to merge into a deeply transformative, popularly based, Third Wave feminism. We review two different assessments of today's post-Second Wave situation, outline the core elements that together can shape a new upsurge, and point to the impact such a development might have for the social justice movement.

Chapter 12

Patriarchal Roots

One unifying theme in U.S. history is the patriarch – the white ruling class male: "the man." Our approach here will not be to look deeply into this social figure – as Ronald Takaki, for example, does so effectively in *Iron Cages*. Rather, we need to acknowledge the white patriarch's dominant presence in shaping the lives of all the other people in the United States, historically and up to the present. We will survey some of the ways patriarchy has distorted the relationships between men and women, turned sex and race into a dangerous mixture, and shaped politics and culture to keep women and peoples of color oppressed.

Patriarchy is the systematic limitation and control by men of women's sexuality, reproductive capacity, labor, social roles, and political participation. It links sexual pleasure to the domination of other human beings; and in doing so, patriarchy breeds rape, sexual torture – including of men, as at Abu Ghraib prison in Iraq in 2004 – and the abuse of children.

Historically, as Marxist social anthropology has shown, the control of women's sexuality and labor became firmly established only with the rise in antiquity of state powers. These hierarchical societies brought with them social classes, standing armies, and private property passed from one generation to the next. Over time, patriarchy adapted as society changed from one type of class society to another – be it slave, feudal, dynastic, capitalist, or socialist. In each case, the system drew on tradition and personal habits, cultural practices and appeals to the natural order to remain in place – all backed up by violence and the threat of violence.

Patriarchal relations shape what it means to be a man – the socially constructed male gender – at the same time that they contain and constrain women. And in this process patriarchy imposes heterosexuality on both women and men. It polarizes human beings into rigid gender roles and denies the existence of identities lying between the masculine and feminine – identities that some less hierarchical societies have made room for.

In the United States patriarchy has served well to maintain the all-around dominance of white ruling class men – while feeding divisions among everyone else in society. The system affords privileges to all men, regardless of their social class. For working class men, however, these male privileges – as with white privileges – undermine solidarity and help bind people to their oppressors.

Forms of dominance and division

Indigenous cultures

Patriarchy has been around for a long time. Many early societies were matrilineal – meaning that families traced their descent through their mother from one generation to the next. This type of social organization usually went with being a "hunter and gatherer" society, where the men hunted and the women controlled the home and village life. Often when groups settled down in one place and took up agriculture, the role of women changed and the men became more dominant in the shared village space. Matrilineality and matrilocality – living in the household of the mother's line – can continue as social holdovers, however, even as patriarchal relations become established in a settled civilization.

At least some of the societies the Europeans encountered on arriving in the Americas were of the matrilineal type – the Cherokee people, for example, and the Zuñi in the Southwest.[1] Among Plains Indians women treated the sick and took on the role of holy people. Other indigenous peoples privileged men in the social organization and public councils, but a feeling of mutual respect and recognition marked the division of labor between the sexes.

The Europeans brought with them their own ideas of how things should be organized. Missionaries were often the first people to live closely with the native peoples. Guided by patriarchal interpretations of Biblical scripture, they projected their own male supremacist and Eurocentric outlook onto the societies they found here. Most missionaries felt that men should make decisions without concern for women's opinions. Farming was seen as men's work; and men should either produce the necessities of life themselves or trade – say, animal skins – to provide for their families.

Also, the indigenous nations' freer attitudes toward sexuality often clashed with the missionaries' strict views. The Indians usually accepted divorce, for example, and it often consisted of little more than the man or the woman moving out of their shared living space. For some peoples –

the Crow, Mohave, and Arapaho, for example, out of more than a hundred others – alternative gender roles could be adopted voluntarily regardless of sex. Biological men could take on the social roles of women, organizing the household and taking care of children. And some women rode with the men as fighters.

While sometimes referred to as "berdache" – a word of French origin – or, in the past decade or so, as "two-spirited" people, both these categorizations tend to be marked by Western dualism. Rather, children were allowed to choose an ambiguous, but unified male/female gender identity – and might then marry either a man or a woman. The society made a place for such individuals – while at the same time not recognizing the existence of relationships between people of the same gender category. Two berdaches, for example, would not live together. Stories are told of women who took on a mix of gender roles, but no personal histories exist comparable to the studies of the biologically male berdache. This absence could be due to an anthropological blindspot, or possibly from the native peoples' adoption of a Western male/female division after conquest. Also, women warriors and leaders more often were likely to marry biological men and raise their own families.[2]

In cultural matters, the grasping selfishness of the European invaders contrasted with the system of gift-giving and mutual obligation that many Indian nations – among them the Powhatan and Iroquois – used to regulate relations among themselves. Europeans brought into this balanced world their greed, their guns, and their alien germs. Disruption and death followed them everywhere.

Under these conditions native women stood out in their resistance to the European attack on traditional ways. A study of nations in the Great Lakes area makes clear that women were less likely than men to convert to Christianity or to go along with European mission policies.[3] Trade with Europeans tended to undermine women's economic position in the community by devaluing their craft skills. And Europeans tended to deal with and only make agreements with men. This corrupting influence worked to undermine the mutual respect between the sexes in native communities.

After a century and more of European influence, observers noted that an undercurrent of hostility and bickering came to mark men's and women's attitudes toward each other in a number of Great Lakes communities. And more generally, the warrior image continues to influence relationships to this day, burdening indigenous women with the bulk of responsibilities at home.

The colonial era

As we saw in Chapter 1, in the early to mid-1600s, some men of African origin in Virginia were able to own property and vote. Once the plantation rulers put the slave system in place, however, only white men of property held the franchise. The 1691 Virginia law that banned intermarriage singled out white women for punishment when they married African or Indian men. By contrast, from the 1660s on, children of a slave woman fathered by a white man became the property of the slave owner. As a result of this legal structure, the rape of African women became a widespread practice within Southern slave culture for two hundred years.

Slaves were property, and being white was a kind of property as well – with legal rights accorded to its owner and passed on as an inheritance to his children.[4] Being male gave men the right to control women and children, just as whiteness came with privileges that could be defended in court. For the laboring classes, being white included the obligation to defend the slave system and its plantation oligarchy. A man's control over the women and children in his life assured that his labor power, and that of the next generation, would remain a part of the slave economy. Even as poor white farmers scraped out a living at the margins of society, they helped sustain the way of life of the local plantation patriarch.

White women passed their lives under the control of first their father, and then their husband. Howard Zinn captures the essence of patriarcal dominance with this quote from an 18th Century publication, *The Spectator*: "Nothing is more gratifying to the mind of man than power or dominion; and…as I am the father of a family…I am perpetually taken up in giving out orders, in prescribing duties, in hearing parties, in administering justice, and in distributing rewards and punishments….In short, sir, I look upon my family as a patriarchal sovereignty in which I am myself both king and priest."[5]

Women who broke out of this pattern became loose women – labeled prostitutes, spinsters or old maids, and sometimes witches, while even widows lived on the margins of society. Especially vilified were European women who shared their lives with men of color – and more generally, people who gave up their whiteness to live with native people or to struggle alongside Africans. Control of white women's bodies – and the color of their offspring – was essential to maintaining the unnatural system built on racial difference.

Meanwhile, as Angela Davis points out, African people – both slave and free – experienced the harsh, forced equality of oppression.[6] The mutually respected roles of African village life had broken down under slavery; and people struggled to preserve family ties in a setting where all aspects of their lives were subject to the patriarch's intervention. It is little wonder that when the hard-fought-for freedom from slavery finally arrived, women eagerly devoted themselves to their homes and children, and liberation in broader society became publicly identified with male assertiveness and pride.

Cult of domesticity

Within the dominant relations of patriarchy, a certain rough equality and mutual respect between white men and women marked the hard life of early farming families. By the beginning of the 1800s, however, this situation began to change. Owners were building factories and looking for a source of cheap labor, and they turned to young women, especially in the textile and garment industries. Long hours and hard conditions together yielded only low wages – as the mill owners, the press, and clergy promoted the view that women were not real workers. Rather, young women were said to be marking time until they could find a husband. So even as new opportunities opened up, the dominant culture stressed that women's rightful place was in the home. This "cult of domesticity" – especially when combined with low wages – undercut any potential for women to achieve independence in their lives.

Later, at various points over the next 150 years, controlling white women's bodies by keeping them at home remained critical to maintaining white male supremacy. For example, challenges to patriarchal relations occurred:

- *during the social turmoil after the Civil War*, as women shaped by abolitionism and the early suffrage movement made a place for themselves in the Freedmen's schools in the South;
- *as the women's-place-is-in-the-home system started breaking down* under the pressure of industrialization – and, in reaction, the first women's prison, built in 1874, stressed training in household skills;[7]
- *in the mix of new immigrants, Mexicans, and free black people* that accompanied urban expansion in the late 1800s, thereby threatening white men's exclusive access to white women; and
- *after the two world wars*, as the economy struggled to provide work for returning soldiers, including soldiers of color who felt emboldened by their military service and the respect shown them by European men and women.

Chinese domestic workers

In California, too, the cult of domesticity took hold. The mostly male society of the early years of Anglo settlement – with its cult of the Western Hero – began disappearing after the Civil War.[8] In its place developed a dangerous (to white supremacy) mix of white women and white, Mexican, Chinese, and native men. While promoting family values for white women, the authorities also moved to effectively exclude Chinese wives from entering the United States to join their husbands. The passage of the Page Act in 1870 required "lengthy and humiliating interrogations of [a Chinese wife's] character prior to being issued a visa in China."[9] This restriction, however, did not prevent many thousands of Chinese women being purchased in China and sold into slavery in West Coast brothels in the following decades.

While popular culture pictured Chinese men as lascivious and craftily seeking to seduce helpless white women – all the more reason to keep them at home – a public world of prostitution serving white men thrived in the West Coast cities. Chinese women had no voice in the dominant culture, even though they became the target of outraged moral censure. Their voicelessness, Robert G. Lee comments, fit with the Victorian era's overall sense of propriety and "seemed to confirm the claim to the passionless true nature of womanhood in general."[10]

Lee describes how Chinese men during the 1870s and '80s, forced out of both manufacturing and agriculture, fell back on becoming household servants – or on occupations like running laundries that were extensions of women's work. Chinese men then took on a new representation in popular culture as a "third sex" – which helped manage the tension of having another man in the white man's house. In this way the lines defining sex and color became blurred. Racism and male supremacy worked together both to confine white women to the home and to subjugate men of color.

Anti-miscegenation

Despite laws barring intimacy between white people and people of color, white males were unrestrained in their violent access to black women. By the decade between 1850 and 1860, "the mulatto slave population increased by 67 percent; in contrast, the black slave population increased by only 20 percent."[11]

California expanded its early law against mixed marriages to include Chinese, or "Mongolians" in 1880, two years before the exclusion of all Chinese immigrant laborers from entering the country. Then in 1884, with the Page Act providing insufficient control, the state legislature prohibited wives of Chinese immigrants from joining their husbands. The goal was the prevention of a new generation of Chinese being born – thereby eliminating the "Chinese problem," as open violence had earlier dealt with the "Indian problem."[12]

Later waves of anti-Japanese and anti-Filipino sentiment in California resulted in further legal restrictions on interracial marriages. Countrywide the number of states with anti-miscegenation laws peaked at 38 around the time of the eugenicist-backed Johnson-Reed Immigration Act of 1924. That year also saw passage of the Virginia Racial Integrity Act. Eugenics expert Lothrop Stoddard declared, "White race-purity is the cornerstone of our civilization." And Walter Plecker, who was responsible for implementing Virginia's law, proudly declared in 1943, "Our own indexed birth and marriage records, showing race, reach back to 1853. Such a study has probably never been made before...Hitler's genealogical study of the Jews is not more complete."[13]

By the 1950s, almost half the states still had anti-miscegenation laws. Then under the influence of the civil rights movement, the Supreme Court ruled against Florida's harsh penalties for adultery involving mixed-race couples. Finally, in 1967's *Loving vs. Virginia,* Chief Justice Earl Warren wrote for the majority, "Under our Constitution, the freedom to marry or not marry a person of another race resides with the individual and cannot be infringed upon by the State."[14]

Sex and Jim Crow

The cult of domesticity, anti-miscegenation laws, and the social neutering of Chinese domestic workers helped keep white women under patriarchal control. But the unnaturalness of these arrangements both assured their eventual breakdown and, given this underlying reality, supercharged the personal dynamics across the color line – especially in the defeated Southern states bent on reasserting white patriarchal power after the Civil War.

Lynching and rape

In the decades after the violent suppression of Reconstruction, opinion leaders nurtured a simmering rage directed at African Americans' sense of entitlement to their freedom. Ida B. Wells estimated in the 1890s that 10,000 lynchings had occurred in the first 30 years after the Civil War. The great bulk of these were the result of white nightriders, Klu Klux Klan terror, and election violence in the years up to 1877. Then the killings settled into a pattern of roughly 100 people a year murdered by white vigilante violence over the next 50 years. This record translates to one person killed every three and a half days for assault, murder, and rape – as well as for "wanting a drink of water," "sassing a white lady," "being troublesome," or for "nothing."[15]

Despite this reign of terror, as we saw in Chapter 5, black people organized and defended themselves – refusing to accept the abuse. During the 1880s in Memphis, Tennessee, Ida B. Wells contested the tightening hold of segregation after the Supreme Court ruled Sumner's Law, the 1875 Civil Rights Bill, unconstitutional. When ordered out of a ladies' railroad car, Wells resisted the conductor's physical attempt to remove her by biting his arm. She finally was dragged from the car only with the assistance of two other men. Wells sued the Chesapeake & Ohio Railroad, winning a $500 settlement in a Memphis court. The judgment was later overturned on appeal, however, and the incident ended up costing Wells $200 in court costs.

When Wells described her experiences in a church newsletter, the story quickly spread. Soon she was asked to write on a range of topics for the black press in Kansas City, Detroit, Indianapolis, and Louisville. Newspapers had sprung up in all the urban areas where black people lived – serving as a lifeline that nourished a shared sense of racial community. Philip Dray comments, "Newspapers and other periodicals were ubiquitous, a result of fast-growing literacy among blacks and a keen interest in the current events that affected their lives."[16] In 1889 Wells purchased a share of a newspaper and took on the roles of writer and editor for the *Free Speech and Headlight*. Typical of Wells's stand was an editorial in 1891 in response to a lynching in Georgetown, Kentucky: "Of one thing we may be assured, so long as we permit ourselves to be trampled upon, so long we will have to endure it. Not until the Negro rises in his might and takes a hand resenting such cold-blooded murders, if he has to burn up whole towns, will a halt be called in wholesale lynching."[17]

What is remarkable is that it was not until 1892 that Wells came to realize that overwhelmingly the charges of rape used to justify up to two-thirds of all lynchings had no basis in reality. Wells's investigations undercut her earlier belief that "unreasoning anger over the terrible crime of rape...[suggested] perhaps the brute deserved to die anyhow and the mob was justified in taking his life."[18] On reflection, however, certain questions came to mind: Why had there not been an epidemic of rapes during the Civil War, when white women were left to the care of black slaves? Or especially during Reconstruction, when black people held political power and yet there were no reports of rape? When Wells drew the appropriate conclusions in a *Free Speech* editorial, her days in Memphis were numbered: "Nobody in this section believes the old threadbare lie that Negro men assault white women. If Southern white men are not careful they will over-reach themselves and a conclusion will be reached which will be very damaging to the moral reputation of their women."[19] Frederick Douglass commented during this period that until he read Wells's articles he, too, "had begun to believe it true that there was increased lasciviousness on the part of Negroes."[20]

Charges of rape actually had very little to do with sexual assault – and everything to do with shoring up white supremacy in the South. Lynching was not about meting out justice, since the courts were totally controlled by white people and any legal proceeding would have yielded the desired punishment. Rather lynching – which often included sexual mutilation – aimed to terrorize a whole people into submission, to emasculate black men while defending the pinnacle of white male privilege, access to white women.

The violence of the period also had an inverted counterpart in Southern culture. The "Mammy" figure emerged as part a warm, nostalgic dream of earlier times – when black people "knew their place" and lovingly cared for white people. Philip Dray points to other conditions that compounded the white South's resentment at a new generation of audacious and independent-minded black people: "the sexual anxiety of the Victorian era," "the region's historic emphasis on protecting personal honor," "warm memories of vigilantism of the Reconstruction era," "widespread religious fundamentalism," and "economic depression." Also, Christian teachings claimed that black people – as "the children of Ham – were beings of darkness." Finally, lynching served as "a form of tribal sacrifice…a form of painful spasm a community 'needed' in order to regain a feeling of normalcy."[21]

Together, all these conditions and the brutal bloodfests they supported succeeded in creating an image in people's minds that connected the word *rape* with black men – and black men raping white women, in particular. The reality, however, was just the opposite: white men, who feared neither legal nor communal retaliation, could act on their sexual urges against women of color with impunity. The image of the black rapist justified lynch mob terror repeatedly between 1880 and 1930. It arose again in the 1930s case of the Scottsboro Boys. It lurked in the background in the killing of Emmett Till in 1955, and in the 1970 murder of Henry Marrow, described by Timothy B. Tyson in *Blood Done Sign My Name*. These dates come uncomfortably close to the present and suggest that the image still haunts us today – as does its real counterpart, white male violence in the military, in women's prisons, and at fraternity and team parties on or off campus.

Making homosexuality abnormal

As the color line became harshly defined, homosexuality for the first time came to be identified as a scientifically abnormal social category – as a particular defect in character with racial overtones.[22] Two trials during the 1890s focused people's attention, first, on Oscar Wilde, charged with sodomy in England; and second, on Alice Mitchell, accused of killing her lesbian lover in the United States. During this same period, Havlock Ellis published the first textbook on sexology in which he claimed that "the question of sex – *with the racial questions that rest on it* – stands before the coming generations as the chief problem for solution."[23] This text proved to be helpful for some gay people of the era, as it helped to validate their sense of identity. At the same time, Ellis paved the way for homosexuality to be categorized as a medical pathology, a type of mental disease.

In earlier years sexual "inversion" – taking on opposite sex roles – was one thing, while committing particular criminalized sex acts was another. "Sodomy" involved any act not connected to procreation – and ranged from masturbation all the way to bestiality. Same-sex physical love was condemned by the Hebrew Bible and considered a sin by the early Christian Church. Even so, man-boy intercourse was a staple of ancient Greek society – although not the man-man variety – and part of growing up in certain parts of Melanesia require the passing of semen from young men to boys, thereby enabling them to develop into men. In Europe the persecution of sodomy increased during the 12th and 13th centuries, including executions and imprisonment, as the church extended its hold over the common people. Later, the rising bourgeoisie associated homosexuality with decadent manor life in order to help mobilize public opinion behind their revolutionary objectives.[24]

By the late 1800s, authorities in Europe had been conducting occasional raids for centuries on underground all-male gathering places. Women by contrast generally were not considered sexual beings in their own right – outside of a relationship with a man. Largely confined to private spaces, women experienced same-sex love in the settings where men had before the rise of the capitalist cities – in extended family networks and with and among servants in large households. As white women were brought together in factory dormitories and later in girls' schools, passionate friendships with varying degrees of physical expression were not uncommon. But these relationships largely passed unnoticed in public discourse, given women's assumed lack of sexual interest. The contrast with the earthy sensuality attributed to women of color – used to justify white men's violent attraction – highlights the society's profound confusion around race and gender.

During the Jim Crow era, this confusion took on a more defined character – as homosexual relationships came to be associated with interracial ones, and both received the label "abnormal." This linked assessment continued in psychiatry into the 1970s. Only with the rise of the gay and lesbian movement after the Stonewall Rebellion* in 1969 did mental health experts take homosexuality out of the category of mental illness (1973) – six years after state anti-miscegenation laws had been ruled unconstitutional.

The uneasiness with sexual roles in the early 1900s showed up in the popularity of cross-dressing in Vaudeville acts, and in the gender-bending farce *A Florida Enchantment* that both toyed with lesbian love

---

* In the early morning hours of June 28, 1969, gay and transgender men and lesbians for the first time stood up and defended themselves, instead of meekly, and even shamefully, accepting harassment from the police and criminal underworld. The Stonewall Inn, a mafia-controlled gay bar on Christopher St. in Greenwich Village, became the site of several evenings of street fighting by patrons and community supporters in response to a police raid. This rebellion marked the start of the gay – later to become the lesbian-gay-bisexual-transgender/questioning (LGBTQ) – liberation movement. *(Martin Duberman,* Stonewall*)*

while projecting the starkest racist stereotypes. In Archibald Gunter's original novel published in 1891, the main character Lillian, who experiences being transformed into a man, ends up marrying her woman friend – with whom she had flirted while still dressed as a woman. By the time the 1915 movie version came out, however, this ending proved too risky, so everything was short-circuited by the heroine's "waking up" from her suggestive dream.

Siobhan Somerville reports that attitudes toward women's passionate relationships with other women were mixed at the turn of the 20th Century, as these relationships had not yet been pathologized. Popular fiction of the time – including the stories of African American writer Pauline Hopkins – reflects this ambiguity. Overlapping themes center on light-skinned characters "passing," on cross-dressing, and on romantic relationships between women – while often couched as tragedies or safely isolated in a stage world separate from heterosexual culture.

The Jim Crow era drew a sharp line between white people on the one side and people of color on the other. On the basic human level, the unnaturalness of this division led writers to focus on the margins – where one color blends into another, or where either-or sexual identities break down. In the larger social context of the period, as discussed in Chapter 6, the United States was emerging as a new and energetic imperialist power. The virile white male and the purity of his line represented imperial power and civilization in an increasingly multi-colored world.* Meanwhile, European immigrants, pressured into dropping their old-world identities and class-consciousness, gained factory employment. But along with it came harsh working conditions, crowded tenements, immigrant bashing, and deportation – as well as battlefield death and injury in the inter-imperialist rivalry of World War I. In this process of acculturation to the realities of white privilege, clearing up ambiguities required pathologizing any deviance from the heterosexual, white norm.

Political uses of patriarchy

Jacksonian Democracy

In the 1830s Andrew Jackson extended the vote to all white males as part of his effort to preserve the slave system and crush remaining indigenous resistance. Jackson solidified his base in the Democratic Party; strengthened grassroots allegiance to white supremacy and the slave system; and mobilized a base for the expulsion from the South of the "Five Civilized Tribes"– the Cherokee, Chickasaw, Choctaw, Creek, and Seminole.[25]

---

* Harvard trained lawyer and eugenicist Lothrop Stoddard's *The Rising Tide of Color Against White World-Supremacy* (1920) clearly represents this outlook.

The progressive challenge to Jackson during this period came from opponents of the slave system, reflected in David Walker's Appeal (1829), Nat Turner's Rebellion (1831), and the abolitionist movement beginning in the early 1830s. Women began to speak out publicly, gaining experience that later carried over to the early women's suffrage movement. Maria W. Stewart, a free black woman, gave talks in Boston between 1831 and 1833.[26] And two white women from a former slaveholding family in South Carolina, Angelina and Sarah Grimké, toured the Northeast lecturing against the slave system.[27] All three women faced criticism for stepping outside the bounds of what was then considered women's proper role.

Jackson's reactionary policy of white male enfranchisement succeeded, however. And as the Southeastern native peoples struggled to survive the forced march west over the Trail of Tears – or fled to form isolated settlements in the Appalachian Mountains – white settlers moved in to take over the dispossessed nations' land in Georgia, Alabama, and the Carolinas. "The Democracy," as the Jacksonian movement came to be called, distributed white male privileges in the form of political power and land in order to consolidate the Southern patriarchs' hold on federal power for another generation and more.

The Wilmington Riot

Some sixty years later, the Democratic Party moved to reassert its power in North Carolina, using a variation on the same methods. In the run-up to the 1898 elections, the Democrats consciously linked "black rule," as they called the racially mixed state and local fusion governments, with rape.[28] Campaigners went about North Carolina rallying white farmers who had voted for the Populist Party to rise up in defense of white women. Not only were the Democrats able to undercut the class solidarity of the Populists with this racist appeal, they also dealt a blow to women's aspirations for the vote. In place of suffrage, the racists offered protection. Some white women took advantage of this backward movement to enter the public arena, baiting white men to stand up and show their manhood. Others stood next to their husbands on the campaign circuit, representing the pure and passive ideal at stake in the struggle.

In Wilmington Alfred Moore Waddell transformed himself from an old, poor, ex-Confederate colonel into the leader of the white supremacist mob that seized power from the city's elected authority. Waddell's family, Glenda Elizabeth Gilmore reports, "could scarcely believe the manly vigor that now gripped the old colonel…For Alfred Waddell, the hypermasculine trappings of the white supremacy campaign provided an opportunity to act out his redemption upon a public stage."[29]

On Election Day Democrats won all across the state. The Republicans hardly put up a fight – and in Wilmington the Republican governor had withdrawn all the Republican candidates from the contest. Nonetheless, the day after the election the Democrats called a mass meeting and drew up a "white declaration of independence." They demanded the resignation of the police chief and the mayor, who had a year left on his term of office. They called on employers to fire their black employees. And they ordered Alexander Manly, the outspoken editor of Wilmington's black newspaper, the *Daily Record*, to get out of town.

The next morning Waddell led a mob in hunting down black leaders and property owners – shooting people and chasing them out of town. As reported in the press, the number of people killed that day was about a dozen. Folk accounts, however, ranged into the hundreds, with images of carts passing through town loaded with bodies. Waddell took over the mayor's office. And in the wake of the riot, some 1,400 African Americans fled Wilmington – while white people once again moved in to take over their property. The governor and Republican President William McKinley refused to intervene. And the next state convention of the Republican Party – the Party of Lincoln – was a "whites only" gathering.

Restriction, upsurge, and counter-"Reconstruction"

A third example of patriarchy's political usefulness is the counterattack on the "Second Reconstruction" of the 1960s and '70s. Wini Breines, in her study of the 1950s, shows that white women's restricted horizons during this decade clashed with the real opportunities that were opening to them in society.[30] As a result of this contradiction, the repressive '50s actually laid the groundwork for the women's liberation movement of the 1960s. As described by Micaela Di Leonardo and Roger Lancaster, this broad upsurge in consciousness and organization, which later came to be identified as feminism's "Second Wave,"[*] achieved a number of lasting gains:[31]

- *making a distinction between sex* – the biological configuration people are born with – *and gender* – the patterns of behavior, trained capacities, and roles society constructs for women vs. men;
- *affirming that "the personal is political"* – particularly in relation to women controlling their own lives in the areas of reproduction, household tasks, child rearing, and sexual fulfillment;
- *pulling away the ideological veil* that hides women's true potential behind a fixation on body type and particular images of beauty,

[*] The First Wave extended from the pre-Civil War women's movement – often identified with the Seneca Falls Convention of 1848 – to August 26, 1920, when the 19th Amendment giving women the right to vote became law.

"mother-blaming" as the source of people's psychological problems, and women's "sexual passivity," "frigidity," and "neuroses";

- *working to rebalance the sexual revolution* of the 1960s to counter its bias toward men;
- *revealing and taking steps to correct* the medical profession's orientation to men and male diseases by stimulating "better research on breast cancer, contraceptive methods, the physiology of menopause, and the elimination of unnecessary hysterectomies, Cesarean sections, and radical mastectomies"; and
- *broadening the understanding of work* and women's (and men's) relationship to it – by validating women's efforts in the reproduction of labor power in the home, as well as by demanding equal pay for equal work in all sectors of the economy, and especially in those traditionally identified with women.

In the next three chapters we will broaden this assessment by discussing some of the shortcomings of Second Wave feminism. Here, however, we want to emphasize the movement's lasting impact on people's thinking and social practices – as part of the popular upheaval of the 1960s that many call the "Second Reconstruction."

Sheila Collins provides a measure of the broad challenge to the U.S. social system at the end of the 1960s:

- "Between 1958 and 1972...the percentage of those who thought that government was run for the benefit of a 'few big interests' rose from 17.6 percent to 53.3 percent.
- "In 1960, 18 percent of the people polled thought the government was spending too much on defense. By 1969 that figure had climbed to 52 percent, and
- "By 1970, 58 percent in a Harris poll thought that defense spending should be cut."[32]

Collins goes on to show sharply dropping confidence in the president, in Congress, business leaders, educators, and the military. At the same time, by the early 1970s people were open to considering a real shift in national priorities:

- "44% favored direct public ownership of natural resources.
- "Ninety percent...favored a federal program to give jobs to the unemployed,
- "83 percent favored more federal funds for pollution control, and
- "76 percent favored more federal funds for education."[33]

Collins then shows how the conservative counterattack took as its initial target the weak link in white progressive thinking – namely, the black woman. Liberal sociologist Daniel Moynihan in his *The Negro Family: The Case for National Action* focused on what he called the "pathology" of the black family. Collins notes that in the 1965 Moynihan Report "the black matriarchal family is made the scapegoat for the ills of the black lower class."[34]

Then in the early 1970s the media began beating the drums of the "white backlash" – taking advantage, in particular, of the progressive movement's failure to recognize and struggle through with white workers their sense of deteriorating privileges. Emblematic of this effort was the TV program *All in the Family* (1971-1979), whose liberal-oriented goal was to expose and defuse class, race, and gender tensions. While ridiculing embattled dockworker Archie Bunker for his racist and anti-woman attitudes, the program at the same time indelibly imprinted on millions of minds an image of backward white workers.

The real-life efforts of revolutionary activists of the period to move into white communities and organize among white workers came too late.* Then the closing of union plants in the North undercut the social base of the oppressed nationality movements – as in Detroit with its League of Revolutionary Black Workers and huge NAACP. Patriarchal practices of male leaders undermined internal solidarity in the movement. And the government moved violently against Black Panthers, American Indian Movement activists, and Puerto Rican and Chicano nationalists.

Together with the media offensive, deindustrialization, and counterinsurgency measures, the offensive against the Second Reconstruction also had its more subtle side. Cooptation of leading movement forces operated in two directions to preserve, even if in modified form, the white male dominated social structure. On one side, some individuals in the national movements found their way to a middle class life-style – professionals, academics, and a few at the margins of corporate management. Political power brokers from these sectors also gained a role in overseeing the cities for regional ruling elites – and from these positions helped chill out grassroots dissent. On a second front, affirmative action resulting from the 1964 Civil Rights Act tended to benefit white women disproportionately – since better-off women had access to resources that allowed personal advancement through education. As a result the leading sector of the white women's movement largely separated off from its potential base among the masses of working class women of all nationalities.

---

* See Chap. 19, pp. 289-292, for a discussion of the New Communist Movement of the 1970s.

Then as the economic crisis of the early 1970s took hold – the devaluation of the dollar, rising gas prices, the decline in average wages (which continued for 20+ years), and stagflation – industry moved south and men of color in the rust belt lost out overall. In subsequent decades, with the increase in service industries, women of color were able to make some gains, but the trend toward more equal treatment in the workplace also had much to do with men's deteriorating situation. Meanwhile white male union workers, who had largely ridden out the 1960s in their privileged and apparently secure economic positions, came under attack as well. By 1981 the popular movements were in retreat, and Ronald Reagan turned on the white male workforce. His mass firing of the air traffic controllers sent a signal that the period of privileged accommodation with organized labor was over. Reagan counterbalanced his real attack on white workers with an appeal to patriarchy and white supremacy: He opposed the Equal Rights Amendment; used Clarence Thomas to dismantle the Equal Employment Opportunity Commission; filled his administration with anti-abortion advocates, including Chief of Staff, Patrick Buchanan; and bonded with his supporters by labeling poor women on welfare "welfare queens."[35]

The Second Reconstruction, as with the first, fell to a combination of attacks on people of color and privileges distributed to white people – this time, to white women as well as men. After the Civil War, women were denied inclusion under the 14th and subsequent amendments that assured black men the right to vote. It took another 50 years to achieve this goal. In the 1960s, by contrast, patriarchy bent to allow better-off women into the educated elite, while continuing to restrain advancement with glass ceilings and old-boy networks. At the same time, certain oppressed nationality individuals were able to achieve a measure of economic and political power. Effectively split off from their social bases, both these social elites still maintained sufficient standing to confuse people and hold out hope for individual advancement. The majority of working class people, however, found themselves no better off – and white patriarchal capitalism successfully reconstituted itself after this most recent revolutionary challenge.

Chapter 13

Three Faces of Male Supremacy

Male supremacy maintains its hold through a system of male privileges, embedded in a race- and class-divided society, and backed up with violence and the threat of violence. Abuse of women and children, murders of estranged partners, and rape all have their place in this degrading system. Culturally, male chauvinism poisons relations at the personal level and reinforces in social life a male-centered "hegemony" – or overwhelming dominance of images and ideas. Structurally, the conditions of life for many oppressed nationality and working class women remain difficult – despite the benefits of Second Wave feminism to the corporate, professional, and academic elite.

Violence toward women is shocking and offensive, but so common that many are neither shocked nor offended. The softer and more pervasive side of oppression can be harder to see – as is true as well for the varieties of experience at different positions in society's race/class structure. Ingrained habits of thought and action disguise the unacceptable as normal. And, as with white supremacy, the ideas and practices of male supremacy can work their way into the minds and behavior of the oppressed, causing victims to collude in their own oppression.

Male violence

Violence is the raw, open sore of male supremacy. It can be directed at strangers – as when rape becomes a weapon of war or in a gay-bashing attack – or at the most intimate people in one's life. It destroys people physically and emotionally, and survivors carry deep scars even when healed. Post-Traumatic Stress Disorder (PTSD) is most often associated in the public mind with war; but the greatest number of PTSD sufferers are women who have been physically attacked – raped or beaten –

most often by someone they know. Such attacks make a person feel helpless, uncertain of where one's personal boundaries are – or even who, at bottom, one really is. And then there is the ongoing fear – of strangers and of people who say they love you – feeling trapped yet moving on, often like nothing ever happened, but deeply uneasy, hating oneself for letting it happen.

Rape and domestic violence

Here are some of the facts related to men's attacks on women:

- *In the United States more than 3 women each day die from domestic violence.*[1] One estimate suggests there are over 2 million incidents of battering each year[2] – which works out to a women being hit somewhere in the country every 15 seconds. The National Coalition Against Domestic Violence reports 691,710 cases for 2001 – which reduces the rate to about 1 attack every 45 seconds. The same source indicates 25% of women will experience battering in their lifetime.[3]
- *Men sexually attack women at the rate of about once every two-and-a-half minutes,*[4] and less than half of the attacks are reported to the police.[*5] Some 67% of rapes are carried out by people whom the victim knows – even more when incest, spousal rape, or rape by people in authority, like prison guards, is taken into account. This number has dropped from the 80 to 85% range since the early 1990s, in part due to increased awareness around date rape and prevention. The image of the random attacker, though real enough in its own way, is unrepresentative of the majority of assaults. And since most people in our informally segregated society associate mainly with people of their own race, cross-racial rape is a small percentage of what actually occurs.
- *About 17% of women in the United States have been the victim of rape or attempted rape.* Data from the National Crime Victimization Survey show that, bad as the numbers are today, sexual attacks were five times more frequent in 1973 than they were in 2003 – with rates per thousand people (men and women) over age 12 being 2.5 in 1973, 1.5 in 1993, and .5 in 2003.[6]
- *Rape is the most underreported of all crimes.* In part non-reporting results from the feelings of shame and helplessness that accompany being attacked – along with an unwillingness to relive the experi-

---

* One study for the period from 1992 to 2000 found only 24% of sexual assaults were reported, while the number for "intimate partner violence" was 54%. *(National Coalition Against Domestic Violence [NCADV])*

ence in public, or to have one's personal life probed by police and defense lawyers. But many women, even today, do not realize that the pressure, intimidation, or the inability to give consent due to alcohol or drugs, adds up to rape. Since the majority of women know their attackers – and in some cases go on to date them again – there is also concern over what the allegations might have on the man's life. In the military – either in schools or in service – there is also the problem of higher-ups not taking charges seriously, or retaliating in ways that affect the woman's career.

- *A survey by Ms. magazine of men who sexually attacked women* shows that violators tended to drink more than others, were raised in a strict family environment, experienced violence in their family once or twice per month, talked with friends about what a woman would be like in bed, read pornography "very frequently," approved of having sexual relations regardless of how long two people know each other, believed myths like "*no* means *yes*," saw "woman as adversaries, endorsed sex role stereotypes, saw rape prevention as women's responsibility, and considered the mingling of aggression with sexuality as normal."[7] Particularly problematic are single men in groups – in the military, in fraternities, and on team sports – where some of the above characteristics are combined with male competitiveness, macho posturing, and the release of inhibitions in a group setting.[8]
- *Violence toward women also can result from "postcolonial rage"* directed out of self-hatred onto one's own community. Eduardo Duran and Bonnie Duran cite the incidence of internalized violence among native peoples that shows up in high rates of suicide and death from alcoholism. When externalized, "we encounter a level of violence within the community that is unparalleled in any other group in the country....The authors can attest to the astronomical incidence of domestic violence within the Native American nuclear family.[9]

Domestic violence had the informal backing of law through much of U.S. history. Also, the Freudian theory of women's supposed masochism helped justify public inaction during the early to mid 20th Century. New York State passed the first protection order law in 1962 – with the aim of saving marriages – but judges failed to follow through by issuing orders. Only after the women's movement organized the first residential shelters for abuse victims in the mid-1970s, and followed up with suits against the police, did concerted lobbying force states to pass laws making domestic violence a crime.[10]

The public acceptance of abuse – of bruised women and belt-whipped and spanked children – is not just a behavior of some marginal subculture. Personal testimonies make clear that the progressive movement during the 20th Century had its share, too, of violent households.[11] And LGBTQ activists today recognize the problem also exists in their communities.[12] The problem of male violence – and its carryover into male and female violence against children – is all around us and close to home. A critical step in confronting this situation is to find ways to make public the private spaces where abuse occurs – removing the partitions that isolate families into consuming and reproduction centers of patriarchal capitalism. Then communities can provide supportive networks to prevent violence – and hold offenders accountable when it occurs.

Remedies and shortcomings

An important outcome of Second Wave feminism has been the bringing to public awareness of rape and domestic violence and the creation of an extensive institutional system of response. Driven more by the radical wing of the movement in the 1970s, "Take Back the Night" demonstrations, Women Organized Against Rape, and the setting up of secret sanctuaries for abused women and children – these actions marked a clear break with the oppressive, desperate silence that had characterized abused women's lives. This period included, also, the Supreme Court's *Roe vs. Wade* decision, ending women's forced recourse to illegal abortions and the life-threatening dangers they involved. Over time there developed a professionalized and institutionalized network of rape crisis centers, women's centers, abortion clinics, and domestic abuse counseling and support programs. The movement also targeted the police and criminal justice system, demanding more sympathetic and responsive investigators, and pushed to hold men accountable for their actions. Finally, in 1994 the movement succeeded in passing the federal Violence Against Women Act (VAWA)* – most recently reauthorized in January 2006 – which helped consolidate many of the gains of the struggle.

Despite these groundbreaking advances, however, the movement suffered at each step, from a certain blindspot with regard to race and class.

---

* After 10 years VAWA counted among its accomplishments:

1) passage of more than 650 state laws, with all states now recognizing stalking as a crime and rape by someone known to the victim as equal to that by a stranger;

2) receiving more than 16,000 calls a month on the National Domestic Violence Hotline;

3) encouraging businesses to adopt programs that assist employee victims of domestic violence; and

4) increasing rates of reporting domestic violence to 59% in 1998 compared to 48% in 1993.

At the same time, however, legal conditions vary significantly from state to state, and local prosecutors still face resistance from police in gathering evidence and in meeting the burden of proof in court. *(National Task Force to End Sexual and Domestic Violence Against Women, "The Violence Against Women Act")*

- "Take Back the Night" marches often passed through the downtown areas of cities or in better off, frequently university-related urban communities. With the marchers usually being white women and their male supporters, a hidden if unintended message tended to reinforce the white woman/black rapist image of earlier times.
- Over the years rape-crisis and domestic abuse centers – overwhelmingly white staffed and directed – found themselves unable to respond to the real-life conditions of poor women, women of color, Spanish speakers, and immigrant women with their different languages, economic needs, and cultural traditions.
- While the reproductive rights movement successfully pressured to end the conditions that made back-alley abortions necessary, they failed to address the legal practice of sterilization abuse. For much of the 20th Century, eugenics-inspired thinking promoted sterilizing women in circumstances of economic and physical stress – when on welfare or living in poverty, and at the time of giving birth. Victims of this practice were primarily people of color – Puerto Rican and indigenous women, and African American women in the South, in particular.[13]
- In the more recent period, divisions have centered on the call by women of color activists for "Reproductive Justice" in place of reproductive rights. The language of rights can leave open the question of whether a person is in a position to take advantage of a particular right. For many activists of color, the core problem is *access*, not *rights* – to affordable reproductive services, to sufficient income to make raising children possible, to decent housing, education, and health care. Divisions in the April 2004 "March for Women's Lives" in Washington, DC, centered on this theme. March organizers, responding to well-organized pressure by women of color organizations, took significant steps toward being inclusive; and women of color activists mobilized in unprecedented numbers. But the conditions of life facing many Third World women are not yet fully part of the outlook of the mainstream women's movement.[14]
- By not having anti-racism be integral to its outlook, the mainstream movement has discounted the system's abuse of men of color – inside and outside the courts; before, during, and after their time in prison. And many immigrant women have felt themselves held hostage to the threat of deportation – a situation ad-

dressed, in part, by a revision to VAWA in 1996.* As a result of these realities of life in a white supremacist society, the silence of many women of color persists to the present. People simply refuse to risk deportation or offer up those closest to them to the oppressor.

- The argument that male violence cuts across all races and classes 1) has helped build a broader constituency for actions like the passage of VAWA, and 2) undercuts stereotypes that link abuse to men of color and to workers in "wife-beater" undershirts. But this argument also obscures data that show that the stresses of working class life and white supremacy do, in fact, take an added toll in women's suffering. By not recognizing this situation, the specific needs and strengths of working class women and women of color drop from sight. In addition, when race and class are not part of the picture, the problem of violence ends up being seen only as an inherent character defect of men.

Patriarchal relations exist within an all-encompassing system of white supremacist capitalism. The competitive, dog-eat-dog character of this system both feeds men's dependency on male privilege and tears them down at the same time. Family members – women and children – often feel directly the consequences of these tensions. Given the history of Second Wave efforts to overcome male violence, to really meet the needs of all women, women of color and working class women must be central to the movement's analysis and action.

Community-based solutions

The Color of Violence Conference in 2000 marked a new phase in the struggle against male violence. Spearheaded by Andrea Smith, an indigenous anti-domestic violence activist at the University of California, Santa Cruz, the conference addressed the inadequate attention given to women of color in the program of mainstream feminism. Keynote speaker Angela Davis focused on the problematic role of the state in holding men accountable for their behavior toward women. Given the history of white supremacy and its enforcement by the criminal justice system, a policy of criminalization is hugely contradictory for women of color. It often results in women's needs being suppressed in the interest of community solidarity. Moreover, this model has not worked: while

---

* People on A-3, G-5, and B-1 visas – working for diplomats and international agencies, or in business but with permanent residence outside the United States – these groups are not covered by the VAWA revision and remain vulnerable to being battered. *(Joy Mutanu Zarembka, "Maid to Order")* The same is true for H-4 visas – see the discussion on Kiran, below.

arrest rates are high in communities of color, violence against women and children continues to damage and destroy people.[15]

Two main action paths became clearer in the wake of the conference. First is the development of nationality- and culturally-specific women's centers across the country. For example:

- ***Korean American Women in Need*** in Chicago finds shelters for battered women, seeks out understanding counselors, and translates materials for Korean women. The organization's analysis sees power relations at the heart of women's experience of violence – and not just power relations in the home, but in society as well. Founding board member Inhe Choi comments, "domestic violence stems from power injustice in society. Society is creating this issue, but the quick remedy, and the remedy that is most used, is the police and the courts. But in some ways, the state itself is an oppressor....Our goal is to make sexual violence a community issue."[16]
- ***The Esperanza Peace and Justice Center*** in San Antonio sees itself as a feminist organization and uses a holistic approach to combat violence against women. Marissa Ramírez explains, "It's hard to pinpoint one specific project that deals only with violence against women. A lot of projects deal with a wide range of issues, including violence, immigration, and all those things that affect violence: racism, sexism, and homophobia."[17]
- ***Kiran*** is a North Carolina organization that provides services to South Asian women, particularly those whose husbands work at the Research Triangle near Raleigh on H-4 visas. Since women on these visas are excluded from the Battered Spouse Waiver that was added to VAWA in 1996, they are particularly vulnerable to deportation if they speak up about abuse. Mainstream services tend not to understand immigration-related issues, and some women find themselves racially stereotyped and pressured to conform to American cultural norms to receive help. Kiran staffers have found that it is the level of traditionalism a woman feels bound to that can keep her from seeking help – not so different from some of the white Southern working class women they have met in their work.[18]
- ***Arkansas Women's Project*** Executive Director Judy Matsuoka explains the organization's broader definition of violence against women: "A lot of violence against women comes from the social belief that women are inferior, and the need for them to be controlled through violence and discrimination... We saw those connections and we monitored violence against women, and initially we drew a lot of flack from other domestic violence groups. They

said we were diluting the message....[But] groups are now saying, 'Of course hate crimes can be gender-based.'[19]

- ***Indigenous women*** can be caught in a bind because men who commit sexual violence can hold high status in the community. Also, some tribal councils call on the police for outside intervention. Other councils, by contrast, rely on the exercise of sovereignty by native courts to follow traditional methods – mediation and in extreme cases banishment from the community – as has been carried out by the Pit River Nation in California.[20]

A second direction is represented by the organization INCITE! – Women of Color Against Violence, which came out of the 2000 conference and then reconvened people several times in subsequent years. In

CARA's approach to community accountability

Community accountability begins with a recognition that criminalization has failed and calls on progressive organizations to adopt a set of policies and procedures that are appropriate for their particular community. One participant group, a collective of women from Communities Against Rape and Abuse (CARA) in Seattle, provides these ten steps from their model of community intervention:

- Recognize the humanity of everyone involved.
- Prioritize the self-determination of the survivor.
- Identify a simultaneous plan for safety and support for the survivor as well as others in the community.
- Carefully consider the potential consequences of your strategy.
- Organize collectively.
- Make sure everyone in the accountability-seeking group is on the same page with their political analysis of sexual violence.
- Be clear about what your group wants from the aggressor in terms of accountability.
- Let the aggressor know your analysis and your demands.
- Consider help from the aggressor's friends, family, and people close to her*.
- Prepare to be engaged in the process for the long haul.

Each step includes explanations and examples based on CARA's own experience in implementing community accountability. Such summations of practice give depth to the direction recommended for the anti-violence movement by INCITE!'s working group on community accountability.

—source: Bierria, et. al., "Taking Risks"

* The text alternates between male and female pronouns throughout.

July 2005 INCITE! produced a working paper "Community Accountability within the People of Color Progressive Movement." This program's goal is to support survivors and rehabilitate their attackers – holding men accountable for their actions, while finding a way to heal the community.

INCITE!'s approach recognizes the hardships faced by men of color in the United States, as well as the role women often fill as "shock absorbers in capitalist society."[21] To survive, women may pick tough men to partner with – whose rage then may end up being displaced onto the people nearest them, thereby reenacting abuse men experience in their own lives and forcing others to feel the same sense of shame and worthlessness. Meanwhile, cross-cultural studies have shown that where women have collective power – whether economic or based in social solidarity – battering is less common. Community accountability models seek to encompass this complex reality and heal people who have been damaged by patriarchal capitalism, returning them to a supportive and mutually attentive social network.

Cultural hegemony

Male violence against women helps enforce a whole system of male privileges – the same way lynching aimed to subordinate all black people, and the U.S. prison system enforces a social order that keeps profits flowing for the owning class. Violence lurks in the background of each system of oppression – while the normal functioning depends on habit, customary thinking, and a whole cultural apparatus that reinforces and makes acceptable the ordinary, daily relations of domination. This structure of overwhelming power, or hegemony, operates along each dimension of oppression – along the axes of race and class, as well as gender. Here we briefly survey some of the ways U.S. culture embeds and nurtures violence in defense of patriarchy:

- *Capitalist culture:* Beatings, rape, and murder are only the most extreme forms of abuse directed at women, lesbian-gay-bisexual-transgender/questioning (LGBTQ) people, and others in our society. Domestic abuse includes psychological and emotional cruelty and manipulation; just as gay bashing includes name-calling, taunting, and social isolation. And as verbal abuse can lead to violence, the social investment in creating and reinforcing a male image – one that equates maleness with winning, aggression, and control – prepares the ground for both. At the heart of capitalist culture, which glories in getting over and surviving at others' expense, is the spirit both of "manifest destiny" – conquest and genocide – and of brutality in personal relations.

- ***Military culture:*** The military is a concentrated example of the link between culturally supported violence and what it means to be a man. Linda Bird Francke reports on the way cadences in army training became more clearly anti-woman in the 1980s as the military integrated women into its normal operations.[22] Men needed to be more clearly set apart – by tearing down women – so as not to appear weak or passive. The military culture, in its informal banter as well as in its more formal training routines, nurtures a desire for control, male camaraderie, sexual access to women, and the use of force to resolve problems. The effects appear in the records of sexual harassment inside the military; in domestic violence against women and children in U.S. military towns; in the distorted lives of women sex workers living near military bases in the United Sates and in other – especially poorer, darker-skinned – countries around the world; in the abuse and abandonment of wives from such countries brought back to the United States; and in the rape and murder of mostly darker-skinned women in war zones.
- ***Men in groups:*** The macho culture of the military is a specific instance of the more general problem of rape culture in men's groups – including fraternities, sports teams, and traditionally men's workplaces.
- ***Gay bashing:*** The defense of the male self-image turns not only women into adversaries but other men as well. Heterosexual men in caring roles, men attracted physically to other men, or transgender folks who opt to change their sexual identity – all can upset a heterosexual man's fragile sense of who he is. The deaths of Jake Gyllenhahl's character in *Brokeback Mountain* or Hillary Swank's in *Boys Don't Cry* dramatize this reality – a reality experienced all too directly by Gwen Araujo, Sakia Gunn, and Matthew Shepard.* As often happens in trials of anti-gay murderers, Shepard's killers put forward a "gay panic" defense, which, while ruled out by the court during the trial phase, was allowed to be presented at sentencing. Such official countenancing of male prejudice also shows up in school districts' slow adoption of poli-

---

* A group of men beat and strangled Gwen Araujo, a 17-year old transgender Chicana, in October 2002 and then buried her body in the woods. A man at a bus stop stabbed Sakia Gunn, a 15-year old African American lesbian, to death in May 2003. In October 1998 Matthew Shepard, a 21-year old white gay college student, was beaten, robbed, and tied to a fence in rural Colorado and left to die. Other victims include Native American Fred Martinez (Colorado, 2001), and African American teenagers Ukea Davis and Stephanie Thomas (Washington, DC, 2002), and Nikki Nicholas (Detroit, 2003). *(Hernández, "Young and Out"; Cullen, "Quiet bombshell in Matthew Shepard trial")*

cies aimed at preventing harassment based on sexual orientation. The routine acceptance of name-calling and gay-baiting by young men builds up powerful fears and insecurities at an age when youths are just discovering who they are and how to manage their sexuality. As child psychiatrist Lynn Ponton states, "This really affects all of our children – this name-calling, this prejudice, this stigma – not just the 7-8% that will finally identify as gay or bisexual."[23] When carried over into adulthood, the fear of being labeled gay, particularly among black men who feel that social acceptance demands they live up to the "strong black man" image, can result in "living on the down-low." Men marry and raise families while meeting their sexual needs secretly with other men – and in some cases then passing HIV along to their female partners. In this way, a dominant culture that supports gay bashing ends up increasing the hardships of black women.[24]

- ***Violence against children:*** bell hooks points out that the culture of violence also affects women in their relations with their children.[25] Not only men abuse children; and the culture generally supports a "spare the rod, spoil the child" attitude toward child-rearing. That this attitude flows from deep, systematic conditioning is shown by the absence of violence toward children in, for example, California's native cultures before contact with Europeans.[26]
- ***Popular culture:*** From old-time westerns to today's war stories, sci-fi, or fantasy epics – *Black Hawk Down, Star Wars, Lord of the Rings* – violence is glorified. And the story is often a thinly veiled allegory of imperialist conquest over – sometimes literally – the darker forces of the earth. The Indians of yesterday have become the "mud people" in *Lord of the Rings*, just as the United States today seeks to turn Central Asia into an updated version of the Wild West. This dominant picture, along with the stereotypical images of foreign terrorists and urban street life on the police and spy shows, sets people up – especially, but not only white people – for a fortress-outlook on the world, and violent suppression as the only solution.
- ***Hip hop:*** When stacked up against the hegemonic brainwashing by mainstream culture, the sometimes violent, sometimes misogynistic lyrics of hip-hop music fit all too comfortably – but also at times can carry a subversive edge. As Mark Anthony Neal points out, songs and near pornographic videos, while exploiting black women's bodies also promote a beauty standard that contrasts with the Hollywood/glamour magazine version. Also, the suggestion of violence by the oppressed is always unnerving to the oppressor – even if it is as misdirected toward self-gratification

as most contemporary music is. Noteworthy in hip-hop culture, however, is the undercurrent of rebellion and resistance by women of color. Aya DeLeón, for example, uses hip hop to reject sexism and reclaim a positive vision of collective struggle against white supremacy.

- ***Deeper currents:*** Pearl Cleage's *Mad at Miles*, written in 1990, takes on with righteous anger musicians like Miles Davis and Ike Turner who boasted of their abuse of women – while people kept on listening to their music. Cleage wrote to counter Shahrazad Ali, whose *The Blackman's Guide to Understanding the Blackwoman*, an underground bestseller of that period, called for slapping and restraining women and dealing with them as untrained animals. Cleage cites statistics on women's treatment by people who claim to love them – four killed each day at that time – and provides a survival guide to help women prepare for the domestic violence struggle. She points out 1) the patterns of behavior – name-calling, intimidation, throwing things – that the culture encourages from men; and 2) how to go about challenging men to change, while giving priority to women's own safety. Cleage also calls on women – and men – to stop supporting public figures who abuse women.
- ***Objectification:*** Turning women into objects – treating people as things – traps women in roles that constrain their creative inner power, the essence of a person's humanity. This modern version of the old Chinese practice of binding women's feet, while less outwardly deforming, still aims at controlling and crippling women's potential. In resurgence after the radical critique of Second Wave feminism, objectification shows up in the way today's culture defines women's bodies as – and confines women to being – objects of desire for men. Hair products, beauty creams, fashion magazines, sitcoms, romantic comedies, and an epidemic of pornography all frame women narrowly – in part to counterbalance women's actual increased role in all aspects of public life. In a similar way, groups like the Promise Keepers call for women to be at home with the children, and for men to live up to their "true role" as providers and protectors – a course that narrows social expectations, locks women in, and justifies discrimination at the workplace. The religious right's stress on "family values" fits with this mindset in a particularly hypocritical manner. The image of the ideal family blocks out the real hardships many women face, especially single parents and the working poor. In addition, the call comes at a time when 1) more women must work outside the home to maintain the family's standard of living, and 2) social

supports that would actually help provide for a decent family life have been cut.

Cultural hegemony in the interests of male supremacy impacts all aspects of people's lives in the United States – from the character of personal relationships, to the way men and women see themselves, to the roles people carry out in society. Patriarchal culture breeds violence – just as patriarchy is embedded in and serves the interests of an exploitative class society.

Class and women's oppression

In looking today at the lasting outcomes of Second Wave feminism, one clear result is the opening of the world of paid work to women. At the same time, however, the benefits of this change have been distributed unevenly. As Stephanie Luce and Mark Brenner comment, "the majority of working women are still in low-wage, insecure jobs with little prestige and stability and no benefits."[27]

Who works where

The data for women's **participation in the labor force** show that rates for:

- *all women* almost doubled from about 33 percent in 1950 to 60 percent in 2004;
- *married women* went from 24 percent to 61 percent in the same period;
- *women with children under age six* increased from 39 percent in 1975 to 62 percent in 2004.

While women of color historically have had a higher proportion of women in the workforce, the increases indicated here have affected women of all races, although the data is insufficient to track the specific gains of Latina and Asian-Pacific Islander women.

A second change is in **who does what type of work**. The greatest increase occurred among managerial and professional workers, where by 2004 women made up half of the category. A third improvement has been the **increase in earnings for women with college degrees**. Between 1973 and 2003, salaries for this group of employees increased 31 percent after taking inflation into account. At the same time, however, professional women 1) still face a "glass ceiling" that makes advancement difficult, and 2) in effect work two jobs, given the effort required to manage both a career and work at home.

On examining wages, the distribution of college degrees, and professional occupations more closely, one finds:

For wages,

- half of all women earned less than $12.50/hour in 2005 – with this number being only 60 percent higher than the poverty wage for a family of three ($7.81);
- almost 60 percent of African American women and 67% of Latina women earned less than this cut-off.

For college degrees,

- by 2004, only 23 percent of working age women (25 to 64) held college degrees;
- the numbers for African Americans and Latina women were 14 and 9 percent, respectively.

For managerial and professional workers,

- 39 percent of white women and 44 percent of Asian/Pacific Islander women held these positions;
- for African American and Latina women, by comparison, the rates were 31 percent and 22 percent.

For women without college degrees, the opportunities for nontraditional jobs at high wages are few. As dramatized in the movie *North Country*, women who try to break into such jobs often face harassment and many leave. As a result, Luce and Brenner note: "The occupations that are most common for women workers today are remarkably similar to what they were in the 1940s: nurses, nurses' aids, typists, and secretaries."[28]

Other data show that while the gender wage gap has closed to a 23 percent deficit, much of the improvement came about because of the decreasing level of men's wages. Women continue to earn unequal wages for comparable work; and women lose substantial income during the childbearing years. Over the span of a lifetime, women's income gap compared to men increases to 38 percent.

When considering work at home, women continue to carry the greatest burden. Among working women, compared to their husbands women with small children put in:

- *more than twice* the time in child care activities;
- *nearly twice* the time on household maintenance tasks.

The combination of low wages and greater time spent caring for children, along with the decreased earning ability during the child-rearing years, leads to high poverty rates for women: "Today over 20 percent of white female-headed families and almost a third of female-headed families of all races are living in poverty."[29]

Meanwhile reduced caretaking supports through the 1996 Temporary Assistance for Needy Families (TANF) welfare program devalues the work of raising children. It also encourages the belief that the source of poverty is sexual activity and bearing children – as opposed to 1) domestic abuse, given that some 50 to 65 percent[30] of recipients have been battered; and 2) the system's inability to provide adequate jobs and a way out of poverty for women through education and job-training. While TANF calls for screening, along with provision of assistance to survivors of domestic violence, this policy is not enforced. As a result, many women, seeing no way out, remain in abusive relationships. Also, the enforcement of workfare provisions of the law, requiring recipients to do public service work in return for benefits, undermines public employment – a stronghold of people of color and unionization since the 1960s. Overall welfare policies restrict poor women's opportunities to achieve independence. Instead they create increased competition for low-wage jobs – which in turn undercuts pay scales for full-time workers and minimizes the social pressure to raise the minimum wage.[31]

Causes and outcomes

Luce and Brenner point to a series of causes leading to the distribution of jobs and income outlined above. They include:

- Most fundamentally, the **reliance on individualized strategies** to improved employment; namely, by way of college education and legal challenges aimed at opening up occupations – with the result that "women who have benefited from these individual solutions have been disproportionately white and those with prior access to resources"[32]
- **Systematic institutionalized racial preferences** that affect every aspect of a people's lives – from where a person lives, to the educational resources available, to the opportunities for employment and promotion.*
- A woman's **class position**, since class mobility is very limited
- **Having children**, since doing so impacts a woman's earning power – contributing to a situation where "75% of poor families have children under eighteen years of age"[33]
- The presence of **strong unions,** as shown by the significantly higher wage increases gained by teachers and nurses – although some job categories like teacher assistants, and child care and kindergarten workers still lag the average despite higher than average rates of unionization

---

* See Chapter 16 for a detailed accounting of such preferences for white people.

- Working in a **caring profession,** an extension of women's traditional unpaid work in the home and therefore having a lower wage level
- An **absence of good jobs** for the majority of women, who are not in a position to take advantage of either the individual pathway to highly skilled employment or the organizational support of a hard-pressed trade union movement
- **Government welfare policies** that fail to address the economic vulnerability of poor women, undercut the wage level of employed workers, and discredit the role of government entitlement programs[34]
- The **social arrangements for reproducing and sustaining the labor force,** which systematically lock women into traditional roles – both at home and in underpaid employment – and thereby subsidize capitalism with women's unpaid labor
- The **absence of a strong feminist movement** able to force structural changes around the worth of women's time, access to the full range of employment, and social and cultural supports[*] – both public and private – that address women's needs and make possible outcomes that are on a par with men's
- The lack of **collective consciousness and struggle** that pushes beyond questions of equal access and equal treatment within the structure of capitalism

Limiting demands to achieving equality within the class system assures that the majority of women will continue living lives marked by hardship and uncertainty. "In the end, capitalism cannot provide sustainable, living-wage jobs for all….Individual solutions based on market access won't be enough: women also need class-based solutions. In fact, individual solutions have only exacerbated the problem for many women."[35]

Finally, the unequal impact of feminist gains at the workplace has carried over to the international arena.[36] The impact of U.S. culture has

---

[*] For example, industry could recognize the debilitating effects of menstrual cramps for many women and make allowances for this natural condition. Where men and women are alike – as with the need for sleep, for example – accommodations are made for the sleep cycle. There is also a weekly work cycle. Why not for the monthly menstrual cycle? Gloria Steinem wondered what the situation would be like if men menstruated: "Men would brag about how long and how much. Young boys would talk about it as the envied beginning of manhood. Gifts, religious ceremonies, family dinners, and stag parties would mark the day. To prevent monthly work loss among the powerful, Congress would fund a National Institute of Dysmenorrhea." *(Emily Martin, "Premenstrual Syndrome, Work Discipline, and Anger," quote on p. 71)*

helped pave the way for women to work in highly exploitative export industries, as in the *maquiladora* factories along Mexico's border with the United States. It has also fed the growth of microcredit grants to mostly women entrepreneurs throughout the Third World, as a highly suspect route to economic development. By dissolving the bonds of tradition and the structures of family and community support, First World feminism has helped liberate better-off women – while facilitating international capital's access to vast reserves of low-wage women's labor. This process of capitalist primitive accumulation* holds out the prospect of women's broadening their horizons and developing a new sense of personal identity. But it does so at a heavy personal cost for the majority of women: long work days, low pay, and no social protections. As in the United States from the early 1800s to the present, if there is no organized movement that can embody the collective strength of this workforce – a development that is ferociously repressed by local agents of finance capital – the individual route to emancipation becomes a dead end for most women. At the same time, however, the United States can still pose as a champion of women's rights – even using the issue, as in Afghanistan, to justify imperialist war – while the reality for the majority of women worldwide remains oppressive, albeit increasingly in a new, more modern form.

---

* See Chapter 10, p. 137, for a discussion of primitive accumulation.

Chapter 14

Intersectionality

Male supremacy – the system of patriarchy – is a powerful and corrosive force. It divides and pigeonholes people into polar categories – male/female, homosexual/heterosexual, even white (active, virile)/not white (passive, dependent). The either/or patriarchal mindset seeks to lock people in and lock them down – separating and labeling people according to gender, race, class, and other social criteria. Then the heterosexual white male remains as the standard that others have to measure up to – an integral whole, normal.

Going against this negative classifying power, a more recent "counter-hegemonic" initiative aims to heal the fragmentation and validate each person's unique identity. This *intersectional* viewpoint does not pile up oppressions – stacking race on class on gender on sexuality to come up with, say, a black + working class + lesbian identity. Rather, it affirms each person's specific social reality and history, in all its complexity. This affirmation starts by fully recognizing – really seeing each person – as an integral whole.

Here the question might be raised: But doesn't this approach mean more, not less fragmentation? Now each grouping, each individual, has a claim to authentic representation. If people spend all their time trying to grasp so many particular histories – not forgetting regions, countries of origin, and the differently abled – everyone ends up lost in the details. This danger is real – as the evolution of *postmodernism** during the 1980s

* *Postmodernism* originally was a critical approach to literature that called on theorists to look past a particular text or story to the social context the author writes from. In this way, critics were able to identify biases in the text and read deeper meanings, or the subtext, shaped by the author's socially constrained perspective. The name *postmodern*ism comes

and '90s demonstrates. This outlook's focus on social particularities and the rejection of "totalizing narratives," including Marxism, tends to leave postmodernists cut off from broad social struggles having the potential to transform society.

As Second Wave feminism has affirmed, the personal *is* political. Individual confrontations with patriarchal power, or with the habits and assumptions of white privilege, are critical to the broader struggle, as well as to people's own personal transformation. Socially conscious individuals build the future society as they go. But broad movements of masses of people require broader theoretical perspectives as well – ones that reintegrate an understanding of people's particular realities in ways that can challenge for power in the public arena.

Paying attention to the individual stories of a wide range of people can help people in the United States internalize a sense of the intersections of oppression. For example, the writings of bell hooks (*Killing Rage: Ending Racism*), Cherríe Moraga and Gloria Anzaldúa (*This Bridge Called My Back*), Ward Churchill (*Perversions of Justice)*, Frank H. Wu (*Yellow*), Mab Segrest (*My Mama's Dead Squirrel*), and many other voices found in the bibliography of this book – as well as in music, film, and other spoken and visual arts – together give a sense of the rich reality of the country's many peoples.

At the same time there is the need to probe for the larger fault-lines of society. Such zones of tension suggest alliances that have the potential to crack open the whole structure of white supremacist patriarchal capitalism. Third World feminism is one such strategic alliance. Its birth and

---

from the method's challenge to *modernism*, an outlook dating back to the Enlightenment of the 1700s. The modernist worldview holds that reality can be examined and understood straightforwardly, if incompletely, by developing ever more complex theoretical structures that reflect the inner dynamics of development and change – from the atom to the cosmos, and including society in between. Postmodern theorists call these over-arching analytic perspectives "totalizing narratives." They claim that such understanding is compromised by the socially situated, and therefore biased, nature of all human perception.

For feminists, postmodernism provided a powerful tool to lay bare the sexist assumptions that permeate the art forms society uses to reflect and understand itself. Given social conditioning of such monstrous proportions, it is no wonder women's oppression has been seen as the normal, or natural order of things.

Starting from this liberatory initial impulse, however, postmodernism then lost its moorings, breaking from reality completely. All writing and analysis came to be seen as socially situated, and therefore tainted. The socially determined framework people bring to their study unavoidably conditions their understanding. As a result, all thinking must be seen as a text that requires interpretation, and endless reinterpretation – with no fundamental grounding anywhere to anchor the analytic process.

For many postmodernists external reality and its patterns of operation get lost in the swirl of theory. And conscious social activity or social practice – individual, organized, or scientific – no longer serves as the vital link between reflective thought and the evolving material reality humanity is part of. Postmodernism ends up being radically disempowering – as it undermines the potential for emancipatory action – despite its origins as a socially engaged, subversive tool of analysis.

development grew in response to the primarily white Second Wave women's movement of the 1960s. By the early 1970s new voices began to emerge that challenged a "one-size-fits-all" vision of women and feminism.

First steps

Early initiatives tended to develop within or emerge from organizations active in the oppressed nationality movements. But splits also occurred in the broader social movements and germinated in the background among independent activists before taking organizational form.

- ***The Third World Women's Alliance*** grew out of the Student Non-Violent Coordinating Committee (SNCC) toward the end of the 1960s. Asian Sisters in LA developed out of the Asian American Political Alliance. Elaine Brown became the Chair of the Black Panther Party in 1973 and moved women into a number of important positions within the party during her three-year tenure. And Women of All Red Nations (WARN), founded in 1974, included many women who were also members of AIM, the American Indian Movement.[1]
- ***Struggles developed in the reproductive rights movement*** around the particular needs of women of color. The organization NARAL (National Abortion and Reproductive Rights Action League) opposed calling for guidelines that would help protect women of color from unwanted sterilizations. NARAL feared that such restrictions would impinge on reproductive freedom and limit access to sterilization for the mostly white, better-off women who were having trouble getting doctors to perform this procedure. Later conflicts also emerged over certain longer-lasting contraceptives – Norplant and Depo-Provera – whose side-effects were downplayed in an effort to target oppressed nationality communities. An opposing trend developed – and in New York City included the Coalition for Abortion Rights and Against Sterilization Abuse (CARASA). Multinational – though predominantly white – and anti-imperialist in its outlook, CARASA benefited from the leadership and inspiration of women like Puerto-Rican activist, Dr. Helen Rodriguez-Trias. Eventually the larger critical trend took national form at the 1983 National Conference on Black Women's Health Issues – and later in similar health initiatives in other communities of color during the 1980s and '90s. The emphasis on "reproductive justice" that became so much a part of the struggle around the 2004 March for Women's Lives was already a unifying theme of NBWHP conference 20 years earlier.[2]

- ***After the Stonewall Rebellion in June 1969,*** the Gay Liberation Front (GLF) – and later the narrower, single-issue Gay Activists Alliance – became an active presence in the general upsurge of that period. The GLF mobilized for the Black Panther's Revolutionary People's Constitutional Convention in the fall of 1970 – responding to party chairman Huey Newton's statements of support for gay liberation. Then on May 1, 1971, gay activists made up a large, spirited, and multiracial, though mostly white, contingent in the Washington DC anti-Vietnam War effort to "shut down Washington." Besides the internal struggle over allying broadly or focusing on specifically gay issues, other tensions manifested in 1) the formation of the Third World Gay Liberation Front by Puerto Rican and black activists, and 2) the emergence of a new activist lesbian movement. Mainly seeing themselves as part of the women's movement – as woman-identified women – lesbian activists and their allies struggled to find the balance between their identity as women, as sexual beings, and as social activists. Eventually a new voice of black lesbian feminism helped give clarity to the struggle when the Combahee River Collective issued "A Black Feminist Statement" in 1977.[3]
- ***Within the black cultural nationalist movement*** the Black Women's United Front (BWUF) began to assert a new role and identity for women within Black Nationalism.[4] Initiated by the Congress of African People, five hundred women from organizations like the All African Peoples Revolutionary Party, National Welfare Rights Organization, Pan African Students of America, Youth Organization for Black Unity, and others joined to found the BWUF in Detroit on January 25, 1975. Local chapters later organized around 1) upholding the right of woman to self-defense – linked to the cases of Cheryl S. Todd and Dessie X. Woods, who had killed attackers while defending themselves against rape; 2) raising consciousness around black women's oppression by class and gender, as well as race; 3) educating community people on the leading role of women in 19th Century Black Nationalism; and 4) giving recognition to women leaders in the current struggle, as well as to the fact that "black women at the grass roots were the main force of the Modern Black Convention Movement.*"[5] These

* The pre-Civil War Black Convention Movement began with a gathering in Philadelphia at Mother Bethel AME Church in 1830. Delegated annual conventions took place over the next five years, and then again in 1843, 1847, 1848, 1853, and 1855. In the 1960s and '70s organizers of the Modern Black Convention Movement convened national meetings in Detroit and Washington DC (1966), Newark (1967), Philadelphia (1968), and Gary (1972). Out of this motion came the Congress of African People, the African Liberation Support

developments also had their impact on cultural nationalist leaders, as "Amiri Baraka, Haki Madhubuti, and Maulana Karenga began to repudiate sexism and male chauvinism in Black America."[6]

Nationalism and male privilege

Nonetheless, the struggle against male supremacy and heterosexism in the national movements was uneven. Elaine Brown in *A Taste of Power* describes how male alliances within the Black Panther Party poisoned the organization's internal norms and eventually forced her from leadership – just as the party was enjoying its greatest influence in Oakland and California. Within the cultural nationalist movement, some activists opposed both 1) the creation of the BWUF as a separate organization, and 2) having the fight against sexism be a point of unity of this new formation.

As the nationalist movement began to break apart in the mid-1970s, the BWUF succumbed to sectarian conflicts. Still, the larger process of women's self-assertion had a lasting impact. Dating back to the 1800s, male leaders had tended to project a vision of national liberation with a patriarchal character, often equating *freedom* with *manhood*. "Whether we are reading Delaney, DuBois, Douglass, Garvey, Cleaver, George Jackson, King or Malcolm X, often they suggest that the wounds of white supremacy will be healed as black men assert themselves not as decolonized free subjects in struggle but as 'men,'" writes bell hooks. "The equation of black liberation with black manhood promotes and condones black male sexism."[7]

Mark Anthony Neal sees the "Strong Black Man" image of the civil rights era as a damaging legacy that today's hip-hop generation is struggling to shake free of. Criticism of the in-your-face thuggism of some mainstream hip hop can actually be a cover to protect, and a call to return to, the male privilege inherent in the Strong Black Man image. Neal comments: "Despite seemingly positive attributes, the figure of the Strong Black Man can be faulted for championing a stunted, conservative, one-dimensional, and stridently heterosexual vision of black masculinity that has little to do with the vibrant, virile, visceral masculinities that are lived in the real world."[8] Neal characterizes the nationalism of the 1960s and '70s as "Reactionary Black Nationalism" – based in part on the movement's sexism and homophobia. But he also targets the historic figures listed above by bell hooks, and directs particular criticism at hypocrisy and male privilege in the religious community, both Christian and Muslim.

Committee, the National Black Assembly, and the Black Women's United Front. (*Lerone Bennett, Jr.,* Before the Mayflower; *Komozi Woodward,* A Nation within a Nation.)

In similar fashion, Elizabeth Martínez comments, "during the Chicano liberation movement of 1965-'75, open challenges to sexism began to be heard from Chicana participants....The contradiction of encountering male-supremacist practices within a movement supposedly fighting for social justice spurred many Chicanas to new consciousness."[9] Later articles by Martínez, like "Chingón Politics Die Hard" and "Building New Roads to Liberation," drive home the view that the nationalism of the 1960s-'70s Chicano movement had a close association with male chauvinism. The vision of Aztlán was "macho nationalism," from the identification of the movement with its four main male leaders;* to the macho style of its public presence; to the sexualized imagery of oppression as "castration" and of male salutations, "*carnal*"; to the lack of attention to women's oppression inside the movement. By contrast, Martínez highlights women's central role in the struggle and the appropriateness of women's dedication to empowering others.

Laura Pulido's study of three 1960s organizations – the Black Panther Party (BPP), the Chicano organization CASA (*El Centro de Acción Social y Autónomo*), and the Asian/Pacific Islander collective East Wind – draws a similar conclusion. Comparing the three organizations, Pulido concludes: "While East Wind had nationalist overtones, it did not compare to CASA and the BPP, both of which, because of their relatively more homogeneous constituencies, developed more deeply entrenched nationalist ideologies and practices. In short, the lack of a strong nationalist orientation helped to erode the power of Asian American patriarchy."[10] Pulido goes on to indicate that gender relations were the "Achilles' heel of the Third World Left," at the same time that it was "a site for men and women to engage questions of gender equality and for women to develop as political leaders."[11]

Third World Feminism

Women of color were active not only in the various national movements but also in the primarily white, middle class, feminist movement of the 1960s. There people struggled to broaden the movement's perspective to include demands that reflected the needs and aspirations of women of color. Given the uniformity of the image of women the movement projected, however, and its single-minded focus on sexism – thereby discounting race and class oppression – it is not surprising that participation lagged. Some white women who took seriously the charges of racism in the movement also found the setting stifling and moved to other forms of activism. Later, once Third World feminism had established itself in the 1980s, these women found ways to reintegrate them-

---

* César Chávez (United Farm Workers), Corky González (Crusade for Justice), José Angel Gutiérrez (La Raza Unida Party), and Reies López Tijerina (*La Alianza Federal de Mercedes*)

selves into this more inclusive feminist movement.[12] Nonetheless, the primarily white movement of the '60s had its positive impacts across race/national lines. It helped stir awareness of new possibilities among broad masses of women. And it helped train a group of activists who were then able to take their skills and practices – including consciousness-raising circles, as one example – into the women of color movement.

Toward a new political subject

An early women's organization with wide influence was the National Black Feminist Organization (NBFO), founded in 1973. Becky Thompson notes that "although its members employed the tool of consciousness-raising...the content of these sessions was decidedly black women's issues: stereotypes of black women in the media, discrimination in the workplace, myths about black women as matriarchs, and black women's beauty and self esteem."[13]

During this same period, and sparked by the example of the NBFO, black women in Boston formed the Combahee River Collective. An important forerunner of the autonomous Third World Women's movement, their 1977 "Black Feminist Statement" asserted *identity* as the motivating factor in the struggle for liberation. "We believe that the most profound and potentially most radical politics come directly out of our own identity, as opposed to working to end somebody else's oppression."[14] They also drew out the interconnection among oppressions: "We believe that sexual politics under patriarchy is as pervasive in black women's lives as are the politics of class and race. We also often find it difficult to separate race from class from sex oppression because in our lives they are most often experienced simultaneously."[15]

Noteworthy during this period is the key role that lesbian women of color played in the emerging movement. The Combahee River Collective's statement stressed the importance of alliance building – at the same time that it validated an autonomous black women's movement: "Although we are feminists and Lesbians, we feel solidarity with progressive black men and do not advocate the fractionalization that white women who are separatists demand. Our situation as black people necessitates that we have solidarity around the fact of race...We struggle together with black men against racism, while we also struggle with black men about sexism."[16]

For many 1981 marked, in the words of Angela Davis, "the development of women of color as a new political subject."[17] In this year Cherríe Moraga and Gloria Anzaldúa, both lesbians, published *This Bridge Called My Back: Writings by Radical Women of Color*. In the introduction to the 1988 Spanish edition, Moraga states: "This book tries to reach to the other side, by making a bridge over the differences which historically have defeated women of color, to the point of silencing them, erasing them, and fragmenting them."[18] She summarizes the development of this new political subject, noting the leading role that black women had played during the 1970s – and the Combahee River Collective statement is included in the collection. Moraga also notes the origin of the term describing this political subject: "At the end of the 1970s, Asian, Latin American, native North American and African women began to reclaim the term 'women of color' (regardless of our actual color), as a term of political identification to distinguish us from the dominant culture."[19]

In the introduction to the 2001 edition Moraga reflects, "The established race-based politics [of the 1970s] was not radical enough. It did not go to one fundamental root of injustice, which some of us believed to be the gender-defined divisions of labor and loving." By contrast, an intersectional standpoint advances such a radical analysis by stressing the fundamental interpenetration of gender and sexuality with race and class.

Becky Thompson notes other events that made 1981 a turning point in the emergence of Third World feminism. Kitchen Table Women of Color Press, founded that year, made *This Bridge Called My Back* one of its first publications. The multiracial protest at the West Coast Women's Music Festival drove home the point that movement events had to be built on coalition politics from the start, not brought in at the last minute. And in 1981 bell hooks published her first book, *Ain't I a Woman*; and Latin American feminists met for the first time in Bogotá, Colombia.

Global feminism

A similar intersectional perspective informs what has come to be known as "global feminism" – where the particularities of women's oppression around the world are taken as the starting point for analysis and struggle. Examples are:

- ***Highlighting the phenomenon of disappearing men,*** who migrate to seek work, abandon family responsibilities, or are drawn into military conflict; and the associated feminization of poverty worldwide "due to declining concern with reproducing the labor force"[20]
- ***Developing an international human rights approach*** to reproductive rights, universal access to health care, and preventing gender-based violence; and grounding these demands in policies around national budgets, reducing debt, fair trade, and international standards for corporations[21]
- ***Attacking the hypocrisy of formal equality*** that keeps private spaces and their relations of power off-limits – and so allows the ongoing terrorizing and torture of women[22]

- ***Making clear how women workers' conditions differ worldwide*** and focusing on 1) the logic and operation of capital, 2) the indigenous hierarchies women find themselves in, and 3) the varying ideologies around gender, technology, development, and skill levels that shape the specific content of "women's work"[23]
- ***Supporting sex worker organizing*** and thereby empowering women to transform their lives; opposing debt-bondage, trafficking, and child labor, along with laws that exclude sex workers from society[24]
- ***Countering the neo-colonialist attitudes*** of "enlightened advocates of the North" who seek to impose their ideologies and moralities, marginalize and silence Third World women, push technological solutions for presumed "backwardness," and imply that people are incapable of self-determination and need to be rescued.[25]

Strategy and tactics

In recent decades global feminism and women of color feminism in the United States have shared many themes and stimulated each other's development – at international meetings like those in Beijing (1995) and in Durban, South Africa (2001), for example. In 2000, Chela Sandoval's *Methodology of the Oppressed* drew on the words of Moraga and Anzaldúa to express what she calls the "differential consciousness" that characterizes Third World feminist struggle. Moraga had written: "Our strategy is how we cope [on an everyday basis], how we measure and weigh what is to be said and when, what is to be done and how, and to whom...daily deciding/risking who it is we can call an ally, call a friend (whatever that person's skin, sex, or sexuality)."[26] And paraphrasing Anzaldúa, Sandoval comments: "[We are] women who do not share the same culture, language, race, sexual orientation, or ideology, 'nor do we derive similar solutions' to the problems of oppression. But when the differential form of U.S. third world feminism is deployed, these 'differences do not become opposed to each other.'"[27] Instead, quoting black lesbian poet Audre Lorde from the pages of *This Bridge Called My Back*, "Only within that interdependency, acknowledged and equal, can the power to seek new ways of being in the world generate the courage and sustenance to act where there are no charters."[28]

What comes through clearly in Sandoval's summary is an affirmation of the free-flowing tactics and creativity used by women of color on a daily basis to resist white supremacist, patriarchal capitalism. A similar emphasis linking personal interactions to broader social movements is found in Patricia Hill Collins's *Black Feminist Thought*, also published in 2000. Collins stresses an "inclusive perspective [that] enables African-

American women to avoid labeling one form of oppression as more important than others, or one expression of activism as more radical than another...Viewing the world as one in the making...shows that while individual empowerment is key, only collective action can effectively generate the lasting institutional transformation required for social justice."[29]

Chapter 15

Toward a Third Wave Women's Movement

The two previous chapters highlighted critiques of Second Wave feminism that center primarily on race and class – questions that weakened the movement's transformative capacity and set it up for co-optation and counterattack. This approach to evaluating the recent history of feminism can help mark distinct periods in the "longest revolution" – at least as it has developed in U.S. history. As an example, Susan Archer Mann and Douglas J. Huffman suggest four current trends that do "not seek to undermine the feminist movement, but rather to refigure and enhance it so as to make it more diverse and inclusive"[1]:

- ***Intersectionality theory,*** developed primarily by women of color as we saw in Chapter 14, focuses on systematic oppression centered on a person's own identity and unites with others from this standpoint.
- ***Feminist postmodernism,*** emerging primarily from academia, moves analysis off the dominant story lines of mainstream culture to include marginalized voices and validate the experiences of everyday life.
- ***Post-colonial theory,*** included in the previous chapter as "global feminism," emphasizes the variety of experiences of Third World women, and calls for "historic specificity" in discovering the commonalities of women's oppression and resistance worldwide.
- ***Young feminists,*** encompassing a range of perspectives, include 1) a critique of "austere 'missionary feminism' that entailed self-policing, confession through consciousness-raising groups, and salvation through political action"[2]; 2) web-zines and blogs that

present an unstructured array of personal experiences; 3) lived cultural critiques like wearing party dresses with combat boots to undermine images of the feminine; and 4) a fluidity of sexual identity that lays bare the social construction of gender.

Mann and Huffman also mention certain trends among younger feminist-identified activists that push so far that they can take on an anti-woman character. Included here are "girlie feminists" that exult in maxing out on stereotypical feminine dress and make-up; "power feminists" who promote getting ahead by deploying their sexual charms; and, more generally, the individualistic emphasis on "do-it-yourself" feminism, which "reverses the second wave's notion that the personal is political as the political becomes totally personal."[3]

For Mann and Huffman, these different trends together make up today's Third Wave feminism – which they then contrast and compare with Marxist, or socialist feminism. Pythia Peay, who works with the organization Sacred Circles in Washington DC, takes a different approach. Peay identifies the Third Wave with "women in their 20s and 30s who still advocate for women's rights while embracing a 'girlie culture' that celebrates sex, men, gay culture, and clothes."[4] She then points to a new feminism, a Fourth Wave that has been growing for at least a decade. Peay's Fourth Wave feminism unites women in the face of today's dominant conservative agenda – revealing a "political activism that's guided and sustained by spirituality."[5] This trend has a global dimension identified with the Global Peace Initiative of Women Religious and Spiritual Leaders, the September 2004 Women & Power conference in New York, the V-Day movement aimed at stopping global violence against women, and a U.N. Resolution aimed at including women in all peace negotiations. At the heart of the movement is the desire to transcend differences through "collaboration, not conquest…When you get Jewish, Catholic, Buddhist, Hindu, and Sufi women all practicing their faith in the same room, another religion emerges, which is feminine spirituality."[6]

While valuing these writers' identification of the trends within today's feminism, our sense is that conditions have not yet developed to the point where a Third Wave can be identified. The sheer variety of critiques of the Second Wave speaks to both the potential for a new wave's emerging, and the absence of a clearly defined leading edge to the struggle. Our approach by contrast, is to take as given the currents of feminism identified by Mann, Huffman, and Peay, but to then add still other perspectives and trends evident in society. In time, and with conscious organizing effort, a new historic feminist wave can take shape, one with a depth and transformative potential that will clearly set it apart from the class and race-bound movements of earlier periods.

Elements of the next wave

The review below includes 1) the five feminist currents mentioned Mann, Huffman, and Peay, 2) perspectives highlighted in previous chapters, and 3) some new elements not previously mentioned. The goal is to suggest inclusiveness – since a social movement requires a multitude of heterogeneous impulses to grow and adapt to changing conditions. But we also begin with a core set of four priority components, since to be successful a transformative project must also have direction.

Third World feminism and global feminism

Given 1) the continuing strength of white supremacy in the United States, as well as 2) the weaknesses of both First and Second Wave feminism in confronting this reality, a Third World feminist outlook almost certainly needs to be at the center of the next wave. Linda Burnham suggests, however, that making this goal a reality will require that Third World feminism:

- ***Develop a national organizational infrastructure*** that can mobilize large numbers of people to shape national policy;
- ***Reacquire the movement's earlier "critical, political edge*** and sense of connection to a broader social justice movement."[7]

Socialist feminism

While never achieving the level of a movement in its own right, socialist feminism has been a persistent voice for the past three decades and more – dating back to the 1940s Communist Party-organized Congress of American Women and the writings of Claudia Jones and Mary Inman.[8] The publication in 2002 of *The Socialist Feminist Project* (*SFP*) by Monthly Review Press reaffirms the importance of this viewpoint – as do articles since 2002 in the left journal *Science & Society*. We have drawn on many of these writers for the analysis in the previous two chapters.

In her introduction to *The Socialist Feminist Project*, Nancy Holmstrom brings the history of the women's movement up to the present: "feminist theorizing of the last decade was of a highly academic sort – postmodernism – while the dominant politics have been the most local and particularistic form of identity politics. Moreover, of course, we have to appreciate the context in which all this has taken place: namely, the general rightward political drift throughout the world during the 1980s and much of the 1990s."[9] The absence of an analysis addressing this larger social context provides an opening for an outlook centered on class – but also inclusive of race, gender, and sexuality. In a sense, this left intersectional perspective comes from the standpoint of class, while Third World feminism starts from gender and racial oppression. A synthesis of these two variations in outlook is already in the making, given the inclusion in *SFP* of writers like Angela Davis, Cherríe Moraga, and Elizabeth Martínez; as well as Leith Mullings, co-founder of the Black Radical Congress; Johanna Brenner, longtime feminist and member of the left organization Solidarity; Dorothy Allison, author of *Bastard Out of Carolina*; and social scientist and welfare policy analyst Mimi Abramovitz.

Claudia Jones (1915-1964)

Claudia Jones and her three sisters arrived in Harlem from Trinidad in 1922, joining their parents who had come the year before. Their movement was part of the Great Migration, when people of African descent relocated from the U.S. South and the Caribbean to Northern cities in search of work. World War I had made life difficult, and returning veterans faced a recession and demanded jobs and resources. Meanwhile, employers in the North were looking for cheap labor.

Harlem was both a place of desperate poverty and, at the same time, the center of an African-African cultural renewal – the Harlem Renaissance. Jones experienced both sides of this social reality. She contracted tuberculosis at age 17 from living in a cold-water flat and coming home exhausted from long hours working in a laundry. She also found her life transformed by the cultural and activist climate of the period.

The Scottsboro case captured Jones' energy and enthusiasm. Nine young African American men from Alabama had been charged in 1931 with raping two white girls. Although one of the girls later recanted, all the young men spent at least six years in prison. A series of appeals managed to keep the young men alive, while all white juries repeatedly handed out death sentences. Four of the nine eventually received pardons in 1937. The other five survived the brutality of the prison system and, though deeply scarred by the experience, either escaped or were finally set free by 1950.

The Communist Party took up the Scottsboro case when other groups, including the NAACP, refused to get involved. Historian David Oshinsky wrote in 1994, "the youths and their families chose to be represented by the party's International Labor Defense because, as one mother noted, 'They are the only ones who put up a fight to save these boys and I am with them to the end.'" [20]

Based on this record of advocacy, Jones joined the Young Communist League (YCL) in 1936. She became a Harlem organizer for the YCL and later served as the YCL state education director, state chair, and member of the national council. Meanwhile Jones also helped staff the Communist Party's *Daily Worker* newspaper and became editor of the YCL's *Weekly Review*.

In responding to critics of Marx and the left, Holmstrom notes that "feminists are justified in wanting a social theory that gives a fuller picture of production and reproduction than Marx's political economic theory does, that extends questions of democracy not only to the economy but to personal relations. They are also justified in wanting to pay attention to the emotional dimensions of our lives, both to understand how oppression manifests itself in the most intimate aspects of our lives and also, most importantly, to give a more complete vision of human emancipation."[10]

Claudia Jones' greatest impact on the CP came in the area of women's rights. In 1948 she became editor of the *Daily Worker's* Negro Affairs Desk and then executive secretary of both the CPUSA National Negro Commission and its National Women's Commission. She toured every state in the union speaking passionately from personal experience on the struggles to end race and women's oppression.

Jones' 1949 essay, "An End to the Neglect of the Problems of Negro Women" was a wake-up call for the party. While the CP campaigned vigorously to end white chauvinism, it paid much less attention to women's concerns. There was not yet a shared understanding of the interconnections among race, class and gender – or "super-exploitation," as Jones called this intersection of oppressions. "Negro women – as workers, as Negroes, and as women – are the most oppressed stratum of the whole population," she wrote.

Jones understood that black women had always been leaders in their families and communities. Harsh circumstances had prepared women for difficult battles and for leadership roles in mass struggles. At the same time, Jones pointed clearly to the source of the problem, "The responsibility of overcoming these special forms of white chauvinism rests...squarely on the shoulders of white men and white women. Negro men have a special responsibility particularly in relation to rooting out attitudes of male superiority as regards women in general."

Jones's outspokenness and political activism cost her personally. During the McCarthy anticommunist campaign of the early 1950s, the courts jailed her three times and finally deported her. She arrived in Great Britain in 1955 and quickly linked up with the Caribbean people who had newly immigrated there. Although Jones thought of herself as an American, in her new home she became a Caribbean immigrant once again. Jones started a newspaper, the *West Indian Gazette.* Then after race riots erupted in 1958, Jones helped found and promote what is now known as the Notting Hill Carnival, London's largest street fair.

—sources: Watson-Crosby, "Claudia Jones"; Weigand, Red Feminism; *Linder, "The Trials of The Scottsboro Boys"; Oshinsky, "Only the Accused Were Innocent"; Wheeler, "*The New York Times: *Turning truth on its head"*

Revolutionary organization

Kjersti Ericsson's *Sisters, Comrades!* provides another dimension to the socialist-feminist perspective. Writing from a Marxist perspective, Ericsson, too, analyzes women's experiences laboring in the market economy, working at home, dealing with male privilege in family life, combating media stereotypes, and connecting to women's struggle worldwide. But then Ericsson carries the analysis a step further to the *organizational* consequences of women's situation.

Ericsson draws on her experience in Norway's Workers' Communist Party (AKP). This party has a daily newspaper, holds leadership positions in a number of trade unions, and achieves respectable showings in national and local elections. As a significant revolutionary party in an industrial country, the AKP has much to teach organizers in the United States. At the same time, conditions in Norway are clearly different from those in the United States, where racial oppression and imperialist expansion have a long history. Until the immigration of the 1970s, Norway was a relatively homogenous society; and there is only one oppressed nationality, the Sami, or Laplanders, living in an isolated region of the north. The AKP supports this nation's right to self-determination and has Sami people among its members. The challenge for activists in the United States is to learn what they can from Ericsson and the AKP, while grounding the U.S. movement's analysis and program on this country's history and current situation.

Ericsson makes the following three main points in relation to women and organization in the social struggle in Norway:

- *women's organization* is the "key link" in the struggle for socialism;
- *a strategic alliance* is required between the "two vanguards" – broad organizations of women and of the working class;
- "women must conquer" the working class party.[11]

Women as key link: Drawing on experience from around the world, Ericsson cites women's:

- *differing relationship to time* compared to men, since women are caught in the "squeeze between job and family";
- *struggling to break out of being paid "supplementary wages"* – in order to earn an income sufficient to support themselves and raise children;
- *centrality to struggles in the public sector* – around day care and services for the elderly, for example.

Ericsson comments: "Female workers…play a leading role by virtue of the fact that they, as an oppressed sex, are forced to start a number of battles which have fundamental importance for the entire working class.

Therefore, we see women leading the way in the battle for working hours, in the battle for the public sector and in the battle for wages."[12]

Women as vanguard: At the same time, Ericsson sees the traditional working class vanguard as playing "a leading role by virtue of the value they produce, by virtue of being concentrated in large workplaces, by virtue of being well-organized and having strong fighting traditions." So an "alliance between the two vanguards is called for." Steps toward building such an alliance include:[13]

- *Building an autonomous women's movement,* including women's unions, and allying women in the working class with women teachers and others in the lower professional sector. "The most important prerequisite for an alliance is...that the new "vanguard," the female workers, show their strength and fight their way out of invisibility."
- *Raising women's issues consistently in male dominated arenas,* like trade unions and professional organizations. This task requires also that women who work in male-dominated, "core proletarian" jobs be organized and given the support they need to survive and to withstand the "pressure to become one of the 'guys.'"
- *"Getting tough" courses* that "take their starting point from the perspective that women's 'personal characteristics' such as a lack of self-confidence, perfectionistic demands of herself, fear of shaming those she is representing, are created by society and can be fought against through collective effort.... To 'toughen up'... breaks down the concept that some are, in some magical way, 'strong,' can 'fight' and 'lead,' while others are not 'made that way.' And it strengthens women's responsibility for each other."
- *Allying with women-conscious men* who take up women's struggles and fight male chauvinism in the movement. This task also requires *carrying on struggles to raise men's consciousness about women's conditions* in order to "break down the barrier that male chauvinism represents."
- *Building mutual support around the struggles taken up by each of the two vanguards,* and working out differences as they develop in order to avoid divisions in the struggle.

Women as revolutionary leaders: The third strategic step Ericsson points to is for women to capture the leading revolutionary party. In her view, the "two vanguards" are broad, mass organizations of the traditional working class on the one hand, and of women – both workers and lower-level professionals – on the other. The leading revolutionary organization remains, for her, a single, unified party, comprised of people from the two vanguards, as well as from broader society. With her goal of capturing the party in mind, Ericsson lays out a program for struggle within the party:[14]

- *Fight for a program that makes women in the working class visible,* and which can serve as a basis for party policy and struggle from a woman's perspective.
- *Challenge the mechanisms that push women's concerns to the background:*
  - **systematic coincidences** that keep women's issues off the agenda – people getting sick, understaffing, "urgent business requires our attention..."
  - **men's blind spot** that relegates women's concerns to invisibility
  - **personal interactions** that give power to men while silencing women – it is necessary to "make interactions between the sexes a political theme"
  - **men's posturing** in taking up women's issues
  - individual women **holding formal positions** in place of women holding real power in the organization
  - women leaders **"leading on men's terms"**
  - **women leaders not given the support** to function as leaders
- *Recruit women in large numbers* into the organization.
- *Hold separate internal meetings* of women as needed.
- *Show strength in women's mass struggles.*

We have presented Kjersti Ericsson's points on organization in some detail because there is so little material on organizational questions in the writings of the women's movement in the United States. One could say that this absence is in itself a statement – implying that women's struggles and alliances already do take place and, in fact, should take place outside the confines of traditional left organizations. But for socialist feminists, where the need for organization is usually a given, the lack of focus on such questions may reflect the writers' social position in academia, their main identification with local grassroots organizing, or the overall weakness of the left in the United States.

Criticizing white privilege

The emergence of Third World feminism out of the upsurge of the 1960s contributed, in complementary fashion, to a beginning awareness of what it means for European women and men in the United States to be identified as white.

A number of books by white women can help white people move beyond their being socially constructed as white. *White Women, Race Matters,* by Ruth Frankenberg; *Memoirs of a Race Traitor,* by Mab Segrest; *The Wall Between,* by Anne Braden; and *A Promise and a Way of Life,* by Becky Thompson, are a few that stand out. In addition, Dana Frank, in "White Working-Class Women and the Race Question," shows the deep roots of white privilege among Southern working class women and among women union members as well. These analyses make clear the distorting effects of white supremacy on the development of women's solidarity historically. At the same time, just by their very existence, they also point to the potential for women to lead in criticizing and overcoming divisions based on racial privilege.

We will go into more detail in Chapters 20 and 24-26 on ways to put the insights of these authors into practice. For now we want to highlight several points they seem to be in agreement on:

- *White people need to be proactive in developing personal relationships with people of color* – as one way to establish a personal connection to oppressed nationality struggles.
- *Examination of one's life is important* to get deeper insights into how race privilege affects one's thinking and actions – but this essential reflection should not be cut off from being actively engaged in social struggles to change the world. Otherwise, the personal can stop being political and become a self-centered indulgence instead.
- *White activists have an obligation to not just dismiss their family members* or other white folks as being "racists" or "backward." Rather there is a need to deeply understand how people arrive at their understanding of the world – in both its positive and negative aspects – so as to struggle in appropriate ways over time to transform oneself and others in a positive direction. In this country, it can safely be said that no white person is born an anti-racist.
- *The struggle to move beyond a white identity is a process* – and one that all white folks will be grappling with for the foreseeable future and beyond. Keeping in mind the long-term character of the struggle can help a person remain modest and reflective, as well as motivated to continue being active through all the temporary, often surprising, setbacks along the way.

Other components of the next wave

- ***Grassroots women's organizations***
  - *Workplace-based* – such as the workers' center movement described in Miriam Ching Yoon Louie's *Sweatshop Warriors;* as

well as more established organizations like the Coalition of Labor Union Women (CLUW), and unions of hospital and child care workers, flight attendants, and nurses

- *Community-based* – such as the *Esperanza* Peace and Justice Center in San Anton
Third World women
landria, VA; the DC
land, whose cleaning
tice"; and Global Wc

- ***Women's peace organiz***
with spirituality, such a
lowship, Code Pink, W
like Women's Interna
(WILPF)

- ***Other progressive trenc***
Mann and Huffman a
new generation of activ

- ***Lesbian-Gay-Bisexual-***
compassing in particu
and people of color c
ACT-UP (AIDS Coaliti

- ***Feminist and socialist***
lowing examples from

  - *Feminist theory* – ce
the "production an
enting" in patriarc
explain the persiste
one mode of produ
another; and 2) to understand the ways capitalism might weaken certain aspects of oppression while permitting new adaptive forms to develop[16]

  - *Marxist theory* – focusing on the reproduction of labor power and women's unpaid labor in lowering the subsistence wage, thereby increasing capitalists' surplus value[17]

  - *Social regulation theory* – theorizing the specifics of local labor markets based on the working out of contradictions in the productive and reproductive spheres, with the government setting the regulatory conditions in which development takes place[*][18]

---

[*] Jon Liss of Tenants and Workers United comments: This perspective "structurally links gender and the struggle for 'social wages' as a key arena of struggle – moving way beyond

- ***Lessons from 20th Century socialism*** – drawing on Margaret Randall's analysis of the Cuban and Nicaraguan experience,[19] for example, or Maxine Molyneux's identifying the "acid test" of women's strategic interests in revolutionary societies as:[20]
    - *abolishing the sexual division of labor*
    - *lifting the burden of domestic labor*
    - *ending institutional discrimination*
    - *political equality at all levels of society*
    - *reproductive access and choice*
    - *clear policies directed at ending male violence and control*
- ***Institutional infrastructure created out of the Second Wave*** – including Women's Studies programs, rape crisis centers, women's economic development projects, and the networks of women in political and professional circles; and recognizing that some in this last sector will give first allegiance to their current class or racial privileges, while others will respond positively to a new upsurge and will be in a position to provide resources, training, and political support
- ***Ally groupings of feminist men*** – such as Men Against Rape Culture in North Carolina; here, too, most solidly oriented when composed primarily of men from oppressed nationalities and the working class, and taking leadership from women with these same class and racial/national backgrounds

Re-centering the social justice movement

Step by step over the first four sections of this book we have built up an analysis that began with 1) a focus on the white race, and then moved in turn to 2) oppressed nations and the resistance to imperialism, 3) race and class, and now 4) patriarchy and white privilege. At each step, the analysis took on a new dimension, and the interrelations became more complex. When viewed separately, each type of oppression has its own form of resistance struggle: self-determination for national struggles, working class rule for the class struggle, and an end to patriarchy for women and people excluded from the male/female dichotomy. But as each contradiction gets layered over the one before, the resulting intersectional analysis of U.S. society and its dynamics comes closer to reflecting the reality people actually live each day. The struggle against patriarchy, though persisting the longest through history, has only taken shape

---

the male proletarian/factory model that still undergirds much left orientation." *(Personal communication)*

as a thoroughly liberatory project in the last 30 to 60 years.* As a result, once grasped, its effect almost certainly must be to recenter the way social justice activists view the long-term struggle to transform society.

Patriarchy interpenetrates with race and class. Understanding one oppression requires an awareness of all three – and the profound impact each has on people's lives. In any given situation, one contradiction may be primary and need the most attention, while the others are secondary. But all contribute to the unique reality of the moment. And each contradiction is central to creating a core strategic alliance among the oppressed nationality, working class, and women's and LGBTQ anti-patriarchy movements. Only such a historic bloc of forces will allow all

Tenants and Workers United: Putting Sisters at the Center

One approach to building a working-class community organization is to put "sisters at the center." The idea here is that if working class women of color can achieve their liberation, this same process will also liberate the rest of society. A good example in northern Virginia is the Women's Leadership Group (WLG) of Tenants and Workers United (TWU).

During the spring of 1995 a half dozen women met regularly at the TWU to discuss community concerns – particularly the needs of women. To facilitate the discussion, each member of the WLG drew a picture to represent an aspect of community life. Catalina Zeleda drew a picture of children playing in the street. People questioned her about this and she talked about her children having nowhere else to play. Many of the other women agreed with this assessment. But what could be done about the lack of recreational facilities? The WLG started by gathering the facts – documenting the recreational resources in the Latino and African-American neighborhood and comparing these with the adjacent more affluent, predominantly white neighborhoods.

After locating a large map of the area, the women walked block by block, marking every playground and outside grill that they saw, both public and private. In the TWU neighborhood they found just one public grill and two small playgrounds. And these facilities belonged to the Arlandria/Chirilagua Housing Cooperative, where the WLG was based. Clearly, the needs of the 9,000 residents of Arlandria were not being met.

When the WLG drove through the adjacent neighborhoods, it was a different story. They marked down several semi-private parks located at churches and three large public parks, each with several grills. They also noted privately owned grills behind almost every house, and privately owned swing sets behind many homes.

---

* The Combahee River Collective circulated their "Statement" in 1977. Simone de Beauvoir's *The Second Sex*, an influential early work of Second Wave feminism, came out in 1949.

oppressed peoples – and each such person taken individually – to feel they are included in the movement's vision of the future. And only such a broad-based alliance will have the moral and political strength to challenge for political power – and then be able to use it to achieve national liberation, end the class system, and carry social transformation through to the complete elimination of racism and patriarchal oppression.

Patriarchy damages everyone – by limiting and prescribing how people act and think, and whom they can love. A revolutionary feminist project has the potential to free men as well as women – as well as everyone on a continuum of genders in between. Four elements from the preced-

The WLG then turned to the Parks and Recreation budget, analyzing it with the help of the TWU staff. Together they found $75,000 in unspent/reserved money for area tennis courts. Armed with this information and their map of recreational resources, the women met with the Alexandria City Director of Parks and Recreation in November 1995. Once the WLG presented their evidence, the director quickly agreed to change the budget and address the community's needs. Although it took more than a year, by the spring of 1997 the Arlandria neighborhood had a new $30,000 playground, plus two new public grills in their local park. In addition, the city installed a $75,000 multi-purpose court in the spring of 1998 – where area young people now play basketball, mini-soccer, tennis and volleyball.

In winning this victory the WLG and the TWU summed up several important lessons:

The WLG made a political decision not to differentiate between public, private and semi-private playgrounds. This allowed the disparity between the middle class and working class neighborhoods to really stand out.

Investigation with hard facts, data, and maps provided the WLG with critical ammunition. The women produced all this knowledge using a direct, hands-on approach. Prior to the women's mapping, most of the TWU members and staff had not really observed the city carefully.

A democratic internal process was a key aspect of the struggle – just as the WLG/TWU was fighting to win popular democratic rights at the city level.

The struggle helped develop women's leadership skills – and it strengthened the TWU at the same time.

Putting working class women and their issues at the center had direct and long-lasting benefits for the entire community. The women's power came from their organization, their social base in the Arlandria/Chirilagua Housing Cooperative, and their intimate understanding of the need for playgrounds and grills in the community. This knowledge and organizational strength proved decisive in meeting with city officials – resulting in neighborhood improvements valued at more than $100,000.

—source: Tenants and Workers United, "Report"

ing discussion will likely characterize such a transformative movement:

- ***an autonomous Third World women's movement*** – at the center of a broad working class (including women working at home) and professional women's movement – evolving in time into a distinctive Third Wave revolutionary feminism;
- ***heightened awareness and struggle around women's conditions of life and their reflection in culture*** – in people's personal relationships, and in their families, organizations, and society at large;
- ***internal practices*** within both popular and revolutionary organizations ***that work to overcome male privilege and empower women***, particularly women of color, thereby making women's leading role in the struggle both a well-grounded reality and widely recognized;
- ***personal norms of relating that are direct and open***, rather than charged with power dynamics, as part of the process of building over time internally, as well as externally through social struggles, the beloved community we all aspire to be part of.

In the closing chapters of the book, we will return to these themes and to the practical steps necessary to make them real. Now we move from an analysis of the core contradictions of race, class, and gender to an examination of the social forces and strategic alignment required to end the system of white supremacy in the United States. The next two sections assess the roadblocks and potential for white people's participation in the struggle. Then we consider the conditions and prospects for organizing a broad united front against white supremacy – and offer specific steps for building such a front. We conclude with a reminder of the historic costs of white privilege – and point to the emancipatory alternative prefigured by today's social justice movement.

WHO NEEDS
NIGGERS

The white farmer has not always been the lazy, slipshod, good-for-nothing person that he is frequently described as being. Somewhere in his span of life he became frustrated. He felt defeated. He felt the despair and dejection that comes from defeat. He was made aware of the limitations of life imposed upon those unfortunate enough to be made slaves of sharecropping. Out of his predicament grew desperation, out of desperation grew resentment. His bitterness was a taste his tongue would always know.

In a land that has long been glorified in the supremacy of the white race, he directed his resentment against the black man. His normal instincts became perverted. He became wasteful and careless. He became bestial. He released his pent-up emotions by lynching the black man in order to witness the mental and physical suffering of another human being. He became cruel and inhuman in everyday life as his resentment and bitterness increased. He released his energy from day to day by beating mules and dogs, by whipping and kicking an animal into insensibility or to death. When his own suffering was more than he could stand, he could live only by witnessing the suffering of others.

—Erskine Caldwell and Margaret Bourke-White, 1937,
You Have Seen Their Faces

V

WHITE PRIVILEGE, WHITE CONSCIOUSNESS

We now want to look more closely at the system of racial preferences at the start of the 21st Century. The goal of the discussion in this and the following two sections is to get a sense of the social forces that potentially can unite against the system of white supremacy and racism. Here we describe the reality of white privilege – as well as white people's attitudes toward their privileged position. We point to some of the barriers that keep the majority of white people on the sidelines – or to varying degrees supportive of the system. And we also suggest a process where, in response to challenges, these barriers can break down – freeing people to see their situation more clearly and to act effectively based on their new understanding.

In Chapter 16 we lay out the specific details of white privilege today. Contrary to the way the majority of white folks see things, the data demonstrating continued racial inequality is overwhelming. We sketch in the lifeline of statistically typical white people, highlighting how white privileges impact their lives from birth to the grave. We provide data that compares this approximately working class white experience to that of working class black and Latino peoples primarily, but also to Asian/Pacific Islander and native peoples as the data permit.

Then in Chapter 17 we review the contradictory ways white people understand their privileged position, as well as the toll it often unknowingly takes on their lives. The dynamics of privilege work to maintain the class system and, at the same time, intersect with and reinforce gender oppression.

Chapter 18 concludes the section by pointing to the choice white people have – either to continue reproducing the system or to break free from it. People's energy can go into maintaining the social and psychological defenses that support racial oppression. Or it can power a new awareness that turns privileges into tools of the multiracial struggle against white supremacy.

Chapter 16

The Reality of White Privilege

Many white people might say that things were bad a hundred years ago during Jim Crow segregation, or even fifty years ago before the civil rights movement, but now all that is in the past. Things are different now. In support of this view are the images we see every day – people of color as sports figures, movie and TV stars, religious leaders, authors, and politicians. The reality, however, is that once you get past these mostly media shaped public images, the lives that the majority of people live in the United States remain largely separate and unequal.

The table beginning on page 236 outlines a "life story" of white privilege. The data there describe the material advantages favoring an average white person – sometimes more, sometimes less – starting at birth and running through to retirement.

Social class

We are trying to get a sense of white racial privileges – distinct from the surplus taken by the white ruling class through exploitation. To do so, we want to focus as much as possible on differences within the broad working class. As described in earlier chapters, the white owning class in the United States exploits both white workers and workers of color. At the same time, the system affords white workers certain racial privileges that they have often jealously defended despite their exploitation. The white ruling class *exploits* both white workers and workers of color – and uses racial privileges to sustain their rule. White workers *benefit* – in comparison to workers of color – while at the same time being exploited for their labor power. This distinction is crucial. It points to the fact that ending exploitation – and the system of racial privileges that supports it

– is in the interests of white working class people as well as people of color.

With this framework in mind, it would be best if we could remove the top 1% of the population from the data. By taking this approximation to the white owning class out of the picture, we would come closer to capturing the amount of material privileges that white workers benefit from. Taking another 10% of the population would account for upper middle class managers and professionals – but would also include a larger number of people of color. Another 25% would eliminate the lower middle class of shop owners, foremen, schoolteachers, and others – but the racial mix now would be even more varied. Unfortunately, the government does not guide their data collection by the same analysis of class and race we use. As a result, we are forced to rely on numbers that in a less direct way take into account the high representation of white people at the top of society. For this purpose, as one example, the *median*, when it is available, works better than the *average*.* When the median is not available, or when percentages across races are compared, some mental reduction of the number associated with white people is called for to get a more accurate measure of differences within the working class.†

---

* The *average* or *mean* of a group of numbers tends to get stretched upward by any very large values in the group. The *median*, by contrast, tends to remove the impact of these exceptional values. Take, for example, a group of children aged 2, 2, 2, 2, 3, 3, 3, and a couple 14 year-olds – these last being an older brother and a friend doing homework in the corner until they get picked up later. If you wanted to characterize this group with one age value, you'd find the *average age* to be 5 years old (add up all the ages and divide by the total number of kids: 45/9 = 5). Since at early ages one year makes a big difference, characterizing the group as a bunch of 5 year olds is misleading. By contrast, the *median age* is 3, obtained by putting the numbers in order from lowest to highest and then picking the number in the middle. In this case, since there are 9 children, you count in five numbers from either end and you end up with a 3. Describing the group with one number, the median value – in this case, 3 – comes closer to reflecting the ages in the room than the average age, 5.

As another example, take housing in a town: 10 homes valued at $20,000; 26 at $50,000; 15 at $80,000; 2 at $150,000; and then the factory owner's mansion with a spread of land, $2 million. The average value of the housing in the town is then $100,000 – greater than all but three of the homes in the town. By contrast, the median house is worth $50,000, right at the middle value of the workers' homes. If what we're after is one number that approximates working class home values, the median is clearly preferable.

† Take a comparison of home ownership, for example. In 2003, the rates were white, 72.1%; black, 48.1%, and Latino, 46.7%. Taking the top 1% of white households out of the picture would mean that now 71.1 out of every 99 white households owned their own homes, or a rate of 71.8% – reflecting only a .3% decrease in the white ownership rate. So the impact is smaller than one might initially expect. Taking 10 percent out – removing the white upper middle class – reduces the rate to 62.1 out of every 90 households, or 69%. This approximation is only 2.3% less than the original 72.1%.

Differences favoring a working class white person in the early 21st Century

(See note at end for key to abbreviations.)

Heritage

246 million acres of **land** *distributed to white homesteaders during the 19th Century (only .3% were black),* affecting about one quarter of today's population [BC, 3]

Trillions in **accumulated earnings differences** *favoring white people, as a result of slavery, segregation and contemporary discrimination* [BC, 3]

Effects of Federal Housing Administration and Veterans Administration **redlining and home loan restrictions,** *from the 1930s through the 1960s favoring white homeowners' asset building* [SFC, 2; HC, 190]

Effects of GI Bill after World War II favoring white **employment advancement** [HC, 190]

White people's **inheritances:**

3.6 times the likelihood of **receiving an inheritance:** 28% of white families vs. 7.7% for African Americans [2004, UFE, 17]

4 times greater **parental median net worth** (assets minus debts): $198,700 (w) vs. $47,000 (A) [2004, UFE, 17]

At *birth*

Less than half the chance of **dying as an infant:** 5.7 per 1,000 live births (w) vs. 14.0 (A) [2001, WIR, 103]; just under half the rate (n) [2003, APH]

Greater **life expectancy:**

male: 74.8 years (w) vs. 68.2 years (A) [2003, APH]

female: 80.0 years (w) vs. 74.9 years (A) [2003, APH]

Youth

Less than half the chance of **growing up in poverty:** 14.3% of children (w) vs. 34.1 %(A) and 29.7% (L) [2003, SWA, 319]

About half the chance of growing up in a family that is **"asset poor"**†*:* 26% (w) vs. 52% (A) and 54% (L) [1999, HC, 40]

If arrested, twice as likely to be **processed as a juvenile,** *and not as an adult:* 66% (w) vs. 31% (A) [2000, MM, 6]

When **arrested the first time,** *one ninth the chance of being sent to juvenile prison:* compared to African Americans [2000, MM, 6]

When arrested **on a drug charge,** *1/48th the chance of being sent to juvenile prison:* compared to African Americans [2000, MM, 6]

Overall less likely to be **held in juvenile jails** *or placed in* **adult prisons:** compared to the African American youth, who make up 44% and 58% of the youth in these facilities, while being about 15% of the youth population [2000, MM, 6]

Spend less time in prison for ***violent offenses:*** 193 days on average (w) vs. 254 (A) and 305 (L) [2000, MM, 6]

Less likely to be ***under correctional supervision:*** 1 in 15 young males (w) vs. 1 in 3 (A) and 1 in 10 (L) [2003, MM, 5]

Education

Higher chance of ***completing high school:*** 88.7% (w) vs. 79.2% (A) [2002, WIR, 214]

More likely to ***attend a racially segregated school:*** percentage of students of own race at their school, on average, 80% (w) vs. a little over 50% (A and L, taken together) [2001, HC, 143]

More likely as a white student to: [HC, 144-145]

- *begin school* ***without a "cognitive skills" gap***
- *attend a* ***higher quality school***
- *be taught by* ***higher paid teachers***
- *be tracked into a* ***higher-level ability grouping***
- *have more access to* ***special program*** *opportunities*
- *have more access to* ***technology***
- *have* ***more money spent*** *on you, both as capital investment and operating costs*
- *have* ***questions on the SATs*** *favor you:* "every question chosen to appear on every SAT in the past ten years has favored whites over blacks" [2003, *Nation*, 24]

College

More likely to ***complete four or more years*** *of college:* 29.4% (w) vs. 17.2% (A), as percent of the group's adult population [2002, WIR, 103]

More than a third more likely to ***graduate in six years:*** 59% (w) vs. 37 % (A), as percent of group entering college [1998, BP, 6]

More likely to have a ***professor of your own race:*** compared to African Americans, who are 11.1% of students and 5% of faculty [1998, BP, 6]

One third the chance of being a ***victim of a hate crime*** *on campus:* compared to African Americans [2000, BP, 4]

Employment and unemployment

Less likely to be ***unemployed:*** 4.8% (w), 10.9% (A), 6.8% (L) [2004, SWA, 222]

Less likely to hold a ***low-wage job:*** white people are 58.4% of low-wage workers and 69.6% of the overall population, or 58.4% / 69.6% (w) vs. 14% / 11.2 % (A) and 21.9% / 13.4 %(L) [2003, SWA, 341]

More likely to be ***interviewed and hired*** *by someone of your own race* [COOS, 60]

Less likely to be subjected to ***special hiring tests*** [COOS, 60]

(Differences favoring a working class white person, continued)

More likely to ***use computers*** *at work:* 51.3% (w) vs. 39.9% (A) [1997, SWA, 211]

More ***favorable employment position****, shown by smaller gain from unionization:* 13.8% wage premium when unionized (w) vs. 20.9% (A) and 23.2% (L) [2003, SWA, 191]

Have a greater chance at **higher paying jobs** in: [1999, COOS, 55-59]

- *advertising:* <2% African American
- *largest law firms:* .01% African American [1990]
- *media:* TV writers, movies, publishing houses, news reporters, and editors

or in ***positions*** *as:*

- *sales representatives*
- *engineers*
- *magazine staff,* including "liberal" or left media like *The Nation* or *Rolling Stone*
- *police*
- *firefighters:* <2% African American

During a recession ***less likely to lose***:

- *your* ***job****:* job loss from 2001-2003, 1.9% (w) vs. 3.4% (A) [2003, SWA, 251]
- *a* ***long-tenure job****:* during 2001-2003 recession, 5.6% (w) vs. 7.3% (A) [CEPR, 4]

Much less likely to be a ***target of racial harassment*** *on the job* [2000, BW]

Income and poverty

Bring home more ***income*** *in a year:*

- *about 40% higher median family income:* $55,768 (w) vs. $34,369 (A) and $34,272 (L) [2003, SWA, 48]
- *higher women's hourly wage:* $12.94 (w) vs. $11.14 (A) and $9.75 (L) [2003, SWA, 167]
- *higher men's hourly wage:* $16.82 (w) vs. $12.23 (A) and $10.67 (L) [2003, SWA, 167]

Be cushioned against ***income loss*** *during recessions:* -1.7% average income loss from 2001 to 2003 (w) vs. -3.5 % (A) [WIR, 96]

Less than half as likely to:

- *be* ***poor****:* 10.5% (w) vs. 24.4% (A) and 22.5% (L) [2003, SWA, 316]; 8% (w) vs. 26% (n) [2001, WIR, 42]
- *experience* ***food hardship****:* 17.1% (w) vs. 37.6% (A) and 43.7% (L) [2002, REEW, 3]
- *experience* ***housing hardship****:* 10.0% (w) vs. 23.5% (A) and 19.6% (L) [2002, REEW, 3]

Housing and homelessness

Less likely to be **homeless***:* white people are 35% of the homeless and 70% of the overall population, or 35% / 70% (w) vs. 50% / 12% (A), 12% / 12% (L), and 2% / <1% (n) [2001, CL, 26]

More likely to be offered: [1995-1997, COOS, 39]

lower **rents**

more **incentives**

more **choices**: "60 to 90 percent of housing units shown to whites are not made available to blacks"

More likely to **own your own home***:* 72.1% (w) vs. 48.1% (A) and 46.7% (L) [2003, SWA, 295]

More likely to have **help from your family** *to make down payment:* 46% (w) vs. 12% (A) [1991-1995, HC, 113]

Half as likely to be **turned down** *for a mortgage or home improvement loan* [2004, UL]

Pay a lower **interest rate** *on your mortgage:* 8.12% (w) vs. 8.44% (A) [1999, HC, 111]

Have more **equity** *in your home:* median $58,000 (w) vs. $40,000 (A) [1994, HC, 109]

Less likely to live by a **toxic waste** *dump* [1999, EF, 2]

More likely to live in a **segregated** *community* [2003, BCGI, 4]

Have the value of your house **secured by segregation** *and threatened by integration* [HC, 121]

Have your home be more **highly valued** *on the market:* by 22% compared to African American homeowners [2001, HC, 121]

Household wealth and asset poverty

Ten times as much **wealth** (assets minus debts):

median household: $106,400 (w) vs. $10,700 (A) [2001, SWA, 285]

single woman headed household: $56,590 (w) vs. $5,700 (A) and $3,900 (L) [2001, WIR, 65]

Twice as likely to own **stocks, bonds or mutual funds** [BCGI, 5]

Have more than 5 times the **savings** *in IRAs, thrifts, and future pensions:* $63,506 (w) vs. $11,890 (A) and $9,904 (L) [2001, WIR, 14]

Less than half the likelihood of:

living in a household with **debts** *equal to or greater than your assets:* 13.1% (w) vs. 30.9% (A) [2001, SWA, 285]

being **asset poor***:* 25% (w) vs. 54% (A) [1999, HC, 39]

having **trouble paying** *rent or mortgage* [BCGI, 5]

Greater **ability to bounce back** *from economic recession:* between 1996 and 2002, wealth up 17% (w), down 22% (A), back to original level (L) [BC, 1]

(Differences favoring a working class white person, continued)

Health

More likely to:

be in ***good health****:* 92% (w), 86% (A), 87% (L), 83% (n) [2003, APH]

have ***health insurance****:* 88.3% (w), 79.8% (A), 67.6% (L) [2002, APH]

have a ***regular doctor****:* 80% (w), 67% (A), a little over 50% (L) [2003, APH]

be able to ***choose your medical provider****:* 84% (w), just over 70% (A and L) [2003, APH]

see a ***doctor of your own race****:* compared to African Americans and Latinos, who make up >25% of the population but have just 11% of medical school graduates [2005, GDN]

receive ***higher quality*** *health care* [2002, HA, 314]

If insured:

one third the chance of having ***public insurance,*** like Medicaid, which some doctors refuse to accept [2002, APH]

50% more likely to ***receive authorization*** *for an emergency room visit:* compared to African Americans [2002, APH]

Less likely to:

have ***trouble communicating*** *with your doctor:* 16% (w), 23% (A), 33% (L), 27% (API) [2003, APH]

suffer from ***hypertension and diabetes****:* compared to African Americans [2000, LH]

die from ***coronary disease, stroke, prostate, and breast cancer****:* compared to African Americans [2002, HA, 313]

Half the likelihood of dying from ***diabetes****:* compared to Native Americans and Latinos [2003, APH]

One-sixth the chance of being the victim of a ***homicide****:* compared to African Americans [2003, APH]

One-seventh the chance of dying from ***AIDS****:* compared to African Americans [2003, APH]

Justice system

Less chance of ***going to jail:*** 160 out of 100,000 residents of the same race (w) vs. 765 (A) and 262 (L) [2004, BJS]

Much less chance of:

being stopped by police as a result of ***racial profiling*** [1999, AI]

*being subjected to "****police brutality, unjustified shootings and deaths in custody****"* [1999, AI]

being sentenced to ***death and executed*** [2003, AI2]

Half as likely to be ***stopped and searched*** *for drugs,* if a white male, while twice as likely to have drugs when searched [2002, TW, 13]

Far less chance of going to prison for a **drug charge**: compared to African Americans, who are 14% of drug users, 35% of drug arrests, 55% of drug convictions, and 75% of those sent to prison on drug charges [2003, MM, 5]

Serve a year **less time** *on average when convicted:* compared to African Americans [Debt, 214]

Elections

Less likely to be **disenfranchised**: in 23 states more than 10% of African American males cannot vote; in AL and FL the number is above 30%; and in MI, VA, and NM it is about 25% [2003, MM, 6]

More likely to have **your own race vote for you** *if you run for office* [2001, BCGI, 80]

Retirement

Have more than 5 times the **retirement and pension assets**: average value $65,411 (w) vs. $12,247 (A) and $10,206 (L) [2001, UFE, 18]

Less likely to have **retirement income** *under half your current income:* 25.4% (w) vs. 40.0% (A or L) [2001, SWA, 297]

---

* Letters in parentheses signify (w) = white, (A) = African American, (L) = Latino, (n) = native, (API) = Asian/Pacific Islander Year, source, and page number of data are in brackets.

Abbreviations are as follows, with full citations listed in the bibliography: AI= Amnesty International, 1999; AI2=Amnesty International, 2003; APH=American Public Health Association; BC=*Black Commentator*; BCGI=*Breaking the Code of Good Intentions*, Bush; BJS=Bureau of Justice Statistics; BP=BlackPressUSA, Edney; BW=*BusinessWeek*, Bernstein; CEPR=Center for Economic and Policy Research, Schmitt; CL=*ColorLines*, Talvi; COOS=*By the Color of Our Skin*, Steinhorn and Diggs-Brown; EF=Earth First, Schweizer; GDN=*Greater Diversity News*, Curry; HA=*Health Affairs*, Lavizzo-Mourey; HC=*Hidden Cost of Being African American*, Shapiro; LH=Leslie Harris; MM=Manning Marable, "Abolishing American Apartheid, Root and Branch"; *Nation*, Rosner; REEW="Race, Ethnicity, and Economic Well-Being," Finegold and Wherry; SFC=*San Francisco Chronicle*, Adelman; SWA=*State of Working America*, Mishel; TW=Tim Wise, "White Racism in the Present Era"; UFE=United for a Fair Economy, Leondar-Wright, et. al.; UL=Urban League, Ferguson; WIR=*Wealth Inequality Reader*, Collins, et. al.

† Asset poverty results when household wealth (assets minus debts) is insufficient to maintain the family at the poverty line for three months ($4,175 in 1999) when no income is coming in.

Labor market and non-labor market discrimination

As a result of the civil rights movement, discrimination in hiring and pay is now illegal. In a very uneven manner, major institutions have taken action to balance their hiring and promotion practices in a way that is less exclusionary today than, say, fifty years ago. Formal discrimination still occurs, however, and the Equal Employment Opportunities

Commission (EEOC) is responsible for examining charges and enforcing penalties, at least for documented workers with valid Social Security numbers. Under these circumstances, a person of color and a white worker with similar credentials are more likely to be treated with formal equality in hiring and promotion than in years past. Thanks to the civil rights movement, labor market discrimination no longer gives European American workers the same, explicit level of affirmative action advantage at the job site that was the custom for hundreds of years.

But research has shown that more subtle versions of entry-level discrimination are still common. When identical applications carry a name associated with African Americans, like Tamika or Shafik, they are less likely to receive a callback from employers. When actually interviewed, white applicants land the better-paying receptionist job, while people of color tend to be steered to back office clerical positions. Employers tend to rationalize white people's mistakes on qualifying tests and give them a second chance. Also, stereotypes about people of color remain common, which can lead to targeted recruitment in whiter communities. And applicants of color often have to prove their competence up front, while white workers only receive focused attention once they are known to make mistakes.[1] Even if hired in a time of economic upswing as in the late 1990s, once the downturn comes, the impact on quality jobs can be devastating. Dwight Kirk comments: "55% percent (or 166,000) of the union jobs lost in 2004 were held by black workers," and "African American women accounted for 70 percent of the union jobs lost by women in 2004."[2]

Unequal institutional practices also show up as non-labor market discrimination, which the workplace then magnifies. The law says that discrimination in hiring is not allowed, so white supremacy works to exclude people of color from the training required to get hired. The law says that discrimination in promotion is illegal, so internal corporate culture acts to isolate and undermine the career path of oppressed nationality employees.

Emblematic of the gulf between people's life at home and the dominant workplace culture is the commute to work: "Mass transit use tends to be overwhelmingly minority, and when it isn't, whites and blacks either get on at different stops or take bus and subway routes that originate and pass through racially separate neighborhoods." Or when traveling by car: "The commuting story is a common one among blacks, who describe how their drive is fueled by the sounds of jazz, gospel, or urban contemporary music until just a few blocks from work, when they turn down the volume and prepare themselves mentally to face yet another day as the very visible minority in the office."[3]

Differences in the quality of grade schools, high school graduation rates, admissions to leading universities, and incarceration rates all tend to favor white people. Cross-generational wealth holdings and segregated living arrangements contribute to and reinforce these patterns. As a result, African Americans, Latinos and native peoples for the most part do not have to be discriminated against in the personnel offices: they never get in the door. Similarly, the figures on incarceration rates testify to the lack of viable options open to young people of color as they grapple with how to make their way in society. And the military's disproportionate numbers of oppressed nationality volunteers tells the same story. Society fails to provide openings for its young people of color, so they turn to the military as a way to move ahead.*

Racial profiling

In schooling and employment, white people are privileged by not being weighed down by racial stereotypes. White people tend to be viewed as just normal folks. When carried over into law enforcement, stereotyping becomes racial profiling, and once again white people get a pass. Nobody racially profiles white people. Yet white folks for the most part are completely unaware of this privilege of being presumed innocent. In addition, the favoritism continues throughout all levels of the criminal justice system.

Henry Louis Gates, the distinguished Harvard professor, commented on the times he has been stopped by the police for being at the "wrong place at the wrong time" – or more accurately, as a result of racial profiling. His experience fits with the unfunny joke: "What do you call a black Ph.D.?" "A n_____." Similarly, while the O.J. Simpson case showed that wealthy defendants can pay their way out of even the most heinous charges, it also showed that a prominent black person can have evidence manipulated by racist police – just as readily as the ordinary people arrested in Philadelphia and LA during the 1990s whose cases were eventually reversed for the same reason.

Frank H. Wu, a professor at Howard Law School, describes in his book *Yellow* how racial profiling tilts arrest records against black and Latin motorists, as well as against Asian youths labeled as gang members. Wu shows that profiling is a perfect example of a self-fulfilling prophecy. You expect to find criminals among the oppressed nationality population, so you devote disproportionate resources to this area and then make arrests there. Meanwhile criminals in the European American community slip by. The statistics look good and reinforce the discriminatory practice. When backed up by laws that favor white people, the im-

---

* During the Iraq War military recruitment has particularly targeted Latino youth. By contrast, African American enlistment dropped sharply in the years after 2003 compared to the pattern from the Vietnam War onward. By 2006 rates for African Americans were roughly equal to the proportion of black people in U.S. society.

pacts can be dramatic. The courts treat crack users, living mostly in the inner cities, much more harshly than people caught with powdered cocaine, the drug of choice for white suburbanites. Combining this legal distinction with racial profiling has resulted in a pattern where African Americans, while using drugs at just a little over their population rate (14% vs. 12%), are arrested at almost three times this rate. Then they are found guilty and incarcerated at even higher rates – 4½ times and 6¼ times their population rate, respectively.[4]

Unquantifiable benefits of being normal

The statistics listed in the life history above are only the surface evidence of the color line in the United States. Underlying them is the whole texture of daily life. Here, for white people, color is an asset that goes unnoticed. Being white is taken for granted. Yet once you take a look, as Peggy McIntosh encourages white people to do in "Unpacking the Invisible Knapsack," the contributions of racial privilege to white folks' lives appear everywhere. Here are a few examples based on McIntosh's exercise:

Family Wealth – The Unequal Playing Field

Thirteen years ago, my parents sold the house I grew up in. After turning 65, my father wasted no time retiring. He'd purchased our house back in 1952 for $20,000 thanks to a 3 percent mortgage made possible by the Veterans Administration. Now he was considering an offer of $300,000.

Ten years later, my colleague, Cornelius, sold the house he grew up in. Cornelius' folks had also purchased a place in the early '50s in Chester, just outside Philadelphia. A few years ago, after Cornelius' father died, his mother wanted to move back to Virginia. Cornelius sold the house in 2000; he received all of $29,500.

That $270,500 gap reveals a microcosm of race in America. My family is white and Cornelius' is black. Cornelius and I have worked together for 20 years, always making an identical salary, yet my net worth is several times his. My two brothers and I enjoyed good schools, parks and libraries because of rising property values. My parents' growing home equity not only provided for retirement but also sent us to private colleges – and even helped with the down payments on our own homes.

Today, thanks to them, my house is paid off and my 21-year-old daughter is about to graduate college with a nest egg of her own. When my parents pass away, we stand to inherit a tidy sum. Cornelius had no such help.

As American manufacturing declined, Chester became increasingly black and populated by people on fixed incomes, who faced higher taxes to maintain public services and schools. Cornelius' parents' expenses climbed as their city deteriorated. Cornelius attended college on scholarship, but

- Opportunities for housing, financial credit, employment, and public accommodations – which may then be closed due to class, gender or other prejudices, but not because of your race
- Seeing in the media – TV, newspapers, movies – members of your race prominently and predominantly displayed, and often linked to positive accomplishments
- Protecting your children from people who might make them feel bad about themselves
- Sending your children to quality schools where most of the students and teachers tend to look like them
- Having your children taught history throughout the school year in a way that highlights your race's accomplishments
- Being hired and promoted by people of your race
- Being confident that your race won't get in the way of medical and legal services
- Not having your actions credited to or charged against your race

worked his way through school. Today, rather than look to his mother for financial help, Cornelius helps support her.

What's this got to do with race? It goes back to the postwar suburbs and the government policies and subsidies that made them possible – and guaranteed they'd be segregated. A set of New Deal programs led by the Federal Housing Administration allowed millions of average white Americans to own a home for the first time. Down payment requirements were reduced from up to 50 percent to 10 or 20 percent and the time to pay off the remaining mortgage was extended from five years to 30 years. Federal investigators evaluated 239 regions; communities with a mere one or two black families were deemed *ipso facto* financial risks ineligible for low cost home loans. Government appraisal maps colored those communities red – hence the term "redlining."

Between 1932 and 1962, the federal government backed $120 billion of home loans; more than 98 percent went to whites. Barred from purchasing a home in the new suburbs, Cornelius' parents had to buy in one of the few communities where black people could live.

Many whites who grew up middle class in the suburbs like to think we got where we are today on merit – hard work, intelligence, pluck and maybe a little luck. We wonder why non-white parents didn't just work hard, buy a home and pass on the appreciated value like our parents did. We tend to be blind to how the playing field has been – and continues to be – tilted to our advantage.

—from: Adelman, "The Houses that Racism Built"

when you screw up – or do well

- Being able to ignore other people's languages – both inside the United States and outside – and assume others will have to learn yours
- Not thinking twice about going into a store, eating at a restaurant, hailing a cab, trying on clothes before buying them, or driving through rural areas or on the interstate.

International comparisons

The discussion to this point highlights the fact that the average white person in the United States today – the median, working class white person – rides through life on a cushion of racial privilege. That this fact is true does not mean, however, that working class white people's lives are free from exploitation, tension, contradiction and suffering. Rather, *it assures that this outcome is the case.* Privilege distorts people's perceptions. It drives their choices away from uniting along class lines – and toward living in separate neighborhoods, sending children to all-white schools, working as much as possible with and around white people, and hanging out and vacationing with other white people in overwhelmingly white spaces. This tightly woven tapestry of life screens out both the worse-off life conditions of people of color – but also that part of oneself that knows that "an injury to one is an injury to all."

The color line still exists in the United States at the beginning of the 21st Century. Compared to ordinary white people, the life conditions of black, Latino and native peoples are much worse. Yet despite all the white privileges, and in spite of the vast wealth that the U.S. ruling class owns and controls around the world, the average white working class person in the United States does not compare well with workers in other industrialized countries. In the box on the next page you will see how the United States stacks up – and its white people in particular, where the data is available – against the other 14 top industrialized countries in the world.*

---

* Top 15 countries based on Gross Domestic Product (GDP) per person and having a population greater than 5 million: Australia, Austria, Belgium, Canada, Denmark, Finland, France, Germany, Italy, Japan, Netherlands, Sweden, Switzerland, United Kingdom, United States. *OECD2, "GDP per capita"*

Note for box on next page: US/w stands for white people in the United States. Year, source, and page number for the data are in brackets. Source abbreviations, in addition to those listed in the box on p. 241, are: AI2=Amnesty International, 2003; CB=U.S. Census Bureau; CEPR2="Give me a break," Jorgensen; CIA=*World Fact Book*; COE=Council of Europe; DAWN="Global Military Spending," Deen; EI="Canada vs. the OECD," Boyd; HCS="Health Care Systems", Docteur; ILO="Ageing of Labor Force," Auer; OECD="Society at a glance"; UN=UN Office on Drugs and Crime; WA="World Atlas," geographyIQ.com

United States compared to other industrialized countries

(Key to abbreviations in note on previous page)

Mortality

Highest rate of ***infant mortality:*** [2001, WIR, 103 (US/w); 2000, HCS (other 14 countries)]

overall: 6.9 per 1,000 live births (US), running down to a low of 3.2 in Japan

white people: 5.7 per 1,000 live births (US/w) (next highest of 14 countries Britain at 5.6, down to a low of 3.2 in Japan)

Lowest ***life expectancy:*** [2003, APH (US/w); 2004, CIA, WA (other 14 countries)]

overall: 77.1 years, running up to 81.5 in Japan [2001, OECD]

white males: 74.8 years (only Finland has a lower rate; running up to Sweden's 78.12)

white females: 80.0 years (only Denmark has a lower rate; running up to Japan's 84.51)

Working life

Second from top in ***average hours worked*** *by those employed:* 1,815 (US) surpassed only by Australia (1,824) (no data for Austria or Switzerland) [2002, SWA, 415]

Third from top in ***retirement age:*** 63.6 (US) surpassed only by Japan (66.5) and Switzerland (64.6) [1995, ILO]

Worst legally mandated ***paid vacation:*** none (US), and running from a low of 2 weeks in Canada to 30 days in five countries (no data for Australia, Japan, Switzerland) [2000, CEPR2]

Worst ***total leave*** *(vacations and holidays) in manufacturing sector covered by collective bargaining:* average 23 days (US), running up to 45 days in Italy (no data for Australia and Canada) [1999, CEPR2]

Wage inequality

Greatest ***wage inequality*** *among workers:* comparing total earnings of the top 10% of workers to that of the lowest 10% (no data for Denmark) [SWA, 398]

Highest ***poverty rates*** *for:* [2000 (US, at peak of upturn); other countries 1999 and 2000 OECD]

children: 21.7% (next highest Britain at 16.2%, down to a low of 2.4% for Denmark)

elderly: 24.6% (next highest Australia at 23.6%, down to a low of 1.6% for the Netherlands)

total population: 17.1% (next highest Japan at 15.3 %, down to a low of 4.3% for Denmark)

Continued on next page

(United States compared to other industrialized countries, continued)

Tied for 3rd worst ***gender wage gap****:* 75.8 cents on a dollar of male earnings, running up to 89.1 cents for Belgium [SWA, 400]

Greatest ***inequality in family income****:* using two measures, the Gini coefficient and the ratio of total earnings of the top to lowest 10% of families [SWA, 401]

Top 0.1% of families *take in 7.4% of all income earned:* compared to 3.3% in Britain and 2.0% in France – up from lows of 2% or below for all three countries in the 1960s to the 1980s. [1998, SWA, 407]

Social support

Worst ***maternity/child care policies****:* [2004, SWA, 410]

paid maternity leave*:* 0 weeks, matched only by Australia; running up to a high of 52 weeks in Britain (no data for Sweden)

maternity income*:* 0% of regular earnings; running up to a high of 100% in six countries (no data for Sweden or Switzerland)

unpaid maternity/child care leave*:* 12 weeks; running up to a high of 160 weeks in Austria, 156 weeks in Germany, and 144 weeks in France and Finland

Lowest:

coverage by ***public health insurance****:* 25.3% (US), next lowest Netherlands at 75.7 %, all others 99 or 100% [2001, HCS]

"bang for the buck" in ***health*** *spending, measured by* years of life *gained for every percent of GDP going to the health care industry:* 5.5 (US), running up to 11.2 (Finland) [2001, CB; OECD]

pension *payments:* 6.1% of GDP, better only than Canada and Australia, running up to 13.8 (Italy) [2001, OECD]

public ***social spending****, as percentage of Gross Domestic {Product:* 14.8% (US), running up to almost double that amount in Sweden and Denmark [2001, OECD]

Quality of life

Worst in average of 25 ***environmental indicators*** [2001, EI]

Worst ***incarceration rates****:*

overall: over 5 times the rate in Britain per 100,000 population, running up to 15 times the rate in Sweden (no data for Austria or Belgium) [2000, UN, 269-271]

for white people only: about 50% higher than Britain, up to 4.5 times as high as Sweden [2000, UN; 2000, BJS]

Military spending *equal to all the rest of the world combined* [2004, DAWN]

Only ***death penalty*** aside from Japan [2002, AI2]

Only ***juvenile death penalty*** [2001, COE]

The international comparisons in the table on the previous pages describe U.S. society as a place where people work harder and have less time off, die younger, have fewer social supports, live in a worse environment, and feel fearful and insecure as they devote huge resources to imprisoning people and policing the empire. Yet we live in the richest country in the world.

Economic inequality

Part of the reason for the harshness of life in the United States is that the country's wealth is obscenely unequal in its distribution between the very small owning class and the rest of us. The *Wealth Inequality Reader* reports that the top 1% of households in 2003 owned 32.7% of all household wealth, and the top 5% together owned more than the other 95% of the people combined. The number of billionaires more than doubled between 1992 and 2002 (from 92 to 205), and the number of people owning $10 million or more in assets went up 8 times. Meanwhile more than a quarter of the people in 2002 had a net worth (assets minus debts) of less than $5,000. Similar sharp contrasts exist around stock ownership.

Along with wealth holdings comes a controlling interest in corporations, domination of the government, a network of private schools, clubs and vacation homes – all of which together, as William Domhoff classically described in *Who Rules America?*, make up a close network of ruling class institutions. This systematic, entrenched, gross inequality typifies U.S. capitalist society at the start of the 21st Century. And we have not even mentioned here the billions of people around the world – a world dominated by the United States – who survive on just dollars a day. Making all this inequality and suffering possible, as demonstrated throughout this book, is the system of racial preferences inside the United States. It prevents people's uniting to take control of U.S. society and then running it by and for the vast majority – the working class with its various races and nationalities, along with allies from other classes.

We have sketched in above the material reality of white privilege. Pointing out these facts does not suggest that all white people are racist, or that on average they are. As Ohio State University Professor John Powell comments, "The slick thing about whiteness is that whites are getting the spoils of a racist system without themselves being personally racist."[5] But we have also suggested that there is a price paid in social outcomes in comparison to other large industrial countries – for people of color especially, but also for white working people. White privilege is a curse on all working people – but to get rid of it, white people will first have to recognize that it exists.

Chapter 17

White Consciousness

Many white people will not agree with the description of white privileges outlined in Chapter 16. When polled, European Americans tend to feel the problem of racial inequality has mostly been solved as a result of the civil rights movement. Compared to the reality of privilege outlined on pages 236-241, a study in 2001 showed that 61% of white people believe black people have "equal or better access to healthcare," 49% believe there are "similar levels of education" across the races, and 42% believe there are "similar earnings."[1] Along the same lines, a 2003 national poll found that "40 to 60 percent of all whites say that the average black American fares equally or better in terms of jobs, incomes, schooling, and healthcare than the average white person."[2]

Maria Krysan and Amanda Lewis in "Racial Discrimination is Alive and Well" further describe white folks' understanding: "A Gallup poll found that 79 percent of whites believed that blacks had as good a chance as whites in their community at securing employment. A poll done by the Kaiser Family Foundation in 1997 found that ...more whites than in the past believe there is very little racial discrimination and that blacks have as good a chance as whites of succeeding today." By comparison, large percentages of black people disagree on each count. As one person of African descent commented, "White people don't have a clue as to what's going on. And a lot black people out there too – they're just angry."[3]

Krysan and Lewis, as well as Howard Winant in "Racial Dualism at Century's End," stress the contradictory character of white people's consciousness. On the positive side, most white people believe all children should be able to go to the same schools. The majority sees no inborn differences between the races, they view segregation as wrong, and feel racial equality is the right policy. At the same time, many white people believe that black people are lazy, prefer to be on welfare, and tend toward violence. White people agree that there should not be discrimination in hiring or in the real estate market. Yet they tend to discount evidence or complaints of discrimination and choose to live in segregated communities. Many white youth internalize aspects of African American and Latin culture – high-fiving, dress and dance styles, street phrases (What up?, Bro', joint) – and together with their parents accept and even at times support people of color in visible social roles. At the same time, the political right manipulates white people's contradictory consciousness by using code words like "welfare," "illegal aliens," and "gang violence" – to tap their racist side. The result is the continued ascendancy of white power – and this is true even where faces of color may appear in more prominent roles.

Winant surveys some of the competing trends in today's political culture. There are flashbacks to earlier periods of history in today's extreme right and their vulgar defense of white supremacy: the Klan marching against immigrants, or white supremacist militias training for a future race war. Racism based on bad science keeps cropping up as well – through the incorrect use of IQ and other biased statistics. In an attempt to appear more moderate, racists also package their message as a populist appeal to equality, reverse discrimination, and the defense of white rights.

The dominant form of racial reaction, however, has depended on a reinterpretation of the 1960s experience. This appeal upholds formal equality and the myth of a colorblind society. Under this guise, neoconservatives have rolled back affirmative action, redefined the phrase *special interests* to target people at the grassroots in place of corporate entitlements, and promoted individual over collective advancement. Winant sums up: "Thus from the late 1960s on, white identity has been reinterpreted, rearticulated in a dualistic fashion: on the one hand egalitarian, on the other hand privileged; on the one hand individualistic and 'colorblind,' on the other hand 'normalized' and white.…Yet a refusal to engage in 'race-thinking' amounts to a defense of the racial status quo, in which systematic racial inequality and yes, discrimination as well, are omnipresent."[4]

The consequences of white privilege in politics came through again in the 2004 reelection of George W. Bush. One African American woman organizer wrote: "Many…white progressives…can't see that the fundamental issues of racism and white privilege are at the core of middle Amerikkka's identification with the Bush white male patriarchal swagger."[5]

The role of the media

Advertisers and the media project images of multiracial unity when there's a multiracial audience, as with football, for example. But aside from sports, shows with diverse casts still feature people of color in subordinate roles – as with *Cold Case*, and the *CSI* and *Law and Order* shows. The overlap between white and black favorites has been increasing, although a Nielsen report in March 2005 had six of black audiences' top ten shows – like *Half and Half, Girlfriends*, and *Cuts* – not appearing on the white viewers' list. Meanwhile Latino, Asian and native roles remain scattered at best, and usually locked into stereotypical characters. The media's practices can to some extent popularize cross-racial images and associate positive roles with people of color. But they come up short as a reflection of social reality. The effect is to reinforce both sides of white folks' contradictory perspective: the appearance of equality – even though white male actors continue to dominate the leading roles – and, at the same time, a violent undercurrent associated with black and Latino street culture.

Melanie Bush, in *Breaking the Code of Good Intentions*, highlights six ways that the media support the continuing reality of racial inequality in everyday life:

- The images and lifestyles projected as applying to everyone actually reflect a white experience.
- The stress on interpersonal relations focuses attention on individuals and not on the institutions that structure inequality.
- Stories of people of color who have "made it," as well as images of interracial friendships, tend to deny the continuing existence of racial inequality.
- Not reflecting the reality of racial inequality undermines people's ability to analyze the structural patterns of institutional racism.
- Who is included and excluded from representation, and how they are portrayed, conveys a sense of who is really "American."
- Stories and themes suggest that there is no need to take collective action to correct systemic inequality.

These points reflect primarily the role of the so-called liberal media. At the same time, the syndicated call-in talk shows and their hosts are more direct – targeting crime, welfare, single mothers, and hip-hop culture for particular, color-coded abuse. By and large there is little cultural crossover – especially by white people. People still tend to watch different TV shows, and white folks seldom go to movies that open a window into black life. Meanwhile movies that really reflect Latino, Asian or native communities in the United States are rare to non-existent. Yet there are enough TV shows, supporting actors, sidekicks, and headliners in "colorblind" roles to keep the illusion going that segregation is a thing of the past. Reality is something else entirely: "No longer are there separate water fountains for blacks and whites. But in their place are the separate water coolers that we stand around while we discuss the different shows we saw on television the night before."[6]

Segregation and white bonding

An important reason for white people's blindspot about other races is the almost entirely white worlds people live in. People of color usually appear in controlled and predictable ways – the landscapers, the people behind the counter, the maintenance crew, the co-workers who blend in or keep to themselves. In the mid 1990s Andrew Hatcher described this situation in his *Two Nations: Black and White, Separate, Hostile and Unequal,* followed a few years later by Leonard Steinhorn and Barbara Diggs-Brown's *By the Color of Our Skin: The Illusion of Integration and the Reality of Race.* Both books make clear the need to take a hard look at social reality in the United States – and separate it out from the media images and self-justifications that fill peoples' heads.

Steinhorn and Diggs-Brown describe everyday life with subheads that read "Living, Learning, Working Apart" and "Praying, Playing, Entertaining Apart." They discuss "How the Integration of the Mass Media Undermines Integration." There are the racial stereotypes – "Noble Negro, Angry Black, Urban Outlaw" – and the yearly rituals repeating "I Have a Dream" and presenting "Black History" as if it is not at the heart of U.S. history. These authors see white fear and black rage as the driving forces behind modern segregation. And what often appears to be a model of diversity can, in fact, be something very different. For example, at the workplace, "because blacks and whites who work together must depend on each other to make a product or finalize a sale, rarely is overt racial tension tolerated. Interaction uncommon outside work happens regularly here. But just as with mixed neighborhoods and schools, there is much less integration at work than meets the eye, for it is in the workplace that we most confuse racial intersection with racial integration. Nowhere is the integration illusion more at work than at work." And even there the intersection is limited: One study showed that 90% of the supervisors and managers in their sample had no black co-workers with comparable duties. For all workers, the study found that 60% worked in completely segregated workplaces, and another 30% were almost completely segregated.

The flipside of the surface familiarity and guarded speech in mixed settings is the white bonding that Tim Wise talks about in *White Like Me.* At a bar after work or on the weekend, in conversations with friends over coffee or at the union hall, someone makes a comment, uses the n-word, or tells a joke. No one has to say anything, but everyone knows that what just happened was a white thing. It cements the unity of the group – and confirms its voluntary, conscious separation from people of color. And at the same time this white bonding reinforces the whole structure of separation that feeds white people's fears – and maintains the system of racial privileges in place.

A deeper form of bonding takes place in white families. Here the whole family culture can rest on mostly unspoken assumptions about who the neighbors are or should be, who goes to the neighborhood school, who plays what sports, who attends which church and, finally, who dates whom. It does not take much to rock this world – a family of color moving into a suburban town, for example, or into the next city block. The depth of the common assumptions makes the pressures to conform intense – within and across families and among young people growing up in the same neighborhood. Challenging these assumptions can be very threatening. In some respects things haven't changed much since Lillian Smith quoted this letter from a missionary friend from the South written in 1947:

> I wanted to stay in the South and help rid it of lynching and segregation. That is what I really wanted to do. But there was Mother…you know how disgraced she would have felt had I stayed and helped here. She would have died if she had seen me eating with a Negro…But she is proud of me now, going to Africa as a missionary…And the president of the U[nited] D[aughters] of the C[onfederacy] in our town is giving me a party next week; she's proud of me too. I am the only one ashamed…I don't think I'm afraid for myself…it's Mother. I love her; I can't hurt her. How do you learn to hurt the people you love, even when you know they're wrong, for something you know is right? That is so hard.[7]

In white people's segregated communities, the overall illusion of normalcy can go on for decades. Nonetheless, reality has a way of breaking in. Sons and daughters go off to war. Plants close down and the workers are either unorganized or too divided to mount a fight. Children turn to drugs, suicide – suicide rates run double those for black youth, but trail rates for native peoples – or shooting up their schools. While apparently unrelated to race, the knowing wink among white friends that sustains a racist fantasy world, raises questions about the community's ability to handle its internal contradictions. Failure to address racial tensions gets carried over into class, gender, and cultural antagonisms that divide the community. These suppressed contradictions, given the surface illusion of racial unity, then erupt into violence from time to time. The fortress mindset also fits neatly into the demands of empire. Conformity, together with a fear of terrorists identified with immigrants of color, help bring white youths into the U.S. military – not to mention the Border Patrol and their vigilante supporters.

International blind spot

The white blindspot has a close relation to white people's international blindspot, when it comes to understanding what it means to be an "American"* and the role of the United States in the world today. Melanie Bush discusses the opinions of students she interviewed at Brooklyn College, a part of the City University of New York. Her students were both native born of all races and immigrants from around the world. Some of her findings are:

- 58% believe that "the United States can't be multicultural and American at the same time." Another 21% were uncertain. In other words there is a sense that you have to give up your ethnic heritage to become fully an "American."
- The experience of immigrating to the United States is racialized. European immigrants are more than twice as likely to feel themselves to be American (29.3%) compared to foreign-born black people (12.7%). This experience goes along with Toni Morrison's observation: "Deep within the word 'American' is its association with race. To identify someone as a South African is to say very little; we need the adjective 'white' or 'black' or 'colored' to make our meaning clear. In this country it is quite the reverse. American means white."[8]
- White native-born students tend to expect various privileges as part of their heritage. These include 1) material benefits from living in the "homeland of the world elite," as well as 2) a psychological boost from feeling that "we are the 'best.'" In line with this perspective is Eric Hobsbawm's comment that the United States "has no collective identity except as the best, the greatest country, superior to all others and the acknowledged model for the world."[9]
- When white students experience economic hardships, there is a tendency to see themselves as victims compared to other groups of people. For example, one student who had trouble getting enough financial aid blamed scholarships given to people of color. This sense of victimization is a theme running through U.S. history: "Most whites consider themselves to be, somehow, victims of African Americans, just as they feel set upon and victimized for no good reason by dark Islamic forces in the world, and for the same

---

* Throughout this book we have avoided using the term *American* to refer to a citizen of the United States, since rightfully this word applies to anyone living in North, South, or Central America. The Spanish language, in contrast to English, uses the term *estadounidense* – basically "United-Statesian" – to describe a U.S. citizen.

reasons that they constructed a national mythology of victimization at the hands of 'savage' Indians."[10] Bush quotes a firefighter after the events of 9/11/2001: "We in the United States take care of everyone all over the world and this is what we get?"[*]

- The American Dream is a powerful image. It centers on freedom and opportunity achieved through hard work – and failure rests with the individual for not measuring up. Only 11.4% of Bush's students fully disagreed with the statement: "The American Dream can be achieved by anyone who works hard." By contrast, those who resist this dominant perspective tend to be viewed as anti-U.S. and ungrateful. The implication also is that one should not focus too much on past history – particularly on events that reflect negatively on how the United States rose to world supremacy.

Psychological wage

It is true that many white people live in poor housing, depend on welfare, and feel alienated from the world pictured on TV. But through it all, in the United States European Americans remain white. They speak English and can dream of succeeding in the way the movies, TV and magazines picture the possibilities. White folks can hang out in settings where no person of color would feel comfortable and feel that this space is normal – not related to race in any way.

European Americans can get a job where more often than not the boss or supervisor is the same color as they are. Most people have a leg up on positions by virtue of their network of friends and family, or because of the broader community they belong to. There is a certain psychological security associated with having these informal structures of support. And if there happen to be co-workers or even a supervisor who is of a different race, white workers will often console themselves that the person only got his or her job because of affirmative action.

W.E.B. DuBois referred to this aspect of privilege, available to even the worst-off white person, as a "psychological wage."[†] The sense of su-

---

[*] In fact, U.S. aid trails that of all other top industrial countries. *(See footnote on p. 246 for the list of countries.)* For the United States, Official Development Assistance (ODA) as a percentage of Gross National Income (GNI) is the *lowest* of the 15 industrial countries used for comparison in this chapter. In 2003 the U.S. ODA/GNI came in at 0.15%, while the highest country in the group was Denmark with 0.84%. *(Globalis-Indicator)*

[†] "It must be remembered that the white group of laborers, while they received a low wage, were compensated in part by a sort of public and psychological wage. They were given public deference and titles of courtesy…[and] admitted freely with all classes of white people to public functions, public parks, and the best schools. The police were drawn from their ranks, and the courts, dependent upon their votes, treated them with such lenience as

periority is an illusion born of hardship, alienating people from reality while making that reality bearable. It also alienates people from their class brothers and sisters. In place of struggling in solidarity with others, "the drug of white supremacy," as Lillian Smith called it, substitutes empty dreams and prideful individualism. Smith commented half a century ago: "Nobody could take away from you this whiteness that made you and your way of life 'superior.' They could take your house, your job, your fun; they could steal your wages, keep you from acquiring knowledge; they could tax your vote or cheat you out of it; they could by arousing your anxieties make you impotent; but they could not strip your white skin off of you. It became the poor white's most precious possession, a 'charm' staving off utter dissolution. And in devious, perverse ways it helped maintain his sanity in an insane world, compensating him – as did his church's promise of heaven – for so many spiritual bruises and material deprivations."[11]

For men, the investment in the fantasy of superiority can carry over and be reinforced in domestic relations, resulting in a domineering and abusive attitude toward one's wife and children. Racism and women's oppression have always been closely connected. When the reality does not measure up to the dream, others can be blamed – the nagging wife, people of color, gay people, or foreigners and the government that supposedly makes things easy for everyone else. It is a potent delusion.

Economically comfortable white people do not have to work very hard to maintain a sense of superiority – and more likely than not, will deny that they are privileged. The illusion is that their experience is neutral. White people live a normal life, while failure to live up to the norm is deviant – and that deviance is responsible for all the negative experiences in the lives of people of color and poor people. White people work hard, struggle with the contradictions of family and work life, and have no consciousness that their relatively comfortable existence is tightly linked to the oppression that exists in the nearby city, across the tracks, down by the river, or across borders and oceans. Public institutions – the schools, trash collection and other services – for the most part work the way they are supposed to, and the police are seen as friends. If something needs improving, you know whom to call, or you can bring it up at the next PTA meeting. And while there may be some presence of people of color in the area, comments usually range from 1) "they pretty much keep to themselves," to 2) "they're just like us," or 3) "isn't a shame…." In

---

to encourage lawlessness. Their vote selected public officials…[which] had great effect upon their personal treatment and the deference shown them. White schoolhouses were the best in the community…[and] newspapers specialized on news that flattered the poor whites and almost utterly ignored the Negro except in crime and ridicule." *(DuBois,* Black Reconstruction, *pp. 700-701)*

Lillian Smith (1897-1966)

Lillian Smith was one of the first prominent white southerners to denounce racial segregation openly and to work actively against the entrenched and often brutally enforced world of Jim Crow. From as early as the 1930s, she argued that Jim Crow was evil ("Segregation is spiritual lynching," she said) and that it leads to social moral retardation.

Lillian Eugenia Smith was born into a large, respectable, prosperous family in Jasper, Florida, on December 12, 1897. When the family business collapsed in 1915, her family moved to their cottage in Clayton, Georgia, and started Laurel Falls Girls Camp. Smith studied at Piedmont College in Demorest (1915-16) and then left to help run the family camp. Pursuing her great love of music, she also did two stints at the Peabody Conservatory in Baltimore, Maryland (1917, 1919). In 1922 she went to China to offer musical instruction at a Methodist missionary school. When her parents' health began to fail in 1925, Smith came home and eventually took over the running of the camp, which in time she converted into a place for serious discussion of social issues. Her longtime partner, Paula Snelling, a school counselor, assisted her.

Smith gained national recognition – and regional denunciation – by writing *Strange Fruit* (1944), a bold novel of illicit interracial love. Five years later she hurled another thunderbolt against racism in *Killers of the Dream (1949)*, a brilliant psychological and autobiographical work warning that segregation corrupted the soul; removed any possibility of freedom and decency in the South; and had serious implications for women and children in particular in their developing views of sex, their bodies, and their innermost selves.

From her home in Clayton, atop Old Screamer Mountain, Smith openly convened interracial meetings; and she toured the South, talking to people from all races and classes. She was unsparing in her criticisms of "liberals" and "moderates" and refused to join groups such as the Southern Regional Council until they could oppose segregation as well as racism. In her own psyche Smith struggled with intensely conflicting desires: to write creatively, following her heart's passions, or to respond to her stern conscience and the intellectual voice of duty.

Smith greeted the historic 1954 Supreme Court decision outlawing school segregation as "every child's Magna Charta." The following year she wrote *Now Is the Time*, a tract appealing for compliance with the high court's decision. Her other writings were diverse – from *The Journey* (1954), a book on her ordeal with breast cancer, to *One Hour* (1959), an attack on McCarthyism thinly disguised as a novel.

Smith battled cancer from the early 1950s until her death in 1966, but to the end she remained devoted to her dream of a South liberated from the "ghosts" of southern traditions. Her last published work was *Our Faces, Our Words* (1964), which applauded nonviolence in the civil rights movement.

—from: Clayton, "Lillian Smith"

any case, there is little or no community of interest based on mutual understanding and respect.

The presence of a psychological wage often goes unnoticed – though it can pop up in sayings like the young male mantra, "I'm free, white and 21!" – but its loss can have serious repercussions. With white men's wages trending downward, as they have over the past couple decades, people's responses to job loss can angrily target people of color. This anger helps feed the allegiance of white working class men to the anti-labor policies of the Republican Party and their center-right Democratic Party allies. The Republican's "Southern Strategy" aligns the party tacitly, if not openly, with the most backward elements in the South – the Thurmonds, Lotts, and DeLays. Its racial content is clear and speaks loudly to white workers who hold tightly to their whiteness. While psychological wages bind workers to their oppressors, their real wages continue to move downward as a result of ruling class investment, tax, and anti-labor policies.

Chapter 18

Holding On, Breaking Free

White consciousness, with all its self-justifying illusions, helps perpetuate the system of racial preferences. Racial and international blindspots, white bonding, media images of a fantasy world, and psychological gratifications – all work to reproduce a very real world of segregated and unequal lives. By being satisfied with an imaginary world, white working class people close off all possibility of building a world that can really meet their needs – through struggling together with and alongside workers of color. When it comes to white consciousness, people really face a clear choice: either hold onto it tightly or break free.

Fortunately, there is some good news in this review of white consciousness – some hopeful aspects that can be built on as we seek a way out of the thicket of racial antagonism that characterizes U.S. culture. First there is the relatively large minority of white people in the various surveys who recognize that white people actually are better off than people of color. Second, there is the contradictory character of white consciousness itself. People's conflicted understanding provides an opening that is much closer to the surface now than in the years prior to the civil rights movement.

When confronted with the evidence of white privilege, white people tend to react in a variety of ways. Having a sense of the process that people go through in coming to terms with their whiteness can help organizers deal with these various reactions in a rational and supportive way. It is surprising how much the process parallels what people go through in confronting the prospect of imminent death. In this case it is the death of the white self that people must deal with.

There are five recognized stages in dealing with the likelihood of death: denial, anger, bargaining, depression, and acceptance. Here we should emphasize that the goal of *acceptance,* as is the case also with physical death, "is NOT doing nothing, defeat, resignation or submission. Acceptance IS coming to terms with reality."[1] Analyzing the death of white consciousness is not an exact analogy, but it provides a way to organize white people's responses – to see the positive potential at each stage, as well as the danger of getting stuck at any point along the way.

Denial

Denial of white privilege is the most common response and shows up in a variety of ways:

- "I'm not a racist" – *which may well be true, but it is beside the point*
- "My family hasn't oppressed anyone. We've worked hard for everything we've got and we're proud we did it on our own."
- "Look at the Jones down the street. They're black and they're better off than we are."
- "That used to be true, but now the problem is 'reverse discrimination.' Unqualified people [of color] get all kinds of preferential treatment these days compared to white folks."
- "Who are you to suggest I'm privileged? I sure don't feel privileged!"
- "That's just some liberal [left, communist, PC] crap. You must not be listening to Rush [Limbaugh] or watching Fox News."
- "This is just some white guilt. Get over it."
- "There was a lot of hatred of white people there" – *heard after a meeting that mentioned white privileges*
- "There aren't any people of color where we live, so we don't have any racial problems."
- "We've fought for our way of life in Iraq [Vietnam, Korea, Panama, Grenada...]. Freedom [i.e. privilege] isn't free." – *which is true: there is a cost, but folks have been fighting on the wrong front*
- "It's really a question of class. Once the working class takes power, all these issues will disappear."
- "I'm on it. I know the history. I have good friends who are black [my husband/wife is Latino/a or Asian, we've adopted a black child, or I've written a book on white privilege]. Everything is cool."

Sometimes the denial is less direct. Here people acknowledge that there is a gap – they see the differences but point their finger at other people. In this way white people retain their sense of being normal, rather than privileged:

- "It's their own fault that they can't make it. They're not willing to work hard" – *blaming the victim*
- "Welfare mothers keep having babies with different fathers" – *citing usually second- or third-hand examples of others' deviance*
- "The solution is education" – *which is at least partially true with respect to white people, but here reflects a sense of distance from people of color.*

As is suggested by these examples, the ways people express their denial can vary – from flat-out rejection, to rationalization, personal attack, resentment, ridicule, labeling, or haughty one-upsmanship. Whatever the packaging, the common feature is an unwillingness to confront social reality – not necessarily their particular corner of it, but the whole picture.*

Why not calmly talk things out instead? Rather than trying to appear aware, why not be open to some new information? Unfortunately, the fact is that white privilege is a bedrock feature of our culture and of people's psyches – and has been for 300 years. It gets inside people and

---

* Some people have argued that the white mountain people of Southern Appalachia have not received white privileges. One way to think through this position is to review the following checklist: 1) *Land* – how did people historically get their land? 2) *The vote* – weren't Appalachian men enfranchised as part of the Jacksonian Democracy? 3) *Relation to slavery* – weren't there slave owners as well as poor white people in the mountains? *(See Dunaway,* Slavery in the American Mountain South.) Were the mountains a safe refuge for run-away slaves? 4) *Culture* – did the mountain folk reject Indian fighter imagery and racist minstrelry? 5) *Reconstruction* – were people in the mountain states supporters of Reconstruction? 6) *Descendants* – were the Scots-Irish who migrated from Appalachia to Oklahoma, and from there to California, particularly known for their anti-racist outlook? *(See Dunbar-Ortiz, "One or Two Things I Know about Us.")*

On each count, the facts do not support the view that Southern Appalachian people have not benefited from white privilege. It is true that there were stations on the underground railroad and an abolitionist current in the region – as was the case, for example, in North Carolina as well. And the mountain people tended to break with the South during the Civil War, which was no small thing. But Free Soil Oregon also opposed slavery – while banning black people from the state. *Living separate, basically segregated lives, does not demonstrate a lack of privilege.* Poverty, brutal exploitation by mine companies and absentee landowners, a powerful history of struggle, including armed resistance to the coal operators, a distinctive culture derived in part from African roots – these together do not remove people from the racial contradictions of the dominant society. Rather, as discussed in Chapter 10, these larger social divisions *make possible* the deepened class oppression of all workers.

Many European immigrants have gone through a period of dehumanization and harsh exploitation on the way to becoming accepted as white people. Yet white working class people in the United States today still suffer from class oppression. The key question then is, are white people willing to turn their privileges around – instead of denying them – and proactively join with others in taking on the system of white patriarchal capitalism?

shapes their understanding of the world, of other people, and themselves. As Steinhorn and Diggs-Brown comment: people "are not making... choices consciously because of race...They are merely accommodating their lives to a culture influenced and in many ways determined by race." It is easy to get stuck at the level of denial. In fact, that is just where the majority of white people can be found – reinforced by separate lives, white bonding, and a media that hides more than it clarifies.

Anger

Anger can occur when the message is actually starting to break through the defenses. In that sense it can be positive, especially if met with a calm response that sticks to the facts. Defensiveness is a lower level form of this response. A person's voice can take on an edge as s/he inquires into the particulars or the implications of white privilege in their own lives. It is a warning that basic beliefs are being challenged. Or it can be a reaction to a perceived attack:

- "Are you saying I'm privileged and that I'm a bad person?"
- "What are you really saying – that I'm a racist?"
- "Privilege, OK. But you're suggesting I'm somehow responsible for this situation?"
- "What exactly is it that you're implying I should be doing about all this?"

If the conversation can get through the defensiveness to this last question, then the door is open to a potentially fruitful exchange. In any case, one message of this book is that confronting the fact of one's privilege is not a question of blame or moral failing. The issue is systemic – people are born and raised into this condition. The structure of society and the way it operates constantly reinforce the apparent naturalness of segregated lives and the illusions that sustain them. It can be frightening to call all this, the very fabric of one's life, into question – what you learned in school, what you have picked up from your family and friends, your everyday sources of information, the patterns of daily life in your community and at work, all the structures of understanding that up to this point helped you make sense of an otherwise pretty crazy world.

Fortunately, what most white people have going for them is the positive side of their contradictory consciousness. Despite everything, people also pretty much share a value system that opposes racism and recognizes the basic humanity of people of other races. It can still be a terrifying prospect to challenge the established social order where you live. But at least there is a basis for constructing a new outlook on the world: one grounded on people's shared humanity, on the shared experience of capitalist oppression – even if only in the upside-down form of white privilege – and on the natural desire to join forces against a common threat. And the system of racial preferences is just such a threat – for white people as well as for people of color.

Anger, then, can actually be a positive sign that a person's defenses are being challenged. It can also signal, however, a white consciousness aroused in response to difficult times – with the anger displaced onto people of color, immigrants, liberals or leftists, or gay people. Here is denial with a vengeance, and with challenges to white manhood often mixed in. Direct loss of white privileges can also be a factor – when people find themselves living or working side by side with people of color. The sense of shame that can accompany this loss feeds white violence and the hate groups that thrive on it.

Bargaining

Bargaining is the stage where a person accepts the reality of whiteness but seeks to neutralize its significance. Here, the response probably starts with "All you're saying is true" and then continues:

- "...and that's why we donate to the NAACP." Or, to use one of Tim Wise's examples: that's why he struggled during the 1980s to end apartheid in South Africa.[2]
- "...but there are parts of town [restaurants, stores, and so on] that I can't go into either, because they're Latino [black, native] and I'm not welcome."
- "...but when I talk to people of color about these questions, they act like they don't want to hear it."
- "...but there's nothing I can really do about it."
- "...and now I suppose you want us to sell everything we have and give to the poor."

Unlike actual dying, which at some point is unavoidable for everyone, the death of whiteness can be delayed indefinitely. You can bargain forever – recognizing the existence of privilege on the one hand, yet looking for the best deal to do something about it on the other; giving up something here, but holding on to it over there.

Depression

Depression, including deep feelings of guilt, can result when a person finally takes in the whole picture and sees where they fit in. All of a sudden people realize that during their whole life they have been part of a system that oppresses people of color, even though they may have done nothing personally to offend or suppress anyone. Just by having white skin, you benefit, whether you like it or not. It can be an overwhelming experience. It can leave a person with a sense of helplessness, even despair. All of life's training up to that point has left you unprepared for this new reality, and for many people it is not clear what to do about it.

The positive aspect of this new sense of vulnerability is that it can open people up to a whole new world of possibilities. By realizing for the first time all there is to learn, one can begin to listen better, be more modest in working with others, and take initiative to fill in all the new-found gaps in understanding. The negative side is that one can become paralyzed, withdraw from efforts to bridge the color line, and retreat into a kind of privileged cocoon. This course of action, as with the three previous steps, can lead to a dead-end:

- "This society's racial problems are really terrible. But they're just too much for me to deal with."
- "I'm going to provide for [take care of] my family and leave these social problems for other people who know better what to do about them."

Another response to being overwhelmed by the reality of white supremacy is to deny one's whiteness altogether and take on the ways of a person of color – "go native," as the saying goes. The positive thing here is that in taking this route, people can begin to learn something about the culture they submerge themselves into. Sometimes the lessons can be painful, however, as people come up against a reality that differs from their media-conditioned images. The negative side of taking this path is that suppression of one's white identity is not the same as the death of white consciousness. It only buries it. To move past whiteness, to preside over the death of the white self, one must fully accept its reality.

Acceptance

Acceptance means coming to terms with one's privileged status – and then turning that privilege around, directing it toward ending the system of racial preferences. Only in this way is it possible for white people in the United States to finally be rid of their white selves. European Americans cannot escape the reality of their white skin – and all that it entails. But skin color does not determine consciousness – as the heroic example of John Brown showed 150 years ago. Under conditions today that are much more favorable than in Brown's time, white people have a clear choice to break free of white consciousness. Rather than being stuck with their denial, anger, equivocation, and guilt, white people can accept who they are and commit to ending the system that has chained them to their privileges.

Just how to go about taking up this struggle is the subject of Chapters 24 to 27. But first, in Chapters 19 -20, we want to look at the times in history when white people have allied themselves with the struggles of people of color. The goal is to draw lessons that can help build a united fight against the system of white privileges today. Then in Chapters 21-23 we look at current alignments among people of color, with similar goals in mind. White people cannot hope to end white supremacy on their own, as individuals, no matter how sharp their personal break with white consciousness. Understanding how to link one's personal transformation to the organized social forces capable of transforming the whole system is a key strategic question. The final section of the book then provides specific suggestions to help people put these strategic insights into practice.

Outside His Whiteness

I told this guy that he should
step outside his whiteness.
            And he did.
But he felt odd at first.

Everything began to look
      strangely different.
Truths suddenly became lies.
The rich got richer,
      the poor got poorer,
            there was no justice.

Wow! He exclaimed.
Everything is clearer now!
He began shouting with excitement.
Everything was blurred before!
      I couldn't tell right from wrong.
            I felt no compassion for people
            who cried about oppression.
Now my heart hurts for
all people who suffer.

Oh my god! he shouted.
All of this clarity is
making my head spin.
It's giving me a headache!
I just realized that Black
people were enslaved!
And Indians were nearly annihilated!
Mexicans were forced off their lands!
Did you know that they
made laws against Chinese?
Japanese were locked up for
Being Japanese!

Wow! He shouted again.
He then open-handedly
grabbed his temples
      and squeezed his head
            tightly, as if it were
                  preparing to explode.
I stared at him,
not knowing what to do.

Then his eyes turned up
into his head, showing only
      the whites of his eyes.
Then he fell back into
      his whiteness.
I asked if he was okay,
to which he unfortunately
responded, Oh yeah
      I'm back to normal again.

—Joe Navarro

VI

WHITE ALLIES – SOLIDARITY AND BETRAYAL

There is a huge weight of accumulated baggage burdening U.S. society. But there is also a reserve of strength people can draw on to shed that weight and stand up together as freely associating communities – in whatever form that may take. The main source of strength is the democratic sentiments of the oppressed nationality peoples. Class, color, nationality and gender contradictions crisscross this broad front, and money flows to support rising elements within it – business people and politicians, conservative columnists, academics, and preachers. The color line becomes blurred as a Condoleeza Rice or an Alberto Gonzales moves within the white power structure – as well as through intermarriage and the potential assimilation of national groups outside the black/white color axis. Contradictions between Latinos, African Americans, and Asians in LA, or between Lumbee Indians and black youth in North Carolina's Robeson County also tear at the potential alliance of oppressed nationalities. Gang violence and drugs, at times with the complicity of the police, can also take their divisive toll, as rage turns inward.

Progressive forces within communities of color are struggling to overcome these contradictions and redirect people's anger at the white supremacist system. Once a movement gets rolling, many of the more middle forces will likely start to see things more clearly and join in the struggle – as happened during the Civil War and, to a lesser extent, in the 1960s. Allowing for the small percentage of people who never will break with the system, the oppressed nationality core of the united front opposing white supremacy potentially represents some 25 to 30% of the U.S. population.* A truly broad movement against white supremacy will, therefore, also require a significant number of white people to be reliable allies in the struggle – with a much larger number being at least pas-

---

* In July 2005 the U.S. population included Latino/Hispanic, 14.4%; African American, 12.8%; Asian, 4.5%; indigenous, 1.0%; and two or more races, 1.5% – for a total of 34.2%. The value for "White alone, not Hispanic" was 66.9%. *(U.S. Census Bureau, "Selected Age Groups for the Population by Race and Hispanic Origin")*

sively open to change, or not working actively against it. White activists' primary responsibility is to build this sector of the united front – showing independence and initiative, while orienting to the overall leadership of the oppressed nationality forces in the front.

History shows, however, that when white people are in alliance with oppressed nationality peoples, they tend to go only so far, and no farther. *So far* here refers to the point where white people feel their own particular concerns have been met – and anything more would threaten some reserve of white privilege. End slavery? – OK, but not full social equality. Organize a union? – OK, but not affirmative action to equalize seniority rights. A country of immigrants? – maybe, but not language equality. Voting rights? – OK, but not for ex-felons. As a result, there are two key elements to the task of winning a sector of white people to the struggle:

- white people must understand that destroying white supremacy is in their own personal interest, so that they do not stop half way;
- leadership needs to be centered among people of color, so that the movement remains firmly oriented to its goals.

In Chapter 19 we look at the historical record when white folks fought side by side with oppressed nationality peoples. The objective here is to understand the conditions that favor unity across the color line. Then in Chapter 20 we take a more personal approach to understanding the circumstances that contribute to individual white people becoming firm allies in the struggle, as well as freedom fighters in their own right.

Chapter 19

The Historical Record

As we have seen in earlier chapters, racial privileges repeatedly undercut alliances that formed between European Americans and oppressed nationality peoples. When united struggles developed, they often occurred out of necessity – white leaders looking for additional support when they found themselves in difficult circumstances. The dropping away of one-time white allies is also a common theme. Fortunately, however, there are many examples of principled solidarity in history that today's activists can build on.

Highlights from the period before 1900*

New York slave conspiracy of 1741

In New York City during 1741, a series of fires and robberies led to a State Supreme Court investigation that resulted in the arrest of 160 black people, mostly slaves, and 21 European immigrants, mostly indentured servants – but also including a hostelry owner and an itinerant teacher. New York at the time was on edge because of the Stono Rebellion two years earlier in North Carolina – where some white people had been accused of being in sympathy with the slaves.[1] Also, the war between Britain and Spain at that time encouraged fears that Catholics were spying for Spain. Trials led to the burning of 13 black people at the stake, the hanging of 16 others, and the transporting of 70 to plantations in the Caribbean. Four European immigrants were hung, and seven were banished.[2]

---

* See also the discussions of Bacon's Rebellion (Chap. 1), the War for Independence (Chap. 3), and the periods of Reconstruction and the Populist movement (Chap. 5).

Later slave conspiracies

Herbert Aptheker in his book *Abolitionism* mentions a number of white opponents of slavery in the South: Joseph Wood, executed in 1812 for leading a slave rebellion in Louisiana; George Boxley, who escaped before being hanged for plotting with slaves in Virginia in 1816; four men in Charleston, South Carolina, who received fines and jail sentences for encouraging Denmark Vesey's conspiracy in 1822; three men in Louisiana in 1790 convicted of supporting slave unrest and jailed; James Mumford, forced out of Virginia in 1802 for encouraging revolt; Judge Jabez Brown, in 1804, excoriated in the Georgia press and forced to relocate to the North for upholding the right of slaves to rebel...and many others.[3]

Mexican American War

Noteworthy in the 1846-48 war with Mexico was the formation of the *San Patricio* (St. Patrick) Battalion of Irish immigrants, who fought on the side of anti-slavery Mexico. Angered by the U.S. Army's discrimination against Catholics – and by anti-Catholicism generally in U.S. society – a platoon of Irish immigrants led by Captain John Riley went over to the Mexican side. Once the war started, some 200 additional Irish and German immigrants joined the battalion, dismayed by the greed and brutality of the U.S. army's seizure of land from Mexican civilians. The *San Patricios* fought fiercely, especially at the decisive battle of Churubusco in 1847, and they received promises of land in return for their service. When captured, many were hung as deserters, despite widespread protest in Mexico. Capt. Riley survived, though branded with a "D" for *deserter* on his face* because he had joined the Mexican side before the war began. Mexico honors the *San Patricios* twice a year – on the anniversary date of their hanging, and on St. Patrick's Day. And since 1993, the Irish people in Riley's hometown in County Galway celebrate the *San Patricios'* memory.[4]

Abolitionism

John Brown was probably the most consistent white anti-racist fighter of the pre-Civil War period. Contemporaries remarked at the basic naturalness of his relations with black people, undistorted by the racism of the times. By contrast, the white abolitionist William Lloyd Garrison tended to have a patronizing manner, particularly in his relationship with the escaped slave and abolitionist orator, Frederick Douglass. In 1847 Douglass founded his own newspaper, *The North Star*, commenting

---

* Or possibly branded twice – once on each cheek – as shown in the movie *One Man's Hero*, starring Tom Berrenger, which tells the story of the *San Patricios*.

that black people "must be our own representatives and advocates, not exclusively, but peculiarly; not distinct from, but in connection with our white friends."[5] In contrast to Douglass, Garrison guided his followers toward a dead-end by insisting on pacifism and rejecting electoral politics – while single-mindedly focusing on propaganda opposing slavery. Garrison's life holds both positive and negative lessons for today's activists – his principled and active public stand over the course of three decades, his willingness to go to jail for his beliefs, and his nearly being lynched in Boston in 1836. Over against these qualities, however, stand a certain rigidity and an unwillingness to listen to or take leadership from the majority black membership of the movement.

Aside from Garrison, there were many white people, both North and South, who risked social isolation, mob violence, prison, and death to oppose slavery. The Quakers, though pacifists, were steadfast station agents on the Underground Railroad. Prudence Crandall had her school in Connecticut burned and a special law passed prohibiting her from teaching a young black woman in a class with white children. Proslavery mobs drove the Reverend Joel Parker from New Orleans and George Frederick Simmons from Mobile, Alabama, in the 1830s. And two men originally from Illinois, last names Fuller and Bridges, were whipped and transported from Missouri for helping slaves to escape. During 1835-36, Aptheker reports, "Mississippi especially was the locale of mass executions of slaves, and whites, too, were lashed and hanged in this state. Others met similar fates in Virginia, Georgia and South Carolina."[6]

Aptheker recounts other stories from the 1840s and 1850s – including the conversion of Ralph Waldo Emerson to abolitionism after passage of the Fugitive Slave Act in 1850 – and caps these stories with a retelling of John Brown's raid on the federal arsenal at Harper's Ferry in 1859. Aptheker makes clear the soundness of Brown's plan – aimed at stocking up with sufficient arms to be able to hold out in the Appalachian Mountains and provide a guerilla army refuge for escaped slaves. W.E.B. DuBois praised Brown in these words: "John Brown worked not simply for the Black Man – he worked with them, and he was a companion of their daily life, knew their faults and virtues, and felt, as few white Americans have felt, the bitter tragedy of their lot."[7] And from Brown's friend and fellow abolitionist, Frederick Douglass, came this eulogy:

> With the statesmanship, civilization and Christianity of America, the Negro is simply a piece of property, having no rights which white men are required to respect, but with John Brown and his noble associates, the NEGRO IS A MAN, entitled to all the rights claimed by the whitest man on earth. Brave and glorious old man! Yours was the life of a true friend of humanity, and the triumphant death of a hero. The friends of freedom shall be nerved to the glorious struggle with slavery by your example; the hopes of the slave shall not die while your name shall live, and after ages shall rejoice to do justice to your great history.[8]

The final act of abolitionism was the Civil War. The heroic role and fighting spirit of the former slaves during the war won many white people to a conscious anti-slavery stance – including the conversion of Gen. John Logan from an Illinois exclusionist to a staunch supporter of Congressional Reconstruction. White people from the laboring classes joined the Union army in large numbers and hundreds of thousands gave their lives in the struggle. The image of trainloads of troops singing "John Brown's body lies amolderin' in the grave" speaks to the solidarity-forging character of the struggle. The reality is that black and white working people together brought down the slave system.

White Southern opposition to the planter class

Many white people in the South were not willing to fight in defense of the slave system, and others actively fought a rearguard action against the Confederacy. Timothy Tyson notes that in 1864, General George E. Pickett had 22 young white men hanged in Kinston, North Carolina, for disloyalty. Also, the Heroes of America, a network of guerrilla fighters totaling some 10,000 people, harassed Confederate forces across the state. Then in 1862, when the Union army captured parts of eastern North Carolina, nearly a thousand white men joined up.[9] Even North Carolina governor Zebulon Vance commented in 1864, "the great popular heart is not now and never has been in this war. It was a revolution of the politicians and not the people."[10]

After the war white teachers helped staff the new freedom schools, while white and black Union troops together helped enforce the new power relations. Northerners demobilized from the army and stayed in the South, while others ventured there for much the same reason that settlers headed west. White Southerners, labeled "scalawags" by the defenders of white supremacy, joined with black Republicans and the Northern "carpetbaggers" to gain power across the Deep South. Some, like John Prentiss Matthews in Mississippi, eventually gave their lives for defying Democratic Party intimidation at the polls.[11] Others fought against the Ku Klux Klan from its founding in 1867 through its final suppression by Federal Law and prosecution in 1872. Albert Parsons, for example, who was later executed as one of the anarchist leaders in the 1886 Haymarket Affair, fought on the Confederate side during the war but later became a Radical Republican and helped put down the Klan in Texas in the early 1870s.* Even some ex-Confederate officers, like General

---

* Parsons married Lucy Waller, a woman of African, Cherokee, and Mexican descent, and the two were active in socialist and anarchist organizing in East Texas. Racists shot Parsons in the leg and threatened him with lynching for registering black people to vote. The couple also received threats because of their mixed marriage and left Texas for Chicago in 1872. After Parsons's execution, Lucy continued as an outspoken labor organizer for more than 50 years. She fought for free speech in the repressive climate after Haymarket, helped

James Longstreet, played an honorable role in the fight to preserve and expand democracy in Louisiana.

Eric Foner notes that at no point did a majority of white people in the South support the Republican Party, but that "what is remarkable is not how few whites supported the party but, in some states, how many."[12] There were some prominent planters who joined, as well as former Whig politicians, hill country Unionists, and city and town skilled workers who resented the former plantation owners' rule. Opponents branded these people "white negroes" – and despised them even more than the Northerners. Scalawags came to control six states stretching from North Carolina to Texas. Carpetbaggers, in turn, played a leading role in Florida, South Carolina, and Louisiana, where a native scalawag base of opposition among white people was more limited. Meanwhile, the planters, like every defeated ruling class in history, used every means at hand – electoral, economic, religious, and, especially, paramilitary – to claw their way back into power.

Reconstruction had its white heroes and more than a few martyrs. But it also had its compromisers and inconstant friends. White Georgia Republicans failed to oppose a Democratic campaign to expel black legislators from the state government – in the hopes of building a Republican majority based on economic issues and white supremacy. The result was that Reconstruction never really took hold in Georgia. This same concessionary attitude showed up in Mississippi as well, where Governor James L. Alcorn appointed Democrats to key positions. His campaign had argued for modernization – a "harnessed revolution" that could "lead and direct the colored vote."[13] Here black Republican support was strong enough to be able to turn Alcorn's faction out of office in 1873 and win half the elected positions throughout the state.[14] In South Carolina the electorate rebuffed a similar pattern of paternalism – by winning half the executive offices, three Congressional seats, and a State Supreme Court appointment. For the most part, white Reconstruction political leaders rode the post-war revolutionary wave, but then at key junctures failed to follow through – refusing to use the state militia against the Ku Klux Klan*, remaining passive rather than mobilizing to protect black voting rights, and caving in to power grabs by white mobs.

---

found the International Workers of the World in 1905, and edited the IWW's newspaper, *The Liberator*. From 1925 on Lucy Parsons supported the work of the Communist Party USA, aiding in the defense of the Scottsboro Boys and joining the party in 1939. She maintained a revolutionary outlook throughout her life, and on dying in 1942 at age 89, the FBI confiscated all the 1500 books in her library. *(Women's History Information Project, "Lucy Parsons: Woman of Will")*

* As we saw in Chapter 5, Governors Powell Clayton in Arkansas and E.J. Davis in Texas, were the exception in this regard.

Women's suffrage movement

Black women played a leading role in the abolitionist movement, along with black men. But many white women were staunch allies in the struggle, in part due to the developing consciousness of women's oppression that the anti-slavery movement helped nurture. White women served as anti-slavery authors, editors, lecturers and fundraisers – and stood firm in the face of mob attacks. They worked for unity in the movement by opposing personal feuds and factionalism; and they opposed racist ideas and policies, targeting in particular the treatment of black women under slavery. White women also set a moral tone for other white abolitionists, as evidenced by the resolution initiated by the wealthy Southern abolitionist Sarah Grimké, who had grown up in a slave-owning family: "It is the duty of Abolitionists to identify themselves with these oppressed Americans, by sitting with them in places of worship, by appearing with them in our streets, by giving them our countenance in steamboats and stages, by visiting with them in their homes, and encouraging them to visit us, receiving them as we do our fellow citizens."

Frederick Douglass addressed the 1848 Women's Rights Convention at Seneca Falls, NY, and supported the campaign for equal rights. Douglass stated, "Let woman *take* her rights, and then she shall be free." In similar fashion, abolitionist orator Wendell Phillips upheld women's claim to full citizenship, education, professional work, and equal pay.[15]

A turning point for the two allied movements came, however, during the debate over the 14th Amendment in 1866, whose central tenet was "equality before the law, overseen by the national government."[16] While the amendment started out upholding equal suffrage, during the course of the debate the word *male* came to be introduced into the Constitution for the first time. Foner summarizes the situation: "In politics, it was indeed the 'Negro's hour.' A Civil War had not been fought over the status of women, nor had thirty years of prior agitation awakened public consciousness on the issue. Yet the dispute over the Fourteenth Amendment marked a turning point in nineteenth-century reform…[l]eaving feminist leaders with a deep sense of betrayal."[17]

Frederick Douglass continued to struggle to win over the movement's leaders. But once the 15th Amendment gained approval in 1869 – "prohibiting federal and state governments from depriving any citizen of the vote on racial grounds,"[18] but remaining silent on women's right to vote – the movement split. Elizabeth Cady Stanton and Susan B. Anthony formed the National Woman Suffrage Association, while supporters of the two amendments formed the American Woman Suffrage Association, led by Lucy Stone, Henry Blackwell, and Julia Ward Howe. In 1890 the two organizations merged to form the National American Woman Suffrage Association. Then with the influx of Southern women in the years around 1900, the movement became more explicitly white supremacist. Segregated parades, discouraging black women's organizations from joining the association, and refusing to speak out about the racial subordination of black women – all marked the movement's public stance.[19]

By the time the 19th Amendment passed in 1920, the fact that white women in the movement had originally stood against white supremacy was a distant memory. W.E.B. DuBois and Ida B. Wells spoke out forcefully for women's right to vote – but the white-led movement overall moved comfortably with the times. These were the years when the KKK grew rapidly – with an added boost from President Wilson in the White House – and the government targeted immigrants for deportation and socialists for jail. Suffragette speakers argued that a block of white women voters in the South would strongly support the current social order. And they suggested that black women could be disenfranchised as readily as black men had been.

Only in the late 1960s did that early fire against white supremacy again begin to burn at the heart of the women's movement.

Leadership by the left and labor

By the early 1900s only two labor organizations defied the reign of racism and privilege among white working people. They were the International Workers of the World (IWW) and the United Mineworkers (UMWA). The Knights of Labor had degenerated into a racist sect, and the dominant AFL, under Samuel Gompers's leadership, focused mainly on keeping Asian workers out of the craft unions. While small in relation to the social players of the times, both the IWW and the UMWA were forerunners of two important oppositional forces as the 20th century progressed: the Communist Party USA and the Congress of Industrial Organizations (CIO).

The IWW to the CPUSA

Beginning in 1908 the IWW put out a call to form "One Big Union" and focused organizing on workers in the lowest-paid, hardest, and dirtiest jobs of the period. By bringing in agricultural, lumber, and mine workers, saw and textile mill hands, and laborers on the railroads and docks, the IWW developed a culture of multiracial organizing throughout the country. Organizers recruited Mexican miners, welcomed women and Asian members, and helped African American and white workers struggle together in the Louisiana sawmills and on the docks of Philadelphia. The IWW viewed World War I as a contest among the colonial powers to divide the world – so they opposed U.S. participation. By the end of the war, a combination of heavy government repression and difficulties maintaining their base – as organizers moved from struggle to struggle – led to the eroding of the IWW as an effective organization. Then in the wake of the Russian Revolution in 1917, leading activists like Big Bill Haywood became part of the Communist Party USA (CPUSA) after its founding in 1919.

The revolutionary left made a complicated transition during the 1920s, and by the early '30s – as we saw in Chapters 6, 7, and 9 – the CPUSA had developed a commitment to fighting black national oppression. Examples of the party's multiracial organizing during this period include: setting up Unemployed Councils, building independent unions as part of the Trade Union Unity League*, campaigning to free the Scottsboro Boys, bringing sharecroppers into the Southern Tenant Farmers Union, opposing Italian aggression in Ethiopia, and helping to launch the National Negro Congress (NNC) in 1936. The party also carried out internal campaigns aimed at rooting out white racism in its ranks.

In the history of the United States, there had never been anything like it. Here was a majority white organization that by the end of the 1930s had changed the composition of its membership, developed leaders in the black freedom movement, and gained credit for their leading role among African American workers.

In the 1940s, however, much of this reputation faded. Two shortcomings in the CPUSA's practice cost it dearly. First, there was the tendency of the party to orient its work around directives from outside the country. The party had benefited from international consultation in developing its 1928 position on the Black Nation in the South. In addition, the international united front against fascism in the mid-1930s encouraged the party to work with broader social forces like the NNC. But then international tensions began to mount prior to WWII. The Western powers refused to support the fight against fascism in Spain and dragged their feet on forming an anti-fascist alliance with the Soviet Union. When Stalin made a tactical decision to bloc with Germany so as to avoid being isolated and attacked by Hitler, the CPUSA blindly followed along – switching out of its anti-fascist stance and jettisoning the work in popular front organizations like the NNC. This one-sided response demonstrates the party's second shortcoming: an all-or-nothing approach to carrying out the organization's political line. This practice had hurt the party earlier in the South. In the effort to build united front organizations

* From 1929 to 1935 the Trade Union Unity League (TUUL) promoted industry-wide organizing, supported the formation of Unemployed Councils, and established unions independent of the dominant AFL. The TUUL reached a peak membership in 1934 of about 125,000. It led important organizing battles during the early years of the Great Depression that contributed to later CIO campaign victories. The TUUL's shortcomings included sectarianism, due to its close identification with the CPUSA, and a failure to continue work within the AFL unions, thereby falling into dual unionism. *(Foster,* American Trade Unionism*)*

with white liberals – mostly unsuccessful, it should be noted – the party had abandoned its independent organizing among black tenant farmers and sharecroppers.

When Germany attacked the Soviet Union in June 1941, the CPUSA jumped whole-hog back into the anti-fascist war effort. Now seeking to project itself as the staunchest anti-fascist fighters, the party gave up all political independence. Leaders reveled in the acceptability that came with the U.S.-Soviet alliance against world fascism. The party backed Roosevelt's internment of the Japanese during the war. It opposed A. Philip Randolph's March on Washington and the demand that war industries be opened to African American workers. The over-zealous enforcement of the wartime no-strike pledge – with party members acting as shop floor bosses during a time of speed-ups and profiteering – contributed to workers' later abandonment of the party during the Cold War purges. Finally, in May 1944 the CPUSA went so far as to dissolve the party itself – and, along with it, the party's revolutionary position on the Black Nation in the South.*

These developments took a huge toll on the CP's standing in the oppressed nationality movements. First, as Robert Allen points out, the party destroyed its credibility with Japanese Americans for a generation and more.† As for the African American freedom movement, "the Communist Party had revealed itself as a highly unstable ally of black freedom: alternately embracing and rejecting black reformers, sometimes abandoning the black struggle altogether, and then reacting with breast-beating campaigns against white chauvinism that disrupted its own organization more than it diminished prejudice among the members. The party had certainly made positive contributions to the struggle for racial equality, but its erratic behavior and compulsion to dominate the black movement lost it many friends."[20]

It is important to recognize and learn the lessons – both positive and negative – from this tumultuous period in CPUSA history. Courageous organizers worked under incredibly difficult conditions during the 1930s, learning from their experience and from the new people joining their ranks. The party trained thousands in a revolutionary working class outlook and fought racist policies and practices inside as well as

---

* The CPUSA reconstituted itself a little over a year later, after a letter by Jacques Duclos, a leader of the Communist Party of France, gave expression in April 1945 to widespread criticism of the party's dissolution. The CPUSA's revolutionary position on the African American nation in the South never regained the standing and influence of the pre-war years. (*Isserman,* Which Side Are You On?; *Haywood,* Black Bolshevik)

† In the early 1950s, the party's denunciation of Puerto Rican patriots' armed attacks on Blair house and the U.S. Congress also undermined its following in the national movements, as did its later criticism of the nationalism of Malcolm X during the 1960s.

outside the organization. With few exceptions, party life came the closest to capturing a vision of a non-racial future as any social setting in the United States up to that time. The contrast with the dominant Jim Crow society was striking – and not lost on the black recruits who joined the party in large numbers.

Yet it can also be said that the CPUSA was not able to follow through on the organizing gains made during this period. Breakthroughs like Benjamin O. Davis's New York City Council victory in 1943 were the exception. The party's views tended to flip-flop and implementation was often one-sided. Some grassroots leaders were able to buffer the impacts of the changes and apply the party's positions in a way that made sense in terms of their local conditions. Trade union leaders in particular were less likely to be pulled one way or the other because of their solid grounding among their members. Overall, however, the party leadership did not consult closely with their rank and file members and close supporters. As a result, the CPUSA lost its leading role and was unable to follow through on its revolutionary commitment to the freedom movements.

The mineworkers and the CIO

Black workers played a leading role in forming the United Mineworkers Association (UMWA) in the Appalachian coalmines of the South in the late 1800s. Ten years after its founding in 1890, the union had 20,000 African Americans among its 100,000 members. The UMWA organized on an industrial basis and maintained a multiracial staff both nationally and in the South. The union's top leadership was white, however; and in the North, among anthracite miners in Pennsylvania for example, many locals refused to accept black members.

In the broader labor movement the pattern of racial exclusion created deep animosity between the races. Factory owners turned the unions' policies to their advantage by importing African American workers from the South to break strikes. Union organizers, even progressive ones like William Z. Foster after the 1919 Steel Strike, tended to blame defeats on black workers – often attacking them more viciously than other, non-black strikebreakers.

Then as the Great Depression set in during the early 1930s, conditions finally began to change. Under John L. Lewis's guidance the UMWA broke with the AFL leadership in 1936 and then formed the Congress of Industrial Organizations (CIO) in 1938. Lewis hired communists, with their anti-racist consciousness and years of organizing in the South, to help build the movement. A second generation of African Americans now worked in the packinghouses and steel mills; the depression had leveled the playing field to some extent for all workers; and the political climate – even President Roosevelt came out in support of unions – encouraged workers to organize.

The AFL organizing model centered on elite craft unions had shown itself inadequate to the times. Production conditions coming out of World War I had concentrated huge amounts of capital in the textile, auto, steel and other industries. To offset the power of the owners, everyone in an industry had to be brought into the union. This industrial form of unionism – as carried out earlier by the Knights of Labor, the IWW, and the CPUSA-led unions of the independent Trade Union Unity League – required "wall to wall" unity of workers in all job categories. As a result, African American laborers in shipping, housekeeping, and other positions at the fringes of an industry began to enter the unions. In doing so, the trade union movement developed a new spirit of racial solidarity. Previously, employers had consciously viewed their multiracial workforce and its hierarchy of privilege as a way to keep workers divided – a kind of "strike insurance." The new movement broke through these barriers – at least to the extent that everyone in a workplace belonged to the same union. Along with membership came a degree of protection on the job and at least some input into the collective voice that bargained with the employer.

One condition that favored black workers' support for the new unions was an alliance between the mostly white CIO and the National Negro Congress. A. Phillip Randolph headed this broad, multi-class African American united front, which solidly backed the CIO organizing drives. The NNC included community, church and intellectual leaders, as well as communists, the NAACP and the Urban League. The receptivity to union organizing evidenced by the NNC's broad social base gave black workers the encouragement they needed to join the movement in significant numbers.

In a certain sense, however, the CIO organizing wave of the late 1930s remained a struggle between capital and white workers – given the largely segregated industrial relations at the start of the decade. Even after the sit-down strikes and the pitched battles to organize "Little Steel," black workers in the early 1940s still could not work in many basic service and war-related industries. It took A. Philip Randolph's threatened March on Washington in 1941 to force President Roosevelt to open these jobs. Then when black workers responded to the war's labor shortage and moved into these new positions, they often faced work stoppages and other protests by white workers.

The unions with the best record fighting for racial equality were those that had a strong presence – if not a majority – of oppressed nationality members. A second favorable condition, often overlapping the first, was a strong presence in leadership by the revolutionary left. The UCA-

PAWA* union advanced the rights of Latino and women workers in the Southwest during the 1930s and '40s. The United Packinghouse Workers of America (UPWA) became an integral part of the black freedom movement in Chicago. While the UPWA was majority white and had white leadership, it also had a strong African American presence in the four flagship meatpacking companies in Chicago. In the late 1940s, unable to improve conditions at the bargaining table, the UPWA turned to the community. The leadership encouraged members to join the NAACP, and together the UPWA and the NAACP campaigned to desegregate the restaurants and other service establishments in Chicago. They also compelled the large corporations based in the city to begin hiring African Americans.

In other unions the record was uneven. The communist-led National Maritime Union ran an internal education program on racism. The predominantly African American Tobacco Workers enjoyed a rich, multiracial social life. In most of the CIO and AFL unions, however, where a white majority dominated, the commitment to racial equality stopped at the level of basic membership rights. Here black and other oppressed nationality workers often found themselves restricted to particular job classifications.

The auto industry is one example that shows how these various tensions played out. The GM plant in Flint, MI, where the great 1937 sit-down strike took place, had an overwhelmingly white workforce, many of whom were transplanted southerners or "mugwumps." Among the demands of that struggle, once the union won recognition and a conservative electoral majority replaced the communists who led the sit-down, was a call to restrict black employment.[21] Later, black workers during World War II moved into the industry and advanced to skilled positions. White autoworkers, however, repeatedly walked out in protest, and management used this opposition as an excuse to deny promotions to African Americans. James Loewen describes how in this situation UAW president R. J. Thomas steadfastly fought the racist outbreaks. "This problem must be settled or it will wreck our union," he told booing white workers at Packard in 1943. When 25,000 walked out, Thomas threatened to kick anyone out of the union who did not return to work. Thomas was willing to move ahead, "even if it requires that large numbers of white workers out there lose their jobs." Eventually most of the strikers returned to work.[22]

After the war ended in 1946, Walter Reuther challenged Thomas for the position of union president. Since his election in 1939, Thomas had been able to count on the backing of a strong left presence in the union. Reuther also had depended on CPUSA backing. He won the leadership

---

* United Cannery, Agricultural, Packing, and Allied Workers of America. See box on p. 130.

of Detroit's amalgamated West Side Local 174, shortly after returning with his brother from working in the Soviet Union in the mid-1930s. By 1939, however, Reuther had distanced himself from the party, except when they joined together to back Thomas for president in opposition to the rightwing Homer Martin. Then in 1946 Reuther narrowly defeated Thomas through a campaign of redbaiting – attacking his support by the communists. Reuther's election marked a huge shift in the CIO. He helped defuse the largest strike wave in U.S. history in 1946; supported the purging of communists from the unions during the McCarthy years; and after becoming CIO president in 1952, brought the CIO back into the AFL fold – forming the AFL-CIO.

It is clear that the left played a key role in supporting a progressive stance on race in the UAW during World War II. Also clear, by contrast, is Walter Reuther's anti-communism and how it matched up with racism in the auto industry and the union – later targeted by the League of Revolutionary Black Workers in the 1960s.

The UAW is just one example showing the adaptation of white supremacy to postwar conditions in the labor movement. As discussed in Chapter 9, departmental seniority in the steel industry locked black workers into the harshest conditions in the foundries. Also, hiring and firing patterns by employers – often linked to technological change and reserved as a "management prerogative" in negotiated contracts – went unchallenged. By the 1970s black miners – who in 1900 made up 20% of the union – counted for only a small fraction of the UMWA membership. And in 2005, meatpackers working at the huge Smithfield hog-processing plant in Tar Heel, NC, once again struggled to overcome differences around race – this time between black, Latino and native workers – in order to unionize.

Leadership by oppressed nationalities

In the wake of the revolutionary left's suppression during the McCarthy years and the bureaucratization of the labor movement in a merged AFL-CIO, new historical actors arose during the 1950s and '60s. Actually, they were not really new – but rather embodying in new form a very old tradition, but now with a higher level of self-consciousness. Cedric Robinson speaks of a "Black Radical Tradition" extending back to Africa – a culture of resistance embodied in slave revolts throughout the African diaspora, in the heroic struggles of African American soldiers during the Civil War, and in the outpouring of national pride through the Garvey movement at the close of World War I.

The fight for desegregation and voting rights mobilized support from much of white America, especially among youth and the religious community. White people were present – though in relatively small numbers and mostly in supportive roles – in the lunch counter sit-ins, the Freedom Rides, and the voting rights campaign. Doctors and lawyers volunteered their services. White students canvassed with SNCC – and a few individuals, like Bob and Dorothy Zellner, were there from the start. A number of northern unions provided material support for desegregating the South, and at times leaders joined in marches led by Martin Luther King. But as the struggle moved north, the union support fell away. A much-weakened UPWA was the only union on the podium with King when he opened his campaign in Chicago in 1966. A hint of the UPWA's earlier, working-class approach to the freedom struggle reappeared briefly in the 1968 Memphis sanitation workers strike. But a sniper killed Dr. King just at the point when he was connecting the issues of war, poverty, worker organizing, and black liberation.

Meanwhile, urban rebellions shook the cities of the North – the deadliest being Watts (1965), Newark (1967), Detroit (1967), and Washington (1968) – with more than 60 outbreaks occurring in the days after Martin Luther King's assassination. Gunmen shot down Malcolm X in February 1965, but his teachings on Black Nationalism bore fruit in subsequent years under the slogan "Black Power." The process of urbanization, as black people moved from the South to urban centers of the North and West, had developed among African Americans a heightened sense of national identity. Various classes and sectoral forces struggled for leadership internal to the movement – struggles that the white power structure took advantage of to provoke splits and deadly antagonisms. But the movement took on the whole range of nation-building concerns: economic, social, cultural, political, and military. Welfare mothers demanded respect. Students pushed for ethnic studies programs and increased faculty – striking at San Francisco State College, seizing Hamilton Hall at Columbia University, and a year later carrying out the armed occupation of Straight Hall at Cornell. Cultural expression flowered – exemplified in the plays of Amiri Baraka, the songs of Nina Simone, and the pre-rap teachings of Gil Scott Heron. Revolutionary working class consciousness emerged with the Black Panther Party in California and then with the League of Revolutionary Black Workers in Detroit. And a series of Black Power conferences sought to house the movement and give it political expression.

The various perspectives in the movement were not necessarily antagonistic, but police, with federal backing through the FBI's COINTELPRO program, fostered divisions in the movement – murdering and imprisoning dozens of organizers. Even the harshest penitentiaries were sites of struggle – Attica, in New York, taken over for five days, before Rockefeller's bloody suppression; and George Jackson's organizing, alleged escape attempt, and killing by guards at Soledad prison in California. Money suddenly became available to buy off grassroots leaders or promote their political careers. And then capital systematically dismantled the industrial base that underpinned the movement, shifting production to the South, Southwest, and overseas.

An early attempt to undercut the movement through the War on Poverty actually fed revolutionary consciousness. As Rodolfo Acuña points out[23], thousands of grassroots people – the majority of them women – served on local anti-poverty boards. And together with Martin Luther King's Poor People's Campaign, the program brought an awareness of poverty to the broader public. At the same time, local white elites moved quickly to close off any real access to power by the dispossessed, thereby blocking the reformist road to correcting grievances. The deeper consciousness that resulted helped nurture the social movements of the period, although mostly in partial and unfocused ways.

Chicano people

Inspired by the African American freedom movement and anti-colonial struggles worldwide, other oppressed nationalities in the United States gathered strength. A broad-based upsurge among the Chicano people began with union organizing among farmworkers and a grape boycott launched in 1964. Two years later Mexican and Filipino worker organizations merged to form the United Farm Workers Organizing Committee, led by César Chavez, Dolores Huerta, and Gil Padilla. Militancy spread to the Midwest, as Báldemar Velásquez formed the Farm Labor Organizing Committee (FLOC) in 1968.

This same period saw the land struggle break out, as Reies López Tijerina led sit-ins by *La Alianza Federal de Mercecdes* to reclaim historic land grants taken by force, fraud, and government appropriation.

In Denver and Los Angeles poet and former professional fighter, Corky Gonzales, led the Crusade for Justice in actions on behalf of urban youth – targeting police brutality, in particular. The Crusade reached out to support the American Indian Movement, black political activist Angela Davis, and movements in Mexico. In 1968 high school students walked out – first in LA, where police attacked a march of 10,000 students, and then in Denver, San Antonio and other cities across the Southwest. Students primarily focused on racism in education – reflected in overcrowded, run-down schools, a lack of Chicano teachers, and suppression of Chicano culture. Then in 1969 The Crusade hosted the First National Chicano Youth Conference, which established the movement goal as self-determination for the Chicano people. And in California, university and community activists formed the student organization MEChA (*El Movimiento Estudiantil Chicano de Aztlán*), which continued to be active into the 21st Century.

Also formed during this period were 1) the Brown Berets – allies of the Black Panther Party – whom LA police targeted for repression after the student walkout; 2) the women-staffed publication *El Grito Del Norte*, founded by author and former SNCC activist Betita Martínez and others; and 3) the *La Raza Unida Party* (RUP), sparked by electoral victories in Crystal City, Cotula, and Carrizo Springs, Texas. A cultural awakening also took place – in music, visual arts, and poetry. And in theater, Luis Valdez formed the *Teatro Campesino* as an extension of the farmworker movement.

On August 29, 1970, the various sectors of the Chicano movement came together in the Chicano Moratorium demonstration in LA. Over 20,000 people marched to protest the war in Vietnam and the disproportionate number of Chicano soldiers killed there. Later in the day, police attacked a peaceful post-march gathering in Laguna Park and killed two people, Angel Diaz and Lynn Ward. Then in the evening, TV reporter Rubén Salazar died after being shot directly in the head with a tear gas canister while resting at a bar. Following the Moratorium, activists from the RUP in California formed the August 29th Movement, which later went on to become part of the League for Revolutionary Struggle (LRS).[*]

Puerto Rican people

The Young Lords Party developed out of the Puerto Rican communities in Manhattan and spread to *barrios* in Philadelphia, Bridgeport, and other cities along the East Coast – as well as to Chicago in the Midwest. The Young Lords allied themselves with the Black Panthers, Brown Berets and other revolutionary community organizations. For a time, they captured the imagination of young people, and helped convert former gang conflicts into political alliances.

This period also saw an upsurge in the Puerto Rican independence struggle. The *Movimiento Pro Independencia*, led by Juan Mari Bras, formed the Puerto Rican Socialist Party (PSP) in 1971. Armed resistance groups began operating: the *Fuerzas Armadas de Liberación Nacional* (FALN) in 1974; and the *Ejército Popular Borícua*, also known as *Los Macheteros*, in 1976. The FBI targeted both groups, leading to the arrest and jailing of the political prisoners mentioned in Chapter 8. In the late 1970s activists established a network of community newspapers, among them *El Enfoque Communal* in Philadelphia, and set up the National Congress for Puerto Rican Rights.[†]

Indigenous peoples

In Chapter 7 we sketched the pattern of land struggles that began with the seizure of Alcatraz Island in 1969 and culminated with the occupation of Wounded Knee in 1973 and the subsequent reign of terror at the Pine Ridge Reservation through 1975. The FBI and its allies among

---

[*] See the box on pp. 291-292 for a discussion of the League of Revolutionary Struggle.

[†] Also see the discussion of the Puerto Rican resistance struggle on pp. 78-82.

the Pine Ridge tribal authorities killed more than 60 people in the course of this protracted struggle. Two FBI agents, Jack Coler and Ron Williams, died in a confrontation at the Jumping Bull Ranch, and with little evidence to go on the police and courts fixed the blame on Leonard Peltier. In 2005, Peltier remained in jail – in bad health, made worse by official mistreatment over the years – despite a worldwide campaign calling for his release.

Asian peoples

The early 1960s civil rights movement brought attention to the racist character of U. S. immigration policies, including the exclusion of Asian peoples. The Immigration and Nationality Services Act of 1965 corrected many of the worst aspects of earlier policies. As Asian immigrants began entering the country, they found established communities – Chinatowns, Japantowns – built around the descendents of people who had entered the country generations earlier. These long-time residents shaped the character of the upsurge in Asian organizing linked to other oppressed nationalities. At the same time, energy also came from the new arrivals, who brought with them organizing skills and a heightened sense of national consciousness linked to liberation struggles worldwide.

Organizing targeted conditions in Chinatowns, as one example – pushing for improved housing and educational opportunities. In one landmark struggle thousands marched to save the International Hotel in San Francisco – home to an older generation of Manongs, or Filipino laborers, who had filled the ten blocks of Manilatown up until the era of redevelopment in the 1960s. This struggle lasted 37 years – from the first eviction notice in December, 1968; through the massively protested expulsion of 50 community elders in 1977; to a finally rebuilt I-Hotel with housing for 105 seniors completed in July, 2005. Out of the many community struggles of the 1960s and '70s came organizations like I Wor Kuen, which joined in the formation of the League of Revolutionary Struggle (LRS); and Workers Viewpoint, a forerunner of the Communist Workers Party, the organization attacked by the KKK and Nazis in Greensboro, NC, in 1979, killing five people and paralyzing a sixth.

Each of these national movements had contending forces, and the state resorted to various combinations of cooptation and violent repression to bring them under control. While impacting conditions in the United States, the upsurge also helped broaden internationalist consciousness. People formed links with pro-independence parties in Puerto Rico and opposed the war in Vietnam. They connected with worker and farmer struggles in Latin America, joined Venceremos Brigades to Cuba, and learned from revolutionary movements in Africa and China.

Broad popular activism of the period

With the national movements forming the central dynamic of the 1960s and '70s, other social sectors became active as well. Here white people tended to play a predominant role.

Anti-Vietnam War movement

15,000 people marched against the escalation of the Vietnam War in April, 1965. Then over the next ten years, hundreds of thousands took part in biannual mobilizations in Washington, DC, and New York City. The primarily African American student organization SNCC (Student Nonviolent Coordinating Committee) came out against the war in 1966, as did Martin Luther King with his historic speech at Riverside Church in New York City on April 4, 1967 – exactly a year before his assassination. Muhammad Ali refused the draft and was stripped of his boxing crown. Militant anti-draft actions, draft card burnings, and the jailing of resisters eventually ended the draft. Stolen FBI files revealed the federal COINTELPRO program, and publication of the Pentagon Papers laid bare the deception behind the war. Coffee houses sprang up near army posts, resistance by soldiers increased both in Vietnam and at home, and the GI movement finally helped bring the war to an end.

Second Wave feminism

Early writings by Simone de Beauvoir, *The Second Sex*, and Betty Friedan's, *The Feminine Mystique*, nurtured stirrings of feminist consciousness and led to the formation of the National Organization for Women in 1966. NOW focused primarily on equal rights with men, reproductive rights, and the cultural representations of women. Parallel critiques emerged, first within SNCC and then among other oppressed nationality and antiwar forces, resulting in the formation of a "radical" trend in the women's movement. Here issues of race, class, and eventually sexual orientation came to the fore – with actions and analysis targeting patriarchy, white supremacy, and capitalism. Women's caucuses and consciousness raising groups sprang up everywhere. Books, magazines, and underground papers, women's centers and health collectives, networks supporting victims of rape and domestic violence – all helped create an institutional infrastructure for the movement.

Gay and lesbian movement

The Stonewall Rebellion* of June 28, 1969, launched the modern gay and lesbian movement. Consciousness raising and direct action methods challenged the oppressive conditions of the times – including homophobia in NOW and in other progressive and left organizations. Militant

* See note on p. 183 for a description of the Stonewall Rebellion.

picketing, chanting, and disruption of American Psychiatric Association (APA) meetings sparked an internal debate that led to the removal of homosexuality from the APA's list of pathologies in 1973. Radical lesbians challenged both the women's and the gay men's movement, carving out a space and a social identity for themselves. When combined with the perspective and social reality of oppressed nationality women, as described in Chapter 14, the whole array of social movements in a sense became recentered: socially, around Third World feminism, and analytically, around what was later to be called intersectionality.

Other social movements

This period also saw an upsurge by *disability activists* pushing for public access and nondiscrimination in housing and employment. The *environmental movement* took off with the first Earth Day celebration in 1970. Former *mental patients* and their allies organized to target the medieval practice of lobotomy and to reign in the use of electroshock therapy. *Senior citizens* found a new voice – one example being the Gray Panthers, founded in 1970 – and spoke out about poverty among the elderly, the lack of facilities to aid senior networking, and job discrimination.

The New Left

Starting with Students for a Democratic Society (SDS) in 1960 and its *Port Huron Statement* two years later calling for "participatory democracy," a new, mostly white and young social force began to take shape with a critical and vaguely anti-capitalist outlook. Student rebellions at Berkeley in 1965 and at Columbia in 1968 – resonating with a huge student-led movement in France that same spring – echoed through other colleges and universities across the country.

As the 1960s proceeded, a range of organizations emerged with a more explicit socialist and worker-centered analysis – often inspired by the Chinese Revolution and its critique of the Soviet model of socialism, especially after the 1968 Soviet invasion of Czechoslovakia. African American organizations took the lead here, too – as with the Revolutionary Action Movement, inspired by the example of Robert Williams and his armed defense against nightriders in Monroe, NC. Among other vanguard groups of the period, the Black Panther Party targeted the lower sector of the working class, whom they called the "lumpen," and the League of Revolutionary Black Workers focused on autoworkers, directing demands at both the employers and the United Auto Workers union. Meanwhile independent white leftists who took seriously the charge to organize within white communities, formed organizations like People for Human Rights, the Jobs or Income Now (JOIN) campaign in Chicago, and the October 4th Organization in Philadelphia. Out of this ferment of activism, increasingly linked to the multinational working class, came the New Communist Movement of the 1970s.

The organized working class for the most part remained on the sidelines of these struggles. Exceptions were mainly smaller unions with roots in the communist-influenced struggles of a generation before: the United Electrical Workers and the Hospital Workers Union, Local 1199, being two examples. Mainly however, union leaders like the United Auto Workers' Walter Reuther fought the manifestations of national consciousness in their own bureaucratic domains. And overseas, the AFL-CIO worked hand-in-glove with the CIA to disrupt authentic, popular trade union organizing.

The all-around upsurge in the national and social movements split white people into opposing camps. A significant number of radical women, students, returning soldiers from Vietnam and other working class youth, ex-Peace Corps volunteers and academics – all moved in varying degrees toward a deeper understanding of U.S. imperialism and national oppression. White people marched, were beaten and tear-gassed, went to jail, provided material support, risked social isolation, and gave their lives for the struggle*. At the same time, however, the sacrifices among oppressed nationality freedom fighters were many times greater. The point here is not to raise these courageous white people above the principal victims of state and rightwing repression. Rather, it is to underscore that 1) white people also made sacrifices in the struggle, and 2) the revolt of oppressed nationality people at home and abroad sparked their activism.

Overall, however, the majority of white workers remained passive – riding out the period on a cushion of relative privilege as the earth shook around them. Given the hegemonic white supremacist outlook in this sector, many simply did what came naturally – trying to keep a toehold in a changing world. At the same time, however, millions voted for the openly racist third-party candidate George Wallace in the 1968 elections; unions worked to keep people of color out of the skilled trades; construction workers attacked anti-Vietnam War protesters in New York City; union teachers resisted African American parents' efforts to control their children's education in Oceanhill-Brownsville; and white working class neighborhoods violently protested integrated housing and school busing.

---

* Among those who died were Andrew Goodman and Michael Schwerner, murdered together with African American James Chaney (1964); Jonathan Daniels, Viola Liuzzo (1965); Allison Krause, Jeffery Miller, Sandra Scheuer, William Schroeder (1969); Diana Oughton, Ted Gold, Terry Robbins (1970); Mike Nathan, Bill Sampson, Jim Waller – gunned down together with African American Sandi Smith and Cuban-born César Cauce (1979).

League for Revolutionary Struggle (LRS)

Most histories of the 1960's and '70's ignore the new revolutionary organizations that emerged during this period – collectively known as the New Communist Movement (NCM). Or else they treat them as crazy offspring and nothing but trouble for the social movements of the time. But facts are very stubborn things, and the fact is that the NCM established a significant base in the labor and oppressed nationality movements, and had a following in the tens of thousands.

The League of Revolutionary Struggle (Marxist-Leninist) – or the LRS – was one of those groups. Like other NCM organizations, the League looked primarily to the Third World rather than to North America or Europe for its inspiration. Its Marxist framework was shaped in large part by the perspectives of Amilcar Cabral, Fidel Castro, Che Guevara, Ho Chi Minh, and Mao Zedong – as much as by Marx and Lenin. In taking this path, the LRS developed a critique of the Soviet Union and the pro-Soviet stance of the Communist Party USA. The League was one of the few NCM organizations primarily rooted in the oppressed nationality movements, rather than in the anti-war or white student movements of the period.

The LRS came out of a merger in October 1978 between I Wor Kuen (IWK), an organization of primarily Asian American labor and community organizers, and the August Twenty-Ninth Movement (ATM), mainly Mexicano/a-Chicano/a revolutionaries from the La Raza Unida Party who had a focus on worker organizing. A year later Amiri Baraka brought in his Revolutionary Communist League, mostly black activists from the Newark-based Congress of Afrikan People. Throughout its more than 10-year history, more than 80% of the LRS membership were from oppressed nationalities, and a majority of the organization's leadership were women.

A major difference between the League and other new communist organizations centered on the "national question" – or how revolutionaries should assess national liberation struggles inside the United States, like those of the African American and Chicano/a peoples. Beyond opposition to white supremacy and racism, the League upheld then – as does the Freedom Road Socialist Organization today – that national rights include the right to self-determination. Self-determination means the right to self-government in the historical territories of the Black Nation in the South and the Chicano Nation in the Southwest. This right to political power, including autonomy in areas of concentration elsewhere in the country, carries with it the right to full sovereignty and national independence if the people so choose. The LRS developed this analysis further in what came to be called "The Sunbelt Strategy."

Most of the League's time and resources went into organizing, rather than into theoretical debates. The LRS worked in traditional sectors for communist organizing like the auto and steel industries. It also was active in the cannery and service industries, with their concentrations of African Ameri-

Continued on next page

Continued from previous page

cans and Asian Pacific Islander and Latino immigrants, many undocumented. The League was active in labor unions, but it also helped establish worker-based community organizations across the country. A central goal of LRS organizing was to help oppressed nationality workers understand their dual role – as fighters for both working class power and national liberation.

This perspective comes out clearly in the key struggles led by the LRS, such as the incredible 18-month strike of mostly Chicano/a-Mexicano/a cannery workers in Watsonville, California. In this battle for job security, benefits and social respect, the workers came to recognize their campaign as 1) a fight for workers rights, 2) a component of the Chicano Liberation Movement, and to a lesser extent, as 3) part of women's fight for equality.

Another significant LRS campaign centered on building the Rainbow Coalition during the 1984 and 1988 Jesse Jackson presidential campaigns. The LRS understood that the Jackson campaign and the Rainbow Coalition that supported it had emerged from the Black Liberation Movement. They saw it as a mass-based challenge to the right-wing politics of the Ronald Reagan regime. The Jackson campaign was an out-front challenge to the white supremacy at the core of Reagan's appeal to white Southern voters and working class white "Reagan Democrats." The Rainbow Coalition/Jackson campaign pushed mainstream Democrats to stand up against the right-wing agenda whether they wanted to or not. The League, along with other NCM organizations and many independent socialists, worked to build the Rainbow Coalition by helping to organize and mobilize support in the Latino and Asian Pacific Islander communities, and among progressive students of all nationalities. The campaign also garnered support from African American leaders like Ron Daniels and Congressman Ron Dellums. And it struck a responsive chord among broader sectors of people – white farmers, sections of the labor movement, the peace movement, Native Americans, Arab Americans, and LGBTQ activists.

A couple of years after the second Jackson campaign, the League voted to dissolve itself. Internally, there had been a growing lack of democracy, as well as sectarian attitudes toward other left organizations. Externally, sustained redbaiting and political attacks had accompanied the League's growth. The 1989 attack on students in China's Tiananmen Square, along with the collapse of the Soviet Union, also helped bring the organization to a crossroads. A majority of the leadership proposed that the LRS drop Marxism, abandon revolution, and transform the organization into a loose network working for a program of radical reforms. A minority faction vigorously disagreed. At a special congress on September 8, 1990 a large majority voted to dissolve the League.

The minority faction formed the Socialist Organizing Network and later merged with the Freedom Road Socialist Organization in 1992. A central component of this merger was unity on the importance of the national liberation movements to revolution in the United States.

—*Bill Gallegos*

Despite the counterattacks and the media-orchestrated backlash described in Chapters 3 and 12, the period of the 1960s and '70s registered important gains for oppressed nationalities and other social movements. Many young people.became socially active and learned how to organize. And the repercussions of the upsurge in national consciousness impacted all sectors of society. The movement built its institutional capacity; pushed open access to jobs, education and services; transformed cultural images around race and gender; and forced the state to implement affirmative action measures to correct historic wrongs.

Summarizing the lessons learned

From this brief review of U.S. history we want to draw out the following conclusions concerning white people's role in opposing white supremacy:

- **A dominant theme through World War II is that European Americans only brought oppressed nationality people into their struggles when victory could not be assured without them.** If forced by necessity to broaden their ranks, white leaders would make limited concessions – first by forming segregated units, and later by restricting access to certain job categories and leadership positions. These practices appear in the Union army during the Civil War, in the U.S. armed forces through World War II, and more informally, in the Special Forces after the Vietnam War. In union organizing the pattern of inclusion by necessity predominates through the CIO organizing drives of the 1930s , '40s, and into the 1960s – and in some unions continues to the present.
- **Oppressed nationality people have made use of contradictions among European peoples to advance their own freedom agendas.** Certain approaches have been more successful than others – for example, black people's decisive role in defeating the slave system during the Civil War, and their participation in the armed forces in World Wars I and II. Another example is black and Chicano participation in building the CIO during the 1930s and '40s. By contrast, Southern Populism in the late 1800s was pretty much a dead end – as was the recruitment of people of color to be strikebreakers during the early 20th century.
- **An important condition for progress is that oppressed nationality peoples have their own independent organizations closely linked to the grassroots.** The period of the mid-20th century freedom struggles is probably the best example of an across-the-board upsurge in oppressed nationality organizing. But the roots go deep into the past – as recounted earlier in Chapters 5-7.

Here too, however, the record is uneven. The post-WWI Garvey Movement marked a milestone in the development of African American national consciousness, but it eventually collapsed under government repression and mismanagement. Also, the various national movements of the 1970s succumbed to FBI and police attacks, cooptation, internal divisions, and economic restructuring.

- **A second condition that can allow solid gains to be made is when the revolutionary left grounds its outlook and practice among the oppressed nationalities.** The CPUSA's experience during the 1930s testifies to this possibility. Here, however, history shows that the mostly white leadership of the party became cut off from its base among the oppressed nationalities and lost its revolutionary orientation.

- **These two conditions – oppressed nationality organization and a well-grounded left – played out clearly in the trade union movement during the time of its greatest upsurge.** The all-black Brotherhood of Sleeping Car Porters provided an independent base for A. Philip Randolph – as he presided over the National Negro Congress in 1935, led the March on Washington Movement in 1941, and later formed the Negro American Labor Council in 1960 to combat continuing racism in the AFL-CIO. Organizations like the UPWA, UCAPAWA and later the FTA, where the left and oppressed nationality workers both held strength, actually became institutions of the freedom movements. And where the left held influence pretty much on its own – even in an overwhelmingly white organization like the UAW – the leadership took a progressive stance on race. Only for a brief time, however, during the first years of the CIO, did these forces come anywhere near determining the overall direction of the workers' movement.

- **Individual white people have joined in the struggle against white supremacy throughout U.S. history.**

- **White people have taken part in larger numbers and with the greatest effectiveness and clarity of mind when oppressed nationality peoples were the leading force in motion.** The movements 1) against slavery, 2) during the 1960s and '70s, and even 3) in the Jesse Jackson electoral campaigns of the 1980s – all demonstrate this point.

- **White people can also come to the freedom struggles from the left, as shown by the social battles of the 1930s and '40s.** Here progressive thinking arises out of the fight against monopoly capital and for working class power. By coming to see the national movements in the United States as integral to the fight against U.S. imperialism, white revolutionaries in the '30s were able to play a role in supporting the development of the national movements, the African American freedom struggle in particular.

- **The movements of the 1960s and '70s ultimately lacked a unifying and broadly influential leading organization.** Grounded among the working class of the oppressed nationality peoples, such an organization would have had to be non-patriarchal, inclusive, and thoroughly democratic in its internal culture in order to sustain the struggle through periods of advance and retreat.

In later decades, many white people who initially became involved during the upsurge of the 1960s tended to gravitate to the left as their understanding of the social system deepened. The social left in various forms – socialist, feminist, pacifist, anarchist – has served as a kind of refuge for white folks with anti-white supremacist consciousness. During the 1980s such people supported the Jackson Campaigns. In the 1990s they protested police brutality, welfare cuts, and English-only campaigns; worked to defend affirmative action and bilingual education; and helped advance "jobs with justice" and immigrant rights.

There is no central orienting force today in the United States comparable to either 1) the national movements of the 1960s or 2) the CPUSA and its leading role in the labor struggles of the 1930s. The challenge for activists of all nationalities is to help set the conditions for a new upsurge – together this time – of the workers' movement and the national freedom movements. In addition, as we saw in Chapters 14-15, to be successful this strategic line-up will also need to include a women's movement centered on Third World feminism, whose form has taken shape only in recent decades.

Chapter 20

Personal Transformation

Activists in the United States today benefit from a long history of struggle against white supremacy. At the same time, people live their own particular lives – with their own particular ups and downs and lessons learned. It is one thing to look at times of upsurge in the past – the abolition movement and the Civil War, the 1930s or 1960s – and something else to confront the conditions in 2006 where the possibility of fundamental change in our social system seems so distant. Social movements help to bring forward revolutionaries – but what happens in their absence? How then do people find their way?

To gain insight into this problem, while being mindful of the dominant white consciousness in the country today as discussed in Chapter 17, we want to examine the two following questions:

- Where do white people who actively oppose white privilege and racism come from?
- What does it mean to be a "good ally" in the struggle?

In seeking answers to these questions, we hope to find ways to 1) be proactive in helping European Americans come to grips with their particular social reality; and 2) set the goal high for what white activists can aspire to become, while keeping the bar low for people to join in the struggle.

Where do white opponents of white racism come from?

There are a number of books available that are helpful in understanding how individual white people have come forward as fighters against white supremacy. Some contain short biographies describing a range of activists, like *A Promise and a Way of Life, White Men Challenging Racism,*

Refusing Racism: White Allies and the Struggle for Civil Rights, and *Through Survivor's Eyes*.[1] Others are individuals' own stories – for example, books by Anne Braden, Roxanne Dunbar-Ortiz, Myles Horton, Mark Naison, Mab Segrest, Tim Tyson and Tim Wise.[2] Beyond these resources there are the lessons readers can recall from their own experience or from the lives of people they have known.

In the next few pages we will present seven short biographies by people involved in writing this book. They are typical of many other European Americans, also generally unknown to the public, who are active in the struggle against white supremacy. These stories are meant to give a sense of the variety of ways folks can come to an anti-white supremacy perspective.

Michelle, age 32, bookkeeper

I was raised in Littleton, Colorado, a suburb of Denver shaped by white flight and the accumulation of wealth by working and middle class whites.

My first truly conscious memory of race and class was in 9th grade, following an incredibly sheltered childhood where whiteness and the "American Dream" were the norm, the neutral. I became friends with Angela, a working class Chicana whose parents had made it to the suburbs despite the exclusion and through many years of hard work and involvement in the labor movement. (Both were rank and file members of the UFCW [United Food and Commercial Workers] at a grocery store in Littleton.)

Angela asked me to spend the night at her house. I went to my mom asking for permission to stay over and my mom, with a pause, said, well how do we know that her family is OK? Although I couldn't put fancy words or an articulate analysis to it, I knew immediately that this was about race and class. She had never asked such things about my other friends' families.

I never told Angela about that question from my mom. I talked my mom into letting me spend time with her and her family – much to my benefit. I learned some good boxing moves from Angela's dad; and over the 4 years that we were friends, I was exposed to what a union was and why it's important for working people. All this, in addition to having a really good friend.

I went to college at the University of Colorado (CU) in Boulder. A year before finishing high school I began to identify with "activism" and to understand that there's much more to the world than the very narrow view I had been exposed to in life. I immediately threw myself into student activism at CU Boulder – in particular, working with the Student Environmental Action Coalition (SEAC), a national student group that was about to hold a conference on environmental justice at CU. Working within SEAC allowed me to connect with student organizers, many of whom did not even primarily identify as environmental activists, but rather as social and racial justice activists. I was challenged in all sorts of ways. Dhoruba Bin Wahad, a Black Panther who had just been released from prison after being wrongly imprisoned for 19 years, opened the conference, only because of the strong anti-racist politics of the organizers. That talk alone by Bin Wahad challenged me in more ways than I can go into here.

In 1994 after many years of all kinds of student activist work, I was fortunate to be involved in a student struggle – which culminated in a hunger strike – for the tenure of a Chicano professor and for a full-fledged ethnic studies program at the university. Conditions and relationships came together in a way that allowed us to wage a successful and broad based struggle that I believe helped shape the national fight for ethnic studies on campuses. United Mexican American Students/MEChA and the Asian Pacific American Coalition were the primary student of color organizations who led the fight. Other independ-

Speech by Dhoruba Bin Wahad

Michelle comments: "Looking back, it is really interesting to see how this long-time Black Revolutionary would address a very white and privileged crowd of young people. Rereading it, i can see why i was so challenged and inspired by it."

I want you to understand that you are at the University of Colorado because the United States of America has created a system of white-skin, male privilege and supremacy. And that this university, this citadel of higher learning, is a racist institution from the top to the bottom. That its function, and its objective is not to teach you how to think, but to teach you what to think. What it wants to teach you to think is that as a white person, you are somehow better than any person of color. That you come from a European heritage that has enlightened the world and advanced the world in terms of civilization and culture. I have come here tonight from the bowels of the American dream to tell you something. To tell you that if you do not understand the connection between the mindset which rapes the Earth, and that has raped my people, you are cashing in on your white-skin, male privilege.

Don't think that you are not being funded and helped by foundations and corporations who finance you precisely because you will not challenge white-skin, male privilege. Because you will fight for a forest, fight for a tree, fight for a whale, but you won't support Black people, you won't support Puerto Rican people, you won't support the oppressed of the Earth – that is your father, that is your mother, that are your ancestors – against the oppressor. You won't do that. I know you don't want to hear it, but it's true.

What I'm saying to you is that the most difficult struggle you have will not

ent students of color – who for one reason or another had decided not to work through the more established student of color groups – and progressive white students filled out the coalition. Together we succeeded in getting an Ethnic Studies Department and tenure for Estevan Flores in the department. Upon reflection, I believe the white students in the coalition made plenty of mistakes – and we weren't the only ones. But all and all we were fairly principled and willing to make those mistakes in order to be the kind of allies and equal partners in the struggle that we needed – and continue to need – to be.

I remember at the end of the fight in one of our last meetings before the end of the school year, one Chicana student said, "Before this struggle I had given up hope, I was simply just ready to get out of this racist town, this racist school. These two months completely changed my experience here, in this school. I will never be the same after this." Nor will I. Although a college is not a microcosm for the larger world, I learned that we could fight and win. We were able to build trust together, develop sophisticated strategies that worked, and fight to

be against lumbering companies, it will not be against multinational corporations which pollute the Earth. The most difficult struggle you'll have will be to cleanse your heart of racism – from the assumption that what you have to say is so important. You are a minority in the world – you need to really understand that for you to grow. For you to become a powerful movement...You should understand that you have to become like John Brown. You have to become like all of those revolutionaries, and all of those people in your history that have stood up against tyranny and that have fought with their lives to destroy the oppressor. You must become the new citizen of the world. You must empower yourself.

I think we can build a movement in this country that will bring to a screeching halt the raving lunatics who control this society today. I think that we can build the type of coalitions that will not only educate us about each other, but will also empower us. We can build organizations where women really lead, and are not just figureheads. We can build organizations that accept Black and Third World leadership as a matter of course. We can build organizations that confront racism with courage, with dignity, and with principle. We can build movements in this country that are very, very strong. We can build a movement like this, but we will not build that movement if you do not confront white-skin, male privilege, if you do not question the assumptions that you have, coming from the socialization that you come from. You have to do that if you want to make the environmental movement a serious movement that will radically change the power relationships in this country.

—from: Speech by Dhoruba Bin Wahad to the Student Environmental Action Coalition's national conference, October 1991

maintain those wins. This experience gives me the hope that those same wins. This experience gives me the hope that those same kinds of working relationships, based on multiracial organizing with an understanding and respect for self-determination, are both possible and absolutely critical if we are to bring about the kind of world we want to build.

Charlie, age 62, union organizer

I was born in 1943 and raised on a small dairy farm in central Virginia. My parents were anti-New Deal, Southern Republican pioneers, forbade the use of the "N" word or offensive characterizations, but clearly were comfortable with Jim Crow. As a highschooler in the '50s, my only rebellion in the segregated school system was from the right – I was the first Goldwaterite I knew and thought all civil rights agitation was an international communist plot. I considered any display of subservience from African Americans indicated genuine acceptance of the superior social status of whites and a racial timidity, not a survival strategy.

The first major challenge to my acceptance of the status quo happened in May 1962, while working in Huntsville, Alabama. The firebombings and near fatal beatings of Freedom Riders in nearby Anniston, Birmingham, and Montgomery convinced me that I didn't have the stomach for killing defenseless communists; that I could kill only armed communists in a military situation. So I joined the army. In basic training, it was forcefully and painfully impressed on me that timidity and a reluctance to fight were not part of a Black racial psyche. This was a significant revelation.

The three years I spent in the military presented a few more challenges to my simplistic worldview, but that process really took off when I took an overseas discharge and I spent 12 months in SE Asia, India, and the Middle East. Smug anti-communism simply could not explain the world as I experienced it away from the cocoon of likeminded comrades. I began a slow realization that I was on the wrong side of a titanic struggle against an empire of the rich and powerful. The degree to which I could shed my ideological ignorance in order to understand what was going on around me was the degree to which I could make sense of the Black Liberation struggle back home. I remember my excitement at reading Malcolm X's biography, and realized that three years prior, I had witnessed my fellow team members grin with satisfaction at the news of his assassination. The struggles of the '60s gave rightwing Southern whites many opportunities to discard a totally useless prism and perspective, but many chose not to look elsewhere for the means to really interpret the events of their world. I consider myself one of the luckiest people in the world that I didn't suffer that fate.

Bryan, age 26, high school teacher

Before I ever bounded into Mrs. Eno's 1st grade class, Doug E Fresh had beatboxed his way into my little small-town California world. My older cousin hit me with a Slick Rick mixtape, and I was trippin. My sister and I would sit by the radio, waiting for Run DMC's newest single to play, so we could tape it and "let the tape rock 'til the tape popped." We made our parents take us to the video store to rent *Breakin*, then broke down cardboard boxes and lamely attempted break moves on our driveway.

See, I grew up as far from the South Bronx ghettos of Hip-Hop's birth as one could be, but I always knew that Black people were human beings. While that might not sound particularly profound, I think it's the key piece of my anti-racist foundation. I didn't grow up on minstrel shows with my "mammy" chasing me out of the kitchen; I didn't have to wonder if Black people used that water fountain or went to that school because they weren't actually as good as me. I came of age as the civil rights gains of "The Cosby Show," and "A Different World," laid out the complexities of (at least middle class) Black life, and Public Enemy and N.W.A. replaced CNN as my generation's news source.

So when I showed up on the public court to play pick-up ball, I didn't have caricaturized images of Black people in my head. These dudes were people just like me, and in fact, I was actually in *their* space now and would have to prove *my*self… "check out the whiteboy." They were *better than me*, and if I wanted to hang, I would have to figure out how they talked, how they interacted, how to survive in what was, for the moment, *their world*. Otherwise, I'd never even get on the court.

I don't think that most white kids have this experience, and it had sort of a DuBoisian "Double Consciousness" effect on me. Clearly, there were two worlds where I lived, and if I wanted access to both, I was going to have to transition smoothly, because exclusion was always one slip away.

By the time I finished high school, it was Malcolm X, and Spike Lee flicks, and freestyle cyphers on the back of the bus home from basketball games, and getting called a "whigger" for always confronting my white friends on their racism, and, and, and…

So when I finally interacted with organized anti-racism, or any kind of theoretical manifestation of it, it all seemed pretty common sense. I was a bit shocked by some of the institutional constructs that held white supremacy together (Prison industrial complex? Word?!), and, of course, I still wasn't even close to comprehending the extent of the privileges my whiteness afforded me every day. But still, if the basic premise was human rights, well, I never had to struggle to see Black people, or any people of color for that matter, as humans.

I've learned a lot since then. I'm constantly struggling to stay conscious, stay vigilant, every second of every day. Sometimes it makes me crazy, but I figure it's not a tenth of the craziness that people of color are forced to endure. So I'll bear it gladly. And I'll keep fighting, and keep messing up, fighting and messing up, until I die. It's a lifetime commitment, and like Big Daddy Kane said, "it ain't no half-steppin."

Stan, age 56, writer

I didn't know when I was a kid that *National Geographic* was racist, but I liked the maps. I've always loved maps; and I loved to read omnivorously. Those *National Geographics* were about as close as I ever got to anyone except white people until my parents were pushed by the economy into an aircraft factory in St. Louis. Suddenly I was going to school with people who were not white. By then it was the sixties.

My parents had cautioned me never to use the word "n_____," not out of any anti-racist impulse, but because my Mom thought it sounded common. It reminded her of her own poor-white roots in Arkansas, which she always wanted to leave far, far behind. She substituted sanitized versions of the past for the reality of the Depression she grew up in, clothed in her siblings' hand-me-downs.

I really didn't start hanging out with any Black folk until I was 17, when I got myself an apartment in the Pruitt-Igo slum in St. Louis and found a roommate who went by the nickname, Skeeter. Skeeter, who was 19, and I had one thing in common, and that was that we liked to drink beer. The advantage of living in St. Louis back then was that no one ever carded us when we wanted to buy beer. So Skeeter and I had a pretty good thing going – no supervision, plenty of beer, and just sitting around, listening to music.

That year Martin Luther King declared his opposition to the war in Vietnam, and my father began to use the word "n_____" when he shouted at the television. He did this even though about half the people he worked with driving rivets into the fuselages of F-4 Phantoms at McDonnell were Black. That was also the year that Richard Nixon unveiled his Southern Strategy – though I knew nothing about this – which my parents went for hook, line, and sinker. Black people looked very dangerous to them that year, and Nixon's campaign managers worked very hard to fan those fears.

I had been expelled from school the year before for "rebelliousness." But then I got permission to go back and finish high school in 1969, so I went home. I was very confused and self-absorbed, and was hanging around with bikers and their ilk, so I pretty much missed all the political winds that were blowing around me. One thing led to another, and by December of that year, I had joined the Army on the Delayed Entry Program. In January, I went to Basic Training at Ft. Leonard Wood and by the end of that year, my life had been turned upside down. My first assignment in the Army was as an infantryman in the 173rd Airborne Brigade in what was then called the Republic of Vietnam.

Just like in Iraq in 2005, there was pretty widespread opposition to the US occupation there and a lot of people were fighting against us. A lot more people were supporting the people who were fighting against us. I was shocked when during my initial days there, my unit murdered an old woman just because she was Vietnamese. I was even more shocked when I suddenly discovered a few months later that I now felt perfectly prepared to shoot someone because that person was Vietnamese. In order to adjust myself to my circumstances as an occupying soldier, I had to reduce the Vietnamese to something less than human in my own mind in order to do my job. The politics I had ignored at home, which was a lot about white supremacy, had invaded my life in Vietnam.

That was when I first became aware of racism, and I never forgot it. It has consequences. Racism seals off your conscience while you burn down someone's home.

In many ways, the struggle against white supremacy – even before I knew what it was – was the catalyst that would eventually take me out of a military career and into revolutionary politics. There is not a day that goes by in my life that I do not think about that old woman my platoon murdered.

Now, these decades later, I have raised three Black children; and this, more than anything, helped me to understand that white privilege has to be exposed if we are to understand what this thing – whiteness – means. I've had to tell my kids, you cannot afford to give white people you don't know the benefit of the doubt. And I've had to tell other white people, that instruction is not racist... it's survival. Don't take it personal.

Elly, age 59, retired autoworker

"So how did a nice Jewish girl like you end up like this?" I don't know how many times I've heard that question – but it seems almost constantly, especially when it comes to the question of race.

I was raised in luxury and never wanted for a thing. I was a rebel, but mostly without a cause. It took me until I was 14 to begin to figure it all out. The tip-off, of course, was growing up in the U.S. apartheid system – first in Texas and then in Baltimore – during the 1950s. While others around me accepted without question "the natural order of things" – black servants for all white families, even those without much; separate neighborhoods enforced by laws; separate, and inferior, schools; separate water fountains and playgrounds; separate everything – for some reason it just didn't seem right to me. Even my family's inability to live where they wanted because of their religion didn't phase them. They didn't overtly mistreat the folks who made their life, and mine, easy – nannies, maids, laundresses, gardeners – like I'd seen at my grandparents, with the yelling and snide asides. They treated people as if they were invisible.

Two events – coincidences of history really – coming almost simultaneously, helped me put things together. One night after dinner, our family was sitting in the parlor in a "Leave it to Beaver" moment. My father was getting ready to read the paper; my mother was on the phone; my brother and I were watching TV. Our maid – actually surrogate mother since she was the one who really raised us – was walking by. My father, the complete Southern gentleman, called out in a most pleasant voice, "Althea, can you hand me that newspaper, please?" It was at his feet.

This was just a few months before my parents and I had an "appointment" with the headmaster at my new school – a private, progressive institution in the John Dewey tradition. By the luck of the draw, my teacher gave me the development of child labor laws in England as the first research assignment in European history. You can probably imagine the rest, given that it was 1959. During my research I found all my modern sources referring back to something written in the mid-1800s by a guy named Karl Marx. This hot-shit 9th grader decided to go right to the source. The research paper I handed in was based on *Capital*, and sprinkled liberally with terms like "reserve army of labor" and "wage slavery," along with details of the conditions of the English working class. It all made perfect sense to me. I could see that the servants in my house – I had been to their homes over the years – had a remarkable amount in common with the English working class, only worse. The rather large "F" on my paper, along with the note to my parents to "see the headmaster" sent shock waves through my Republican family. As did the "did you know you are breeding Bolsheviks in your bathroom" chat with Mr. Vogel.

Chip, age 63, activist/writer

I grew up in the white suburbs of Philadelphia, in a mostly middle class section surrounded by more wealthy areas of the Main Line. The only black people I can remember while growing up were two women clerks, one in the town hardware store and the other at a local pharmacy. For my town, the one Jewish kid was what diversity amounted to, along with an "Italian section" and the Catholic Church and its school, St. Margaret's. At age eight I bunked for two weeks with a black kid at a YMCA camp. Yet even without any exposure to people with different skin colors – or probably because of it – there was plenty of racist name-calling, "Your mom (this and that)," and the like.

High school wasn't much different really. There my anti-Semitism came to the fore, and after offending any number of people I finally became more aware of what I was doing. My parents' attitudes weren't much help. In high school the black kids tended to be the athletes, except for the one guy who quietly made it into the college prep courses – although I never spoke with him. Along with being clueless about race went anti-communism – "I'd rather be dead than a communist," religious narrow-mindedness, and an overall ignorance about the world – all while graduating at the top of my class.

In college, the pattern continued – even though the civil rights movement was unfolding during those years, 1960 to '64. There were a couple black guys in my fraternity, and that was a plus – although I remember my racism coming out in a somewhat drunken pledge party we had for one of the new black pledges. Malcolm X spoke at our campus and I didn't attend. When Martin Luther King was there one time, it struck me that I couldn't honestly sing "We Shall Overcome." During the summer of 1963, however, I did help out with an NAACP tutoring project in Philadelphia; and I remember listening to a part of the March on Washington and being impressed with the community/celebratory feeling that came from the event.

Key for me, probably, was the unavoidable reality of people struggling – African Americans at home and Vietnamese in Southeast Asia. After college I took a two-year break from the academic grind and went to Laos with the International Voluntary Service. There I spent a lot of time reflecting on things and in occasional discussions with other volunteers. Also, the CIA and US military were all around us – flying overhead to bomb the Ho Chi Minh Trial, making mistakes and bombing friendly villages – while the invasion of the Dominican Republic added to the evidence of U.S. aggression. For the first time I came to a political decision on my own – opposition to the Vietnam War.

Between opposing the war, cheering on the Berkeley student rebellion, reading Malcolm X's autobiography, and consulting with that same black fraternity brother and former pledge about the various civil rights organizations – he spelled out the positive things about each of the groups – I was kind of on my way. That doesn't mean I don't still shudder at the racist things that came out of my mouth in subsequent years.

By and large my path was one of hit and miss, floundering from med school to a lab tech job and eventually to working as a lathe operator in a gear factory for ten years. At one point in my cross-class journey, I even ended up on a mental ward for ten days. There was also trial and error – many errors – in finding my way in 1979 to what felt like a political/organizational home. If there's been one mentor in my life, it's been the collective mentoring of this group of activists, since 1985 called the Freedom Road Socialist Organization. It's the difference between wandering in the dark by yourself and having a kind of collective light to help point the way and keep you company. In time, it even helped me come to feel that I'm just one of the ordinary, basically healthy human beings out there who are trying to make a better world.

Anna, age 28, union organizer

I was born and raised in Memphis, TN in a part of town that is predominantly African American. In spite of that, or maybe because of it, my parents did a good job of ensuring that I understood that black people were different from me. We might have all been poor, but I was different because I was white. Even now it is hard for me to admit that about my folks whom I love. On a conscious level, I never bought that we were somehow better, smarter, or more civilized because we were white. On a subconscious level, it was ingrained in me.

I was 5 years old when I remember hearing the word "racist" for the first time. I didn't know what it meant, but I instinctively knew by the tone in which it was spoken that I didn't want it applied to me. I was on the school bus, and someone told a joke. Everyone laughed, and I wanted to be the next to entertain the crowd. I told a joke that I had overheard one of my uncles telling my dad. No one laughed. In fact, some kids were angry, others were in shock, and LaKesha, my best friend, began to cry. I asked her what was wrong, and she said, "How can my best friend be racist?" I told her I didn't know what that word meant. She explained that it meant that I thought I was better than her because I was white. I started to cry, and I told her that I didn't think I was better and that I didn't want to be or mean to be racist. I asked her forgiveness and told her I would never be racist again. From that day on, I began to challenge myself and to question everything I was taught.

What I didn't know at the time was that racism is more than just not liking someone because of his/her race. It is about being denied privileges, resources, and access because of your race. I saw evidence every day of how I was granted these privileges because I was white. There were only a handful of white kids in my elementary school. In fact, I was the only white person in the entire 6th grade. We were automatically smarter and better behaved because we were white. We were given access to the "smart kids" magnet program, even by a teaching staff that was predominantly African American. There were some African American kids that slipped through into the program, but out of twenty kids that were in the program, only four were African American. I soon came to realize that this was the way to keep the white parents happy and to show that our school wasn't a "black" school. I felt guilty and wanted to drop out of the program, but my parents wouldn't allow it.

I attended a magnet school for international studies for both middle and high school. It was full of folks of different races, ethnicities, languages, and religions. Even in this environment, the white and the Asian kids were the ones in the honors/ college-bound courses, and everyone else took the vocational/regular courses. I was the kid who tried to break boundaries, who never felt as though I fit. I never liked what I saw and wanted to do something to change it.

I began to challenge myself as well as others around the issue of racism and white skin privilege. I decided that in everything I did I would try and correct this wrong that I didn't choose to be a part of. I challenged my family and my friends. It was very difficult and tumultuous at times. We would have scream fests at each other. No one likes to be called racist and everyone will deny that they somehow contribute to racism. Eventually we stopped yelling and started listening, and we have come to some understanding with each other. It is still a challenge, but one that I am dedicated to overcoming. I figure if we want to overcome racism, we have to start with ourselves and with our families as well as the political and social institutions we are a part of. Maybe if enough of us start pushing, we can break down some boundaries and help people get to the root of what's wrong.

So where, then, *do* white activists come from?

Based on these examples, white activists come from just about anywhere – from the North, South, and West; from the working, middle, and upper class; from grade school, college, high school, and the military – and even from gay and heterosexual folks, although this aspect did not come through in the bios as written. And this is just a sampling of seven activists who happen to be helping out with this book. Taking these short biographies together with the longer accounts in the books mentioned at the start of the chapter, we can identify a number of common features in folks' life stories. Each point has a name or two associated with it as examples:

- **No white person is born with anti-white supremacy consciousness** – or perhaps people are, but it quickly gets socialized out of them. Everyone has made mistakes and is constantly learning – a reason to be patient with family, friends, and co-workers, as well as with the white people we have yet to meet. (Anne Braden*, Mab Segrest)
- **Getting to know people of other races and nationalities personally** is incredibly important – probably the single most important experience that can help clarify white folks' understanding. This fact is one reason why the increasing segregation of U.S. society in

* A full name without a footnote marker refers to the autobiography by that person listed in the endnotes for Chapter 20. Where only a first name appears, the reference is to one of the seven bios in the text.

recent decades is so damaging. (Charlie, Stan, Bryan; Tim Wise, Mark Naison, and many others)

- **Parents, friends, lovers and spouses – in a word, a *mentor* – can help open up a world** different from the one drummed in by the media, daily culture, and most school history books. (Anne Braden, Carl Braden*, Rose Marie Cummins*)
- **Belonging to an organization that is socially active** can foster a collective learning process and an environment that nurtures personal growth. (Chip; Betty Liveright*)
- **Engaging in social activism can open people to new ideas,** as reality forces them to confront questions that come up in the course of a campaign. (Michelle)
- **Seeing first hand the conditions in which people live** and the way people are treated can be a starting point – especially if there is someone there to help the person make sense out of what they are seeing. (Herbert Aptheker†, Stan Markowitz†)
- **Being confronted by someone** – be it friend, acquaintance, teacher or stranger – can raise to consciousness the contradictions in a person's life and force a reevaluation of how one thinks and how the world works. (Anna; Virginia Durr‡, Susan Burnett*, Tim Wise)
- **Reading books, taking a class, hearing a speech** can all have a life-changing effect if they come at the right time – when people are really receptive, open to listening and challenging their preconceptions. (Elly, Michelle)

Other contributing factors can also be important in preparing the way toward deeper understanding and activism around white supremacy:

- **Drawing on religious roots** – to sort through hypocrisy and make a commitment to social justice (Horace Seldon†, Pat Cusick*, Myles Horton)
- **Breaking with a religious or family outlook that keeps a person's thinking narrowly focused** (Bonnie Kerness*, Betty Liveright*)
- **Feeling like an outsider** – for example, as a gay, lesbian or transgendered person – and therefore being more open to understand-

---

* In Becky Thompson, *A Promise and a Way of Life*

† In Cooper Thompson, *White Men Challenging Racism*

‡ In Brown, *Refusing Racism*

ing the conditions faced by other outsiders and the powerless (Mab Segrest)

- **Experiencing and resisting class or gender oppression directly** – and then making the connections with racial oppression (Roxanne Dunbar Ortiz, Myles Horton)
- **Living in times when social movements are on the rise** (Bill Walsh[†] and almost everyone else over 50)
- **Taking initiative in a socially meaningful way** – and feeling good about the experience, whether that first effort is successful or not (Tim Tyson, Herbert Kohl[‡])

The goal of making lists like this – and learning from other people's

John Howard Griffin (1920–1980)

John Howard Griffin wrote and was the main character in *Black Like Me*, a graphic account of 1950s life in the Jim Crow South. The story follows a middle-aged, white Southern man who became black for six weeks in order to understand what it meant to be black under segregation. What Griffin experienced changed his life.

Griffin grew up in Texas during the 1920s, and at the age of 15 he moved to France to get a classical Benedictine education. Over the next six years Griffin completed studies in French, music, literature, and medicine, and worked as an intern conducting experiments in the use of music as therapy for the criminally insane. At the outbreak of WWII he joined the French Resistance before spending three years with the U.S. Army Air Corps in the South Seas, where he was decorated for bravery. In later years Griffin reflected, "I made no connection between the racism that was murdering the Jews of Europe and the racism that afflicted the minority people of America.. . [I] heard the Nazis say the same thing about Jewish people that I had grown up hearing about black people but I did not recognize the similarities."

In 1959, after shaving his head and using skin dyes, drugs and ultraviolet light to darken his skin, Griffin spent six weeks traveling through Louisiana, Mississippi, Alabama, and Georgia posing as an itinerant black man. Griffin's account of his experiences, first published in the magazine *Sepia*, and later as the book *Black Like Me*, is a gripping tale of degradation and cruelty. As Griffin remarked, he wasn't treated as a second-class citizen, but more like a tenth-class one. Griffin's experiences take the daily evils of racism and thrust them in your face, just as they were thrust in his: the ever-present use of "n_____"; the rudeness of the clerk when he tried to pay for a train ticket with a big bill; the difficulty he had in finding someone who would cash a traveler's check for a Negro; the driver who would not let black riders off the bus to use the restrooms; the white man who followed him at

Continued on next page

experience as recounted in their biographies – is to find ways to help white people come to terms with the reality of white privilege in their lives. When that happens, people can then find themselves freed up – the door now open to further transformation of their thinking and actions.

What does it mean to be a "good ally"?

The aim here is not to come up with a blueprint or script for being a good ally. Rather it is to identify an approach – a state of mind or orientation – that will help people discover for themselves what is appropriate to do or say in various situations. An assumption here is that since the process is ongoing and lasts a lifetime, it is OK to jump in anywhere – right where you happen to be at the moment. There is no entrance exam

Continued from previous page

night and threatened to mug him.

In general, Griffin found that conditions for blacks were appalling, with black communities physically run-down and, at least on the surface, appearing defeated. He even noticed a look of hopelessness on his own face, after only a few weeks as a black man. Griffin found positive signs, however, in Montgomery, Alabama, where the black community, under the leadership of Martin Luther King, Jr., had become energized by using civil disobedience to challenge the racist system.

Weary of life as a black man, Griffin stopped taking his medication and lightened his skin back to its normal color. He then began alternating back and forth between races, visiting a place first as a black man and then as a white man. When his skin was black, black folks welcomed Griffin with generosity and warmth, while white people responded to him with hostility and contempt. When his skin was white, white people treated him with respect and black people responded with suspicion and fear. Griffin concluded that the races did not understand each other at all, and that a tolerant dialog would be needed to bridge the gap separating them.

The publication of the *Sepia* article in 1960 rocketed Griffin to fame. Congratulatory mail rolled in from all over the world. But back home the town of Mansfield, Texas, greeted him with hate mail and reprisals. On Main St. people burned an effigy of him painted half white and half black. They lit up a cross in a Negro schoolyard and targeted Griffin with threats, including one to castrate him. By August, things were so bad that he decided to move his family to Mexico.

Griffin continued to speak out until a heart attack disabled him while on an extended speaking tour in 1976. He died four years later from the illnesses that had plagued him for many years. Griffin's experiences as a black man, however, followed him into the grave. Rumors circulated that the treatments he underwent while writing *Black Like Me* had eventually led to his death.

—*sources: Philips,* SparkNote; *Quasar, "Review"*

or bar people have to climb over. At the same time, there are some aspects of being an ally that white folks can strive for, as they self-monitor their actions and reactions in different situations over time. A few of these characteristics are the following:

- **Recognizing that you know next to nothing about almost everything.** This state of mind is very important since it opens a person up – to questioning all that society has taught them, and to listening to and observing carefully what other people say and do. It can also prevent folks from using the little bit of knowledge they do have to justify "speaking for" other people. The point is not, however, to throw out one's ability to reason along with all the excess baggage. And feeling guilty is not a substitute for clear thinking. People have to reach their own conclusions about what is right and wrong, true and false, and go from there.
- **Learning the histories of oppressed nationality peoples.** Take responsibility for grappling with the history of the color line in the United States – to see how it came to be, and how it has impacted people in the past and continues to do so today. "Taking responsibility" means doing it on one's own – and not expecting people of color to be one's teachers. Once this rich history is understood and internalized, it can help empower a common struggle against the system of racial preferences.
- **Building personal relationships with oppressed nationality peoples.** Through personal relationships white people can arrive at a more intimate sense of common purpose and an identification with the concerns of people colored differently from themselves. Doing so, however, requires the recognition that people of color have good reason to test white people, and that mutual trust takes time to establish. Not recognizing this larger context can lead to over-personalizing a situation – and then to getting hurt or becoming self-righteous and blaming others when a relationship does not work out.
- **Orienting to the struggles and leadership of oppressed nationality peoples.** Many white folks live and work in segregated conditions in U.S. society – often voluntarily. White activists in these situations should seek to be intentional about linking up and, where necessary, adjusting their local struggles to be in the flow with those of oppressed nationalities either in nearby locations, statewide, or nationally.
- **Being open to criticism from oppressed nationality people.** This point is linked to the first one above. It speaks specifically, however, to the more personal aspect of relationships that develop in

life and struggle. The obligation is to listen deeply and to grapple with the points people raise – and to recognize the effort required and the care being expressed when such criticism is offered. At the same time, a person should not blindly accept whatever someone else says. The goal is to attain clarity and purpose flowing from one's own understanding. It is only as someone who is freely acting and comfortable with her/himself that a person can be of real use in the struggle.

- **Taking responsibility for being active, raising issues, and organizing among white people in ways that challenge white supremacy.** This emphasis on work among white people complements the points above about seeking out personal relationships among and orienting to the struggles of oppressed nationality peoples. One can draw on the energy, insight, and direction provided by these movements. But the organizing effort needs to be with white people – understanding and uniting with their concerns, building struggle, and linking those struggles in a natural way with those of oppressed nationality peoples. It basically comes down to caring enough about folks to be willing to connect with them through the fog of white consciousness that is all around us. Friends, family members, even casual acquaintances deserve this type of patient, gentle but persistent attention.
- **Taking initiative and playing a leadership role where appropriate.** Being a good ally does not imply that a white person cannot be a leader in a multiracial organization. If the group's culture is democratic and there is adequate representation – if not a majority – of oppressed nationality members, white people can contribute and be held accountable as leaders. Organizations where white folks only function in subservient roles distort the idea of oppressed nationality leadership and tend to play on white guilt.
- **Not giving up.** When the contradictions seem to be overwhelming, take the time to work things through. Let the injuries heal and then get back into the struggle again – maybe in new conditions with a fresh slate. People are bound to come up against conditions where their socially conditioned responses cause pain to others. And people may also find themselves misguided and heading down a dead-end street somewhere. Being honest and facing up to the social roots of these actions can help folks renew their commitment at a higher level.

There are no doubt other characteristics that go into being a good ally, some of which you will find in Paul Kivel's section on "Being Allies" in his *Uprooting Racism*. Also, the books mentioned at the beginning of this chapter give rich, concrete examples of ways that white folks have struggled against white supremacy.

There are two additional aspects of being a good ally that can push the boundaries of this social role out farther. The term "ally" is particularly on target when referring to white people struggling alongside oppressed nationality peoples in their fight for national liberation. The analysis in Section II on the national movements in the United States gives a theoretical and historical basis for this understanding of the word *ally*. The key point here centers on recognizing the imperialist character of the U.S. social structure – and the impact this accumulation-driven system has on oppressed nationalities both inside and outside the country. Active support for self-determination for the African American, Chicano, and indigenous nations is a critical aspect of opposing the U.S. system of white supremacy – as is the defense of Cuba's independence and support for the Puerto Rican, Filipino, and Iraqi peoples' struggles to control their own countries.*

The second aspect speaks to white people's direct relationship to white supremacy and, in particular, the inherently oppressive character of systematic white privileges. The previous section, Chapters 16-18, describes the white consciousness that dominates so many people in the United States. There we posed the choice as "holding on or breaking free"...from white privilege. It is in this sense that white people can be more than simply allies in the struggle. They can be *freedom fighters* in their own right. White people can struggle to break down the barriers – many of them internal – that divide people from their brothers and sisters with darker skin. It is this sense of being personally driven to overturn the system that is most likely to keep white people steady and reliable through all the ups and downs of the struggle.

Solidarity...or betrayal

The problem remains, however, that historically white people have not been particularly good allies, much less freedom fighters against white supremacy. It is important to emphasize positive examples from history and today, as we have done in these last two chapters. And as we hold out the real possibility that white folks can transform themselves, the nagging fact remains that there is a whole lot of negative history to face up to.

We described in Chapter 5 how the Republican Party after the Civil War and the Populists in the 1890s were particularly graphic examples of betrayal by former white allies. Someone like Tom Watson, the Georgia Populist of the 1890s, embodied this "friend of black people" turned

---

* This list is not inclusive. Many other countries and nations throughout Latin America, Africa, and Asia could be mentioned here as well.

rabid segregationist. Short of betrayal, however, there are a range of other forms of inconstancy – reflected, for example, in the warnings over the years by oppressed nationality observers that "white activists can always return to their homes in the suburbs." Such temporary, friend-of-the-moment relationships – where interests coincide and then pass into indifference – make up the more common form of unreliability over time. Abolitionists, who put their lives on the line to end slavery, parted company during the Reconstruction period. The Communist Party USA dug deep roots in the South and Southwest during the 1930s – but then made a wholesale shift in its organizing strategy with the approach and onset of World War II. Many white civil rights activists tended to drop away or focus on anti-Vietnam War activism when the movement shifted to the North and to the question of Black Power and self-determination.

There are also the small, daily betrayals that seldom make it into our personal accounts or even into consciousness. There are the broken relationships that occur as life pulls people in different directions. For example, Tim Wise in *White Like Me* talks of his childhood friendships that gave way to his privileged path of academic tracking and then college. There are the guilty silences, the discomfort when personal worlds intersect, going with the flow, turning away from the pain of injustice, and a thousand other ways that people can betray their deepest good nature – as well as their brothers and sisters under the skin. Looking at these experiences straight in the face and seeing them for what they are is an important step in understanding how privilege breeds betrayal.

People get swept up in social movements. They can get carried along for a while and then drop away once the social momentum passes or their particular concerns are met. For the individual white person the reasons usually make sense: "I signed up to help end slavery," or "capitalism," or "segregation." Once that particular contradiction gets resolved, or the overall orientation shifts, the alliance can dissolve and the allies go back to being… well, white people. Wars are won – from the Revolutionary War through the Civil War to World War II – or lost, as in Vietnam. Social structures shift and the United States emerges as the sole superpower in the world. But white supremacy remains intact – this system of racialized capitalism, with its hegemonic culture rooted in slavery, conquest, and patriarchy. Its strength flows from centuries of malign existence at the center of the social set-up in the United States. And for this reason, those who struggle against white supremacy are forced to learn humility, consistency, resiliency, and forgiveness – including of themselves. White activists committed to ending the system of racial preferences must face up to this inescapable reality.

Meanwhile throughout history forces within the oppressed nationality communities have been clear and consistent in their demands – depending on the period – for freedom, equality, and self-determination.

White folks who paid attention to Metacom, Benjamin Banneker, or Harriet Tubman; to the *Plan de San Diego*, W.E.B. DuBois, or Ella Baker; to A. Philip Randolph, AIM, or Lolita Lebrón; and to many others – these white folks willing to listen and learn, coming from whatever social class, would have known how to proceed to end white supremacy. Today white people can benefit from these same insights from history, as well as from contemporary analysis emerging from today's oppressed nationality movements. In addition, people can develop a heightened understanding of the ways white privilege distorts and restricts their own lives – the cost to white people themselves of their own privilege. Together these two keys can open the door to becoming freedom fighters on their own behalf – as well as reliable allies in the struggles for national liberation. *Leadership by the oppressed nationality peoples* and a *deep understanding of how white supremacy harms white people, and white working class people in particular* – together these two conditions can help assure solidarity, rather than betrayal, by white allies over the long haul.

Most people get involved as a result of being hailed by a visible political movement...If there had been no movements to hail me, I have no idea what I would have done or would be doing today. If you are one of those organizers capable of pioneering initiatives, and we need such organizers in women of color movements today, and you want to activate youth, make sure you combine the political content with forms and styles of presentation that can dramatically hail young women and men.

—Angela Davis, "Coalition Building Among People of Color"

VII

Social Forces and Leadership

In earlier sections of this book we reviewed 1) the state of national consciousness among oppressed nationalities (Chapter 8); 2) a proposal to organize the South and Southwest by building a working class movement centered on the oppressed nations of that region (Chapter 11); and 3) the prospects for a Third Wave women's movement with women of color at the center (Chapter 15). Chapters 16 through 20 then took on the question of white people's ability to function as allies in the struggle to end white supremacy and racism. Together, these assessments point to a strategic alliance, or a united front, where oppressed nationality forces – with women and working class people in the lead – form the core of the front.

The question then becomes: How realistic is this rather grand strategic plan? It identifies the large fault lines of U.S. society – race, class, and gender. And it suggests a line-up of forces that, if well organized and united around a shared vision, could take power and transform society. To what extent can we say that such a front – or even the potential for such a front – exists?

The three chapters in this section examine this question. We move from a theoretical approach – focusing on the key fault line for this book, race – to a concern with the real life conditions organizers face in building a united front of oppressed nationalities.

In Chapter 21 we look at the color line at the start of the 21st Century. In particular, we consider 1) whether the color line is currently being redrawn, and 2) the conditions where blurring the color line is a positive development.

Chapter 22 assesses the broad prospects for unity among the oppressed nationalities. We review the contradictions that organizers confront in working to build unity internal to and among the various national movements. In the end, the larger social fault lines are only suggestive. Reality is far from monolithic when it comes to the actual people who make up a particular race or nationality. Progressives and revolutionaries count on that variation when it comes to organizing a sector of white people to fight against white supremacy. In similar fashion, the social system survives by fostering contradictions within communities of color that undermine unity despite experiencing shared oppression.

Chapter 23 then looks at gender, class, and organization. In particular, we highlight the importance of women taking a leading role in the united front against white supremacy. We conclude by drawing out some implications of the overall analysis for transforming movement organizations.

Chapter 21

Redrawing the Color Line?

There is a sense in which we all know where the color line is. Each of us can tell if a person is white or if they are not – at least, for the most part we think we can. Yet everyone's assessment is not always the same. Some people consider Asians to be white – or figure they might as well be, based on income, education and property ownership. Yet what about darker skinned South Asians or Pacific Islanders? Or Vietnamese boat people, Laotians, or Cambodians – many of whom are fisherman, farmers, and other working people living at or near the poverty level. Some Latino people have only a last name or maybe a slight shade of brown that points to their heritage. A movie starring Jennifer Lopez, for example, can unfold without even a reference to her being Latina. And a native person in a work setting, away from family and community life, can be taken to be white in impersonal interactions. For very light-skinned black people, "passing" can be an option. But regardless of the situation, to pass as white – to become assimilated into whiteness – in our culture still carries with it the shadow of the color line. It remains something that has been passed over.

What it takes to be white

One response to the question, "What does it take to be white?" is... white skin. But that answer is clearly not enough, since a common tendency today is to lump all Spanish-speaking people together – be they light-skinned, *mestizos/as,* or people of Indian or African heritage. Then everyone under the heading Hispanic or Latino is considered to be "brown." One example is when a commentator points to the year 2050 and says that then is when people of color will be a majority in the

United States. But to make such a prediction requires that all Latinos will still be brown on the strange U.S. color scale.

The Irish

Previous waves of immigrants to the U.S. had to go through a trial period in order to earn their whiteness. Noel Ignatiev's book *How the Irish Became White* discusses this transition period during the mid-1800s when there was a struggle over how the Irish would align themselves.

The fiery nationalist leader and first Irish Member of the British Parliament, Daniel O'Connell, challenged his ex-countryman living in the United States to stay true to their hatred of oppression and to take up the abolitionist cause. Some 60,000 Irish people in 1841 signed the *Address from the People of Ireland to their Countrymen and Countrywomen in America,* drafted by a group of U.S. and Irish abolitionists, including the African American Charles Lenox Remond. The statement concluded: "Irishmen and Irishwomen! *Treat the colored people as your equals, as brethren.* By your memories of Ireland, continue to love liberty – hate slavery – CLING BY THE ABOLITIONISTS – and *in America you will do honor to the name of Ireland.*[1]"

Meanwhile, as mentioned in Chapter 3, the popular image in the U.S. of the Irish people among native-born citizens of European background was only a notch better than free black people. Irish workers preformed the most menial work, and their low pay undercut African Americans in service positions – in restaurants, hospitals, trash collection and personal service. But when given the opportunity to unite with the abolitionists against slavery, as William Lloyd Garrison lamented, "not a single Irishman has come forward, either publicly or privately, to express his approval of the *Address*."[2] The highly influential Archbishop John Hughes of New York urged Irish Catholics – despite Pope Gregory the XVI's antislavery stance – to "merge socially and politically with the American people," by which he meant the country's white people.[3]

Mobs from Irish neighborhoods then sealed the decision in blood during the New York draft riots of 1863. Though partly motivated by class hatred, due to rich people's option to buy their way out of the Civil War draft for $500, the protesters opposed the war itself. Rioters targeted black people as the cause of their problems – killing hundreds and destroying black sections of the city. In doing so, the main section of the Irish people showed that their loyalties lay with the white supremacists rather than with the oppressed. In return, Irish workers over time gained a piece of the government in big cities, as well as work in the mines and skilled trades where employers excluded black people. But they also got corruption, death for union organizing (the Molly Maguires[*]), and depressed wages, as the Robber Barons gained control of the country's industry.

Eastern and Southern Europeans

The next great wave of European immigrants in the late 19th and early 20th centuries went through a similar transition period. The white ruling class feared that the influx of socialist-leaning Southern and Eastern Europeans would carry their revolutionary ideas into the workers struggles of the period – and potentially break through the wall that kept black, Chinese, and Mexican American workers out of the movement. As a result, the European immigrants found the carrot of assimilation dangled before them. In exchange for chasing this dream, newcomers received classes in Americanism, beatings by nativists,[†] crowded tenement buildings, suppression of their native languages, long hours and hazardous work – all backed up by the threat of deportations, jail and even execution, as in the case of Sacco and Vanzetti.

The Palmer raids at the end of World War I kicked many socialists out of the country. The Johnson-Reed Act of 1924 restricted immigration of Southern and Eastern Europeans – linking quotas to the much smaller population proportions that existed in 1890. Some workers later gravitated to the Communist Party USA, while others played a role more broadly in the labor upsurge of the 1930s. Eventually, however, most moved into the middle class as fully assimilated white people. The question is: Will today's Latino and Asian immigrants follow a similar trajectory? And might a sector of upper class African Americans possibly join them?

---

[*] The Molly Maguires were a secret organization of Irish mineworkers in eastern Pennsylvania who fought the mine owners – along with the police and courts they controlled – between 1865 and 1875. In 1875 the Mollies managed to form a union and called a strike. The head of the Reading Railroad, Patrick Gowen, then hired Pinkerton Detective James McParlan to infiltrate the mines. Resistance ended with the hanging of ten movement leaders in 1877.

[†] An anti-immigrant and anti-Catholic movement arose in the 1840s in response to people from Ireland and Germany coming into the country. This *nativist* current, claiming priority for earlier generations of immigrants and having nothing to do with the indigenous peoples, took political form in the Know Nothing Party of the 1850s. Nativism later characterized the Klu Klux Klan, the anti-Chinese mobs of the 1870s and '80s, the eugenics movement of the 1920s, and today's anti-immigrant campaigning by groups like FAIR (Federation for American Immigration Reform) and the Minutemen border vigilantes.

Blurring the color line

If the goal is to get rid of the color line, then why be concerned if people try to become assimilated? Isn't it good if the line gets blurred out? One way to approach this question is to consider different ways that people can move across the color line – and in doing so seem to make the line disappear. Hip-hop culture is one place where we can see at least two different types of "crossing over."

Hip hop culture

The book *Can't Stop, Won't Stop*, by Jeff Chang, gives an accounting of the origins of hip hop in the 1960s and '70s – linked to Jamaican Reggae music, gangs in the South Bronx becoming political, and new forms of expression by excluded youth through graffiti, break dancing, DJ-ing and, eventually, rap. During the 1970s the new sounds swept across neighborhoods and gang turf and eventually found their way to more upscale venues in downtown Manhattan. The new culture served as a solvent that helped cut through contradictions, much as 20 years later hip hop would set a tone for the peace-making initiatives of the early '90s among youth gangs in LA.

Albums like *The Message* and *Planet Rock* helped launch the 1980s, when Ronald Reagan came into power. Along with him came a right-wing program to reverse the gains of the civil rights era – which in time resulted in criminalizing youth of color. What had been a bridge between cultures in the '70s now became an expression of resistance from the grassroots – reflecting the harsh reality of oppressed nationality youths' lives. Mainstream critics targeted the messengers – the rappers and other hip hop artists – and left unacknowledged the social reality the performers gave voice to. Public Enemy and its hallmark *It Takes a Nation of Millions to Hold Us Back* became the anthem of the new post-civil rights generation. As Chuck D, a central voice in the group famously commented, "Hip hop is the CNN of black youth."

In this setting, the few white youth who found their way to hip hop and embraced it felt that their involvement was a political act – that they were taking a stance in solidarity with youth of color against a violent and racist system. These same fans ridiculed the white rapper of the period, Vanilla Ice – based on his lack of skills and, more generally, a transparent attempt to be what he was not.

Similar divisions had characterized earlier musical periods – as with jazz in the 1930s and '40s. Phil Rubio cites Milton Mezzrow, Red Rodney, and Johnny Carisi as jazz musicians who worked under black bandleaders during this period.[4] He tells how Mezzrow, arrested for marijuana possession in 1940, "insisted on being classified as 'colored' and assigned to the 'colored' cell-block. From then on he began referring to himself as a 'colored musician' and 'voluntary Negro.'" By contrast, Rubio also recounts how some white bandleaders would secretively attend black performances to steal ideas for their arrangements. In time jazz audiences became overwhelmingly white – as did, later, the consumers of rhythm and blues. Elvis Presley drew on R&B roots to become a rock-and-roll star. But later, as he rose in popularity, the King distanced himself from the culture he had exploited. Crossing the color line has a long history in the music world. The main lesson, however, is that while a few individual white people may genuinely cross over, power relations in the industry and society have remained essentially unchanged.

As the 1980s moved into the '90s, increasing numbers of white youth moved to connect with the rising hip-hop culture. Bakari Kitwana[5] notes that by 1994, Billy Wimsatt, a white graffiti artist and general hip-hop head from Chicago pointed to three kinds of white hip-hop fans[6]: 1) the hard core, who were deep into the culture and had close ties with youth of color; 2) the majority, who pretty much lived in their own world but responded to the music's beat and its rebellious attitude; and 3) a section of suburban and ex-urban youth who adopted the clothes, language and music but had no contact to speak of with youth of color. A fourth grouping, but in a different category altogether, were the white owners and managers of the music industry who controlled what went into the mainstream. This group presided over the shift from the political message of Public Enemy in the late 1980s to the commercialized gangster image of the mid-'90s and beyond.

By the early 2000s, surveys showed that some 70% of hip-hop's audience was white. The culture had become solidly mainstream, and artists like Nelly and 50 Cent set the pace with CDs going "multi-platinum" – selling several million copies of each release. Socially conscious rap remained, but mostly in local markets and distributed by independent producers. White rapper Eminem, like the Beastie Boys to a lesser extent before him, had gained respect for their rapping skills. But there is little doubt that their popularity also got an extra boost from their skin color.

One question that comes out of this almost forty years of cultural development straddling the color line is: to what extent can it be said to have contributed to overcoming, or at least undermining, white supremacy? One way to gauge the impact is to see two different ways to blur the color line: 1) crossing over into the dominant white capitalist and patriarchal culture, or 2) crossing over into a culture of resistance centered among oppressed nationality peoples. The first changes nothing – nothing but the skin color of a few performers who are making more money and a bunch of listeners who are giving it up. It is good that performers are not excluded as in the past and that white youth have some cultural icons with skin colors different from theirs. But white folks still run the music industry; and white youths who buy hip-hop CDs passively consume the culture.

By contrast, those white young people in the 1980s who found their way to hip hop crossed over into a culture of resistance. The degree to which they became conscious of their whiteness and its privileges and signed on for the long haul varied. But their initial motion was in the right direction. It is this question of conscious alignment with the struggles and conditions of oppressed nationality peoples that determines whether the color line is genuinely being erased by a pixel or two – or whether it is just taking on a new disguise.

During the rightward shift since Reagan took office, the dominant forces in society have reversed earlier gains in the struggle – by targeting affirmative action, criminalizing youth, pushing down the wage floor, gentrifying the central cities, and shifting employment to the South, Southwest and overseas. During this same period, hip hop moved into the mainstream, its open political message pushed down and out – into local areas and projected worldwide. There hip hop lives on as an oppositional culture closely tied to struggle. White youth can still genuinely cross the color line and become politically active through hip hop. But they are most likely to do so by connecting with people of color at the grassroots – and joining there with cultural forces targeting white supremacy.

Even after making such a move, however, the question remains whether transitioning white youths will be leaving their white privilege behind. Kitwana seems to suggest so in his *Why White Kids Love Hip Hop*. There he points to hip hop's potential as a new kind of political movement – with its hip hop conventions, registering youth to vote, and efforts to repeal repressive drug laws in NYC.[7] In proposing this idea, Kitwana draws a sharp distinction between the positive motion of today's youth and the race-conscious politics of the civil rights era. Meanwhile, coming at the question from the other side, Glen Ford, who writes as the *Black Commentator*[8], presents a different view. He points out that the basic demands of the earlier movement have still not been met – good jobs, living incomes, and quality housing, health care and education. In addition, huge amounts of corporate funds have gone into making the current generation of youth feel that they are "unique." Ford emphasizes that during the current extended period of political reaction, identification with past struggles must be strengthened, not denied.

A non-race conscious politics based in hip hop, as proposed by Kitwana, draws its appeal from the culture's rebellious attitude and its identification with artists of color. But today the dominant "gangsta" culture is mainstream and the majority of the audience is white – with industry leaders shaping the product to the tastes of this predominantly white audience. A contrasting image of a progressive hip-hop movement comes from the opening pages of *The Future Five Hundred*. This survey of youth organizations in the United States in 2002, and specifically its pictures and bios of 25 young organizers – the "Future 25" – captures the energy and hope of the hip-hop generation. Almost all the people included here are youth of color. But even more noteworthy is the fact that the white youth represented make it a point to note their privilege as white people – and their commitment to turning this advantage to the service of the movement.

Intermarriage and adoption

Intermarriage also can be seen as helping to blur the color line. And cross-racial adoptions also challenge the color line in the most intimate family setting. There is no doubt that these relationships are an advance over the anti-miscegenation laws that remained on the books in 16 states as late as the 1960s. And there is no reason to question the genuineness of the relationships that people of different races enter into – unlike psychiatrists of not so long ago who considered such pairings similar to homosexuality and, as such, labeled them both "abnormal." At the same time, however, one can ask whether these kinds of family arrangements, in and of themselves, challenge the existence of the color line in the United States today. In the movie *Bulworth* Warren Beatty as the transformed hip-hop senator calls for everyone to intermarry. That way over time, he says, the country's population will all be brown and racism will disappear.

The actual pattern of intermarriage, however, tends to move people away from "brownness" and toward whiteness. According to the 2000 census[9], some 16% of Asian Americans are in mixed marriages; and for those under age 35, 50% have non-Asian spouses.[10] Native people marry outside their race more than half the time, mostly to white people. Puerto Ricans lead all Latinos at a rate of 21%, with Mexicans and Cubans coming in at 12%. Finally, over 80% of mixed-race marriages include a white spouse – even where one partner is black. Given the way race works, then, children in families with one parent of African descent tend to be "of color" – and black trumps white. In other situations with a white spouse, the children tend to move toward full assimilation into white society. These patterns point to the continuing polarity of black-white social relations, with the status of Asian, Latino and native peoples lying in contested terrain.

There is no doubt that for more than two centuries anti-miscegenation laws were a bulwark of white supremacy. In particular, such laws targeted women in order to protect white patriarchal bloodlines. As discussed in Chapter 1, one of the first measures in legalizing slavery declared that the children of a slave woman were slaves – regardless of the race of the father. Another targeted white women, banning mixed relationships to prevent the offspring's challenge to the racial hierarchy. With the evolution of white supremacy to include other peoples of color, anti-miscegenation laws expanded to preserve the fiction of the white race – while reinforcing its harsh reality in real life.

Nonetheless, by the start of the 21st Century, with anti-miscegenation laws ruled unconstitutional in *Loving vs. Virginia* (1967) almost forty years earlier, the system of white supremacy and its color line continues. The struggle over the color line shows up in the categories included on the census every ten years; in the debates within the American Sociological Society over whether black children should be adopted by white parents; and in the opposing political positions taken by organizations of multiracial people – as in the case of California's Proposition 209 aimed at ending affirmative action in education. Such disputes are a clear advance over the tragic images historically assigned to "half-breeds," mulattos and uprooted Eurasians. As Sasha S. Welland comments in her *ColorLines* article "Being Between,"[11] such figures were "continually used to reinforce norms of racial segregation." In similar fashion, getting a handle on the social meaning of multiracialism today gives insights into the current, and evolving, structure of white supremacy.

Daniel HoSang reports in "Hiding Race" on the support given to anti-affirmative action campaigner, Ward Connerly, by a number of organizations of self-identified multiracial people: Interracial Voice, Project RACE, the Multi Racial Activist, and a few other online networks. These groups have joined Connerly in blaming racism on the "belief in 'race' itself" – suggesting that it is the boxes on the census forms that divide people. These groups' goal is to eliminate public data collection identifying people by race. By so doing, they also hope to undermine policies that target the historic – and current – injustices caused by white supremacy. While the groups' statements oppose racial discrimination, they reject "any relationships with civil rights or racial justice organizations, often dismissing them like Connerly does as seeking only to profit from a 'racial spoils system.'"[12]

Countering such organizations – and Connerly – are groups that celebrate their mixed heritage while recognizing the ongoing reality of white supremacy. Originating mostly on college campuses, groups like the Association of Multiethnic Americans, the Hapa Issues Forum and the Mavin Foundation have spoken out against Connerly's attempt to use multiracial families as proof that racial categories no longer have social meaning. And student members of MISC at Smith College "assert that anything naming itself a multiracial movement has to move beyond identity issues to include anti-racist politics as an integral part of its agenda."[13]

As with hip hop culture, then, mixed race relationships at the family level can impact the color line in sharply different ways – even as they physically blur out the margins of whiteness. To the extent that people recognize the reality of color in U.S. society – even if they personally straddle the line in some respects – they then can identify with its darker side and, as such, with the social forces in contradiction to white supremacy. In similar fashion, white parents who raise their cross-race adoptive children to understand the social realities of race will enable them to align more smoothly with movements opposed to white domination. Only superficially does such training appear to divide people within the same family. Rather, it demonstrates white parents' ability to act as allies across the color line in the most intimate fashion – by raising nationality and race conscious freedom fighters.

But people also have the option to move in the opposite direction – toward assimilating themselves or their cross-race children into white society and its privileges. Here the downside, the hook, of white privilege is even sharper than for straight-up white folks. The culture encourages people to gravitate toward whiteness and its privileges, while seeking – often unconsciously – to avoid the consequences of having darker-than-white skin. But in doing so, people can leave themselves disarmed in the face of a social reality that continues to be color conscious and white supremacist.

For multiracial relationships on the oppressed nationality side of the color line – where neither partner is white – the situation is less charged but still contains its own contradictions. Here racial categories tend to get broken down and cross-cultural identities, rooted in resistance to white supremacy, can gather strength. People with these kinds of multiracial backgrounds can still be attracted by the colorblind politics of a Ward Connerly – after all, Connerly himself is of African descent. And there can be a certain "exoticism" that comes with a mixed heritage, which can tend to set people apart. Nonetheless, there is a greater possibility in these situations to both recognize and accept social differences in a deep and historically rooted way. Doing so is what really allows people to see and relate to each other fully as unique individuals. And this ability, in turn, is a key element in building a movement capable of transforming the system of racial preferences.

Who's on which side of the line?

The color line can be difficult to see because of the amount of energy expended – in popular culture and social denial – to keep it out of public consciousness. As we have seen in earlier chapters – Chapters 3 and 16 in particular – the dominant discourse uses the language of formal equality to promote a rightwing colorblindness that denies the continuing existence, not to say the strengthening, of racial and national oppression. Today, after decades of budget cuts and tax give-aways to the rich, the reality is that many working people live stressful, insecure, and fragmented lives – very much in line with the dominant free market picture of society as a collection of isolated individuals. Popular forms of self-organization – from grassroots union organizing to community-based movements – are generally at a low point, although the massive spring 2006 mobilization of Latino immigrants and others provides hope of changes to come. And the public sphere – including a threadbare safety net – has been systematically defunded in favor of war and empire.

In the fall of 2005, all of these tendencies came together in hurricane Katrina's man-made devastation of New Orleans: lack of public resources, official incompetence, public disorganization, and racist denial. And then in the wreckage of Louisiana and Mississippi, military recruiters moved in to recruit soldiers to kill and be killed in Iraq. Corporations took advantage of below market wages paid – and often left unpaid – to undocumented immigrants brought in from Central America. And at the same time, Fox News and CNN analysts – not to mention the rightwing radio talk shows – fed anti-immigrant fears nationally by opposing driver's licenses and college aid programs for undocumented workers and youth.

The color line runs through all these issues – from the 70% of New Orleans who were black, poor and then dispersed to undercut their ability to organize; to the military's hunger for black soldiers to kill brown people in Central Asia; to the targeting of brown-skinned workers as the root cause of the country's job loss, declining wages, and shortage of public resources.

Even though the United States in 2006 is the dominant power in the world, there are challenges on all sides:

- *internationally*, rebellion and resurgence from Central Asia to the Philippines, and throughout Latin America; and
- *at home*, incompetence, corruption, spiraling international debt, and a spineless political opposition.

The times are uncertain. And historically – as we have seen in Chapters 3, 5 and 9, for example – such times are when the dominant social forces operate in a way that strengthens white privilege. Wedges get driven between white workers and peoples of color. Doors open that allow new sectors – like the Irish, Italians, Eastern Europeans, or Jewish people – to join the privileged ranks of the solid white front. Similar dynamics can be seen at work in the United States in the current period.

Latinos/as

The situation is very complex when looking at the various Latino peoples in relation to the color line. Dominating the situation are two color schemes – one all white, the other having a range of hues but in a sense anchored in black. There is the whiteness of George Bush and the U.S. Chamber of Commerce. And then there are the multiple shades of ordinary Latino people – *la raza*: descendants of people from the annexed portion of Northern Mexico; Puerto Rican U.S. citizens, living on the island or in North American urban *barrios;* and generations of immigrants with indigenous, African and European backgrounds. One side offers, to varying degrees, the illusion of acceptance, integration and, ultimately, whiteness – on a par with Europeans. The other lives the reality of race.

George W. Bush began his first administration in 2001 with an eye to bringing at least a section of middle class Latinos into the white camp. He made a point of speaking Spanish and promoted his personal relationship with Mexico's president, Vicente Fox. There was also talk of normalizing immigration relations between the two countries, though the particulars remained murky. Then came 9/11 and a sharp change in U.S. policy. Border patrols and resources increased – but hundred of migrants continued to die trying to enter the country through the mountains and deserts of the Southwest.* The flow of undocumented workers also continued undiminished. By 2005 internal checkpoints had been set up in a 100-mile zone running along all the country's borders.

Bush found himself pulled one way by agribusiness interests and the U.S. Chamber of Commerce, who still demand a steady supply of low-wage labor, and pulled the other way by his anti-immigrant, white supremacist popular base. Arizona's Proposition 200, passed in November 2005, requires proof of citizenship to receive public benefits and to vote. And at the end of 2005, in response to the chorus of immigrant bashers, the Congress passed the "Border and Immigration Enforcement Act of 2005," making it a felony to offer assistance to an undocumented immigrant and calling for a double fence to run along 700 miles of the border with Mexico. In response, Vicente Fox charged, "This wall is shameful," and compared it to the Berlin Wall, torn down in a popular rising in 1989.[14]

Despite this record of attacks on brown people, the ruling class still offers the hope of assimilation to people currently living inside the country – in line with Linda Chavez's neoconservative viewpoint in *Out of the Barrio: Toward a New Politics of Hispanic Assimilation*. Overall the policy seems clear: clamp down on the border; provide businesses with their low-wage workforce through a new *bracero* – or temporary worker – program; and offer the upper classes the privileges of whiteness by way of assimilation into the white supremacist structure. Supporting this program are arguments that distance "brown" from "black" – seeking to separate Latinos from African Americans at the opposite extreme from whiteness.

One commentator reflects this reactionary vision of the 21st Century: "There is not going to be a non-white majority in the 21st century [in the

---

* A new record of 460 deaths occurred during the period from October 1, 2004, through September 29, 2005. (Science Daily, *Oct. 4, 2005)*

United States]. Rather there is going to be a mostly white mixed-race majority...[W]hat seems to be emerging in the United States is a new dichotomy between blacks and non-blacks. Increasingly, whites, Asians and Hispanics are creating a broad community from which black Americans may be excluded."[15]

Helping to justify this redrawing of the color line are writings like Nicolás Vaca's *The Presumed Alliance* and Richard Rodriguez's *Brown*. Reviewer Ed Morales[16] dubs these authors "brownologists" for lumping all Latino people together as brown and drawing a line of separation with African Americans. Their argument stresses two main points: first, the distinctive histories of Latinos/as and black people in relation to white supremacy; and, second, the economic and political tensions that have divided the two peoples in recent decades. Morales grants the kernel of truth in both these claims. But then he zeroes in on the key question – what about the blackness that is part of being brown? Some ten percent of Latinos are very dark skinned – and there are many more who identify with the resistance struggles of black people. There are the Afro-Latin roots of people from Caribbean countries and Brazil – from Puerto Rico, and the Dominican Republic, to Venezuela, Colombia, Panama and Mexico itself. There are the common cultural roots of hip hop originating in neighboring communities in the Bronx and Harlem; as well as the last line of Pedro Pietri's poem, *Puerto Rican Obituary*: "Aquí to be called negrito means to be called LOVE." Morales also notes, "After a few generations many Latinos start to look more and more like African-Americans," and asks, "Aren't we always cooperating and competing with everyone we love?"

Morales concludes: "Vaca's book might be helpful in clearing the ground for future cooperation between blacks and Latinos by acknowledging points of contention. But the book is more likely to have the effect of reinforcing what generations of immigrants have been taught: that estrangement from blackness is the key to success in America."

A counter perspective suggests that while a sector of the Latino population might be pulled into the white orbit, the masses of Latino people, unlike the European immigrants in previous waves, will likely continue to be treated as outsiders. One reason is the organic connection to the great Latin American land mass, population and culture to the south. Puerto Rico is an example – neither set free from its colonial status nor brought in as a state, mainly because of its Spanish speaking populace. In similar fashion, the Latin *mestizo* people and culture, with its historic ties to the Chicano national territory of the Southwest, will likely remain indigestible by the white body politic.

Second, despite the debates going on over people's heads, a 1995 study showed that "educational outcomes of Chicano/a youth are the lowest of any major racial/ethnic group in the United States."[17] Also, among students in LA colleges and high schools, as researcher Marc Pizarro reports, "Race is by far the most dominant facet of these students' identities."[18] Racial confrontations and the experience of discrimination directed at students and their family members shape these youths' sense of who they are and how they fit into society.

Third, as Ted Allen points out[19], the assimilation of the Latino middle class would likely undermine their role as social control agents, a function the white supremacist system depends on. This sector in a sense would then disappear as a buffer separating the white ruling class from the Latino masses. By denying their roots and becoming white, Latino leaders risk losing their legitimacy as authentic popular spokespeople. What fits better with the logic of the system is that here and there a Latino individual succeeds – Attorney General Alberto Gonzales, for example, in the same way as Clarence Thomas, Colin Powell, and Condoleeza Rice have among African Americans. There is then the appearance of multiculturalism and equal opportunity; and the middle class continues to aspire to lead the majority of Latino people struggling with the reality of white supremacy.

An Open Letter to our African American Sisters and Brothers

Note: Peoples of color are being hurt more than ever today, thanks to the "Permanent War on Terrorism" and the War at Home. It, therefore, seems more important than ever to build alliances between our peoples who have similar struggles for liberation from poverty and racism, for peace with justice. This Open Letter is offered in that spirit . . .

—Institute for Multiracial Justice, San Francisco

The media have been full of it this year, with such headlines as "Hispanics Now Largest Minority," "America's Ethnic Shift...," "Latinos pass blacks unless you count black Latinos...," "Hispanics Pass Blacks..."

As Latino/a teachers, activists, community people, students, artists and writers, we stand fiercely opposed to anyone making those numbers a reason to forget the unique historical experience of African Americans, the almost unimaginable inhumanity of slavery lasting centuries, the vast distance that remains on their long walk to freedom. We cannot let whatever meager attention has been given to the needs of Black people up to now be diminished by those new statistics.

In the Latino community we will combat the competitiveness that could feed on those headlines and blind some of our people to the truth of this society. We will combat the opportunism that is likely to intensify among Latino politicians and professionals. We celebrate the unique resistance by African Americans over the centuries, which has provided an inspiring ex-

Continued on next page

Continued from previous page

ample for our communities as shown by the Chicano movement of 1965-75. We affirm the absolute necessity of standing with you against racist oppression, exploitation, and repression – the real axis of evil – and of supporting your demand for reparations.

Latinos who may find it hard to see beyond their own poverty, their own struggles against racism – are indeed, real – need to think about one simple truth. Only solidarity and alliances with others will create the strength needed to win justice.

Those newly announced statistics emphasize difference and pit brown against black like athletes racing against each other in the Oppression Olympics. But other numbers show how much we share the same problems of being denied a decent life, education, health care, all human rights. In times of war, look who fights and dies for the U.S. out of all proportion to our populations: Black and Brown people.

To put it bluntly: we are both being screwed, so let's get it together!

History makes the message clear. It is worth recalling a major reason why George Washington –the invader who wasn't our Great White Father any more than yours – became president. He made a name for himself by successfully using the tactic of Divide and Conquer against different native nations and tribes. Divide and Conquer, later Divide and Control, has sustained White Supremacy ever since. It will continue to do so unless we cry out a joint, unmistakable, thunderous NO.

That will not be easy. Our peoples have different histories and cultures, together with great ignorance about each other. Competition for scarce resources, from jobs to funding for university departments, can be real. Latinos do not always see how in a nation so deeply rooted in racism, they may have internalized the value system of white supremacy and white privilege.

As Latinos, we are committed to help build alliances against our common enemies. We oppose the divisiveness encouraged by statistics about who is more numerous than who. As activists, we urge our community to support Black struggles and to fight together at every opportunity for our peoples' liberation. As teachers, we work to educate Latinos about both Black and Brown history, and our past alliances. As men and women, we can never do too much to assert our common humanity across color lines.

Last, but hardly least, Latinos are a very diverse people with many different nationalities and histories. Latinos also have various roots. In particular, we should recall that more Africans were brought to Mexico as slaves than the number of Spaniards who came, as can be seen by the all-African villages in Mexico today. The African in us demands proud recognition.

—Signed by 37 Latino activists, artists, and academics.[29] *Reprinted from* La Voz de Esperanza. *Initiated by the Institute for Multiracial Justice in San Francisco, cofounded in 1997 by Elizabeth (Betita) Martínez and Phil Hutchings.*

Finally, the increasing cultural identification with indigenous peoples, or *indigenismo*, marks a heightened consciousness of *la raza*'s ties to communities throughout the hemisphere – including the Zapatista rebel movement in Chiapas, Mexico. Young people have drawn on this identity, as well as on the spirituality of the native peoples, as a way to ground their opposition to the dominant power structure. While not all aspects of *indigenismo* have been positive – Betita Martínez raises questions about certain male chauvinist practices, for example[20] – this development has the potential to strengthen relations between the Chicano and native peoples.

The complexity of such trends is evident, however, in an apparently similar development in Puerto Rico in the form of "indigenous revivalism."[21] Supported by a mitochondrial DNA study from the National Science Foundation, proponents claim a majority of the island's inhabitants are descended from the Taíno people – the Arawak nation all but extinguished by Columbus's mad search for gold 500 years ago. By promoting this predominantly indigenous perspective, the mixed race alternative, *la raza cósmica*, tends to fade – and with it, in particular, the Puerto Rican people's connection to Africa. As described by Christina Verán, critics of Taíno resurgence see it as "a too-convenient, less racially-problematic alternative to the island's African-derived culture and gene pool. Indigenous revivalism is seen as pitting a more mythologized Indian identity against a black reality."

Asian/Pacific Islanders

The relationship of Asian/Pacific Islanders (API) to the color line is also complex – but in its own distinct way. The apparent social distance of API people from "blackness" is not the main dynamic here. Instead of the well-publicized economic conflicts between Asian merchants and black community organizations, the main problem actually rests with the power of myth* – namely, the usefulness to white supremacy of viewing API people as a so-called "model minority." Picturing Asian immigrants as super-smart and super-achieving because of their race – in other words, their genetic make-up – reinforces the racist perception that the difficult social conditions facing black, brown, or native peoples are their own fault. "Chinese, Japanese, or Koreans can make it in the United States – so what are you complaining about?" is how the reasoning goes. At the same time, this same myth works against the ordinary API per-

---

* For the power of myth to shape public opinion in lasting ways, see *The Decision to Use the Atomic Bomb*, by Gar Alperovitz, on the view that "dropping the A-bomb on Japan saved many thousands of U.S. soldiers lives"; and *The Spitting Image*, by Jerry Lembcke, on the belief that "anti-Vietnam war protesters spat on returning GIs."

son, who faces both unrealistic expectations and discrimination based on the stereotype.

A higher proportion of Asian immigrants entering the United States since 1965 have been professionals compared to other racial communities. These voluntary immigrants contrast with 1) Latino workers driven to leave their country by economic necessity, or 2) other API immigrants forced from their homes by war. Frank Wu, in his book *Yellow*, explains that once the presence of a highly trained mother and father are taken into account, the success rate of API students is no longer remarkable. The same results are true for any racial grouping with similar backgrounds. And the same goes for API students' study habits. When students of other races study together – as in college programs aimed at increasing retention rates – the results are the same: higher rates of success. Meanwhile, the real poverty among Hmong or Cambodian refugees goes largely unnoticed. As does the sharp class differences between, say, garment sweatshop owners and their workers, or large restaurant owners and their employees in the Chinatowns across the country.

Even the near equality of API and white income levels breaks down when looked at more closely. Asian households tend to be larger than white households, with more of the extended family living together. When broken out individually, Asian incomes tend to trail whites. Asians are more likely to be self-employed – putting in longer hours, with fewer benefits, and with all the risks that small businesses entail. Being more urban based than white people, and residing in markets with higher costs of living – Hawai'i, California and New York, for example – are also factors that drive down APIs' real wages, once the higher price levels are taken into account. Finally, averages increase because hundreds of well-paid managers from Japan, though temporarily in the country, are counted as Asian Americans.

At the upper income levels, a review study discussed by Wu shows that Asian men with doctorates are paid about 18 percent less than comparable white men. Also, North Carolina activist Milan Pham observes that it is only after graduation when the elite stratum of API young people "hit the workforce…[that] they finally begin to see that there are real differences and they're being treated differently." Up to that point students tend to reason: "'I'm definitely not African American, so I must belong to this other group.' And so it takes us until [we're] out of college to figure out that we're not white."[22]

At the bottom end of the income distribution, Vietnamese, Hmong, Montangnards, and Cambodians all have rates of poverty well above white levels. Even South Asian Indians, with a median income of $49,696 (compared to $55,768 for white people in 2003), have a poverty rate of 25% – greater than that of both African Americans (24.4%) and Latinos (22.4%).

Discrimination is also important in shaping people's lives. It forces people to live together in the same neighborhoods, to open up their own businesses, or to work as employees for a relative or countryperson. Children of working class immigrants deal with school administrators and ESL (English as a Second Language) teachers who are slow to adjust to their language needs. High dropout rates and problems in the job market follow. Also, the model minority myth can lead to Asian youths' becoming the targets of other young people's violence. On defending themselves, the image flips and the talk turns to Asian street gangs – and police build up photo catalogs of Asian youths with no criminal records.

Despite this myth-busting reality, other oppressed nationality people can continue to believe the image – and people remain divided. Sociologist Clara Rodriguez comments, "What does the term 'non-white' mean?... Non-white is to New York Puerto Ricans what Puerto Ricans and blacks are; 'white' is what Puerto Ricans and blacks are not."[23] The implication is that for many people of color Asians are firmly on the white side of the line.

The model minority myth persists despite the long history of racial oppression and exclusion suffered by Asian Americans – from the anti-Chinese Union Label on cigar boxes of the 1870s, through eighty years of near total immigration restriction, to Japanese internment and confiscation of property during World War II. It persists despite the feelings expressed by Asian playwrights and authors who relate the common API experience of being treated as "perpetual foreigners" – whether or not they were born in the United States. And most important, the model minority myth persists because of the role this amalgam of Asian nationalities – from India in the west through China, Japan and Korea in the east – plays within the tortured logic of the white supremacist system. On the one hand API people are raised up as proof that racism does not exist. And at the same time, these same people are kept at arms length and kept available for stirring up fears: fear of being "taken-over" – as in the John Huang* 1996 campaign contribution flap[24]; fear of being betrayed by an "internal enemy" – as in the Wen Ho Lee† nuclear spying outrage[25]; or fear of being victimized by terrorists – as with the Indians and Sikhs murdered, harassed, and arrested after 9/11.

---

* Senate hearings investigating Huang and others' money-raising practices opened, according to Frank Wu in *Yellow*, with committee chairman Fred Thompson of Tennessee claiming "'hard evidence' of a Chinese scheme to influence the presidential elections." These claims were never substantiated. *(Wu,* Yellow, *p. 107)*

† Nuclear physicist Wen Ho Lee, charged with spying for China, was held in solitary confinement for the better part of a year. When released in September 2000, Lee received an extraordinary apology from Judge James A. Parker, a Republican, citing the case as "an embarrassment to the nation."*(Wu,* Yellow, *p. 184)*

Asian/Pacific Islanders seem to straddle the color line – neither black (brown or red) nor white – in the same way as Palestinians and Arab people. These populations' life conditions vary widely. Large numbers of professionals work in the United States and contribute to a brain drain from Third World countries. At the same time, subsistence farmers on the losing side of the U.S. war in Southeast Asia, Korean army brides turned out on the street, low paid sweatshop and restaurant workers, expatriate factory workers from Palestine... all make up the underbelly of the empire's multiculturalism. The media keeps the spotlight on those who succeed, while the overall social reality remains one of cultural "otherness." This contradictory position fits right in with the fragmentation and unresolved tensions around color that characterize white supremacy.

The scholars of the Association of Asian American Studies, unfortunately, do not seem to be providing many answers to this situation. Jeff Chang notes the association's overall turn toward cultural studies might be seen as "a wholesale retreat from the social problems of the time."[26] His review of Claire Jean Kim's study of the 1990 Korean grocery boycott in the Flatbush neighborhood of Brooklyn, New York, draws out two important points: 1) the Korean community organizers were unable to gain the support of Asian American and younger Korean organizations to oppose the black community coalition; and 2) the author sides with the black boycotters, sending the message that API folks should "acknowledge your privilege, learn your racial context, and play fair." Unfortunately, as Kim recognizes, the dominant powers do not play fair – and the voice of protesters "is consistently garbled, distorted, and then silenced." Kim's stance suggests that, despite the boycott, Asian Americans and black people are on the same side of the color line.

Frank Wu presents a similar outlook. In *Yellow* he analyzes the problems that API people face – while taking full account of other peoples of color in the country. As the first Asian professor at Howard Law School, Wu often was asked why he chose to teach at a predominantly black school. He notes: "Paradoxically, it takes the race conscious act of forming a group to beget the color blind ideal of being judged on one's merits. When people of color are numerous enough, we form a critical mass. We cease to bear the burden of being representative, and we can relax as our race recedes into latency." Then Wu suggests, "Working in multiracial coalitions of equal members, united by shared principles, we can create communities that are diverse and just. Together, we can reinvent the civil rights movement. And that possibility is why I teach at Howard."

In contrast to Wu's sense of certainty, Chang suggests there is a void that intellectuals working in Asian studies are failing to address. "A new generation of APIs," he says, "dies to answer the questions: where do we stand? What are we fighting for?"

Overview

W.E.B. DuBois said at the beginning of the last century, "The problem of the 20th century is the color line."[27] That statement remains true today – despite all the changes – but includes, as well, the more explicit interweaving of race with structures of class and gender oppression. A hundred years ago court cases repeatedly sought to gain citizenship for Japanese, Middle Eastern and Indian people based on culture and achievement instead of color. Eventually, the Supreme Court resolved the uncertainty in *U.S. vs. Thind* (1923) by appealing, in startlingly unscientific fashion, to the "common understanding ... of who is white."[28]

Today, uncertainty reigns again. Given intensified white supremacy and the weakness of the oppressed nationality movements, all kinds of confusion around race, color and nationality coexist in people's minds. Most people in the United States, whether white or oppressed nationality, suffer from a kind of divided consciousness – aspiring to varying degrees to live in a non-racist society, yet confused about why the issue of race keeps intruding and never gets resolved. The U.S. ruling class benefits from this confusion, as it keeps natural allies within the working class and among the oppressed nationalities apart.

In this light, there are three reasons we have looked at the question of the color line in this chapter:

- **Strategy:** In thinking about the forces potentially aligned against white supremacy, a first approximation is to think in terms of the color line. Who is included among the direct targets of racial oppression? And who, therefore, is most likely to become active in opposing this system?
- **Leadership:** We suggested at the end of the last chapter, Chapter 20, that white people should look to people of color for leadership in the struggle to transform U.S. society. To whom, then – to what social forces – should they be looking? And how inclusive is the category *of color*? Also, who does the color *white* encompass – when activists look to organize a sector of potential white allies?
- **Social construction of race**: It is important to reaffirm the socially constructed nature of racial categories and to recognize that there is ongoing struggle over how these categories are perceived. To overcome the structure and practices of white racial preference, people first have to see that such a system actually exists in the real world. It is not enough to wish it away – to simply be "colorblind" in one's personal relationships. Carried to the level of social policy, a colorblind outlook denies the need for corrective action

and thereby locks in systematic white privileges throughout society.

This discussion has not provided any firm answers to the question of the color line – this group is white, for example, or that one is not. What we have tried to do, however, is describe the terrain where the struggle over color is unfolding. Also, we have tried to give a sense of the forces at work and the overall stakes involved in the outcome. In the next chapter we look at one side of the color line – examining the prospects for unity among the core forces directly impacted by white supremacy.

Chapter 22

Prospects for Unity

For white people, the color line is there to be crossed. It is also there to suggest where to look for leadership. Once there is a sense of where the line runs, the next question is: Which forces among the oppressed nationalities should people look to for leadership? And a related question: To what extent can it be said that these forces form, or are in the process of forming, a united front against white supremacy?

In Chapter 8 we discussed the state of nationalist consciousness among oppressed nationality peoples at the start of the 21st Century. The main focus here, by contrast, is on efforts to build unity among these forces – viewing such work as essential to the emergence of a broad and massive struggle against white supremacy. We will briefly outline examples in a range of areas to suggest the scope of these efforts. Then we will survey some of the barriers to unity before venturing an overall assessment of the situation.

The material reviewed in this chapter requires at least another book to do it justice. The number of different nationalities, the complexity of each people's history, and the particularities of each group's relations with others are rich and important topics – and they receive all too little attention from the dominant culture.

Building unity

Coalitions and alliances

The ***Root Cause*** coalition participated at the anti-FTAA* mobilization in Miami in November 2003[1]. Root Cause brought together groups throughout South Florida that had been developing their own particular critiques of corporate globalization – the Miami Workers Center, Haitian Women's Organization, Coalition of Immokalee Workers, Low Income Families Fighting Together (LIFT) and Power U for Social Change. These groups together built three days of activities based in the Latino, Haitian and African American communities – including a march that joined up with an AFL-CIO-organized anti-globalization demonstration in downtown Miami. There were speeches and chants in multiple languages – Spanish, English, and Haitian Creole – as well as black and Latin hip-hop music and spoken word performances. The coalition targeted global justice issues connected to long-term organizing work in communities of color:

- *public housing* – which is currently being privatized;
- *immigrant rights* – with a focus on the imprisonment of Haitian immigrants; and
- *the Taco Bell boycott* – aimed at improving wages of workers on tomato farms.

White people were welcome to join the activities, but they did so in a supportive role, forming contingents at the rear of the Root Cause march. The coalition also carefully managed relations with the city authorities – given Miami's reputation for police violence. Later this concern proved to be on target, as AFL-CIO president Sweeney condemned the "obstruction, intimidation, harassment, and violence at the hands of police in Miami."[2]

A second example is the ***National People of Color Environmental Leadership Conference***, which in 1991 brought environmental organizers together from across the United States, as well as from six foreign countries.[3] Participant groups included Concerned Citizens of Tillery NC, Southwest Network for Environmental and Economic Justice (SNEEJ), Indigenous Environmental Network (IEN), and Asian Pacific Environmental Network (APEN). Speaking to the power that flows from shared experiences, Tom Goldtooth, an Ojibwe organizer from Minnesota, commented that the testimonies from other people of color "just kind of hit me – that it's a life-and-death situation that's going on. It's not just the

---

* Free Trade Area of the Americas – a policy aimed at reducing trade barriers in the all the Americas, often referred to as "NAFTA on steroids." For more on NAFTA, see Chapter 8.

communities...in Minnesota, it's not just Native people, but it's all people of color." During the 1990s the movement successfully defended itself from a corporate counteroffensive. In 1998 the Sierra Club defeated an anti-immigrant resolution – and then in 2004 rejected an anti-immigrant slate trying to take over the national board. The movement is decentralized, but sustained by deep roots in local organizing, as well as by an infrastructure that includes the Environmental Justice Fund and the Environmental Justice Resource Center.

Labor organizing

There are many examples where labor organizing brings together workers of color – especially where people of color predominate. Here we highlight several different forms of organizing connected to labor activism:

- ***San Francisco hotel strike:*** The main goal of the strike by UNITE HERE Local 2 against the major hotels in San Francisco in the fall of 2004 was to synchronize contracts nationwide.[4] But the union also made a point of demanding that the hotels form a Diversity Committee and employ an ombudsman to help increase the percentage of African American workers in the industry. A 1963 sit-in at the San Francisco Sheraton forced the industry to employ African Americans in front-of-the-house positions. Over the years, however, the hotels started replacing black workers with immigrant employees. Economist Steven Pitts comments: "Blacks aren't perceived [by employers nationwide] as compliant, and therefore when many employers make hiring decisions, they simply don't hire them."[5] The aim of Local 2 is to win a structural reform – a kind of affirmative action consent decree – that can open new possibilities for African American employment and further black-Latino unity both in the hotels and in the community.
- ***Organizing the unorganized:*** In 1999 the Service Employees International Union (SEIU) succeeded in winning bargaining rights for some 80,000 home care workers, mostly Latina and African American women. This was the largest single organizing victory by the labor movement since 1937.[6]
- ***Joint organizing campaigns:*** The Stamford Organizing Project (SOP) in 1998 brought together four union locals* to organize low-wage workers and, in doing so, mobilize support from the communities where the workers lived.[7] Non-workplace issues came to the fore, with a particular focus on housing, followed by involve-

---

* Hospital Workers Union 1199, Hotel Employees and Restaurant Employees (HERE), Service Employees International Union (SEIU), and United Auto Workers (UAW).

ment in local political campaigns. The range of workers included Haitian taxi drivers, Latino janitors, and workers in health care and Head Start child care programs. In three years the SOP organized more than 4,700 workers in the Stamford area.[8]

- ***Immigrant Rights Freedom Ride:*** Caravans traveled across the country to Washington, DC, in the spring of 2004 to promote amnesty for undocumented workers. Initiated by the merged unions UNITE HERE, and sponsored by the AFL-CIO nationally, the Immigrant Freedom Ride built on the history of bus riders traveling through the South and challenging segregation during the African American-led civil rights movement of the 1960s. Organizers in 2004 made sure the campaign's push for legalization also focused attention on the uncompleted – and ongoing – black freedom struggle. Some black commentators, however, such as former civil rights leader Rev. Joseph Lowry, reminded the organizers of labor's historic lack of reciprocity with regard to the black freedom struggle. While not disagreeing with this record, other leaders urged black people to support the immigrant workers. TransAfrica president Bill Fletcher commented: "joining hands with immigrant workers helps build the power that we need to bring us closer to the justice that we have always demanded."[9] Removing the fear of arrest and deportation can help encourage full participation by immigrant workers in union organizing campaigns – to the advantage of all nationalities at the workplace.
- ***Workers centers:*** A community-workplace form of organizing, workers' centers target mostly immigrant workers to help promote organization and power on the job. Some centers, such as those reviewed in Miriam Ching Yoon Louie's *Sweatshop Warriors*, focus primarily on women workers. Workers centers have had both mutually supportive and sometimes contentious relations with organized labor. There is a sense that the centers fill a strategic need that rightfully a creative labor movement would already have addressed. At the same time, some workers' suspicions of organized labor can at times be eased by intermediaries that deal directly with individual problems – while at the same time encouraging solutions based on collective action. As of August 2003, there were 118 such centers in 30 different states[10]. Also, there are local formations that bring together multiple centers, like MIWON (Multi-ethnic Immigrant Workers Organizing Network) in Los Angeles, mentioned in Chapter 11.

Organizing Korean and Latino Restaurant Workers

The Koreatown neighborhood in Los Angeles is home to about 300 Korean-owned restaurants, most of them small. Powering these restaurants is an underground workforce of almost 2,000 Latino and Korean cooks, servers, busboys and dishwashers working in sweatshop conditions for sub-minimum wages. Days are 12-14 hours, 6-7 days a week, with a monthly take home pay of $600 to $700. Even with tips, which are shared, wages do not reach the minimum wage.

Waitresses are 30% of the restaurant workforce. They tend to be Korean women who are often the sole support of their families. The other 70% are immigrant Latino men, many of whom have families depending on them in their home countries. In addition to inadequate pay and hothouse working conditions, people have to put up with abusive treatment from employers – name-calling, baby-sitting the boss's kids on days off, and doing the bosses' laundry.

Since its founding in 1992, the Korean Immigrant Workers Association (KIWA) has responded to these conditions – first, through individual advocacy, and since 1997 by helping to organize the Restaurant Workers' Association of Koreatown (RWAK). KIWA's approach all along has been to stress workers' collective initiative, emphasizing 1) involvement of large numbers of people, and 2) the potential to bring about long-lasting changes in the industry. In this process, KIWA has worked to develop multiracial class-consciousness across LA's race, class and gender lines.

KIWA's first big campaign to organize Latino restaurant workers came in 1998 at the Baek Hwa Jung Restaurant. This boycott over back wages for three Latino employees signaled an important message to Koreatown residents: KIWA would advocate for all low-income workers in the area, regardless of nationality. In response, local restaurant owners accused the organizers of being "traitors." After five months of weekly pickets, the restaurant met the back pay demands.

The larger goals of the boycott were to change restaurant conditions and, in the process, to deepen workers' consciousness. In this effort KIWA faced several challenges. First, they had to break down racial and ethnic perceptions among the workers, while building up a shared class identification. To this end, KIWA built a collaborative relationship with a group rooted among Latinos/as – the Workers' Rights Project at the Coalition for Humane Immigrant Rights of Los Angeles (CHIRLA).

Since most of the waitresses in the industry are Korean women and the other employees Latino men, gender plays a critical role in organizing. Tip sharing is a good example. Latino workers had complained that Korean waitresses would not share their tips. KIWA headed off a potentially damaging cultural rationale that pictured Korean women as selfish and prejudiced against Latino men. Instead, KIWA focused on the boss's refusal to pay all the workers better wages.

Continued on next page

Women of color

As mentioned in Chapter 13, some 1,500 indigenous, African American, Latina, Asian and other women came together in the spring of 2000 at the ***Color of Violence: Women of Color Against Violence Conference*** – and another two thousand were turned away.[11] The conference goal was to counter "the professionalization of the anti-violence movement and its marginalization of women of color." Presenters and workshops featured anti-domestic violence activists from around the world. Themes included women's role in the international economy, rape, war and militarism, and grassroots organizing and political action. Out of the conference came ***INCITE! Women of Color Against Violence,*** a national organization based in local chapters that targets violence against women in the prison system, in the experience of colonialism by native women, and in war, the welfare system, and immigration.

A second example is the ***Women of Color Resource Center*** in Oakland, CA, founded in 1990 by Linda Burnham and Miriam Ching Yoon Louie.[12] Through a combination of local activities and international conferences, the center brings a human rights perspective to its focus on welfare, reproductive rights, and the criminalization of the poor. The center has an eight-part training series on women in the global economy; publishes a newsletter *Sister to Sister*, linking activists inside and outside the

Continued from previous page

The Korean waitresses had to overcome cultural and gender barriers that kept them from interacting with men as coworkers – especially men from another race. Korean culture tends to restrict women's employment to Koreatown, so the waitresses feared being blacklisted. This fear made it difficult for them to take collective action and join the RWAK.

Latino men presented their own special challenge. Though first-generation immigrants like their Korean coworkers, Latino men had more opportunities to leave Koreatown and work elsewhere. Their mobility in the industry gave the men a personal way out in place of the collective struggle to build the workers' association.

Logistics presented another big problem. Meetings had to be scheduled at 8 am on Sunday mornings – late enough for Korean women to get their families up and fed, and early enough for everyone to get to work on time. The language barrier made it necessary to have headsets and written agendas, with everything being translated into both Korean and Spanish.

When KIWA started restaurant organizing in 1997 the restaurants had a 97% rate of non-compliance with labor laws. A KIWA survey in 2001 indicated a drop to about 41% non-compliance. The struggle continues.

—sources: Nguyen, "Showdown in K-town"; Park & Park, "Korean and Latino Restaurant Workers Organize in Koreatown, Los Angeles"

United States; and each year updates a national directory listing more than 200 women of color organizations. The center also sponsors events in the Bay Area and annually presents "Sisters of Fire" awards to outstanding activists.

Youth

The ***Community Youth Organizing Campaign***, based in South Philadelphia sent a delegation of Asian young people and adult advisers on a 23-day trip to the West Coast and back during the summer of 2004. They visited organizations like the Emmanuel Baptist Church in Winston-Salem, NC; La Fuerza Unida in San Antonio, TX; the Pilipino Workers Center in LA and Khmer Girls in Action in Long Beach, CA; and the Committee for the Political Resurrection of Detroit, MI. The youths' goal was to learn from other grassroots activist organizations – particularly those not constrained by the funding treadmill of the non-profit world. The experiences they shared drove home two main lessons: 1) "Divided we fall [is] a universal strategy," and 2) "People are struggling. Everywhere." They concluded "It's up to us to redraw those borders [that divide people] so that those of us fighting for our right…to expect a 'richer and fuller life' – are on the same side of that barbed wire fence."[13]

Overview of other joint work

In addition to the examples reviewed above, many other initiatives demonstrate the wide scope of joint investigation, work, and struggle by oppressed nationality peoples. Here are a few such examples:

- **Media:** *ColorLines* magazine, a major movement resource since 1998 – and the source of many of the examples in this chapter
- **Immigration rights:** African American congressional representative Sheila Jackson Lee's introducing HR 2092, the "Save America Comprehensive Immigration Act of 2005"[14]
- **Education:** the ERASE (Eliminate Racism and Advance School Equity) initiative, helping oppressed nationality organizations take on racism in their local schools[15]
- **LGBTQ activism:** women of color organizing to oppose the elitist leadership of the Human Rights Campaign's Millennium March on Washington in 2000 and its failure to interweave issues of race, class, and gender into its call for gay rights[16]
- **Community organizing I:** the primarily African American organization Mothers on the Move (MOM) in the South Bronx, advocating for immigrant rights and supporting the May 1 2006 national boycott – based on shared needs around clean streets, jobs, education, and housing[17]

- **Community Organizing II:** the Institute for MultiRacial Justice in San Francisco, CA, analyzing problems in coalition building as the main way to overcome white supremacy, and forming alliances among communities of color to fight racism and oppose imperialist war
- **Language barriers:** the community organization DARE in Providence, RI, setting up a Spanish-speaking committee in order to be able to organize Latina, as well as black day-care providers[18]
- **Trainings:** the National Network for Immigrant and Refugee Rights developing BRIDGE, their popular education trainings "to find common ground with others fighting for economic, social, and racial justice"[19]
- **Law:** the Critical Race Theory movement of law students and faculty that works to expose "the historical centrality and complicity of law in upholding white supremacy"[20]
- **Ethnic studies I:** programs dating from the 1960s showing new life in the 1990s with the increase in students of color on campuses – including hunger strikes and sit-ins, with women playing a more central role[21]
- **Ethnic studies II:** the "Beyond Chicanismo" program at Metropolitan State College Denver 1) hosting speakers from the Puerto Rican, African American, and Chicano freedom movements, and 2) forming a "Women of Principle Speakers Series" to bring in Congresswoman Cynthia McKinney, historian Roxanne Dunbar Ortiz, and others[22]
- **Culture:** black and Latino street youth's creation of hip hop and artists like Mos Def, Kanye West, Diamonique, Ursula Rucker, Massive Monkees, Sarah Jones, and La Bruja feeding a positive undercurrent that cuts across cultures and plays against the dominant gangsta/b___/consumption/porn[23]
- **Multiracial left organizations and gatherings:** groups like Freedom Road Socialist Organization and the antiwar coalition United for Peace and Justice having people of color caucuses and internal affirmative action that assures a leading, and often majority, role for oppressed nationalities
- **Theory:** Omi and Winant's influential theory of "racial formation" (see Chapter 3) broadened to a race/ethnicity/nationality formation perspective – one that takes into account the particularities within and among various people of color groupings in a context of white supremacy[24]

- **Politics:** the victory of Antonio Villaraigosa in the Spring 2005 mayoral election in Los Angeles – the first Latino mayor there in more than a century – overcoming some of the divisions between "black and brown" that allowed white candidate James Hahn to win in 2001[25]

This broad array of examples suggests that there is a trend toward building unity among the various oppressed nationality peoples. At their best, these efforts represent "points of departure" – as Angela Davis characterizes this objective[26] – starting points rooted in identity but developing a core unity that is politically based and non-exclusionary. At the same time, forms of participation and support by white allies can vary from direct membership in an organization, to support groups and ally caucuses, or to a more a formal relationship in a temporary coalition or longer-term alliance. The main point here is that the potential for a broad united front among oppressed nationality peoples seems to have a basis in 21st Century reality.

Obstacles

Having pointed to these positive examples of unity and joint struggle, we now need to review some of the problem areas that hold back the formation of the united front of oppressed nationality peoples. We will touch on these points more briefly – not because of their lack of importance, but because doing justice to the topics is beyond the scope of this book.

External barriers

First there are the barriers placed directly in the path of oppressed nationality organizing by the power of the state – immigration penalties, criminalization of youth, welfare programs that beat down women, and right-to-work laws that disempower workers. Another example is the official dispersion of Katrina survivors out of New Orleans that took place in the fall of 2005. These forms of legal restriction and division are then magnified by the power of the media to stigmatize each targeted group – immigrants, young people, women, workers, and even, after a time, Katrina survivors.

To be active in building a movement, people must be able to see beyond the structurally imposed fears and dependency that control their lives. If you are at risk of being separated from your family and deported, if you are in jail, scrambling to survive with your children on welfare, or holding down two or three jobs to get by, there is much less likelihood that you can step out and become active in fighting oppression. Progressive and revolutionary organizations face the task of opening up space – in society and in people's minds – that will free people to become full social actors in their own right.

At a deeper level, through a process the Italian Marxist Antonio Gramsci called "hegemony," ruling class culture works to keep people fragmented and passive. The dominant value system promotes:

- *competitiveness* rather than cooperation,
- *individualism* and getting ahead versus concern for the community,
- *buy-it-now materialism* in place of grassroots activism,
- *war and violence* instead of working things out based on mutual respect, and
- *common sense white supremacist assumptions* rather than critical thinking.

Much of this capitalist-oriented outlook overlaps with a male-centered, patriarchal value system. Human agency, or the ability to act with others to change the world, is often missing from the teachings of religious leaders, as well as from the schools and popular culture. Schools teach students to be entrepreneurs but not organizers. Working class people, especially workers of color, are devalued in movies and TV. Meanwhile middle and upper class life styles appear to be the norm.

This whole system of values – this *ideology* of me-first, get-it-while-you-can and any-way-you-can thinking – contrasts sharply with the basic needs of working people for solidarity and community. In the absence of a worldwide wave of national liberation movements, as existed in the 1960s and '70s, the ruling class taunt "There is no alternative"* tends to set the framework for people's thinking. To make headway, the left will need to replace this perspective with a value-system centered on people's ability to take initiative and be mutually supportive. Values like "an injury to one is an injury to all" and "we'll all rise together" reflect this type of working class outlook.

Internal divisions – within nationalities

Other divisions are not so directly linked to ruling class power and policies, although often they can be traced back to the same source. We review, first, tensions that can appear *within* an oppressed nationality, and then follow these with problem areas that develop *between* different peoples.

Internalized oppression: A hundred years ago, at a time when African Americans had only the most distorted representation of themselves

---

* A phrase identified with Prime Minister Margaret Thatcher and her rightwing supporters in Britain during the 1980s – later shortened to TINA. It is the core slogan of neoliberalism and suggests that free markets, free trade, and capitalist globalization are the only way forward for modern societies. By contrast, "another world is possible" is the rallying theme of the anti-capitalist global justice movement.

in public life, W.E.B. DuBois in the *Souls of Black Folk* (1903) characterized the United States as "a world which yields [the African American] no true self-consciousness, but only lets him see himself through the revelation of the other world. It is a peculiar sensation, this double-consciousness, this sense of always looking at oneself through the eyes of others, of measuring one's soul by the tape of a world that looks on in amused contempt and pity. One ever feels his two-ness – an American, a Negro, two souls, two thoughts, two unreconciled strivings, two warring ideals in one dark body, whose dogged strength alone keeps it from being torn asunder."[27]

Today, one part of the mind takes in the TV shows, sports and movies – with their macho images and Eurocentric assumptions. The other side draws on real-life family and community relationships, and on a current of resistance in grassroots culture and the spoken word. The stresses from contrasting self-images can be greatest for young people, who often depend on older siblings or strong adults in their lives to help sort out who they are and where their allegiance lies.

Children of color and poor white children alike can come to see where they live and who they are through the distorted lens of corporate mass media. The result is a kind of colonization of people's minds. For white people the psychological boost they get from being white can intercept their sense of shame and defensively heighten instead their sense of racial pride. For oppressed nationality people the shame and self-hatred can lead to behavior directed at themselves and at their own people. Suicide, drug use, gang war, and sexual predation can be the outcome – all of which reinforce the negative images projected by white culture.

Color: The white, light-skinned beauty standard is a legacy of white supremacy and colonialism worldwide. In the California Newsreel movie *A Question of Color* both dark-skinned and light-skinned African Americans tell of their being slighted or commented about, particularly in growing up, because of their skin tones. Light skinned people can be viewed as having an edge because their features more closely approach the white social norm. And they tend to be favored on magazine covers and in the *telenovelas* (Latin soap operas). Dark-skinned people, by contrast, can experience the downside of those norms – being seen in a negative light on the beauty scale, and carrying over to expectations around intelligence and moral character.

Skin tones can be a factor in the pecking order in some churches and social clubs, and can affect assessments of potential partners by parents and friends. These hurtful divisions are one more example of internalized oppression – here reflecting the dominant culture's fixation on whiteness – even as white people fill the tanning salons and flock to beaches to get some color.

Social Class: National movements are by their definition multiclass formations – since nations are made up of several classes. But the vast majority of African American, Latino and native peoples are working class – although specific communities like the Cuban enclave in Miami have a higher proportion of business owners and other property holders. Also a larger proportion of Asian Americans tend to be professionals and small businesspeople.[28]

W.E.B. DuBois at one point in his career spoke of the "talented tenth" – the educated elite whom he saw at that time as key to the fight against white supremacy. The system itself, however, also targets this sector for recruitment – more so today than a hundred, or even forty years ago. During the 1960s, college students, intellectuals and clergy people played leading roles in the freedom struggles. Yet it was also from this sector that accommodating politicians, corporate careerists, and a new sector of conservative spokespeople emerged. In addition, while the talented tenth often have useful skills, their approach to organizing can be very individualistic – overvaluing their own role in comparison with that of ordinary people. Comedian Bill Cosby's attacks on the black poor, starting with his 2004 NAACP awards speech, are representative of this elite outlook. "He [Cosby] unerringly and wrongly blames the poor," comments Ronald Walters, director of the African American Leadership Institute. "He seems to think that if they would only change their minds, all their problems would go away."

Due to the current decades-long period of social reaction, the elite sector today tends to be more closely tied to white capital than at any time in the past. As one example, George W. Bush put new restrictions on non-profit organizations, seeking to limit their use as an avenue for independent activism. Instead, the administration increased support for conservative, church-based services. In similar fashion, the promotion of rightwing intellectuals of color in the media, politics and academia all work to bind opinion leaders to the dominant agenda.

Gender: An important lesson from the 1960s upsurge of the national movements is the degree to which patriarchal, or *chingón*, styles and organizational practices weakened the popular forces. We discussed this period and the subsequent rise of Third World Feminism in Chapter 14, and we will look at the strategic implications of this lesson in the next chapter, Chapter 23.

Homophobia: The power of homophobia to divide people showed up clearly in the 2004 presidential election. Rightwing strategists focused on the issue of gay marriage, tying it closely to their base in the fundamentalist Christian churches. Meanwhile the Democrats, generally lacking any concept of running on principle, scrambled to find ways to deflect the issue. As it turned out, only a relatively small number of oppressed nationality people changed their vote at the polls. The percentage of black voters opposing Bush, for example, dropped just two points, from 91% to 89% between 2000 and 2004.[29]

Even more insidious are the built-in heterosexual assumptions of everyday life – where no conscious exclusion is intended. Patterns of relating when folks are, or should be, most relaxed and at ease – at parties, in bars, and at each other's homes – often leave no room for people whose most intimate relationships are outside the male-female pattern. This lack of awareness tends to exclude potential activists, who feel the progressive vision has no place for them. Or it forces people to dissemble, wage an often solitary fight, or organize separately in order to be part of the movement. Fortunately, on the positive side there is evidence that young people today are beginning to develop a more clear-sighted anti-heterosexist outlook and practice.

Country of origin: On coming into the United States, immigrants from Africa or the Caribbean can seek to distance themselves from being considered black or African American. Haitians, Arubans, or Cape Verdeans, for example, come to the United States knowing that the racial hierarchy here places black people at the bottom. Under such circumstances, who would willingly choose to be subjected to such a status? Community activist Gloria Andrade comments: "In America the further away from 'black' you get, the better.... If you've got that African heritage that comes out in the skin color, or in the hair, you're fighting even harder to distance yourself from it because of what black means in this country."[30] As a result, people can hold on to the identities of their birthplace and keep at arm's length the issues and activism of the community where they eventually settle – a community where, given the segregation of U.S. housing patterns, most people will likely have the same skin color.

For Mexican, Nicaraguan or Honduran immigrants the hold of one's native country often centers on family and the desire to return home. People displaced by war, like the Vietnamese, Cambodians, and Hmong, in turn seek to preserve something of their home countries' ways – through their culture and self-employment as fishermen or farmers.

Among Mexican immigrants, whole communities can move together – recruited to come north by a labor contractor from the same village. Farm owners along the Pacific Coast seek to maintain an excess supply of farm labor. That way wages are kept low and working conditions kept marginal at best. The result can be conflict with workers who arrived in the same area in a previous recruiting wave. For most of its history, organized labor in the United States took a hard stand against undocumented workers. Fortunately, since 2000 the AFL-CIO, responding to pressure from unions of farmworkers and service employees,* has called for organizing all the workers in the United States, both documented and undocumented.

Immigrants coming to this country can have a strong positive impact on the level of struggle here. Ted Allen points to the experience early in the 1900s when West Indian immigrants came to the U.S. and refused to accept the social status forced on them as they became African Americans.[31] In the English-speaking Caribbean Islands, as described in Chapter 1, the European population historically was so small that middle-class sectors and the armed forces were mostly people of African descent. On coming to the United States, such immigrants found the U.S. system something of a shock and became an important force in fighting against it. Marcus Garvey came from Jamaica, for example, and the family of Malcolm X was of West Indian origin.

Likewise, immigrants from Latin American countries tend not to understand, at least initially, the racial categories at work here in the United States. As David Bacon reports[32], when whole communities move north – say, directly from Oaxaca, or perhaps after some time working in Northern Mexico – they bring a sense of community and tradition of struggle with them. The Indigenous Front of Binational Organizations, for example, organized by Triquis and Mixtecs from Oaxaca, later formed an alliance with the United Farm Workers. In Nebraska, Qanjobales and Mams from Guatemala have used their networks to help organize meatpacking plants. A real problem for the ruling class is the possibility that Latino immigrants, like their Caribbean predecessors, will draw on experiences from their home country to help dismantle the system of racial privileges.

Internal divisions – between different nationalities

Language differences: Unless progressive organizations make a conscious effort, they usually follow the dominant society's practice of privileging the English language. The result is a reflection of that privilege inside the movement – together with, at a minimum, a second-class status accorded to non-English speakers, or, at worst, a continuing divide among activist communities.

Stereotyping: People know their own histories mainly from their families and the culture they grow up in. If left to the schools, no one would know much of anything worthwhile about the history of the subject peoples in the United States or the popular classes. This being the case, how realistic is it to expect, say, Latinos or African Americans to

---

* United Farm Workers (UFW), Farm Labor Organizing Committee (FLOC), Service Employees International Union (SEIU), and Hotel Employees and Restaurant Employees (HERE)

know much about each other's histories? Or about that of Asian Pacific Islanders or the First Nations? Many immigrant peoples, for example, do not understand the terrible history of slavery or its impact on U.S. culture. In this respect, people of color can be similar to white folks in not grasping the deep historic roots that feed current conditions. Not knowing contributes to stereotyping, misperception, and fears based on media images and rumors – at least some of which trace back to bosses of various stripes. Sweatshop owners, foremen, labor contractors, and local politicians all can have a stake in keeping their countrymen isolated and, as a result, more readily controlled.

Narrow nationalism: Sharp boundary lines drawn between different nationalities encourages distrust instead of solidarity. Also, reactionary nationalism often promotes men, or a man, as part of a leader-centered group culture. It undermines efforts toward forming a united front that can advance common demands.

Meeting separately or developing an agenda for a particular community are not in themselves evidence of narrow nationalism – as we saw in Section II, Chapters 5-8. Consider the Black Radical Congress, for example, and its *Freedom Agenda*: "The struggles of peoples of African Descent are inextricably linked to the many diverse struggles of oppressed people and nations across the globe."[33] And the nationalism evident in the 2006 immigrant upsurge – in Los Angeles, in particular – resonated with, and drew inspiration from, earlier African American freedom struggles.

Also Milan Pham comments: "I think we have to have a little bit of stability in our house before we're like, okay, let's make a neighborhood....[I]t's important to coalition with other people of color, but it's not time yet....The southeastern United States is not there yet." [34] The implication is that unity requires clarity on the program of one's own community, as well as a willingness to work with others to achieve common goals.

Economic competition: Economic tensions run deep and they are particularly difficult because of the dependent positions in which oppressed nationality people generally find themselves. In other words, the white power structure and its allies of all colors hold a monopoly of financial and industrial power. Everyone else is left to fend for themselves – and encouraged by the capitalist culture to compete in whatever way they can, to view others with suspicion and worse, and to justify whatever it takes to get an edge on others. Examples include:

- **Workers:** Latino immigrant workers in agriculture, construction, landscaping, meatpacking and other industries, where African Americans previously made up a sizeable section of the workforce; or within a company, like the huge Smithfield hog-processing plant in Tar Heel, NC, African Americans being moved into supervisory positions overseeing mainly Latino workers, so that tensions around work end up playing out in terms of race.

- **Small owners:** so-called "middle men" – often Korean, South Asian, or Dominican – owning businesses in communities of a different nationality and, at times, lacking a sense of commitment to that community
- **Students:** parents from one racial grouping – Asian parents at the Lowell school in San Francisco, for example[35] – opposing affirmative action at magnet schools, the loss of which negatively impacts other oppressed nationality peoples
- **Youth:** brown on black violence (and vice versa), as well as tensions being carried into schools and the prison system, thereby hardening racial divisions

Political competition: As the numbers of Latinos grows in particular cities – for example, in Houston, Los Angeles, or Providence – the community's push for political power can end up targeting African American political leaders. Since black people succeeded in moving into these positions only recently, challengers can come across as stand-ins for the white power structure. As Congressman Joe Almeida, an African American from Providence, RI, commented: "Every Latino who ran [in 2000] is light- or white-skinned." As people of color, he added, "We're more apt to run against ourselves than someone who is white" – so as not to take on the white power structure directly.[36] Meanwhile, the poor living conditions in many Latino neighborhoods can get blamed on black political leaders. The contradictions and concerns on both sides are real. In the absence of a functioning alliance between peoples – not to mention with indigenous and Asian Pacific Islanders, as well – the potential power of a united political front goes untapped. Harold Washington's 1983 mayoral campaign in Chicago demonstrates perhaps best the progressive potential of such a united effort in the political arena.

These areas of conflict among oppressed nationality peoples are real and carry severe consequences for the individuals and groups caught up in them. Meanwhile there is little or nothing the dominant culture does to help people overcome their differences. Gloria Anzaldúa suggests approaching problems between races/nationalities "*con corazón en la mano*" – with your heart in your hand. "What we need is a more compassionate, empathetic way of being with each other."[37]

Another approach that seeks to resolve deep contradictions in the context of opposing white supremacy is presented in Eric K. Yamamoto's *Interracial Justice*. Yamamoto lays out both a theory and set of principles that can provide a basis for mediating conflicts – which he then uses to analyze cases of historic land seizure and economic conflict. This restorative approach to community healing serves as a complement to the more forward-looking, pro-active examples outlined at the beginning of this chapter.

Overview

We began this chapter by pointing to instances where oppressed nationality people managed to break through the many barriers that can divide people. Those examples, as well as the more nationalist-oriented and global struggles reviewed in Chapter 8, point to people's resilience and resourcefulness in coping with the very difficult conditions people face inside the United States. After all, it is important to remember that we are talking about the home country of the sole superpower in the world today – and the greatest military power in world history. At the same time, 1) the historic breakthrough of the Reconstruction period (Chapter 5), and 2) the progressive advances throughout society in the wake of the civil rights and national movements of the 1960s (Chapters 3, 12, and 20) – these historical periods suggest the tremendous transformative potential when oppressed nationality movements are able to take the lead.

Much is at stake then in the contest over whether unity among oppressed nationalities will eventually prevail. Activists of all nationalities have a role to play in helping set the conditions where such unity can flourish and eventually predominate. Recognizing the great social fault line created by white supremacy is a start. But, in the scope of things, it is only a first step, and a relatively small one at that. It is in the particularities of organizing – in confronting day-to-day the nearly infinite intersections of oppression and resistance – that a truly leading social force among the oppressed nationality peoples will emerge. With a new upsurge of struggle almost certain at some point in the future, there is cause for optimism that today's scattered efforts at building unity will come together in a broad front and benefit from wide popular support – including a sector of white allies won to the struggle.

Chapter 23

Gender, Class, Organization

We have traced white supremacy's major fault line and assessed the potential for unity among the leading social forces in opposition to the system. Now we want to round out this discussion of strategy – first, by bringing gender and class briefly into focus and, second, by pointing to implications of the analysis for left and progressive organizations.

Sisters at the center

Cutting across all the national movements is the question of gender – or, more specifically, male privilege. The discussion in Chapters 12-15 on "Patriarchy and Privilege" pointed to the need to put women's interests and concerns at the center of the fight against white supremacy.

There are different ways to understand the word *center* as the strategic goal. One is in the sense of women being at the social heart of a campaign or movement. The 1930s organizing drive among California farmworkers is one example, as described in the box on the next page. There women organized the workers camp, struggled to make sure food supplies were sufficient during the strike, and went into the fields to challenge the scabs. In a sense this role both accords with and pushes beyond the historic division of labor where women hold things together at home while men are active in the world of work and public life.

A second sense of being central is when women are the social base of the movement, the first to go into motion, and the core force moving things forward. Here the civil rights movement in Mississippi during the early 1960s is an example, as described by Charles Payne in *I've Got the Light of Freedom*. In contrast to the 1940s and '50s when men led through their positions in the NAACP, women active in the churches tended to respond more readily to the voting rights campaign of the 1960s.

A third meaning is when women have a key role in leadership; a fourth, when the program of the movement centers on women's needs; and finally, when women represent the public face of the movement. We touched on a number of these aspects of women's centrality in Chapter 15.

Working class women of color

The normal functioning of white supremacy leads to large numbers of oppressed nationality men being tied up in the criminal justice system, forced out of the home by provisions of the welfare system, dying from AIDS, or – particularly on Indian reservations – committing suicide. (For the data, see Chapter 16.) As a result, social stresses centered on the home can end up being carried by women. Harsh labor market conditions, especially for people without a high school diploma or facing lan-

Mrs. Valdez and the 1933 Cotton Strike in California: a Mexican women's perspective

Mexicanas were a vital part of the [1933 California cotton] strike, and about half of the strikers at Corcoran were women. They ran the camp kitchen, cared for children, and marched on picket lines. They distributed food and clothing. Some attended strike meetings, and a few spoke at the meetings. And it was the women who confronted Mexican strikebreakers. In short, women were essential to this strike, though they have been largely obscured in accounts of its history. Mrs. Valdez went on strike and was on the picket lines. She was not a leader, but one of the many women who made the strike possible.

Mrs. Valdez remembered a collectivity of Mexican women. By 1933, Mexican women worked alongside men in the fields. Like the men, they were paid piece-rates and picked an average of two hundred pounds per ten-hour day. Picking required strength, skill, and stamina... [W]omen faced hardships in caring for their families: houses without heat, which contributed to disease, preparing food without stoves, and cooking over fires in oil barrels. Food was central to her memory, reflecting a gender division of labor. Getting enough food, a problem at any time, was exacerbated by the Depression, which forced some women to forage for berries or feed their families flour and water. Food was an issue of survival.

While Mrs. Valdez described the abysmal conditions under which women labored, the women were active, not passive, participants in the strike. Women's networks that formed the lattice of mutual assistance in the workers' community were transformed during the strike. The networks helped form daily picket lines in front of the cotton fields. Older women still sporting the long hair and *rebozos* of rural Mexico, younger women who had adapted the flapper styles of the United States, and young girls

Continued on next page

guage barriers, then amplify instability in both households and the community.

Since child rearing – which most often falls to women – is not a valued occupation in this society, compensation for this service through the welfare system is abysmal and, after 1996, limited to five years in a person's lifetime. Child care services also are grossly underfunded, so availability of quality care at a decent cost is a big problem for mothers seeking work. And the flipside is that child care workers – often oppressed nationality women themselves – make little better than poverty level wages even with college training. The lack of decent public transportation systems, which poor women often use to get to jobs, only worsens this situation. The upshot is that in 2005 21% of oppressed nationality women and 28% of oppressed nationality children were living in poverty.[1]

Continued from previous page

barely into their teens rode together in trucks to the picket lines. They set up makeshift child-care centers and established a camp kitchen.

With the spread of the conflict, these networks expanded and the women's involvement escalated from verbal assaults on the strikebreakers to outright physical conflict. When, after three weeks, growers refused to settle, women organized and led confrontations with Mexican strikebreakers. According to Mrs. Valdez, the women decided that they, not the men, would enter the fields to confront the strikebreakers. They reasoned that strikebreakers would be less likely to physically hurt the women.

In organized groups, the women entered the field, appealing to strikebreakers on class and national grounds – as "poor people" and "Mexicans" – to join the strike. Those from the same regions or villages in Mexico appealed to compatriots on the basis of local loyalties, denouncing as traitors those who refused.

Exhortations turned to threats and conflict. The women threatened to poison one man who had eaten at the camp kitchen – an indication again of the centrality of (and their power over) food. But women had come prepared. Those armed with lead pipes and knives went after the strikebreakers. One ripped a cotton sack with a knife. Others hit strikebreakers with pipes, fists, or whatever was handy. Although strikers had felt that the women would not be hurt, the male strikebreakers retaliated, and at least one woman was brutally beaten.

Mrs. Valdez recalls the strikebreakers justifying themselves to the women in terms of the need to feed their families. But the striking women's ultimate rebuke was also expressed in terms of this need: "*Si ... nosotros también tenemos que comer y también tenemos familia. Pero no somos vendidos!*" [Yes, we too have to eat and we also have families. But we're not sell-outs!]

—from: Weber, "Raiz Fuerte"

These disadvantages in homes and communities tend to offset the gains made by women of color in education, job quality, and income levels in recent decades. Also, the narrowing gap between men's and women's wages is not exclusively a product of women's gains. Rather it results in large measure from oppressed nationality men's losses in the wake of deindustrialization. As Angela Davis points out in "Reflections on the Black Woman's Role in the Community of Slaves," there continues to be a certain forced and distorted version of equality experienced by oppressed nationality men and women. Both are denied their traditional patriarchal roles – men not able to be providers and protectors, women required to labor outside the home for their families to survive. The increase in service job openings since the 1970s – in jobs traditionally identified with women – has reinforced this pattern. The result is increased employment and wage gains for some women of color. Men's position in industry meanwhile has deteriorated, ratcheting up the stresses on families. Extended family networks provide an important support system, but they also add burdens to an already weary older generation.

Whether working in garment sweatshops, in hotels and restaurants, or taking care of one's own or others' children; whether trapped in the sex trade, in an abusive relationship, or forced to maneuver every day to avoid sexual harassment on the job, on the street, in prison, or in the military – the conditions facing working class women of color are a measure of the quality of U.S. society. Quoting Angela Davis: "According to a time-honored principle advanced by Marx, Lenin and Fanon, and numerous other theorists, the status of women in any given society is a barometer measuring the overall level of social advancement. As Fanon has masterfully shown, the strength and efficacy of social struggles – and especially revolutionary movements – bear an immediate relationship to the range and quality of female participation."[2]

The centrality of women in the struggle to transform U.S. society flows directly from these observations:

- The condition of women reflects the backwardness of the U.S. social order today – just as it will be a measure of the advancement in any future society that the social justice movement is able to bring about.
- In order to assure that women's needs are met – as a fundamental condition of social progress – there must be a high level of participation of women at all levels of the movement.
- In order to assure broad participation, women must share equally, if not predominate, in the movement's leadership and be fully represented in its social program and public face.

The forced equality of oppression can be a help or a hindrance to this process. The movement can draw on the strengths of more open social roles and fill them with progressive content – empowering an intentional equality. Or people may react to their current conditions by trying to recapture their traditional roles – thereby reinforcing patterns of male dominance and holding back women's participation and leadership. Fortunately the experience of the 1960s movements helped open new space for women. One example is the widespread participation of women in the Chicano student activism of the 1990s. When asked in 1999 about the role of Chicanas in the movement, Gloria Anzaldúa commented, "Oh yeah, the *movimiento* has become what I call a *movimiento macha*, female."[3]

The Davis/Fanon perspective suggests also the importance of keying on issues of special concern to women – among them, domestic violence, reproductive rights, including sterilization abuse, child care, and unequal pay. Doing so has the prospect of freeing women so that they can be active in the movement, develop themselves, and lead. In the meantime, internal to the movement, organizations can provide resources for child care and transportation, pay attention to unequal relationships in the home, and – within this wider support system – prioritize women's leadership development. Such conscious policies serve the current requirements of the struggle – but they also point to, or prefigure, the type of society the movement hopes to build.

SNCC

An example from the history of the civil rights movement can help make some of these ideas more concrete. The Student Non-Violent Coordinating Committee (SNCC) of the early 1960s brought some of these aspects of women's centrality together in a way that can serve as a partial model for organizing today. As already mentioned, the social base of the movement in Mississippi at that time tended to be women. But it was also the outlook and organizing style of SNCC that helped to bring these women into motion. Ella Baker was a moving spirit, trainer, and adviser of the SNCC field staff – starting from the organization's formation in the summer of 1960.[4] Her presence helped set a tone for organizers and the people these young folks identified as potential local leaders. SNCC's organizing style, as described by Payne, contrasted sharply with the approach of the Southern Christian Leadership Conference (SCLC), an organization consisting almost exclusively of male preachers. Baker had helped set up that organization, too, in 1957, but she found herself excluded from leadership despite her on-the-ground accomplishments in building the movement. The clash of styles between SNCC and SCLC, and between Baker's emphasis on grassroots organizing versus Martin Luther King's more charismatic approach, formed one of the key contradictions within the civil rights movement during the early 1960s.

Finally, in addition to 1) the social base among Southern church-women, 2) the contribution of women organizers,* and 3) Ella Baker's influential role in the movement, Fannie Lou Hamer of the Mississippi Freedom Democratic Party came to represent the public face of the Southern voting rights struggle. Hamer first tried registering to vote in 1962 after attending a SNCC voter education meeting. It took her three times because registrars required interpretation of sections of the state constitution. On joining the movement, Hamer lost her job, endured constant harassment, and had to separate from her family so her husband would not be fired. She became a SNCC field organizer and at one point received a beating that affected her physically the rest of her life. In the summer of 1964, Mrs. Hamer headed the Mississippi Freedom Democratic Party challenge to the racist, all-white state delegation being seated at the Atlantic City Democratic Party Convention. When offered two seats "at large" without the right to vote, Hamer rebuffed the so-called compromise and led her delegation out of the convention. The delegates and their SNCC supporters learned a powerful lesson that summer in the ways of Democratic Party manipulation.[5]

This experience with Democratic Party politics, along with the passage of the Civil Rights (1964) and Voting Rights (1965) Acts, pushed SNCC and the black freedom movement in new directions. Organizers wrestled with the uncertainty of the period and the next stage of the struggle. Confronting the segregated cities in the North, putting forward the demand for "Black Power," and directing white supporters to take up organizing in their own communities – all marked this decisive shift. In the process, SNCC moved away from the grassroots organizing methods that had marked its early years, especially after the election of Stokely Carmichael as national chairman in 1966.[6] The tensions that had characterized the SNCC/SCLC style differences eventually crystallized in 1968 when SNCC women set up their own organization, the Black Women's Liberation Committee. Then in 1970, the BWLC joined with Puerto Rican activists to form the Third World Women's Alliance. This step marked the beginning of what became the Third World women's movement discussed in Chapter 14.

Despite – or perhaps because of – women's impact on SNCC's work and its organizing style, SNCC also produced one of the first statements by women challenging male chauvinism in the movement. Drafted anonymously in 1964, the position paper "Women in the Movement" by Mary King and Casey Hayden, listed 11 examples of clear-cut chauvinist

---

* Women seldom held top leadership positions in SNCC, but people like Diane Nash, Ruby Doris Smith, Muriel Tillinghast, Dorie Ladner, Prathia Hall, Donna Moses and many others played important roles as local movement leaders. *(Robnett, Reader's Companion to U.S. Women's History)*

practices – from decision-making and leadership assignments, to women being called "girls" and routed to clerical positions. The statement forced discussion within SNCC and found its way into other organizations and publications over the next several years.

Looking back at these early years of SNCC helps give substance to the call to put sisters of color at the center of the struggle. There is a sense of the social base, the grassroots and veteran leadership, and the public face – as well as of women's internal monitoring of movement norms around gender. And along with these aspects of women's participation came an organizing style aimed at building a "movement of leaders," rather than a "leader of the movement," as Ella Baker put it.

A strategic view that puts women at the center does not flow from what is often called an "essentialist" perspective – one that draws on the supposed innate traits of women as women. Rather it comes from an assessment of the way patriarchal white supremacy oppresses women – and Third World women, in particular – in the United States. Women have been at the core of their communities – dealing intimately with the system and raising children to survive within it. Women generally are socialized to be relation-centered, which is key to building a movement based on strong interpersonal ties – one that is able to neutralize competition and rigid polarities while managing disagreements and building consensus. And in this time of impoverished public resources, women are well positioned to lead struggles around the conditions of labor reproduction and the social wage. Nonetheless, men today still predominate in the public sphere, and women still carry the weight of working both inside and outside the home. Under these conditions, the challenge to the movement is to provide, or shake loose from the system, the social supports necessary for women to come into their own as organizers and leaders.

Fighting patriarchy, leading together

Sisters being at the center of the movement does not deny the importance of men in the struggle. In fact, it opens new possibilities in addition to the traditional roles where men have excelled – as warriors, initiators, planners and public spokespeople. The movement can encourage men to take on nurturing roles as well, as part of a social infrastructure that supports women in leading and public positions. Both men and women benefit when a full range of social roles is open to them. This breakdown of patriarchal roles and attitudes also has the benefit of making space for lesbian women to fully participate at all levels of the movement. Given the powerful role lesbian women played in shaping the Third World women's movement (see Chapter 14) – as well as, unfortunately, the continuing existence of male chauvinism among gay men – such a move assures strong leadership in a merged struggle against both patriarchy and white supremacy. At the same time, the movement benefits by having the widest possible participation and the full development of everyone who joins it.

Finally, "sisters at the center" gives a sense of the bridge formed by white women attracted to the Third World Women's movement – and who thereby work to unite white allies with oppressed nationality struggles. As an example, Becky Thompson in *A Promise and a Way of Life* mentions white women who became disenchanted with Second Wave feminism because of its inability to connect with women of color but who later reengaged with the movement after the rise of Third World Feminism.

Working class base

Implicit in our discussion of strategic forces is this book's underlying orientation toward the working class – as pointed out in the overview of race and class at the end of Chapter 11. The very large majority of oppressed nationality people belong to the working class – but with a higher percentage of professional and small business people among Asian Pacific Islanders for historic reasons.* National movements are multi-class in character. And working class movements have to make efforts to win over middle class people in order to reduce the class alliance around the big capitalists. In each case, however, the role of middle class forces can be contradictory – standing against national oppression and monopoly power, but uneasy with the energy, demands, and abilities of grassroots people. To assure maximum participation at the base and to keep the struggle true to its emancipatory goals, the core character of the movement needs to be, or become, working class.

The historic role of the working class results also from the close connection of white supremacy to the setting up of the colonial slave system (see Chapter 1). Since that time, as discussed throughout this book, white privilege has played a key role in maintaining the divisions within the working class – and thereby assuring the dominance of the white patriarchal rulers. Just as white supremacy is integral to maintaining the United States as a capitalist superpower today, so the working class – with a united front of oppressed nationality workers and women at its center – has a key role to play in overcoming racial and national oppression.

---

* As Bob Wing explains in "Crossing Race and Nationality," immigration restrictions on Asian working class people resulted in a higher proportion historically – about 40% – of that community being professionals and small business people. Since the immigration reforms of 1965, family reunification plus the brain drain of highly educated technical workers has continued the pattern.

Organizational transformation

In Chapters 16 to 20 we looked at the potential for a section of white people to become allies in the struggle – as well as freedom fighters in their own right. In the last three chapters we then assessed the leading oppressed nationality forces – their potential for unity and the central role of women in the united front. Combined with the survey of the national movements in Chapter 8, these discussions help bring into focus just who it is that activists of all colors, but white folks in particular, can look to for leadership. And not just look to – since organizers can play a role in developing that leadership, as well.

One place to begin is at home, so to speak – in the popular and revolutionary organizations of the progressive movement. As one example, the Freedom Road Socialist Organization in 1998 set the strategic goal of transforming itself so that the membership would become majority-oppressed nationality by the end of 2001. By early 2002, an organization that began in 1985 with less than 10% oppressed nationality members, had reached a level of 46% – not quite, but almost achieving its goal.

Setting an objective of this kind may appear to be simply a matter of "counting heads" – lacking a deeper political motivation. But it actually carries broad implications for an organization's work – the struggles taken up, the people prioritized in recruitment, the supportive internal culture required so that everyone feels comfortable, and the kinds of internal education carried out. One way to capture this transformation objective is to focus on the organization's *composition, consciousness* and *culture.*

Also important in making concrete the overall strategic outlook presented here is to place the fight against patriarchy at the center of organizational life. Examples are 1) developing studies on gender and LGBTQ (Lesbian-Gay-Bisexual-Transgender/Questioning) oppression; 2) organizing activities around preventing male violence and rape; 3) setting up safeguards – meeting monitors, women's and LGBTQ caucuses – related to internal norms and processes; and 4) prioritizing women and LGBTQ folks for recruitment.

Finally, organizational transformation requires renewed attention to the working class base of the movement. Here the focus can be on workers of color opposing war and empire abroad and its consequences for people here at home. For example, many themes come together in the organizing around Hurricane Katrina. Katrina underscored 1) the importance of organizing in the South; 2) the centrality in the struggle of African American and other oppressed nationality peoples – such as Vietnamese fishermen and laborers from Central America; 3) the added dimension of male violence that women had to contend with in the middle of the crisis; 4) the federal anti-worker policies that targeted prevailing wages, the minimum wage, and basic health and safety standards; and 5) the overall market-driven response of the ruling circles that rewarded established wealth and made the poor of all races carry the weight of the disaster.

It is in the course of such struggles that the movement can strengthen the leading front of oppressed nationality peoples – but only if conscious organizers keep this strategic goal in mind as they work to address people's immediate needs. Internal transformation of movement organizations can be both a stimulus to and a consequence of building the leadership of oppressed nationality peoples in the broader social movement.

At the end of Chapter 20 we suggested that leadership by the oppressed nationality peoples is the surest way to keep the movement against white supremacy true to its goal. For hundreds of years the ruling class – plantation-based, industrial or, as today, imperialist – has used the system of white privilege as a kind of "revolution insurance." By transforming the composition, culture, and consciousness of their organizations, left and progressive activists can establish an organizational guarantee against white folks' historic unreliability – "betrayal insurance" is one way to think of it. With this orientation guiding today's organizing, the movement will then be ready for the next upsurge in the struggle. Around the core leadership of the oppressed nationality united front, masses of white people from the youth and a section of the working class – most likely with women in the lead – will once again come to see that their self-respect and sense of social solidarity is at stake in the struggle. In time, with the eventual defeat of U.S. imperialism, democratic and human rights will have full sway – developing out of the alignments, internal practices, and leadership built by the popular movement in the course of struggle.

The efforts at organizational transformation that activists carry out today are a critical example of what Ella Baker called "building the road while walking it." In doing so, the movement not only prepares itself to mount an ultimately successful challenge to white, patriarchal capitalism; it also lays the groundwork for the future, post-revolutionary society. One assessment of 20th Century socialism concludes: "The central political problem is therefore how to ensure that revolutions do not transmute into their opposite and become the basis for a new kind of oppression and exploitation."[7] By transforming movement organizations today around nationality, gender and class, activists help put in place a guarantee against future reversals – whether by white people, men, or old or new economic elites. Such efforts are the best way to honor the sacrifices of past generations.

The strategic outlook presented here is both optimistic and historically based. Both these aspects are important: *optimistic* – so that people's spirit will move them to add their energy and initiative to the struggle; and *historically based* – so that people's efforts are grounded in and accord with reality. By contrast, a number of perceptive critics of racial oppression in the United States seem to be overwhelmed by the weight of the evidence of racial divisions around them. Derrick Bell (*Faces at the Bottom of the Well*), Andrew Hacker (*Two Nations: Black and White, Separate, Hostile Unequal*), Leonard Steinhorn and Barbara Diggs-Brown (*By the Color of our Skin: The Illusion of Integration and the Reality of Race*), and even Becky Thompson (*A Promise and a Way of Life: White Antiracist Activism*) all convey a sense that the system of racial inequality is so much a part of the U.S. character that it can never be changed.

These authors' insights have contributed greatly to the analysis in this book, and we value their work. Nevertheless, the historical account brought together here suggests that this group of authors' pessimism is misplaced. There is sufficient evidence, both in U.S. history and in activists' own personal experience, to support a more positive outlook. A movement 1) rooted in the working class, grassroots forces of the oppressed nationalities, 2) with women at the center, and 3) having a significant sector of European Americans in motion around it – such a movement could bring sufficient forces into motion to challenge and then transform the system of privilege. Once holding the initiative, the internal character of the movement can help create and define the social content of liberation. The quality of the relationships people build today, along with the social norms they establish, provide a foretaste of the future society. One advantage of "prefiguring" or "modeling the life we seek to build" is that it works both ways. Not only does prefiguring shape the future, but it also allows people today to get a taste of what the future transformed society will be like.

The struggle to overcome white supremacy in the United States is a huge undertaking, and there are certain to be setbacks and painful losses along the way. But the rewards are great, appearing often in the smallest events of everyday life – in people's relationships with friends and movement comrades, and in the ever-widening circle of new people attracted to the struggle for social justice.

We now turn to a practical program that flows from the strategic perspective outlined in the preceding pages. It is an approach to organizing that we hope anyone seeking to end the system of privileges will be able to apply in their own lives.

A Revolutionary Vato Loco

Are you a veteran?
She asked
Yeah, I said
Soy veterano,
A revolutionary vato loco
A barrio warrior
In the people's army
Soy veterano de
La lucha contra el
Yanqui imperialismo
I'm a guerrilla fighter
En las calles de Aztlan
I'm one of the many,
The proud

I'm a resistor
Refusing to accept
The occupation army
And being treated as a foreigner
On the lands of
My ancestors
Si, yo soy veterano
De la causa
Struggling for the dignity
Of poor and working class
Families
I've waged a war
Against ignorance
And have battled for peace

—Joe Navarro

VIII

TAKING ON THE SYSTEM

Step by step over the course of earlier chapters, we have moved toward a strategy for overcoming white supremacy and racism. Section I described the origins of the white race as a social control mechanism that emerged at the same time as chattel slavery in the British colonies of North America. We showed how this mechanism reinvented itself over the centuries, distributing privileges to white working people – and severely punishing those who resisted – in order to bind people into a white front with the ruling class. All the while these same workers were abused and exploited. But they turned their anger on more accessible targets – Indians, slaves, Mexicans, or Asian immigrants – rather than on their oppressors.

In Sections II through IV we showed how the conflict around race deepened into national oppression at home and abroad; and we drew out some of the interconnections between race and class, and between race and patriarchy. On this historical basis, we then developed a line-up of social forces capable of opposing white supremacy today. We started in Section V by presenting the pattern of privilege as it exists in the early 21st Century, along with its accompanying white consciousness. Section VI examined whether a sector of white people can be brought into the struggle as reliable allies – and as fighters in their own right. Then in Section VII we looked at the core forces in a potential united front against white supremacy, and their interconnections around race, class, and gender.

Overall the analysis points to the need for organizers of all races and nationalities inside the U.S. to build a broad united front against white supremacy and racism that:

- is rooted in the working class of the oppressed nationalities,
- has women at the center of the movement, and
- brings a section of white people – workers, students, and other progressive-minded people – into the struggle.

The question remains, how can people go about building this front? Each of the preceding sections of the book points to a piece of an answer, which we summarize now with the section numbers in parentheses:

- Learn about the origins of white privilege and its historic development (I)
- Respect, nurture, and organize around the revolutionary national sentiments of the oppressed nationality peoples (II)
- Prioritize working class organizing in the South and Southwest and tie it to developments in the Global South (III)
- Build an autonomous women's movement centered on Third World feminism (IV)
- Provide support – through encouragement, and criticism where necessary – to white people coming to terms with their privileged position in U.S. society (V)
- Look to the movements of oppressed nationality people for leadership in the struggle – and help build those movements (VI)
- Promote unity and help work through contradictions – which can become quite sharp – among the oppressed nationality peoples (VII)
- Make women's participation and leadership central to the social justice movement (VII)

The rationale behind each proposal appears in the section indicated, and we do not want to repeat those discussions here. Rather our goal is to fill out this program of action – and bring it down to earth – by discussing the personal, organizational, and social dimensions of putting the plan into practice. We draw here primarily on the organizing experience of the people involved in writing this book. At the same time, insights from the many writers cited in previous sections have helped shape our thinking over the years.

Chapter 24 presents ten ways that people can personally become involved in the struggle against white supremacy and racism. Since everything ultimately comes back to how all of us – you the reader, we the writers, and everyone else – actually conduct our lives, this personal perspective is fundamental to movement building.

In Chapter 25, we look at the internal organizational aspects of the struggle against white privilege. Organization is essential to empowering working class people of all races and their allies. Not having access to material resources, the dispossessed depend on each other to build relationships and institutions for the long haul. This chapter lays out some of the organizational measures that can help groups be true in their internal practices to both their short- and long-term goals.

In Chapter 26 we suggest ways to go about engaging in the social struggle so that activism can be most effective in building the united front against white supremacy. Here the focus is on looking outward –

on building the movement in the course of struggle, and on deepening people's consciousness and their commitment to fundamental social change.

Finally, in Chapter 27 we situate this book within the larger public discussion on ending white supremacy. We encourage wide-ranging exchanges among activists and with the broader public on how to end the U.S. system of racial privileges – while keeping the discussion closely linked to on-the-ground organizing work.

Chapter 24

The Personal is Political

Being involved in the struggle against white supremacy is, first, a personal decision. But how to connect one's everyday activities to the large-scale plan of action proposed in this book is not always clear. Doing so is essential, however, to building a movement – person by person, in a widening circle of activity and commitment.

Here are ten ways people can jump into things right where they are – wherever that might be – and, if already involved, how they can deepen that engagement:

1) Become aware of privilege and internalized oppression. Peggy McIntosh has a well-regarded exercise, "White Privilege: Unpacking the Invisible Knapsack," which helps European Americans understand how they are privileged by being white. McIntosh points out that people can be aware that others are worse off than they are; but these same people remain unaware – and the culture keeps them unaware – of how this situation translates into their benefiting from privileges themselves.

"White privilege is like an invisible weightless knapsack of special provisions, maps, passports, codebooks, visas, clothes, tools and blank checks," comments McIntosh. She asks people to take stock of what they have in their own personal knapsacks and offers more than 25 examples – such as, "I can arrange to protect my children most of the time from people who might not like them," or "I am never asked to speak for all the people of my racial group." McIntosh notes that some items everyone in a decent society should be entitled to – things like "the expectation that neighbors will be decent to you, or that your race will not count against you in court." Other privileges confer power, like "My skin color [is] an asset for any move I ...want to make," or white people are "morally neutral, normative, and average, and also ideal, so that when we work to benefit others, this is seen as work which will allow 'them' to be more like 'us.'"

A similar exercise can be conducted by men, non-working class people, and heterosexuals to get at the specifics of male, class and hetero privileges. Coming from the opposite side, popular education methods developed by the Brazilian educator Paolo Freire, such as *Pedagogy of the Oppressed*, can help oppressed people gain insights into the social system where they live. Anger at oppressive conditions – which may be deeply internalized or bubbling near the surface – can turn into positive energy to transform society. Regardless of color or nationality, the common objective of these exercises is clarity – an awareness of social reality as it is and one's place in it. Without this kind of clarity, people's attempts to bring about change will likely remain unfocused and only occasionally effective.

2) Build intentional relationships based on equality with people of other nationalities. We discussed this point in Chapter 18 as an essential part of white folk's "breaking loose" from white privilege. It is implied as well in Chapter 22's emphasis on building unity among oppressed nationality peoples. Similar considerations apply to heterosexuals developing friendships and working relations with LGBTQ folks; to men, with women in non-sexual contexts; and to middle and upper class individuals, with people in the working class.

A key element for these relationships to be beneficial for everyone is that they be based on equality. The burden here is on those with privilege to be primarily in a learning mode – being willing to examine the reality of their privilege together with others in the relationship. Ultimately the goal is to turn privilege – be it in education, social access, or material wealth – to everyone's advantage by making it available for use by the social justice movement.

Educated people can help write grants. More connected folks can do fundraising. Those with extra resources can help get a project off the ground, take care of mailings, or help with transportation. The issue is not so much a matter of personal handouts – although friends help out friends in a crunch. Rather, a group might use a "Health and Welfare Fund" to allocate resources, as one example. Here everyone contributes what they can to the fund based on their situation. And the whole group then decides which project or individual receives how much and under what circumstances.

Privilege also affects relationships through the deeply internalized feelings of confidence that people with privilege have – and which other very competent people sometimes lack. Important to building up this sense of confidence is the actual experience of struggle – fighting back, taking leadership – as well as coming to understand the historical and social roots of powerlessness

3) Study and discuss the history of peoples of color, as well as of white working class people. We mentioned this point in Chapter 18, particularly as it applies to white people in relation to people of color. But it applies more broadly, since different nationalities tend to be steeped in stereotypes about each other. Developing personal relationships is essential; but there is also an obligation to learn other folks' history – and to do it on one's own time, so to speak, and not expect to be spoon-fed by friends.

All these considerations apply to questions of class and gender as well. One goal of this book has been to approach these varied aspects of people in an intersectional way. We encourage readers to turn to the studies included in the bibliography to learn more, particularly the starred items that are the main sources for each section. The movement is only beginning to create a common history of struggle that people of all nationalities can identify with. Learning each other's histories, and drawing on all our varied experiences, is essential to creating a collective memory appropriate to the emerging society the movement hopes to build.

4) Question, talk about, and challenge the evidence of white supremacy all around us. Simply putting into words an observation or a question can help people see more clearly what is going on – the composition of a meeting, people's body language, or who is interrupting whom. Questions are good because they leave the answer open and allow folks to respond freely. At the same time, when someone asks a question back, there is the opportunity to "tell it like it is" – or at least as it appears to you – simply and directly.

Resistance or non-cooperation are options when other people voice a snide comment about a certain part of town, a put-down of a particular class of people, or a color-coded joke. Ted Allen suggested one way to respond in this situation: "Oh, you must think I'm white?"[1] Another is to point to a personal relationship with the targeted group – "Just so you know, my wife is a Chinese immigrant." And however one responds, the goal can be more than just silencing the speaker. Most desirable is being able to turn the conversation into a straightforward discussion of race and its role in society. Tim Wise gives an example from a conversation in a bar, when working to defeat David Duke in his campaign for governor of Louisiana in 1991, and concludes: "There are ways to talk to people, even truly tough cases, and make some headway, break down some defenses, get people to at least begin to question the things they have always taken for granted precisely because they have *never been challenged before* by anyone who looked like them."[2] Finally Noel Ignatiev calls for people to become "race traitors":

> White skin is the official currency of this society. It buys admission to neighborhoods, to schools, and so on....Now if there were five or ten percent counterfeit whites around – people who looked white but really weren't – then, I think, the white skin would lose its value. The judge, the school principal, the cop, the social worker, the personnel officer at the plant – and all of the other people who implement and carry out the racial tracking of our society – would no longer be sure about how to perform their function.[3]

In this spirit, one can be proactive by crossing the color line to hear a speaker, attend a holiday celebration, volunteer one's time, go to church, or take part in a discussion. At the same time, it is important to be sensitive about spaces that people of color reserve for themselves – but not jumping to such a conclusion based on little or no information. Discovering what is possible, and what is not, can feel a little risky, but being willing to step out of one's comfort zone is necessary to break down the social barriers that divide people. Still, the invasion and domination of other people's spaces is a real concern – and verges over into the larger issues of gentrification of neighborhoods and cultural appropriation.

Finally, the direct rejection of privilege can make sense at appropriate times – usually combined with organizing others to do the same. Examples include 1) a group of workers who turn down a raise aimed at undercutting their support for a union contract; or 2) the officers in the Civil War movie *Glory* refusing their pay until black soldiers received the same wages as the white soldiers.

5) Take a good look at your home. Paul Kivel, in *Uprooting Racism*, notes that people's homes are their most intimate spaces and they reflect who we are. One useful exercise is to look around and see what our home tells us about ourselves. The pictures on the walls, the books or magazines lying around – or their absence; the sound of conversations, TV shows, or music; the traffic in and out of children, friends, or activists; the smells of food, coffee or farmland – all these aspects of people's homes say something about who we are. There is no pre-judgment implied here, because homes depend in part on how much money folks have, their ages, and whether they live in the city, the suburbs, or the country. The point is, however, that if people profess to be against white supremacy, yet everything in their home reflects a white culture, then there is a disconnect. At the same time, there can be a downside here, too, in collecting – or appropriating as commodities – others' cultures. Consciously altering the home environment, however, can reflect movement in a new direction – and can reinforce efforts to be consistent in one's values and to identify with a shared history of struggle. As Kivel notes, engaging children in this project can make it a learning experience for the next generation, too.

6) Challenge white supremacy (sexism, homophobia) in family life. A lot of emotional energy goes into maintaining the structure of relationships in a family. Raising questions about the internal culture – the humor, the assumptions about peoples of other races, or who does what tasks around the house – can stir up people's defenses. The challenge is to find ways to address these topics while still maintaining a connection with folks. For white people who become anti-racist activists – and in doing so break with their families to varying degrees – facing up to this responsibility is often difficult.

Two women from the South who broke with the white supremacist environment in which they grew up make this point. Mab Segrest, in *Memoirs of a Race Traitor*, tells how she came to accept her obligation to her family at the urging of African American mentors in North Carolina. Anne Braden, in *The Wall Between*, reflects on her own struggles with family members and the slow, almost imperceptible changes she saw in her father's attitudes over decades of loving struggle. Neither woman regrets her rejection of the dominant Southern ways and their values; and each sees her personal transformation as a necessary and liberating step forward. At the same time, by re-engaging with their families, both women were able to understand better the social sources of their parents' prejudices – and, in doing so, come to accept their folks' humanity, while continuing to hold up a mirror to offensive words and practices. Just as the family has a powerful ability to shape and contain a person; so too, once free from its negative influences, one can bring that same power to bear to reshape the family culture. The lessons learned in this most intimate struggle – and the sense of personal wholeness achieved – can radiate outward in relationships with friends, coworkers, and other activists.

7) Take an inventory of activism in the community. It can be helpful to look around to see who the grassroots activists are in the community – and then plug into what is going on. By being supportive, putting in the time, and establishing ties on the basis of joint work, people can learn the skills needed to bring about change. Building relationships with folks from different oppressed nationalities helps foster understanding and unity. And if of European descent, orienting oneself in this way helps ground a person's activism – providing a base from which to reach out and organize other white people.

If the community is homogeneous – as is the case with many white people, who overall tend to live in segregated communities – the basic approach can still be the same: seek out those who are active in a progressive way and then link up with them. The problem, however, is that when organizations are racially isolated – as in white suburbia or small-

Anne Braden

We lost one of our best today y'all.

We stood on her shoulders. All of us race traitors, us "whiggers," us "n----- lovers," and white folks that decided that we'd rather cast ourselves into the identity oblivion than sit one more minute comfortably on the porch of white supremacy. She was a worker, and so we knew we had to work. She loved the South because she knew what it could be, and so we did. She sat and talked with us, and so we shared. She never backed down.

Anne Braden died today.

Many of you reading this won't even know who Anne Braden was. Like the Grimké sisters, and John Brown, and, and, well...damn, see, the names just don't come that easily...Anne chose to eschew the plunder of whiteness for a lifetime of struggle for racial justice. This struggle had high and low points, as it spanned over 50 years of activism and organizing, and it deserves to be memorialized.

You can bet we're not going to find her name gracing a textbook, street sign, or holiday any time soon though. Anne rejected white supremacy flatly, then spent her life working to dismantle it. They can't tell us white kids what it was that she was doing. We might see the sense in it and follow along. We might search for the last remaining bits of humanity they've trained us to cloak so deeply and struggle to make them manifest. We might be mad that they hid it from us for so long. We might have to destroy their system.

They have to erase her existence. Or color her crazy like ole John Brown.

I only met Anne Braden once. Anne had been invited to speak on a panel with other "firestarters" like Dolores Huerta, Tim Sampson, Elizabeth Martínez, and Mandy Carter. I ended up in a workshop with her later on in the day. Anne's graceful fire consumed the whole room. I sat on the floor because the space was so full, and I felt like a small child at the foot of Jesus. Who was this woman laughing deadly serious about not trusting a roomful of white people to do anything good on their own? Her charm was magnetic, and I hung on every word. White supremacy was a sham. The only way out was organization. White people had to step aside and follow the leadership of people of color. White people could redeem ourselves, could make our lives worth living, if we were willing to fight. Young whiteboys don't get to hear this too often, you know?

Her humility was startling. And as I spent the workshop, and the 2-3 hour conversation with her, the organizers of the workshop, and 2 other inspiring organizers that followed, it became clear that I was in the presence of greatness. She needed to know everything about what they were doing, how they were doing it, and how the rest of us could use it. She patiently prodded me for conclusions about organizing dilemmas that I was facing back in North Carolina. She was the honored guest, and she spent the af-

Continued on next page

town rural areas – they can drift in directions that end up setting people against other grassroots folks. Efforts to improve suburban schools can pit people against the needs of oppressed nationality children in a nearby city. Or the children of immigrant farmworkers can be viewed as a drain on the state's education resources, rather than the asset they actually are to the community. For white organizers who do not have oppressed nationality people to orient themselves to, the challenge to stay ideologically grounded increases. Under such conditions, seeking out activists and movements of color – even if at some distance from where an person lives – can be important to keeping one's bearings.

8) Be intentional about building a base for activism at the workplace. For most people who want to be active, it has to be right where they happen to be at that moment in their lives. For others, especially students or youth who are not already tied to a job or a community, there can be an element of freedom to shape where they spend their working life. One possibility is to select a workplace based on its potential as an organizing site – by considering the make-up of the workforce, its history of struggle, and the degree to which the workers share connections to a particular town or neighborhood. Then, rather than getting a job, say, as a union

Continued from previous page

ternoon asking us questions like we were.

Anne Braden was tireless. She had long ago earned the right to retire and rest, but she woke each morning to create a list of things that needed doing that day, and went to bed each night knowing that there was still more to do. Anne Braden was a leader. She, along with her good friend Ella Baker, influenced and facilitated the growth of multiple generations of young people in Southern freedom movements. Anne Braden was humble enough to admit that she was part of the problem and determined enough to put her life on the line every day as part of the solution.

White people need to know Anne Braden. We need to know that we have options, that the spoils of whiteness come up short when measured against the soul of struggle. We need heroes and examples and teachers. We need to know that resistance to white supremacy is a lifelong journey that you can never leave. We need her grace and her enthusiasm and her humility.

White people fighting for the end of white supremacy have been standing on the shoulders of Anne Braden for over 50 years now. Many of us without even knowing it. Because of her resistance, many of us have found our humanity, have woken up each day with a purpose, and dug in for the long haul. The strength of her foundation has helped us to know that we are not crazy, we are not alone, and that we will win.

Thank you Anne. You've made us all a little bit taller. May you at last find rest.

—from: Bryan Proffitt, "If a Tree Falls in the Forest..."

staffperson – where the relationships with workers are less direct – one can hire on as a rank-and-file worker for the long haul.* On this basis of equality with others, an organizer can then build ties with co-workers over time in a way that fits with the strategic front against white supremacy discussed in Chapter 23. An extension of this approach is the call to organize the South and Southwest described in Chapter 11.

9) Examine other aspects of life to see if changes would favor increased activism.

- **Where you live:** perhaps a house or apartment in a different community would enable the building of intentional relationships and a social base for activism.
- **The church, synagogue, sangha, or other religious institution you might attend:** possibilities for increased social engagement might flow from proposing a project or, where necessary, by making a change to a different gathering.
- **The amount of TV watched:** maybe a different pattern of activity would free up some time for activism, for a progressive book club, or for a class at the local community college.
- **One's physical condition:** working out, a basketball league, karate or other activity can help keep a person physically fit and more prepared to take on the challenges of an activist's life. Also, the older a person gets, the more important such activity is so that one can bring all the accumulated wisdom of a lifetime to bear for social change.
- **Where and with whom one socializes:** one of the most segregated spaces in the United States – along with people's religious activities – is where folks relax and enjoy leisure activities. Perhaps other options are available – new places to visit, or new friends to go out with or have over.
- **Learning a new language:** with the increase of immigrants of color in the United States, learning a second language like Spanish, Tagalog, or Haitian Creole is nearly a necessity for anyone who wants to be effective in opposing white supremacy.

---

* Consciously taking on a working class job is most effective when there are others to help make the adjustment to the new conditions, provide feedback, and offer other forms of emotional, and sometimes financial, support. On one's own the organizing work can be frustrating – even as the on-the-job experience contributes to personal growth. One example of a support group is the Rank and File Youth Project, which helps college-age students make the transition to the workplace. The R&FYP has a newsletter, regular conference calls, and by the fall of 2006 had held two *Inside Organizer* training schools. *(Parsons, "A New Generation of Youth Labor Activists)*

Generally, the idea is to look at all the ways one might free up time and develop the ability to be more intentionally engaged with others. Having an overarching political perspective is important, too, since it can help a person see the link between everyday activities and the long-term goal of social transformation. The challenge is for people to take responsibility for their lives, be aware of how they spend their time, and make the best use of whatever freedom – or privilege – they may have.

10) Finally, what if people are just too busy or overwhelmed by trying to hold everything together? What if they feel they can't change anything, that they will never be effective as a change agent, or that everyone out there is already doing about what they can anyway? The key here is probably not to "do" anything, but just to be open – to people's history, to really seeing what is going on in one's life, to new relationships, and to new kinds of conversation. This society being the way it is, just about everything a person does is tied in somehow with color, class, and gender. A starting point is to keep one's eyes and ears open – along with one's heart and mind – and see what happens.

Chapter 25

Organizational Measures

A central message of this book – in the historical chapters as well as in those focused on current conditions – is that organization is necessary to bring about change in society. It is good for people to join with others in trade unions, community organizations, service groups, or wherever else folks are working to improve themselves and society. And where no organizations exist, people can form their own. Gaining experience working collectively with others is a skill that folks have to learn mainly on their own, since the society provides little training in organizing skills. Once people recognize that social change requires collective action, then the question of what kinds of organization and how they should function becomes important. Here we want to address some of these questions as they relate to the struggle against white supremacy and racism.

Enabling personal development

One way organizations can advance the struggle is to foster the kinds of personal engagement outlined in the preceding chapter. For example,

- **Develop awareness of privilege and internalized oppression.** An organization can hold a workshop – at a conference, for example – that deals with racial privilege and brings in gender and class in appropriate ways. Another possibility is to offer a training program to the organization's members – such as a workshop by the People's Institute's ("Undoing Racism") or the Catalyst Project ("Anti-Racism for Collective Liberation"). Also, valuable training resources are available at the "Challenging White Supremacy Workshop" website, http://cwsworkshop.org/workshops.html.

- **Build relationships across the color line.** A group can prioritize outreach and recruitment – and conduct the kinds of discussions internally that will prepare people to be successful in this effort. Such activities help achieve the goal of transforming the composition, consciousness, and culture of movement organizations – as discussed in Chapter 23.
- **Study and discuss the history of peoples of color, as well as of white working class people.** Organizations can conduct internal studies, hold forums and film showings for the broader community, and generally encourage a culture of discovery. Popular education methods can decrease the dependence on written materials – by using music, role-playing, video clips, and exercises that get folks physically engaged with a topic.* Educational methods should take into account people's range of abilities and learning skills so that people do not feel excluded. And in a multilingual setting, having appropriate written materials, as well as translators and translation equipment, are essential.

For each of the other personal activities suggested in Chapter 24, similar organizational implications follow:

- **Encourage folks to talk about their personal experiences involving race, class, and gender.** Such shared lessons are an effective approach to learning, since they are so direct and personal in their impact.
- **Engage the group in carrying out an inventory of community activism and area workplaces.** Such a project can encourage members to be intentional about where they live and work, and about their outreach efforts and the activities they engage in. Where organizational resources are available, it may be possible – and necessary – to provide financial support to folks who move into new areas or take on new jobs that include a step-down in pay. Such considerations are important when implementing a strategic plan like "Organize the South and Southwest," which calls for folks to move to the Sunbelt and to be strategic in considering where to settle and what jobs to take.
- **Develop a supportive internal culture.** Recognize people's varying needs – related to their different languages, different stages of

---

* Two examples: "Step forward, step back" helps a group of people become aware of who is in the room – "Step forward if you've experienced real hunger; step back if both parents went to college." The "Ten Chairs" activity, developed by United for a Fair Economy, assigns people to sit on chairs representing equal divisions of the national wealth based on who owns how much of that wealth. Most people end up crowded onto the last few chairs.

life, different family responsibilities, and different types of personal relationships. The culture can also encourage timeliness, good practices around personal organization and communication, and a friendly, direct approach to resolving contradictions.

- **Encourage openness to new people.** By recognizing the validity of everyday interactions as a form of social struggle, an organization can counsel patience in handling disagreements with other people. The overall weakness of the social justice movement in the early 21st Century brings with it an often unrecognized benefit. It requires activists to learn how to talk to people who may disagree with them. Discovering areas of unity and keeping them primary, while clarifying and managing differences, is an important skill for activists and organizations to develop.

Internal processes

We now want to focus on aspects of internal functioning that can help an organization 1) achieve transformation goals around race, gender, and class (see Chapter 23); and 2) prefigure the type of society the movement seeks to bring about:

1) Take affirmative action to select and develop leaders. Affirmative action helps demonstrate an organization's commitment to internal transformation. Quotas or separate candidate lists are two mechanisms that can be used to elect leadership – as is bringing additional people onto the leadership body to balance out its representation. Who chairs meetings, who leads in planning major events, and who the presenters are in workshops – all are examples of leadership roles that deserve such attention.

Along with a commitment to filling positions of influence in an organization comes the need to first develop people's leadership skills. In their absence, folks get set up to fail by being pushed too far too fast – or they end up as figureheads for others in the group with the real power. Affirmative action to promote leaders of color, women, LGBTQ, and working class folks works its way back through leadership development to the recruitment priorities of the organization. To develop new leaders, the organization must assure that new people join who can become part of the process. At the same time, having leaders who are representative of a strategic constituency assists in recruitment – by providing a public face that folks can identify with, by helping to shape a welcoming internal culture, and by serving as mentors for new people coming in.

2) Promote a culture of planning and evaluation. By developing plans for campaigns or for periods of a year or more, and then by regularly evaluating the work, the group can systematically pay attention to recruitment, retention, and leadership development. Such planning and evaluation skills can also carry over into members' lives as well, helping people to be more focused and productive in their work.

3) Encourage a climate of directness in dealing with contradictions that arise. Group processes benefit by having a round of comments at the end of each meeting to evaluate how the discussion went. If there is a commitment to overcoming divisions around race, gender, and class, comments can address behavior that others find annoying or offensive: catch phrases that may have a racist connotation; people who tend to speak too long or too often – often men; or conversations that assume a certain level of education or a male-female pattern of socializing.

A person who says or does things that are offensive in a group usually is not conscious of their impact on others. If the actions were intentional, the person probably would not be in the group to begin with. For the benefit of the person being criticized, as well as to make the space safe for whoever is raising the criticism, there needs to be a group norm that people first listen to criticism – and not jump to an immediate defense. If in a group setting, others can help clarify points and provide a social cushion to support the process of listening and reflection. Over time, differences can then be resolved in the course of working together to achieve common goals. If a climate that allows direct criticism does not exist, then patterns of behavior by white folks, for example, are likely to drive people of color out of the organization. And similar dynamics can take their toll on women, as well as working class and LGBTQ folks.

It should be noted, however, that no one should accept criticisms that are not on target. Criticism can be very helpful – after all, who wants to go around offending or annoying people you want to work closely with. But people need to make up their own minds – using their own judgment after taking into account everything that others are saying. Simply giving in to group pressures undermines the integrity of the whole organization.

4) Pay attention to group dynamics. Since so much of what people do is shaped by the dominant culture, it can be helpful to pay attention to the organization's dynamics – who speaks too much, who gets up and moves around and when, who makes a face or shakes their head when another person is speaking. These patterns may sound nit-picky, or they might simply reflect personal mannerisms. But people from dominant groupings have a way of unconsciously throwing their weight around; and such patterns of behavior should be brought to group consciousness. People who are standing can add a sense of importance to their words. Making a face can undermine what another person is saying – just as nodding can either indicate support, or turn the speaker into a mouthpiece for the person nodding. Someone may pay close attention to one speaker – to a man, say, or a leading person in the group – and then get up, move around, or leave the room for another.

One way to deal with these kinds of behaviors is to have a "process monitor" assigned to keep track of who talks, who's listening, and whatever other little tricks, if any, people may be pulling to dominate, or ignore, the discussion. Other ways to assure a balanced conversation, especially in a large group with limited time, are:

- After a man has spoken, wait a little while before recognizing another male speaker. By providing some space, people who are reluctant to jump into a conversation may find themselves willing to speak.
- From time to time invite those in the group who have not spoken to express themselves, if they so choose.
- Go around the room one by one, with folks having the option to pass if they like and then allowing them another chance after the circuit is complete.
- Have a rule that no one speaks twice before everyone has spoken once – or at least has had the opportunity to speak.

These kinds of structured practices can be very empowering to folks who are not skilled at speaking, or who are a minority of one kind or another in the room. And the group benefits by hearing from everyone – and not just from the college-educated or other more skilled speakers. Needless to say, however, going overboard on dynamics should be avoided, as with any group activity taken to excess. The goal is not the process itself, but the full contribution of everyone in the room to the group's mission.

5) Provide space for caucuses based on race or nationality, gender, sexuality, and class. People in the socially oppressed grouping can decide if there is a need for a caucus or not. Caucuses should meet at a convenient time and place; and ally groupings should meet at the same time. These two provisos help assure that the caucuses are not just for show and that the whole organization focuses on the concerns of the affected groups. Issues that come up within the caucuses and ally groupings can then be brought before the whole organization for consideration.

Caucuses make possible a collective process to work through differences inside the organization. It might be difficult for an individual to raise criticisms 1) of someone with standing in the group, 2) of a man, where the person affected is a woman, or 3) of a person who does not take criticism well. In such situations the support and affirmation of other people of color, or other women, can be crucial in clearing up a problem. Similarly if the matter concerns a more general cultural practice

Examples of White Supremacy & Privilege within the NYC Peace & Justice Movement

Refusing to acknowledge and accept leadership from activists and organizations of color:

- refusing to participate in people of color-led events
- refusing to participate in broad anti-war activities with strong people of color participation or leadership
- white groups starting coalitions without input from, or honest outreach to, organizations of color and then calling their groups "citywide." One activist dismissed the lack of input and outreach, saying "I long ago gave up paying attention to skin color… On such matters, I'm with Dr. King.... What's important about people is not the color of their skin, but the content of their character."
- white activists making strategy decisions without consulting activists of color, whose work is critical to implementing the decisions
- white activists using their greater financial or volunteer resources to attract resources, and to dominate leadership or staff positions and decision-making ("do it my way, and I'll raise the dollars")

Promoting positions that challenge the impact of war on more privileged populations, while ignoring or even justifying its impact on people of color and immigrants:

- refusing to recognize the centrality of white supremacy and racism in the war drive at home and abroad. One long-time peace activist in reference to the U.S. war against Afghanistan, "A racist war? It isn't. Vietnam was. But the Afghans for the most part are not dark skinned. A criminal war, yes. An illegal war, yes. An unconstitutional war, yes. But a racist war? B---s---."
- denying the impact on people of color of the war at home and abroad
- denying that non-Arab people of color within the U.S. are particularly targeted by the war
- appealing to racism or national chauvinism in opposing the war

Discrediting, ignoring or minimizing the history and prominent roles of people of color in the peace and justice movement:

- "dissing" or discrediting people of color organizations
- dismissing the roles of people of color in anti-war movements: One movement activist claimed that Angela Davis and Muhammad Ali were not serious anti-war activists during the Vietnam War.

Engaging in the politics of privileged projection: Some white activists, comfortable with a "white" peace movement, claim that activists of color are "too busy with domestic issues" to do anti-war work. This perception can be a cover for the white person's enthusiastic involvement in activism against the war abroad, but indifference to opposing the wars at home – which, after all, primarily target communities and people of color. Apparently, it hasn't occurred to this activist that his/her whiteness, along with class privilege, both enables and influences the luxury of choosing on which issues s/he will focus.

Creating an atmosphere of marginalization, disrespect or neglect towards people of color in anti-war meetings and events:

- white activists tending to dominate discussions and favoring the most "articulate"
- not calling on activists of color to speak and chair meetings
- white people assuming that their experiences are the norm, and viewing people of color's realities as the "other" or "the exception"
- judging what political approach will work with "the average person" by the experience in white neighborhoods
- using terms like "us" and "them"

Creating an environment in meetings, through certain actions, that is threatening to, or uncomfortable for, immigrants

- exposing immigrants and other people of color to the risk of arrest in civil disobedience (CD) actions, or promoting CD in communities of color without understanding that immigrants risk jail, deportation and/or police violence that could lead to serious injury or death
- insensitivity to immigrants' religious and cultural practices

Such practices reproduce in our movement the white supremacy that permeates U.S. society. A similar dynamic involves class: those with greater access to education, wealth and power often marginalize working people... and involves gender: male supremacy creates unfavorable conditions for women's equal participation. Most white activists don't see how "whiteness" privileges them and perpetuates white supremacist social relations in movement work. White activists have a responsibility to struggle against white supremacy, a struggle that includes:

- sharing leadership with, and being willing to follow the lead of, people and organizations of color;
- maintaining an attitude of collectivity and not dominating discussion;
- challenging racist language and actions (especially within movement spaces); and
- prioritizing the issues, experiences and struggles of people of color.

—from: "An Open Letter To Activists Concerning Racism In The Anti-War Movement," with 15 co-signers[4]

or leadership style, a collective recommendation can more quickly get to the bottom of the situation than a single voice.

6) Learn how to contain differences within the organization. Discussion and debate are essential to a group's learning process and to its ability to adapt to new conditions. At the same time, differences of opinion can sometimes lead to hard feelings, can turn off new people, and can result in internal divisions, inaction, and even the splitting or destruction of an organization. Being able to contain and work through differences over time is critical to an organization's vitality. The problem is that U.S. society encourages people to dream of liberation in the form of owning their own small business or becoming a professional. Managing differences so as to build large, democratic organizations capable of transforming society, by contrast, is not a skill supported by the power structure.

Corporations and the military have a chain of command to assure unity of action. And trade unions in the United States have often functioned in a similar fashion, with entrenched leadership using the call to be a "team player" as an excuse to silence opposition. Movement organizations aspire to function democratically, but unfortunately there are very few models of effective organizations to look to. The experience of socialism in power during the 20th Century too often turned "democratic centralism" into democracy for the elite and centralism for everyone else. The result of this situation is that the movement in the United States has a long way to go to discover and implement forms of organization that are both democratic and able to function effectively on a large scale.

The inability to manage both aspects of this contradiction undermines the fight against white supremacy. Internal debate is crucial; but hair-splitting and setting up multiple competing organizations is a dead end for the struggle. Grassroots folks – working class people of all nationalities – have little patience for this kind of "small business" mentality, where every so-called leader wants to lord it over a private movement fiefdom.

Here are a few organizational measures to help deal with this concern:

- **Minimize the fundamental questions** that everyone in an organization either agrees to or agrees to live with. These "bottom lines" should be as inclusive as possible while still upholding the defining aspects of the movement – the central importance of opposing white supremacy being one such example.

- **Speak in terms of "themes"** that characterize a period rather than micro-specifying the fine details of the organization's official position. Having folks oriented to a theme – like "opposing empire," for example – allows them to carry out work that is true to the conditions where the live and work, while still fitting in with the organization's overall perspective.

- **Be willing to trust the group process – up to a point.** There is a balance between the individual and the group, and between a single organization and a group of organizations. No one has total insight into reality; so even if an organization gets something wrong, there needs to be patience and trust that in time everyone will learn from the experience. If the group persists in its wrong direction, people can still look for ways to disassociate themselves while maintaining unity around central questions. The ultimate authority for decisions must be a person's own judgment – but informed, as much as possible, by an all-sided openness to what grassroots voices are saying.
- **Prevent individuals from becoming entrenched in leadership.** There is a balance, too, between continuity of leadership and an organization's ability to be flexible and adapt to changing conditions. As much as possible an organization should strive for 1) a collective, or group, leadership with input from many sources; and 2) the movement of individuals in and out of leadership positions, so that people do not become rooted in place. Term limits of some kind can encourage two things: First, they compel the organization to bring forward new leaders to fill the positions left open by people rotating out. And, second, the former leaders bring to their status as rank and file members their knowledge of how the organization works. They can share this understanding and be a force for greater participation by ordinary members in groupwide decision-making.

7) Don't overlook questions of security. It may seem strange to speak of security concerns, since everything we have mentioned here is legal and above board. Unfortunately, however, history shows that legality and a righteous cause have not been enough to prevent violent attacks of either the official or unofficial kind in the United States. From the original Klu Klux Klan and White Leagues at the end of the Civil War, through the Palmer Raids after World War I, the McCarthy attacks on the trade unions after World War II, and the FBI's COINTELPRO program during the 1960s and '70s – the United States has consistently suppressed movements that fundamentally challenge the status quo.

Recognizing this history and taking into account the relative vulnerability of the sectors of people involved – people who historically have been lynched, deported, beaten, raped, and murdered – require that the movement be serious about protecting its own. Most basically this obligation calls for organizing that is both broad and deep, so that large numbers of people can be brought out to defend anyone who comes under attack. It also means taking precautions so that the movement's campaigns, organizations, and membership are transparent to people at the base, while being obscured from forces who want to destroy the movement. In particular, people's jobs need to be protected from reprisals. And tactics should take into account the higher vulnerability of people of color, women, lower sector workers, and LGBTQ folks to police and reactionary violence.

Security is an underrated area of concern for the social justice movement. This situation reflects, in part, the overall weakness of the movement, as well as its rightful primary focus on organizing and mobilization. Nonetheless, having a mindset that looks reality square in the face requires that people recognize the deeply violent character of the U.S. social system – and that the victims of that violence are distributed unequally, depending on race, gender, and class.

There are many other aspects of organizational life that are worth paying attention to as part of developing new, more direct, and open ways of relating to one another. For example, there are:

- *decision making processes* that draw on consensus, voting, and a mix of both
- *communication practices and etiquette* around phone calling vs. email and hard copies
- *methods of summing up* and otherwise processing the group's experience
- *balancing formal activities* and the informal life of the group
- *balancing individuals' organizational life* with their lives at home and at work
- *providing mutual support* – be it emotional, financial, or general mentoring

Too often people do not realize all that is involved in building an organization, and they tend to fall back on ingrained habits combined with unrealistic expectations of other people. Just as with raising children, however, most people eventually figure out how to do it, and they get better with practice. Being basically friendly, listening well, and paying attention to detail will get a person a long way.

We have highlighted points that can help an organization be both effective and internally consistent in its struggle against white supremacy. The aim is for people to look squarely at this essential task and not to lose heart when troubles crop up. We also want to encourage organizations in the social justice movement to share their experiences in organization building. That way a collective expertise in time can emerge to help sustain a variety of influential democratic organizations, anchored in the grassroots freedom movements.

Chapter 26

Social Struggle

The personal and organizational measures discussed in the two previous chapters address issues of privilege in people's lives and in movement organizations. As people connect with others actively engaged in struggle – and reach out to new forces in creative ways – the movement grows. Organizations gain experience, resources, and influence. The systematic character of oppression becomes clearer. Social forces join together, work through differences, learn how to challenge for political power and carry through social transformation.

Given this overall pattern of struggle, we want to suggest certain steps to help move the process forward. The emphasis here is not so much on the specific issues that people should take up – for two reasons. First, the range of issues is quite large, since the strategic perspective we recommend calls for a merging of the social movements for national liberation, working class power, and an end to patriarchy. Second, we have looked at the specifics of each of these movements and the prospects for unity in earlier sections. Here we want to suggest an approach to organizing that over time will have the greatest chance of bringing into being a strategic front against white supremacy and racism.

Stay centered on self-determination, affirmative action, and internationalism

Self-determination focuses attention on the central demand for political power by the oppressed nationality peoples. Without the fundamental democratic right to political power – including the right of the African American, Chicano, and First Nations to secede if necessary – the system of white supremacy and the racist ideas it generates in people's minds will continue. The struggles to end patriarchy and capitalism also involve questions of power – in personal relations through to the organized power of the working class to reshape society, with leadership centered among the oppressed nationalities and women's.

Affirmative action in its broadest sense is simply another way to talk about ending privilege. It emphasizes the historic roots of race and gender privilege and calls for proactive policies to set matters straight – affirmative action on the job, in the home, in popular culture, in the criminal justice system, in politics and throughout society. By orienting to the struggles of people of color at any particular moment, white organizers can distinguish the specific form the struggle is taking at the moment – be it for reparations, Katrina reconstruction, or immigration rights; or for an end to right-to-work laws or male violence.

Internationalism is a third bedrock perspective, because of the imperialist role of the United States in the world. This standpoint allows people to see clearly the underlying forces driving an issue like immigration, for example, or the war in Iraq, the "War against Drugs" in Colombia, and the "War on Terror" generally. It helps one be mindful of the material benefits – and associated racial and national prejudices – that come from living in a superpower in the Global North. Armed with this awareness, one can then – as a simple act of solidarity and with no special recognition due – turn that privilege around and target U.S. imperialism from the inside. The prescription to "Think globally, act locally" is sound – but it can be broadened to "Think globally, act globally," as well. Struggles at home weaken U.S. imperialism – and are the primary form of internationalism for activists inside the United States. Then by consciously linking with people in other parts of the empire, the U.S. movement can maximize its strategic impact, while countering the inevitable distortions that come from living inside the world's only superpower.

Start where people are at

"Starting where people are at" is a truism of organizing – but it has two aspects. The first is the obvious call to listen to what people say without prejudgment and without pushing one's own views on others. In particular, for white people organizing among white workers, it means not leading with a rap on white privilege. The perspective of this book holds that white working class people are oppressed by capitalism. So the first step in organizing is to get a concrete feel for the ways people experience their lives and understand their situation. This listening aspect can help organizers appreciate both the problems people face and the ways they have to resolve them. Some individuals will be more active; others will be more passive – but observing all the while what is going on. And a few may be a source of issues themselves. By sorting out what the concerns are and who is dealing with them in what ways, an organizer can begin to get a sense of which folks to connect up with in a supportive way, and around which key issues.

The second aspect of this approach is less obvious. It comes down to being a true friend to folks you are working with. If the United States is white supremacist; if white folks are privileged simply by virtue of their skin color; and if this privilege has negative consequences for white people themselves, as well as for others – then there is an obligation to share this understanding and discuss it through with people. What makes the conversation possible is the underlying unity established by working together on issues of recognized importance. The overall learning process is two ways – but the main responsibility in connecting with people is the organizer's.

As to the particulars of white privilege itself – by choosing the right issue, the right allies, and the right targets, each step can work to undercut privilege. White folks' linking up with people of color undercuts privilege – particularly when it occurs in a supportive rather than a "come join our organization" way. Joint efforts to form a union, to oppose mandatory minimum sentences or the death penalty, or to demand quality public education for everyone – such struggles can help keep an organization of predominantly white folks on the right track. By contrast, if the majority of a U.S.-born group decides to oppose immigrant rights rather than advance them – say around access to driver's licenses or education benefits for immigrant children – then it is probably time to part ways. By letting people know clearly why continued support is impossible, others may be influenced in their thinking and help form a nucleus for a more progressive organization in the community.

By summing up such experience – both positive and negative – and viewing the lessons in the larger framework of U.S. society, the reality of white privilege and how to fight it become clearer. Concrete lessons, learned in the course of struggle, and starting from where people are at – these are the steps that enable people to learn about privilege, come to terms with it, and then turn it to good use in the struggle.

Go broader and deeper

When engaging in struggle, the challenge often is to broaden the ranks of the forces fighting around an issue – take ending the war in Iraq, as one example. Two different approaches are possible for primarily white organizations in this situation: One amounts to activists' asking people of color to "come join our..." coalition, demonstration, or organization. As a way to entice a new constituency to take part in a demonstration, for example, the peace group might invite a speaker, include a slogan, or encourage an information table at their event. None of these steps is bad in itself, and the result can be a richer learning experience for the people who attend the demonstration. But the likelihood of large-scale participation by the new constituency is small at best.

A second approach is more long term in its outlook but carries with it the prospect of real unity of action in the future. Here the organizers identify issues of concern to the new constituency – perhaps by first bringing a speaker to the peace group's organizational meeting. The second step is then to offer organizational support to one or several groups within the new constituency that are active – say, around police violence, domestic abuse, or LGBTQ rights. By actually following through on the commitment of support, the original peace group develops new ties with people in the community, learns the kinds of pressures people are experiencing in their lives, and in the course of join activity gains some first-hand understanding of people's attitudes toward the war. Over time, these relationships generate a new, richer common language of resistance to oppression at home, as well as to the war. The peace folks bring their people out to demonstrations against police abuse. And when the next peace demonstration comes along, new community forces may now decide to be part of the planning process – helping to shape the event in a way that resonates with their community. By actively linking up in this way, primarily white organizations can transform their outlook and put their relative privilege to work – through their personal connections and networks or fundraising skills – to oppose the concrete, material disadvantages being experienced by folks of color.

Develop consciousness, theory, values

People learn best from their own experience. People can hear all the arguments about why gay and lesbian folks are the same as everyone else and should enjoy the same rights. But until heterosexual folks meet and become friends with real human beings, the issue remains abstract. Personal relationships are critical – across the color line, among different oppressed nationality peoples, or with women in positions of leadership.

On becoming socially active, people are often open to new ideas as they search for ways to advance their issues. Engaging in struggle helps a person understand who holds power and what it takes to bring about a favorable result – what arguments work, in what settings, and with how many people mobilized to get the point across. No amount of discussion or study conveys a sense of popular power better than taking part in a campaign – win or lose. But people draw the clearest lessons through evaluating their collective experience together with others.

The struggle for summation

While people learn from direct experience, the lessons – particularly from setbacks – are not always immediately clear. The problem is that in any struggle, there are actually two struggles: what happened and what people think happened. If a union loses the first election in an organizing campaign, the company will have its summation: "The workers don't want a union. They showed their confidence in the company, etc., etc." The organizers' summation is likely to be very different: There may have been intimidation by the company. There were not enough Spanish speaking organizers to win over the Mexican and Honduran workers. There was not enough attention to community issues to show that the union was there for the long haul and for all the issues that workers confront in their lives.

The company's summation leads to a real defeat – to a loss of hope and to workers' falling back into passivity. The second summation points to specific problems that can be addressed. Struggling to win people to this second viewpoint is critical. The summation needs to be grounded in reality and take into account the whole situation – the balance of power inside the plant, the amount of support in the community, the resources and staying power of the union. When everything is seen in this larger perspective – and assuming it rings true – people can be won to a deeper, more strategic, and longer-term fight.

The role of theory

Social theory essentially consists of summation raised to the next level: 1) take experience gained either directly or by way of other people's reports, 2) examine it with the help of an analytic and historical framework like the one used in this book, and then 3) draw out the lessons in a way that gives deeper insights into how the society functions and how to go about achieving movement goals. By sharing these summations with other people and being open to criticism and revision, the lessons gain clarity, have a wider impact, and help build unity. This type of theoretical work is essential to keep a movement on the path toward its goals, while adapting to changing circumstances.

Not paying attention to the deep structure of society and to long-term principles, by contrast, almost always leads people and organizations to conform to the system, even if they start out in militant opposition. The Populist Movement at the end of the 19th Century is a good example, as discussed in Chapter 5. Failure to have a principled stand against white supremacy left the movement open to race baiting, division, and defeat. Also, work that remains local in its outlook is likely to drift aimlessly or in relatively narrow channels. A community struggle around a school can turn into a platform for someone to run for city council – OK as far as it goes. But if that person's career becomes the goal instead of empowering the community, the campaign goes off track.

In general, campaigns can be summed up from three standpoints:

- What were the immediate benefits or losses from the struggle?
- To what extent did the broader popular movement gain strength?

- Were forces won to a deeper understanding of society, to the need for revolutionary organization, and to committing for the long haul?

A fourth criterion that overlaps the first two can be drawn out as well: Was there an advance in the battle for the minds of the broader public? Contesting the hegemony of ruling class ideas is critical to developing conditions where a mass movement can take hold and flourish.

By evaluating experience collectively along these dimensions, a movement deepens its theoretical understanding of the system and how to oppose it effectively. Also, individuals' summing up their personal experiences using these criteria can help people stay on course – by gaining insight into their strengths and weaknesses and clarifying how best to contribute to the struggle.

Philosophical outlook

Carrying the process of social activism and reflection more deeply can bring people to a philosophical outlook that embraces change and the power of ordinary people to transform the world. Seeing oneself in the flow of a constantly changing reality empowers people to relax into their role as change agents. Otherwise their activism can seem exceptional – passivity being the normal state – and required only by temporary difficulties in their lives. The Marxist philosophy of dialectical materialism, Liberation Theology, Engaged Buddhism, and other religious outlooks that embrace change can help sustain people's deepest commitment to social justice and ending white supremacy.

Social justice values

The social justice movement embodies a set of values that can be brought to consciousness, validated, and taught to others. These values are secular in origin, emerging out of the concrete conditions of contemporary struggle. At the same time they overlap with the teachings of many religions, without requiring a specific accompanying belief system. Examples of such values are:

- ***Solidarity:*** realizing that "an injury to one is an injury to all"
- ***Confidence in the power of ordinary people:*** trusting grassroots people's ability to learn, struggle, and transform both the world and themselves
- ***Openness and commitment to learning:*** being skilled at listening, putting effort into study, and being willing to examine oneself and one's actions
- ***Being active and useful:*** being intentional about one's life; taking responsibility to understand the world and one's place in it, and to work to change things for the better

- ***Courage:*** being willing to take a stand and act on it – not only in relation to the dominant forces in society, but also in relation to ones family, friends, and comrades
- ***Being all-sided:*** striving to base judgments on the whole picture, while recognizing that all the information is usually not available
- ***Commitment to shared effort:*** rejecting privileges, and turning those that one must live with – like being white or male – to the advantage of the struggle
- ***Being good at uniting:*** seeing differences clearly while, at the same time, uniting wherever possible to broaden the movement and increase its impact
- ***Reliability:*** having one's words and actions be in accord with each other
- ***Seeing clearly and acting appropriately:*** being able to find one's bearings independently; making proper distinctions between who is a friend and who is not
- ***Being principled, yet flexible:*** knowing where one stands, while not being rigid
- ***Valuing life:*** having a sense of oneness with other people and the environment, and a commitment to their protection

There are many other such standards – such as valuing children and their development, and honoring elders. In real life, moral judgments often depend on the conditions people find themselves in – and to some extent the ethical guidelines counter-balance each other. For example, it is important to be honest with other people in the movement. But as any slave narrative shows, survival as a human being under the U.S. slave system required a highly refined ability to dissemble and deceive the white plantation owners and their henchmen. Such situations are covered by the admonition to see conditions clearly and act appropriately. Another example is in handling criticism: people should be open to listening and to changing their behavior when made aware of their shortcomings. But if the criticism is an unprincipled attack by vested interests, aimed solely at tearing the person down, then courage becomes primary. Such attacks need to be withstood, deflected, or countered – while still paying attention to the kernel of truth they may contain.

Values should not be the exclusive property of the religious right, as they often seem to be today. The list above points to the powerful ethical system inherent in the revolutionary struggle to transform society. It also foreshadows the standards that are likely to guide behavior in the future – at least until people develop their moral outlook further under the new conditions of social liberation.

Nurture the strategic alliance where you are

In Chapters 22-23 we described a united front centered among oppressed nationalities, with women at the core, and with a section of white people forming a broad popular movement against white supremacy. Similar alignments make sense for the struggle against monopoly capitalism, where the multinational U.S. working class forms the core of the united front, and against patriarchy, where an autonomous Third Wave women's movement will likely be the leading force. While each movement has its own strategic configuration, priorities, and plan of action, the target is the same – a single, integral oppressive system that must be transformed to meet the needs of all three movements. This complex balance between independence and joint action in a strategic alliance can be expected in time to give way to a merger of the three movements.

Being guided by such an awareness has implications for the way activists conduct their organizing work today. While engaging in a particular struggle, one can keep in mind the larger systemic reality of race, gender, and class oppression. By doing so, one can then look for intersections and ways to connect with other strategic forces. For example,

- ***within the oppressed nationality movements*** – people can work to promote working class leadership and the centrality of women in the struggle;
- ***in the workers movement*** – organizers can link their unions to oppressed nationality struggles in the community and promote the centrality of women in both; and
- ***in the fight against patriarchy*** – women's and LGBTQ organizations can focus on issues of concern to working class people of all races, while supporting efforts to achieve political power in areas of oppressed nationality concentration.

Wherever people are, they can help build the strategic alliance of these independent but interrelated social forces. In so doing, they lay the groundwork for an eventual single merged movement – and at the same time help shape the relationships of the new society that will emerge from the struggle.

Increase ties among organizations

As discussed in Chapter 25, there is much to learn to enable people in groups to function effectively together. The points made there about managing differences while uniting to carry out work applies also to groups of organizations – in the form of coalitions, federations, and fronts. In order for one group to join in united action with another, both groups have to first exist – so the first responsibility is to the health of one's own organization. But once this aspect is taken care of, it is good to find ways to link up with others. Organizations together can magnify each other's impact, deepen understanding of the issues, and learn important lessons on how to keep decision-making power at the base.

The dominant culture works overtime to keep people fragmented – focused solely on their own personal and small group issues. Part of building a movement, and then a movement of movements, is learning how to keep all the many relationships among individuals and organizations working in a positive way – handling differences, allowing space for independence and initiative, and maximizing impact in a way that is flexible and adaptive to changing circumstances.

Build revolutionary organization

A central conviction developed and defended throughout this book is that ending white supremacy and racism requires transforming the social system currently in place in the United States. White supremacy, capitalism, and patriarchy form a single, unified three-headed monster. To defeat one, you must defeat them all. And, as with any human project beyond the scope of a single individual, people must organize to make it happen. To build a house, you call on a construction crew. To hold a conference, bargain collectively with an employer, or repulse an invader, people must organize appropriately for the task – set goals, devise a plan, marshal resources, and recruit, train and deploy people to carry out the work. Social revolution is no different. It is just bigger and more complicated, with more intermediary stages, likely setbacks, and unexpected challenges. It is multi-generational in scope and confronts, here and now, the most powerful ruling class in world history. No wonder people shy away from looking this reality square in the face.

But facing the monster is both necessary and unavoidable. The struggles of everyday life make clear the features of the system. Basically, it comes down to being willing to accept this reality and then doing what is necessary to overcome it. In particular, to make a social revolution there must be a revolutionary organization.

In this spirit, initiatives are underway in the United States to "refound the left" – efforts aimed at bringing conscious movement forces into a formation that can contest for power.* For our purposes, however, it is the overall outlook activists have in their organizing work that we want to stress. As people engage in social struggles, they can keep in mind the need to bring everything together in an organizational form that can contest for political, economic, and social power. Overcoming

---

* Freedom Road Socialist Organization has played a role in this effort and readers can go to their website <www.freedomroad.org> and publications for more information.

white supremacy and racism requires 1) an uncountable number of individual actions every day, 2) a multitude of organizations struggling around the issues that grassroots people deal with daily in their lives, and 3) a wealth of experience flowing out of the specific conditions in every community across the country. It also requires a revolutionary organization – party, alliance, front, or federation – that can concentrate people's vast experience and put it back out to them in a way that keeps the movement growing, struggling, learning, and moving forward together.

Movement activists can strive to embody and represent this outlook in their own lives and organizing work. In doing so, each person becomes a center of initiative. And the old Buddhist saying, "the universe in a grain of sand," becomes "the social justice movement in each individual."

And just as each individual is an integral whole made up of many parts, so too the social justice movement is the same – not just a collection of oppositional trends, tendencies, and competing initiatives, but a movement foreshadowing a different world, a new way of living together.

The long-time Southern freedom fighter, Anne Braden, who passed away as this book was being written, called this alternative social reality "the other America."* People are sinking roots, grounding themselves in the rich history of struggle in this country and in the complex social realities where they find themselves – or choose to be. People are developing dense interpersonal connections that reflect an intersectional understanding of race, gender, and class. People are organizing themselves – in local, state, national and international formations; around political, economic, and social issues; and in single-issue, identity-based, popular groups, coalitions, alliances and revolutionary organizations. Taken together, all this ferment is a movement in the making – but for the most part not yet conscious of itself. It is like the different parts of a body, carrying out their independent yet interrelated tasks – an integral whole in its own right, against which the dominant social structure, with its own internal processes and ruling class, stand in opposition. In this sense, the Buddhist saying is true in both directions: the social justice movement – like any individual – is a living, contradictory, and growing social entity. As such, it requires self-awareness and self-direction – and a leading, influential, and grounded revolutionary organization to make such consciousness possible.

---

* Michael Harrington used the phrase "the other America" to describe the lives of people living in poverty in the United States – in his 1962 book of that name. Braden, by contrast, speaks of "offering…a great opportunity, the possibility of finding a whole 'other world' or other community to live in." *(Braden, "Finding the Other America")*

Chapter 27

Advancing the discussion

There are many ways to advance the public discussion around white supremacy and racism – despite the weight of the mainstream media and consumer culture in people's lives:

- *Public actions*, picket lines, and vigils help deepen activists' commitment while being a visible public presence.
- *Major mobilizations* and, depending on conditions, militant actions can break through to a wider audience by way of TV, radio, the press, and word of mouth.
- *Letters to the editor*, op-ed pieces, and participation in community gatherings of various kinds – a labor legislative breakfast, a listening meeting on police-community relations, or a local candidates' night – all can help move a community conversation forward. By participating in such events, activists learn how to connect with people and engage directly with their everyday concerns.

Many resources are available to help people develop their message and then take it out to the public:

- *Ethnic and women's studies programs*; progressive think tanks; movement magazines, newspaper, pamphlets, and non-profit newsletters; Indy media outlets; websites, web-'zines, and blog-spots; and a few exemplary radio and TV programs – all provide ways to access and share information about what is really going on in society.
- *College professors and teachers* can often shape the content of their classes in ways that help students gain insight into social reality.

Even more latitude is possible for conference organizers, workshop facilitators, and popular education trainers.

- *Public forums and speakers tours*; study group, book club, and online discussions; guest speakers at membership meetings and organization-to-organization exchanges – all help circulate ideas and deepen understanding outside the usual channels. While helping to grow the circle of engagement, these efforts also promote activism and help build greater unity among movement forces.
- *Researchers, commentators, and activist intellectuals*, especially when they write in an accessible style, open a window to current reality and the past. Together they provide the movement with both a history and a present worth remembering and building on.

Our goal in this book has been to draw on such resources in a way that is unifying and intersectional in its outlook. The bibliography for each section represents only a small part of the resources available – a richness of studies, analyses, and practical experience that reflects a social movement in the making. There is a tremendous amount to learn and digest – and then turn into informed social action. There is much to unite with and, at the same time, much to disagree with. Several writers we have relied on heavily are not in agreement with each other – or with us, for that matter – on all questions. Ted Allen, for example, whose historical research informs the understanding of white privilege set out in Chapter 1, did not consider African Americans or the Chicano people to be nations with the right to self-determination. He also drew a distinction between his "social control" analysis and the work of "social constructionists" like David Roediger – with whom he otherwise shared many views. Anne Braden, who demonstrated a life-long commitment to anti-racist struggle once she broke with the Southern society that raised her, was often labeled a "communist." Nonetheless, she never made building a revolutionary organization a priority – a position that this book advocates.

When it comes to the theoretical and practical balance between race and class, there are wide divergences among anti-racist fighters. Chapter 10 presents a critique of the different positions in the debates within the New Communist Movement of the 1970s. That analysis can also be helpful when looking at the positions of organizations today. But our perspective in this book has been more to learn from what we view as the strengths of the various positions, rather than to pry them apart and catalog the differences. Perspectives like those advanced by Adolph Reed – author of *Class Notes* and a partisan of the U.S. Labor Party – have much to teach about class dynamics in the United States. The same is true for Michael Zweig, author of *The Working Class Majority* and convener of the conference series "How Class Works," sponsored by the

Center for Working Class Life at SUNY Stony Brook. The divisive character of racism comes through clearly in these writings, as does the importance of working class power in overcoming it. A very different analysis comes from J. Sakai, who sees oppressed nationalities as the only constituents of the U.S. working class – or "proletariat," as she calls this revolutionary social force. Sakai views white workers as fatally compromised by their complicity with white supremacy. Her writings draw out important lessons of betrayal from the history of the U.S. working class – and all activists should take them into account. In addition, Sakai allows for organizing among white workers in the same way that activists pay attention to allies from other non-proletarian sectors. The differences between writers like Sakai and Reed are sharp – and there are many other viewpoints in between among the sources we have drawn on. Regardless of these differences, however, each is an anti-racist fighter that we can and have learned from. In our view, the best approach is to 1) look for aspects of truth even where we mainly disagree, 2) clarify differences of analysis and strategy through frank and respectful discussion of divergent views, and 3) unite as broadly and fully as possible to organize against oppression.

The best assurance of all-sidedness is the ferment of the discussion itself – especially when linked to on-the-ground organizing experiences – as each person and group struggles to get a sense of the real-life contradictions, their interrelations, and their constant development and change. Recognizing this reality is essential, we believe, to developing a broad, inclusive debate that can help the movement gain clarity, higher levels of organization, and a more influential social practice.

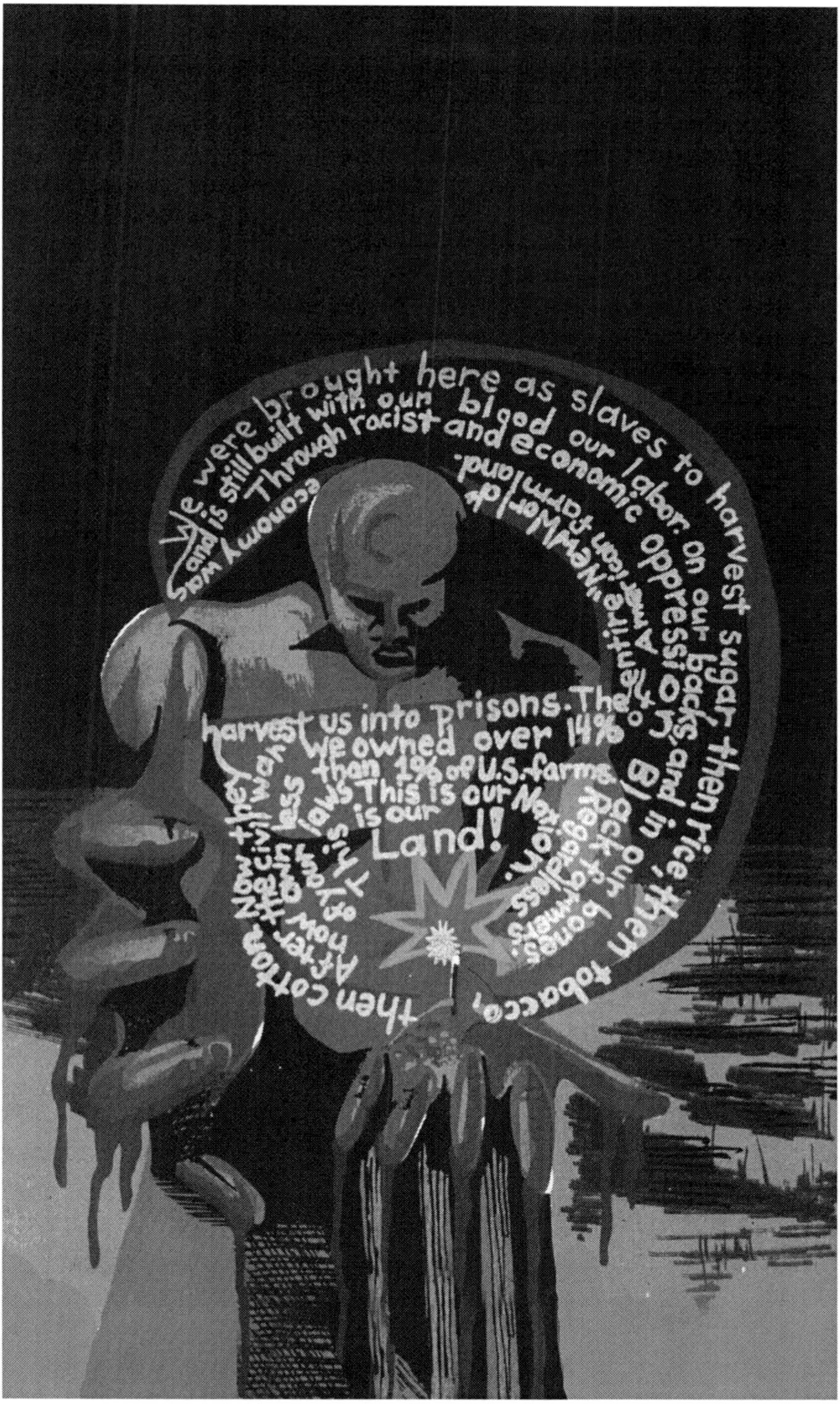

We were brought here as slaves to harvest sugar then rice, then tobacco, then cotton. Now they harvest us into prisons. The entire New World economy was and is still built with our blood our labor on our backs and in our bones. After the civil war we owned over 14% of America's farmland. Through racist and economic oppression

now own less than 1% of U.S. farms.

This is our Nation. This is our Land!

Privilege

With his *Eyes Wide Shut*
He cruised through life
This tom
"Uncle'd" his success by connecting it to perception
So he sought twin peaks
Connected at opportunity the Fore-fathers fought to keep him from
His skin
Worse than a scarlet A
So he wrote his story in the image of upper class
Now we read it like novels
And the critical analysis is he's to blame
But it's not true
The truth lies somewhere buried under constitutions and declarations
Of independent contracts and corporate mergers
The truth is a cable plugged into a network
Of Good Ole Boy broadband
That's got America Online
And we enter the net of Privilege
Given to the white light built on the backs of so many people of color
His mind
Works overtime like sweatshops
No union because we won't save him
But buy into this idea of ignorance that makes him sell out
Look at it
I don't need Peggy McIntosh to *Unveil The Invisible Knapsack*
That I know holds all of the goods and commodities
Tell me what is he to do?
When he sees that white supremacy isn't radical, it's reclusive
Not blond hair and blue eyed
It is Heirs and Heiresses and blue blood
His blood is red
And the only inheritance he can leave behind
Is how to punch in and out, be micromanaged, and stay underpaid
Imagine hearing the term White Privilege for the first time
From a supposed scholar overlooking that any academic understanding
Is both a product and result of privilege
Because this man lives it everyday
Much more than a case study, more than research
Because it isn't funded
And it's not supported, but rather attacked by an institution

An institution called the "American Way"
Imagine him
Trying to hammer his way through the class ceiling
Do we cast him aside as foolish?
Or do we band together to help him
One man's pocket holds hammer funding
One community's collection plate holds Lowe's purchase power
So let's go to work
And possibly Depot revolution into their upper echelon
Until we can make it our Home, our Office
It's easy to point sellout from the other side of the street
But let's imagine owning the block
Let's change it from moving on up to moving in
Understand that our fore-fathers are foster parents
We were taken from our birth homes
So we need new movements to step in like Social Services
A custody hearing
That gives back our right to self determination
Don't look at him sideways or cock-eyed
Let's look at the White boys club that cast aside their origins
Made their jacket the standard
Set rules that benefit some and deficit others
Club white balls across greener pastures into holes of security
And a higher credit score
While we fall strokes behind and into negative debt
So don't Tiger Woods our *Lost Boys*
Let's do a Corey Haim intervention
Before they are overcome by the lure of bright white lights
And fade forever
I say let's be rowdy like Roddy Piper
When John Carpenter tells us *They Live* to overcome us
Wear sunglasses at night like one hit wonders
Protect our eyes from the glare
And see this for the maliciousness it truly is
I don't want my share of the American Pie
Because my Life says I have to steal it off the window sill
I want the full course meal
And the sweet tea of rebellion, not the white wine of aged imperialism
So my comrade, put on your best clothes
We busting into his house to eat tonight

—*Dasan Ahanu*

IX

The Cost of Privilege

What final tally can we make of the cost of white privilege? The largest entries, the ones that dominate the balance sheet and overwhelm any assessor of the past or present, reflect the pain and suffering of the darker skinned people in U.S. history: the indigenous peoples of North America, subject to dispossession and genocide; the African peoples, rounded up and transported to slavery, and their descendants imprisoned behind the color line; the *mestizo* peoples of the Southwest and Puerto Rico, robbed of their homelands and segregated by color and language; the Asian peoples who immigrated, labored and suffered exclusion; and the modern immigrants of color who continue to labor and live largely separate and unequal lives. Add in, finally, the international human toll of white supremacy, and the cost becomes truly immeasurable. People today can only begin to comprehend its meaning – as we struggle to encompass this reality with our compassion.

At the same time, however, the balance sheet also shows another entry – smaller, no doubt, but significant nonetheless. It is the cost paid by white people – factory and service workers, farmers, women laboring at home or for unequal wages in industry, small tradesmen, teachers, and others working with their minds – a cost paid unknowingly for the most part, but a cost nonetheless. The relative advantages that white working people hold in society continue today – as spelled out in detail in Chapter 16. But here we want to shift attention to the cost side of the ledger – to draw out what people have lost and continue to lose by being made subject to a privileged status. By looking more closely at the balance sheet, white people – and white working people in particular – can come to see the compelling reasons to take action on their own behalf to overturn the system of racial privileges.

Because white folks in the United States have been so unaware of this aspect of their existence, we want to look at the cost of privilege with the help of three different standpoints – the past, the present, and the future. We have waited to the end of the book to draw up this summary, because now we can highlight points that already appear in earlier pages. In a sense, this tally sheet puts together the final piece of the strategy to transform the white supremacist system – a material basis for white people to engage in the struggle. White privilege has been the linchpin of the U.S. capitalist system since the beginning of slavery some three hundred years ago. By finally acting in response to this cost to themselves and others, a section of white people can assure that the struggle centered among peoples of color becomes a broad, truly mass movement

A look at the past

Some of the ways white people in the past behaved appears shocking and offensive today, no matter the color of the person's skin. Dressing up in black face or as Indians to unleash an other-worldly mob violence against black communities; semi-official militias and slave patrols; the sickeningly common rape of slave women; night riders hunting down and murdering grassroots leaders of color; state-sponsored massacres of Indian villages; lynching parties poisoning young people minds; violent attacks on Chinese laborers – all these are examples of the dehumanizing ways working class white people violently enforced the color line. And then there was the day-in, day-out mental deformity required to block out people's existence – and to deny people's humanity when avoidance was impossible: treating people as children, belittling and ridiculing their abilities, denying people's sexuality while at the same time creating fantastic oversexed images to justify rape and murder. While this culture of terror can ultimately be tied back to the plantation and industrial rulers, to politicians, clergy, and the press, nonetheless ordinary white people willingly took part in these abhorrent activities and sustained this white supremacist mindset from generation to generation.

It can be said that the worst aspects of this type of behavior are no longer tightly interwoven with what it means to be a white person today. And, as reviewed in Chapter 19, characterizing the U.S. culture of the past as a terror culture for people of color does not mean that there were no white allies who resisted this culture. But it is also true that the great mass of white people, who did not take part in the atrocities, nonetheless stood by and let them happen. That no anti-lynching law was ever passed by the U.S. Congress, despite the communal murders of some 5,000 people between 1882 and 1968, attests to this fact. On June 13, 2005, the Senate finally passed a resolution of apology for this criminal inaction.

Is it not true, then, that these white people of the past – participants and observers alike – paid a cost for their meager, but significant, material and social privileges? What, one might ask, is the worth of one's soul?

In addition to this fundamental question, there are other costs that people paid. Here are a few:

- Despite the misery and harsh conditions of life for poor white people in the South, once slavery was put in place, white folks in the South never again rebelled against the planter class. Bacon's Rebellion in 1676 was the last such uprising, and it was multiracial.
- People were frozen out of friendships and marriage with people across the color line.
- Often the worse off people were, the more vicious the defense of their psychological wage – and the more susceptible to recruitment to blood fests of various kinds in its defense.
- Solidarity with all the workers at a workplace or in an industry was impossible. Bosses could recruit strikebreakers from across the color line and, in highly circumscribed and unreliable ways, pretend to be a friend of the colored races.
- Minstrel-show racism deformed 19th Century culture and filtered out contributions by people of color. At the same time, spirituals and Latin rhythms worked their way up from the grassroots and, without acknowledgment, impacted songs and popular language – giving a hint of what white society was missing out on.
- Collusion in shutting down Reconstruction robbed many white children of their chance to become educated. It also replaced a commitment to social uplift – in the form of public expenditures for hospitals and asylums, for paving streets and helping the poor – with public stinginess and prideful, isolated individualism.
- White working class people fought and died in the country's wars of expansion – and only belatedly, mainly in Vietnam and after, made way for people of color to sacrifice themselves in numbers disproportionate to their presence in society.

Despite all these costs borne by white working class people, if asked at the time, very few would have understood how much they were paying for their white supremacist way of life. People attended church, they married and raised children, they socialized, had friends, and considered themselves decent folk. Society reinforced their view of the world, and anyone who countered it found themselves isolated – labeled eccentric or crazy – and if they persisted, run out of town, imprisoned, or worse. This look at past history has two aspects to it: First, there is the cost to white people living in these earlier periods that becomes clearer with the benefit of hindsight. And second, there is the realization that those white folks who acted so terribly for the most part "knew not what they did."

Which raises the question: Do white folks today know what they are doing?

Experiences today

Getting a feel for the cost of white privilege today is like going a second round on Peggy McIntosh's exercise "Unpacking the Invisible Knapsack," discussed in Chapter 24. There we recommended this exercise as a way for white people to discover the privileges in their lives – in comparison with the lived experience of people of color. Now we want to rummage around a little deeper in the knapsack, and pull out the bricks at the bottom – the ones that are actually weighing down white people without their being aware of it. By gaining some clarity on this invisible burden, folks can hopefully gain the motivation to toss out the whole knapsack.

The data cited in Chapter 16 show that white working class people in the United States come up short compared to their counterparts in other industrial countries – in health care, maternity leave, vacation time, retirement age, and overall life expectancy. Many white people are unaware of their country's second-rate performance in these areas and how they and their loved ones lose out. Or, if vaguely aware, people may blame workers of color or immigrants for dragging the United States down, rather than the capitalist system that exploits working people of all colors.

The cost of privilege can be seen in the faces of family members when they receive news that their son or daughter has died in Iraq. It fills the wards at Walter Reed where disfigured soldiers are kept alive by the most modern methods only to face a future with meager public support for veterans. And the costs of maintaining a world-spanning empire drain resources that otherwise could be directed to human services at home – like education or child care, for example. Meanwhile capitalists undercut the jobs and pay of white workers by shifting good jobs overseas – where the International Monetary Fund backed by the U.S. Army helps keep wages low. In turn, foreign workers flee the conditions imposed on their home countries by U.S. imperialism and arrive here ready to work just about anywhere, for just about anything. Given people's traditions of resistance at home, however, these newcomers also arrive as potential recruits in the struggle against white supremacy. Until white workers learn to welcome these new arrivals as allies, however, illusions of greatness in being white and "American" will help make bearable actual lives of overwork, insecurity, and anger.

International comparisons make a clear case that white working class people pay a cost for buying into white supremacy. But personal experience is still the best teacher. Tim Wise gives some examples of the toll of privilege in his personal story *White Like Me*. Here are three:

- **Loss of family history:** Wise tried to learn something about his European roots from his grandfather, who emigrated to the United States as a teenager. He found that the experience of becoming a white American – the pressure to adapt and conform – had totally erased the experience of the early years from his grandfather's mind.
- **Being unconsciously dominated at the base of your being by racism:** Wise's grandmother was a progressive person throughout her adult life and actively opposed racism in her interactions with people. But in her last years she lost many of her mental faculties and required skilled nursing home care. What remained, however, was enough to be able to call the nursing home staff all kinds of racist names – despite her inability to even recognize the people in her own family. She was betrayed in old age by social experiences that had shaped her earliest identity as a white person.
- **Being scorned and reprimanded for identifying with people of color:** When in the sixth grade, Wise began expressing himself with the mannerisms and language of the black youths he hung out with in school and in the neighborhood. His white teacher immediately started treating him with hostility – not calling on him in class, putting him down both verbally and with her attitude. Fortunately Wise's mother intervened when his tuning out of school in response to this treatment became evident after a couple weeks. Other young people are not so lucky. Children of color can remain disconnected out of self-defense; while white youths learn a hard lesson – and end up putting distance between themselves and kids of color they normally would be friendly with.

Here are a few other personal experiences that white folks often have to deal with as a result of living in this society:

- **Discovering racist language coming out of your mouth:** People who normally consider themselves decent, friendly, and open to everyone can suddenly find themselves in situations where they participate in offensive behavior: when they are drunk or in a party atmosphere – where men can also unleash unexpected violence against women; or during incidents of white bonding, when people exchange looks and comments that knowingly put down people of color. While these experiences can be repressed, they also linger as a guilty reminder of who a person really is.
- **Disruption of family life:** Antagonism can develop among loved ones when a family member breaks with the family culture and consciously struggles to cross the color line.

- **Shock when racial divisions become clear:** Sometimes the reality of racial divisions breaks through into consciousness in a disturbing way – the rebellions in 1992 in response to the freeing of police attackers videotaped while beating motorist Rodney King; the sharply opposing reactions to the exoneration of O.J. Simpson in his double-murder trial; or the reality of black poverty – and official neglect – laid bare when the levees broke in New Orleans after Hurricane Katrina.

The increasing segregation of community life also comes with a price. Many white people in the United States live in white cocoons, having only the most incidental, or highly structured contact with people of color. The consequences for white people are:

- **No close personal relations with people of color:** Everything related to race and color remains abstract – filtered through the media and the buzz of daily conversation.
- **Fear:** People resist traveling to a nearby city, riding public transportation, or stopping or visiting in communities of color. The media feed an image of color-coded crime, and all youths of color arouse suspicion. Antennas go up at the sight of a person of color in the neighborhood, and security companies thrive off people's unease.
- **Inability to handle situations that involve people of color:** Contradictions can become nasty in a minute – as the Academy Award winning movie *Crash* demonstrates. Unfortunately, like most mainstream treatments of racial contradictions, *Crash* contains nothing to suggest what to do about this edgy, antagonistic society.
- **Feeling like you are walking on eggshells:** Lack of experience results in a person not knowing what to say or how to say it when around people of color. This situation has its positive side in that white folks might listen and learn something, but mostly it just reinforces a desire to live separately.
- **Feeling suspicious with strangers:** The author had an experience when studying Spanish in Cuba in 1999. While sitting at an ice cream shop, three dark skinned young men came up and sat down at a nearby table. They asked how the ice cream was and how much it cost – and immediately I began wondering how these guys were trying to get over on me. As it turned out, they simply didn't know what was up with this shop, and we ended up having a relaxed and friendly conversation.

- **Having distorted personal relationships across the color line:** The lack of comfort in relationships can set white people up to 1) bend over backwards in a way that runs counter to their true feelings, 2) be attracted by what is "exotic" in another person and not by who they really are, and 3) act in awkward and even semi-weird ways around people of color. Sometimes the experiences work themselves through to real intimacy or friendship. Other times it just leaves a bad taste and confirms folks' desire to live in their separate worlds.

These tensions are the price white folks pay for being channeled into segregated lives. The resolution of this situation requires the empowerment of people of color – either 1) through a merged struggle that includes white people, or 2) through a consolidation of oppressed nationality strength in areas of concentration. Regardless of how the struggle unfolds, however, white people who cannot find it in themselves to cross the color line will continue to suffer the fears that come with self-imposed isolation.

Ultimately two main costs of privilege stand out as central to white working class people in the United States today – one material, the other spiritual:

- **White people's lack of understanding prevents united action to correct shared grievances:** Antagonism in the workplace or across neighborhood boundaries often centers on favoritism of some kind that is accepted as normal by white workers. There is the extra bit in the paycheck as a reward for "keeping an eye on things," or for being a "good example." There are the personal ties with the boss's family – perhaps when they attend the same church – or the connections with this person or that in the city or county government. While feeling normal in many cases, and not a conscious act of class treachery, this acceptance of favoritism acts as a knife in the heart of united action across race lines. As mentioned in Chapter 10, the lowest regional pay scales for white workers have occurred where the greatest differentials existed between the pay of white workers and workers of color. In other words, the greater the companies' apparent generosity in the way of white privileges, the lower the average rate of pay that white workers actually received – compared to other regions of the country where worker solidarity was greater. Post-Reconstruction governments in the South and big city political machines have both worked with this same logic – the more divided people are at the grassroots, the lower the overall level of services and the more favoritism runs rampant.

- **White people's inability to identify with the suffering and struggles of people of color, both historically and today, leaves people rootless and spiritually stunted:** Because of distorted racial thinking reinforced by material privileges, white working people often feel a chasm between themselves and their darker skinned brothers and sisters. The torment of slavery, genocide, expropriation, and exclusion all happened to "other" people. The truth, however, is that this vast toll taken by white supremacy from peoples of color at home and abroad ought to be felt – by any measure of human decency – as white folks' own loss as well. By not incorporating into themselves this sense of sacrifice, white people lose their share in the redemptive history of struggle against white supremacy that underlies any reasoned hope for the future. The pale, Eurocentric version of U.S. history fed schoolchildren – and recounted as justification for today's expansion of empire – is no replacement for this spirit-nurturing heritage of struggle.

White working people end up floating along, manipulated into fighting their brothers and sisters of color, and subject to the whims of the ruling class capital accumulation process. They are employed one day and tossed on the scrap heap the next. They are called on to police the empire and face the rage of oppressed people at home and abroad. In this sense the slave patrols of the past take a modern form, but now in uniform.

Yet everything just seems normal to most white people. Not recognizing the terrible cost paid over the centuries and up to the moment by their class brothers and sisters of color dulls the moral sense. And it keeps many white workers from realizing that they too are being sacrificed, as generations have been before them. Three hundred years of white privilege and counting...how does it feel to stand by and let a brother or sister be tortured, raped, beaten, murdered, and worked to the bone?

Back from the future

The last way to get a handle on the cost of white privilege is to look back from the conditions in the future that people today are struggling to bring into existence. The time machine we can use to get a glimpse from this perspective is to place ourselves within the culture emerging out of today's social justice movement.

The movement's ability to prefigure the future gives a hint of what a society committed to overcoming racial privileges might be like. By contrasting this future reality with the present, we have a third perspective on the cost to white people of passively going along with their advantaged position in society.

At its best today's movement foreshadows a future society where:

- The conscious attention to race, class, and gender help people be aware of the social forces that shape who they are.
- Relations among people are direct and open. People's common commitment to ending oppression allows them to work through contradictions around race, class, and gender.
- People work together so that privileges that carry into the movement from outside or from the past can be turned to society's advantage and to advancing the struggle. Affirmative steps to rectify social inequalities help build a sense of mutual trust.
- People discover that addressing issues forthrightly enables them to see and interrelate with each other as they really are. The veil of social distance that now separates people disappears.
- Mutual acceptance and respect make possible an all around struggle for mass, democratic empowerment in all aspects of society – for national liberation, working class power, and an end to patriarchal oppression.
- Social isolation declines. Mutual support and solidarity replace fragmentation. Popular culture encourages social engagement, enriches people's lives, and contributes to society addressing issues in constructive ways. Personal salvation comes through the uplift and deliverance of the whole community. Charity is the giving of oneself and one's resources to the struggle.
- Because everyone's contribution is valued, people become active and help shape the conditions of their own lives. People learn how to organize and effect change, how to reflect on experience together and correct mistakes, and how to carry out and defend their newly won social power.
- Since people are highly valued and the struggle to shape society to meet people's needs is a work in progress, the attitude toward crime becomes one of prevention and restorative justice. People's transgressions against the community are understood to be failings of the community, as well as of the person. Taking responsibility for this situation means 1) getting to the source of people's criminal actions, and 2) working to bring folks back into the community as contributing members. There is no social scrap heap or execution ground.
- Personal relationships are deep and varied. There is time to reflect and time to be friendly with each other – in two's and three's, as well as in larger gatherings. The moral outlook consistent with a life of struggle and solidarity – as outlined in Chapter 26 – holds

sway throughout society. And new, higher forms of moral practice develop, emerging out of the new conditions of life that people find themselves in.

- The obscene economic inequality of today fades to a bad memory from the past. People on the bottom are empowered to shape their lives and their community. Those with resources – who still benefit from economic, racial or gender privilege – contribute as they can to the struggle. In doing so, the relatively privileged do only what is in keeping with being an equal member of the community. Their actions are not considered particularly exceptional or worthy of praise.
- Public life makes a big comeback. People do things together – rather than just watching or paying for their entertainment prepackaged. Sports, plays, musical performances, and poetry slams receive generous public support. Schools become community centers. Educational resources come to the people and are accessible to everyone.
- People in the United States see themselves as world citizens and act in a way that advances social welfare around the world. The lessons learned in dealing with privilege internally are applied as part of the world community. Just as reparative acts are required to heal historic injustices around race, class and gender inside the United States, so too do centuries of colonialism and imperialism require a sharing of the country's privileged bounty with the oppressed around the world. In time the United States becomes a respected and valued member of the community of nations.

All these elements of a future transformed society can be seen to varying degrees in today's social justice movement. It is the projection forward of these qualities that makes possible a look back from the future to assess the present cost of privilege for white working class people. Every bulleted point above identifies something that is missing from most folks' lives today. And while the future is a long way off, the social justice movement is alive and advancing the struggle in the here and now. The motivation for folks to take the step and become part of the struggle comes from recognizing the cost that privilege extracts today by holding back a united movement for social transformation. Alcohol and drugs provide short-term relief from pain, but at a huge personal and long-term cost. The drug of white privilege – to paraphrase Lillian Smith – works the same way.

Perspectives from the past, present, and future, help bring the costly weight of white privilege into focus in an all-sided way. Once this burden is clear, it then becomes a question of what to do about it – how to transform one's privilege into an asset for the popular struggle. In following through on this question, white people can help lift society's foot off the necks of oppressed peoples of color at home and abroad – and, at the same time, they can save their own souls. History, strategy, a sense of where the movement is headed and why folks should care – these ideas can help people of all races become true and effective freedom fighters. The struggle needs and has a place for everyone.

Notes

(See bibliography for complete information on cited works.)

I. The White Race
[1] Main sources for the discussion of slavery in Europe and the slave trade throughout Section I are *The Slave Trade*, by Hugh Thomas, and *The African Slave Trade*, by Basil Davidson.

Chapter 1: Origin of the White Race
[1] Chapter 1 follows the argument of Theodore W. Allen in *The Invention of the White Race*, Vols. I and II, and Lerone Bennett, Jr. in *The Shaping of Black America*
[2] Bennett, Jr., op. cit., pp. 40-41
[3] Quoted by Allen, Vol. II, op. cit.
[4] Howard Zinn, *Peoples' History of the United States*, p. 40
[5] Ibid., p. 42
[6] Allen, Vol. II, op. cit., p. 250
[7] Ibid.
[8] Ibid., pp. 250-251
[9] Bennett, Jr., op. cit., p. 68
[10] Allen, Vol. II, op. cit., p. 248

Chapter 2: Shades of Whiteness
[1] Material on the enslavement of Indians is drawn from *The Indian Slave Trade*, by Alan Gallay.
[2] Main sources throughout Section I on indigenous peoples and their struggles are *The Earth Shall Weep*, by James Wilson, *Facing East from Indian Country*, by Daniel K. Richter, and *Atlas of the North American Indian*, by Carl Waldman.
[3] The discussion of Indians and whiteness is based on "How Indians Got to Be Red," by Nancy Shoemaker, and "From White Man to Redskin," by Alden Vaughn
[4] Main sources for the discussion of Mexicans in the Southwest include *Occupied America*, by Rodolfo Acuña, *Racial Fault Lines*, by Tomás Almaguer, and *Anglos and Mexicans in the Making of Texas, 1836-1986*, by David Montejano
[5] Bill Uzgalis, "Bartolomé De Las Casas"
[6] The discussion of the California mission system follows *Junípero Serra, the Vatican, and Enslavement Theology*, by Daniel Fogel
[7] Robert G. Lee, *Orientals*
[8] Ruth Frankenberg, *White Women, Race Matters*, p. 75

Chapter 3: Images of Whiteness
[1] Alexander Saxton, *The Rise and Fall of the White Republic*; David Roediger, *The Wages of Whiteness;* Michael Omi and Howard Winant, *Racial Formation in the United States*, and Ruth Frankenberg, *White Women, Race Matters.*
[2] Bennett, Jr., op. cit., p. 71
[3] Ibid, p. 73
[4] Zinn, op. cit., p. 110

[5] Benjamin Banneker, "Letter to Jefferson"
[6] Peter Kolchin, *American Slavery*, p. 78
[7] The discussion of the pre-Civil War period follows Saxton, op. cit.
[8] W.E.B. DuBois, *Black Reconstruction*, p. 727
[9] Karl Marx and Fredrick Engels, *Manifesto of the Communist Party*
[10] The discussion of the 1960s changes in ideology is based on Omi and Winant, op. cit.

Chapter 4: Beyond the White Race
[1] The anthropological discussion draws primarily on *Biological Anthropology*, by Barbara King, and *What It Means to Be 98% Chimpanzee*, by Jonathan Marks.
[2] National Institutes of Health, "Understanding Human Genetic Variation"
[3] Jonathan Marks, op. cit., pp. 81-82

II. Race, Nations, and Empire
[1] W.E.B. DuBois, *The Souls of Black Folk*

Chapter 5: Reconstruction
[1] The main sources for the discussion of Reconstruction are Eric Foner's *Reconstruction* and Lerone Bennett, Jr.'s *Before the Mayflower*.
[2] Foner, op. cit., p. 364-365
[3] Bennett, Jr., op. cit,, p. 236
[4] Foner, op. cit., p. 367
[5] Ibid., p. 95
[6] Ibid., p. 95
[7] Ibid., p. 586
[8] The discussion of the post-Reconstruction period mainly draws on Steven Hahn's *A Nation at Our Feet*.
[9] Hahn, op. cit., p. 333
[10] Ibid., p. 382
[11] Ibid., p. 437
[12] Robert Allen, "Self-Interest and Southern Populism," in *Reluctant Reformers*
[13] Hahn, op. cit., p. 440
[14] W.E.B. DuBois in *Souls of Black Folk*, quoting a freedman's comment to his former owner
[15] Bennett, Jr., *Before the Mayflower*, p. 252

Chapter 6: Imperialism and National Oppression
[1] V.I. Lenin, *Imperialism*
[2] Howard Zinn, *People's History of the United States*, p. 408
[3] Lerone Bennett, Jr., *Shaping of Black* America, pp. 115-116
[4] Ibid., pp. 126, 128
[5] David Walker, *Appeal*
[6] 1928 Comintern Resolution, "Resolution on the Negro Question in the United States"
[7] Ibid.
[8] W.E.B. DuBois, "A Negro Nation within the Nation"
[9] Gilberto López y Rivas, *The Chicanos*, p. 24
[10] Clark S. Knowlton, "Causes of Land Loss Among the Spanish-Americans in Northern New Mexico"
[11] Juan Gonzalez, *Harvest of Empire*, p. 101
[12] Knowlton, op. cit., p. 120
[13] Ibid., p. 121
[14] James Wilson, *The Earth Shall Weep*, p. 308
[15] Ibid., p. 303
[16] Quoted in Wilson, op. cit., p. 315
[17] Ibid., p. 316

[18] Vine Deloria, Jr., *Custer Died for Your Sins*, p. 172
[19] Zinn, op. cit., pp. 313-314
[20] UN Special Committee on Decolonialization, Press Release GA/COL/3102
[21] Gonzalez, op. cit., p. 249
[22] Don Young, "Report on H.R. 856: United States-Puerto Rico Political Status Act"
[23] Juan Gonzalez, "Another battle over Puerto Rico"
[24] United States of America, "The Insular Areas"

Chapter 7: The Right of Self-Determination
[1] Josef Stalin, *Marxism and the National Question*. It is worth noting that this definition was so widely accepted that even a bitter opponent of Stalin in the United States, Max Shachtman, a Trotskyist, offered an almost identical definition for a nation in 1933. *(Shachtman,* Race and Revolution, *p. 71)*
[2] Komozi Woodard, *A Nation within a Nation*, pp. 5-6
[3] George Breitman, ed., "Message to the Grassroots," in *Malcolm X Speaks*, p. 9
[4] Bob Wing, "*Indio Claro o Oscuro*?"; and Calpotura, Francis, "A Journey Home"
[5] Barbara Ceptus, "Growing Up Haitian, Growing Up Black"
[6] Carl Waldman, *Atlas of the American* Indian, p. 234; Paul Wong, "Introduction" in *Race, Ethnicity, and Nationality in the United States*; and Milan Pham, "Beyond the Model Minority"
[7] Russell Means, quoted in James Wilson, op. cit., p. 408
[8] James Wilson, op. cit., p. 422
[9] Ward Churchill, "The Crucible of American Indian Identity," in *Perversions of Justice*, *p.*221
[10] Ibid., p. 223
[11] Ibid, p. 224
[12] Ward Churchill, "Stolen Kingdom: The Right of Hawai'i to Decolonialization," in *Perversions of Justice*, p. 99
[13] Ibid., p. 105
[14] Carl H. Marrs, "ANCSA: An Act of Self-Determination"
[15] Willie Hensley, "The Land is the Spirit of the People"
[16] Mike Wicks, "Short History of Big Mountain – Black Mesa"; Waldman, op. cit., p. 237
[17] Inbal Sansani, "American Indian Land Rights in the Inter-American System"
[18] Western Shoshone Defense Project, "Western Shoshone Victorious at United Nations"
[19] Indianz.com, "Cobell legal team awarded fees for trust fund fight"; Gray, Louis, "No one should prejudge trust fund settlement figures"

Chapter 8: National Struggles and the Fight for Global Justice
[1] Robert Frank, "US Led a Resurgence Last Year Among Millionaires World-Wide
[2] Steven Rattner, "Inured to Inequality"
[3] Robert Hunter Wade, "Does Inequality Matter?"; and Martin Hart-Landsberg, "Neoliberalism: Myths and Reality"
[4] Hart-Landsberg, op. cit., p. 10
[5] Russell Mokhiber, and Robert Weissman, "The Age of Inequality"
[6] Analia Penchaszadeh, "World Social Forum 2003: U.S. Activists in Porto Alegre"
[7] Peter Graves-Goodman, "Another World is Possible (World Social Forum) Discussion at Miami Workers Center"
[8] Bill Gallegos, "Immigrants fight for freedom"; and Joaquín Bustelo, "Making Sense of the Latino Uprising"
[9] Malcolm Suber, keynote speaker at the Black Workers For Justice 25th Annual Martin Luther King Support for Labor Banquet on April 1, 2006
[10] Saladin Muhammad, "African Americans and Latinos Unite"
[11] Stu Schneider, "Victories for Home Health Care Workers"
[12] Million Worker March, http://www.millionworkermarch.org
[13] David Solnit, "The New Face of the Global Justice Movement"

[14] Bryan Proffitt, "Breaking the Silence: Katrina and Sexual Assault"
[15] Chris Nisan, "Black farms continue struggle for land, justice, rights"
[16] Glen Ford and Peter Gamble, "Unions Seek Path to Economic Development"
[17] Pakou Hang, "Hmong-town, USA"; and Vijay Prashad, "An Indian American Election"
[18] Jill Johnston, "Project Regeneration Update"
[19] Susan Gooding, "Recognizing Indigenous America in Times of War"

III. Race and Class
Chapter 9: Missed Opportunities
[1] W.E.B. DuBois, *Black Reconstruction*, p. 353, quoted in Michael Goldfield's *The Color of Politics*, p. 113
[2] Charlie Orrock provided an early draft of parts of this chapter.
[3] Much of the first half of this chapter is based on Michael Goldfield's *The Color of Politics* and Philip Foner's *Organized Labor and the Black Worker*. Additional material on the National Labor Union, National Colored Labor Union, and the Liberal Republicans comes from Eric Foner's *Reconstruction* and David Montgomery's *Beyond Equality*. Throughout this chapter, discussions of the Southwest draw on Rodolfo Acuña's *Occupied America*.
[4] Philip Foner, op. cit., p.21
[5] Ibid., p. 20
[6] *Boston Daily Evening Voice*, January 13, 1866
[7] Philip Foner, op. cit., p. 23
[8] Philip Foner, op. cit., p. 34
[9] Quoted in David Montgomery, *Beyond Equality*, p. 409
[10] DuBois, op. cit., p. 353, 367 and quoted in Goldfield, op. cit., p. 133
[11] Goldfield, op. cit., p. 148, citing Herbert Hill, "Anti-Oriental Agitation and the Rise of Working-Class Racism"
[12] John R. Commons, *History of Labor in the United States*, quoted in Goldfield, op. cit. p. 149
[13] Acuña, op. cit., p. 78
[14] Quoted from the Memphis *Watchman* in Philip Foner, op. cit., p. 57
[15] Ibid., p. 61
[16] Acuña, op. cit., p. 101
[17] Ibid., p. 234
[18] Diane McWhorter, "Carry Me Home"
[19] Interview with Ray Henderson, *Birmingham-Pittsburgh Traveler*
[20] Quoted in George Stoney, Judith Helfand, and Susanne Rostock, *Uprising of '34*
[21] Michelle Brattain, *The Politics of Whiteness*, p. 78
[22] Ibid., p. 144
[23] Ibid., p. 145
[24] Ibid.
[25] Bill Fletcher and Fernando Gapasin, "The Politics of Labour and Race in the USA"

Chapter 10: Race, Class, and Privilege
[1] Karl Marx, *Capital*, p. 715
[2] Ibid., pp. 714, 751
[3] The discussion in the remainder of Chapter 10 follows the argument of *A House Divided: Labor and White Supremacy* (*AHD*), by Roxanne Mitchell and Frank Weiss.
[4] Quoted in Robert L. Allen, *Reluctant Reformers*, p. 213
[5] Quoted in Earl Ofari, "Black Activists and 19th Century Radicalism," cited by Mitchell and Weiss, op. cit., p. 4
[6] Marx, op. cit., p. 301
[7] W.E.B. DuBois, "Socialism and the Negro Problem," quoted in Mitchell and Weiss, op. cit., p. 3
[8] Jeffrey B. Perry, ed., *A Hubert Harrison Reader*, pp. 59, 71, and quoted in John Alan, "The Socialism of Hubert Harrison"

[9] Quoted in Fletcher and Gapasin, op. cit.
[10] V. I. Lenin, "Socialist Revolution and the Right of Nations to Self-Determination", p. 2, and quoted in Mitchell and Weiss, op. cit., p. 13
[11] The list (originally appearing in Ted Allen's *Can White Radicals be Radicalized*) and the additional quotes are taken from the following works of William Z. Foster, as listed by Mitchell and Weiss: *From Bryan to Stalin,* pp. 44-45, 337-338; *American Trade Unionism,* pp. 62-74; *Twilight of World Capitalism,* p. 62; *The History of the CPUSA,* pp 542-549, as noted in Mitchell and Weiss, pp. 8-9
[12] Mitchell and Weiss, op. cit., p. 9
[13] Ibid., p. 10
[14] CPUSA, "Introduction" to *The Communist Position on the Negro Question,* quoted in Mitchell and Weiss, p. 4
[15] Mitchell and Weiss, op. cit., p. 9-10
[16] V.I. Lenin, *Left-Wing Communism,* Collected Works, p. 90, quoted in Mitchell and Weiss, op. cit., p. 27
[17] See the analysis in Michael Reich, *Racial Inequality*
[18] Mitchell and Weiss, op. cit., p. 61
[19] Ted Allen or Noel Ignatiev, exact source unknown
[20] The references listed for Ted Allen and Noel Ignatin in the 1960s and early 1970s are *The White Blindspot* (A&I, 1967), *Can White [Radicals] be Radicalized?* (Allen, 1969), *Without a Science of Navigation We Cannot Sail in Stormy Seas* (Ignatin, 1969), *The Most Vulnerable Point* (Allen, 1972), "Preface" to the republication of *The White Blindspot* (A&I, 1972), *White Supremacy in U.S. History* (Allen, 1973): Mitchell and Weiss, op. cit., ft, p. 105
[21] Mitchell and Weiss, op. cit., pp. 110-111
[22] Quoted in ibid., p. 108
[23] Ibid., p. 109
[24] Ibid.
[25] Quoted in ibid., p. 113

Chapter 11: The Sunbelt Strategy
[1] The analysis developed in the 1980s is drawn from "A Southern Strategy," by Gordon Dillahunt (January–February 1988 issue of *Forward Motion*) and "The 'Sunbelt Strategy' and Chicano Liberation," by William Gallegos.
[2] Material on the economic importance of the South, not cited elsewhere, comes from Saladin Muhammad's "Organize the South in the Context of Globalization"
[3] U.S. Census Bureau, "Population Estimates for the Fastest Growing Cities with Populations over 100,000"
[4] Dart, Bob, 2005. "Heading South: Population boom shows region's clout"
[5] *Occupational Outlook Quarterly,* "Large metropolitan areas that had the fastest employment growth, 1998-2003"
[6] Joel Kotkin, "Top 25 Cities for Doing Business in America"
[7] Quoted in Liz Sidoti, "Base Plan Would Alter Military Landscape"
[8] Source for the two maps comparing 1983 and 1999 union density: *Common Sense Economics,* AFL-CIO
[9] Barry T. Hirsch and David A. Macpherson, "Union Membership, Coverage, Density and Employment" by state and nationally for 1983, 2005
[10] First Union Bank, *Regional Economic Review*
[11] Saladin Muhammad, "Organize the South in the Context of Globalization," p. 7
[12] Fernando Gapasin, unpublished discussion paper
[13] *BusinessWeek,* "Jobs: The Lull Will Linger"
[14] Betsey Leondar-Wright, "Black Job Loss, Déjà Vu"
[15] James Petras and Henry Veltmeyer, "Argentina: Between disintegration & revolution"
[16] UE-150 Public Workers Union, "Proposed Resolution for BRC Support for the International Worker Justice Campaign"

[17] Speech at 2000 BWFJ Martin Luther King Support for Labor Banquet
[18] The approach taken in this section is based on Fernando Gapasin, op. cit., together with additional suggestions by Bill Gallegos
[19] DuBois, *Black Reconstruction*, p. 700

IV. Patriarchy and Privilege
Chapter 12: Roots of Patriarchy
[1] Zuñi and Plains Indians examples from Howard Zinn, *People's History of the United States*
[2] Lauren Wells Hasten, "In Search of the 'Berdache'"
[3] Carol Devens, "Countering Colonization"
[4] Cheryl I. Harris, "Whiteness as Property"
[5] Zinn, op. cit., p. 108
[6] Angela Davis, "Reflections on te Black Woman's Role in the Community of Slaves"
[7] Angela Davis, "Public Imprisonment and Private Violence"
[8] This discussion draws on Robert G. Lee, "Orientals"
[9] Ibid., p. 89
[10] Ibid., p. 91
[11] Bárbara C. Cruz and Michael J. Berson, "The American Melting Pot?"
[12] Ruth Frankenberg, *White Women, Race Matters*
[13] Both Plecker and Stoddard quoted in "Eugenics in America," *Facing History and Ourselves*
[14] Cruz and Berson, op. cit.
[15] Philip Dray, *At the Hands of Persons Unknown*, p. x-xi
[16] Ibid., p. 57
[17] Quoted in Dray, op. cit., p. 59-60
[18] Ibid., p. 63
[19] Ibid., p. 64
[20] Ibid., p. 67
[21] Ibid., pp. 74-79
[22] This discussion follows Siobhan B. Somerville, *Queering the Color Line*
[23] Quoted in ibid., p. 15, italics in original
[24] Micaela Di Leonardo and Roger Lancaster, "Gender, Sexuality, Political Economy"
[25] Alexander Saxton, *The Rise and Fall of the White Republic*
[26] Lerone Bennett, Jr., 1993. *Before the Mayflower*
[27] Zinn, op. cit.
[28] Patriarchy in the Wilmington riot draws on Glenda Elizabeth Gilmore, *Gender and Jim Crow*
[29] Gilmore, op. cit., p. 110
[30] Wini Breines, *Young, White, and Miserable*
[31] List of topics and quote drawn from Di Leonardo and Lancaster, op. cit., pp. 47-48
[32] Sheila Collins, *The Jackson Campaign and the Future of U.S. Politics*, p. 54
[33] Ibid., p. 55
[34] Ibid., p. 63
[35] Pam Chamberlain and Jean Hardisty, "Reproducing Patriarchy"

Chapter 13: Three Faces of Male Supremacy
[1] NCADV, "Domestic Violence Facts"
[2] Mimi Abramovitz, "Still under Attack"
[3] NCADV, op. cit.
[4] RAINN, "Every Two and a Half Minutes"
[5] RAINN, "Statistics"
[6] Ibid.
[7] List and quote in Robin Warshaw, *I Never Called It Rape*, p. 84
[8] Linda Bird Francke, "Women in the Military"
[9] Eduardo Duran and Bonnie Duran, *Native American Postcolonial Psychology*

[10] Marjory D. Fields, "Combating Domestic Violence"
[11] Clancy Worthington, "Stopping Battering in Our Own Ranks"
[12] Ramon Johnson, "Gay Abuse"
[13] Jael Silliman, et. al., "Women of Color and their Struggle for Reproductive Justice"; Duran and Duran, op. cit.
[14] Ziba Kahef, "Toward Reproductive Freedom"
[15] Patrisia Macias Rojas, "Rebuilding the Anti-Violence Movement"
[16] Quoted in Bernice Yeung, "Fighting the Many Faces of Violence"
[17] Ibid., p. 29
[18] Shivali Shah, "South Asian Americans in the American South"
[19] Yeung, op. cit., p. 28
[20] Luana Ross, "Our Lands, Our Bodies: Native Justice"; Janice Haaken, "Stories of Survival"
[21] Haaken, op. cit., p. 110
[22] Francke, op. cit.
[23] Adam Wilkenfeld, "Gay Bashing"
[24] Juba Kalamka, "How Can I Be Down?"
[25] bell hooks, *Feminism is for Everybody*
[26] Daniel Fogel, *Junípero Serra, the Vatican, and Enslavement Theology*
[27] Stephanie Luce and Mark Brenner, "Women and Class," p. 83. The data and discussion of differing class impacts of Second Wave feminism are based primarily on this article and Hester Eisenstein, "A Dangerous Liaison?"
[28] Luce and Brenner, op. cit., p. 85
[29] Ibid., p. 84
[30] Abramovitz, op. cit., p. 224
[31] Ibid.
[32] Luce and Brenner, op. cit., p. 86
[33] Ibid.
[34] This bullet point drawn from Abramovitz, op. cit.
[35] Luce and Brenner, op. cit., p. 91
[36] This discussion follows Eisenstein, op. cit.

Chapter 14: Intersectionality
[1] Becky Thompson, *A Promise and a Way of Life*
[2] Jael Silliman, et. al., op. cit.
[3] Barry D. Adam, *The Rise of a Gay and Lesbian Movement*
[4] Komozi Woodard, *Nation within a Nation*
[5] Ibid., p. 197
[6] Ibid., p. 183
[7] bell hooks, *Killing Rage*, pp. 64-65
[8] Mark Anthony Neal, *New Black Man*, p. 24
[9] Betita Martínez, *De Colores Means All of Us*, pp. 163-164
[10] Laura Pulido, *Black, Brown, Yellow, and Left*, pp. 213-14
[11] Ibid., p. 214
[12] Thompson, op. cit.
[13] Ibid., p. 146
[14] Combahee River Collective, "A Black Feminist Statement," p. 212
[15] Ibid., p. 213
[16] Ibid.
[17] Quoted in Thompson, op. cit., p. 151
[18] Cherríe Moraga, "Introducción," p. 1, author's translation
[19] Ibid.
[20] Temma Kaplan, "Disappearing Fathers," p. 156
[21] Rosalind P. Petchesky, "Human Rights, Reproductive Health, and Economic Justice"

[22] Martha Nussbaum, "Legal Weapon"
[23] Chandra Talpade Mohanty, "Women Workers and Capitalist Scripts"
[24] Kamala Kempadoo, "Globalizing Sex Workers' Rights"
[25] Tram Nguyen, "North-South Differences Challenge Women at UN," Kempadoo, op. cit.
[26] Quoted in Chela Sandoval, *Methodology of the Oppressed*, p. 59
[27] Quoted in ibid., p. 60
[28] Quoted in ibid.
[29] Patricia Hill Collins, *Black Feminist Thought*, pp. 289-290

Chapter 15: Toward a Third Wave Women's Movement
[1] Susan Archer Mann and Douglas J. Huffman, "The Decentering of Second Wave Feminism and the Rise of the Third Wave," p. 57
[2] Ibid., p. 69, discussing Dent, "Missionary Position"
[3] Ibid., p. 74
[4] Pythia Peay, "Feminism's Fourth Wave," p. 59
[5] Ibid.
[6] Ibid., p. 60
[7] Ibid., p.25
[8] Lise Vogel, ed., "Symposium on Red Feminism"
[9] Nancy Holmstrom, "Introduction," p. 7
[10] Ibid.
[11] Kjersti Ericsson, *Sisters, Comrades!*, pp. 77, 81, 107
[12] Quotes in this paragraph, ibid., p. 77
[13] Quotes and five points, ibid., pp. 81-83
[14] Quotes and five points, ibid., pp. 84-88
[15] Joy Mutanu Zarembka, "Maid to Order"
[16] Ann Ferguson, "On Conceiving Motherhood and Sexuality"
[17] Ericsson, op. cit.
[18] Jamie Peck, *Workplace*
[19] Margaret Randall, *Gathering Rage*
[20] Maxine Molyneux, "Conceptualizing Women's Interests"
[20] David Oshinsky, "Only the Accused Were Innocent"

V. White Privilege, White Consciousness
Chapter 16: The Reality of White Privilege
[1] Maria Krysan and Amanda Lewis, "Racial Discrimination is Alive and Well"
[2] Dwight Kirk, "Can Labor Go Beyond Diversity Lite?"
[3] Leonard Steinhorn and Barbara Diggs-Brown, *By the Color of Our Skin*
[4] Manning Marable "Abolishing American Apartheid, Root and Branch"
[5] California Newsreel, *Race – The Power of an Illusion*

Chapter 17: White Consciousness
[1] Melanie Bush, *Breaking the Code of Good Intentions*, p.5
[2] Ibid, p. 176
[3] Andrew Bryant, Jr., personal comment to author.
[4] Howard Winant, "Racial Dualism at Century's End"
[5] Amadee Braxton, personal communication
[6] Steinhorn and Diggs-Brown, op. cit, , p. 87
[7] Lillian Smith, *Killers of the Dream*, p. 214
[8] Bush, op. cit., p. 109
[9] Ibid, p. 107
[10] *Black Commentator*, 10/21/04
[11] Smith, op. cit., p. 164-165

Chapter 18: Holding On, Breaking Free
[1] Barbara Gould, "Five Stages of Dying"
[2] Wise, op. cit.

VI. White Allies – Solidarity and Betrayal
Chapter 19: The Historical Record
[1] Herbert Aptheker, *Abolitionism*, p. 95
[2] R. Brian Ferguson, "The Witch Hunt You Never Heard Of"
[3] Aptheker, op. cit. pp. 95-96
[4] Vivasancarlos.com, "San Patricios – The Irishmen who Died for Mexico"
[5] Aptheker, op. cit., p. 66
[6] Ibid., p. 103
[7] Quoted in ibid., p. 123
[8] Quoted in ibid., p. 140
[9] Timothy B. Tyson, *Blood Done Sign My Name*, p. 171
[10] Ibid., p. 172
[11] James W. Loewen, "Forward," p. xxi
[12] Eric Foner, *Reconstruction*, p. 297
[13] Ibid., p. 298
[14] Ibid., p. 347
[15] Aptheker, op. cit., p.87
[16] Foner, op. cit., p. 256
[17] Ibid., p. 255
[18] Ibid., p. 446
[19] Robert L. Allen, with Pamela P. Allen, *Reluctant Reformers*
[20] Ibid., p. 226
[21] J. Sakai, *The Myth of the White Proletariat*
[22] Loewen, op. cit., p. xxvii
[23] Rodolfo Acuña, *Occupied America*, p. 335

Chapter 20: Personal Transformation
[1] *A Promise and a Way of Life*, by Becky Thompson; *White Men Challenging Racism*, by Cooper Thompson, Emmett Schaefer, and Harry Brod; *Refusing Racism: White Allies and the Struggle for Civil Rights*, by Cynthia Stokes Brown; and *Through Survivors' Eyes*, by Sally Avery Bermanzohn
[2] *The Wall Between*, by Anne Braden; *Red Dirt* and *Outlaw Woman*, by Roxanne Dunbar-Ortiz; *The Long Haul*, by Myles Horton; *White Boy*, by Mark Naison; *Memoir of a Race Traitor*, by Mab Segrest; *Blood Done Sign My Name*, by Tim Tyson, and *White Like Me*, by Tim Wise.

VII. Social Forces and Leadership
Chapter 21: Redrawing the Color Line?
[1] Noel Ignatiev, *How the Irish Became White*, p. 9
[2] Ignatiev, ibid., p.23
[3] Theodore W. Allen, *The Invention of the White Race*, Vol. 1, p. 181
[4] Phil Rubio, "Crossover Dreams"
[5] Bakari Kitwana, *Why White Kids Love Hip Hop*
[6] William Upski Wimsatt, *Bomb the Suburbs*
[7] Nicole Davis, "Motion to Repeal"
[8] Glen Ford, "Powerful Illusions,"
[9] Sharon M. Lee and Barry Edmonston, "New Marriages, New Families"
[10] Frank H. Wu, *Yellow*
[11] Sasha Welland, "Being Between"
[12] Daniel HoSang, "Hiding Race"
[13] Welland, op. cit.

[14] Boston.com, "Fox Raps U.S. on Plan for Fence"
[15] Theodore W. Allen, "'Race' and 'Ethnicity,'" pt. 55, quoting Lind
[16] Ed Morales, "Brown Like Me?"
[17] Marc Pizzaro, "Racial Formation and *Chicana/o* Identity," p. 191
[18] Ibid., p. 193
[19] Allen, "'Race' and 'Ethnicity,'"
[20] Betita Martínez, De Colores *Means All of Us*
[21] Cristina Verán, "Born Puerto Rican, Born (Again) Taíno?"
[22] Hong-An Truong and Christina Chia, "Beyond the Model Minority"
[23] Allen, "'Race' and 'Ethnicity,'" ft. 92
[24] Wu, op. cit., p. 107
[25] Wu., op. cit., p. 184
[26] Jeff Chang, "Where Do We Stand"
[27] W.E.B. DuBois, "The Souls of Black Folk"
[28] Mae M. Ngai, *Impossible Subjects*
[29] Signers of the "Open Letter to our African American Sisters and Brothers": *Dr. Rodolfo Acuña*, historian and author, California State University, Northridge, Calif.; *Gloria Anzaldúa*, writer, scholar, spiritual activist, Santa Cruz Calif.; *Ricardo Ariza*, director, Multicultural Affairs, Creighton University, Omaha, Neb.; *Frank Bonilla*, professor, University of California-Riverside, professor emeritus, Hunter College, NY; *Antonia Castaneda*, associate professor history, St. Mary's College, San Antonio; *Dr Raoul Contreras*, associate professor Latino Studies, Indiana University NW, Gary, Ind.; *Kaira Espinoza*, student, activist, San Francisco State University, San Francisco; *Cesar Garza*, graduate student, Loyola University, Chicago; *Dr. Yolanda Broyles-Gonzales*, professor, department of Chicano Studies, University of California-Santa Barbara; *Francisco Herrera*, community singer, activist San Francisco; *Aya de León*, writer, performer, activist Berkeley, Calif.; *Emma Lozana*, director, Centro Sin Fronteras Chicago; *Jennie Luna*, Ed.M., teacher, danzante, activist, New York; *Roberto Maestas*, executive director, co-founder, El Centro de La Raza, Seattle; *Frank Martín del Campo*, president, Labor Council for Latin American Advancement, San Francisco; *Elizabeth "Betita" Martínez*, author, activist, teacher, San Francisco; *Adelita Medina*, freelance journalist, New York; *Roberto Miranda*, editor in chief, Spanish Journal, Milwaukee; *Carlos Montes*, board president, Centro Community Service Center, Los Angeles; *Richard Moore*, executive director, Southwest Network for Environmental and Economic Justice, Albuquerque, N.M.; *Cherríe Moraga*, author and playwright, San Francisco; *Aurora Levins Morales*, writer, historian, educator, organizer, Berkeley, Calif.; *Ricardo Levins Morales*, artist, educator, organizer, Minneapolis; *Estela Ortega*, director of operations, co-founder, El Centro de la Raza, Seattle; *Joe Navarro*, schoolteacher, poet, activist, Hollister, Calif.; *Jose Palafox*, Ph.D. candidate, filmmaker, University of California-Berkeley; *Eric Quezada*, housing activist, San Francisco; *Marianna Rivera*, educator, Zapatista Solidarity Coalition, Sacramento, Calif.; *Dr. Julia E. Curry Rodríguez*, assistant professor, San Jose State University-San Jose, Calif.; *Graciela Sánchez*, executive director, Esperanza Peace & Justice Center, San Antonio; *John Santos*, musician, author, educator, founder of the Machete Ensemble, Oakland, Calif.; *Renee Saucedo*, activist-attorney, director Day Labor Program, San Francisco; *Olga Tallamante*, executive director, Chicana/ Latina Foundation, Pacifica, Calif.; *Luis "Bato" Talamantes*, human rights activist, former political prisoner, poet, San Francisco; *Piri Thomas*, author, poet, activist, Albany, Calif.; *Dr Mercedes Lynne de Uriarte*, professor of journalism, University of Texas, Austin; *Leonard Valdez*, director, Multicultural Center, California State University, Sacramento, Calif.

Chapter 22: Prospects for Unity
[1] Manuel Pastor and Tony LoPresti, "Bringing Globalization Home"
[2] John Sweeney, "Letter to Governor Jeb Bush"
[3] Jeff Chang and Lucia Hwang, "It's a Survival Issue"
[4] David Bacon, "Strike Force"

[5] Ibid.
[6] Fernando Gapasin, "Beyond the Wage Fight"
[7] Daniel HoSang, "All the Issues in Workers Lives"
[8] Janice Fine, "Building Community Unions"
[9] Francis Calpotura, "Riding with the Wind"
[10] Janice Fine and Jon Werberg, "Workers Centers"
[11] Patrisia Macias Rojas, "Rebuilding the Anti-Violence Movement"
[12] Women of Color Resource Center
[13] Community Youth Organizing Campaign, *Crossing Borders*
[14] David Bacon, "Uniting African-Americans and Immigrants"
[15] Terry Keleher, "ERASE – Towards a New Model of School Reform"; and Traxler, "ERASE Racism"
[16] Kim Diehl, "Here's the Movement, Let's Start Building"
[17] Michelle García, "A Bronx Tale"
[18] Rinku Sen, "Building Black-Brown Unity"
[19] Eunice Hyunhye Cho, "BRIDGE: Creating Tools for Education and Social Change Across Communities"
[20] Cornel West, "Forward," p. xi
[21] Bob Wing, "Educate to Liberate"
[22] Elizabeth Martínez and Max Elbaum, "Building Roads to Liberation"
[23] Davey D, "U.S. artists missing the boat as global movement coalesces"
[24] Paul Wong, "Introduction"
[25] Gary Phillips, "The Battle of Los Angeles"; and Morales, "Brown Like Me?"]
[26] Angela Davis, "Coalition Building Among People of Color"
[27] DuBois, op. cit.
[28] Quoted in Paul Harris, "The paradox that divides black America"
[29] Bob Wing, "The White Elephant in the Room"
[30] Shannah Kurland, "Brown Power vs. Black Power"
[31] Allen, *Invention of the White Race.*
[32] David Bacon, "Communities Without Borders"
[33] Black Radical Congress, "A Black Freedom Agenda for the 21st Century," Section XIV
[34] Truong and Chia, op. cit.
[35] Jeff Chang, "On the Wrong Side"
[36] Kurland, op. cit.
[37] Mónica Hernández, "With Heart in Hand/*Con Corazon en la Mano*"

Chapter 23: Gender, Class, Organization
[1] U.S. Census Bureau, "Annual Demographic Survey"
[2] Angela Davis, "Reflections on the Black Woman's Role in the Community of Slaves"
[3] Hernández, op. cit.
[4] Barbara Ransby, *Ella Baker and the Black Freedom Movement*
[5] Ibid.
[6] Charles Payne, *I've Got the Light of Freedom*
[7] Yiching Wu, "Rethinking 'Capitalist Restoration' in China"

VIII. Overcoming White Supremacy and Racism
Chapter 24: The Personal is Political
[1] Ted Allen, speaking at Bryn Mawr college, *circa* 1993
[2] Tim Wise, *White Like Me*, p. 103
[3] Danny Postel, "An Interview with Noel Ignatiev"
[4] The 15 cosigners of the "An Open Letter To Activists Concerning Racism In The Anti-War Movement" are Steve Bloom, Jean Carey Bond, Humberto Brown, Saulo Colón, Bhairavi Desai, Cherrene Horazuk, Randy Jackson, Hany Khalil, Ray Laforest, Ngô Thanh Nhàn, René Francisco Poitevin, Merle Ratner, Liz Roberts, Juliet Ucelli, Lincoln Van Sluytman

Bibliography

(principal sources starred)

Sources used in more than one section [section numbers in brackets]

* Acuña, Rodolfo, 2000. *Occupied America: A History of Chicanos* (Addison Wesley Longman: New York) [I-IV, VI]

* Adam, Barry D., 1995. *The Rise of a Gay and Lesbian Movement* (Simon & Schuster Macmillan: New York) [IV, VI]

* Allen, Robert L., with Pamela P. Allen, 1983. *Reluctant Reformers: Racism and Social Reform Movements in the United States* (Howard University Press: Washington, DC) [II, III, VI]

Allen, Theodore W., 2001. "'Race' and 'Ethnicity'": History and the 2000 Census," *Cultural Logic.* http://clogic.eserver.org/3-1&2/allen.html [I, VII]

* ________________, 1994. *The Invention of the White Race, Vol. 1: Racial Oppression and Social Control* (Verso: New York) [I, II, VII]

* ________________, 1997. *The Invention of the White Race, Vol. 2: The Origin of Racial Oppression in Anglo-America* (Verso: New York) [I, II, IV]

Almaguer, Tomás, 1994. *Racial Fault Lines: The Historical Origins of White Supremacy in California* (University of California Press: Berkeley) [I, III]

* Bennett, Jr., Lerone, 1991. *The Shaping of Black America*, rev. ed. (Penguin Books: New York) [I, II]

* __________________, 1988. *Before the Mayflower: A History of Black America* (Penguin Books: New York) [II, IV]

Braden, Anne, 1999. *The Wall Between* (The University of Tennessee Press: Knoxville) [V, VI, VIII]

Cecelski, David S. and Timothy B. Tyson, eds., 1998. *Democracy Betrayed: The Wilmington Race Riot of 1898 and its Legacy* (University of North Carolina Press: Chapel Hill) [II, IV]

Davis, Angela, 1971. "Reflections on the Black Woman's Role in the Community of Slaves," in *The Angela Y. Davis Reader*, 1998, edited by Joy James (Blackwell Publishers: Malden, MA) [IV, VII]

DuBois, W.E.B.,1969 (1935). *Black Reconstruction in America: An Essay Toward a History of the Part Which Black Folk Played in the Attempt to Reconstruct Democracy in America, 1860-1880* (Atheneum: New York) [II, III]

Duran, Eduardo and Bonnie Duran, 1995. *Native American Postcolonial Society* (State University of New York Press: Albany) [IV, VII]

Foley, Neil, 1997. *The White Scourge: Mexicans, Blacks, and Poor Whites in Texas Cotton Culture*, (University of California Press: Berkeley) [I, II]

* Foner, Eric, 1988. *Reconstruction: America's Unfinished Revolution, 1863-1877* (Harper-Collins: New York) [II, III, VI]

Foster, William Z., 1947. *American Trade Unionism: Principles and Organization, Strategy and Tactics* (International Publishers: New York)

* Frankenberg, Ruth, 1994. *White Women, Race Matters: The Social Construction of Whiteness* (University of Minnesota Press: Minneapolis) [I, V]

* Gonzalez, Juan, 2001. *Harvest of Empire: A History of Latinos in America* (Penguin Books: New York) [I, II, IV]

Hacker, Andrew, 1995. *Two Nations: Black and White, Separate, Hostile and Unequal* (Ballantine Books: New York) [V, VII]

Kelley, Robin D. G., 2002. *Freedom Dreams: The Black Radical Imagination* (Beacon Press: Boston) [II, IV]

Kivel, Paul, 2002. *Uprooting Racism: How White People Can Work for Racial Justice* (New Society Publishers: Gabriola Island, BC, Canada) [VI, VIII]

Kolchin, Peter, 2003. *American Slavery: 1619–1877* (Hill and Wang: New York) [I, VI]

* Lee, Robert G., 1999. *Orientals: Asian Americans in Popular Culture* (Temple University Press: Philadelphia) [I, IV]

Louie, Miriam Ching Yoon, 2001. *Sweatshop Warriors: Immigrant Women Workers Take On the Global Factory* (South End Press: Cambridge, MA) [IV, VII]

* Martínez, Elizabeth, 1998. De Colores *Means All of Us* (South End Press: Cambridge, MA) [II, IV, VII]

_______________, 1997. " *Chingón'* Politics Die Hard: Reflections on the First Chicano Activist Reunion," in *Living Chicana Theory*, Carla Trujillo, ed. (Third Woman Press: Berkeley) [IV, VII]

* McIntosh, Peggy, 1988. "White Privilege: Unpacking the Invisible Knapsack," excerpted from "White Privilege and Male Privilege: A Personal Account of Coming To See Correspondences through Work in Women's Studies," Working Paper 189. Wellesley College Center for Research on Women. Available at http://www.antiracistalliance.com/Unpacking.html [V, VIII]

Montejano, David, 1987. *Anglos and Mexicans in the Making of Texas, 1836 –1986* (University of Texas Press: Austin) [I, II]

* Saxton, Alexander, 1990. *The Rise and Fall of the White Republic: Class Politics and Mass Culture in Nineteenth-Century America* (Verso: London) [I, IV]

Schechter, Patricia A., 2001. *Ida B. Wells Barnett and American Reform, 1880-1930* (University of North Carolina Press: Chapel Hill) [II, IV]

Schmitt, John, 2004. "Recent Job Loss Hits the African-American Middle Class Hard," *Briefing Paper*, Center for Economic and Policy Research, October. http://www.cepr.net [III, V]

Segrest, Mab, 1994. *Memoir of a Race Traitor* (South End Press: Boston) [IV, VI, VIII]

Solomon, Mark, 1998. *The Cry Was Unity: Communists and African Americans, 1917-36* (University Press of Mississippi: Jackson) [II, III]

* Steinhorn, Leonard and Barbara Diggs-Brown, 1999. *By the Color of Our Skin: The Illusion of Integration and the Reality of Race* (The Penguin Group: New York) [V, VII]

* Thompson, Becky, 2001. *A Promise and a Way of Life: White Antiracist Activism* (University of Minnesota Press: Minneapolis) [IV, VI, VII]

Truong, Hong-An and Christina Chia, 2005. "Beyond the Model Minority: Interview with Milan Pham," *Southern Exposure*, Vol. 33, Nos. 1-2, Summer [II, VII]

Tyson, Timothy B., 2004. *Blood Done Sign My Name* (Three Rivers Press: New York) [IV, VI]

Waldman, Carl, 2000. *Atlas of the North American Indian*, rev. ed. (Checkmark Books: New York) [I, II]

* Wilson, James, 1998. *The Earth Shall Weep: A History of Native Americans* (Grove Press: New York) [I, II]

* Wise, Tim, 2005. *White Like Me: Reflections on Race from a Privileged Son* (Soft Skull Press: Brooklyn) [V, VIII]

* Woodard, Komozi, 1999. *A Nation within a Nation: Amiri Baraka (LeRoi Jones) and Black Power Politics* (University of North Carolina Press: Chapel Hill) [II, IV, VI]

* Wong, Paul, 1999. "Introduction," in *Race, Ethnicity, and Nationality in the United States: Toward the Twenty-First Century*, Paul Wong, ed. (Westview Press: Boulder) [II, VII]

* Wu, Frank H., 2002. *Yellow: Race in America Beyond Black and White* (Basic Books: New York) [IV, VII]

Zinn, Howard, 1999. *A People's History of the United States*, 20th Anniv. Ed. (HarperCollins: New York) [I, II, IV]

I. The White Race

Allen, Theodore W., 1998. "Interview," *Cultural Logic*. http://eserver.org/clogic/1-2/allen%20interview.html

Banneker, Benjamin, 1791. "Letter to Jefferson." Available at http://afroamhistory.about.com/library/blbanneker_letter.htm

Becker, Eddie, current. *Chronology on the History of Slavery and Racism*. http://innercity.org/holt/chron_1790_1829.html

Bennett, Herman L., 2003. "Soiled Gods and the Formation of Slave Society," Chap. 1 of *Africans in Colonial Mexico: Absolutism, Christianity, and Afro-Creole Consciousness, 1570–1640* (Indiana University Press: Bloomington) pp. 14–32. http://www.indiana.edu/~iupress/books/0-253-34236-8.pdf

Craven, James M., "Native Americans." http://www.home.earthlink.net/~blkfoot5

* Davidson, Basil, 1980. *The African Slave Trade*, rev. ed. (Little, Brown and Co.: Boston)

DeLoria, Philip J., 1998. *Playing Indian* (Yale University Press: New Haven)

Equiano, Olaudah, 1789. *The Interesting Narrative of the Life of Olaudah Equiano, or Gustavus Vassa the African* (London). http://history.hanover.edu/texts/equiano/equiano_contents.html

Finkelman, Paul, 1993. "Jefferson and Slavery: Treason Against the Hopes of the World," in *Jeffersonian Legacies*, Peter S. Onuf, ed. (University Press of Virginia: Charlottesville) pp. 181–221. Available at http://csd.k12.nh.us/%7Ecbour/slavery

Fogel, Daniel, 1988. *Junípero Serra, the Vatican, and Enslavement Theology* (Ism Press: San Francisco)

* Gallay, Alan, 2002. *The Indian Slave Trade: The Rise of the English Empire in the American South, 1670–1717* (Yale University Press: New Haven)

* King, Barbara J., 2002. *Biological Anthropology: An Evolutionary Perspective* (The Teaching Co.: Chantilly, VA)

Knight, Franklin W. and Clayborne Carson, current. "The Slave Trade." http://www.caribbeanlime.com/the%20slave%20trade.htm

Kolchin, Peter, 2003. *American Slavery: 1619–1877* (Hill and Wang: New York)

Lewontin, Richard, 1995. *Human Diversity* (Scientific American Library: New York)

Loewen, James W. 1996. *Lies My Teacher Told Me: Everything Your American History Textbook Got Wrong* (Simon & Schuster: New York)

Lynch, Jack, ed. 2003. *Samuel Johnson's Dictionary* (Walker and Co.: New York)

Manning, Patrick, 1992. "The Slave Trade: The Formal Demography of a Global System," in *The Atlantic Slave Trade: Effects on Economies, Societies, and Peoples in Africa, the Americas, and Europe*, Joseph E. Inikori and Stanley L. Engerman, eds. (Duke University Press: Durham)

* Marks, Jonathan, 2002. *What it Means to Be 98% Chimpanzee: Apes, People, and Their Genes* (University of California Press: Berkeley)

Claude McKay, 1953. "Tiger," in *Selected Poems* (NY: Bookman Associates)

McNabb, Donnald and Louis E. "Lee" Madère, Jr. "A History of New Orleans." http://www.madere.com/history.html#002

Morgan, Edmund S., 1975 *American Slavery/American Freedom: The Ordeal of Colonial Virginia* (WW Norton & Co.: New York), quoted and discussed in Theodore Allen, *The Invention of the White Race*, Vol. II.

National Human Genome Research Institute. "Understanding Human Genetic Variation," National Institutes of Health. http://science.education.nih.gov/supplements/nih1/genetic/guide/genetic_variation1.htm

* Omi, Michael and Howard Winant, 1986. *Racial Formation in the United States: From the 1960s to the 1980s* (Routledge: New York)

Richter, Daniel K., 2001. *Facing East from Indian Country: A Native History of Early America* (Harvard University Press: Cambridge, MA)

Roediger, David R., 1991. *The Wages of Whiteness: Race and the Making of the American Working Class* (Verso: New York)

Shoemaker, Nancy, 1997. "How Indians Got to Be Red," *American Historical Review*, June 1997, pp. 625–644

Takaki, Ronald, 1989. *Strangers from a Different Shore: A History of Asian Americans* (Penguin Books: New York)

* Thomas, Hugh, 1997. *The Slave Trade: The Story of the Atlantic Slave Trade: 1440–1870* (Simon & Schuster: New York)

U.S. Census Bureau, 2001. "The Hispanic Population: Census 2000 Brief." http://www.census.gov/prod/2001pubs/c2kbr01-3.pdf

Uzgalis, Bill, 2003. "Bartolomé De Las Casas," Oregon St. University. http://oregonstate.edu/instruct/phl302/philosophers/las_casas.html

Vaughn, Alden T., 1982. "From White Man to Redskin: Changing Anglo-American Perceptions of the American Indian" *American History Review*, Vol. 87, October, pp. 917–53

Wagner, Phillip, 2002. "Sugar and Blood: The Story of the African Slave Trade in Brazil," *Brazzil Magazine*, April. http://www.iei.net/~pwagner/brazarticles/April2002.html

West, Jean M. "Slavery and Sanctuary in Colonial Florida." http://slaveryinamerica.org/history/hs_es_Florida_Slavery.htm

Wright, Ronald, 1992. *Stolen Continents: The "New World" Through Indian Eyes* (Houghton Mifflin Company: Boston)

Yale Bulletin and Calendar, 1996. "The historic tradition of 'Black Election Day' explored in symposium and cultural festival," Nov. 4-11, Vol. 25, No. 11

II. Race, Nations and Empire

Becker, Marc, 2003. "Vieques." http://www.yachana.org/reports/vieques/report.html

Brown, Carolyn M. and David A. Padgett, 2005. "Top Cities for African Americans." http://www.blackenterprise.com/ExclusivesEKOpen.asp?id=850

Bush, Rod, 2000. *We Are Not What We Seem: Black Nationalism and Class Struggle in the American Century* (New York University Press: New York)

Bustelo, Joaquín, 2006. "Making Sense of the Latin@ Uprising." Available at http://stangoff.com/?p=277

Calpotura, Francis, 2003. "A Journey Home," *ColorLines*, Vol. 6, No. 2, Summer

Cavanaugh-O'Keefe, John. "Introduction to Eugenics," *Eugenics Watch*. http://www.eugenics-watch.com/index.html

Ceptus, Barbara, 2005. "Growing Up Haitian, Growing Up Black," *ColorLines*, Vol. 8, No. 3, Fall

Communist International, 1928. "The 1928 Comintern Resolution on the Negro Question in the United States." Available at http://www.marx2mao.com/Other/CR75.html

* Churchill, Ward, 2003. *Perversions of Justice: Indigenous Peoples and Angloamerican Law* (City Lights: San Francisco)

Deloria, Jr., Vine, 1969. *Custer Died for Your Sins: An Indian Manifesto* (University of Oklahoma Press: Norman)

DuBois, W.E.B., 1947. "The Pan-African Movement," in *History of the Pan-African Congress*, George Padmore, ed. Available at http://www.etext.org/Politics/MIM/countries/panafrican/padmorefifthpac1947.html

DuBois, W.E.B., 1935. "A Negro Nation Within the Nation," *Current History* 42, June, in *The Oxford W. E. B. DuBois Reader*, 1996 (Oxford University Press: New York)

Elbaum, Max, 2002. *Revolution in the Air: Sixties Radicals turn to Lenin, Mao and Che* (Verso: New York)

Ford, Glen and Peter Gamble, 2006. "Which Way for Black Labor?: Unionists Seek Path to Economic Development," *Black Commentator*, Issue 184, May 18. http://www.blackcommentator.com/184/184_cover_black_labor.html

Frank, Robert, 2004. "US Led a Resurgence Last Year Among Millionaires World-Wide," Wall Street Journal, June 15. http://www.globalpolicy.org/socecon/inequal/2004/0615millionaires.htm

Frey, William H., 2001. "Migration to the South Brings U.S. Blacks Full Circle." http://www.prb.org/Content/NavigationMenu/PT_articles/April-June_2001/Migration_t_the_South_Brings_U_S__Blacks_Full_Circle.htm

FRSO/OSCL, 2005."They can kill a revolutionary, but they can't kill the revolution." http://freedomroad.org/content/blogcategory/140/82/lang,english/

Gallegos, Bill, 2006. "Immigrants fight for freedom," April 26. Available at http://freedomroad.org/content/view/390/45/

García, Ignacio M., 1997. *Chicanismo: The Forging of a Militant Ethos among Mexican Americans* (University of Arizona Press: Tucson)

Georgia Office of Planning and Budget, Census Data Program. "Georgia Population Trends 1990 to 2000." http://www.gadata.org/

Gonzalez, Juan, 2006. "Another Battle over Puerto Rico," *New York Daily News*, February 21. http://www.nydailynews.com/02-21-2006/news/wn_report/story/393209p-333430c.html

Gooding, Susan, 2006. "Recognizing Indigenous America in Times of War," *Political Affairs*, Vol. 85, No. 6, June

Grassroots Global Justice, current. "Mission." http://www.ggjalliance.org/mission

Graves-Goodman, Peter, 2006. "Another World is Possible: (World Social Forum) Discussion at Miami Workers Center," March 19. http://miami.indymedia.org/news/2006/03/3997.php

* Hahn, Steven, 2003. *A Nation Under Our Feet: Black Political Struggles in the Rural South from Slavery to the Great Migration*, (Harvard University Press: Cambridge, MA)

Hang, Pakou, 2003. "Hmong-Town, USA," *ColorLines*, Vol. 5, No. 4, Winter

Hart-Landsberg, Martin, 2006. "Neoliberalism: Myths and Reality," *Monthly Review*, Vol. 57, No. 11, April

Hensley, Willie, 1980. "The Land is the Spirit of the People," keynote speech at Alaska Federation of Natives Convention, Anchorage, Alaska

Husband, Bertha, 1999. "A Look at the Movement to Free Puerto Rico: Ronald Fernandez' Prisoners of Colonialism," book review. http://sandpaper.tripod.com/99-Spring/PrisonersofColonialism.html

Indianz.com, 2005. "Cobell legal team awarded fees for trust fund fight," December 20. http://www.indianz.com/News/2005/011820.asp

Johnston, Jill, 2004. "Project Regeneration Update," *Newsletter*, Military Toxics Project, Spring

Knowlton, Clark S., 1963. "Causes of Land Loss Among the Spanish-Americans in Northern New Mexico," in *The Chicanos*, Gilberto López y Rivas.

Lenin, V.I., 1916. "Imperialism: The Highest Stage of Capitalism," *Selected Works*, Vol. 1, pp. 667-766. Available at http://www.marxists.org/archive/lenin/works/1916/imp-hsc/

* López y Rivas, Gilberto, 1973. *The Chicanos: Life and Struggles of the Mexican Minority in the United States* (Monthly Review Press: New York)

Marrs, Carl H., 2003. "ANCSA: An Act of Self-Determination," excerpt from *Cultural Survival Quarterly*, Fall

Martínez, Elizabeth and Arnoldo García, 2001. "What is 'Neo-Liberalism'? A Brief Definition." http://www.globalexchange.org/campaigns/econ101/neoliberalDefined.html

Mokhiber, Russell and Robert Weissman, "The Age of Inequality." http://www.inequality.org/mokhiberfr.html

Muhammad, Askia, 2005. "CBC panel hears Tulsa 'massacre' victims' appeal." finalcall.com, June 1. http://www.finalcall.com/artman/publish/article_2026.shtml

Muhammad, Saladin, 2006. "African Americans and Latinos Unite: Build a United Democratic Front," panel presentation at Workers World Party conference.

National Immigration Forum, 2006. "The Sensenbrenner-King Bill's 'Greatest Misses." http://www.immigrationforum.org/documents/PolicyWire/Legislation/SenseKingGlance.pdf

Nisan, Chris, 2003. "Black farms continue struggle for land, justice, rights," *Minnesota Spokesman-Recorder*, March 30. http://afgen.com/black_farmers11.html

Nussbaum, Lydia R., 2002. "From Paternalism to Imperialism: The U.S. and the Boxer Rebellion." http://www.arts.cornell.edu/Knight_nstitute/publications/Discoveries%20Fa2002/as.pdf

Ofari, Earl, 1970. *The Myth of Black Capitalism* (Monthly Review Press: New York)

Penchaszadeh, Analia, 2003. "World Social Forum 2003: U.S. Activists in Porto Alegre," at *Economic Justice News Online*, Vol. 6, No. 1, April. http://www.50years.org/cms/ejn/story/77

Prashad, Vijay, 2004. "An Indian American election," *World Affairs*, Vol. 21, Issue 14. http://www.flonnet.com/fl2114/stories/20040716000706300.htm

Rattner, Steven, 2003. "Inured to Inequality", *Washington Post*, June 16

Sansani, Inbal, 2003. "American Indian Land Rights in the Inter-American System: *Dann v. United States*," *Human Rights Brief*, Vol. 20, No. 2. Available at http://www.wcl.american.edu/hrbrief/10/2indian.cfm

Shachtman, Max, 2003 (1933). *Race and Revolution* (Verso: New York)

Schneider, Stu, 2003. "Victories for Home Health Care Workers," *Dollars and Sense*, September/October

Simkin, John. "Radical Republicans," at Spartacus Educational. http://www.spartacus.schoolnet.co.uk/USASradical.htm

Simmons, Aishah Shahidah, 2006. "Words on the Duke Rape Case." http://www.feministing.com/archives/005022.html

Solnit, David, 2005. "The New Face of the Global Justice Movement: Taco Bell Boycott Victory – A Model of Strategic Organizing." http://houston.indymedia.org/news/2005/09/42978.php

Special Committee on Decolonization, United Nations, 2004. "Decolonization Committee Calls for Expediated Process of Self-Determination for Puerto Rico," press release GA/COL/3102, June 6, 2004. http://www.un.org/News/Press/docs/2004/gacol3102.doc.htm

______, 1998. "Special Committee on Decolonization Reaffirms Inalienable Right of People of Puerto Rico to Self-Determination and Independence," Press Release GA/COL/2992, August 11, 1998. http://www.un.org/News/Press/docs/1998/19980811.gaco2992.html

Stalin, J.V., 1913. *Marxism and the National Question*. Available at http://www.marxists.org/reference/archive/stalin/works/1913/03.htm

Torres, Andrés, 1999. "*Cien Años de Lucha*: The Fight over the Status of Puerto Rico," *ColorLines*, Vol. 1, No. 3, Winter

United States of America, 1994. 'The Insular Areas' and 'Native Americans' from "Consideration of Reports Submitted by State Parties Under Article 40 of the Covenant, Initial report of State parties due in 1993, Addendum," U.N. Doc. CCPR/C/81/Add.4. http://heiwww.unige.ch/humanrts/usdocs/1994.html

U.S. Census Bureau, 2003. "The Black Population in the United States: March 2002," *Current Population Reports*, April. http://www.census.gov/prod/2003pubs/p20-541.pdf

Wade, Robert Hunter, 2005. "Does Inequality Matter?" *Challenge*, Vol. 48, No. 5, Sept.-Oct.

Walker, David, 1829. David Walker's Appeal, excerpts. Available at http://www.pbs.org/wgbh/aia/part4/4h2931t.html

Western Shoshone Defense Project, 2006. "Western Shoshone Victorious at United Nations: U.S. found in Violation of Human Rights of Native Americans – Urged to Take Immediate Action," at Shundahai Network, May 10. http://www.shundahai.org/3-10-06Western_Shoshone_UN_Press_Release.htm

Wicks, Mike, 2006. "Short History of Big Mountain – Black Mesa," at American Indian Cultural Support. http://www.aics.org/BM/bm.html

Wing, Bob, 2001. "*Indio Claro o Oscuro*?" *ColorLines*, Vol. 4, No. 2, Summer

Young, Don, 1997. "Report on H.R. Act 856: United States-Puerto Rico Political Status Act." http://www.congress.gov/cgi-bin/cpquery/T?&report=hr131p1&dbname=cp105&

III. Race and Class

AFL-CIO, 2000. *Common Sense Economics*, Economics Education Program (AFL-CIO Department of Education: Washington)

Alan, John, 2004. "The Socialism of Hubert Harrison," *News and Letters*, January-February

Allen, Ted, 1972. *The Most Vulnerable Point*. Unavailable. Inquire with Jeffrey B. Perry and the Theodore W. Allen Scholar Program at the State University of New York, Stony Brook.

Black, Bob, 1998. "Beautiful Losers: The Historiography of the International Workers of the World." http://www.inspiracy.com/black/beautifullosers.html

Boisson, Steve, 2002. "*Salt of the Earth*: The Movie Hollywood Could Not Stop," *American History*, February. http://historynet.com/ah/blhhollywoodmovie/index.html

Boston Daily Evening Voice, 1866. Organ of the Boston Trades Assembly, January 13.

* Brattain, Michelle, 2001. *The Politics of Whiteness: Race. Workers, and Culture in the Modern South* (Princeton University Press: Princeton)

Carrington, Yolanda, 2004. "Stemmer."

Dart, Bob, 2005. "Heading South: Population boom shows region's clout," *The Atlanta Journal-Constitution*, April 21

Davis, Daniel S., 1972. *Mr. Black Labor: The Story of A. Philip Randolph, Father of the Civil Rights Movement* (E.P. Dutton: New York)

Dillahunt, Gordon, 1988. "A Southern Strategy," *Forward Motion*, Jan.-Feb.

DuBois, W.E.B., 1995 (1913). "Socialism and the Negro Problem," in *W.E.B. DuBois: A Reader*, David Levering Lewis, ed. (Henry Holt & Co.: New York)

EEOC, 2004. "Focusing Enforcement Efforts on Systemic Discrimination." http://www.eeoc.gov/abouteeoc/35th/1970s/focusing.html

Executive Committee of the AFL. "Minutes, Part 2: 1925-1955," at University Publications of America. http://www.lexis-nexis.com/academic/guides/labor_studies/afl/afl2.asp

First Union Bank, 1998. *Regional Economic Review*, July

Fletcher, Bill, Jr. and Fernando Gapasin, 2002. "The Politics of Labour and Race in the USA," in *Socialist Register 2003: Fighting Identities: Race, Religion and Ethno-Nationalism*, Leo Panitch and Colin Leys, eds. (Monthly Review Press: New York)

* Foner, Philip S., 1976. *Organized Labor and the Black Worker, 1619-1973* (International Publishers: New York)

Foster, William Z., 1952. *History of the Communist Party of the United States* (International Publishers: New York)

________________, 1949. *The Twilight of World Capitalism* (International Publishers: New York)

________________, 1937. *From Bryan to Stalin* (International Publishers: New York)

Foster, William Z, et. al., 1947. *The Communist Position on the Negro Question* (New Century Publishers: New York)

* Gallegos, William, 1987. "The 'Sunbelt Strategy' and Chicano Liberation," photocopy

Georgia State University Library, 2004. "Background Reading on the General Textile Strike of 1934." http://wwwlib.gsu.edu/spcoll/Labor/work_n_progress/34Strikebackground.htm

Goff, Gary, 1997. "We Need to Reject Those Things That Divide Us," *Forward Motion*, No. 62, Vol. 15, No. 2

* Goldfield, Michael, 1997. *The Color of Politics: Race and the Mainsprings of American Politics* (New Press: New York)

* Griffith, Barbara S., 1988. *The Crisis of American Labor: Operation Dixie and the Defeat of the CIO* (Temple University Press: Philadelphia)

Hill, Herbert, 1973. "Anti-Oriental Agitation and the Rise of Working-Class Racism," *Society*, January-February

Hirsch, Barry T. and David A. Macpherson, 2006. "Union Membership, Coverage, Density and Employment" by state and nationally for 1983 and 2005. http://www.trinity.edu/bhirsch/unionstats/

Hudson, Hosea, 1991 (1972). *Black Worker in the Deep South: A Personal Record*, 2nd ed. (International Publishers: New York)

Ignatin, Noel, and Ted Allen, 1969. *White Blindspot* and *Can White Radicals Be Radicalized?* Detroit Radical Education Project

Jobs with Justice, Washington State, 2003. "Victory on the Puget Sound Waterfront and for our Entire Labor Movement!" http://www.wsjwj.org/news_2002/longshore_2002.asp

Kelley, Robin D.G., 1990. *Hammer and Hoe: Alabama Communists During the Great Depression* (University of North Carolina Press: Chapel Hill)

Kenyon College Seminar Program, 2000. "Interview: Ray Henderson," *Birmingham-Pittsburgh Traveler*. http://northbysouth.kenyon.edu/2000/Fraternal/Ray%20Henderson.htm

Kotkin, Joel, 2004. "Top 25 Cities for Doing Business in America," *Inc. Magazine*, March. Available at http://www.tampachamber.com/ci_viewnews.aps?id=99

Korstad, Karl, 1992. "Black and White Together: Organizing in the South with the Food, Tobacco, Agricultural and Allied Workers Union (FTA-CIO), 1946-1952," in *The CIO's Left-Led Unions*, Steve Rosswurm, ed. (Rutgers University Press: New Brunswick, NJ)

Lenin, V.I., 1920. *Left-Wing Communism: An Infantile Disorder*. Available at http://www.marxists.org/archive/lenin/works/1920/lwc/

__________, 1916. *Socialist Revolution and the Right of Nations to Self-Determination*. Available at http://www.marxists.org/archive/lenin/works/1916/jan/x01.htm

Leondar-Wright, 2004. "Black Job Loss, *Déjà Vu*," *Dollars & Sense*, No. 253, May-June. http://www.dollarsandsense.org/archives/2004/0504leondar.html

Lyons, Thomas, 1999. "Review of Timothy Minchin, *Hiring the Black Worker: The Racial Integration of the Southern Textile Industry*," Economic History Services, June 18. http://eh.net/bookreviews/library/0163.shtml

Mandel, Michael J., 2004. "Jobs: The Lull Will Linger," *BusinessWeek*, October 25

Martínez, Elizabeth and Arnold García, 2001. "What is 'Neoliberalism'?: A Brief Definition," *Global Economy 101*. http://www.globalexchange.org/campaigns/econ101/neoliberalDefined.html

Marx, Karl,. 1968 (1871). *The Civil War in France*, in *Karl Marx and Frederick Engels: Selected Works* (International Publishers: New York)

__________, 1967 (1867). *Capital: A Critique of Political Economy*, Vol. 1 (International Publishers: New York)

McWhorter, Diane, 2002. *Carry Me Home: Birmingham Alabama – The Climactic Battle of the Civil Rights Revolution* (Touchstone: New York)

* Mitchell, Roxanne and Frank Weiss, 1981. *A House Divided: Labor and White Supremacy* (United Labor Press: New York)

Montgomery, David, 1981. *Beyond Equality: Labor and the Radical Republicans, 1862-1872* (University of Illinois Press: Chicago)

Muhammad, Saladin, 2000. Speech at Black Workers for Justice Martin Luther King Support for Labor Banquet, April

* Muhammad, Saladin, 1998. "Organize the South in the Context of Globalization," speech to the First Southern International Workers' School, Brisbane Institute, Morehouse College, Oct 1-4

Occupational Outlook Quarterly, 2003. "Large metropolitan areas that had the fastest employment growth, 1998-2003." http://www.bls.gov/opub/ooq/2003/summer/oochart.pdf

Ofari, Earl, 1974. "Black Activists and 19th Century Radicalism," *Black Scholar*, February

Perry, Jeffrey B., ed., 2001. *A Hubert Harrison Reader* (Wesleyan University Press: Middletown)

Petras, James and Henry Veitmeyer, 2002. "Argentina: Between Disintegration and Revolution," *Covert Action Quarterly*, No. 74, Fall

Pontecorvo, Gillo, dir., 2005 (1968). *Burn*, MGM

Reich, Michael, 1981. *Racial Inequality: A Political-Economic Analysis* (Princeton University Press: Princeton)

Rosengarten, Theodore, 1974. *All God's Dangers: The Life of Nate Shaw* (Avon: New York)

Ruiz, Vicki L. 1998 "United Cannery, Agricultural, Packing, and Allied Workers of America/Food, Tobacco, Agricultural, and Allied Workers of America (UCAPAWA/FTA)," in *Readers' Companion to Women's History*, (Houghton Mifflin Co.: New York). Available at http://college.hmco.com/history/readerscomp/women/html/wh_019613_unitedcanner.htm

Sidoti, Liz, 2005. "Base Plan Would Alter Military Landscape," *Associated Press*, May 15

Stoney, George, Judith Helfand and Susanne Rostock, 1995. *Uprising of '34*. P.O.V. series, Public Broadcasting System. http://www.pbs.org/pov/pov1995/theuprisingof34/

UE-150 Public Workers Union, 2005. "Proposed Resolution for BRC Support for the International Worker Justice Campaign," mimeograph, passed June 16

U.S. Census Bureau, 2006. "Population Estimates for the Fastest Growing Cities with Populations over 100,000: July 1, 2004, to July 1, 2005," June 21. http://www.census.gov/Press-Release/www/2006/cb06-95table1.pdf

United States Department of Defense, 2003. "Percent Distribution of DoD Military and Civilian Personnel by State." http://web1.whs.osd.mil/mmid/m02/FY00/M02_2000_census.PDF

Vogel, Richard D., 2006. "The NAFTA Corridors: Offshoring U.S. Transportation Jobs to Mexico," *Monthly Review*, Vol. 57, No. 10, February

________________, 2005. "Wal-Mart's End Run around Organized Labor – Aided and Abetted by the State of Texas," at *MR-zine*, July 15. http://mrzine.monthlyreview.org/vogel140705.html

Weisbord, Vera Buch, 1974. "Gastonia, 1929: Strike at the Loray Mill," *Southern Exposure*, Vol. 1, No. 3-4, Winter. Available at http://www.weisbord.org/Gastonia.html

Women's International League for Peace and Freedom (WILPF), current. "Study Packet VI: People's and Workers' Resistance Movements." http://www.wilpf.org/corp/VI/VI-all.pdf

IV. Patriarchy and Privilege

Abramovitz, Mimi, 2002. "Still under Attack: Women and Welfare Reform," in *The Socialist Feminist Project*, Nancy Holmstrom, ed.

Amott, Teresa and Julie Matthaei, 1991. *Race, Gender, and Work: A Multicultural Economic History of Women in the United States* (South End Press: Boston)

Baxandall, Rosalyn, 2003. "Precursors and Bridges: Was the CPUSA Unique?" *Science & Society*, Vol. 66, No. 4, Winter

Beauvoir, Simone de, 1989 (1949). *The Second Sex* (Vintage: New York)

Bierria, Alisa, et. al., 2005. "Taking Risks: Implementing Grassroots Community Accountability," unpublished, excerpted in INCITE!'s "Gender Oppression, Abuse, Violence: Community Accountability within the People of Color Progressive Movement," pp. 35-38

Breines, Wini, 1992. *Young, White, and Miserable: Growing Up Female in the Fifties* (Beacon Press: Boston)

Brenner, Johanna, 2000. *Women and the Politics of Class* (Monthly Review Press: New York)

Brown, Elaine, 1992. *A Taste of Power: A Black Woman's Story* (Doubleday: New York)

Burnham, Linda, 2001. "Doing Double Duty," *ColorLines*, Vol. 4, No. 3, Fall

Cleage, Pearl, 1990. *Mad at Miles: A Blackwoman's Guide to Truth* (The Cleage Group: Southfield, MI)

Chamberlain, Pam and Jean Hardisty, 2000. "Reproducing Patriarchy: Reproductive Rights Under Siege," *The Public Eye Magazine*, Vol. 14, No. 1, Spring

Collins, Patricia Hill, 2000. *Black Feminist Thought: Knowledge, Consciousness, and the Politics of Empowerment* (Routledge: New York)

Collins, Sheila D., 1986 *The Rainbow Challenge: The Jackson Campaign and the Future of U.S. Politics* (Monthly Review Press: New York)

Combahee River Collective, 1977. "A Black Feminist Statement," in *This Bridge Called My Back: Writings by Radical Women of Color*, Cherríe Moraga and Gloria Anzaldúa, eds. (Kitchen Table: Women of Color Press: New York)

Cruz, Bárbara C. and Michael J. Berson, 2001. "The American Melting Pot? Miscegenation Laws in the United States," *OAH Magazine of History*, Organization of American Historians, Vol. 15, No. 4, Summer.
http://www.oah.org/pubs/Magazine/family/cruz-berson.html

Cullen, Dave, 1999. "Gay panic lite," at Salon.com, November 2.
http://www.salon.com/news/feature/1999/11/02/shepard

Davis, Angela, 2002. "Public Imprisonment and Private Violence: Reflections on the Hidden Punishment of Women," in *The Socialist Feminist Project*, Nancy Holmstrom, ed.

____________, 2000. "The Color of Violence Against Women," *ColorLines*, Vol. 3, No. 3, Fall

Dent, Gina, 1995. "Missionary Position," in *To Be Real: Telling the Truth and Changing the Face of Feminism*, Rebecca Walker, ed. (Anchor Books: New York)

Devens, Carol, 1992. *Countering Colonization: Native American Women and Great Lakes Missions, 1630-1900* (University of California Pres: Berkeley)

Di Leonardo, Micaela and Roger Lancaster, 2002. "Gender, Sexuality, Political Economy," in *The Socialist Feminist Project*, Nancy Holmstrom, ed.

Dray, Philip, 2003. *At the Hands of Persons Unknown: The Lynching of Black America* (Modern Library: New York)

Duberman, Martin, 1993. *Stonewall* (Plume Books: New York)

Eisenstein, Hester, 2005. "A Dangerous Liaison? Feminism and Corporate Globalization," *Science & Society*, Vol. 69, No. 3

Enloe, Cynthia, 2002. "Militarizing Women's Lives," in *The Socialist Feminist Project*, Nancy Holmstrom, ed.

* Ericsson, Kjersti, 1993. *Sisters, Comrades!* (Workers Communist Party of Norway: Oslo)

Facing History and Ourselves, current. "Eugenics in America: Anti-miscegenation Laws."
http://www.facinghistorycampus.org/Campus/rm.nsf/0/6279243C0EEE444E85257037004EA259

Fields, Marjory D., 2005. "Combating Domestic Violence: A History."
http://www.law.dv.edu/castlerock/Fields%20Services%20US%20History%2003-06.pdf

Fogel, Daniel, 1988. *Junípero Serra, the Vatican, and Enslavement Theology* (Ism Press: San Francisco)

Francke, Linda Bird, 2004. "Women in the Military: The Military Culture of Harassment – The Dynamics of the Masculine Mystique," in *America's Military Today: The Challenge of Militarism*, Tod Ensign, ed. (The New Press: New York)

Frank, Dana, 1998. "White Working-Class Women and the Race Question," *International Labor and Working Class History*, No. 54, Fall

Friedan, Betty, 2001 (1963). *The Feminine Mystique* (W.W. Norton & Co.: New York)

Gilmore, Glenda Elizabeth, 1996 *Gender and Jim Crow: Women and the Politics of White Supremacy in North Carolina, 1896-1920* (University of North Carolina Press: Chapel Hill)

Haaken, Janice, 2002. "Stories of Survival: Class, Race, and Domestic Violence," in *The Socialist Feminist Project*, Nancy Holmstrom, ed.

Harris, Cheryl, 1995. "Whiteness as Property," in *Critical Race Theory: The Key Writings that Formed the Movement*, Kimberlé Crenshaw, et. al., eds. (The New Press: New York)

Hasten, Lauren Wells, 1998. "In Search of the 'Berdache': Multiple Genders and Other Myths," Department of Anthropology, Columbia University. http://www.laurenhasten.com/berdache.htm

Hernández, Daisy, 2004. "Young and Out: Anything But Safe," *ColorLines*, Vol. 7, No. 4, Winter 2003-2004

* Holmstrom, Nancy, ed., 2002. *The Socialist Feminist Project: A Contemporary Reader in Theory and Politics* (Monthly Review Press: New York)

____________________________. "Introduction," in *The Socialist Feminist Project*, Nancy Holmstrom, ed.

hooks, bell, 2000. *Feminism is for Everybody: Passionate Politics* (South End Press: Cambridge)

_________, 1995. *Killing Rage, Ending Racism* (Henry Holt & Co.: New York)

* INCITE! Women of Color Against Violence, 2005. "Gender Oppression, Abuse, Violence: Community Accountability within the People of Color Progressive Movement." http://www.incite-national.org

James, Joy, ed., 1998. *The Angela Y. Davis Reader* (Blackwell Publishers: Malden, MA)

Johnson, Ramon, current. "Gay Abuse: Same-Sex Partner Domestic Violence," at Your Guide to Gay Life. http://gaylife.about.com/od/abusedomesticviolence/a/gayabuse.htm

Kalamka, Juba, 2004. "How can I be down? A bisexual black man's take on "the down low," *ColorLines*, Vol. 7, No. 4, Winter 2003-2004

Kaplan, Temma, 2002. "The Disappearing Fathers under Global Capitalism," in *The Socialist Feminist Project,* Nancy Holmstrom, ed.

Kashef, Ziba, 2004. "Toward Reproductive Freedom," *ColorLines*, Vol. 7, No. 4, Winter 2003-2004

Kempadoo, Kamala, 2002. "Globalizing Sex Workers' Rights," in *The Socialist Feminist Project,* Nancy Holmstrom, ed.

Lee, Butch, 2000. *Jailbreak Out of History: The Re-Biography of Harriet Tubman* (Solidarity Publishing)

Linder, Douglas O., 1999. "The Trials of 'The Scottsboro Boys," part of *Famous American Trials: "The Scottsboro Boys" Trials, 1931-1937.* http://www.law.umkc.edu/faculty/projects/FTrials/scottsboro/SB_acct.html

Luce, Stephanie & Mark Brenner, 2006. "Women and Class: What Has Happened in Forty Years," *Monthly Review*, Vol. 58, No. 3, July-August

Mann, Susan Archer and Douglas J. Huffman, 2005. "The Decentering of Second-Wave Feminism and the Rise of a Third Wave," *Science & Society* Vol. 69, No. 1, January

Marable, Manning, 1983. *How Capitalism Underdeveloped Black America* (South End Press: Cambridge)

Martin, Emily, 2002. "Premenstrual Syndrome, Work Discipline, and Anger," in *The Socialist Feminist Project*, Nancy Holmstrom, ed.

Martin, Patricia Yancey and Robert A. Hummer, 1993. "Fraternities and Rape on Campus," in *Violence Against Women: The Bloody Footprints*, Pauline B. Bart and Eileen Geil Moran, eds. (Sage Publications: Thousand Oaks, CA)

Mies, Maria, 1986. *Patriarchy and Accumulation on a World Scale: Women in the International Division of Labor* (Zed Books: London)

Mohanty, Chandra Talpade, 2002. "Women Workers and Capitalist Scripts: Ideologies of Domination, Common Interests, and the Politics of Solidarity," in *The Socialist Feminist Project,* Nancy Holmstrom, ed.

Molyneux, Maxine, 2002. "Conceptualizing Women's Interest," in *The Socialist Feminist Project*, Nancy Holmstrom, ed.

Moraga, Cherríe, 2000 (1983). *Loving in the War Years* (South End Press: Cambridge)

*____________ and Gloria Anzaldúa, eds. 1984 *This Bridge Called My Back: Voices of Third World Women in the United States* (Kitchen Table Press: New York)

____________ and Ana Castillo, eds., 1988. *Esta Puente, Mi Espalda: Voces de mujeres tercermundistas en los Estados Unidos* (Ism Press: San Francisco)

National Coalition Against Domestic Violence, current. "Domestic Violence Facts." http://www.ncadv.org/files/DV_Facts.pdf

National Task Force to End Sexual and Domestic Violence Against Women, current. "The Violence Against Women Act: 10 Years of Progress and Moving Forward." http://www.vawa2005.org/history.pdf

* Neal, Mark Anthony, 2005. *New Black Man* (Routledge: New York)

Nguyen, Tram, 2001. "North-South Differences Challenge Women at the UN," *ColorLines*, Vol. 4, No.3, Fall

Nussbaum, Martha, 2006. "Legal Weapon" Review of *Are Women Human? And Other International Dialogues*, by Catharine A. MacKinnon, *The Nation*, July 31/August 7

Oshinsky, David, 1994. "Only the Accused Were Innocent," *New York Times*, April 3. http://query.nytimes.com/gst/fullpage.html?res=9F07E5DA133CF930A35757C0A962958260

Peay, Pythia, 2005. "Feminism's Fourth Wave," *Utne Reader*, March-April

Peck, Jamie, 1996. *Work*-Place*: The Social Regulation of Labor Markets* (Guilford Press: New York)

Petchesky, Rosalind P., 2002. "Human Rights, Reproductive Health, and Economic Justice: Why They Are Indivisible," in *The Socialist Feminist Project*, Nancy Holmstrom, ed.

Pulido, Laura, 2006. *Black, Brown, Yellow, and Left* (University of California Press: Berkeley)

RAINN, 2005. "Every Two and a Half Minutes," Rape, Abuse, and Incest National Network. http://www.rainn.org/statistics/minutes.html

____________. "Statistics." http://www.rainn.org/statistics/index.html

Randall, Margaret, 1992. *Gathering Rage: The Failure of Twentieth Century Revolutions to Develop a Feminist Agenda* (Monthly Review Press: New York)

Rojas, Patrisia Macias, 2000. "Rebuilding the Anti-Violence Movement," *ColorLines*, Vol. 3, No. 3, Fall

Ross, Luana, 2001. "Our Lands, Our Bodies: Native Justice," *ColorLines*, Winter 2000-2001

Sanders, Joshunda, 2004. "Taking the Rap: Poet Aya de Leon Tackles Sexism and Reclaims Hip-Hop in Her New Play," *San Francisco Chronicle*, March 14. http://sfgate.com/cgi-bin/article.cgi?file=/chronicle/archive/2004/03/14/PKG8R5HFQ41.DTL

Sandoval, Chela, 2000. *Methodology of the Oppressed* (University of Minnesota Press: Minneapolis)

Segrest, Mab, 1985. *My Mama's Dead Squirrel: Lesbian Essays on Southern Culture* (Firebrand Books: Ithaca)

Shah, Shivali, 2005. "South Asian Americans in the American South," *Southern Exposure*, Vol. 33, Nos. 1-2, Summer

Silliman, Jael, Marlene Gerber Fried, Loretta Ross, and Elena R. Gutierrez, 2004. "Women of Color and Their Struggle for Reproductive Justice," Chapter 1 in *Undivided Rights: Women of Color Organize for Reproductive Justice* (South End Press: Cambridge). Available at Center for American Progress, http://www.americanprogress.org/

* Somerville, Siobhan B., 2000. *Queering the Color Line: Race and the Invention of Homosexuality in American Culture* (Duke University Press: Durham)

Takaki, Ronald, 1990. *Iron Cages: Race and Culture in 19th-Century America* (Oxford University Press: New York)

TWU (Tenants and Workers United, formerly Tenants and Workers Support Committee), 2004. "Report: Women's Leadership Group," 3805 Mount Vernon Ave., Alexandria, VA 22301

Vogel, Lise, et. al., 2003. "Red Feminism: A Symposium," *Science and Society*, Vol. 66, No. 4
Warshaw, Robin, 1994. *I Never Called It Rape: The Ms. Report on Recognizing, Fighting, and Surviving Date and Acquaintance Rape* (HarperCollins Publishers: New York)
Watson-Crosby, Jessica, 2004. "Claudia Jones – Dynamic champion of equality," *People's Weekly World*, Feb. 28. http://www.pww.org/article/articleview/4854/1/204/
Wheeler, Tim, 1997. "*The New York Times*: Turning truth on its head – the Scottsboro case," *People's Weekly World*, February 15
Weigand, Kate, 2002. *Red Feminism: American Communism and the Making of Women's Liberation* (John Hopkins University Press: Baltimore)
Wilkenfeld, Adam, 2003. "Gay Bashing," at Connect with Kids. http://www.connectwithkids.com/tipsheet/2003/121_apr23/bash.html
Worthington, Clancy, 1995. "Stopping Battering in Our Own Ranks," *Forward Motion*, Vol. 14, No. 1, January
Yeung, Bernice, 2001. "Fighting the Many Faces of Violence," *ColorLines*, Vol. 3, No. 4 Winter 2000-2001
Zarembka, Joy Mutanu, 2001. "Maid to Order," *ColorLines*, Vol. 4, No. 3, Fall

V. White Privilege, White Consciousness

Adelman, Larry, 2003. "Affirmative Action for Whites: The houses that racism built," *The San Francisco Chronicle*, June 29
American Public Health Association, 2004. "Fact Sheets: Racial/Ethnic Disparities." http://www.apha.org/NPHW/facts/RaceEth-PHW04.Facts.pdf
Amnesty International, 2003. "United States of America: Death by discrimination – the continuing role of race in capital cases." http://web.amnesty.org/library/print/ENGAMR510462003
____________________, 1999. "United States of America: Race, Rights and Police Brutality." http://www.amnestyusa.org/countries/usa
Auer, Peter. 2002. "Ageing of the Labour Force in OECD Countries: Economic and Social Consequences." http://www-ilo-mirror.cornell.edu/public/english/employment/strat/publ/ep00-2.htm#4
Bernstein, Aaron, 2001. "Racism in the Workplace," *BusinessWeek*, July 30
Black Commentator, 2004. "Wealth of a White Nation: Blacks Sink Deeper in Hole," October 21. http://www.blackcommentator.com/110/110_cover_white_wealth.html
Boyd, David R., 2001. "Canada vs. the OECD: An Environmental Comparison." http://environmentalindicators.org
* Bush, Melanie E. L., 2004. *Breaking the Code of Good Intentions: Everyday Forms of Whiteness* (Rowman and Littlefield Publishers: Lanham, MD)
Bureau of Justice Statistics, 2005. "Demographic trends in jail populations." www.ojp.usdoj.gov/bjs/glance/jailrair.htm
Caldwell, Erskine and Margaret Bourke-White, 1937. *You Have Seen Their Faces* (University of Georgia Press: Atlanta). Available from Spartacus Educational, "Lynching." http://www.spartacus.schoolnet.co.uk/USAlynching.htm
CIA, 2004. *World Factbook*. http://www.odci.gov/cia/publications/factbook/index.html
Clayton, Bruce, 2002. "Lillian Smith (1897-1966)," *The New Georgia Encyclopedia* http://www.georgiaencyclopedia.org/nge/Article.jsp?id=h-463
* Collins, Chuck, et. al., eds., 2004. *The Wealth Inequality Reader* (Dollars and Sense – Economic Affairs Bureau: Cambridge, MA)
Council of Europe, 2001. "Abolition of the death penalty in Council of Europe observer states." http://assembly.coe.int/Documents/WorkingDocs/doc01/EDOC9115.htm
Curry, George E., 2005. "Health Disparities Called a 'National Embarrassment," *Greater Diversity News*, March 10-March 16
Deen, Thalif, 2004. "Global military spending to surpass $1 trillion, says UN report." http://www.dawn.com/2004/08/22/int11.htm

Docteur, Elizabeth and Howard Oxley, 2003. "Health-Care Systems: Lessons from Reform Experience," OECD Health Working Paper #9. http://www.oecd.org/dataoecd/5/53/22364122.pdf

Domhoff, William, 1967. *Who Rules America?* (Prentice-Hall: Englewood Cliffs, NJ)

Dunaway, Wilma A., 2003. *Slavery in the American Mountain South* (Cambridge University Press: New York)

Dunbar-Ortiz, Roxanne, 2002. "One or Two Things I Know about Us: Rethinking the Image and Role of the 'Okies," *Monthly Review*, July-August. http://www.monthlyreview.org/0702dunbar.htm

Edney, Hazel Trice, 2002. "Racist Attacks Increase on College Campuses." http://www.BlackPressUSA.com

Ferguson, Chaka, 2004. "Report lists disparities between blacks and whites," *Fayetteville Observer*, March 24

Finegold, Kenneth and Laura Wherry, 2004. "Race, Ethnicity, and Economic Well-Being." http://www.urban.org/url.cfm?ID=310968

GeographyIQ.com, 2005. "World Atlas." http://www.geographiq.com

Globalis-Indicator, 2005. "Net ODA as % of GNI – 2003." http://globalis.gvu.unu.edu/indicator.cfm?IndicatorID=104#row

Gould, Barbara, 2001. "Five Stages of Dying." http://oldfashionedliving.com/dying.html

Harris, Leslie M., 2006. "African Americans: Contemporary Issues," at Microsoft Corp. http://encarta.msn.com/msn/encyclopedia_761587467/African_American.html

Jorgensen, Helene, 2002. "Give Me a Break: The Extent of Paid Holidays and Vacation," at Center for Economic and Policy Research. http://www.cepr.net/give_me_a_break.htm

Kirk, Dwight, 2005. "Can Labor Go Beyond Diversity Lite?" *Black Commentator*, Issue 127, February. http://www.blackcommentator.com/127/127_think_labor.html

Krysan, Maria and Amanda Lewis, 2005. "Racial Discrimination Is Alive and Well," *Challenge*, May-June, Vol. 48, no. 3

Lavizzo-Mourey, Risa, et. al., 2005. "Forward: A Tale of Two Cities," *Health Affairs*, Vol. 24, No. 2.

Leondar-Wright, Betsy, et. al., 2005. "State of the Dream 2005: Disowned in the Ownership Society" United for a Fair Economy. http://www.FairEconomy.org

Loury, Glenn C., 2002. *The Anatomy of Racial Inequality* (Harvard University Press: Cambridge, MA)

Marable, Manning, 2003. "Abolishing American Apartheid, Root and Branch," *Dialogue and Initiative*, Winter

* Mishel, Lawrence, et. al., 2005. *The State of Working America 2004/2005* (ILR Press: Ithaca)

Nielsen Media Research, 2005. "Latest TV Ratings – In Black and White," March 24. http://www.eurweb.com/printable.cfm?id=19528

OECD, 2005. "Society at a Glance." http://www.oecd.org/els/social/indicators

_____, 2005. "GDP per capita." http://www.oecd.org

_____, 2004. "Quarterly Labor Force Statistics." http://www.oecd.org

Robinson, Randall, 2000. *The Debt: What America Owes to Blacks* (Penguin Putnam: New York)

Rosner, Jay, 2003. "On White Preferences," *The Nation*, April 14

Schweizer, Errol, 1999. "Environmental Justice: An Interview with Robert Bullard," *Earth First! Journal*, July. http://www.ejnet.org/ej/rwc.html

* Smith, Lillian, 1961. *Killers of the Dream*, rev. ed. (WW Norton: New York)

Shapiro, Thomas M., 2005. *The Hidden Cost of Being African American: How Wealth Perpetuates Inequality* (Oxford University Press: Oxford)

Talvi, Silja J.A., 2002. "No Roof Over My Head," *ColorLines*, Summer. http://www.colorlines.com

UN Office on Drugs and Crime, "Seventh United Nations Survey of Crime Trends and Operations of Criminal Justice Systems, covering the period 1998-2000." http://www.unodc.org/pdf/crime/seventh_survey/7s.pdf

U.S. Census Bureau, 2004. "Comparative International Statistics." http://www.census.gov/prod/2004pubs/03statab/intlstat.pdf

* Winant, Howard, 1997. "Racial Dualism at Century's End," in Wahneema Lubiano, ed., *The House that Race Built: Black Americans, U.S. Terrain* (Pantheon: New York)

Wise, Tim, 2003. "White Racism in the Present Era," *Dialogue and Initiative*, Winter

VI. White Allies – Solidarity and Betrayal

Anthony, Louise, 1997. "Feminists: Bourgeois vs. Radical Perspectives," in *The Prism*, March. http://www.ibiblio.org/prism/Mar97/feminist.html

* Aptheker, Herbert, 1989. *Abolitionism: A Revolutionary Movement* (Twayne Publishers: Boston)

Bagget, James Alex, 2003. *The Scalawags: Southern Dissenters in the Civil War and Reconstruction* (Louisiana State University Press: Baton Rouge)

Beal, Thomas D., 2005. "Review: The Great New York Conspiracy of 1741: Slavery, Crime and Colonial Law." http://222.findarticles.com/p/articles/mi_m0SAF/is_1_29/ai_n9772269

Bermanzohn, Sally Avery, 2003. *Through Survivors' Eyes: From the Sixties to the Greensboro Massacre* (Vanderbilt University Press: Nashville)

Bin Wahad, Dhoruba, 1991. Speech to the Student Environmental Action Coalition's national conference, October

Brown, Cynthia Stokes, 2002. *Refusing Racism: White Allies and the Struggle for Civil Rights* (Teachers College Press: New York)

Dunbar-Ortiz, Roxanne, 1997. *Red Dirt: Growing up Okie* (Verso: New York)

Ferguson, R. Brian, 2003. "The Witch Hunt You Never Heard Of," at History News Network. http://www.hnn.us/articles/1571.html

Fletcher, Bill, Jr. and Peter Agard, 1987. *The Indispensable Ally: Black Workers and the Formation of the CIO, 1934-1941* (Kramer Communications: New York)

Goldfield, Michael, 1993. "Race and the CIO: The Possibilities for Racial Egalitarianism during the 1930s and 1940s," in *International Labor and Working-Class History*, No. 44, Fall

Halpern, Rick and Roger Horowitz, 1996. *Meatpackers: An Oral History of Black Packinghouse Workers and Their Struggle for Racial and Economic Equality* (Twayne Publishers: New York)

Harbury, Jennifer, 2005. "The Case of Leonard Peltier: Statement of Fact," for the Leonard Peltier Defense Committee. http://www.freepeltier.org/peltier_faq.htm

Haywood, Harry, 1978. *Black Bolshevik: Autobiography of an Afro-American Communist* (Liberator Press: Chicago)

Hing, Alex, 1983. "On Strike, Shut it Down: Reminiscences of the S.F. State Strike," in *East Wind*. http://userwww.sfsu.edu/~ericmar/hingl.html

Horton, Myles, with Judith Kohl and Herbert Kohl, 1998. *The Long Haul: An Autobiography* (Teachers College Press: New York)

Isserman, Maurice, 1993. *Which Side Were You On?: The American Communist Party during the Second World War* (University of Illinois Press: Urbana)

Lichtenstein, Nelson, 2003. "Reuther the Red?" in *Labour/Le Travail*, No. 51, spring. http://www.historycooperative.org/journals/llt/51/lichtenstein.html

Loewen, James W., 2003. "Forward," in Thompson, et. al., *White Men Challenging Racism*

Naison, Mark, 2002. *White Boy: A Memoir* (Temple University Press: Philadelphia)

Navarro, Joe, 2000. "Outside His Whiteness." Available at http://www.geocities.com/poetajoe/Joe_Navarro.html

Padilla, Marisol and Juan R. Taizán, 2005. "Raza Youth Rise Up: Student Mobilizations in the 1990s." Available at http://freedomroad.org/content/view/340/71/lang,en/

Pangalinan, Erin, 2005. "I Hotel Reborn" in *Philippine News*, August 17-23. http://www.manilatown.org/pdfs/philnews0805sm.pdf

Phillips, Brian, 2005. *SparkNote on Black Like Me.*, March 7. http://www.sparknotes.com/lit/blacklikeme/

Quasar, 2002. "Review of *The Life and Times of John Howard Griffin: A Companion Volume to Black Like Me*," at Epinions.com. http://www.epinions.com/content_73782496900
Robinson, Cedric J., 2000. *Black Marxism: The Making of the Black Radical Tradition* (University of North Carolina Press: Chapel Hill)
Sakai, J., 1989. *Settlers, The Mythology of the White Proletariat: The True Story of the White Nation* (Morningstar Press: Chicago)
Thompson, Cooper, Emmett Schaefer, and Harry Brod, 2003. *White Men Challenging Racism: 35 Personal Stories* (Duke University Press: Durham)
Trelease, Allen W., 1971. *White Terror: The Ku Klux Klan Conspiracy and Southern Reconstruction* (Louisiana State University Press: Baton Rouge)
U.S. Census Bureau, 2006. "Selected Age Groups for the Population by Race and Hispanic Origin for the United States: July 1, 2005." http://www.census.gov/Press-Release/www/2006/nationalracetable3.pdf
Vivasancarlos.com. "San Patricios: The Irishmen Who Died for Mexico," and related links. http://www.vivasancarlos.com/patrick.html
Women's History Information Project, current. "Lucy Parsons: Woman of Will," International Workers of the World (IWW). http://www.iww.org/culture/biography/LucyParsons1.shtml

VII. Social Forces and Leadership

Abdel-Alim, Hesham Samy, 2005. "Hip Hop Islam," at *Al-Ahram Weekly Online*, No. 750, July. http://weekly.ahram.org.eg/2005/750/feature.htm
Acuña, Rodolfo and 36 cosigners, 2003. "An Open Letter to Our African American Sisters and Brothers," Esperanza Peace and Justice Center, in *Voz de Esperanza*, July/August. http://www.esperanzacenter.org/index.html
Bacon, David, 2005. "Divided We Fall," at TruthOut.org, November 23. http://www.truthout.org/docs_2005/1123050.shtml
____________, 2005. "Communities Without Borders," *The Nation*, October 24
____________, 2005. "Uniting African-Americans and Immigrants," *The Black Scholar*, Summer
____________, 2004. "Strike Force," *The American Prospect*, October 22. http://www.prospect.org/web/page.ww?section=root&name=ViewWeb&articleId +8798
Bayoumi, Moustafa, 2004. "Monolithic view of Arabs is dangerous," at Timesunion.com, July 13. http://www.mafhoum.com/press7/202P5.htm
Bell, Derrick, 1992. *Faces at the Bottom of the Well: The Permanence of Racism* (Basic Books: New York)
Black Radical Congress, 1998. "A Black Freedom Agenda for the 21st Century" (Draft). http://www.hartford-hwp.com/archives/450/519.html
Boston.com, 2005. "Fox Raps U.S. on Plan for Fence." http://www.boston.com/news/world/latinamerica/articles/2005/12/18/mexicos_fox_raps_us_on_plan_for_fence/
Burnham, Linda, 2001. "The Wellspring of Black Feminist Theory," Working Paper Series 1, Women of Color Resource Center, 1611 Telegraph Ave., #303, Oakland CA 94612
California Newsreel, 1993. "A Question of Color." http://www.newsreel.org/films/question.htm
Calpotura, Francis, 2004. "Riding with the Wind," *ColorLines*, Vol. 7, No. 1, Spring
Carson, Clayborne and Heidi Hess, 1993. "Student Nonviolent Coordinating Committee" in *Black Women in America: An Historical Encyclopedia* (Carlson Publishing: New York). http://www.stanford.edu/group/King/about_the_projuect/ccarson/articles/black_women_3.htm
* Chang, Jeff, 2005. *Can't Stop Won't Stop: A History of the Hip-Hop Generation* (St. Martin's Press: New York)
____________, 2001. "Where Do We Stand?" *ColorLines*, Vol. 4, No. 3, Fall

Chang, Jeff, 1999. "On the Wrong Side: Chinese Americans Win Anti-Diversity Settlement – And Lose In the End," *ColorLines*, Vol. 2, No. 2, Summer

___________ and Lucia Hwang, 2000. "It's a Survival Issue: The Environmental Justice Movement Faces the New Century," *ColorLines*, Vol. 3, No. 2, Summer

Chavez, Linda, 1992. *Out of the Barrio: Toward a New Politics of Hispanic Assimilation* (Basic Books: New York)

Cho, Eunice Hyunhye, 2004. "BRIDGE: Creating New Tools for Education and Social Change Across Communities," *Network News* (National Network for Immigrant and Refugee Rights), Spring-Summer

Community Youth Organizing Campaign, 2004. *Crossing Borders: Looking Out From the Ground Up*, 1213 Race St., Philadelphia, PA 19107

Cox, Larry and Dorothy Q. Thomas, eds., 2004. "The Women of Color Resource Center," in *Close to Home: Case Studies of Human Rights Work in the United States* (The Ford Foundation: New York).
http://www.fordfound.org/publications/recent_articlers/docs/cose_to_home/p86

Crenshaw, Kimberlé, et. al., eds. 1995. *Critical Race Theory: The Key Writings that Formed the Movement* (The New Press: New York)

D, Davey, 2005. "U.S. artists missing the boat as global movement coalesces," at MercuryNews.com.
http://mld/mercurynews/entertainment/columnists/Davey_D/12825751.htm

* Davis, Angela, 1994. "Coalition Building Among People of Color: A Discussion with Angela Y. Davis and Elizabeth Martínez," in *The Angela Y. Davis Reader*, Joy James, ed. (Blackwell Publishers: Malden, MA)

Davis, Nicole, 2003. "Motion to Repeal," *ColorLines*, Vol. 6, No. 3, Fall

Diehl, Kim, 2000. " Here's the Movement, Let's Start Building': An interview with Barbara Smith," *ColorLines*, Vol. 3, No. 3, Fall

DuBois, W.E.B., 1903. *The Souls of Black Folk*. Available at
http://etext.lib.virginia.edu/toc/modeng/public/DubSoul.html

Fine, Janice, 2001. "Building Community Unions," *The Nation*, January 1.
http://www.thenation.com/doc/20010101/fine

_________ and Jon Werberg, 2003. "Worker Centers," National Study on Worker Centers, August. http://www.labornotes.org/pdf/workercentermap-aug03pdf

Ford, Glen, 2002. "Powerful Illusions," *ColorLines*, Vol. 5, No. 4, Winter

Gapasin, Fernando, 1999. "Beyond the Wage Fight: Social Movement Unionism and Latino Immigrant Workers," *ColorLines*, Vol. 2, No. 2, Summer

García, Michelle, 2006. "A Bronx Tale," *The Nation*, June 19

Harris, Paul, 2005. "The paradox that divides black America," at The Guardian Unlimited/The Observer, October 9.
http://guardian.observer.co.uk/international/story/0,6903,1588158,00.html

Hernández, Mónica, 1999. "With Heart in Hand/*Con Corazon en la Mano*: An Interview with Gloria Anzaldúa," *ColorLines*, Vol. 2, No. 3, Fall

Hill, Herbert, 1996. "Black-Jewish Conflict in the Labor Context," in *Race Traitor*, Noel Ignatiev and John Garvey, eds.

HoSang, Daniel, 2001. "Hiding Race," *ColorLines*, Vol. 4, No. 4, Winter

____________, 2000. " All the Issues in Workers' Lives': Labor Confronts Race in Stamford," *ColorLines*, Vol. 3. No. 2, Summer

Ignatiev, Noel, 1995. *How the Irish Became White* (Routledge: New York)

____________ and John Garvey, eds., 1996. *Race Traitor* (Routledge: New York)

Keleher, Terry, 1999. "ERASE – Towards a New Model of School Reform," *ColorLines*, Vol. 2, No. 1, Spring

Kim, Jee, et. al., 2002. *The Future 500: Youth Organizing and Activism in the United States* (Subway and Elevated Press: New Orleans)

Kim, Jungwon, 2000. "A Luta Continua: The Irrepressible Richie Perez," *ColorLines*, Vol. 3, No. 3, Fall

King, Mary and Casey Hayden, 1964. "Position Paper: Women in the Movement." http://lists.village.virginia.edu/sixties/HTML_docs/Resources/Primary/Manifestos/SNCC_women.html

Kitwana, Bakari, 2005. *Why White Kids Love Hip-Hop: Wankstas, Wiggers, Wannabes, and the new reality of race in America* (Basic Civitas Books: New York)

Krissman, Fred, 1999. "Agribusiness Strategies to Divide the Workforce by Class, Ethnicity and Legal Status," in *Race, Ethnicity, and Nationality in the United States*, ed. Paul Wong

Kurland, Shannah, 2001. "Brown Power vs. Black Power," *ColorLines*, Vol. 4, No. 1, Spring

Lee, Sharon M. and Barry Edmonston, 2005. "New Marriages, New Families: U.S. Racial and Hispanic Intermarriage," *Population Bulletin*, Vol. 60/No. 2, June

Martínez, Elizabeth, 2002. "A View from New Mexico: Recollections of the *Movimiento* Left," *Monthly Review*, July-August.

_________________ and Max Elbaum, 2005. "Building New Roads to Liberation," *ColorLines*, Vol. 8, No. 3, Fall.

* Morales, Ed, 2004. "Brown Like Me?" book review. *The Nation*, March 8

National Network for Immigrant and Refugee Rights, 2001. "The Changing Face of Immigration and Race," *Network News*, Spring

Ngai, Mae M., 2004. *Impossible Subjects: Illegal Aliens and the Making of Modern America* (Princeton University Press: Princeton)

Nguyen, Tram, 2001. "Showdown in K-town," *ColorLines*, Vol. 4, No. 1, Spring

Nieman, Yolanda Flores, 1999. "Social Ecological Contexts of Prejudice Between Hispanics and Blacks," in *Race, Ethnicity, and Nationality in the United States*, ed. Paul Wong

Park, Danny and K.S. Park. "Korean and Latino Restaurant Workers Organize in Koreatown, Los Angeles," *AhoraNow* #4, Labor Community Strategy Center. http://www.thestrategycenter.org/AhoraNow/koreatown_resturant_workers1.htm

Pastor, Manuel and Tony LoPresti, 2004. "Bringing Globalization Home," *ColorLines*, Vol. 7, No. 2, Spring

* Payne, Charles M., 1995. *I've Got the Light of Freedom: The Organizing Tradition and the Mississippi Freedom Struggle* (University of California Press: Berkeley)

Pietri, Pedro, 1973. "Puerto Rican Obituary," in book of the same name (Monthly Review Press: New York)

Phillips, Gary, 2001. "The Battle of Los Angeles," *ColorLines*, Vol. 4, No. 3, Fall

Pizzaro, Marc, 1999, "Racial Formation and Chicana/o Identity," in *Race, Ethnicity, and Nationality in the United States: Toward the Twenty-First Century*, Paul Wong, ed.

* Ransby, Barbara, 2003. *Ella Baker and the Black Freedom Movement: A Radical Democratic Vision* (University of North Carolina Press: Chapel Hill)

Roediger, David R., 2002. *Colored White: Transcending the Racial Past* (University of California Press: Berkeley)

Robnett, Belinda, current. "Student Non-Violent Coordinating Committee (SNCC)," at Houghton Mifflin's Reader's Companion to U.S. Women's History. http://college.hmco.com/history/readerscomp/women/html/wh_035800_studentnonvi.htm

Rojas, Patrisia Macias, 2000. "Rebuilding the Anti-Violence Movement," *ColorLines*, Vol. 3, No. 3, Fall

Rubio, Phil, 1996. "Crossover Dreams," in *Race Traitor*, Noel Ignatiev and John Garvey, eds.

Sen, Rinku, 1998. "Building Black-Brown Unity: Rhode Island's Home Daycare Campaign," *ColorLines*, Vol. 1, No. 1, Summer

Sweeney, John, 2003. "Letter Sent by AFL-CIO President John Sweeney to Florida Gov. Jeb Bush Urging an Independent Investigation into Miami Police Force Tactics During FTAA Demonstrations," December 3. http://www.aflcio.org/mediacenter/prsptm/pr12032003a.cfm

Traxler, Maureen, 2004. "ERASE Racism: Recognizing and Reversing Regional Racism," *Networking Magazine*, February. http://www.eraseracismny.org/news_events/archives/000001.php

U.S. Census Bureau, 2005. "Annual Demographic Survey: March Supplement," tables 1 and 4. http://pubdb3.census.gov/macro/032005/pov/new01_100.htm

Vaca, Nicolás, 2004. *The Presumed Alliance: The Unspoken Conflict between Latinos and Blacks and What It Means for America* (Rayo: New York)

Verán, Cristina, 2003. "Born Puerto Rican, Born (Again) Taino?" *ColorLines*, Vol. 6, No. 3. Fall

____________, 2003. "Riffing on Race," *ColorLines*, Vol. 6, No. 1, Spring

Weber, Devra , 1994. "*Raiz Fuerte*: Oral History and Mexicana Farmworkers" in *Unequal Sisters: A Multi-cultural Reader in U.S. Women's History*. 2nd ed., Ellen Carol DuBois and Vicki Ruiz, eds. (Routledge: New York) http://www.stolaf.edu/people/kutulas/Weber--RaizFuerte.htm

Wellend, Sasha, 2003. "Being Between," *ColorLines*, Vol. 6, No. 2, Summer

West, Cornell, 1995. "Forward," in *Critical Race Theory*, Kimberlé Crenshaw, et. al., eds.

Wimsatt, William Upski, 2000. *Bomb the Suburbs*, 2nd ed. (Soft Skull Press: New York)

Winant, Howard, 1999. "Racism Today: Continuity and Change in the Post-Civil Rights Era," in *Race, Ethnicity, and Nationality in the United States*, ed. Paul Wong

Wing, Bob, 2005. "Crossing Race and Nationality: The Racial Formation of Asian Americans, 1852-1965," *Monthly Review*, December

_________, 2004. "The White Elephant in the Room: Race and Election 2004," at Alternet.org, December 4. http://www.alternet.org/rights/20661

_________, 1999. " Educate to Liberate!': Multiculturalism and the Struggle for Ethnic Studies," *ColorLines*, Vol. 2, No. 2, Summer

Women of Color Resource Center. http://www.coloredgirls.org/

* Wong, Paul, ed., 1999. *Race, Ethnicity, and Nationality in the United States: Toward the Twenty-First Century* (Westview Press: Boulder)

Wu, Yiching, 2005. "Rethinking 'Capitalist Restoration' in China," *Monthly Review*, November

Yamamoto, Eric K., 1999. *Interracial Justice: Conflict and Reconciliation in Post-Civil Rights America* (New York University Press: New York)

VIII. Taking on the System

Bloom, Steve and 14 cosigners, 2003. "An Open Letter To Activists Concerning Racism In The Anti-War Movement," February 13. http://www.ccmep.org/2003_articles/General/021303_an_open_letter_to_activists_conc.htm

Braden, Anne, 2005. "Finding the Other America," *Fellowship*, newsletter of the Fellowship of Reconciliation, January-February. http://www.forusa.org/fellowship/jan-feb_06/braden.html

Catalyst Project. "Workshops." http://www.collectiveliberation.org

Freire, Paolo, 1970. *Pedagogy of the Oppressed* (Continuum International Publishing Group: New York)

Navarro, Joe, 1999. "A Revolutionary Vato Loco," in *Ambidextrous (in two languages): A collection of new and selected poems*. Self-published.

Parsons, Rachel, 2006. "A New Generation of Youth Labor Activists," *Z Magazine*, September, Vol. 19, No. 9. http://zmagsite.zmag.org/Sep2006/parsons0906.html#author

People's Institute for Survival and Beyond. "Undoing Racism/Community Organizing Workshop." http://www.pisab.org

Postel, Danny,1997. "An Interview with Noel Ignatiev," *Z Magazine*, January. http://www.zmag.org/zmag/articles/jan97postel.htm

Proffitt, Bryan, 2006. "If a Tree Falls in the Forest"... Available at http://freedomroad.org/

Index